ROMFORD FOOTBALL CLUB 1876 – 1920

WHERE IT ALL BEGAN

THE WHITE HART HOTEL, HIGH STREET, ROMFORD

Romford Football Club was formed in the above premises on Wednesday, 11th October, 1876

Havering Libraries – Local Studies

ROMFORD FOOTBALL CLUB 1876 – 1920

a comprehensive history

John Haley and Terry Felton

additional material by Linda Rhodes

Heathway Press

First published in Great Britain in 2013 by
Heathway Press
Romford, Essex
www.heathwaypress.co.uk

ISBN 978-0-9566451-1-1

DEDICATION

To the memory of all those mentioned in this publication, without whom it would not have been possible

Contents

FOREWORD

This publication tells the story of a senior football club formed in 1876 to represent the town of Romford in Essex. There are no surviving official club records, so we have delved deep into library and newspaper archives. In these early years of football, newspapers both local and national consisted of very few pages. Space was therefore very limited and sport in general suffered as a result, often any match details provided by the clubs never appearing in the local newspapers.

We have found many discrepancies regarding the number of games played due to results being omitted by the press. On occasions Romford played three games in a single day, and whilst we have been able to decide as to first team and reserve teams, the third game line-up was often a mixture of first and reserve team players. Discrepancies have also been found where the club has issued a summary mid-season which disagrees with the final summary. Maybe the secretary found an error and altered his figures, but this makes life difficult for us statisticians. Some player appearance and goalscoring records have been included, although they are not 100% accurate, again due to the lack of newspaper information.

Reports of some matches (and even published results) differ from newspaper to newspaper on occasion. Maybe one reporter left the ground with a couple of minutes to go and a further goal was then scored. A further difficulty has been that players had no numbers on their kit, and a crowded goalmouth at the opposite end to a reporter would make it difficult to see who scored a goal. Perhaps one reporter clarified the decision with the players, but how do we know which report to believe? Often in match reports fewer than eleven names have been shown, but it cannot be confirmed whether a name or two has been omitted, or the team actually played with an incomplete line-up unless it specifically said in the report.

It appears that when preparing the end of season reports to be presented at the Annual General Meetings, the management occasionally enhanced the club's achievements to present a better picture. Some victories obtained by the reserve team appear to have been accredited to the first team. Today we would call this practice promotional "spin!"

Furthermore, the chairman and vice-chairman referred to in the A.G.M. reports are often not actually named. These reports may state that a certain person took the chair, but not state whether he was the club chairman or just nominated to chair that meeting.

In February 1906 a newspaper article covering the club's first 30 years (see page 344) included a list of Hon. Secretaries and captains. However, the contemporary reports of club meetings contradict this information, so we have disregarded the 1906 list and used the year-by-year reports as our source.

We have tried our best to present a fully accurate description of events. On the odd occasion where some doubt exists and we have a conflict of reports between various newspapers, our common sense has prevailed. We bring you the fullest details available of over **fifteen hundred football matches.**

The seal of the Liberty of Havering, used by the Romford Board of Health in the 19th century. A version of this was adopted by Romford Football Club and sewn onto the players' shirts
Havering Libraries - Local Studies

ROMFORD FOOTBALL CLUB : A BRIEF SUMMARY OF ITS COMPLICATED HISTORY, 1876-1920

Romford Football Club was originally formed in 1876, playing their first season on the cricket ground on Great Mawneys. The ground up to this time had been used by the Romford Cricket Club. In April 1877 farmer Mr John Tiffin, who was landlord at Mawneys, offered the football club use of the ground again for the forthcoming season, but offered the cricket club use of his Lower Field instead, which ruffled a few feathers because the Lower Field did not have a pavilion. The football club played on the same field at Mawneys (by now renamed the Meadow) until 1885, when a speculative builder came to Romford, according to one football club committee member 'To ruin the Place'. The club were forced to find a new home, and made the short move across town to the recently-opened Recreation Ground off Victoria Road. This ground was bordered by Victoria Road, George Street, Upper Richmond Street and the Mill Path.

On 8th October 1887, the Buffaloes Football Club decided to change their name to Romford Olympic to fill the void created by the year's sabbatical of the Romford Football Club. In September of the following season the Romford Club returned to action by merging with Romford Olympic and Romford Y.M.C.A. In 1896 Romford Football Club's local rivals Romford Buffs (not to be confused with the old Buffaloes Club previously mentioned) folded, and their players joined the Romford ranks.

In 1900 the club merged with local rivals St. Edward's Institute. The club kept the Romford name, but this was seen by some as a takeover by the St. Edward's club with headquarters supposedly transferred to the St. Edward's Institute, Market Place, although no evidence has come to light of any meetings being held there. The A.G.M. of that year was held at the White Hart Hotel.

In 1901 the club was notified by the owners of the Recreation Ground that the land had been requisitioned for building purposes. The club had already arranged for their reserve team to play at nearby Brooklands, but due to this ground consisting of no more than open fields, it wouldn't qualify the first team to play there at senior level. The club therefore signed up to play its first team games on the Cricket Ground at Romford Station, which meant a move from one side of what is now South Street, to the other.

In 1906 the club received a proposal of a merger with local rivals Romford United, who had been formed in 1902 and played in the Romford & District League at the Church Lane ground, (approximately 200 yards from where Romford Library stands today). The Romford club agreed to make the United team their reserve side. After just one season Romford United officials decided to de-merge and reinstate their old name, citing a lack of support from the senior club. Following this decision the Romford United team lasted just one more season and folded in 1908.

In the summer of 1909 there occurred a move to take over Romford Football Club with the idea of bringing professional football to the town. Agents were sent into Romford bribing people to sign membership forms and attend the club's Annual General Meeting, with a view to voting off the existing committee. This skulduggery became obvious at the meeting, when six votes more were cast than there were people in attendance! A second vote was ordered, but the result was that popular secretary Charles Heard and various committee members were voted out of office.

The original committee realized there was no way back, so they called a meeting which the majority of the old team also attended, and decided to form a new club in direct opposition to the old one. In their wisdom they decided to resurrect the name of Romford United who had folded only a year earlier.

The officials acquired for the new club a field owned by Mr W. Poel junior situated on the opposite side of Mill Path to the old Recreation Ground, which by this time was being developed for housing. Club supporters and committee members dipped into their own pockets to build a stand and pavilion at the new ground. Alongside the ground on the corner of Victoria Road stood a theatre called the Cosy Corner. The newly-formed football club entered into a business arrangement with the owners of the theatre allowing them to use the football field to hold al fresco concerts in the summer. In return, the football club would receive a share of the theatre's bar profits and their ground would be known as the Cosy Corner Ground. (Was this the first such arrangement for ground naming rights?). Attempts had been made to try to get the old club to reconsider their actions which had led to this debacle, but all was to no avail.

The decision was made, and Romford United was in business. As expected, the majority of the old players considered it a disgrace at the way the old secretary and committee had been voted off, and immediately joined the new setup. So we now had a new club called Romford United run by the former committee of the old club, and represented on the field by the team formerly with the old club; whilst on the other side of South Street, on the Cricket Ground next to Romford Station, the original club was being run by a new committee and represented on the field by a new team! (Confused? You certainly will be).

The majority of Romford supporters showed their allegiance to the newly-formed Romford United club, and the old club seriously declined in direct opposition. The original club was brought to book by the Essex County Football Association for failure to keep proper financial records. Officials were suspended by the County, and the club was expelled from the South Essex League on 16th March, 1911. The club immediately folded, and the futility of their actions a couple of years earlier was exposed.

A further consequence was that the new club expressed a wish to change their name to Romford Football Club, but, fearing they would be made liable for the old club's debts, opted instead to change their name to Romford Town Football Club. They continued to play their games on the Cosy Corner Ground, which because of its shape was also known as the Shoulder of Mutton Ground. This ground was bordered by Victoria Road, South Street, Upper Richmond Street and Mill Path.

By 1915, with the First World War raging and the difficulties of raising a team, the Romford Town Football Club had no choice but to close. In 1919, with the war at an end, the Essex County Football Association appealed for old clubs to restart activities and for new clubs to be formed. Mr. Little, who lived in Brentwood Road, put out feelers to gauge interest in reforming the town club. However, some former players and committee members had lost their lives in the conflict, while others still remained in the forces. In addition the club's Shoulder of Mutton ground had been turned over to allotments! (Not a pretty sight for footballers).

There was not a great deal of interest shown by the locals at first, probably due to the current success of the Great Eastern Railway Football Club, who had joined the Spartan League and were considering adding the Romford suffix to their name. Nevertheless some of the pre-war Romford Town players' and officials' sons and nephews offered their services, and the club re-formed although only at junior club level. The officials acquired a playing pitch on Crown Fields, London Road, but were restricted to running a junior club due to the lack of facilities and the ground not being enclosed.

The team competed in the Romford and District Football League and succeeded in winning the title at the first attempt. The new club was not eligible to enter the moneymaking F.A. Challenge, F.A. Amateur and Essex Senior Cup competitions, and as a result attendances were very low compared to the 'good old days'. Fundraising events were arranged, and in an attempt to improve the club strength they merged with local rivals Romford Ivyleafers prior to the start of the 1920 – 21 season. The newly-merged club played their home games on Brooklands Farm, Medora Road, hoping that the move nearer to the town centre would increase interest and support. Alas, due to the success of the Great Eastern Club competing a mere stone's throw away, this was not to be. The financial struggle continued, good players could not be attracted, and the club folded in late December 1920.

Thus, after nearly 45 years of many changes, including Club names, grounds and headquarters, officials and players, internal wrangles, suspensions and heartaches, the Romford Football Club had ceased to exist.

In the summer of 1921 at Mawney Road Baths the Romford Town Thursday Football Club was formed, entering the West Ham Thursday League so as not to be in direct competition with the Great Eastern Railway Club. The new club secured a pitch at Brooklands, where they were still playing when Romford Football Club was reformed in 1929.

But that is another, and very interesting story...!

ROLL OF HONOUR

ROMFORD FOOTBALL CLUB

1880 – 81	F.A. Challenge Cup	Quarter Final (5th Round)	Away	Darwen	0 – 15
1883 – 84	Essex Challenge Cup	Semi-Final	Neut.	Colchester	1 – 2
1884 – 85	F.A. Challenge Cup	4th Round	Away	Blackburn R.	0 – 8
1889 – 90	Essex Challenge Cup	Final	Neut.	Ilford	0 – 2
1890 – 91	Essex Challenge Cup	Semi-Final (2nd Replay)	Neut.	Harwich & P.	0 – 2
1892 – 93	Essex Challenge Cup	Final	Neut.	Chelmsford	0 – 3
1896 – 97	S.Essex League Div. 1	Runners Up to Leyton			
	West Ham Char. Cup	Semi-Final	Home	W. Ham Garf'ld.	1 – 3
1897 – 98	Essex Senior Cup	Final	Away	Leyton	0 – 3
1900 – 01	R. & D. Lge. Div. 1	Runners Up to Romford St. Andrews			
1902 – 03	S.E.Lge. Div. 2 West	**Champions** **Winners** of Final Play Off.			
1903 – 04	S.E.Lge. Div. 1 B	Runners Up to Southend Athletic			
	R. & D. Lge. Div. 1	**Champions**			
1904 – 05	West Ham Char. Cup	Final **Winners**	Away	Clapton	2 – 0
1905 – 06	Essex Senior Cup	Semi-Final	Neut.	South Weald	0 – 2
1907 – 08	S.E. Lge. Div. 1 A	Runners Up to 4th King's Royal Rifles			
	West Ham Char. Cup	Final	Away	Clapton	3 – 4
	King's Lynn Ch. Cup	Final	Away	Lynn Town	2 – 6
1908 – 09	West Ham Char. Cup	Final **Winners**	Neut.	Leytonstone	4 – 1

RESERVE TEAM

1901 – 02	R. & D. Lge. Div. 2	Runners Up to Romford Alliance
1902 – 03	Romford Char. Cup	Runners Up to Heath Park

ROMFORD UNITED FOOTBALL CLUB

1909 – 10	Essex Senior Cup	Semi-Final	Neut.	South Weald	0 – 3
	West Ham Char. Cup	Final	Neut.	Leytonstone	0 – 4
	Chelmsford Ch. Cup	Final	Away	Chelmsford	0 – 4
1910 – 11	Essex Senior Cup	Semi-Final	Neut.	South Weald	1 – 3
	West Ham Char. Cup	Final **Winners**	Neut.	Leytonstone	3 – 2
	Romford Char. Cup	Final **Winners**	Home	South Weald	1 – 0

ROMFORD TOWN FOOTBALL CLUB

1911 – 12	Essex Senior Cup	Final **Winners**	Neut.	South Weald	1 – 0
	West Ham Char. Cup	Final	Neut.	Custom House	0 – 2
	Romford Char. Cup	Final **Winners**	Home	South Weald	4 – 1
1912 – 13	Essex Senior Cup	Final	Neut.	Ilford	2 – 3
1913 – 14	West Ham Char. Cup	Semi-Final	Away	Clapton	1 – 4
1919 – 20	Romford & D. League	**Champions**			

RESERVES

1911 - 12	Romford Jnr. Ch. Cup	Final (Void)	Home	Mawney Inst.	0 – 2

Romford reserves were defeated in the semi-final but were invited to play in the final as G.E.R. Athletic were unable to fulfil the fixture. On appeal the G.E.R.took their rightful place in the final and the earlier final was declared void.

GLOSSARY

The following abbreviations have been used in match results listings:

FIRST TEAM

Frdly	Friendly Match
FAC	F.A. Challenge Cup
ECC	Essex County F.A. Challenge Cup
ESC	Essex Senior Cup (Renamed)
VCH	Victoria Cottage Hospital Fund
AC	F.A. Amateur Challenge Cup
SEL1	South Essex Football League Div. 1
WHC	West Ham Charity Cup
ECW	Essex County War Fund
RDL1	Romford & District League Div. 1
SEL2	South Essex Football League Div. 2
SEL1B	South Essex Football League Div. 1B
SELPO	South Essex Football League Play Off
SEL1A	South Essex Football League Div. 1A
KLC	King's Lynn Hospital Cup
ICC	Ilford Charity (Hospital) Cup
SFL2B	Southern Football League Div. 2B
CCC	Chelmsford Charity Cup
RCC	Romford Charity Cup
TDF	Titanic Disaster Fund
AFL	Athenian Football League
LLAD	London Football League Amateur Div.
RDL	Romford & District League

RESERVE TEAM

GCC	Grays Challenge Cup
EJC	Essex Junior Cup
SEL2	South Essex Football League Div. 2
RDL1	Romford & District Football League Div. 1
RDL2	Romford & District Football League Div. 2
RCC	Romford Charity Cup
IHC	Ilford Hospital Cup

IN THE BEGINNING

In the early days, football was unrecognisable from the game we know today. In the early 19th century 'folk football' had developed into street football. The authorities at the time feared the impact that mobs under the influence of alcohol who had taken up this pastime were having. There were reports of damage being inflicted on bystanders and their property. The 1835 Highways Act gave magistrates the power to ban street football.

By the 1860s the game had been taken into public schools, from where it emerged as what we now call Association Football. The governing body, the Football Association, was formed in October 1863 and agreed a set of rules for the game.

Under the 1863 rules...

- The maximum pitch dimensions were 200 yards by 100 yards
- Goalposts were 8 yards apart (no tape or crossbar)
- A coin toss determined ends
- Kick-off was to be taken from centre mark
- Sides were to change ends after every goal
- A goal was scored if the ball is kicked between the posts at whatever height
- When a player kicked the ball, any member of his team in front of him was offside
- No running with the ball in the hands
- No hands to throw or pass the ball
- No tripping, hacking or holding was allowed (hacking meant kicking at the opponent's shins)

Those who disagreed with these rules created Rugby Union.

Football was now being played in villages and towns across England. In the autumn of 1876, when Victoria was Queen and Benjamin Disraeli was Prime Minister, the busy market town of Romford, on the ancient London to Colchester road, was about to form a club to join the fray. On Wednesday October 11th 1876 the following notice appeared in the *Essex Times*:

> A meeting for the purpose of establishing a foot-ball club for Romford, will be held at the White Hart Hotel this evening at eight o'clock, to which all gentlemen interested in the movement are respectfully invited.

FORMATION OF ROMFORD FOOTBALL CLUB

This photograph is almost certainly connected with the founding of the Romford Football Club in 1876. The four boys at the back are recognizable from the 1883 team picture (on page 44) as the Clark brothers.
Authors' collection

The first meeting held to form a football club for Romford was initiated by 19 year-old Francis Hugh Thirlwall, a vicar's son who had been educated at Marlborough College and was now employed as a bank clerk. At this meeting Mr Thirlwall in fact argued for the club to play under the rugby code. He was, however, outvoted.

Thirlwall would be a regular playing member of the club for several seasons, being captain in 1877, vice-captain in 1881, and elected to the committee on 1st May 1885. He became secretary of the club in 1894, a position he held for three years. Thirlwall would also be active in the Romford Cricket Club, and would eventually achieve his aim of bringing rugby to the town in 1894. Indeed a very prominent sportsman!

Frederick D'Arcy Richard Clark, 18, another bank clerk, was elected to chair that first meeting, which, as we have seen, was held at the White Hart Hotel, High Street, on 11th October 1876. During the course of the club's first season Mr Clark (who was known as Fred), his three brothers and a cousin would all feature in the team.

So the club was launched, with an initial membership of fourteen. They were mostly very young men fresh from school and employed in offices, with sufficient spare time and pent-up energies to devote to training and playing of matches. Most of them worked for the Ind Coope Brewery, Romford's largest employer, hence the team's nickname 'The Brewers'.

Reports in The *Essex Times* charted the rapid progress of the new venture:

> **Wed. 11th October:** A meeting was held at the White Hart Hotel for the purpose of forming a football club. At this meeting there was an attendance of fourteen people and Mr. Frederick Clark was elected to Chair the meeting. The meeting decided to form a club to play under Association Rules and to use the White Hart Hotel, Romford as the club headquarters. About twenty five names were put forward for membership of the fledgling club.
>
> **Fri. 13th October:** Friday night those members most active in the club's formation, again assembled at the White Hart Hotel, and the rules and regulations drawn up and submitted to the previous meeting, were unanimously confirmed and the following gentlemen elected officers for the opening season. Captain: Mr.E.Champness, Secretary and Treasurer: Mr.F.D.R.Clark. A committee was also appointed and a conversation took place with respect to the grounds on which the club will play. Several places were suggested and the matter was left in the hands of the Committee.
>
> **Mon. 16th October:** A third meeting was held to formalise arrangements for a match to be played on the cricket ground the following Saturday, and the colours to be adopted by the club to be blue and black. Persons intending to join the club were requested to give in their names to the secretary Mr.F.D.R.Clark, of South Street, in order to play in the opening match.

It was the secretary's role to arrange matches and select the players. The job was not always easy. In these early days of football it seems that fixtures were arranged, and players were invited to play, but when assembled for the match the team was often a player or two short. We must remember that they were amateurs with other calls on their time, and had no telephones with which to convey messages quickly. Not the highly organised football of today!

Newspaper reporters when listing the team indicated the positions they played in. We can see that teams in these early days usually comprised a goalkeeper, one full back, two half backs and seven forwards. The fact that the object of the game was to score goals was probably the reason for so many forwards.

Before 1891 the football pitch had a maximum measured size of 200 yards by 100 yards (almost twice the size of modern day pitches), and because of this most of the play took place in the congested centre of the field. Occasionally there was no goalkeeper listed, just eleven outfield players. No doubt goalkeepers got rather cold and lonely and wanted more of the action!

At this early stage of the forming of football clubs, there were no organised leagues. Although the F.A. Challenge Cup Competition started in 1871, Romford did not take part until 1878. The F.A. Amateur and Essex Senior Cups were as yet several years away, and as a consequence clubs were confined to practice matches between club members and friendly matches against other clubs. So Romford did not yet compete in a league, and all fixtures in this inaugural season were friendlies.

It is now time for the first three of the 1500 or so individual match statistics contained in this book. As you will see, as well as date, team names and result, we provide the names of goalscorers and team line-ups when available.

21 Oct	E.Champness Select	0	F.D.R.Clark Select	2
			Clark,Thirlwall	

Messrs. F.H.Thirlwall and F.D.R.Clark both prominent in the winning team, but no details have emerged in relation to the actual team line-ups.

A further game was arranged for 25th November with teams selected by Messrs.G.A.Smith & W.J.Reid.

25 Nov	Reid XI * (W.J.Reid)	0	Smith XI	3
			G.Smith(3)	

* The Reid XI was in fact The Reid IX, as they played with only nine men, and it is not known why the two teams did not have ten men each!

13 Jan	Captain's XI	3	Secretary's XI	2
	Carter(2),Skilton		Roberts(2)	

Captain's XI: E.Champness(Capt),H.W.Palmer,E.Carter,Dennigan,S.W.Skilton,C.Clark,C.Cousens and two others.
Secretary's XI: F.D.R.Clark(Capt),M.Roberts,L.E.Clark,W.D.Heard,C.J.Rawlings,G.A.Smith,F.Stromeyer and two others.
On this occasion it appears that both teams were actually comprised of nine men.

The majority of the club's earliest players worked at Ind Coope's Romford Brewery. This view of the Brewery yard features hundreds of wooden beer barrels neatly stacked in cannonball fashion.
Havering Libraries - Local Studies

Season 1876 - 77

ROMFORD FOOTBALL CLUB

Honorary Secretary and Treasurer: Mr.F.D.R.Clark **Captain:** Mr.E.Champness

Colours: Blue and Black Striped Jerseys, Stockings, and Brewer's Cap and White Knickerbockers

Headquarters: White Hart Hotel, Romford **Ground:** Cricket Ground, Great Mawneys, Romford

COMPETITIONS ENTERED

All Friendly Matches

Match Details

9 Dec Frdly Away Chigwell Grammar School 0 – 0
Romford:
Team details unknown

6 Jan Frdly Home Upton Park 0 – 1
Romford: F.Stromeyer(goal); H.W.Palmer(back);E.Champness(Capt),F.D.R.Clark,E.Carter(half backs);
L.E.Clark,E.C.Matthews,R.H.Lyon,F.H.Thirlwall(forwards).

20 Jan Frdly Away Brentwood Grammar School won
Romford:
Team details unknown

27 Jan Frdly Home Chigwell Grammar School 3 – 1 Scorers unknown
Romford: W.J.Reid(back);E.Champness(Capt),H.W.Palmer(half backs);
F.D.R.Clark,E.C.Matthews,F.H.Thirlwall,G.A.Smith,M.Roberts,E.Carter,R.H.Lyon,H.Gilbey(forwards).

10 Feb Frdly Away Upton Park 0 – 6
Romford: Lucking(goal);W.J.Reid(back)W.D.Heard,E.Champness(half backs);
E.Carter,W.Hitching(right),R.H.Lyon,E.C.Matthews,W.Clark(centre),(forwards).

17 Feb Frdly Away Mars (Hackney Downs) 1 – 2 Thirlwall
Romford: J.H.S.Pitt(goal);H.W.Palmer(back);E.Champness(captain),E.Carter(half backs);
F.H.Thirwall,G.A.Smith,L.E.Clark,E.C.Matthews,R.H.Lyon,C.Clark,C.J.Rawlings(forwards).

24 Feb Frdly Home Brentwood Grammar School 2 – 1 Thirlwall(2)
Romford: H.W.Palmer(Back);E.Champness(Capt),W.J.Reid(Half-backs);
F.H.Thirlwall,M.Roberts,L.E.Clark,G.A.Smith,E.C.Matthews,E.Carter,R.H.Lyon,H.Gilbey(Forwards)

3 Mar Frdly Home Mars (Hackney Downs) 2 – 1 Thirlwall,Roberts
Romford: F.Stromeyer(goal);H.W.Palmer(back);W.J.Reid and E.Champness(captain)(half backs);
F.H.Thirlwall,M.Roberts,L.Carter,G.A.Smith,R.H.Lyon,E.Carter(forwards);

17 Mar Frdly Home Mars (Hackney Downs) 2 – 1 Roberts,L.Clark
Romford: H.W.Palmer(back);E.Champness(captain),C.Lyster(half backs);
M.Roberts,F.H.Thirlwall,L.E.Clark,E.C.Matthews,R.H.Lyon,E.Carter,C.Clark(forwards).

24 Mar Frdly Home Hermits (Victoria Park) 2 – 3 H.Palmer.C.Clark
Romford: F.H.Thirlwall, C.Clark and H.W.Palmer played well.
Remainder of the team unknown

7 Apr Frdly Home Leyton 0 – 2
Romford: H.W.Palmer and E.C.Matthews played well.
Remainder of the team unknown

SUMMARY OF FIRST TEAM RESULTS OBTAINED SEASON 1876 - 77

	P	W	D	L	Goals For	Goals Ag
All Friendly Matches	11	5	1	5	12	18
AGM Report	11	5	1	5	n/k	n/k

Unfortunately we have been unable to trace the score in the away game against Brentwood Grammar School, and the goals for and against in the above summary are therefore incomplete.

First Team Appearances Season 1876 – 77

E.Carter	7	L.Carter	1	E.Champness	7	C.Clark	3
F.D.R.Clark	2	L.E.Clark	4	W.Clark	1	H.Gilbey	2
W.D.Heard	1	W.Hitching	1	Lucking	1	R.H.Lyon	7
C.Lyster	1	E.C.Matthews	7	H.W.Palmer	8	J.H.S.Pitt	1
C.J.Rawlings	1	W.J.Reid	4	M.Roberts	4	G.A.Smith	4
F.Stromeyer	2	F.H.Thirlwall	7			Total	76

First Team Goal Scorers Season 1876 – 77

F.H.Thirlwall	4	M.Roberts	2	L.E.Clark	1	H.W.Palmer	1
C.Clark	1	Unknown	3	Total	12		

Note: The result of the fixture against Brentwood Grammar School and the scorers versus Chigwell Grammar School are of course not included in the above listings.

Post-Season Summary Season 1876 – 77

Following the meetings called to form the Romford Football Club, the first-ever match took place at the Old Cricket Ground, Great Mawneys, Romford, on Saturday 21st October. A team selected by the club captain Elijah Champness, a legal clerk, lined up against one chosen by the Secretary, Fred Clark. An 'exceedingly game' contest ensued, but owing principally to the superior and energetic efforts of Messrs. Thirlwall and Clark, the Secretary's eleven was victorious by two goals to nil.

Five weeks later a second game between sides chosen by players William John Reid and Grimston Abel Smith was played, which the latter team won by three goals to none. The *Essex Times* report on the match states "It is but fair to the losing side to state that they played two short!" No explanation was given as to why they did not play ten a side.

On 9th December, Romford played their first game at Chigwell Grammar School and recorded a goalless draw. The next recorded result was a one goal to nil home defeat against Upton Park, and it appears that they played with only nine men and Upton Park with ten. A week later a match between the Captain's eleven and the Secretary's eleven took place and both teams actually only played with nine men.

On 20th January 1877 the team made the short journey to play Brentwood Grammar School and recorded a win, although the actual score is unknown. Next was a return game at home to Chigwell Grammar School and a three goal to one victory was achieved. The newspaper report indicates seven forwards but does not name a goalkeeper. The return game against Upton Park provided quite a shock and Romford were humbled by six goals to nil! W.Clark, described as a cousin of the four Clark brothers, made his first appearance.

Three games against Mars each ended two goals to one, two of the victories being in favour of Romford. In between these games Romford played a return game at home to Brentwood Grammar School and two goals from Thirlwall secured a two goal to one victory. Both teams played without a goalkeeper! Romford's last two games of the season were both at the Great Mawneys ground and each ended in defeat. Hermits (3-2) and Leyton (2-0) were the successful teams.

Brentwood Grammar School, one of the more salubrious away venues in the early years of the club.
The Chelmsford Chronicle

Annual General Meeting

(as reported in the *Essex Times,* Saturday 5th May 1877)

The annual general meeting, at the end of the season, of the Romford Football Club, was held at the White Hart Hotel, on Tuesday, 1st May, at 8.30 p.m., when there were present Messrs. G.A.Smith (in the chair), Carter, Champness, F.D.R.Clark, Heard, Lyon, Matthews, Palmer, Rawlings, Reid, and Thirlwall. The accounts, having been audited and found correct, were passed. A vote of thanks was given to Mr. Clark for the able manner in which he has conducted the secretaryship, &c., for the past season. In responding, Mr. Clark announced his intention of resigning. Several gentlemen having been asked to take the post, it was finally proposed by Mr.Matthews, seconded by Mr. Palmer, and carried, that Mr.R.H.Lyon be secretary and treasurer during the ensuing season. The club played 11 matches during the season, of which 5 were won, 5 lost, and 1 drawn.

General Meeting

(as reported in the *Essex Times,* Wednesday 19th September 1877)

The annual general meeting of the Romford Football Club was held on Friday evening last, 14th September, at the White Hart Inn. There was a good attendance, and judging from the lively interest evinced in the proceedings, a capital season may be anticipated. Mr.R.Harvey Lyon was re-elected hon. sec., and the committee and treasurer were also re-elected. It was announced with considerable satisfaction that D.McIntosh Esq., had kindly consented to act as President. The club, which is now connected with the Association (London), will play as before on the meadow at Great Mawneys, Mr.Tiffen having again placed it at their disposal.

Note: The above is as reported in the local newspaper the week following the meeting, but as the A.G.M. had been held in May this must have been an Ordinary General Meeting. It is unknown why the secretary and committee were re-elected at this meeting.

It is noted that Romford were connected with the London Football Association, possibly due to the fact that the Essex County F.A. was not formed until 1882. Romford were not permitted to affiliate to the London Football Association in later years, as the ground and headquarters were half a mile outside the limits, and the Essex County F.A. would not give permission for the club to apply.

The club must have been delighted to have as its first President Mr David McIntosh, of Havering Park, whose father had purchased the Manor of the Liberty of Havering-atte-Bower from the Crown in 1828. The manor, established by Royal Charter in 1465, covered the parishes of Havering-atte-Bower, Romford and Hornchurch.

At the end of the club's first season, landlord Mr. John Tiffen had offered them a further season on his meadow by the footpath. The two halves of this pitch were described as the Havering End and the Rifle Butt End. (There was a Rifle Range at Great Mawneys, near the High Street). The pitch was on a slope with the Havering End also known as the top goal. Mr Tiffen decided to offer Romford Cricket Club use of his Lower Field instead for the ensuing season, although objections were raised that this field never had its own pavilion.

In their second season, 1877-78, Romford played the usual formation (goalkeeper, one full back, two half-backs and seven forwards) up to the match against Brentwood School on 3rd November. The following week, against Leyton, they played with two full-backs and six forwards, while their opponents used the usual formation. From this period on it appears that Romford continued with the two backs system, although several teams still used only one. Despite the lack of defenders there were still many nil-nil draws, and games with only one goal scored, but this may have been due to the size of the pitch and congested centre field with twelve to fourteen forwards battling it out! Attack the best form of defence?

Each team provided one umpire who operated in his team's half of the field. A referee was stationed on the touchline on the halfway line and he adjudicated if the umpires disagreed. Each goal comprised two goalposts and a tape connecting them – there were no goal nets or a fixed crossbar. The tape was at an approximate height of eight feet above the ground. At half time both teams changed ends, and after one or two minutes rest, the game was restarted. The call of 'No side!' indicated the end of the match. If a team captain called 'No side!' it seemed to indicate they had suffered enough!

Season 1877 – 78

ROMFORD FOOTBALL CLUB

President: Mr.D.McIntosh

Hon.Secretary and Treasurer: Mr.R.Harvey Lyon **Captain:** Mr.F.H.Thirlwall

Headquarters: White Hart Hotel, Romford **Ground:** The Meadow, Great Mawneys, Romford

COMPETITIONS ENTERED

All Friendly Matches

Match Details

6 Oct Frdly Away Chigwell Grammar School 1 – 1 *Reid or Thirlwall?
Romford: Messrs.F.H.Thirlwall(Capt), M.Roberts and L.E.Clark especially distinguished themselves.
Remainder of the team unknown.

13 Oct Frdly Home Mars (Hackney Downs) 1 – 0 *Reid or Thirlwall?
Romford: J.H.S.Pitt(goal),H.W.Palmer(back),E.Champness,E.Carter(half-backs),
F.H.Thirlwall(Capt),R.H.Lyon,W.J.Reid,C.J.Rawlings,E.Conder,C.Clark(forwards).

20 Oct. Frdly Away Brentwood 0 – 6
Romford: E.Champness(Goal); R.H.Lyon(Back);C.S.Palmer,E.Carter(Half-backs);
F.H.Thirlwall(Capt),W.T.Carter,C.Clark,C.Hardy,L.E.Clark,P.W.Menzies(sub), and another sub,(Forwards).

27 Oct Frdly Home Gresham (South Hackney) 0 – 1
Romford: C.S.Palmer(Goal);H.W.Palmer(Back);E.Carter,E.Clarke(Half-backs);
F.H.Thirlwall(Capt),C.Johnson,E.Conder,E.D.Bacon,L.E.Clark,W.J.Reid,R.H.Lyon,(Forwards).

3 Nov Frdly Away Brentwood Grammar School 0 – 1
Romford: J.H.S.Pitt(goal),H.W.Palmer(back),W.J.Reid,E.Carter(half-backs),
C.S.Palmer,G.Harris(right),F.H.Thirlwall(Capt),C.Clark,E.Champness(centre),R.H.Lyon,H.Gilbey(Left)(forwards).

10 Nov Frdly Home Leyton Reserves 0 – 1
Romford: W.Wright(goal),H.W.Palmer,R.H.Lyon(backs),E.Carter,L.E.Clark(half-backs),
F.H.Thirlwall(Capt),C.Clark,C.S.Palmer,E.Conder,W.J.Reid,G.Harris(forwards).

17 Nov Frdly Away Upton Park 0 – 1
Romford: J.H.S.Pitt(goal),W.J.Reid,H.W.Palmer(backs),A.D.Cornell,L.E.Clark(half-backs),
F.H.Thirlwall(Capt),E.Champness,E.C.Matthews,R.H.Lyon,E.Carter,J.R.Potter,Minter(forwards).

24 Nov Frdly Home Dreadnought (West Ham) 0 – 1
Romford: R.H.Lyon;H.W.Palmer,E.Carter;A.D.Cornell,L.E.Clark;
W.Wright,F.H.Thirlwall(Capt),G.Harris,J.R.Potter,C.S.Palmer.

8 Dec Frdly Home Hermits (Victoria Park) 2 – 0 Roberts(2)
Romford: C.Clark(goal),H.W.Palmer,E.Champness(backs),E.Carter,L.E.Clark(half-backs),
F.H.Thirlwall(Capt),M.Roberts,H.Gilbey,A.D.Cornell,R.H.Lyon,G.Harris(forwards).

15 Dec Frdly Home Union (Islington) 1 – 0 Thirlwall
Romford: F.H.Thirlwall(Capt),W.J.Reid,C.Johnson,C.Clark,E.Conder played well.
Remainder of the team unknown.

5 Jan Frdly Home Spartan Rovers (West Ham) 0 – 0
Romford: C.Couzens(goal),L.E.Clark,E.Carter(backs),H.Gilbey,W.Wright(half-backs),
F.H.Thirlwall(Capt),C.S.Palmer,C.Clark,J.H.S.Pitt,A.D.Cornell,G.Harris(forwards).

12 Jan Frdly Away Mars(Hackney Downs) 0 – 1
Romford: R.H.Lyon(goal),H.W.Palmer,C.S.Palmer(backs),W.T.Carter,L.E.Clark(half-backs),
F.H.Thirlwall(Capt),E.Champness,J.H.S.Pitt,Neville,Harvey,C.Clark(forwards).

19 Jan Frdly Away Pilgrims (Tottenham) 0 – 0
Romford: Chandler(goal),H.W.Palmer,R.H.Lyon(backs),L.E.Clark,S.Vinden(half-backs), F.H.Thirlwall(Capt),E.Champness,A.D.Cornell,C.Clark,J.H.S.Pitt,E.Carter(forwards).

26 Jan Frdly Away Leyton 0 - 13

2 Feb Frdly Home Brentwood Grammar School 0 – 0
Romford: E.Carter(goal);W.J.Reid,H.W.Palmer(backs);L.E.Clark,R.H.Lyon(half-backs); F.H.Thirlwall(Capt),A.D.Cornell,H.Gilbey,E.Champness,E.Conder,C.S.Palmer(forwards).

9 Feb Frdly Away Dreadnought (West Ham) 1 – 4 C.S.Palmer
Romford: H.W.Palmer,E.Champness(backs),F.D.R.Clark,L.E.Clark(half-backs), C.S.Palmer,W.Wright,E.Carter,J.H.S.Pitt,W.Knight,J.R.Potter(forwards).

23 Feb Frdly Home Hermits (Victoria Park) 0 – 0
Romford: E.Champness(goal),W.J.Reid,H.W.Palmer(backs),L.E.Clark,F.D.R.Clarke(half-backs), F.H.Thirlwall(Capt),E.Carter,R.H.Lyon,A.D.Cornell,C.S.Palmer,W.Wright(forwards).

2 Mar Frdly Home Chigwell Grammar School 1 – 0 E.Carter
Romford: J.H.S.Pitt(goal),H.W.Palmer,W.J.Reid(backs),L.E.Clark,E.Carter(half-backs), T.Pool,G.Harris(left),E.D.Bacon,C.S.Palmer(right),A.D.Cornell,R.H.Lyon(centre)(forwards).

9 Mar Frdly Home Finchley Petrels 3 – 1 Pool,Thirlwall,Harris
Romford: J.H.S.Pitt(goal),W.J.Reid,R.H.Lyon(backs),E.Champness,G.Harris(half-backs), C.S.Palmer,T.Pool,H.W.Palmer,L.E.Clark,E.Carter,F.H.Thirlwall(Capt)(forwards).

16 Mar Frdly Away Spartan Rovers (West Ham) 0 – 1
Romford: J.H.S.Pitt(goal);H.W.Palmer,R.H.Lyon(backs);L.E.Clark,G.Harris(half-backs); F.H.Thirlwall(Capt),C.S.Palmer,E.Champness,A.D.Cornell,W.Wright,J.R.Potter(forwards).

23 Mar Frdly Home Brentwood Grammar School 3 – 1 C.Clark,Thirlwall(2)
Romford: W.J.Reid,H.W.Palmer(backs);L.E.Clark,G.Harris(half-backs); F.H.Thirlwall(Capt),C.S.Palmer,C.Clark,A.D.Cornell,E.Champness,E.Carter,R.H.Lyon(forwards).

* It is known from the annual general meeting which players scored all the goals, and it is therefore known that Reid and Thirwall must have scored the goals in these games, but it is not known who scored which goals!

SUMMARY OF FIRST TEAM RESULTS OBTAINED SEASON 1877 – 78

					Goals	
	P	W	D	L	For	Ag
All Friendly Matches	21	6	5	10	13	33
AGM Report	22	7	5	10	13	19

From the A.G.M. press report it appears that a further game was played, a victory. We agree with the number of goals scored, but already have a goal too many conceded. How many were scored in the missing game?

First Team Appearances Season 1877 – 78

E.D.Bacon	2	E.Carter	16	W.T.Carter	2	E.Champness	13
Chandler	1	C.Clark	10	F.D.R.Clark	2	L.E.Clark	17
E.Clarke	1	E.Conder	5	A.D.Cornell	10	C.Couzens	1
H.Gilbey	4	C.Hardy	1	G.Harris	9	Harvey	1
C.Johnson	2	W.Knight	1	R.H.Lyon	16	E.C.Matthews	1
P.W.Menzies	1	Minter	1	Neville	1	C.S.Palmer	14
H.W.Palmer	16	J.H.S.Pitt	10	T.Pool	2	J.R.Potter	4
C.J.Rawlings	1	W.J.Reid	11	M.Roberts	2	F.H.Thirlwall	18
S.Vinden	1	W.Wright	6	Unnamed sub.	1	Total	204*

* Full team details are not known for the away games versus Chigwell G.S and Leyton. plus the home game with Union.

First Team Goal Scorers Season 1877 – 78

F.H.Thirlwall	5	M.Roberts	2	C.Clark	1	E.Carter	1
G.Harris	1	T.Pool	1	C.S.Palmer	1	W.J.Reid	1
Total	13						

Note: The above listing is as reported at the Annual General Meeting.

Post-Season Summary Season 1877 – 78

The club opened the season with a well-earned one all draw at Chigwell Grammar School. In their fixture against Mars on 13th October, Romford secured the winning goal early in the second half. They then suffered two defeats against Brentwood (0-6) and Gresham of South Hackney (0-1). A further four successive one nil defeats followed, among them on 10th November when Romford entertained a strong Leyton team. In favourable weather, except for a five minute shower around half time, Leyton kicked off, playing up the hill. Harrison scored the only goal of the game for Leyton when his shot hit the post and he neatly charged it through at the rebound. At call of 'No side!', Romford had obtained a corner kick, but it was not kicked, as the Leyton team were anxious to get away to catch a train! Leyton called 'No side!' which was cheeky as they were winning at the time.

The following week, with Upton Park having 13 men on the field, Romford agreed to play twelve a side, taking Minter from the Upton thirteen! Unfortunately the game came to a premature end six minutes before time, owing to the regulation of closing the Park gates at 4.30pm. The match against Dreadnought on 24th November was played in pelting rain, and after about an hour's play the game was ended. Romford played with only 10 men and lost by one goal to nil. In the fixture on 8th December Hermits won the toss and elected to defend the Rifle Butt End. There was a very good attendance of both ladies and gentlemen, who witnessed a return to winning ways with M.Roberts scoring both goals for the homesters. The following week Romford made it two wins in a row by defeating the Union of Islington 1-0 courtesy of F.H.Thirlwall.

It was reported that on 29th December at Brentwood, Romford player M.Roberts received a compound fracture of his leg during **a game**. No further information, i.e. result or opponents, has been found. Could this be our one missing match for this season?

On 5th January Romford entertained Spartan Rovers at Great Mawneys, and after one hour's delightful play resulted in a draw, neither side gaining a goal. A week later Romford met Mars on a 'very hard and indifferent ground at Hackney Downs'. Mars secured two goals but one was objected to, and they ran out winners by one goal to nil. On 19th January Romford travelled to Tottenham to play the Pilgrims and earned a 0-0 draw. Seven days later it was a different story when the team travelled to Leyton for the return friendly match, and came home with their tails between their legs following a 13-0 thrashing! The local newspapers didn't provide the result of this match. The result was eventually found in the *Lloyd's London Weekly Newspaper*. We also noted that at the club's Annual General Meeting this game was not included in the summary. Had they been too embarrassed to include it?

The following week Brentwood Grammar School were the visitors and although the home defence held out for a 0-0 draw it meant that Romford had failed to score for five games in a row. Once again, on 9th February against Dreadnought at West Ham Park, the problems of running a football team at that time were only too evident. Romford had to enlist three substitutes, played with ten men and were at a disadvantage once more. Often the team was made up of substitutes from the crowd! A week later Romford were due to play Upton Park but were unable to raise a team and scratched. Upton Park had no such problems, and their first team played instead against their own reserves at West Ham Park.

On 23rd February Romford were at home to the Hermits and the game commenced in most favourable weather. The Hermits brought down a most determined-looking team! Thirlwall kicked off and directly 'Hands!' was called by the Hermits, and this set the example of the childish play of 'Hands!' every time the ball brushed by a player's arm. The ball was in the Hermits' half for almost the entire game but all to no avail as the game ended as a goalless draw. Seven days later Romford were at home to Chigwell Grammar School, and the newspaper report stated that 'Weather was all that could be desired, while a goodly concourse of spectators were present'. Romford played very loosely and only came to life in the final quarter of an hour. Edmund Carter placed the ball between the posts in the last five minutes to secure their first victory in eight games.

On 9th March Finchley Petrels were the visitors and Romford's winning habit continued, with Pool, Harris and Thirlwall doing the needful in a three goals to one victory. A week later Romford travelled to West Ham to meet Spartan Rovers, and experienced some misfortune when both J.Potter and Harry Palmer were hurt. It is not known whether they left the field of play. Spartans won the game with a lucky shot, by one goal to nil. On 23rd March, according to the match report, Romford and the Brentwood Grammar School both played without a goalkeeper and had seven forwards. A determined effort to score goals, regardless of goals conceded. Romford won by three goals to one.

Such were the trials and tribulations in these early years of football, and to compound the problem researchers have to put up with inconsistencies in players' initials and the actual make up of teams as presented in newspaper reports. To be fair, several sets of brothers often played together, which could cause confusion, and if a written team was passed to the match reporter many initials like F and T or C and E could be unclear.

Annual General Meeting

(as reported in the *Essex Times,* Wednesday 1st May 1878)

ROMFORD FOOTBALL CLUB – The general meeting of this club was held at the White Hart Hotel on Friday last, 26th April. G.A.Smith Esq., in the chair, and there was a good attendance of members. The secretary (Mr.R.H.Lyon) read the Balance sheet and report. From which it appeared there was a balance in hand of £2.15s.6d. Twenty two matches had been played during the season, five of which were drawn games, four in favour of, and one against, the club; seven had been won and ten lost; nineteen goals lost and thirteen won. Mr.F.H.Thirlwall kicked five goals, Mr.M.Roberts two, and Messrs. C.Clark, E.Carter, G.Harris, T.Pool, C.S.Palmer and W.J.Reid one each.

D.McIntosh Esq., was re-elected president, and the vice-presidents were all re-elected. Mr. Thirlwall was re-elected captain; Mr.L.Clark was chosen vice-captain, and the secretaryship was left open, Mr.R.H.Lyon having intimated his wish to resign; there is no doubt however that this gentleman will serve again. It was proposed that twenty matches be arranged for next season. Vote of thanks to the chairman, and also to the secretary for his past services terminated the meeting.

Arthur D. Cornell, an influential member of the club for many years.
He became Registrar of Marriages for Romford
Havering Libraries - Local Studies

Percy Meredith Earle, a medical student and Romford footballer
(detail from the photograph on page 52)
Essex County Football Association

Season 1878 – 79

ROMFORD FOOTBALL CLUB

President: Mr.D.McIntosh

Vice-Presidents: Messrs W.H.Pemberton Barnes, Rev. H.M.Burgess, E.Conder, G.Hope, E.H.Lawton, J.G.Matthews, Rev. G.F.Price, Rev. W.J.Skilton

Hon. Secretary and Treasurer: Mr.R.Harvey Lyon

Captain: Mr.F.H.Thirlwall **Vice-Captain:** Mr.L.E.Clark

Committee: Messrs E.Carter, E.Champness, F.D.R.Clark, G.Harris H.W.Palmer, W.J.Reid, M.Roberts, G.A.Smith

Headquarters: White Hart Hotel, Romford **Ground:** The Meadow, Great Mawneys, Romford

COMPETITIONS ENTERED

F.A. Challenge Cup
Friendly Matches

Match details

5 Oct Frdly Away Brentwood Grammar School 3 – 1 Thirlwall(2),Roberts
Romford: C.S.Palmer(Goal);F.B.Nicholson,H.W.Palmer(Backs);G.Barnes,R.H.Lyon(Half-backs);
F.H.Thirlwall(Capt),L.E.Clark,G.A.Smith,W.J.Reid,W.A.Lawton,A.D.Cornell,M.Roberts(Forwards).

19 Oct Frdly Home Leyton 4 – 0 Conden,H.Palmer,E.Carter,Thirlwall
Romford: H.W.Palmer,W.J.Reid(Backs),E.Carter,L.E.Clark(Half-backs);
F.H.Thirlwall(Capt),J.Coleman,R.H.Lyon,E.Conder,G.A.Smith,C.H.Smith,F.B.Nicholson(Forwards).

26 Oct Frdly Away Chigwell Grammar School 0 – 0
Romford: E.Champness(Goal);W.J.Reid,H.W.Palmer(Backs);L.E.Clark,G.A.Smith(Half-backs);
H.H.Barnes,F.H.Thirlwall(Capt),A.D.Cornell,E.Conder,C.S.Palmer,R.H.Lyon(Forwards).

2 Nov FAC1R Home Ramblers (Walthamstow) 3 – 1 Thirlwall,Barnes,Lyon
Attendance: 300
Romford: E.Champness(Goal);H.W.Palmer,W.J.Reid(Backs);L.E.Clark,G.A.Smith(Half-backs);
H.H.Barnes,E.Conder(right),A.D.Cornell,F.H.Thirlwall(Capt)(centre).R.H.Lyon,E.Carter(left).(Forwards).

16 Nov Frdly Away Chelmsford 1 – 1 Scorer unknown
Romford: C.S.Palmer(Goal);L.E.Clark(Capt)(Back);W.J.Reid,E.Carter(Left backs)J.Coleman,G.A.Smith(Right backs);
C.Clark,H.Gilbey,W.A.Lawton,E.Champness,W.Wright(Forwards).

23 Nov Frdly Away Leyton 0 – 0
Romford: C.S.Palmer(Goal);H.W.Palmer,W.J.Reid(Backs);L.E.Clark,G.A.Smith(Half-backs);
G.Harris,C.Reynolds,C.H.Smith,E.Champness,H.H.Barnes,E.Carter(Forwards).

21 Dec FAC2R Away Swifts (Slough) 1 – 3 Lyon
Romford: E.Champness(Goal);H.W.Palmer,W.J.Reid(Backs);C.H.Smith,L.E.Clark(Half-backs);
F.H.Thirlwall(Capt),H.H.Barnes,E.Carter,W.Wright,R.H.Lyon,C.S.Palmer(Forwards).

18 Jan Frdly Away Brentwood 5 – 0 Thirlwall(2)Wright,Roberts,Cornell
Romford: No goalkeeper named;W.Ramsey(Back);L.E.Clark,H.W.Palmer(Half-backs);
H.H.Barnes,W.J.Reid;F.H.Thirlwall(Capt),M.Roberts;A.D.Cornell,W.Wright(Forwards).

8 Feb Frdly Home St. George's College (Croydon) 1 – 0 Andrews
Romford: E.Champness(Goal);W.J.Reid,W.A.Lawton(Backs);C.H.Smith,L.E.Clark(Half-backs);
H.J.Andrews,W.Wright,F.H.Thirlwall(Capt),M.Roberts,H.H.Barnes,C.S.Palmer(Forwards).

15 Feb Frdly Home Chelmsford 1 – 2 Scorer unknown
Romford:
Team details unknown.

8 Mar Frdly Home Union (Islington) 2 – 1 Cornell,C.Palmer
Romford: H.W.Palmer,W.J.Reid(Backs);L.E.Clark,E.Carter(Half-backs); F.H.Thirlwall(Capt), A.D.Cornell,H.J.Andrews,C.S.Palmer,F.B.Nicholson,W.A.Lawton,C.H.Smith(Forwards).

15 Mar Frdly Away Ramblers (Walthamstow) 7 – 0 Thirlwall(4)Wild,Wright,Nicholson
Romford: H.W.Palmer,R.H.Lyon(Backs);L.E.Clark,C.H.Smith(Half-backs); F.H.Thirlwall(Capt), F.B.Nicholson(centre),H.J.Andrews,A.Wild(right),W.Wright,C.S.Palmer,C.Clark((left)(Forwards).

22 Mar Frdly Home Gresham (South Hackney) 0 – 1
Romford: H.W.Palmer,W.A.Lawton(Backs);C.H.Smith,L.E.Clark(Half-backs); F.H.Thirlwall(Capt), E.Champness,E.Conder,F.B.Nicholson,C.Clark,C.S.Palmer,C.Reynolds(Forwards).

29 Mar Frdly Home Finchley 0 – 2
Romford: E.Champness(Goal);F.D.R.Clark,W.J.Reid(Backs),L.E.Clark,R.H.Lyon(Half-backs); F.H.Thirlwall(Capt),C.S.Palmer,A.D.Cornell,W.Wright,F.B.Nicholson,W.A.Lawton(Forwards).

5 Apr Frdly Home Pilgrims (Tottenham) 0 – 2
Romford: W.J.Reid,F.D.R.Clark(Backs);H.W.Palmer,L.E.Clark(Half-backs); F.H.Thirlwall(Capt), R.H.Lyon,C.S.Palmer,F.B.Nicholson,W.A.Lawton,W.Knight,C.Wright(Forwards).

SUMMARY OF FIRST TEAM RESULTS OBTAINED SEASON 1878 – 79

					Goals	
	P	W	D	L	For	Ag
Friendly Matches	13	6	3	4	24	10
F.A.Challenge Cup	2	1	0	1	4	4
Total	15	7	3	5	28	14
AGM Report	15	7	3	5	28	13

CUP RESULTS SEASON 1878 – 79

F.A. Challenge Cup

Final: Old Etonians 1 Clapham Rovers 0

Romford's progress: 1st Round Home Ramblers 3 – 1
2nd Round Away Swifts 1 – 3

First Team Appearances Season 1878 – 79

H.J.Andrews	3	G.Barnes	1	H.H.Barnes	6	E.Carter	6
E.Champness	8	C.Clark	3	F.D.R.Clark	2	L.E.Clark	14
J.Coleman	2	E.Conder	4	A.D.Cornell	6	H.Gilbey	1
G.Harris	1	W.Knight	1	A.W.Lawton	7	R.H.Lyon	8
F.B.Nicholson	7	C.S.Palmer	11	H.W.Palmer	11	W.Ramsey	1
W.J.Reid	12	C.Reynolds	2	M.Roberts	3	C.H.Smith	7
G.A.Smith	6	F.H.Thirlwall	12	A.Wild	1	C.Wright	1
W.Wright	6	Total	153				

The composition of the team for the game against Chelmsford on 15th February is unknown, and it could be that a player other than those listed above may have played in this match, and the above players a game more.

First Team Goal Scorers Season 1878 – 79

F.H.Thirlwall	10	R.H.Lyon	2	A.D.Cornell	2	M.Roberts	2
E.Conder	1	H.W.Palmer	1	E.Carter	1	H.H.Barnes	1
A.Wild	1	F.B.Nicholson	1	W.Wright	2	H.J.Andrews	1
C.S.Palmer	1	Unknown	2	Total	28		

Post-Season Summary Season 1878 – 79

The season commenced with a journey up the Ingrave Road and a fine victory over Brentwood Grammar School in which it appears that both teams were comprised of twelve players. A week later came Romford's first-ever win, over Leyton. This was followed by a drawn game against Chigwell Grammar School.

On 2nd November Romford entered the F.A. Challenge Cup Competition for the first time when they won their home fixture against Ramblers by three goals to one. It was stated that 'Mr.R. Growse of Brentwood acted as Umpire for both teams'. In the match against Chelmsford which was drawn 1-1, Romford played two men short for the first quarter of an hour. It was reported that at the close of the game an adjournment was made to Coval Cottage, where both teams were hospitably entertained by Mr.C.P.Baker! This match was, incidentally, the first-ever game for the newly-formed Chelmsford Football Club.

On 23rd November Romford held their own in a dull nil nil draw at Leyton. After a four week break due to the arctic conditions, the second round F.A. Cup tie took place on 21st December, when Romford were defeated 3-1 by Swifts (Slough) at Kennington Oval. In the 4th Round (Quarter Final) Swifts lost to Clapham Rovers. Clapham Rovers would be defeated by one goal to nil by Old Etonians in the final at Kennington Oval.

On 18th January at last Romford played a game after yet another four week break, on this occasion travelling to Brentwood to play the town team. This was not without some controversy. Due to the previous game being postponed, it was agreed to play the game under any circumstances. Romford arrived at Brentwood three men short at 3.30, with the ground covered with snow, and Brentwood turned up in ones and twos over the next half an hour. The match finally kicked off just after four o'clock. Romford started with eight men and decided to play with no goalkeeper, whilst Brentwood had only seven men! A ninth player joined the Romford team at half time. Due to the late start, play lasted only forty minutes before darkness set in. At the end of the game Romford had obtained a 5-0 victory. The Brentwood club was far from happy, and a letter or two appeared in the local papers.

On 8th February Romford met St. George's College from Croydon and recorded another win. It was reported that the College team were tied for time, so the game was played for only fifty minutes. Time, tide and trains wait for no man! A week later, Romford lost at home to Chelmsford by two goals to one. Despite the game being played at home, Romford started with only six men and it was quite some time before they had a complete team, and to make matters worse the ground was flooded.

Three more weeks without playing due to the match away to Brentwood Grammar School being cancelled, before another win, this time at home to the strong Union team from Islington, albeit by the odd goal from three. A further week saw a resounding seven goals to nil win over the Ramblers from Walthamstow, Thirlwall being at his best with four goals, and Nicholson, Wild and Wright adding to the tally. A week later, on 22nd March, Gresham of South Hackney were the visitors to Great Mawneys, Romford losing by the narrow margin of one goal to nil. Seven days later Finchley came to town and inflicted a 2-0 defeat on the homesters. The newspaper report stated 'One of the Finchley players fell, fracturing his collar bone. Mr.Gaffney and another surgeon were on the ground and at once set the broken bone. This mishap interrupted play for some time!' There is no mention as to whether the man continued playing.

The final game against Pilgrims on 5th April saw Romford's third home defeat in a row, with another two goals to nil reverse.

Annual General Meeting
(as reported in the *Essex Times,* Wednesday 14th May 1879)

The annual meeting of the Romford Football Club was held at their headquarters the White Hart Hotel, on Friday evening, May 9th, at which there were a large number of members present. The President and Vice-President were re-elected to the respective posts for the ensuing year. Mr. Thirlwall was re-elected Captain, and Mr.L.E.Clark, Vice-captain; Mr.W.A.Lawton, Secretary and Treasurer in the place of Mr.R.H.Lyon, who retired.

The report stated that the Club, during the season had won seven matches, lost five, and three well played matches were drawn. Twenty eight goals were won and 13 lost. The season had proved to be a very severe one, the frosts preventing several matches from coming off. The subscriptions had not come in so well as those of the previous year; but owing to the inclement season, &c., the expenses had not been to heavy as formerly, so that a balance of about 12s. remained in favour of the Club. With reference to the matches which were lost, it may be explained that at the very last moment several of the most prominent members were unable to attend; but altogether the Club may be congratulated upon its achievements during the season, as well as with reference to its finances.

Reference is made in the above report to the number of games played by the club during the season. It appears therefore that we have been unable to obtain details of three matches, one win, draw and loss. Romford scored four more goals but conceded two fewer. Unfortunately we do not know which teams played against them in these matches, or the results.

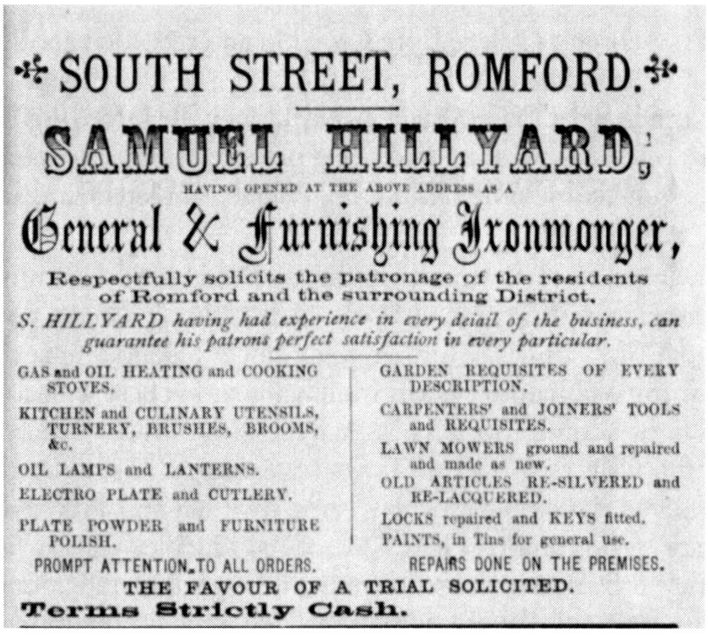

This charming late Victorian advertisement for a Romford business, together with the others in this book, are printed at the end of *The merriest Merry Christmas* by John Freeman (a copy of which is held at the Archives and Local Studies Centre, Valence House, Dagenham)

A rare survival: the 1878-79 season fixture card
Authors' collection

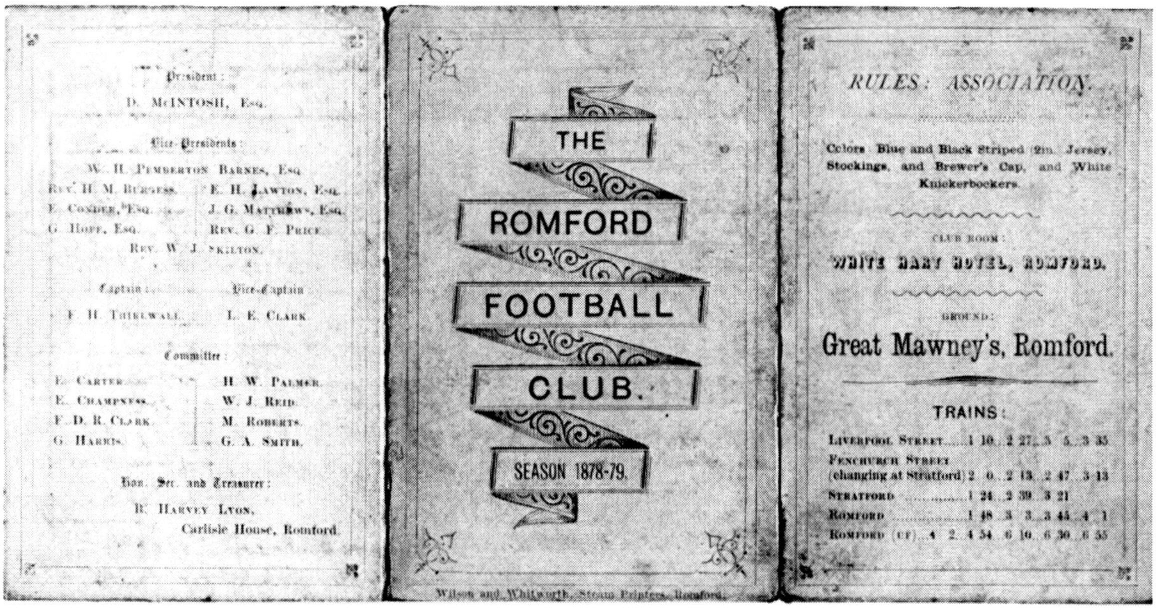

President:
D. McINTOSH, Esq.

Vice-Presidents:
W. H. PEMBERTON BARNES, Esq.
REV. H. M. BURGESS. | E. H. LAWTON, Esq.
E. CONDER, Esq. | J. G. MATTHEWS, Esq.
G. HOPE, Esq. | REV. G. F. PRICE.
REV. W. J. SKILTON.

Captain: F. H. THIRLWALL. Vice-Captain: L. E. CLARK.

Committee:
E. CARTER. | H. W. PALMER.
E. CHAMPNESS. | W. J. REID.
F. D. R. CLARK. | M. ROBERTS.
G. HARRIS. | G. A. SMITH.

Hon. Sec. and Treasurer:
R. HARVEY LYON,
Carlisle House, Romford.

THE
ROMFORD
FOOTBALL
CLUB.
SEASON 1878-79.

Wilson and Whitworth, Steam Printers, Romford.

RULES: ASSOCIATION.

Colors Blue and Black Striped 2in. Jersey, Stockings, and Brewer's Cap, and White Knickerbockers.

CLUB ROOM:
WHITE HART HOTEL, ROMFORD.

GROUND:
Great Mawney's, Romford.

TRAINS:

LIVERPOOL STREET	1 10	2 27	3 5	3 35
FENCHURCH STREET (changing at Stratford)	2 0	2 13	2 47	3 13
STRATFORD	1 24	2 39	3 21	
ROMFORD	1 48	3 3	3 45	4 1
ROMFORD (UP)	4 2	4 54	6 10	6 30	6 55

Front of the card. Note the railway timetable!

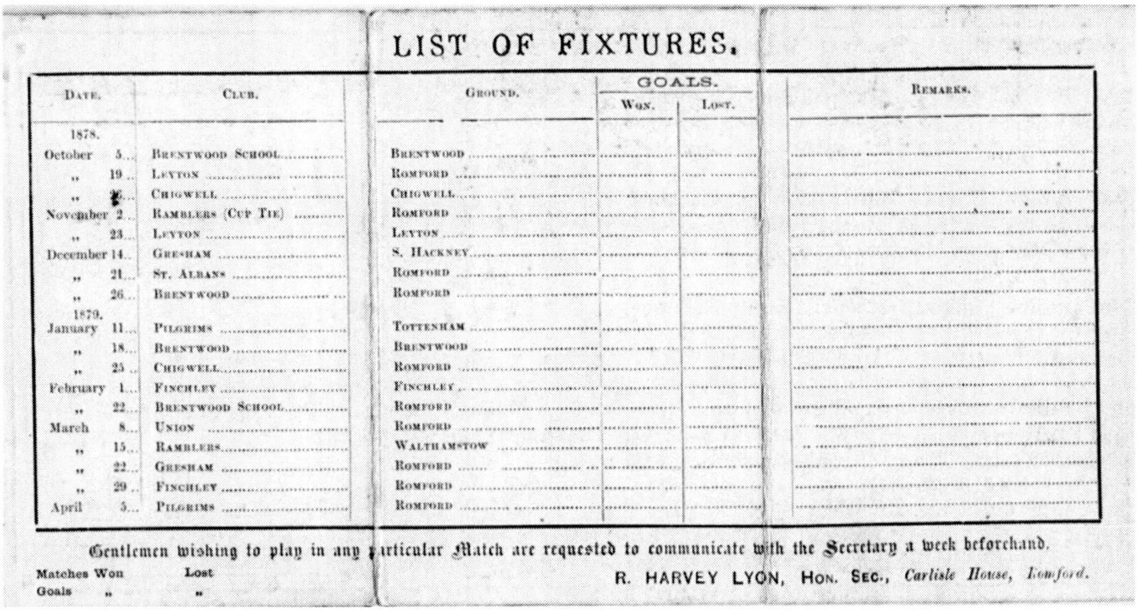

LIST OF FIXTURES.

Date.		Club.	Ground.	Goals Won.	Goals Lost.	Remarks.
1878.						
October	5	BRENTWOOD SCHOOL	BRENTWOOD			
"	19	LEYTON	ROMFORD			
"	26	CHIGWELL	CHIGWELL			
November	2	RAMBLERS (CUP TIE)	ROMFORD			
"	23	LEYTON	LEYTON			
December	14	GRESHAM	S. HACKNEY			
"	21	ST. ALBANS	ROMFORD			
"	26	BRENTWOOD	ROMFORD			
1879.						
January	11	PILGRIMS	TOTTENHAM			
"	18	BRENTWOOD	BRENTWOOD			
"	25	CHIGWELL	ROMFORD			
February	1	FINCHLEY	FINCHLEY			
"	22	BRENTWOOD SCHOOL	ROMFORD			
March	8	UNION	ROMFORD			
"	15	RAMBLERS	WALTHAMSTOW			
"	22	GRESHAM	ROMFORD			
"	29	FINCHLEY	ROMFORD			
April	5	PILGRIMS	ROMFORD			

Gentlemen wishing to play in any particular Match are requested to communicate with the Secretary a week beforehand.

Matches Won Lost
Goals " "

R. HARVEY LYON, HON. SEC., *Carlisle House, Romford.*

Back of the card, with the most important information for supporters

Season 1879 – 80

ROMFORD FOOTBALL CLUB

President: Mr.D.McIntosh **Hon.Secretary and Treasurer:** Mr.W.A.Lawton

Captain: Mr.F.H.Thirlwall **Vice-Captain:** Mr.L.E.Clark

Headquarters: White Hart Hotel, Romford **Ground:** The Meadow, Great Mawneys, Romford

COMPETITIONS ENTERED

F.A. Challenge Cup
Friendly Matches

Match Details

4 Oct Frdly Away Pilgrims (Tottenham) 0 – 5
Romford: L.E.Clark(Goal);H.W.Palmer,W.J.Reid(Backs);F.D.R.Clark,H.Lawton(Half-backs);
F.H.Thirlwall(Capt),A.D.Cornell,E.Champness,Macfarlane major,Macfarlane minor.(Forwards).

11 Oct Frdly Home Hotspur (Shepherds Bush) 0 – 6
Romford:
Team details unknown

18 Oct Frdly Away Finchley 0 – 5
Romford:
Team details unknown

25 Oct Frdly Home Chigwell Grammar School 6 – 0 Thirlwall(2)Cornell(2)Wright(2)
Romford: Fosby(Goal);W.J.Reid,F.D.R.Clark(Backs);L.E.Clark,C.Noad(Half-backs);
W.A.Lawton,W.D.Matthews(right),F.H.Thirlwall(Capt),H.W.Palmer(centre),A.D.Cornell,W.Wright(left)(Forwards).

1 Nov Frdly Home Union (Islington) 4 – 1 Thirlwall,Cornell,Wright,Reynolds
Romford: E.Champness;H.W.Palmer,W.J.Reid;C.S.Palmer,W.A.Lawton;
F.H.Thirlwall(Capt),C.Reynolds,W.Axford,R.H.Lyon,W.Wright,A.D.Cornell.

8 Nov FAC1R Home Clapham Rovers 0 – 7
Romford: L.E.Clark;A.D.Cornell,H.W.Palmer,;W.J.Reid,E.P.Barnes;
W.Wright,F.H.Thirlwall(Capt),C.S.Palmer,C.Noad,E.Champness,H.Axford.

15 Nov Frdly Away Gresham (South Hackney) 0 – 1
Romford: L.E.Clark;W.A.Lawton,-.Morrison;F.B.Nicholson,E.Champness,F.H.Thirlwall;
G.Skilton,E.C.Matthews,W.D.Matthews,C.Reynolds,C.Clark.

29 Nov Frdly Home St.Peter's Institute (Putney) 1 – 1 C.Palmer
Romford: F.H.Thirlwall(Capt),C.S.Palmer,W.J.Reid,E.Champness,C.Magillicuddy,
W.A.Lawton,E.P.Barnes,Dawes,C.Reynolds,C.H.Smith,G.Skilton.

3 Jan Frdly Away St. Albans (Upton) 1 – 1 C.Smith
Romford: F.H.Thirlwall(Capt)(Goal);H.W.Palmer,W.A.Lawton(Backs),C.H.Smith,A.Couzens(Half-backs);
A.D.Cornell,W.Wright,C.S.Palmer,W.Eaton,Hooper,E.Champness(Forwards).

17 Jan Frdly Home Finchley 0 – 1
Romford: W.A.Lawton(Goal);H.W.Palmer,W.J.Reid(Backs);C.Couzens,C.H.Smith(Half-backs);
W.Wright,A.D.Cornell(right),F.H.Thirlwall(Capt),M.Roberts(centre),C.S.Palmer,Hooper (of Woodford)(right)(Forwards).

31 Jan Frdly Home Pilgrims(Tottenham) 0 – 4
Romford: J.H.S.Pitt;F.H.Thirlwall(Capt),M.Roberts,A.D.Cornell,W.Wright,C.Magillycuddy,
W.D.Matthews,A.Couzens,J.H.Ingram,C.Bloomfield,W.Eaton.

14 Feb# Frdly Home Gresham (South Hackney) 0 – 1
Romford: F.H.Thirlwall(Capt)
Remainder of team unknown.

21 Feb Frdly Home Brentwood Grammar School 2 – 1 Matthews,Clark
Romford: W.D.Matthews,C.Clark,
Remainder of team unknown

13 Mar Frdly Away Chigwell Grammar School 2 – 0 Eaton,Wright
Romford: W.A.Lawton(Goal);A.D.Cornell,C.Noad(Backs);C.Couzens,C.H.Smith(Half-backs);
F.H.Thirlwall(Capt),W.Wright,W.Eaton,J.R.Potter,C.Reynolds,H.Axford(Forwards).

On this date, Romford Variety lost at home to Upton Rangers by two goals to one.

The Variety team was : Glover(goal);J.Potter*,A.Martin(backs);C.Couzens*,A.Elms(half-backs);
W.Wright*(Capt),A.Cornell*,W.Eaton*,A.Potter,G.Garnett,S.Reeve(forwards).
* All current or future Romford players!

SUMMARY OF FIRST TEAM RESULTS OBTAINED SEASON 1879 – 80

					Goals	
	P	W	D	L	For	Ag
Friendly Matches	13	4	2	7	16	27
F.A.Challenge Cup	1	0	0	1	0	7
Total	14	4	2	8	16	34
AGM Report	15	4	2	9	17	n/k

It appears that one match has not been traced, which resulted in another defeat.

CUP RESULTS SEASON 1879 – 80

F.A. Challenge Cup

Final: Clapham Rovers 1 Oxford University 0

Romford's progress: 1st Round Home Clapham Rovers 0 – 7

First Team Appearances Season 1879 – 80

W.Axford	3	E.P.Barnes	2	C.Bloomfield	1	E.Champness	6
C.Clark	2	F.D.R.Clark	2	L.E.Clark	4	A.D.Cornell	8
A.Couzens	2	C.Couzens	2	Dawes	1	W.Eaton	3
Fosby	1	Hooper	2	J.H.Ingram	1	W.A.Lawton	7
H.Lawton	1	R.H.Lyon	1	J.A.Macfarlane	1	J.E.Macfarlane	1
C.Magillicuddy	2	E.C.Matthews	1	W.D.Matthews	4	Morrison	1
F.B.Nicholson	1	C.J.Noad	3	C.S.Palmer	5	H.W.Palmer	6
J.H.S.Pitt	1	J.R.Potter	1	W.J.Reid	6	C.Reynolds	4
M.Roberts	2	G.Skilton	2	C.H.Smith	4	F.H.Thirlwall	11
W.Wright	7			Total	112		

First Team Goal Scorers Season 1879 – 80

W.Wright	4	A.Cornell	3	F.H.Thirlwall	3	C.Reynolds	1
C.S.Palmer	1	C.H.Smith	1	W.D.Matthews	1	C.Clark	1
W.Eaton	1	Total	16				

AGM Report states

Wright	5	Thirlwall	3	Cornell	2	Matthews	2
C.Clark	1	C.Palmer	1	H.Palmer	1	Reynolds	1
C.Smith	1	Total	17				

Post-Season Summary Season 1879 – 80

Romford commenced their fourth season on 4th October with a 5-0 defeat at the hands (or rather the feet) of Pilgrims at Tottenham, Bennett securing a hat-trick. A week later worse was to follow with a home defeat to Hotspur by six goals to nil. On October 18th away to Finchley Romford suffered another 5-0 loss. The newspapers gave little space to match reports in these early games, and described the match as follows:

> FOOTBALL: A match between the Romford and the Finchley Clubs was played on the ground of the latter on Saturday, when the visitors scored another grand reverse – by five goals to love. Last year, Romford showed some very good play and won far more goals than they lost; in the three Saturdays which have been devoted to play this season 16 goals have been booked against the club.

The new season was beginning in the same way as the previous one had ended, with three straight defeats. However, Romford closed October with a 6-0 victory over Chigwell Grammar School, and it was reported that 'The Chigwellians were sore pressed, and not five minutes out of the whole time did they succeed in bringing the ball into the vicinity of their opponents' goal'. On 1st November, at their home ground, Romford secured a four goal to one beating of Union and the newspaper reporters were in more encouraging form! The report closed with the news that 'On Saturday next, Romford will be visited by the Clapham Rovers, one of the finest clubs in England, when the first round Cup tie will be played off. It was hoped that the members elected to play against them would fight hard for the honour of Romford'. Sadly, a heavy loss resulted:

> The Rovers had all their own way in the match in the first round of the Challenge Cup Competition, and won easily, by seven goals to nothing. The Home forwards never succeeded in passing the Rovers' backs, and had not darkness set in about half an hour before time, the winning score would probably have been larger. Clark, the Romford goalkeeper, deserves praise for the skilful way in which he stopped many well directed shots…

On 15th November Romford travelled to South Hackney to play Gresham, and came away defeated by one goal to nil. Two drawn matches followed, against St. Peter's Institute and St. Albans (Upton). The return game with Finchley at Great Mawneys, ended in a narrow 1-0 defeat. Then on 31st January the Pilgrims from Tottenham came to town and inflicted a heavy 4-0 defeat on the homesters.

After a two week break and six matches without a win, Romford entertained Gresham in the return fixture, but alas it was to be yet another defeat, this time by one goal to nil. On 21st February Romford managed a 2-1 home win against Brentwood Grammar School. It was played in pouring rain, and with Romford leading by two goals to one it was reported that 'a fine run by Green right down the ground would no doubt have resulted in another goal for the school, but just as he was about making a shot for goal he slipped down, and the ball was sent into neutral ground by the Romford goal keeper'. Three weeks later Romford wound up the season with another victory, this time by two goals to nil, in the return match away to Chigwell Grammar School, Eaton and Wright netting the goals. Thus the team managed to end the season on a high note after such a dismal run of form.

Annual General Meeting

(as reported in the *Essex Times,* Wednesday 28th April 1880)

A meeting of this club was held on Monday evening 26th April, in the Coffee Room of the White Hart Hotel, when there were present – Messrs. F.H.Thirlwall (in the chair), W.A.Lawton (Secretary), E.Champness, L.E.Clark, C.Clark, W.D.Matthews, H.Palmer, J.H.S.Pitt, and C.Smith. –

From the Secretary's report it appeared that 28 matches had been arranged for the past season, out of which fifteen were played, resulting in nine being lost, four won, and two were drawn games. Mr.Thirlwall, the Captain, had played in every match but one; Messrs. Reid, H.Palmer and W.A.Lawton had each played in ten matches: C.Palmer and W.Wright, eight each; C.Smith seven; W.D.Matthews, six; F.D.R.Clark, L.E.Clark, J.H.S.Pitt, and W.Axford, three each.

As to the number of goals obtained W.Wright took the premier position with a score of five; the Captain stood next with three; A.Cornell and W.D.Matthews scored two each; singles being kicked by C.Clark, C.Palmer, H.Palmer, C.Reynolds, and C.Smith. It was to be regretted that during the season it had been found necessary to fall back upon no less than nineteen substitutes, as many as four playing on two different occasions; on another occasion the services of three others were required; whilst there were several matches in which two substitutes helped to make up the required strength of the Romford team.

The accounts, which were audited by W.D.Matthews and C.Clark, showed that the receipts up to the present amounted to £18.0s.5d, and that the expenditure had been £13.15s.5d. Outstanding subscriptions, amounting to £7.8s.0d., had still to be got in, whilst on the other hand, there were further liabilities to be discharged amounting to something like £6; so that it was hoped that the club would be able to start next year's operations with a balance in hand of between five and six pounds. The report so far as it went, was unanimously adopted; but, on the motion of Mr.E.Champness, the further consideration of the subject was adjourned to 28th May, in order to enable the secretary to collect the unpaid subscriptions and present a complete balance sheet.

On the proposition of Mr.L.E.Clark it was resolved that a dinner for members and their friends be held at the White Hart Hotel on the 28th proximo, the necessary arrangements to be left to the Football Committee. A vote of thanks to the chairman concluded the proceedings.

General Meeting

(as reported in the *Essex Times*, Wednesday 29th September 1880)

Fri. 24th Sept a General Meeting was held at the White Hart Hotel at which Mr. G.A.Smith presided. A list of 22 matches arranged for the season was presented by the Hon.Secretary and was approved. Ten new members were elected. Practice commenced on the ground at Great Mawneys on Saturday, when nearly 20 members attended.

Season 1880 – 81

ROMFORD FOOTBALL CLUB

President: Mr.D.McIntosh **Hon.Secretary and Treasurer:** Mr.W.A.Lawton*

Captain: Mr.F.H.Thirlwall **Vice-Captain:** Mr.L.E.Clark

Headquarters: White Hart Hotel, Romford **Ground:** The Meadow, Great Mawneys, Romford

Note* Mr.Lawton was the hon.sec. at the time of the annual general meeting in April, 1880, but at the annual general meeting a year later it was reported that Mr.H.W.Palmer was the hon.secretary. It is unknown when or why this change actually took place.

COMPETITIONS ENTERED

F.A. Challenge Cup
Friendly Matches

Match Details

2 Oct Frdly Away Pilgrims (Tottenham) 1 – 1 Wright
Romford: E.Champness(goal);H.W.Palmer,W.J.Reid(backs);L.E.Clark,C.Couzens(half-backs);
W.Wright,A.G.Martin(right),F.H.Thirlwall(Capt),R.A.Clark(centres),C.S.Palmer,C.Clark(left)(forwards).

9 Oct Frdly Home Dreadnought (West Ham) 0 – 3
Romford: A.G.Martin(goal); W.J.Reid,J.Molineux(backs);L.E.Clark,C.H.Smith(half-backs);
F.H.Thirlwall(Capt),C.S.Palmer,W.D.Matthews,W.Wright,C.Reynolds,J.H.S.Pitt(forwards).

16 Oct Frdly Away Brentwood Grammar School 5 – 0 Scorers unknown
Romford: H.J.Edwards(goal);H.W.Palmer,W.J.Reid(backs),L.E.Clark,C.Couzens(half-backs);
W.Wright,H.Reid(right),F.H.Thirlwall(Capt),G.Garnett(centres),P.M.Earle,W.D.Matthews(left)(forwards).

30 Oct FAC1R Neut# Reading Minster 1 – 1 Wright
Romford: E.Champness(goal);H.W.Palmer,W.J.Reid(backs);L.E.Clark,C.Couzens(half-backs);W.A.Wright,
A.D.Cornell(right),F.H.Thirlwall(Capt),J.Molyneux(centres),P.M.Earle,C.S.Palmer(left)(forwards).

6 Nov Frdly Away Chigwell Grammar School 1 – 1 Scorer unknown
Romford: H.J.Edwards(goal);H.W.Palmer,C.S.Palmer(backs);C.Couzens,R.H.Lyon(half-backs);
W.Wright,A.D.Cornell(right),E.Champness(Capt),C.Reynolds(centres),W.D.Matthews,Harding(left)(forwards).

11 Nov FACRep Reading Minster scratched w/o

13 Nov Frdly Home St.Barts Hospital 3 – 3 Wright, two unknown
Romford: J.H.S.Pitt(goal);H.W.Palmer,W.J.Reid(backs);L.E.Clark,C.Couzens(half-backs); W.Wright,
A.D.Cornell(right),F.H.Thirlwall(Capt),W.D.Matthews(centres),P.M.Earle,C.S.Palmer(left)(forwards).

20 Nov Frdly Away Brentwood 1 – 3 Scorer unknown
Romford: L.E.Clark,C.Couzens,A.D.Cornell,P.M.Earle.
Remainder of team unknown.

27 Nov Frdly Away Chelmsford 3 – 0 Scorers unknown
Romford: E.Champness(goal);H.W.Palmer,W.J.Reid(backs);L.E.Clark,B.J.Smith(half-backs);
W.Wright,A.D.Cornell(right);F.H.Thirlwall(Capt),C.Gooch(centres),C.Couzens,C.H.Smith(left)(forwards).

4 Dec Frdly Home Union(Islington) 1 – 3 Scorer unknown
Romford: E.Champness(goal);H.W.Palmer,W.J.Reid(backs);L.E.Clark,A.Gooch(half-backs);
W.Wright,W.D.Matthews(right),F.H.Thirlwall(Capt),C.Clark(centres),P.M.Earle,C.S.Palmer(left)(forwards).

11 Dec Frdly Home Brentwood Grammar School 2 – 0 Thirlwall(2)
Romford: No goalkeeper;H.W.Palmer,J.J.Barnes(backs);R.H.Lyon,C.Couzens(half-backs);F.H.Thirlwall(Capt),
W.Wright,E.Champness(right),H.A.Edwards,J.Molineux(centres),A.G.Martin,C.H.Smith(left)(forwards)

18 Dec Frdly Away Gresham (South Hackney) 2 – 0 Scorers unknown
Romford: A.D.Cornell(goal);H.W.Palmer,W.J.Reid(backs);L.E.Clark(Capt),B.J.Smith(half-backs); W.Wright,C.Couzens(right),C.S.Palmer,W.D.Matthews(centres),P.M.Earle,J.H.S.Pitt(left)(forwards).

27 Dec Frdly Home Mr.H.Shadwell Select (Wstow) 13 – 0 Scorers unknown
Romford: No goalkeeper;H.W.Palmer,F.D.R.Clark(backs);W.J.Reid,C.Couzens(half-backs); L.E.Clark(Capt), C.Clark(right),P.M.Earle,C.S.Palmer,W.D.Matthews(centres),W.Wright,A.D.Cornell(left)(forwards).

1 Jan Frdly Away Excelsior (Clapton) 5 – 0 P.M.Earle(3)unknown(2)
Romford: No goalkeeper;W.J.Reid,B.J.Smith(backs);J.Elms,J.H.S.Pitt(half-backs); L.E.Clark(Capt),C.Clark(right),R.A.Clark,P.M.Earle,W.D.Matthews(cantres),C.S.Palmer,H.Reid(left)(forwards).

8 Jan Frdly Away St.Barts Hospital 3 – 0 Scorers unknown
Romford: J.H.S.Pitt(goal);B.J.Smith,W.J.Reid(backs);W.Eaton,C.S.Palmer(half-backs); L.E.Clark(Capt),M.Roberts(right),P.M.Earle,W.D.Matthews(centres),W.Wright,A.D.Cornell(left)(forwards).

12 Feb FAC3R Home Reading Abbey 2 – 0 A scrimmage,Cornell
Romford: E.Champness(goal);H.W.Palmer,J.Elms(backs);L.E.Clark(Capt),W.J.Reid,E.P.Barnes(half-backs); W.Wright,A.D.Cornell(right),P.M.Earle(centre),C.Clark,C.S.Palmer(left)(forwards).

19 Feb FAC4R Home Great Marlow 2 – 1 Cornell(2)
Romford: E.Champness(goal);H.W.Palmer,E.P.Barnes(backs);L.E.Clark,W.J.Reid,C.Couzens(half-backs); W.Wright,A.D.Cornell(right),F.H.Thirlwall(Capt)(centre),P.M.Earle,C.S.Palmer(left)(forwards).

26 Feb Frdly Home Chelmsford 7 – 0 Scorers unknown
Romford: No goalkeeper;H.W.Palmer,B.J.Smith(backs);W.J.Reid,E.P.Barnes(half-backs); W.Wright, J.Elms(right),L.E.Clark(Capt),G.Garnett,W.D.Matthews(centres);C.S.Palmer,P.M.Earle(left)(forwards).

5 Mar FACQF Away Darwen 0 – 15
Darwen: Broughton(goal);Brindle,Holden(backs);Fish,Duxbury,Moorhouse(half-backs); Marshall,Rostron,Mellow,Bury,Kirkham(forwards).
Romford: E.Champness(goal);H.W.Palmer,E.P.Barnes(backs);L.E.Clark,C.Couzens,W.J.Reid(half-backs) P.M.Earle,C.S.Palmer,A.D.Cornell,W.Wright,M.Roberts(forwards).
Umpires: Messrs.W.T.Walsh and C.Clark. Referee: Councillor J.Thomas of Stoke.

12 Mar Frdly Home Union(Islington) 2 – 0 Rogers(o.g),Matthews
Romford: P.M.Earle(goal);H.W.Palmer,B.J.Smith(backs);E.J.Barnes,C.Couzens(half-backs); W.Wright,A.D.Cornell(right),W.D.Matthews,R.A.Clark(centres),E.Champness,C.S.Palmer(left)(forwards).

Reading Minsters asked Romford if they would be willing to play the Association Cup tie on a neutral ground at Ealing. Romford readily agreed.

23 Oct Thirlwell's Cup Team 5 – 0 L.E. Clark's Members' Fifteen

On this date Romford were originally scheduled to play Excelsior (of Clapton), who failed to excel themselves as they didn't arrive. Not to disappoint the crowd, Mr Thirlwall suggested that he captain his Cup team against a team of fifteen (to make a match of it!) assembled from players and supporters alike, selected and captained by Mr L.E. Clark.

Season 1880 – 81

SUMMARY OF RESULTS OBTAINED SEASON 1880 – 81

					Goals	
	P	W	D	L	For	Ag
Friendly Matches	15	9	3	3	49	14
Inter-Club game	1	1	0	0	5	0
F.A.Challenge Cup	4	2	1	1	5	17
Total	20	12	4	4	59	31
2nd April Press Report	22	12	4	6	61	35
AGM Report	21	11	4	6	n/k	n/k

CUP RESULTS SEASON 1880 – 81

F.A. Challenge Cup

Final: Carthusians 3 Old Etonians 0

Romford's progress: 1st Round	Away	Reading Minster	1 – 1
Replay	Home	Reading Minster scratched	
2nd Round			Bye
3rd Round	Home	Reading Abbey	2 – 0
4th Round	Home	Great Marlow	2 – 1
5th Round	Away	Darwen	0 – 15

First Team Appearances Season 1880 – 81

E.P.Barnes	5	J.J.Barnes	1	E.Champness	10	R.A.Clark	4
C.Clark	4	F.D.R.Clark	1	L.E.Clark	15	A.D.Cornell	11
C.Couzens	12	P.M.Earle	13	W.Eaton	1	H.J.Edwards	3
J.Elms	3	G.Garnett	2	A.Gooch	1	C.Gooch	1
Harding	1	R.H.Lyon	2	A.G.Martin	3	W.D.Matthews	11
J.Molineaux	3	C.S.Palmer	15	H.W.Palmer	15	J.H.S.Pitt	5
H.Reid	2	W.J.Reid	15	C.Reynolds	2	M.Roberts	2
B.J.Smith	6	C.H.Smith	3	F.H.Thirlwall	9	W.Wright	17
Total	201						

Due to the lack of some information for the away game with Brentwood, players other than those named could have made an appearance in the first team during the season, and the above played an extra game.

First Team Goal Scorers Season 1880 – 81

It is regretted that due to the lack of information in press reports, goal scorers are unknown for a large number of matches and it is not possible to compile a comprehensive summary of the goal scorers for the year.

RESERVE TEAM

Match Details

11 Dec Frdly Away St. Barts. Hospital Reserves 1 – 2 Scorer unknown
Romford: R.A.Clark;H.Reid,L.E.Clark(Capt),G.Guyatt,W.D.Matthews,W.J.Reid, E.Garnett,J.H.S.Pitt(?in goal), C.S.Palmer,C.Reynolds.

8 Jan Frdly Home Rochford Hundred Club 0 – 2
Romford: E.Hammond(goal);E.Champness(Capt),J.Elms(backs);C.H.Smith,C.Couzens(half-backs); R.A.Clark,H.Reid(right),G.Guyatt,G.Garnett(centres);E.Reynolds,A.G.Martin(left)(forwards).

These matches are the only details to hand of reserve team games during the season.

Post-Season Summary   Season 1880 – 81

Romford commenced their season on 2nd October when they travelled to Tottenham to play Pilgrims. Towards half-time Clifford Clark placed the ball between the posts, but the umpires disallowed the point. Romford did succeed through William Wright in scoring before the half-time whistle, but the Pilgrims levelled matters in the second period. The game was considerably interrupted by a storm. A week later Romford were defeated at Dreadnought by three goals to nil, again in most unfavourable weather. This was followed by an easy win against Brentwood Grammar School, by five goals to nil.

October ended with the eagerly awaited F.A. Cup tie with Reading Minster, who sent a telegram asking if Romford would consider playing on a neutral venue at Ealing. Romford readily agreed. Due to darkness setting in early, the match was curtailed to an hour and resulted in a 1-1 draw. The necessary replay never took place as Reading were unable to raise a team on the scheduled day and Romford went into the 2nd round by virtue of a default and were then lucky enough to receive a bye into the 3rd round.

Reverting back to friendly action, Romford then had two drawn games against Chigwell Grammar School and St. Bartholomew's Hospital. A week later Romford met with a 3-1 defeat away to local rivals Brentwood. At half-time the home team led by two goals to one and the second half saw attacks by both teams until two or three minutes from the end. Amidst cries of 'Off side!' from the Romford men, the ball was carried down to the visitors' goal, and kicked through by Growse. It should be added that for some time at the beginning and towards the close of the game Romford played a man short, Thirlwall, the captain, being absent! No reason has been found for his absence.

On 27th November, a 3-0 victory over Chelmsford was followed a week later by a 3-1 defeat at the hands of Union of Islington, before Romford struck a purple patch. Eight successive victories were recorded, with 36 goals scored and only one conceded. In the first of these, against Brentwood Grammar School, Romford played with only ten men and no one in goal! The most prominent victory was against Mr. H.Shadwell's Select from Walthamstow, who arrived in the town like lambs to the slaughter. In a very one-sided game Romford scored 13 and could have had many more. (Against Excelsior, the home team were a man short so Romford's reserve, Guyatt, filled the vacancy. For some reason play lasted only 40 minutes with Romford already five goals to the good).

On 12th February came the long awaited third round of the F.A.Cup. Romford were at home to Reading Abbey 'in the presence of a large concourse of spectators'. With the visitors playing well together Romford were hard pressed for twenty minutes, but they woke up and put on a spurt and the ball was continually in the Abbey half. Just before half time the home team secured a goal from a scrimmage 'amidst a storm of applause'. Before the call of time Arthur Cornell, who was in splendid form, sent the ball flying between the posts and Romford were into the fourth round.

Great Marlow, a team with a well established reputation, were Romford's visitors the following week. A large number of spectators attended the match to see if the locals could progress to the next round. The game was played at a fast pace, and Romford were a goal behind after twenty minutes through Lennon. Thereafter the pace increased and amidst great excitement Romford secured two second half goals through the efforts of Arthur Cornell and proceeded into the quarter finals. Romford celebrated their success by defeating county rivals Chelmsford by seven goals to nil the following Saturday. Unfortunately it is not known who scored the goals.

The eight-match winning streak ended in an abrupt fashion. In the quarter final of the F.A. Cup Romford were drawn against the powerful Lancashire side Darwen, who offered to pay Romford's expenses if they would agree to play the match at Darwen. Romford accepted the offer and travelled northwards on Friday 4th March, with the match taking place at 9.15 (yes, 9.15 am!) the following morning. 3,000 spectators were present, with the ground in bad condition and a very strong breeze.

Alas, the burden of travelling the long distance, and the home club having a large squad from which to choose their team, proved too much for luckless Romford, who found themselves twelve goals to nil behind at the interval. With the wind now in their favour Romford fared a little better, but conceded a further three goals in the second half. Fifteen nil, plus five others disallowed, was the final measure of the defeat. Darwen's goals were scored by Kirkham(4), Marshall(4), Mellor(3), Rostron(4). The Romford team, however, had done the town proud by reaching such an advanced stage in the competition. In the semi-final Darwen lost to Old Carthusians 1-4 at Kennington Oval. Romford wound up the season with a fine 2-0 home victory over their strong rivals, Union, and thus completed an enjoyable and successful year.

Annual General Meeting
(as reported in the *Essex Times,* Wednesday 20th July 1881)

On Saturday evening last, July 16th the annual general meeting of the Romford Football Club was held at the White Hart Hotel, when about 20 members sat down to enjoy the good things provided for them by Mr. Fox. The chair was taken by Mr. Thirlwall, and the vice-chair by Mr.Cliff. Clark. There was also present – Messrs. H.Palmer, C.Palmer, E.Champness, G.Bull, Saville, H.Reid, W.H.Fox, W.D. Matthews, G.A.Smith, R.A.Clark, and others.

After the usual loyal toasts had been duly given and responded to, the vice-chairman proposed the "Healths of the Officers of the Club." coupled with the name of the captain (Mr.Thirlwall), the vice-captain (Mr.L.E.Clark) and the secretary (Mr.H.Palmer). He observed that they could not find a better captain or a more energetic secretary. A better secretary was not to be found in the County of Essex, or a club that was managed in a better manner.

The Chairman briefly acknowledged the toast, as did Mr. Clark, after which, Mr.Palmer read the annual statement, which showed that the receipts amounted to £93.10s.1d., including £4.0s.01d brought over from the previous year. The expenses were £89.10s.1d. thus leaving a balance of over £4 to the good, when the outstanding subscriptions have been gathered in. During the year the club had played 21 matches of which four were withdrawn, six lost, and eleven won. He then read the following summary of each man's number during the matches:- W.Wright, 18; L.E.Clark, W.Reid, and C.Palmer, 17 each; H.Palmer, 15; P.M.Earle and C.Couzens, 14; W.D. Matthews, 13; A.Cornell and E.Champness, 12; F.H.Thirlwall, 10; B.Smith and J.Pitt, 6; C.Clark, R.A.Clark, A.Martin and C.P.Barnes 5 each; which, with other small numbers, brought the total up to 230. (Loud applause). The Secretary apologised for being so inattentive during the past season, but hoped to be more diligent during the coming one….

The Vice-chairman next gave "Success to the town and trade of Romford," coupling with it the name of Mr.H.Fox. He remarked that when the toast was first given to him for proposition, he did not see what the Football Club had to do with the town and trade of Romford, and yet on second consideration he asked them whether the Football Club would be there were there no trade in the town of Romford. For that reason he thought there would be a great interest in connection with the two interests. Mr.Fox in responding said he regretted to say that during the last six months the trade of Romford had been under a considerable cloud in consequence of the depression of agriculture, and the closing of the market; but they were now in hopes of having a good harvest, whilst they had the satisfaction of knowing their market was re-opened and would be re-instated in its former position. He hoped in future that the trade of the town would not fall off, but would go on flourishing and prospering. (Hear, hear). He thanked them for the honour they had done him in coupling his name with the toast and for the manner in which it had been received.

The Vice-Chairman gave "The health of the visitors," and coupled with it the name of Mr.J.Bull, who very briefly acknowledged the compliment, and said he hoped that if he was spared and had the honour of attending the anniversary next year it would be in the character of a member and not a visitor. (Hear, hear, and loud cheers). "The health of the Press" having been given, The Chairman proposed in highly eulogistic terms "the healths of Mr. and Mrs. W.H.Fox" with thanks for the most excellent dinner they had provided for them. It was one of the best he remembered ever sitting down to. (Cheers). Mr. Fox briefly responded to the toast, and remarked that it had given him and Mrs. Fox very great pleasure to know that they had given satisfaction to such a distinguished company. Mr.G.A.Smith gave "The health of the ladies," coupled with the name of Mr.W.Reid, who acknowledged the compliment in a humorous manner. The usual vote of thanks to the Chairman brought the proceedings to a close at a comparatively early hour. During the evening some good songs were given by Messrs. Saville, Fox, Reid, C.Clark, and Matthews, Mr. Saville officiating at the piano.

General Meeting

(As reported in the *Essex Times*, Wednesday 14th September 1881)

Note: As an Annual General Meeting had of course taken place the previous July, this must have been a General Meeting in preparation for the coming season, probably generated by the recent death of the club's President Mr David McIntosh.

ROMFORD FOOTBALL CLUB. – the annual meeting of this club was held at the White Hart Hotel on Friday evening 9th Sept 1881, Mr.R.H.Lyon presiding. The election of officers for the ensuing year was proceeded with. General regret was expressed at the death of Mr.D.McIntosh, the late president, and a resolution embodying this feeling was entered upon the minutes. Mr.R.G.Price was then elected president for the ensuing year, and the vice-presidents were re-elected. Mr.F.H. Thirlwall having resigned the post of captain through having left the town, Mr.L.E. Clark was elected in his place, and Mr. Thirlwall was appointed vice-captain. Mr.H.W. Palmer was re-elected hon.secretary, and thanks were accorded him for his past services. The members of the Committee were also re-elected. The match list was gone through and approved. About 26 matches have been arranged and all the days are full except four. The club, which is in a most satisfactory state as regards members and finances, will commence play on the 1st October.

Season 1881 – 82

ROMFORD FOOTBALL CLUB

President: Mr.R.G.Price **Hon.Secretary and Treasurer:** Mr.H.W.Palmer

Captain: Mr.L.E.Clark **Vice-Captain:** Mr.F.H.Thirlwall

Headquarters: White Hart Hotel, Romford **Ground:** The Meadow, Great Mawneys, Romford

Romford continued to play their home games at the Great Mawneys ground for this season. In October an area of six acres of land abutting Victoria Road (opposite a shop recently opened by Mr. Dart) was put aside for a football ground. A newspaper announcement stated: 'Turf to be laid at once! A bicycle track will also be comprised within the grounds. The work is in the hands of gentlemen who may be relied upon to carry it well through!' It is uncertain when this was completed, but this ground became known as the Romford Recreation Ground.

COMPETITIONS ENTERED

F.A. Challenge Cup
Friendly Matches

Trial Match

24 Sept Earle's Select 4 Wright Select 3
No details available of the team line-ups or goal scorers.

Match details

1 Oct Frdly Home Mosquitoes (Dulwich) 1 – 4 Scorer unknown
Romford: Arthur D.Cornell(goal);H.W.Palmer,W.J.Reid(backs);C.H.Smith,C.Couzens(half-backs);
W.Wright,W.D.Matthews(right),P.M.Earle,C.S.Palmer(Centre),S.W.Skilton,R.A.Clark(left)(forwards)

8 Oct Frdly Away Pilgrims (Tottenham) 2 – 0 Scorers unknown
Romford: F.C.Yardley(goal);C.Couzens,H.W.Palmer(backs);W.J.Reid,C.H.Smith,E.Lloyd(half-backs);
W.Wright,W.D.Matthews(right),A.G.Martin(centre),P.M.Earle,C.Clark(left)(forwards).

15 Oct FAC1R Home Clapham Rangers w/o

22 Oct Frdly Home Dreadnought (West Ham) 0 – 0
Romford: E.Champness(goal); C.Witham,F.D.R.Clark(backs);C.Couzens,H.W.Palmer(half-backs);
W.Wright, W.D.Matthews(right), G.Guyatt,G.Barnes(centre),P.M.Earle,C.Clark(left)(forwards).

29 Oct Frdly Home Union (Islington) 0 – 1
Romford: E.Champness(goal);B.J.Smith,H.W.Palmer(backs);C.Couzens,F.H.Thirlwall(half-backs);
W.Wright,C.S.Palmer(right),W.D.Matthews, G.Barnes(centre),P.M.Earle,A.G.Martin(left)(forwards).

5 Nov Frdly Home St.Barts Hospital 1st XI 1 – 1 Smith
Romford: No goalkeeper;W.J.Reid,H.W.Palmer(backs);C.H.Smith,C.Couzens,L.E.Clark(Capt)(half-backs);
W.Wright,A.G.Martin(right),C.S.Palmer(centre),P.M.Earle,W.D.Matthews(left)(forwards).

12 Nov Frdly Away Chigwell Grammar School 1 – 0 Scorer unknown
Romford: G.Garnett(goal);L.E.Clark,W.D.Matthews(backs);W.J.Reid,C.H.Smith(half-backs);
R.H.Lyon,G.Barnes,R.A.Clark,P.M.Earle,G.G.Hunt,W.Wright(forwards).

19 Nov Frdly Away Brentwood 1 – 1 Wright
Romford: E.Champness(goal);A.D.Cornell,H.W.Palmer(backs);L.E.Clark(Capt),C.Couzens(half-backs);
P.M.Earle,A.G.Martin,C.Clark,G.G.Hunt,W.Wright,J.A.Macfarlane(forwards).

26 Nov Frdly Home Chelmsford 1 – 1 Scorer unknown
Romford: -.B.J.Smith(goal);A.D.Cornell,W.J.Reid,(backs);C.Couzens,W.D.Matthews(half-backs);
W.Wright,G.Barnes,P.M.Earle,A.G.Martin,L.E.Clark(Capt),C.S.Palmer(forwards).

3 Dec FAC2R Away Reading Minster 1 – 3 Wright
Romford: E.Champness(goal);H.W.Palmer,A.D.Cornell(backs);C.Couzens,L.E.Clark(Capt)(half-backs);
P.M.Earle, A.G.Martin,M.Roberts,W.D.Matthews,W.Wright,C.S.Palmer(forwards).

10 Dec Frdly Away Finchley 2 – 1 Scorers unknown
Romford:
Team details unknown

17 Dec Frdly Home Foxes(Edmonton) 2 – 0 Scorers unknown
Romford: A.D.Cornell(goal);H.W.Palmer(back);C.Couzens,W.L.Hitchcock(half-backs);
P.M.Earle,W.Wright,J.A.Macfarlane,A.G.Martin,S.W.Skilton,C.S.Palmer(forwards).

26 Dec Frdly Home Hornchurch 10 – 0 Scorers unknown
Romford:
Team details unknown

31 Dec Frdly Away Chelmsford 4 – 1 Scorers unknown
Romford:
Team details unknown

7 Jan Frdly Away Dreadnought (West Ham) 1 – 1

14 Jan Frdly Home Brentwood 2 – 1 Wright, L.E.Clark
Romford: B.J.Smith(goal);G.R.Hitchcock,H.W.Palmer(backs);C.Couzens,W.L.Hitchcock(half-backs);
W.Wright,A.D.Cornell(right),L.E.Clark(Capt),C.Clifford(centre),P.M.Earle,J.A.Macfarlane(forwards).

21 Jan Frdly Away# St. Bart's Hospital 0 – 2
Romford: A.Cornell;H.W.Palmer,G.E.Hitchcock;C.Couzens,W.J.Reid;
W.Wright,P.M.Earle,C.S.Palmer,C.H.Smith,S.W.Skilton,A.G.Martin.

28 Jan Frdly Home Union (Islington) 1 – 1 Scorer unknown
Romford: B.J.Smith(goal);H.W.Palmer,G.R.Hitchcock(backs);C.Couzens,W.D.Matthews(half-backs);
W.Wright,S.W.Skilton(right),C.Clark,C.S.Palmer(centres),P.M.Earle,A.G.Martin(left)(forwards). Umpire: E.Champness.

4 Feb Frdly Away Brentwood Grammar School 0 – 3

25 Feb Frdly Away Dulwich 0 – 1
Romford:
Team details unknown

4 Mar Frdly Home Brentwood Grammar School 2 – 0 Scorers unknown
Romford:
Team details unknown

18 Mar Frdly Away Foxes (Edmonton) 0 – 2
Romford:
Team details unknown

At the Spotted Dog, Clapton

SUMMARY OF RESULTS OBTAINED SEASON 1881 – 82

	P	W	D	L	Goals For	Goals Ag
First Team Friendlies	20	8	6	6	31	21
F.A. Challenge Cup	1	0	0	1	1	3
Total	21	8	6	7	32	24
AGM Report	24	9	6	9	34	32

CUP RESULTS SEASON 1881 – 82

F.A. Challenge Cup

Final: Old Etonians 1 Blackburn Rovers 0

Romford's progress: 1st Round Home Clapham Rangers w/o
2nd Round Away Reading Minster 1 – 3

First Team Appearances Season 1881 – 82

G.Barnes	4	E.Champness	4	R.A.Clark	2	C.Clark	4
F.D.R.Clark	1	L.E.Clark	6	C.Clifford	1	A.D.Cornell	7
C.Couzens	12	P.M.Earle	13	G.Garnett	1	G.Guyatt	1
G.E.Hitchcock	3	W.L.Hitchcock	2	G.G.Hunt	2	E.Lloyd	1
R.H.Lyon	1	J.A.Macfarlane	3	A.G.Martin	9	W.D.Matthews	9
C.S.Palmer	8	H.W.Palmer	11	W.J.Reid	6	M.Roberts	1
S.W.Skilton	4	B.J.Smith	4	C.H.Smith	5	F.H.Thirlwall	1
C.Witham	1	W.Wright	13	F.C.Yardley	1	Total	141

The above players are known to have played in the first team during the season, but due to the lack of many line-ups towards the end of the season the above summary is far from complete, and others may have played.

First Team Goal Scorers Season 1881 – 82

Again, it is regretted that due to the lack of information in press reports it is not possible to compile a summary of the goal scorers for the year.

RESERVE TEAM

Match details

12 Nov Frdly Home St. Barts Hospital 2nd XI 0 – 1
Romford Reserves: B.J.Smith(goal);A.D.Cornell,C.Charles(backs);A.G.Martin,C.Couzens(half-backs); C.S.Palmer,A.Elms,E.Champness,C.Guyatt,G.Guyatt,W.Knight(forwards).

26 Nov Frdly Away Hornchurch# 2 – 0 Scorers unknown
Romford Reserves: G.Guyatt(goal);J.Adams,H.W.Palmer, plus two substitutes(defence); W.Knight,C.H.Smith,R.A.Clark,T.K.Gayford,C.Couzens(forwards).

31 Dec Frdly Home Buffaloes 0 – 0
Romford:
Team details unknown

4 Feb Frdly Away Hornchurch 10 – 0
\# This was the first-ever game for the Hornchurch club.

Post-Season Summary Season 1881 – 82

Romford had quite a setback when they opened the season as the Mosquitoes stung them with a four goal to one defeat at Romford. It was reported that the Romford team were sadly out of condition, and but for the outstanding goalkeeping by Arthur Cornell, the defeat would have been much heavier.

A week later, Romford were leading the Pilgrims 2-0 when the match ended after an hour due to bad weather. On 15th October Romford were due to play Rangers (Clapham) in the F.A. Cup, but that very morning Harry Palmer, the hon.secretary of the Romford club, received a telegram to the effect that Rangers, being unable to bring their cup team, had withdrawn, so Romford received a bye into the next round.

The following week Romford entertained Dreadnought and a goalless draw was the result. A week later Romford were defeated 1-0 by the powerful Union of Islington team. On 5th November Romford's third home game in a row, against St. Bartholomew's Hospital, ended in a one all stalemate. A week later Romford travelled to Chigwell Grammar School and earned a one goal to nil victory.

On 19th November,there was a thrilling one all draw against local rivals Brentwood, but the game finished ten minutes early due to bad light. Romford then entertained Chelmsford with a weakened team, three men having to be picked up on the ground to complete the line-up. (Romford were the home team, so where were the missing players?) Thankfully, a creditable one all draw was earned.

On 3rd December Romford played Reading Minster in the F.A Cup second round. It was reported that 'Minster scored first and Wright equalised for Romford and Martin after a good run the length of the field was within six feet of goal when he was caught by the arm and pulled down as he was about to shoot for goal'.

Romford claimed a foul, but this was turned down. The Minster's second goal, just before half-time, went in off the crossbar! (Romford were continuing at their own ground to use tapes, rather than crossbars). In the second half Romford pinned their opponents in their own half for long periods. Further attempts to equalize were thwarted by the referee, especially when Percy Earle was about to shoot and had his legs kicked from beneath him but no free kick was given. The decisions by the referee led to Romford considering the question of an appeal after a 3-1 defeat.

A week later, owing to a serious accident on the Great Northern Railway at Canonbury, the Romford men did not reach Finchley until four o'clock and the play therefore was of short duration. Romford played with only eight men and Finchley with seven, and a surprisingly low scoring game ended 2-1 in Romford's favour. On 17th December, in the match at home to Foxes, play was interrupted for a time by a severe thunderstorm. Once more Romford played with a man short, and Foxes had only nine men!

Then came a 10-0 home win over Hornchurch followed by a fine 4-1 victory over Chelmsford (four wins in a row!) and then a one all draw against Dreadnought. On 14th January Romford entertained Brentwood in the return fixture and gained a fine two goal to one victory. A week later, away to St. Bartholomew's Hospital, Romford were beaten by two goals to nil. You could say it was a bitter pill for them to swallow.

On 28th January Romford gained a fine draw in the return game at home to Union. A week later the team played away to Brentwood Grammar School with a depleted team due to some players being unable to find their way to the ground because of the thick fog that had descended over the area, and suffered a 3-0 defeat. On the same day the Romford reserve team, led by Arthur Cornell, hammered Hornchurch by ten goals to nil. It appears that some of them were first team players who had decided that it would be easier to get to Hornchurch in the foggy conditions rather than Brentwood.

At a meeting of the club committee on Saturday evening, 18th February, at the White Hart Hotel, chaired by Fred Clark, it was decided to join the London Football Association and Harry W. Palmer, hon. secretary, was appointed to represent the club at a meeting the following Monday evening.

A week later in the away defeat at Dulwich the match was described as 'played in boisterous weather!' On 4th March, Romford entertained Brentwood Grammar School in a return game and recorded a two goal to nil victory when play ended after one hour. Again Romford played a man short until the latter part of the game!

Two weeks later the curtain came down on the season when Romford lost two goals to nil at Foxes of Edmonton, and the press report stated 'The capital passing of the Foxes gave them victory. Two Romford men failed to put in an appearance and two substitutes had to be secured on the ground!' These two missing players (J.A.Macfarlane and Percy Earle) both happened to be playing for Union at Upton Park.

Annual General Meeting
(as reported in the *Essex Times,* Wednesday 14th June 1882)

ROMFORD FOOTBALL CLUB. – The annual general meeting of the members of the above club was held at headquarters, the White Hart Hotel, on Friday evening, June 9th, when the following members were present: - Messrs. L.E. Clark(capt), W.J.Reid, R. H. Lyon, W. D. Matthews, C. Clark, G. Barnes, E. Champness,B. J. Smith, C.S.Palmer, A.G.Martin, and H. W. Palmer (hon. sec). –

The report detailing the results of last season's play was read by the Secretary, and showed that out of the 29 matches which had been arranged 24 were played, nine of which were lost, a like number were won, six were drawn, while for sufficient reasons, five others had not been played. Goals lost, 32; goals won 34. – The Secretary remarked by way of explaining what he considered a not very glowing result of the year's play that the club last year was in a very healthy state in point of playing members. And as with one or two exceptions the club had arranged for playing only one match per week, it had been necessary to vary the teams in order to give all members an opportunity of playing. Thus it happened that the cream of the club had had but few chances of meeting together, to which was to be attributed the main cause of so many lost laurels. He urged the club to endeavour to put on a better figure next year, and to that end suggested that it play two elevens on as many Saturdays as might be practicable, which arrangement, whilst it would enable the first eleven to be kept well together, would permit every member to enjoy a due share of the season's play. Of course such an alteration would involve increased outlay, travelling expenses being paid by the club, but to meet that he would suggest that the subscriptions be raised from 5s. to 7s.6d. This was unanimously resolved upon. The financial statement showed that when a few outstanding subscriptions should be obtained there would be a small balance to the credit of the club. –

Mr. G. Barnes called attention to the inconvenience caused by members who having promised to play did not put in an appearance, and he instanced the match between Romford and St. Alban's. With a view to putting an end to this inconvenience in future it was resolved that members who, did not put in an appearance, should be fined 2s.6d.

It was further resolved that all members should appear in club colours, and that the dress should be altered from blue and black jerseys to blue and black shirts. – The election of officers were then proceeded with, the only alteration made being that in which Mr. A. G. Martin succeeds Mr. H. W. Palmer as hon. sec. and treasurer, the latter having been elected as vice-captain.

Ordinary Meeting
(as reported in the *Essex Times,* Wednesday 13th September 1882)

At a meeting of the Romford Football Club on Saturday evening, 9th September, held at the White Hart Hotel, Mr. L. E. Clark in the chair, a list of 31 matches arranged by the secretary for the coming season was approved. It was resolved that in consequence of the unbecoming behaviour of a number of the rough element on the ground last season that in future only members and their friends should be admitted.

The circular issued by Mr. J. L. Nickisson as to the proposed match between North and South Essex preliminary to the formation of a county association was read, but as the club had fixed their opening match, general meeting, and annual dinner on that day, it was after considerable discussion resolved not to send the names of any players to represent the Romford Club in that match.

The Essex County Football Association is formed

30th September 1882 - Members of Essex Football Clubs met at the White Hart Hotel, Chelmsford, to form Essex County Football Association. Mr.A.C.Durrant (Chelmsford F.C.) Chairman of the meeting, made the proposal, and Mr.J.L.Nickisson (Brentwood F.C.) seconded the motion, which was approved unanimously. Romford were represented by Mr.P.M.Earle.
(The *Essex Times,* Wednesday 4th October 1882)

Cross bars were now compulsory.

21 Nov Mr.H.W.Palmer was appointed to represent Romford at Essex County F.A. Meetings.

THE WHITE HART TAP
IND. COOPE & CO.'S ALES
Chester Dawson
THE OLD WHITE HART AT ROMFORD, WHICH IS ABOUT TO BE DEMOLISHED.

An 1890s drawing of the White Hart Hotel, Romford, the Club's headquarters for many years
Havering Libraries - Local Studies

Season 1882 – 83

ROMFORD FOOTBALL CLUB

President: Mr.R.G.Price **Hon.Secretary:** Mr.A.G.Martin

Captain: Mr.L.E.Clark **Vice-Captain:** Mr.H.W.Palmer

Essex County Representative: Mr.H.W.Palmer

Headquarters: White Hart Hotel, Romford **Ground:** The Meadow, Great Mawneys, Romford

COMPETITIONS ENTERED

F.A. Challenge Cup
Friendly Matches

Trial Matches

30 Sept Clark Select 0 Palmer Select 5
Clarke Select: W.H.Esnan;C.Couzens,W.J.Reid;A.Couzens,L.E.Clark,W.Wright;
H.Carter,C.Clark,G.Guyatt,C.H.Smith,O.J.Daldy.

Palmer Select: E.Champness;H.W.Palmer,A.Cornell;B.J.Smith,R.Carter,A.G.Martin;
C.S.Palmer,R.A.Clark,A.Hinds,E.J.Carter,S.W.Skilton.

6 Jan C.Clark Select 2 Secretary Select 3
Unfortunately no scorers or team details have come to hand.

3 Feb Hornchurch 1 Romford & Chelmsford United Team 3
Romford & Chelmsford: G.A.Smith;H.W.Palmer,A.N.Other;A.Rayner,C.Couzens,A.Couzens;
C.S.Palmer,A.G.Martin,J.Wright,Taylor(Capt),A.N.Other.

Match Details

7 Oct Frdly Home Olympic (Upton Park) 1 – 1 Earle
Romford: A.D.Cornell;H.W.Palmer;C.Couzens,L.E.Clark(Capt);
P.M.Earle,W.Wright,F.H.Thirlwall,C.Clark,C.S.Palmer,S.W.Skilton,A.G.Martin.

14 Oct Frdly Home Excelsior (West Ham) 4 – 1 Martin(2),Skilton,Thirlwall
Romford: E.Carter;H.W.Palmer(Capt),A.D.Cornell;C.Couzens,A.Cornell.Jnr.;
W.Wright;F.H.Thirlwall,C.Clark,S.W.Skilton,A.G.Martin,R.Oliver.

21 Oct FAC1R Away Eton Ramblers 2 – 6 C.Clark(2)
Romford: G.A.Smith;H.W.Palmer(Capt),A.D.Cornell;C.Couzens,A.G.Martin;
P.M.Earle, W.Wright F.H.Thirlwall,C.Clark S.W.Skilton,C.S.Palmer.

4 Nov Frdly Away Pilgrims (Tottenham) 0 – 4
Romford: A.D.Cornell;H.W.Palmer(Capt),B.J.Smith;C.Couzens,A.Couzens;
C.Clark,R.A.Clark,C.S.Palmer,W.Wright,S.W.Skilton,A.G.Martin

11 Nov Frdly Home St.Brides 3 – 0 Wright(2),Lyon
Romford: R.H.Lyon;H.W.Palmer,L.E.Clark(Capt);C.Couzens,A.Cornell Jnr.;
C.Clark,E.Champness,D.Cobb,P.M.Earle,S.W.Skilton,W.Wright.

25 Nov Frdly Home Chelmsford 3 – 0 C.S.Palmer(2)Wright
Romford: E.Champness;H.W.Palmer,L.E.Clark(Capt);C.Couzens,F.H.Thirlwall;
P.M.Earle,W.Wright;C.Clark,C.S.Palmer,S.W.Skilton,A.G.Martin.

2 Dec Frdly Home Buckhurst Hill 7 – 1 C.Clark(3)C.S.Palmer(2)Earle,Skilton
Romford: L.E.Clark(Capt);H.W.Palmer;W.D.Matthews,E.Champness,C.Couzens;
C.Clark,C.S.Palmer,P.M.Earle,W.Wright,S.W.Skilton,A.G.Martin.

9 Dec Frdly Home Clapton 1 – 0 C.Clark
Romford: C.H.Smith;H.W.Palmer(Capt),B.J.Smith;C.Couzens,E.Champness;
C.Clark,C.S.Palmer,S.W.Skilton,A.G.Martin,D.Cobb,F.Gilbey.

16 Dec Frdly Away Dreadnought (West Ham) 0 – 3
Romford: L.E.Clark(Capt);H.W.Palmer,C.Couzens,D.Cobb,
P.M.Earle,A.G.Martin,C.S.Palmer,S.W.Skilton plus three subs.

23 Dec Frdly Away Buckhurst Hill 3 – 0 C.Clark,Skilton,A.Couzens
Romford: E.Champness;H.W.Palmer(Capt),C.Hitchcock;C.Couzens,G.E.Hitchcock;
R.A.Clark,C.Clark,J.Gibson,A.Hinds,S.W.Skilton,W.Wright.

26 Dec* Frdly Home Clapton 11.30a.m. 3 – 0 C.S.Palmer(2),Cobb
Romford: H.W.Palmer(Capt),C.Hitchcock,G.E.Hitchcock,C.Couzens,C.S.Palmer, G.A.Smith,C.Clark,W.Wright,S.W.Skilton,D.Cobb,A.G.Martin,

26 Dec* Frdly Home Ilford 2.30p.m. 3 – 2 Earle(2)Wright
Romford: H.W.Palmer(Capt)C.H.Smith,C.Hitchcock,G.E.Hitchcock,C.Couzens,
C.Clark,C.S.Palmer,P.M.Earle,W.Wright,S.W.Skilton,A.G.Martin.

30 Dec Frdly Home Foxes (Edmonton) 8 – 0 Earle(4)C.S.Palmer(2)Wright(2)
Romford: H.W.Palmer(Capt);A.D.Cornell,C.Couzens,C.Clark,
P.M.Earle,C.S.Palmer,C.Hitchcock,S.W.Skilton,W.Wright plus one sub.

13 Jan Frdly Home Hornchurch 6 – 0
A.Cornell(2),C.Clark,R.A.Hitchcock, two scrimmages!
Romford: Substitute;H.W.Palmer(Capt),A.D.Cornell;C.Couzens,C.Hitchcock;
C.Clark,C.S.Palmer,R.A.Hitchcock,W.L.Hitchcock,S.W.Skilton,W.Wright.

27 Jan Frdly Home Union (Islington) 3 – 0 C.Clark,C.S.Palmer,Skilton
Romford: C.H.Smith;A.D.Cornell,H.W.Palmer;L.E.Clark,C.Couzens;
W.Wright,S.W.Skilton;C.Clark,C.S.Palmer;P.M.Earle,A.G.Martin.

17 Feb Frdly Home Excelsior (West Ham) 1 – 6 Scorer unknown
Romford: G.A.Smith;H.W.Palmer,B.J.Smith;E.Carter,T.K.Gayford;
P.M.Earle,S.W.Skilton,C.Clark,R.A.Clark,A.G.Martin,W.J.Reid.

24 Feb Frdly Away Olympic (Upton Park) 4 – 3 Goadby(2)L.E.Clark,Mansfield
Romford: A.D.Cornell;H.W.Palmer,F.Webster;C.Couzens,A.Ronald;
L.E.Clark(Capt),C.Clark,J.Goadby,H.Mansfield,S.W.Skilton,W.Wright.

3 Mar Frdly Home Dreadnought (West Ham) 2 – 1 Skilton,Thirlwall
Romford: A.D.Cornell;H.W.Palmer,F.H.Thirlwall;C.Couzens,A.Cornell.Jnr.;
P.M.Earle,S.W.Skilton;L.E.Clark(Capt),C.Clark;W.Wright,R.Oliver.

17 Mar Frdly Away Foxes (Edmonton) 1 – 4 Wright
Romford: A.D.Cornell;H.W.Palmer,W.J.Reid;C.Couzens,W.Knight;
L.E.Clark(Capt),C.Clark,A.G.Martin,C.S.Palmer,S.W.Skilton,W.Wright.

24 Mar Frdly Away Chelmsford 1 – 0 Skilton
Romford: A.D.Cornell;T.K.Gayford,B.J.Smith;C.Couzens,W.J.Reid;
E.Champness,R.A.Clark,R.A.Hitchcock,S.W.Skilton,A.G.Martin(Capt).

31 Mar Frdly Home Heron (Dulwich) Scratched on Friday
A scratch match was played between teams selected on the field. No scores or team details are to hand.

7 Apr Frdly Home Woodford Bridge 1 – 0 Scorer unknown
Romford: A.Cornell;A.D.Cornell,H.W.Palmer;L.E.Clark(Capt),C.Couzens;
S.W.Skilton,C.S.Palmer,F.H.Thirlwall,C.Clark,R.A.Clark,W.D.Matthews.

18 Apr Frdly Home Romford Brewery 2 – 1 Scorers unknown
Romford:
Team details unknown

*Note. The first team played two matches on the same day.

SUMMARY OF RESULTS OBTAINED SEASON 1882 – 83

	P	W	D	L	Goals For	Goals Ag
F.A.Challenge Cup	1	0	0	1	2	6
Friendly Matches	21	16	1	4	57	27
Reserve Team	11	5	4	2	16	13
Grand Total	33	21	5	7	75	46
AGM Report*	34	21	5	8	80	47

* This report again appears to include both first team and reserve team games, but results to hand only show a total of 33 matches with one less defeat and the goals for and against do not agree with the A.G.M. report.

CUP RESULTS SEASON 1882 – 83

F.A. Challenge Cup

Final: Blackburn Olympic 2 Old Etonians 1

Romford's progress: 1st Round Away Eton Ramblers 2 – 6

First Team Appearances Season 1882 – 83

E.Carter	2	E.Champness	6	R.A.Clark	5	C.Clark	19
L.E.Clark	10	D.Cobb	4	A.D.Cornell	12	A.Cornell Jnr.	4
A.Couzens	1	C.Couzens	20	P.M.Earle	11	T.K.Gayford	2
J.Gibson	1	F.Gilbey	1	J.Goadby	1	A.Hinds	1
C.Hitchcock	5	G.E.Hitchcock	3	R.A.Hitchcock	2	W.L.Hitchcock	1
W.Knight	1	R.H.Lyon	1	H.H.Mansfield	1	A.G.Martin	14
W.D.Matthews	2	R.Oliver	2	C.S.Palmer	14	H.W.Palmer	20
W.J.Reid	3	A.Ronald	1	S.W.Skilton	21	B.J.Smith	4
C.H.Smith	3	G.A.Smith	3	F.H.Thirlwall	6	F.Webster	1
W.Wright	16	Substitutes	5			Total	229

The above summary is incomplete due to the lack of team details for the Romford Brewery game.

First Team Goal Scorers Season 1882 – 83

C.Clark	9	C.S.Palmer	9	P.M.Earle	8	W.Wright	7
S.W.Skilton	6	A.G.Martin	2	F.H.Thirlwall	2	A.D.Cornell	2
J.Goadby	2	R.H.Lyon	1	A.Couzens	1	D.Cobb	1
R.A.Hitchcock	1	L.E.Clark	1	H.H.Mansfield	1	Unknown	6
Total	59						

At the AGM it was reported that the leading goal scorers were C.S.Palmer(14), C.Clark(13), P.M.Earle(8), W.Wright(7) and S.W.Skilton(6). It is believed that this list may have included goals scored in the trial matches.

Romford Football Club's first team photographed in the gardens of Mawneys Manor House before the match against Woodford Bridge on 7th April 1883. Some founding members appear in this picture
Havering Libraries - Local Studies

The team consists of: A.Cornell; A.D.Cornell, H.W.Palmer; L.E.Clark(Capt), C.Couzens, S.W.Skilton, C.S.Palmer, F.H.Thirlwall, C.Clark, R.A.Clark, W.D.Matthews. (Unfortunately **not** in photograph order)

RESERVE TEAM

Match details

14 Oct Frdly Away Hornchurch 1 – 2 W.J.Reid
Romford Reserves: E.Champness(Capt);G.A.Smith,H.J.Smith;W.J.Reid,H.J.Reid;
R.A.Clark,A.Couzens,F.Gilbey,A.Hinds,G.Daldy,T.K.Gayford.

21 Oct Frdly Home Olympic (Upton Park) Reserves 4 – 2
A.Clark,Cobb,Gilbey,Oliver
Romford Reserves: W.Heasman;R.J.J.Smith(Capt),A.Cornell,Jnr.;T.K.Gayford,G.Guyatt;
R.A.Clark,H.J.Reid,A.Couzens,F.Gilbey,R.Oliver,D.Cobb.

11 Nov Frdly Away Woodford Bridge Reserves 0 – 0
Romford Reserves: G.A.Smith;B.J.Smith,A.G.Martin(Capt);G.Daldy,R.Carter;
C.S.Palmer,F.Gilbey,R.A.Clark,A.Hinds,T.Reynolds,A.Couzens.

18 Nov Frdly Home Dreadnought (West Ham) Reserves 1 – 5 Scorer unknown
Romford Reserves:
Team details unknown

2 Dec Frdly Away Excelsior (West Ham) Reserves 2 – 2 Scorers unknown
Romford Reserves: G.Guyatt;B.J.Smith(Capt),T.K.Gayford;A.Cornell,Jnr.,G.Daldy;
A.Couzens,F.Gilbert,R.A.Clark,A.Hinds,D.Cobb,T.Reynolds.

16 Dec Frdly Home Excelsior (West Ham) Reserves 1 – 1 A.Couzens
Romford Reserves: E.Champness(Capt);C.Clark,A.Couzens,R.Carter,G.Daldy,
W.D.Matthews,C.H.Smith,W.Wright,R.A.Clark plus two subs.

26 Dec Frdly Home Buffaloes 10a.m. 1 – 1 Hinds
Romford Reserves: C.H.Smith;T.K.Gayford,B.J.Smith;R.Carter,G.Guyatt;
E.Champness(Capt),A.Couzens,R.A.Clark,A.Hinds,G.Daldy.

13 Jan Frdly Away Hornchurch Reserves 1 – 0 R.Carter

SUMMARY OF RESERVE TEAM RESULTS OBTAINED SEASON 1882 – 83

	P	W	D	L	Goals For	Goals Ag
All Friendly Matches	11	5	4	2	16	13

Reserve Team Appearances Season 1882 – 83

J.Bailey	1	R.Carter	6	E.Champness	6	R.A.Clark	9
C.Clark	2	L.E.Clark	1	D.Cobb	2	Alf.Cornell.Jnr.	4
A.Couzens	7	G.Daldy	6	T.K.Gayford	8	F.Gilbert	1
F.Gilbey	7	G.Guyatt	4	A.Heasman	1	A.Hinds	7
A.G.Martin	3	W.D.Matthews	3	R.Oliver	1	C.S.Palmer	2
H.J.Reid	2	W.J.Reid	1	T.Reynolds	4	B.J.Smith	6
C.H.Smith	5	G.A.Smith	2	H.J.Smith	1	R.J.J.Smith	1
F.H.Thirlwall	1	W.Wright	1	Substitutes	3	Total	108

Two matches were played with only ten men, and the team details for the home fixture with Dreadnought Reserves is not known, neither are the names of the substitutes.

Post-Season Summary Season 1882 – 83

In Romford's first match of the season, a home draw with Olympic, Thirlwall was a late arrival and the team took the field a man short for the first 15 minutes. In their F.A. Cup 1st Round tie against Eton Ramblers at Home Park, Windsor on 21st October, Romford were thrashed 6-2. On 4th November Romford were defeated 4-0 away to Pilgrims at Tottenham. A week later St. Brides made their first-ever visit to Romford, the game resulting in a 3-0 victory for the home team. William Wright was on target with two goals and Ralph Harvey Lyon got a solo effort.

A further week later Romford won 3-0 at home to Chelmsford. On 2nd December, at home to Buckhurst Hill, Romford secured a resounding 7-1 victory, Clifford Clark scoring a hat-trick. A week later Clapton played with only eight men and lost to a 40th minute goal from Clifford Clark, making it four wins on the spin for the Romfordians.

The following game, away to Dreadnought, resulted in a 3-0 defeat. Romford won their fixture away to Buckhurst Hill on 23rd December with some difficulty. We are told that the ground played exceedingly heavy! On Boxing Day Romford played three matches, the reserves starting at 10am with a home draw against Buffaloes. At 11.30 on the same ground the first team beat Clapton (who again played a man short) three nil. Then, presumably after a fine Christmas dinner, yet another game kicked off at 2.30 pm against Ilford, resulting in a 3-2 win for Romford.

On 30th December Romford, even with a man short, kept their fine goal scoring run going, when they defeated Foxes 8-0 (Earle scoring four), but it has to be said that their opponents had only eight men!

Romford's scheduled game on 6th January was cancelled as their hosts, Old Merchant Taylors, scratched the previous evening. Romford decided instead to play a 'scratch' match between teams selected by Clifford Clark and the secretary, which the latter won 3-2. A week later, at home to Hornchurch, Romford again defeated their local rivals 6-0. On 27th January the game against Union was won 3-0, but the visitors only had nine men. The game was described as 'fast considering the heavy state of the ground caused by a regular downpour, accompanied by thunder and lightning'.

The Romford and Chelmsford clubs united to play a fixture away to Hornchurch on 3rd February 1883. The combined team, comprised of the following players, C.S.Palmer, H.W.Palmer, A.G.Martin, A.Couzens, C.Couzens, J.Wright, G.A.Smith, Taylor(Capt), Rayner, plus two others, won the match by three goals to one.

On 17th February Romford were thrashed 6-1 at home to Excelsior. The following week away to Olympic they secured a well-deserved 4-3 victory.

On 3rd March Romford played the return friendly at home to Dreadnought. It was reported that 'The weather being beautifully fine a large number of visitors, which included many ladies, assembled at "Mawneys", to witness a match between the first elevens of these clubs. The game was grandly contested'. Romford had been defeated by Dreadnought earlier in the season, but now they turned the tables on their rivals by winning 2-1. The goals were scored by Thirlwall and Spencer Skilton (a son of the Rector of St Andrew's Church, Romford). A clerical influence was certainly pervading the team this season, as no fewer than four sons of the Vicar of St Edward's Church (in Romford Market Place), played for the club! They were William, Charles, Robert and George Hitchcock, sons of the Reverend William Maunder Hitchcock.

On 17th March, away to Foxes of Edmonton, Romford were well beaten 4-1. A week later Romford sent a weakened team to play at Chelmsford, but managed a 1-0 win with only ten men. The following week Heron scratched on the Friday, and a scratch game was played between two teams selected on the field. On 7th April at home against Woodford Bridge Romford won 1-0. Before the match, the members of the Romford team were photographed at their Great Mawneys ground by Mr. Whicker of Romford.

The season came to an end on the 18th April when Romford Brewery were the visitors and the home team were successful by two goals to one. The Brewery team as usual contained a fair sprinkling of Romford players!

Annual General Meeting
(as reported in the *Essex Times,* Wednesday 9th May 1883)

The annual general meeting of the club was held at the White Hart Hotel, Romford on Monday evening 7th May 1883. Mr.F.D.R.Clark was voted to the Chair, and there were present, Messrs. L.E.Clark (Captain), Cliff.Clark, R.A.Clark, E.Champness, A.D.Cornell, G.F.Daldy, T.K.Gayford, G.B.Gilbey, F.Gilbey, W.D.Matthews, A.G.Martin (Secretary), H.W.Palmer (Vice-Captain) C.S.Palmer and B.J.Smith.

From a statement submitted by the secretary, it appeared that during the season just ended the club had played 34 matches, 21 of which had been won, eight were lost, and five were drawn. Another set of figures showed that the club had won 80 goals and lost 47. C.S.Palmer occupied the place of honour as having kicked the largest number of goals, he being responsible for 14; C.Clark followed with a score of 13; P.M.Earle 8; W.Wright 7; and S.W.Skilton 6.

Mr.H.Palmer thought the record was a very satisfactory one. – The Financial Statement showed that when a few outstanding subscriptions had been collected and a few outstanding bills paid, the club would have upwards of £3 to begin next year's season with. On the proposition of Mr.H.W.Palmer seconded by Mr.L.E.Clark, Mr.R.G.Price was unanimously re-elected president, and the following were re-elected as Vice-Presidents, viz.: - Mr.W.Pemberton-Barnes, Rev.H.M.Burgess, Mr.W.Bose, Mr.E.Conder, Mr.F.Green, Mr.H.S.Haynes, Rev.Canon Hitchcock, Mr.G.P.Hope, Rev.A.C.Roberts and Rev.W.J.Skilton. The secretary was also desired to communicate with the following gentlemen with a view to getting their names placed on the list of vice-presidents, viz: - Dr.Cunningham, Mr.O.G.Daldy, Dr. Davey, Dr.Wright, Mr.W.C. Clifton, Mr.Joseph Smith, Mr.A.H.Hunt, and Mr.North Surridge.

Mr.A.G.Martin having announced his intention of resigning the secretaryship, a cordial and unanimous vote of thanks was passed to him for the able manner in which he had conducted the affairs of the club during the past season. – Messrs. W.D.Matthews and C.Clark were appointed joint secretaries for the ensuing season. On the proposition of Mr.L.E.Clark the following new members were unanimously elected: - Messrs. J.A.Macfarlane, J.E.Macfarlane, F.Webster, Goadby, A.Ronald, H.H.Mansfield and S.W.Poulton (all ex-defunct Union F.C).

Messrs.L.E.Clark and H.W.Palmer were re-elected captain and vice-captain respectively, for the year ensuing, and Messrs. B.J.Smith and A.G.Martin were chosen to similar positions in regard to the second eleven team.The following in addition to the six officers of the club were chosen as the Committee, viz: - Messrs. F.D.R.Clark, A.D.Cornell, C.S.Palmer, G.A.Smith, E.Champness, S.W.Skilton, J.A.Macfarlane, F.Webster, J.F.Macfarlane, T.K.Gayford, C.Couzens and F.Gilbey. – The meeting concluded with the usual vote of thanks to the Chairman.

Season 1883 – 84

ROMFORD FOOTBALL CLUB

President: Mr.R.G.Price **Hon.Secretaries:** Messrs.W.D.Matthews and C.Clark

Captain: Mr.L.E.Clark **Vice-Captain:** Mr.H.W.Palmer

Reserve Team Captain: Mr.B.J.Smith **Reserve Team Vice-Captain:** Mr.A.G.Martin

Committee: Messrs. F.D.R.Clark, A.D.Cornell, C.S.Palmer, G.A.Smith, E.Champness, S.W.Skilton, J.A.Macfarlane, F.Webster, J.E.Macfarlane, T.K.Gayford, C.Couzens and F.Gilbey.
Plus the six officers of the club

Headquarters: White Hart Hotel, Romford **Ground:** The Meadow, Great Mawneys, Romford

COMPETITIONS ENTERED

F.A. Challenge Cup
Essex County F.A. Challenge Cup
Friendly Matches

Trial Match

22 Sept Captain's Select (Poulton) 1 Vice-Captain's Select (Wright) 1
Captain's Team: Substitute;E.Simpson,B.J.Smith;H.Mansfield;L.E.Clark(Capt);
C.S.Palmer,R.A.Clark,S.W.Skilton,S.W.Poulton,J.Goadby,F.Gilbey,

Vice-Captain's Team: W.D.Matthews,H.W.Palmer(Capt),A.Cornell.Jnr.,R.Carter,C.Couzens;
A.G.Martin,A.Hinds,W.Wright,R.Oliver,C.Clark,G.Daldy.

29 Sept The first annual general athletic sports meeting in connection with the Romford Cricket and Football Clubs took place on the Recreation Ground (which would two years later become Romford Football Club's home ground). The newspaper announcement read: 'Admission charge sixpence plus sixpence extra to the Enclosure. Occupants of Carriages one shilling each! Tickets for the enclosure if obtained previous to the day of the event ninepence each, children half price. Note: NO DOGS ALLOWED'.

Match details

6 Oct Frdly Home Hornchurch 7 – 0 Scorers unknown
Romford: A.D.Cornell;F.Webster,J.E.Macfarlane(Union);H.Mansfield(Union),G.E.Hitchcock;
W.Wright,P.M.Earle,L.E.Clark(Capt),F.H.Thirlwall,J.A.Macfarlane(Union),S.W.Poulton.

13 Oct Frdly Home Olympic (Upton Park) 5 – 1 Scorers unknown
Romford: A.D.Cornell;F.Webster,H.Mansfield;S.W.Skilton,C.Couzens;
J.A.Macfarlane,J.Goadby,W.Wright,R.Oliver,A.Couzens,L.E.Clark(Capt).

20 Oct Frdly Away Maidenhead 2 – 1 L.E.Clark(2)
Romford: A.D.Cornell;F.Webster,J.E.Macfarlane;H.Mansfield,F.D.R.Clark;
W.Wright,J.A.Macfarlane;L.E.Clark(Capt),J.Goadby;P.M.Earle,R.Oliver.

24 Oct Frdly Away Chatham 1 – 5 Webster
Romford: C.H.Smith;B.J.Smith,J.E.Macfarlane;H.Mansfield,H.W.Palmer;
R.Oliver,W.Wright,A.Hinds,F.Webster,W.D.Matthews,J.A.Macfarlane.

27 Oct Frdly Home Foxes(Edmonton) 0 – 2
Romford: C.H.Smith;W.D.Matthews,J.R.Potter;C.Couzens,A.Connell.Jnr.;
C.Metcalfe,S.W.Skilton;C.S.Palmer,R.Oliver;F.H.Thirlwall,A.G.Martin.

3 Nov FAC1R Home Woodford Bridge 3 – 0 J.A.Macfarlane,Oliver,Earle
Attendance: 500
Romford: Arthur D.Cornell;H.W.Palmer,J.E.Macfarlane;H.Mansfield,C.Couzens;
W.Wright,J.A.Macfarlane;L.E.Clark(Capt),J.Goadby;P.M.Earle,R.Oliver.

24 Nov Frdly Home Buckhurst Hill 5 – 0 Earle(2)Wright,Clark,Goadby
Romford: C.H.Smith;J.E.Macfarlane,F.Webster;H.Mansfield,C.Couzens;
L.E.Clark(Capt),W.Wright;J.Goadby,W.D.Matthews;P.M.Earle,R.Oliver.

1 Dec FAC2R Home Mosquitoes (Dulwich) 3 – 1 Goadby,Cornell(2)
Romford: A.D.Cornell;J.E.Macfarlane,F.Webster;H.Mansfield,C.Couzens;
W.Wright,J.A.Macfarlane;F.H.Thirlwall,J.Goadby;P.M.Earle,R.Oliver.

15 Dec Frdly Away Clapton 1 – 0 Goadby
Romford: E.F.Hooper;B.J.Smith,J.E.Macfarlane;W.D.Matthews,H.Mansfield;
R.Oliver,L.E.Clark(Capt);A.D.Cornell,J.Goadby;J.A.Macfarlane,P.M.Earle.

26 Dec Frdly Away Chelmsford 5 – 0 Scorers unknown
Romford: A.D.Cornell;H.W.Palmer,H.Mansfield;C.Couzens,J.E.Macfarlane;
L.E.Clark(Capt),C.Clark,S.W.Skilton,P.M.Earle,R.Oliver,J.Goadby.

29 Dec FAC3R Home Brentwood 1 – 4 Cornell
Romford: E.Champness;F.Webster,J.E.Macfarlane;H.Mansfield,L.E.Clark(Capt),C.Couzens;
J.A.Macfarlane,W.Wright;A.D.Cornell;P.M.Earle,R.Oliver.

5 Jan Frdly Away Olympic (Upton Park) 0 – 0
Romford: C.H.Smith;J.E.Macfarlane,H.W.Palmer;C.Couzens,H.Mansfield;
R.Oliver,J.Goadby,F.Webster,C.Clark,C.S.Palmer,A.G.Martin.

12 Jan Frdly Home Hermits (Victoria Park) 1 – 1 Scorer unknown
Romford: C.H.Smith;J.E.Macfarlane,H.W.Palmer;H.Mansfield,C.Couzens,W.D.Matthews;
R.Oliver,W.Wright,L.E.Clark(Capt),C.Clark,J.Goadby.

19 Jan ECC2R Away Woodford Bridge 3 – 1 Oliver(2)Cornell
Romford: E.Yardley;H.W.Palmer,B.J.Smith;L.E.Clark(Capt),W.D.Matthews,C.Couzens;
W.Wright,P.M.Earle,A.D.Cornell,C.Clark,R.Oliver. Umpires: H.Betts and W.M.Wood. Referee: F.W.Pack(St.Mary's College)

2 Feb Frdly Home Woodford Bridge 1 – 3 Scorer unknown
Romford: C.H.Smith;J.E.Macfarlane,F.Webster;H.Mansfield,C.Couzens,A.Cornell.Jnr;
W.Wright,J.Goadby,C.H.Clifford;L.E.Clark(Capt),A.G.Martin.

16 Feb Frdly Away Lennox (Dulwich) 4 – 1
J.A.Macfarlane,Thirlwall,L.E.Clark,Mansfield
Romford: C.H.Smith;J.E.Macfarlane,F.Webster;H.Mansfield,T.K.Gayford;
W.D.Matthews,L.E.Clark(Capt),C.Clark,F.H.Thirlwall,C.S.Palmer,J.A.Macfarlane.

23 Feb Frdly Away Buckhurst Hill 8 – 1 Scorers unknown
Romford: C.H.Smith;J.E.Macfarlane,F.Webster;H.Mansfield,W.D.Matthews;
L.E.Clark(Capt),R.Oliver,C.S.Palmer,C.Clark,J.Goadby.

1 Mar Frdly Away Foxes (Edmonton) 3 – 0 Goadby(2)L.E.Clark
Romford: G.A.Smith;J.E.Macfarlane,F.Webster;H.Mansfield,W.D.Webster;
L.E.Clark(Capt),R.Oliver;C.S.Palmer,J.Goadby;S.W.Poulton,C.Clark.

5 Mar Frdly Home Chatham 2 – 5 L.E.Clark(2)
Romford: E.Yardley;F.Webster,J.E.Macfarlane;H.Mansfield,W.D.Matthews;
S.W.Poulton,W.Wright;P.M.Earle,A.D.Cornell,C.Clark;L.E.Clark(Capt),R.Oliver.

8 Mar ECCSF Chsford Colchester 1 – 2 L.E.Clark
Attendance: 400
Romford: E.Champness;H.W.Palmer,B.J.Smith;L.E.Clark(Capt),C.Couzens,A.Cornell.Jnr;
P.M.Earle,W.Wright;A.D.Cornell.Snr;J.H.Matthews,R.Oliver.

15 Mar Frdly Home Clapton 1 – 2 Goadby
Romford: A.D.Cornell;F.Webster,C.Couzens;H.Mansfield,W.D.Matthews;
S.W.Poulton,C.Clark;J.Goadby,E.Champness;L.E.Clark(Capt),R.Oliver.

4 Apr Frdly Home Grove House (Shepherds Bush) 7 – 1 Scorers unknown
Romford:
Team details unknown

9 Apr Frdly Home Romford Brewery 3 – 0 Scorers unknown
Romford: R.Brazier;A.D.Cornell,W.D.Matthews;O.Wheatley,R.Hamshire,R.Oliver;
L.E.Clark,C.Clark,W.Wright,F.Gilbey,J.Farrow.

Romford Brewery: G.A.Smith;C.Couzens,H.W.Palmer;R.H.Lyon,J.Gates,A.Couzens;
F.Brewster,C.S.Palmer,C.H.Smith,A.G.Martin,F.Groves.
Note the number of Romford players in the Brewery team!

SUMMARY OF RESULTS OBTAINED SEASON 1883 – 84

	P	W	D	L	Goals For	Goals Ag
F.A. Challenge Cup	3	2	0	1	7	5
ECFA Challenge Cup	2	1	0	1	4	3
Friendly Matches	18	11	2	5	56	23
Reserve Team	9	5	3	1	19	7
Total	32	19	5	8	86	38
AGM Report	36	20	7	9	90	42

Note: The Annual General Meeting report would appear to include the reserve team games, but even so five results have not been traced.

CUP RESULTS SEASON 1883 – 84

F.A. Challenge Cup

Final: Blackburn Rovers 2 Queens Park 1

Romford's progress: 1st Round Home Woodford Bridge 3 – 0
2nd Round Home Mosquitoes 3 – 1
3rd Round Home Brentwood 1 – 4

Essex County F.A. Challenge Cup

Final: Colchester 3 Braintree 1

Romford's progress: 2nd Round Away Woodford Bridge 3 – 1
Semi-Final Chelmsford Colchester 1 – 2

First Team Appearances Season 1883 – 84

R.Brazier	1	E.Champness	3	C.Clark	10	F.D.R.Clark	1
L.E.Clark	18	C.H.Clifford	1	A.D.Cornell	13	A.Cornell Jnr.	3
A.Couzens	1	C.Couzens	13	P.M.Earle	11	J.Farrow	1
T.K.Gayford	1	F.Gilbey	1	J.Goadby	13	R.Hamshire	1
A.Hinds	1	G.E.Hitchcock	1	E.F.Hooper	1	J.A.Macfarlane	9
J.E.Macfarlane	16	H.Mansfield	18	A.G.Martin	3	J.H.Matthews	1
W.D.Matthews	11	C.Metcalfe	1	R.Oliver	19	C.S.Palmer	5
H.W.Palmer	7	J.Potter	1	S.W.Poulton	4	S.W.Skilton	3
B.J.Smith	4	C.H.Smith	8	G.A.Smith	1	F.H.Thirlwall	4
F.Webster	14	W.D.Webster	1	O.Wheatley	1	W.Wright	14
E.Yardley	2	Total	242				

The above record does not include first team match against Grove House of which team details are not to hand. In the away game against Buckhurst Hill Romford had only ten men, whilst in their second match against Chatham, each team played with twelve men. Rules were not as rigid as they are in the modern era.

First Team Goal Scorers Season 1883 – 84

It is regretted that due to the lack of information in press reports it is not possible to compile a summary of the goal scorers for the year, the scorers of nearly forty goals are unknown!

Special Essex County Commission

(as reported in the *Essex Times*, Wednesday 26th March 1884)

21 March A special meeting of the Committee of the Essex County F.A.to consider the protest made by Romford, on the following grounds. J.L.Nickisson had not been a member of the Colchester Club for a month. He had also played for Middlesex against Norfolk was not qualified to play for an Essex Club in the County Cup Competition. Thirdly, that the game was prolonged beyond the ninety minutes.

The Committee found that the player had been a member of Colchester for a sufficient time, and deferred their decision for a few days regarding his playing for another County. On the third item it was agreed that play lasted one hour and thirty eight minutes, but the extra eight minutes were accounted for by an allowance of two minutes for changing the ball and six minutes for the change of ends and that on this ground the protest must fail. The outcome of the second item is not known but is assumed to have failed as Colchester went on the play Braintree in the final at Chelmsford.

Note: This commission was held as a result of Romford's protest regarding the Essex Cup Semi-Final tie against Colchester on 8th March.

RESERVE TEAM

Match details

13 Oct Frdly Away Olympic (Upton Park) Reserves 3 – 0 Webb,Gilbey(2)
Romford Reserves: W.D.Matthews;T.K.Gayford,B.J.Smith;W.Simpson,A.Cornell.Jnr.;
R.A.Clark,A.Hinds,F.Gilbey,J.Bailey,H.Webb.

20 Oct Frdly Home Buffaloes Reserves 2 – 1 Gilbey(2)
Romford Reserves: C.H.Smith;T.K.Gayford,A.G.Martin;W.Simpson,A.Couzens;
C.S.Palmer,S.W.Skilton,G.Daldy,G.Guyatt,A.Hinds,F.Gilbey.

27 Oct Frdly Away Foxes (Edmonton) Reserves 3 – 1 Scorers unknown
Romford played the whole match with nine men, full details unknown.
At kick-off Foxes had only eight men but soon had a full team.

10 Nov Frdly Home Foxes (Edmonton) Reserves 0 – 0
Romford:
Team details unknown

24 Nov Frdly Away Buckhurst Hill Reserves 4 – 1 Scorers unknown
Romford Reserves: J.Farrow,B.J.Smith,T.K.Gayford,H.W.Palmer,A.Cornell.Jnr.,
A.Couzens,A.Hinds,A.Skilton,F.Gilbey,A.G.Martin.

8 Dec Frdly Away Olympic (Upton Park) Reserves 0 – 1
Romford:
Team details unknown.

15 Dec Frdly Home Clapton Reserves 1 – 1 Scorer unknown
Romford Reserves: W.Wright;G.Daldy,F.Gilbey;A.Skilton,A.G.Martin;
R.Carter,A.Couzens,A.Cornell.Jnr.,C.S.Palmer,C.H.Smith.

2 Feb Frdly Away Woodford Bridge Reserves 4 – 0 C.S.Palmer(2)F.Gilbey,G.Dalby
Romford Reserves: E.Champness;B.J.Smith,T.K.Gayford;W.J.Reid,W.D.Matthews;
C.S.Palmer,R.Carter,F.Gilbey,G.Daldy,A.Skilton.

23 Feb Frdly Home Buckhurst Hill Reserves 2 – 2 Scorers unknown
Romford Reserves: G.Guyatt;B.J.Smith,T.K.Gayford;A.Cornell.Jnr.,R.Carter;
A.Couzens,G.Daldy,A.Skilton,F.Gilbey,E.Champness,W.Wright.

RESERVE TEAM SUMMARY OF RESULTS SEASON 1883 – 84

					Goals	
	P	W	D	L	For	Ag
All Friendly Matches	9	5	3	1	19	7

Note: These are the only details to hand and there is the possibility that the team played other friendly matches. There were no league or cup matches.

Reserve Team Appearances Season 1883 – 84

Although several details are not to hand the following list indicates the number of games known to have been played by individual players, although some names may also be missing.

J. Bailey	1	R.Carter	3	E.Champness	2	R.A.Clark	1
A.Cornell Jnr.	4	A.Couzens	4	G.Daldy	4	J.Farrow	1
T.K.Gayford	5	F.Gilbey	6	G.Guyatt	2	A.Hinds	3
A.G.Martin	3	W.D.Matthews	2	C.S.Palmer	3	H.W.Palmer	1
W.J.Reid	1	W.Simpson	2	A.Skilton	4	S.W.Skilton	1
B.J.Smith	4	C.H.Smith	2	H.Webb	1	W.Wright	2
Total	62						

THE ESSEX TEAM THAT BEAT NORFOLK BY THREE GOALS TO ONE AT NORWICH ON 10th OCTOBER 1883

The Essex County Football Association

Back row: P.M.EARLE (Romford) ROBERT COOK (Chelmsford) H.H.JOHNSON (Old Foresters)

Middle row: C.E.CANT (Colchester) R.H.JOHNSON (Old Foresters) J.L.NICKISSON (Brentwood) ROBERT JOHNSON (Braintree) C.WARD (Maldon)

Front row: R.M.BIRD-THOMPSON (Saffron Walden) J.H.MATTHEWS (Old Foresters)

THE UNION FOOTBALL CLUB

In the newspaper report of the Annual Dinner of the Romford Football Club held on Saturday 29th September, 1883, it was reported that:

> Mr. Mansfield, formerly a prominent member of the now **defunct Union Club** proposed "The Officers of the Romford Football Club." The speaker thought there was every reason to expect that the Romford Club would meet with many successes in the ensuing season. (Cheers). He knew that most, if not all, of its members were determined to "do their level best" to secure for the club a proud position in the Football world. (Cheers) To that end it required no little care in choosing the elevens, a task which he was sure the Committee of the club would discharge with due discretion. (Hear, Hear). On behalf of his brother members of the Union he cordially thanked the Committee and members of the Romford club for their kind welcome, and he hoped that what with the old blood and what with the new, the Romford Football Club would make a name for itself in the coming year. (Applause). With the toast he would couple the name of their hard-working captain, Mr.L.E.Clark. (Cheers). (The *Essex Times,* Wednesday 3rd October 1883)

Thus several former members of Union FC joined Romford for the 1883-84 season.

Post-Season Summary Season 1883 – 84

In the opening friendly against Hornchurch on 6th October, the club introduced an entrance fee and offered season tickets for half a crown. Arthur Cornell kept his goal intact, unlike his counterpart who conceded seven goals. Romford's next fixture saw their opponents (Olympic) only able to field 10 players, and Romford secured another big victory by five goals to one. A week later at Maidenhead the home side fielded a strong team which included E.C. Bambridge, an international footballer. The game was watched by a large crowd, and Romford secured their third win in a row. The midweek game at Chatham was played with a very strong wind blowing across the pitch, which meant an endless number of throw-ins and Romford's first defeat of the season.

The following Saturday, 27th October, the match against Foxes was stopped after an hour's play, reason unknown. Romford were beaten 2-0, having fielded quite a weak team - the regular players were representing the Union club in the first round of the London Association Cup, winning the away tie against Westminster by 19 goals to nil! The following week in the F.A. Cup 1st Round a healthy attendance of 500 witnessed a 3-0 victory over Woodford Bridge (Union players Oliver, Earle and Macfarlane scoring the goals!). Three weeks later Romford were in good form at home to Buckhurst Hill with a 5-0 win.

In the F.A. Cup 2nd Round tie on 1st December, Romford goalkeeper Arthur Cornell changed places with centre forward Thirlwall after about twenty minutes play, Cornell soon scoring a couple of goals. They returned to their usual positions after half time and Romford went on to inflict a first defeat of the season on Mosquitoes by three goals to one! Two weeks later in the away fixture at Clapton which Romford won 1-0, the game ended after an hour's play. The spectators' thoughts are not known!

On Boxing Day Romford travelled to Chelmsford and showed little Christmas spirit by inflicting a 5-0 defeat on their unfortunate rivals, marking five wins in a row. A large crowd gathered at the Romford ground for the 3rd Round F.A. Cup tie against Brentwood. Brentwood's forward Abbott broke his leg and was removed from the pitch. He was takento the White Hart Hotel, where the leg was re-set before he was transferred to St. Bartholomew's Hospital. Despite this, Romford were beaten 4-1. Thus the winning streak was ended.

On 5th January Romford travelled to meet Olympic in the return game at Forest Gate, and came away with a goalless draw. The following week Hermits were the visitors to Mawneys and a one all draw was the order of the day.

19th January and Romford were engaged in the newly-formed Essex Challenge Cup Competition with an away tie to Woodford Bridge which they won 3-1. The press reported that 'Woodford won the toss and elected to play with the slope in their favour. After Romford took the lead they came under pressure and Yardley was forced to use his hands'. (He was the goalkeeper, so what were the rules at the time?) The following week the teams met again in a friendly fixture at Romford and it was recorded that 'the weather was beautifully fine and the field was in splendid condition'. Both teams commenced with nine men, Cornell and Couzens arriving for Romford at half time, but the visitors played virtually throughout with eight men, as Gill was injured in the fifth minute and took no further part in the game. Nonetheless Woodford turned the tables on Romford, reversing the previous week's score.

On 16th February Romford played an away friendly at the Greyhound Pub, Dulwich, against Lennox, which they won 4-1. Bland (of the Lennox team) retired before half time due to injury. A week later at Buckhurst Hill the Bucks won the toss and elected to take advantage of a considerable slope to the pitch. Romford played throughout with only 10 men, but still achieved and eight goals to one victory. Against Foxes on 1st March, receiving from his brother Clifford, 'Tony' Clark scored Romford's third goal with a 'daisy cutter' to compliment Goadby's earlier two goals in a 3-0 win.

On Wednesday 5th March, in the home game against Chatham, both teams played with twelve men. There was controversy in the Essex Senior Cup semi-final three days later. With Romford leading by a goal to nil, Wright was badly injured. Colchester scored twice in the closing minutes with the final whistle being blown immediately after the second goal. Romford protested at the inclusion of Nickisson of Brentwood in the Colchester team, but all to no avail.

A week later in the home friendly against Clapton which was lost by two goals to one, the weather was described as 'being more suitable for cricket than football'. On 4th April Romford were due to play Maidenhead who scratched, and a seven goal to one defeat was inflicted on Grove House who kindly provided the opposition!

The curtain came down on the season on 9th April, a Thursday afternoon, when the Romford Brewery team travelled across the High Street to meet Romford in what was now becoming an annual event. The Brewery team (of course!) included eight regular members of the Romford club. At the end of the season, Percy M.Earle was awarded his Essex Senior Cap for six appearances in the County team.

Annual General Meeting
(as reported in the *Essex Times,* Saturday 14th June 1884)

The annual general meeting of the members of the Romford Football Club was held at the White Hart Hotel, on Wednesday 11th June. Mr.L.E.Clark (in the chair), supported by the joint Hon.Secs. Messrs. W.D.Matthews and C.Clark. and there were also present. – Messrs. F.D.R.Clark, E.Champness, A.Cornell, R.A.Clark, G.F.Daldy, F.Gilbey, C.Harrison, H.Mansfield, H.W.Palmer, C.S.Palmer, J.Patching and B.J.Smith.

The report as read by Mr. Matthews set forth that the past season had been a decidedly successful one for the Club both as regards the number of matches played and the number of new members received into the club both playing and honorary. The Club had managed to work themselves into the third round of the Association Cup, ultimately suffering defeat at the hands of their old friends the members of the Brentwood Club after an exciting contest. For the Essex Cup the Club reached the semi-final of the competition when they were beaten under somewhat peculiar circumstances by the Colchester Club. During the season 36 matches had been played, of which 20 were won, nine lost, and seven drawn. Ninety goals had been scored by the Club, against 42 scored by their opponents. (Applause). Mr.P.M.Earle and Mr.C.S.Palmer were the most successful in scoring, each having kicked 11 goals. Financially the Club was in a good position, the balance sheet shewing that after the payment of all accounts there would be a sum in hand amounting to £2.6s 9d.

Out of this year's funds the Club had had to pay for two years' rent of the ground. The railway expenses amounted to £12.12s 9d. and it was hoped that the Club would be able to considerably reduce this item of expenditure next season. The charges which had been made for admission to the field amounted to £8.8s.4d. - (applause) – and a sum of 17s.6d. had been received for season tickets. The gate money had not only helped the funds of the club, but it had had the effect of keeping out of the field a number of "roughs", but which the Club felt confident that they would outlive. (Applause). – The Chairman congratulated the members on having a balance in hand, which, he said, was in great measure owing to the zeal and energy displayed by the hon.secs. – On the proposition of Mr.H.W.Palmer, and seconded by Mr.B.J.Smith, the report and balance sheet were unanimously adopted.

Mr.R.G.Price was re-elected president, and the vice-presidents were re-elected. Mr.L.E.Clark was re-elected captain, and Mr.P.M.Earle was appointed vice-captain in the room of Mr.H.W.Palmer resigned. For the second eleven Messrs. B.J.Smith and A.Martin were re-elected captain and vice-captain respectively. The Committee were re-elected with the addition of Messrs. H.Mansfield and J.Goadby. Messrs. W.D.Matthews and C.Clark were re-elected joint hon.secs.

Mr.H.W.Palmer proposed a hearty vote of thanks to the Hon.Secs. for the very able manner in which they had performed their duties during the past season. (Applause). He could say from experience that the office of secretary was a most unthankful office, and nobody knew what the work was but those who had it to do. Mr.Matthews and Mr.Clark had thrown their heart and soul into the affair, and, as had been remarked by the Chairman, it was mainly owing to their energies that the Club occupied its present satisfactory position. (Applause)...

Season 1884 – 85

ROMFORD FOOTBALL CLUB

President: Mr.R.G.Price **Chairman:** Mr.G.A.Smith **Vice-Chairman:** Mr.L.E.Clark

Joint Hon.Secretaries and Treasurer: Messrs.W.D.Matthews and C.Clark
(Both resigned at the Annual General Meeting on May 1st)

Captain: Mr.L.E.Clark **Vice-Captain:** Mr.P.M.Earle

Reserve Team Captain: Mr.B.J.Smith **Reserve Team Vice-Captain:** Mr.A.G.Martin

Committee: Messrs. F.D.R.Clark, A.D.Cornell, C.S.Palmer, G.A.Smith, E.Champness, S.W.Skilton J.A.Macfarlane, F.Webster, J.E.Macfarlane, T.K.Gayford, C.Couzens and F.Gilbey were re-elected plus Mr.H.Mansfield and Mr.J.Goadby. Plus the six officers of the club

Headquarters: White Hart Hotel, Romford **Ground:** The Meadow, Great Mawneys, Romford

COMPETITIONS ENTERED

F.A. Challenge Cup
Essex County F.A. Challenge Cup
Friendly Matches

Match details

4 Oct Frdly Home Clapton 2 – 2 J.A.Macfarlane,S.Poulton
Romford: E.Yardley;J.E.Macfarlane,F.Webster;H.Mansfield,C.Couzens,J.A.Macfarlane; S.W.Poulton,W.Wright,W.D.Matthews,R.Oliver,L.E.Clark(Capt).

11 Oct Frdly Home Maidenhead 3 – 0 Scorers unknown
Romford: A,Odgers;F.Webster,J.E.Macfarlane;H.Mansfield,C.Couzens,L.E.Clark(Capt); S.W.Poulton,W.Wright,J.A.Macfarlane,R.Oliver,J.Goadby.

18 Oct Frdly Away Hendon 0 – 6
Romford: Sub in goal;B.J.Smith,L.E.Clark(Capt);C.Clark,R.Oliver, W.D.Matthews,C.S.Palmer,E.Yardley,C.Medcalfe.

1 Nov FAC1R Home Clapton 3 – 2 L.E.Clark,Earle,Oliver
Romford: A.D.Cornell;F.Webster,J.E.Macfarlane;H.Mansfield,L.E.Clark(Capt),C.Couzens; J.Goadby,W.Wright,J.A.Macfarlane,P.M.Earle,R.Oliver.

8 Nov* ECC1R Away Woodford Bridge 0 – 0
Romford: A.Clark;B.J.Smith,H.Hailey;L.E.Clark(Capt),C.Couzens,A.Couzens; M.Phillips,R.Oliver,C.Clark,W.Wright,H.W.Palmer.

8 Nov* Frdly Away Olympic (Upton Park) 4 – 0 Scorers unknown
Romford: W.Horn;F.Webster,J.E.Macfarlane;H.Mansfield,M.H.Walker,J.Goadby; C.S.Palmer,E.Goadby,R.Odgers,J.M.Hanson,M.Phillips.

15 Nov Frdly Home Foxes(Edmonton) 3 – 1 Scorers unknown
Romford: G.A.Smith;J.A.Macfarlane,F.Webster;H.Mansfield,M.H.Walker,J.Goadby; L.E.Clark(Capt),R.Oliver,W.Wright,P.M.Earle,J.E.Macfarlane.

22 Nov LCC###

29 Nov ECCRep Home Woodford Bridge 0 – 3
Romford: E.Champness;A.G.Martin,B.J.Smith;C.Couzens,A.D.Cornell,H.Hailey; W.Wright,P.M.Earle(Capt);C.S.Palmer;R.Oliver,H.W.Palmer.

6 Dec FAC2R Home Dulwich 3 – 0 Oliver(2)Wright
Romford: A,D.Cornell;F.Webster,J.E.Macfarlane;H.Mansfield,B.J.Smith,C.Couzens;
J.Goadby,W.Wright,J.A.Macfarlane,P.M.Earle(Capt),R.Oliver.

13 Dec LCC###

20 Dec FAC3R Bye

26 Dec Frdly Home Clapton 0 – 1
Romford: A.D.Cornell;G.E.Hitchcock,M.H.Walker;C.Couzens,W.D.Matthews,Caubert;
A.G.Martin,C.S.Palmer,W.Wright,R.Oliver,L.E.Clark(Capt).

27 Dec Frdly Away Colchester 0 – 5
Romford: A.Cornell;G.E.Hitchcock,B.J.Smith;C.Couzens, Sub.,C.G.Smith;
A.G.Martin,C.Clark,R.Oliver,E.Bloomfield,E.Yardley.

3 Jan Frdly Home Ivanhoe (West Ham) 6 – 1 Scorers unknown
Romford: Substitute in goal;F.Webster,J.E.Macfarlane;H.Mansfield,G.E.Hitchcock,L.E.Clark(Capt);
A.Couzens,J.A.Macfarlane,R.Oliver,S.W.Poulton,R.Carter.

10 Jan Frdly Away Foxes(Edmonton) 4 – 0 Scorers unknown
Romford: P.Smith;J.E.Macfarlane,F.Webster;H.Mansfield,L.E.Clark(Capt);
S.W.Poulton,R.Oliver,J.A.Macfarlane,J.Goadby.

17 Jan Frdly Home Olympic (Upton Park) 4 – 0 Scorers unknown
Romford:
Team details unknown

19 Jan FAC4R Away Blackburn Rovers (Holders) 0 – 8
Romford: E.Champness;J.E.Macfarlane,F.Webster;H.Mansfield,C.Couzens,F.H.M.Walker;
P.M.Earle,W.Wright,R.Oliver,A.D.Cornell,L.E.Clark(Capt). Referee: Mr.Daft(Nottingham Swifts)

7 Feb Frdly Away Grove House (Shepherds Bush) 2 – 0 Scorers unknown
Romford:
Team details unknown

14 Feb Frdly Away Clapton 0 – 12
Romford: W.D.Matthews;J.E.Macfarlane,F.Webster;H.Mansfield
S.W.Poulton,L.E.Clark(Capt),H.J.Myers.

21 Feb Frdly Home Leyton 3 – 1 L.E.Clark(2)Sayer(o.g)
Romford: A.D.Cornell;F.Webster,J.E.Macfarlane;C.Couzens,J.Goadby,H.Mansfield;
S.W.Poulton,W.Wright,H.W.Palmer,L.E.Clark(Capt),C.S.Palmer.

28 Feb Frdly Home Ivanhoe (West Ham) 2 – 2 Oliver,Wright
Romford: E.Champness;C.Couzens,F.Webster;L.E.Clark(Capt),H.Mansfield,J.Goadby;
S.W.Poulton,W.Wright,C.S.Palmer,R.Oliver,R.A.Clark.

14 Mar Frdly Away Maidenhead 1 – 1 Goadby
Romford: E.Yardley;J.E.Macfarlane,F.Webster;H.Mansfield,L.E.Clark(Capt),J.Goadby;
S.W.Poulton,R.Oliver,-.Myers,W.Wright,R.A.Clark.

19 Mar Frdly Home Colchester 3 – 2 C.Clark(2)Oliver
Romford: A.D.Cornell;F.Webster,Barbour;G.E.Hitchcock,C.Couzens,Bolton;
R.Oliver,F.H.Thirlwall,L.E.Clark(Capt),C.Clark.

* Romford played two first team games on this day whilst the reserves beat Olympic Reserves.

At the Annual Dinner on 25th September, it was reported that "For the London Cup they played well, but unfortunately the referee was hardly unbiased in his decisions, and the game went against them."

On 13th December Old Foresters defeated Union by three goals to two in a second round **replay** amid much controversy regarding the refereeing by Mr.Jackson. Union won the original match by two goals to one. It thus appears that the match referred to at the Annual Dinner was the above replay and Romford had entered a team in the London Cup Competition under the name of the defunct Union F.C! As we have seen, many of their players had joined Romford for the 1883 – 84 season after the Union club folded.

"We do not qualify for the London Challenge Cup. Says who?"

At their A.G.M. on 7th May 1883 Romford had welcomed several players well known to them, joining them from the Union Football Club which had become defunct. The Romford club were prohibited from entering the London Challenge Cup by reason of their headquarters being outside the boundaries of the competition, but nevertheless the officials had always hoped to be accepted at some time.

It seems that Romford club officials now saw the opportunity to compete by somewhat devious means! Although the Union Football Club no longer existed, a team was entered in the London Challenge Cup under the name of Union. Below is a report of the second round tie which was won by Union.

LONDON CHALLENGE CUP

PHOENIX ATHLETIC v. UNION – This tie in the first round of the London Challenge Cup was played at Forest Gate on Saturday, 25th October, 1884. Phoenix Athletic protested to the London Football Association on the grounds that a tape was used across one goal, the bar having been broken whilst the goals were being erected. Union won the match 8-0 and presumably Phoenix lost their appeal as Union progressed to the second round.

Union Team: E.Taylor;F.Webster,J.E.Macfarlane;H.Mansfield,L.E.Clark,B.J.Smith; S.W.Poulton,W.Wright,J.Goadby,J.A.Macfarlane,W.Webster.

> UNION V. OLD FORESTERS – This, the only remaining draw in the second round of the above competition, was played on Saturday, November 22nd, at Snaresbrook. Owing to the late arrival of two of the Old Foresters, play was not commenced until 2.50. For the first few minutes the resources, of the Union backs were tried to the uttermost, repeated onslaughts being made by the home team. A fine run by J.A.Macfarlane on the right, was the means of relieving the visitors; give and take play was now the order of the day, but the aspect of the game was speedily altered, the ball being kept well in front of the Foresters' goal. Earle here made a fine shot, which was cleverly stopped by Denton. Clark, however, was too quick and forced both ball and goalkeeper through the posts. Much to the surprise of the Union, and the evident disapproval of the spectators, the point was disallowed on the plea of offside.
>
> Shortly after half time the boys had their first opportunity of scoring, Horner taking advantage of a faulty kick by J.E.Macfarlane, placed a goal to the credit of the Foresters. From this the Union had all the best of the game. Lush and Goadby rendering good service, and the Union, despite the gallant efforts of the "Old Boys," managed to score two goals (Clark and Wright) before the call of time, thus winning a hardly contested game by two goals to one. (The *Essex Times*)

Teams: **Union:** T.Horne,goal;F.Webster,J.E.Macfarlane,backs;W.Lush,H.Mansfield,halfbacks; J.Goadby,S.W.Poulton,right wing;J.A.Macfarlane,L.E.Clark,centres;P.M.Earle and W.Wright, left wing.
Old Foresters: Denton,goal;L.Horder, and Gay,backs;Fox,Fairclough,R.B.Johnson,Half backs; J.H.Matthews,H.Johnson,Shaw,Horner, and Lewis, forwards.

Union/Romford's delight at winning this encounter was short-lived. Following a protest from the Old Foresters that the winning goal should not have been allowed, as the ball had gone out of play just before the goal was 'scored', the match was ordered to be replayed. The tables were turned when Foresters secured a 3-2 victory with much controversy regarding the referee's decisions. This is the match and associated correspondence as reported in the *Essex Times* of Wednesday 17th December 1884:

> OLD FORESTERS V. UNION – On the first meeting of the Old Foresters and the Union at Snaresbrook in the second round of the London cup competition the Union claimed a victory by two goals to one, but a protest lodged by the Old Foresters on the ground that one of the Union goals was kicked after the ball had been out of touch was decided in their favour, and the clubs had consequently to meet again. The match was played on Saturday (December 13th) at Romford, and an unusual amount of feeling was manifested on the part of a large number of the spectators. The fact that Mr. N. L. Jackson, the referee, had made some comments in *Pastime* reflecting on the Union team served to increase the feeling, and Mr. Jackson was informed on Friday that the Union club would lodge a protest if he again acted as referee. The feeling among the spectators increased as the game proceeded. From all sides the referee was greeted with uncomplimentary remarks, and at the close of the game he was followed from the ground by a large crowd, groaning and hissing.
>
> The Old Foresters having won the toss, played during the first half with the strong cross wind rather in their favour. On the outset they were acting on the offensive, but after a time the play became more even, and Webster by a long shot from the centre of the ground placed the ball in the mouth of the Foresters' goal. Denton knocked it out, but Earle, receiving the ball, passed to Wright, who by a clever shot passed it again into the goal mouth, and, although Denton stopped it, he was unable to get it away before Clark rushed in and shot through. The goal was disputed on the ground of offside, but the objection was overruled. After a capital shot from Matthews had been well saved, the Old Foresters from a corner kick equalised matters, the point being scored by Shaw.
>
> On the change of ends the Union for some minutes attacked their opponents' goal, and several shots were made by Poulton, while the play of Earle and J.A.Macfarlane was very good. Eventually the Foresters were again on the aggressive, and when three times in succession claims of "off-side" by the Union were disregarded a shout of disapprobation went up from the spectators. From a throw-in which was claimed by both sides, and was given to the Foresters, Shaw got on the ball and kicked a second goal. This was disputed on the plea of offside, but was allowed by the referee. After some even play the ball was again taken down, and B.Guy, by a sharp shot, registered a third point, a claim of offside being overruled. A few minutes before the call of time, J.A.Macfarlane, from a pass by Poulton, cleverly worked the ball up in the centre close to the goal, and Denton being unable to get it away, Clark put it through. The Union were again getting the ball up when time was called, the Old Foresters winning a hard-fought game by three goals to two.
>
> The Union have lodged a protest against the second and third goals, on the ground of offside, and also against Mr. Jackson having acted as referee, on the ground that in the face of what had appeared in the journal of which he is editor he

was not an unbiased judge. The Old Foresters showed perhaps better combination than the Union, and their defence was decidedly stronger, but the game on the whole was very evenly contested. For the Union, Earle, J.A.Macfarlane, and Poulton showed the best form forward, Lush played a resolute game at half-back, and Horne kept goal well, while on the other side Matthews, Shaw, and H.W.Guy showed prominently among the forwards, and the backs, and half-backs played a strong game, Borrow's defence, being especially good. Messrs Humphreys and Squire were the umpires and Mr.Jackson the referee.

Sides:- Old Foresters: E.B.Denton, goal;S.W.Borrow and L.Horner, backs;R.B.Johnson, and P.Fairclough, half-backs;J.H.Matthews, and C.J.Horner, rights;R.V.G.Shaw,centre; and H.W.Guy and B.Guy, lefts.
Union: T.Horne,goal;F.Webster and J.E.Macfarlane,backs;H.Mansfield,L.E.Clark, and A.Lush,half-backs;P.M.Earle and W.Wright, rights;J.A.Macfarlane,centre;J.Goadby and S.W.Poulton,lefts.

It appears that one name is missing from the Old Foresters team line-up.

The same issue of the *Essex Times* also printed the following related correspondence:

TO THE EDITOR OF THE "SPORTING LIFE"

Sir, - Kindly allow me the space necessary in your paper to protest against the rulings of the referee, Mr.N.L.Jackson, in the above match. To say the least, it was the worst taste imaginable to act as referee in the game, after his letter of the past week, and his conduct during play was such as to lead everyone to feel that his sympathy was undoubtedly with the Old Foresters, and most unfairly against the Union. Not being connected with either club, and feeling that fair play is a jewel, I am sure you will give this letter publication, as it is, without doubt, the unanimous opinion of all unbiased spectators who witnessed the game. – Yours, &c. JUSTICIA

TO THE EDITOR OF THE "SPORTING LIFE"

Sir, - Will you allow me space in your columns to express on opinion re. this match. I have heard that before it the "Union" had protested against Mr.N.L.Jackson acting as referee, and I consider the decisions arrived at by him fully justified their doing so. Two of the goals scored by the Old Foresters were palpably off-side. Against these two goals the Union have protested, and until the decision of the London Committee is determined, the result will remain in abeyance.
I am, Sir, yours &c., Melbourne Lodge, Romford. G.B.GILBEY.

Did the Old Foresters, Mr.Jackson and the London Football Association belatedly realise that the Union team was in fact the Romford side, and between themselves, decide to get Union out of the competition?

SUMMARY OF RESULTS OBTAINED SEASON 1884 – 85

					Goals	
	P	W	D	L	For	Ag
Friendlies	16	9	3	4	37	34
F.A.Challenge Cup	3	2	0	1	6	10
ECFA Challenge Cup	2	0	1	1	0	3
Reserve Team	12	8	1	3	28	12
Total	33	19	5	9	71	59
AGM Press Report**	36	21	4	11	74	67

** This must also include the reserve team results.

CUP RESULTS SEASON 1884 – 85

F.A. Challenge Cup

Final: Blackburn Rovers 2 Queens Park 0

Romford's progress:	1st Round	Home	Clapton	3 – 2
	2nd Round	Home	Dulwich	3 – 0
	3rd Round		Bye	
	4th Round	Away	Blackburn Rovers	0 - 8

Essex County F.A. Challenge Cup

Final: Old Foresters 7 Woodford Bridge 0

Romford's progress:	1st Round	Away	Woodford Bridge	0 – 0
	Replay	Home	Woodford Bridge	0 – 3

First Team Appearances Season 1884 – 85

Barbour	1	E.Bloomfield	1	Bolton	1	R.Carter	1
Caubert	1	E.Champness	3	R.A.Clark	3	C.Clark	4
L.E.Clark	15	A.D.Cornell	8	A.Couzens	2	C.Couzens	12
P.M.Earle	5	E.Goadby	1	J.Goadby	9	H.Hailey	2
J.M.Hanson	1	G.E.Hitchcock	4	W.Horn	1	J.A.Macfarlane	7
J.E.Macfarlane	12	H.Mansfield	13	A.G.Martin	3	W.D.Matthews	4
C.Medcalfe	1	H.J.Myers	2	R.Odgers	2	R.Oliver	16
C.S.Palmer	6	H.W.Palmer	3	M.Phillips	2	S.W.Poulton	8
B.J.Smith	5	C.G.Smith	1	G.A.Smith	1	P.Smith	1
F.H.Thirlwall	1	F.H.M.Walker	4	F.Webster	14	W.Wright	12
E.Yardley	4	Substitutes.	3				

Note: The above record does not include the match against Olympic on the 17th January for which we have no details, and the names of the substitutes are unknown. In view of the number of matches unaccounted for as indicated at the A.G.M., some of the above named will no doubt have played in these missing games.

First Team Goal Scorers Season 1884 – 85

Due to the lack of information in press reports it is not possible to compile a summary of the goal scorers for the year, and we have been unable to find the scorers of twenty four goals!

RESERVE TEAM

11 Oct	Frdly	Away	St. Peters (Putney)	3 – 0	Scorers unknown
18 Oct	Frdly	Away	St. Albans (Forest Gate)	0 – 3	
25 Oct	Frdly	Home	Buffaloes	6 – 1	Scorers unknown
8 Nov	Frdly	Home	Olympic Reserves	2 – 1	Scorers unknown

Romford Res.: C.H.Smith;T.K.Gayford,R.Carter;D.Gayford,R.A.Clark,G.Daldy; A.Skilton,G.Gingell,T.Glynn,H.Campkin. Romford played with only ten men.

Note: Romford played three games this day - see also Essex Senior Cup & First Team friendlies.

15 Nov	Frdly	Away	Foxes Reserves	2 – 1	Scorers unknown
22 Nov	Frdly	Home	Hermits	4 – 0	Scorers unknown
20 Dec	Frdly	Away	Hendon Reserves	n/k	
26 Dec	Frdly	Home	Buffaloes	n/k	
27 Dec	Frdly	Away	Romford Rovers	0 – 2	
10 Jan	Frdly	Home	Foxes (Edmonton) Reserves	3 – 0	Scorers unknown
7 Feb	Frdly	Home	Grove House Reserves	0 – 1	
14 Feb	Frdly	Home	Clapton Reserves	5 – 2	Scorers unknown
28 Feb	Frdly	Home	Buffaloes	2 – 0	Scorers unknown
14 Mar	Frdly	Home	St. Peter's	1 – 1	Scorer unknown

Post-Season Summary Season 1884-85

Romford opened their season with a home two all draw against the strong Clapton team and followed this with a 3-0 victory over Maidenhead. On 18th October the old bogey struck again, with the failure of players to turn up for the away match with Hendon. Romford sadly had only eight men, obtained a substitute at the ground to play in goal and thus played on with a team of nine but lost 6-0! Two weeks later the club were engaged in the F.A. Cup and secured a fine 3-2 win over county rivals Clapton. This was followed by a 0-0 draw at Woodford in the Essex Cup and successive wins over Olympic of Upton Park (on the same day) and Foxes of Edmonton in friendly matches.

Romford lost the County Cup replay at home to Woodford 3-0 under difficult circumstances. Due to the serious illness of his father, Romford captain L.E. ('Tony') Clark was unable to play. A further setback occurred after 15 minutes, when Harry Palmer and M.Wallis kicked at the ball at the same time, and Palmer was left helpless with his left leg fractured below the knee. He was taken to his home in South Street where his limb was reset. His brother Charles went with him and Romford played the rest of the game with nine men.

A week later, with neither of the Palmers able to play, Romford defeated the strong Dulwich team 3-0 in the F.A. Cup. With help of a bye in the F.A. Cup, and Romford players representing the Union team in the London Challenge Cup, it was almost three weeks before the club played another game. This was on Boxing Day at Great Mawneys when Clapton were the visitors in a festive friendly. The Christmas pudding took its toll and the homesters lost 1-0. This was followed by a 5-0 loss at Colchester. Against Ivanhoe, Romford were forced to enlist the help of a substitute in goal but secured a 6-1 win.

In the following match, despite again fielding only nine players, surprisingly Romford achieved a 4-0 victory over Foxes! Despite the impending long trip to Blackburn for the F.A. Cup tie, Romford met Olympic (Upton Park) on Saturday 17th January and obtained a 4-0 victory. The same evening the team travelled to Lancashire arriving at Preston at 2.30 a.m. and staying until midday on Monday. That day they were defeated by Blackburn Rovers 8-0, made their exit from the Cup, and then endured the long journey home.

Then followed a two nil win over Grove House of Shepherd's Bush. On 14th February Clapton exacted revenge for their F.A. Cup defeat earlier in the season by putting 12 goals past Romford without reply. It must be said that Romford fielded only seven men! The same day the reserve team defeated Clapton Reserves by five goals to nil, presumably with a full eleven! Romford wound up the season with victories over Leyton (3-1) two draws against Ivanhoe and Maidenhead before defeating Colchester 3-2 in the final game of the season, although it appears Romford played the last match with ten men.

Annual General Meeting
(as reported in the *Essex Times,* Wednesday 6th May 1885)

ROMFORD FOOTBALL CLUB. – The Annual General Meeting of the above club was held at the White Hart Hotel, on Friday evening the 1st May. Mr.L.E.Clark (captain) presided, and there was a good attendance of members, including the hon.secs. Messrs.W.D.Matthews and C.Clark. The report, as read by the hon. secretary, pointed out that during the first part of the season the club enjoyed a period of continual success, but towards the end there was less energy displayed by the members. During the season 36 matches had been played, of which 21 were won, 11 were lost, and four were drawn. (Applause). They were credited with 74 goals, whilst 67 had been scored against them.

A still more satisfactory feature was that in the competition for the Association Cup the Club played into the fourth round – (Cheers) – having beaten the Clapton and Dulwich Clubs in the first and second rounds respectively, and drawn a bye in the third round. Under those circumstances the Club's team met the famous Blackburn Rovers in the fourth round, by whom they were beaten by 8 goals to love.

In the Essex Cup competition the Club, after having previously played a drawn game, suffered defeat at the hand of the Woodford Bridge Club, a loss no doubt attributable to the untoward accident which befell Mr.H.W. Palmer in the early part of the game, necessitating his own removal and that of his brother from the field and reducing the players of the home team from 11 to 9.

Financially, the club was in a healthy condition. The subscriptions received amounted to £37.9s., and the gate-money to £10.6s. – (applause) – the latter item being £1.17s.8d. in excess of the previous year, thus showing the increased interest taken in the game by the inhabitants. (Hear, Hear). There were a few more subscriptions to come in which when paid would show a balance to the good of £7.4s., in addition to which the club held a certain amount of realizable property such as goal posts, bars, balls. &c. (Applause). After a few congratulatory remarks from the Chairman, who took occasion to complement the Hon.Secs. for the able manner in which they had conducted the affairs of the club, the report was adopted. – The accounts were next audited by Messrs. E.Champness and G.B.Gilbey, and the treasurer's balance sheet was likewise adopted. –

The next business was the election of officers. – Mr.G.B.Gilbey proposed the re-election of Mr.L.E.Clark as captain, and, in seconding the proposition, Mr.Humphrey said it was no doubt an element of weakness to the club to introduce a new captain. – The Chairman said he had thoroughly made up his mind not to stand again. – Mr.Patching said that being so he thought the club ought to tender a hearty vote of thanks to the Chairman. – (Applause). He had worked very hard, and if he did resign he (the speaker) was sure the whole of the members would be very sorry. (Hear, Hear). – Mr.Champness seconded the proposition, remarking that no man in the club had worked harder or done more for its interests than had their Chairman. (Applause). – The vote of thanks was carried with enthusiasm and was duly acknowledged.

On the motion of Mr.Patching, Mr.Frank Webster was elected captain for the ensuing year, and Mr.L.E.Clark accepted the vice-captaincy. – For the Second Eleven, Mr.W.D.Matthews and Mr.B.J.Smith were elected captain and vice-captain respectively. –

A long discussion, initiated by Mr.G.Humphreys, then ensued as to the advisability of the club granting its honorary secretary an honorarium at the end of each season. The proposal however, met with little or no favour, although the speakers concurred in describing the duties of the office as exceedingly onerous and as deserving something more than merely a formal vote of thanks. – The meeting was then adjourned till Friday evening next.

Adjourned Annual General Meeting
(as reported in the *Essex Times*, Wednesday 13th May 1885)

The adjourned annual meeting was held at Head Quarters on Friday evening last, the 8th May. Mr.George Humphrey occupied the chair, and there were also present Messrs.H.Nettleship, C.H.Smith, A.Clark, G.A.Smith, F.H.Thirlwall, S.Skilton, G.F.Daldy, B.J.Smith, T.K.Gayford, F.Gilbey, J.Farrow, H.W.Palmer, F.D.R.Clark, H.Mansfield, L.E.Clark, J.Patching, J.Hooper, H.Shaye, and the two secretaries (W.D.Matthews and C.Clark). – The Chairman said the chief and most important subject before the meeting was the appointment of hon.sec. for the coming season, Messrs.W.D.Matthews and C.Clark having resigned office to the regret of the whole club. (Hear, Hear). – A long discussion followed, many names being mentioned, but it appeared impossible to fix the office on to anyone, and finally, on the proposition of Mr.G.A.Smith seconded by Mr.B.J.Smith, Mr.W.D.Matthews and the Chairman consented to accept the office *pro.tem.,* in the hope that very shortly some member would come forward as a volunteer for the post.

The Committee were then elected as follows:- Messrs.F.Webster, L.E.Clark, W.D.Matthews, B.J.Smith, E.Champness, F.D.R. Clark, C.Clark, R.Carter, T.K. Gayford, F.Gilbey, G.Humphrey, J.E.Macfarlane, H.Mansfield, C.S.Palmer, S.W.Skilton, G.A.Smith and F.H.Thirlwall. – The questions sent by the National Association as to the recognition of professionalism were considered, and were answered that the club was in favour of recognising professionalism under certain restrictions. – The meeting closed with a vote of thanks to the Chairman.

Note: Mr.L.E.Clark was proposed, at the Annual general Meeting, and seconded as captain for the ensuing year, although it appears he was not re-elected as the election took place at the adjourned meeting.

General Meeting
(as reported in the *Essex Times*, Wednesday 7th October 1885)

A meeting of the Romford Football Club was held at the White Hart Hotel on Friday, 2nd October, 1885. Mr. Grimston A. Smith presiding, referred to the fact they had lost their old ground at Great Mawneys, upon which they had played since the club's formation in 1876. They had lost the old ground through a speculative builder coming to Romford to try and ruin the place. (laughter). The committee have been able to secure the recreation ground, off Victoria Road, for the forthcoming season, at an agreed rent of £12 per annum. Mr. Smith said he thought it would be a good ground though not equal to their old one which was better than the Oval. (hear, hear). The new ground possessed an advantage in that spectators could stand on the dry cinder bicycle track encircling the football pitch to watch matches. This would have the effect of bringing in more visitors. (hear, hear).

THE ROMFORD RECREATION GROUND

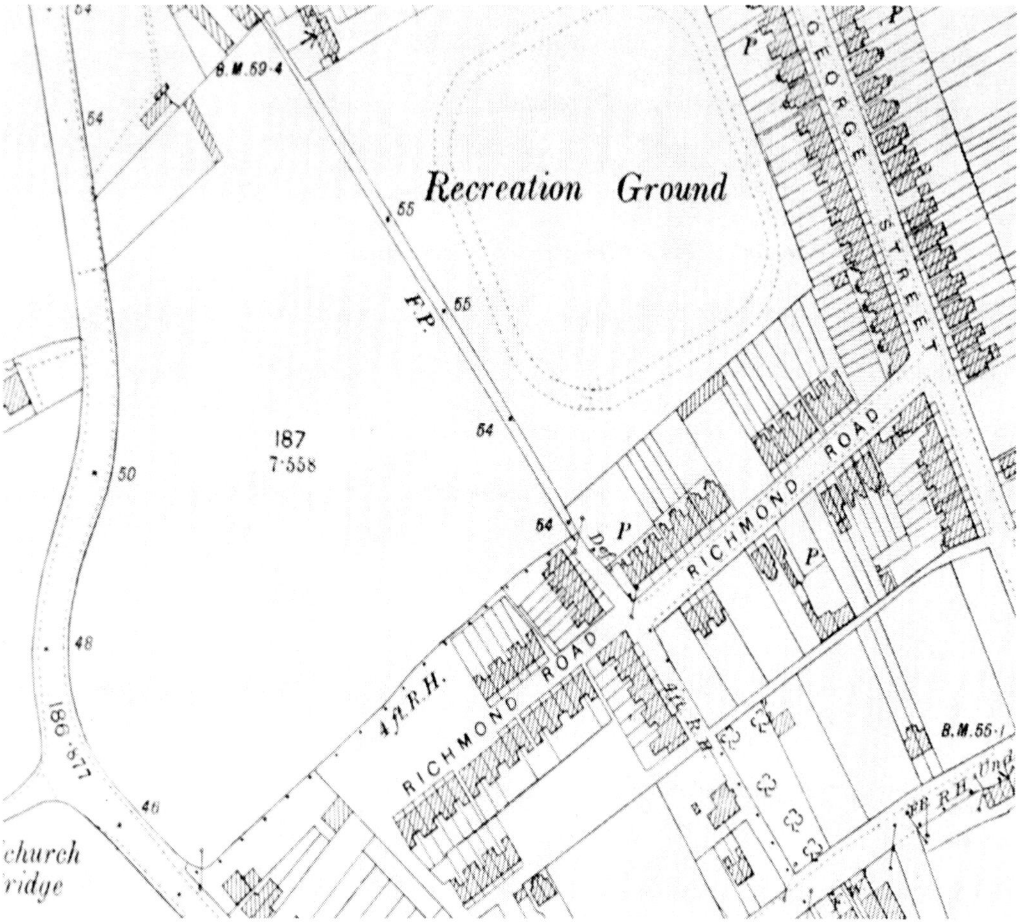

Havering Libraries - Local Studies

The Romford Recreation Ground opened in 1882 as a sports facility accessible to the general public. Romford Cricket Club left Great Mawneys to come here in 1883, followed two years later by the Romford Football Club. This map from c.1898 shows the cycle racing track which encircled the cricket square and football pitch. Athletics also took place here, and it had four tennis courts A small pavilion can be seen at the Richmond Road end of the ground.
(See also the photograph on page 87).

Season 1885 – 86

ROMFORD FOOTBALL CLUB

President: Mr R.G.Price

Hon.Secretary and Treasurer: Mr.W.D.Matthews *pro.tem.*

Hon.Secretary and Treasurer: Mr.W.D.Matthews and Mr.G.Humphrey
(In office at the time of the Annual Dinner on Sept., 25th)

Captain: Mr.Frank Webster **Vice-Captain:** Mr.L.E.Clark

Second Eleven Captain: Mr.W.D.Matthews **Second Eleven Vice-Captain:** Mr.B.J.Smith

Committee: Messrs.F.Webster, L.E.Clark, W.D.Matthews, B.J.Smith, E.Champness, F.D.R.Clark, C.Clark, R.Carter, T.K.Gayford, F.Gilbey, G.Humphrey, J.E.Macfarlane, H.Mansfield, C.S.Palmer, S.W.Skilton, G.A.Smith and F.H.Thirlwall.

Headquarters: White Hart Hotel, Romford **Ground:** Recreation Ground, Victoria Road, Romford

COMPETITIONS ENTERED

Friendly Matches
F.A. Challenge Cup

Match details

3 Oct Frdly Away Maidenhead 0 – 2
Romford:
Team details unknown

10 Oct Frdly Home Grove House (Shepherds Bush) 5 – 2 C.Palmer(2)Wright,Martin,C.Clark
Romford: C.H.Smith;G.E.Hitchcock,F.Webster(Capt));L.E.Clark,H.Mansfield,
W.Wright,J.Goadby,A.G.Martin,R.Oliver,C.S.Palmer.

17 Oct Frdly Away Buffaloes 1 – 1 Champness
Romford: C.H.Smith;B.J.Smith,T.K.Gayford;R.Carter,H.Hailey,C.Couzens;
W.D.Matthews,C.S.Palmer,A.G.Martin,E.Champness,K.Smith. Umpires: A.Cornell(Buffaloes) and F.Gilbey(Romford)

24 Oct Frdly Away Chatham 1 – 0 Matthews
Romford: H.Hailey;F.Webster(Capt),B.J.Smith;H.Mansfield,C.Couzens,W.D.Matthews;
L.E.Clark,R.Oliver,W.Wright,J.Goadby.

31 Oct FAC1R Away Hanover Utd. (Wimbledon) 1 – 1 Oliver
Romford: H.Hailey;B.J.Smith,F.Webster;G.E.Hitchcock,H.Mansfield,C.Couzens;
W.Wright,J.Goadby,C.S.Palmer,L.E.Clark(Capt),R.Oliver.

7 Nov FACRP Home Hanover Utd. (Wimbledon) 3 – 0 C.Palmer,Oliver,L.Clark
Romford: H.Hailey;F.Webster,B.J.Smith;G.E.Hitchcock,H.Mansfield,C.Couzens;
W.Wright,J.Goadby,L.E.Clark(Capt),R.Oliver,C.S.Palmer.

21 Nov Frdly Away Ivanhoe (West Ham) 2 – 1 L.Clark,Goadby
Romford: H.Hailey;F.Webster(Capt),J.E.Macfarlane;H.Mansfield,C.Couzens,J.Goadby;
W.D.Matthews,L.E.Clark,K.Smith,C.S.Palmer,A.Weech.

28 Nov FAC2R Bye

5 Dec Frdly Away Clapton 0 – 2
Romford: H.Hailey;F.Webster(Capt),J.E.Macfarlane;B.J.Smith,H.Mansfield,J.Goadby;
W.Wright,R.Oliver,L.E.Clark,H.W.Palmer.

12 Dec FAC3R Away Old Westminsters 1 – 5 L.Clark
Romford: H.Hailey;B.J.Smith,F.Webster;H.Mansfield,C.Hitchcock,C.Couzens;
J.Goadby,W.Wright,L.E.Clark(Capt),R.Oliver,C.H.Smith.

19 Dec Frdly Away Dulwich 0 – 6
Romford: H.Hailey;F.Webster(Capt),J.E.Macfarlane;H.Mansfield,K.Smith,W.D.Matthews;
W.Wright,J.Goadby,R.Oliver,C.S.Palmer,E.Champness.

2 Jan Frdly Home Ilford 1 – 3 Mansfield
Romford: H.Hailey;B.J.Smith,F.Webster;H.Mansfield,W.D.Matthews,C.Couzens;
R.Oliver,L.E.Clark(Capt),W.Wright,J.Goadby,S.W.Poulton.

16 Jan Frdly Home Clapton 0 – 1
Romford: H.Hailey;B.J.Smith,J.E.Macfarlane;H.Mansfield,C.Couzens,R.Carter;
R.Oliver,L.E.Clark(Capt),J.Goadby,W.Wright,C.Clark.

23 Jan Frdly Home Dulwich 2 – 3 Scorers unknown
Romford: H.Hailey;B.J.Smith,L.E.Clark(Capt);H.Mansfield,Rev.G.E.Hitchcock,A.G.Martin;
J.Goadby,W.Wright,S.W.Poulton,R.Oliver,C.Clark.

6 Feb Frdly Home Dulwich 0 – 3
Romford: C.H.Smith;F.Webster,L.E.Clark(Capt);H.Mansfield,C.Couzens,J.Goadby;
W.Wright,C.Clark,R.Oliver,W.D.Matthews.

13 Feb Frdly Home Ivanhoe (West Ham) 6 – 0 Yardley(3)L.Clark(2),Mansfield
Romford: E.Yardley;F.Webster,B.J.Smith;H.Mansfield,C.Couzens,W.D.Matthews;
L.E.Clark(Capt),R.Oliver,J.E.Macfarlane,H.Farrow,W.Wright.

20 Feb Frdly Home Rochester Invicta 5 – 0 L.E.Clark,C.Clark,Wright,Oliver,Thirlwall
Romford: H.Hailey;B.J.Smith,J.E.Macfarlane;H.Mansfield,C.Couzens,A.Cornell.Jnr;
L.E.Clark(Capt),R.Oliver,C.Clark,W.Wright,F.H.Thirlwall.

13 Mar Frdly Home Maidenhead 0 – 2
Romford: H.Hailey;B.J.Smith,J.E.Macfarlane;H.Mansfield,C.Couzens,A.G.Martin;
A.Weech,W.Wright,E.Yardley,R.Oliver.L.E.Clark(Capt).

SUMMARY OF FIRST TEAM RESULTS OBTAINED SEASON 1885 – 86

	P	W	D	L	Goals For	Goals Ag
Friendly Matches	14	5	1	8	23	26
F.A.Challenge Cup	3	1	1	1	5	6
Total	17	6	2	9	28	32
AGM Report	17	6	2	9	28	33

Note: The press report suggests that Romford conceded one more goal, but our scrutiny of match results has enabled us to collate all seventeen matches but we can only muster thirty two goals conceded.

CUP RESULTS SEASON 1885 – 86

F.A. Challenge Cup

Final: Blackburn Rovers 0 West Bromwich Albion 0
Replay: Blackburn Rovers 2 West Bromwich Albion 0

Romford's progress: 1st Round Home Hanover United 1 – 1
Replay Home Hanover United 3 – 0
2nd Round Bye
3rd Round Away Old Westminsters 1 – 5

First Team Appearances Season 1885 – 86

R.Carter	2	E.Champness	2	C.Clark	4	L.E.Clark	14
A.Cornell.Jnr.	1	C.Couzens	12	H.Farrow	1	T.K.Gayford	1
J.Goadby	12	H.Hailey	13	C.Hitchcock	1	G.E.Hitchcock	4
J.E.Macfarlane	7	H.Mansfield	15	A.G.Martin	4	W.D.Matthews	7
R.Oliver	14	C.S.Palmer	6	H.W.Palmer	1	S.W.Poulton	2
B.J.Smith	12	C.H.Smith	4	K.Smith	3	F.H.Thirlwall	1
F.Webster	11	A.Weech	2	W.Wright	14	E.Yardley	2
Total	172						

Note: The above record does not include the first game against Maidenhead on the 3rd October for which no details are available. On a number of occasions Romford played with only nine or ten men.

First Team Goal Scorers Season 1885 – 86

L.E.Clark	6	C.S.Palmer	3	E.Yardley	3	R.Oliver	3
W.Wright	2	H.Mansfield	2	C.Clark	2	A.G.Martin	1
E.Champness	1	W.D.Matthews	1	J.Goadby	1	F.H.Thirlwall	1
Unknown	2	Total	28				

RESERVE TEAM

Ground: Recreation Ground, Victoria Road

Match Details

3 Oct	Frdly	Home	Dulwich Reserves	1 – 2
10 Oct	Frdly	Away	Grove House Reserves	0 – 1
17 Oct	Frdly	Home	Buffaloes	1 – 1
24 Oct	Frdly	Home	Ilford Reserves	1 – 3
21 Nov	Frdly	Home	Hornchurch Wanderers	5 – 0
5 Dec	Frdly	Home	Clapton Reserves	0 – 0
19 Dec	Frdly	Home	Connaught Reserves	1 – 1
13 Mar	Frdly	Away	Ilford Reserves	0 – 3
20 Mar	Frdly	Away	Ilford Reserves	0 – 3

Romford Res.: T.K.Gayford;W.D.Matthews,R.Carter;E.Patching,H.Porter,H.Davis; S.C.Burgess,C.Clark,W.Lake,R.Edwards.

SUMMARY OF RESERVE TEAM RESULTS OBTAINED SEASON 1885 – 86

					Goals	
	P	W	D	L	For	Ag
All Friendly Matches	9	1	3	5	9	14

Post Season Summary Season 1885 – 86

Towards the end of the 1884 – 85 season the team had a lacklustre appearance and enthusiasm was at a low ebb. The joint secretaries both resigned at the annual general meeting, and player William David Matthews agreed to hold the position of Hon. Secretary and Treasurer on a pro. tem basis. He was elected together with Mr.G.Humphrey as joint hon.secretary and treasurer by the time of the annual dinner at the end of September.

Another setback was the club being forced to leave their home of nine years at Great Mawneys due to building development. They soon, however, found a new home at the Recreation Ground off Victoria Road. To accommodate the club, a new pavilion was erected behind the Richmond Road goal.

Romford commenced playing activities as usual at the beginning of October. The first match was lost 2-0 away to Maidenhead, but a week later, playing their first game on their new home ground, they beat Grove House 5-2. A week later away to Buffaloes a one all draw was achieved. The following week it appears that the team comprised only ten men but a 1-0 win was achieved at Chatham.

Next came the F.A. Cup tie at the Merton Hall Recreation ground at Wimbledon against Hanover United, ending in a 1–1 draw. The following Saturday Romford won the replay 3-0. Good fortune followed as they received a bye for some reason into round three. On 21st November away to Ivanhoe of West Ham, Romford gained a 2-1 victory.

The players then had a two-week break due to the bye in the F.A. Cup but returned to action on 5th December. Romford again played with only ten men and suffered a 2–0 defeat against the strong Clapton team. Worse was to follow as they were soundly beaten 5-1 in the 3rd Round of the F.A. Cup by Old Westminsters.

A massive setback was the death, the following Monday, of Frederick Clark at the shockingly early age of 27. He had chaired the first ever meeting of the club and was still an active member and supporter at the time of his death. His brothers Livingstone ('Tony') and Clifford, both still regular players, took time out for a couple of weeks to mourn their loss. The team then suffered five successive defeats, beginning with a 6-0 thrashing by Dulwich and ending with a 3-0 defeat at the hands of the same team.

On 13th February, quite out of the blue, Ivanhoe came to town but left a dejected side as goalkeeper Yardley recorded a hat-trick in Romford's 6-0 victory. The following week the locals scored five more goals without reply as they made short work of Rochester Invicta. The season closed as it had begun against Maidenhead, this time at home but with the same two goals to nil defeat. It had been a turbulent season, and with the reserve team having a poor year too, things were not so bright. It appears that the loss of Frederick Clark seriously affected the team. Many of the old stalwarts were not present at the annual general meeting, and both the captains and hon. secretaries resigned their positions.

Annual General Meeting
(as reported in the *Essex Times,* Wednesday 21st April 1886)

The annual meeting of the Romford Football Club was held at the White Hart Hotel on Friday evening, 16th April. Mr.G.B.Gilbey in the chair, and there were also present the Rev.G.E.Hitchcock, and Messrs. T.K.Gayford, L.E.Clark, F.Gilbey, F.M.Wilson, A.E.Patching, W.Shave, B.J.Smith, and G.F.Daldy, with Messrs. G.Humphrey and W.D.Matthews, hon.secretaries. – The annual report, read by Mr.Humphrey, stated that the past season had not been as successful as the previous one. This was chiefly through the absence of several prominent players, but apart from this the play all round had not been as good as in past seasons. Seventeen first eleven matches were played, and of these six were won, nine lost, and two drawn. 28 goals were scored for the club and 33 against. The club got into the third round of the Association cup competition. In the first round they defeated Hanover United by three goals to love after a drawn game (one all), in the second round they secured a bye, and in the third they were defeated by the Old Westminsters by six goals to one. Numerically the club was stronger, there being 115 members against 106 last year. The agreement with the lessees of the Recreation ground had expired, and it was for the meeting to decide whether it should be renewed.

Financially the club was in a very satisfactory condition. The balance from the previous year was £6.4s.0d., the subscriptions amounted to £40.0s.6d., the gate money to £8.19s.2d., and season tickets £1, making a total of £56.6s.2d. The expenditure amounted to £50.15s.5d., including £12 for rent of the ground, and a balance remained to the credit of the club of £5.10s.9d. There were outstanding subscriptions to the amount of £10.3s.6d. – On the proposal of Mr.L.E.Clark, seconded by Mr.Gayford, the report was adopted. – The accounts were passed after having been audited by the Rev. G.E. Hitchcock and Mr.Clark. – Mr.R.G.Price was re-elected president, the vice-presidents were re-elected, and it was resolved that Mr.J.Westlake,Q.C.,M.P., the Rev.F.Alban Wyld, Dr.Fraser, and Messrs. J.Ramsey, C.Godfrey, and H.Hollebone be invited to become vice-presidents. – The captains and hon.secretaries tendered their resignations. – On the proposal of Mr.L.E.Clark, it was decided to elect new officers at an adjourned meeting to be held this (Wednesday) evening at 8 p.m., a hope being expressed that there would then be a large attendance.

Adjourned Annual General Meeting
(as reported in the *Essex Times*, Wednesday 5th May 1886)

ROMFORD FOOTBALL CLUB. – The adjourned meeting of the above club was held at the White Hart Hotel, on Saturday evening, the 1st May, Mr.G.A.Smith presiding. There was a fair attendance. The Rev.G.E.Hitchcock was unanimously elected captain, and Mr.L.E.Clark, vice-captain for next season, and Messrs. G.Humphrey and G.B.Gilbey were elected joint hon.secs.

General Meeting
(as reported in the *Essex Times*, Wednesday 26th May 1886)

A meeting of the Romford Football Club was held at the White Hart Hotel on Saturday, 22nd May, 1886. Mr.G.A.Smith presided, to consider the question of a ground. The Lessees of the Recreation Ground, on which the club has played its matches for one season, have intimated that the rent on the ground would rise to eighteen pounds next season as against twelve pounds for the last season, an increase of fifty per cent. It was resolved that the recreation ground be hired for next season at the increased rent. The Caledonians, a Metropolitan club had been offered the ground for a rent of twenty pounds.

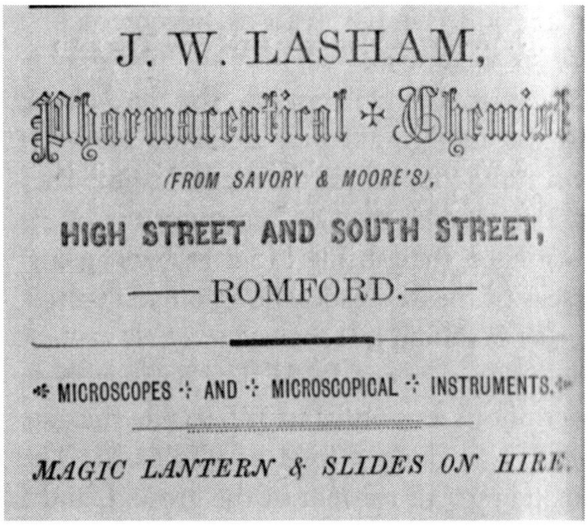

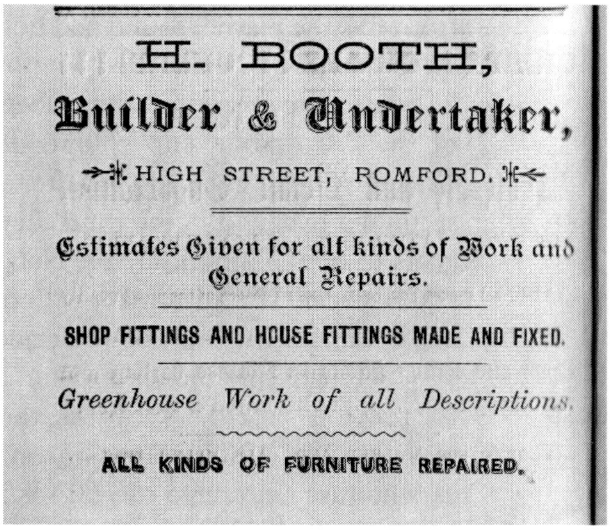

Romford players circa 1886
Havering Libraries - Local Studies

These photographs were discovered among the belongings of Arthur Cornell, who as well as being a very good and long-serving player for Romford, was also a keen photographer. The Romford badge can be clearly seen on the white shirt of the player seated to the right in the first picture. Several players can be recognised from the photograph taken in April 1883 (see page 44), but regrettably we are unable to put names to the players.

Season 1886 – 87

ROMFORD FOOTBALL CLUB

President: Mr.G.A.Smith **Joint Hon.Secretaries:** Messrs. G.Humphrey and G.B.Gilbey

Hon.Treasurer: Mr.W.D.Matthews

Captain: Rev.G.E.Hitchcock **Vice-Captain:** Mr.L.E.Clark

Headquarters: White Hart Hotel, Romford **Ground:** Recreation Ground, Victoria Road, Romford

COMPETITIONS ENTERED

Essex County F.A. Challenge Cup
Friendly Matches

The club did not compete in the F.A. Cup

Match details

2 Oct Frdly Home Olympic (Upton Park) 1 – 1 Clark
Romford: R.Carter;J.E.Macfarlane,B.J.Smith;T.K.Gayford,C.Couzens, G.E.Hitchcock(Capt);
W.Wright,F.H.Thirlwall,R.Oliver,L.E.Clark,T.Sparrow.

30 Oct ECC1R Away Woodville (Upton) 0 – 7
Romford: A.D.Cornell;L.E.Clark,J.E.Macfarlane;R.Carter,G.E.Hitchcock(Capt),C.Couzens;
W.Wright,R.Oliver,E.Champness,R.A.Clark,R.Ford.

6 Nov Frdly Home Ilford Reserves 2 – 0 Scorers unknown
Romford:
Team details unknown.

13 Nov Frdly Home Foxes (Edmonton) 0 – 0
Romford: J.Tetchner;T.K.Gayford,B.J.Smith;G.E.Hitchcock(Capt),C.Couzens,R.Carter;
W.Wright,T.Sparrow,E.Yardley,R.Oliver,W.D.Matthews.

20 Nov Frdly Home Ivanhoe (West Ham) 5 – 0 Wright(2)Matthews,Oliver,Yardley
Romford: J.Tetchner;B.J.Smith,T.K.Gayford;C.Couzens,G.E.Hitchcock(Capt),R.Carter;
W.Wright,T.Sparrow,E.Yardley,R.Oliver,W.D.Matthews.

29 Jan Frdly Home Silesia College (Barnet) 2 – 1 A scrimmage and L.E.Clark,
Romford: J.Tetchner;A.D.Cornell,W.D.Matthews,R.Carter,S.S.Smith,O.Wheatley,
W.Wright,T.Sparrow,E.H.Hinds,R.Oliver,L.E.Clark.

SUMMARY OF FIRST TEAM RESULTS OBTAINED SEASON 1886 – 87

					Goals	
	P	W	D	L	For	Ag
Friendly Matches	5	3	2	0	10	2
ECFA Challenge Cup	1	0	0	1	0	7
Total	6	3	2	1	10	9

Note: Mention is made at the AGM of the few matches that were played but no details were reported, and we have no team line-up for the Ilford Reserves game.

CUP RESULTS SEASON 1886 – 87

Essex County F.A. Challenge Cup

Final: Old Foresters 7 Grange Park 1

Romford's progress: 1st Round Away Woodville (Upton) 0 – 7

First Team Appearances Season 1886 – 87

R.Carter	5	E.Champness	1	L.E.Clark	3	R.A.Clark	1
A.D.Cornell	2	C.Couzens	4	R.Ford	1	T.K.Gayford	3
E.H.Hinds	1	G.E.Hitchcock	4	J.E.Macfarlane	2	W.D.Matthews	3
R.Oliver	5	B.J.Smith	3	S.S.Smith	1	T.Sparrow	4
J.Tetchner	3	F.H.Thirlwall	1	O.Wheatley	1	W.Wright	5
E.Yardley	2	Total	55				

Note: The above summary does not include the Ilford Reserves game for which there are no details.

First Team Goal Scorers Season 1886 – 87

W.Wright	2	L.E.Clark	2	W.D.Matthews	1	R.Oliver	1
E.Yardley	1	Unknown	1	Total	8		

Post Season Summary Season 1886 – 87

It was evident at the Annual General Meeting of the previous season that problems were arising at the club, when both the captains and secretaries tendered their resignations. This was resolved at the subsequent meeting, but the club was struggling to attract new members both as officials and players.

The season opened with a home match against Olympic of Upton Park and Romford secured a 1-1 draw. The next game, four weeks later, was in the County Cup competition – an away game against Woodville (Upton) which proved to be a disaster for the club who were on the receiving end of a seven goals to nil hiding. On the 6th November Romford were at home to Ilford Reserves and gained a much-needed two nil victory.

The following week they renewed conflict with old rivals Foxes from Edmonton and fought out a goalless draw at the Recreation Ground. On 20th November with a near full strength side, Romford excelled when they beat Ivanhoe by five goals to nil, old favourites Matthews and Wright getting among the goals.

Two months followed without a match until Silesia College were beaten by two goals to one, again at the Recreation Ground, on 29th January. We have been unable to find any further results for the season, and indeed do not know if any more were played.

The Annual General Meeting indicated that very few games had been played but gave no indication as to the number, other than to state that eight goals had been scored by the club and eight conceded, which is near to our summary of results.

The Annual General Meeting report also makes it clear that although the club was in a good financial position, it was doubtful, due to the lack of playing members, whether they could continue playing the following season.

Annual General Meeting

(as reported in the *Essex Times,* Wednesday 11th May 1887)

The annual general meeting of the Romford Football Club was held at the White Hart Hotel, on Monday evening, 9th May, when there were present. – Messrs. L.E.Clark (in the chair), G.B.Gilbey, and G.Humphrey (hon.secs)., W.D.Matthews (hon.treasurer), E.Champness, F.Gilbey, T.K.Gayford, H.W.Palmer, B.J.Smith, F.H.Thirlwall, F.M.Wilson, &c., &c. – The report, as read by Mr.Humphrey, stated that last season's play had not been so satisfactory as could have been desired. The usual number of matches had been arranged, but owing to the regrettable illness of the captain (Rev.G.E.Hitchcock) and to other adverse causes comparatively few were played, with the results that eight goals were won and an equal number lost.

Financially things were more satisfactory, the receipts having been £35.16s.0d., as against an expenditure of £31.12s.5d. Taking also into account the sum of £11.11s.6d, representing unpaid subscriptions, the gross balance in favour of the Club was £15.15s.1d. (Applause). The report went on to state that owing to the small number of matches which had been played, the Hon.Secs. had communicated with the lessees of the Recreation Ground with the result that the rent had been reduced from £20 to £16.16s.0d. – On the proposition of Mr.Thirlwall, seconded by Mr.Champness, the report and balance sheet were unanimously adopted. – The Chairman said the next business would be the appointment of officers; but considering the lack of energy on the part of the members in the affairs of the Club, it was a question whether it should longer be carried on.

Mr.Humphrey said that looking over the list of playing members it was very uncertain whether the club could even get an eleven to play every Saturday next season or even every alternate Saturday, and it would be foolish to arrange matches when there were no prospect of playing them. Under the circumstances, it was a question whether – supposing it were decided to continue the club – it should be continued in a dormant state until it found itself in a better position than it appeared to be in at the present moment. –

Considerable discussion ensued, in which the opinion was generally expressed in favour of still carrying on the club, especially considering the position of its finances, and the fact that it could rely on from 12 to 16 playing members. – Mr.Palmer, in proposing a motion to that effect, contended that the club was in quite a flourishing condition. He strongly deprecated showing the white feather just because they had experienced one adverse season, and he equally deprecated the proposal to amalgamate with the Buffaloes. – Mr.Champness seconded the proposition, and suggested that fewer matches than usual be arranged. Referring to the suggested amalgamation with the Buffaloes, he agreed with the remarks of Mr.Palmer. If, however, that club liked to come forward, he (Mr.Champness) thought the Romford Club would be glad to welcome them with a view to an amalgamation.

The proposition was put, and carried unanimously. – The meeting was then adjourned to the 3rd June for the election of officers.

Adjourned Annual General Meeting

(as reported in the *Essex Times*, Wednesday 8th June 1887)

At an adjourned general meeting of the Romford Football Club, at the White Hart Hotel, on Friday evening, 3rd June, Mr.F.H.Thirlwall presiding, Mr.A.Cornell was elected hon.secretary, subject to his acceptance of the post. It was resolved that the club be affiliated to the Essex County Cycling and Athletic Association and Messrs.G.Humphrey and L.E.Clark were elected to represent the club to that association.

Note: It appears that Arthur Cornell was not present at the adjourned meeting and later declined the post, as it is known that Edward Hinds was Hon.Secretary and William D.Matthews, Hon.Treasurer for the ensuing season.

The club ceases playing activity for the season

In late September, Romford Football Club announced that: 'Although this Club is in a healthy condition financially no matches have been arranged for this season. The lack of playing members and the failure to get anyone to undertake the duties of Hon. secretary are the main reasons for this regrettable inactivity'.

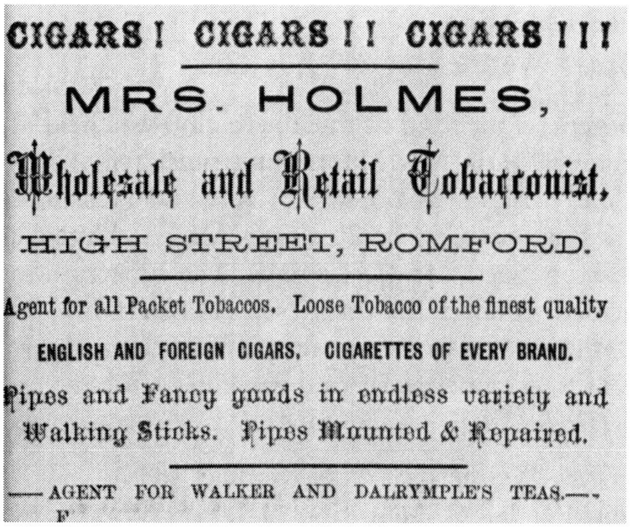

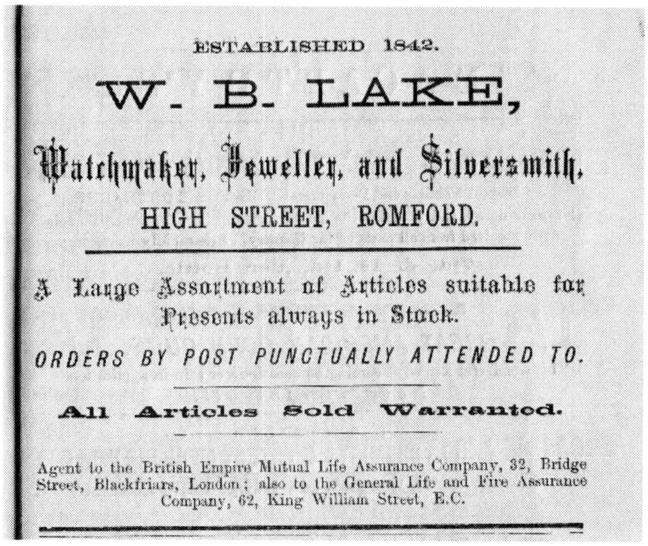

Season 1887 – 88

ROMFORD FOOTBALL CLUB

Hon.Secretary: Mr.E.H.Hinds **Hon.Treasurer:** Mr.W.D.Matthews

Headquarters: Golden Lion Hotel, Romford **Ground:** Recreation Ground, Victoria Road, Romford

Match details

21 Jan	Frdly	Away	Excelsior	P – P

ROMFORD FOOTBALL CLUB - Mr.Hynds [sic], hon. sec. of this club, contradicts the report that they played Excelsior Second Eleven at Chelmsford, last Saturday, and lost by six goals to nil. He says they had arranged to play the Excelsior first team, but were obliged to scratch, as they could not raise a team, and, consequently, not one of their club members went to Chelmsford that day. (The *Essex Times*, 25th January 1888)

The Club suspends playing activities

In February 1888 Romford Football Club suspended operations due to internal wrangles and the difficulty finding anybody willing to take on the responsibility of running the club. The players, determined not to sit around kicking their heels, continued playing on their own home at the recreation ground for three other teams, namely Romford Olympic F.C., Romford Y.M.C.A., and the Nondescripts F.C. All games played were friendly matches.

Resuscitation of the Romford Football Club

On Friday evening 13th July, Mr. George Humphrey presided over a well attended meeting of the members of the Romford, Romford Olympic and Romford Young Men's Christian Association football clubs at the Golden Lion Hotel. It was resolved to amalgamate the three clubs under the title of The Romford Football Club and Messrs. Burrows and Hinds were appointed joint Hon. Secretaries, pro tem. The meeting was deemed very satisfactory. (The *Essex Times*, 18th July 1888)

Annual General Meeting
(as reported in the *Essex Times,* Wednesday 25th July 1888)

ROMFORD FOOTBALL CLUB – A general meeting of the above club was held at the Golden Lion Hotel, on Friday evening 20th July, Mr.G.Humphrey presiding….The officers elected were as follows:- President, Mr.J.Theobald, M.P., Capt., and Treasurer, Mr.W.D. Matthews; Vice-Captain; Mr.J.F.Burrows; Captain 2nd eleven, Mr. F.G.Hudgell; Vice-Captain 2nd eleven, Mr. W.Hynds, Hon. Sec.., Mr. E.H. Hinds. The subscription was fixed at 5s the season. It was decided to enter for the Essex Association Cup, Mr.Humphrey being elected representative to the various county associations. A list of matches was read; the opening fixture to commence second week in October.

CROWD TROUBLE! (The *Essex Times*, Wednesday 7th November 1888)

At a Committee Meeting of the club held at the Golden Lion Hotel on Monday 5th November, attention was drawn to the fact that some individuals witnessing the match against Barking Rovers, did not conduct themselves in a gentlemanly manner and made use of foul and offensive language to the Barking team. It was resolved in the interest of local players and supporters that should this offence be repeated, instructions shall be given to refuse those persons admittance to the ground.

Season 1888 – 89

ROMFORD FOOTBALL CLUB

President: Mr.J.Theobald.M.P. **Hon.Secretary:** Mr.E.H.Hinds **Hon.Treasurer:** Mr.W.D.Matthews

Captain: Mr.W.D.Matthews **Vice-Captain:** Mr.J.F.Burrows

Reserve Team Captain: Mr.F.G.Hudgell **Reserve Team Vice-Captain:** Mr.W.Hynds

Headquarters: Golden Lion Hotel, Romford **Ground:** Recreation Ground, Victoria Road, Romford

Mr.G.Humphrey appointed to represent the Club at Essex County Football Association Meetings.

COMPETITIONS ENTERED

Essex County F.A. Challenge Cup
Friendly Matches

Match details

6 Oct Frdly Home Belhus 1 – 3 Scorer unknown
Romford:
Team details unknown

13 Oct Frdly Home Belmont (Upton) 5 – 1 Clark(3)Wright,Burrows
Romford: T.Davis;B.J.Smith,T.K.Gayford;W.D.Matthews(Capt),S.S.Smith,E.H.Hinds;
J.Amey,J.F.Burrows,W.Wright,C.Clark,R.Oliver.

20 Oct Frdly Away Northamptonshire Regiment 3 – 2 Oliver(2)Amey
Romford: T.Davis;B.J.Smith,W.Brewster;E.H.Hinds,G.Stevenson,C.Couzens;
J.Amey,J.F.Burrows(Capt),R.Oliver,E.J.Ramsey,C.Clark.

27 Oct Frdly Home St. Edward's Church Institute 0 – 0
Romford:
Team details unknown

3 Nov ECC1R Home Barking Rovers 1 – 2* Oliver
Attendance: 500
Romford: T.Davis;A.D.Cornell,C.Couzens;S.S.Smith,G.Stevenson,E.H.Hinds;
J.Amey,W.Wright,R.Oliver,F.Adams,E.J.Ramsay.

10 Nov Frdly Home Leytonstone 2 – 0 Scorers unknown
Romford: T.Davis;B.J.Smith,W.D.Matthews(Capt);C.Couzens,O.Wheatley,R.Carter;
W.Wright,F.Wells,R.Oliver,J.F.Burrows,F.Adams.

17 Nov Frdly Home Buckhurst Hill 3 – 0 E.H.Hinds(2)Oliver
Romford: T.Davis;B.J.Smith,W.Brewster;G.Stevenson,A.Thomson,W.D.Matthews(Capt);
W.Wright,J.Amey,R.Oliver,J.F.Burrows,E.H.Hinds.

24 Nov Frdly Home Old St. John's (Upton Park) 3 – 0 Oliver,Amey,F.Wells
Romford:
Team details unknown

1 Dec ECCRep Away Barking Rovers 1 – 2 Amey
Romford: T.Davis;E.J.Ramsey,C.G.Pullen;W.Wright,J.Amey,E.H.Hinds;
S.S.Smith,C.Couzens,B.J.Smith,A.Cornell,R.Oliver.

8 Dec Frdly Home Upton Rovers 1 – 1 Wells
Romford: H.Tetchner;T.K.Gayford,C.Couzens;R.Carter,O.Wheatley,J.F.Burrows(Capt);
R.Oliver,F.Wells,F.Adams,C.Clark,F.G.Hudgell.

22 Dec Frdly Away Chelmsford 2 – 3 Scorers unknown
Romford: H.Tetchner;T.K.Gayford,C.Couzens;B.J.Smith,H.Heasman,W.D.Matthews;
C.G.Pullen,R.Oliver,C.ClarkE.H.Hinds,F.Wells.

26 Dec# Frdly Home Clapton Melrose 1 – 0 Scorer unknown

26 Dec# Frdly Home Limehouse 4 – 0 Oliver(2)Pullen,Wells

29 Dec Frdly Home Plaistow 4 – 1 Oliver(2)F.Wells.Jnr.,Pullen
Romford: Team details unknown

12 Jan Frdly Home Ilford Park 1 – 3 Scorer unknown
Romford: Team details unknown

2 Feb Frdly Home Grange Park (Leyton) 2 – 0 A Scrimmage,Wright
Romford:
Team details unknown

9 Feb Frdly Away Leytonstone 0 – 2
Romford:
Team details unknown

16 Feb Frdly Home 1st Northamptonshire Regt. 2 – 0 Pullen(2)
Romford:
Team details unknown

23 Feb Frdly Away Grange Park (Leyton) 3 – 2 Scorers unknown
Romford:
Team details unknown

16 Mar Frdly Away Belhus 2 – 3 Scorers unknown
Romford:
Team details unknown

20 Apr CHC Home Ilford 0 – 1
Romford: T.Davis;E.F.Barrow,B.J.Smith;W.D.Matthews(Capt),E.H.Hinds,C.Couzens;
W.Wright,C.Pullen,R.Oliver,F.Wells,E.J.Ramsey.

* Romford protested at the late arrival of Barking Rovers. Match declared void.

Played two games on the same day.

SUMMARY OF RESULTS OBTAINED SEASON 1888 – 89

					Goals	
	P	W	D	L	For	Ag
Friendly Matches	18	11	2	5	39	21
ECFA Challenge Cup	1	0	0	1	1	2
ECFA Chal. Cup (Void)	1	0	0	1	1	2
Cottage Hospital Charity	1	0	0	1	0	1
Total	21	11	2	8	41	26

Note: In some earlier years the A.G.M. report appeared to have included reserve team results in the summary, but this year it was reported that the **first team** played twenty two games. We have obtained eleven results for the reserve team and it is not known whether there were other games played by them.

CUP RESULTS SEASON 1888 – 89

Essex County F.A. Challenge Cup Final: Ilford 2 Somerset Light Infantry 0

Romford's progress: 1st Round Home Barking Rovers 1 – 2*
Replay Home Barking Rovers 1 – 2

*Note: Romford protest at late arrival of Barking Rovers, match declared void and a replay was ordered.

Ilford Hospital Charity Cup
Final: Romford 0 Ilford 1

First Team Appearances Season 1888 – 89

F.Adams	2*	J.Amey	4*	E.F.Barrow	1	W.Brewster	2
J.F.Burrows	5*	R.Carter	2	C.Clark	4	A.D.Cornell	1*
C.Couzens	6*	T.Davis	6*	T.K.Gayford	3	H.Heasman	1
E.H.Hinds	6*	F.G.Hudgell	1	W.D.Matthews	5	R.Oliver	8*
C.G.Pullen	3	E.J.Ramsey	3*	B.J.Smith	7	S.S.Smith	2*
G.Stevenson	2*	H.Tetchner	2	A.Thomson	1	F.Wells	4
O.Wheatley	2	W.Wright	5*	Total	88		

* Played in the game versus Barking Rovers that was declared void.

First Team Goal Scorers Season 1888 – 89

R.Oliver	9	C.Clark	3	J.Amey	3	C.G.Pullen	4
F.Wells	4	W.Wright	2	E.H.Hinds	2	J.F.Burrows	1
Unknown	6	Total	34				

Unfortunately information on goal scorers is limited and the above listing is far from complete.

RESERVE TEAM
Ground: Recreation Ground, Victoria Road, Romford

Match Details

6 Oct Frdly Away Manor Park 2 – 4 Scorers unknown
Romford: Bailey;E.H.Hinds,Thomson;Carter,F.Wells,H.G.Smith;
J.Amey,Wilson,F.Adams,F.G.Hudgell,Guyatt.
13 Oct Frdly Away Belmont (Upton) Reserves 13 – 1 Scorers unknown
20 Oct Frdly Home St. Edward's Church Institute 4 – 4 Scorers unknown
St. Edward's Church Institute: E.Stevenson; ?? , ?? ;W.Swift, ?? ,C.Brown;
M.Sellick,S.Anderson,J.Scott(Capt),G.Enoch,H.Taylor. Umpire: Mr.W.Witherick
27 Oct Frdly Away Cedars 0 – 3
24 Nov Frdly Away St. Olive's (Victoria Park) 0 – 3
1 Dec Frdly Home Cedars 0 – 1
Romford Reserves:
Fielded a very weak team.
29 Dec Frdly Away Chadwell Heath 2 – 1 Scorers unknown
26 Jan Frdly Home Manor Park 1 – 3 Scorer unknown
9 Feb Frdly Home Plaistow 2 – 1 Scorers unknown
23 Feb Frdly Home Chadwell Heath 6 – 0 Scorers unknown

SUMMARY OF RESERVE TEAM RESULTS OBTAINED SEASON 1888 – 89

					Goals	
	P	W	D	L	For	Ag
Friendly Matches	10	4	1	5	30	21

Post Season Summary Season 1888 – 89

The season started on a sad note following the death of the club's President Mr Grimston Abel Smith in April at the age of 45. Mr. Smith, a cashier at the Romford Brewery, had chaired one of the first-ever meetings and in fact played in a few games in the inaugural season. He was for some years a member of the Management Committee before being elected President.

The club reduced season ticket prices from seven shillings and sixpence to five shillings. The season opened with a 3-1 home defeat by Belhus, but a fine 5-1 victory was achieved the following week at home to Belmont (Upton). This was followed by a win over Northamptonshire Regiment, and a draw against St. Edward's Church Institute took the team to the end of October. November commenced in controversy when Barking Rovers arrived late for the Essex Senior Cup Tie, but obtained a 2-1 win over the home club. Romford protested at the late arrival of their opponents, and the County Association declared the match void and ordered a replay. Romford were not happy at the behaviour of some of their own supporters on this occasion! During the rest of November, Romford obtained three successive victories without conceding a goal, including a two goals to nil win over Leytonstone.

Romford got off to a bad start to December when the Essex Cup tie was replayed, and Barking Rovers again won at Romford by two goals to one. Romford had no reason to complain this time, and continued with their friendly fixtures in a 1-1 draw at home to Upton Rovers. On 22nd December, away to Chelmsford, Romford were defeated 3-2.

On Boxing Day Romford played two first team matches as reported in the press. The first against Clapton Melrose commenced at 10 a.m. and ended in a one nil victory. The second game kicked off at 2 p.m. and Romford defeated Limehouse by four goals to nil. They ended the year with a fine four goals to one win over Plaistow.

In the New Year Romford opened with a home defeat by Ilford Park, and a home victory over Grange Park (Leyton) by two goals to nil before losing the return game with Leytonstone by the same score. Two successive victories rounded up the month of February: against the 1st Northamptonshire Regiment and the return game against Grange Park.

Romford then suffered a 3-2 defeat at Belhus, but the team was taken on one of Mr. P. Reynolds' coaches, and we are told that a good day was had by all! The season came to a close on 20th April when Romford entertained Ilford in the final of the Cottage Hospital Charity Cup and Ilford picked up the silverware with a one goal to nil win.

Annual General Meeting

(as reported in the *Essex Times,* Saturday 31st August 1889)

The annual general meeting of the members of the Romford Football Club was held at the Golden Lion Hotel on Thursday evening, 29th August. The chair was taken by Mr.G.Humphreys, and there were also present, Messrs. W.D.Matthews (Captain), R.Carter, L.E.Clark, B.J.Smith, F.Wells, J.Amey, C.A.Wilson, W.Hynds, E.Challenor, J.F.Burrows, G.Barnes, C.Lamprill, R.Wedlake, H.J.Smith, and E.H.Hinds (hon.sec). The hon.sec. read the report, which was of a very satisfactory nature, the balance of the matches played having been won. The first eleven had played 22 matches, of which 13 had been won, seven lost, and two drawn, scoring 47 goals against their opponents' 30, the second eleven having been equally successful. It was suggested that all travelling expenses should be paid to ensure a more representative team playing in the out matches.

The hon.treasurer (Mr.W.D.Matthews) read the financial statement, from which it appeared that the receipts amounted to £51.13s.9d., and the expenditure to £42.16s.4d., leaving a balance in hand of £8.17s.5d...

It was decided to again hire the Recreation Ground for the season, upon the same terms as before, namely £14 per annum. Mr.J.Theobald.M.P., was re-elected president, and the names of Messrs. H.Holmes, E.Bryant, and Captain Darke, were added to the list of vice-presidents. Mr.W.D.Matthews was chosen as captain of the first eleven for the ensuing season, with Mr.L.E.Clark as vice-captain; Messrs. W.Hynds and H.G.Smith being elected captain and vice-captain respectively of the second eleven. Messrs.E.H.Hinds and W.D.Matthews were re-elected hon.sec. and hon.treasurer respectively, and cordially thanked for their services to the club during the past year. Mr.G.Humphreys was elected representative of the club to the associations.

Considerable discussion took place as to whether the subscription should remain the same for players of all ages, and eventually it was resolved to reduce the subscription to 2s.6d. for members 16 years of age and under. It was decided that the Club should enter for the Essex Cup Competition, and the price of admission to the club ground for ordinary matches was fixed at 2d. The following gentlemen were elected on the committee: - Messrs. G.Barnes, E.Champness, C.Clark, G.B.Gilbey, C.Pullen, F.Wells, O.Wheatley, B.J.Smith, C.H.Lamprill, R.Carter, J.Amey, R.Wedlake, J.F.Burrows, and E.Challenor.

Season 1889 – 90

ROMFORD FOOTBALL CLUB

President: Mr.J.Theobald.M.P. **Hon.Secretary:** Mr.E.H.Hinds **Hon.Treasurer:** Mr.W.D.Matthews

Captain: Mr.W.D.Matthews **Vice-Captain:** Mr.L.E.Clark

Reserve Team Captain: Mr.W.Hynds **Reserve Team Vice-Captain:** Mr.H.G.Smith

Committee: Messrs.G.Barnes, E.Champness, C.Clark, G.B.Gilbey, C.Pullen, F.Wells, O.Wheatley B.J.Smith, C.H.Lamprill, R.Carter, J.Amey, R.Wedlake, J.F.Burrows, E.Challenor

County Representative: Mr.G.Humphreys

Headquarters: Golden Lion Hotel, Romford **Ground:** Recreation Ground, Victoria Road, Romford

COMPETITIONS ENTERED

Essex County F.A. Challenge Cup
Friendly Matches

Match Details

5 Oct Frdly Away Buckhurst Hill 4 – 1 Scorers unknown

19 Oct Frdly Home Barking Rovers 3 – 2 Wells(2),Amey
Romford: J.Tetchner;B.J.Smith,W.D.Matthews(Capt);C.Couzens,E.H.Hinds,R.Oliver; W.Wright,C.G.Pullen,J.Amey,E.J.Ramsey,F.Wells.

26 Oct Frdly Away Tottenham Hotspur 0 – 0

2 Nov Frdly Home Ilford Park 2 – 0 Pullan,Amey
Romford: J.Tetchner;B.J.Smith,E.F.Barrow;W.D.Matthews(Capt),E.H.Hinds,W.Gillett; C.S.Pullan,E.A.Gibson,F.Wells,J.Amey,W.Jackson.

9 Nov Frdly Away West Ham Church Institute 3 – 5 Scorers unknown

16 Nov ECC1R Away Grange Park (Leyton) 2 – 0 Amey,Ramsey
Romford: J.Tetchner;E.F.Barrow,B.J.Smith;E.H.Hinds(Capt),R.Oliver,C.Couzens; W.Wright,E.A.Gibson,J.Amey,E.J.Ramsey,F.Wells.

23 Nov Frdly Away Upton Excelsior 2 – 0 Jordison(2)

30 Nov Frdly Home Buckhurst Hill 4 – 1 Jordison(2)Ramsey,Wells
Romford: J.Tetchner;W.D.Matthews(Capt),E.F.Barrow;E.H.Hinds,R.Oliver,C.Couzens; W.Wright,E.J.Ramsey,F.Wells,E.A.Gibson,F.Jordison.

14 Dec ECC2R Home Upton Excelsior 2 – 1 Pullan,Amey
Romford: J.Tetchner;B.J.Smith,E.F.Barrow;C.Couzens,R.Oliver,E.H.Hinds(Capt); W.Wright,C.J.Pullan,J.Amey,E.J.Ramsey,F.Wells.

21 Dec Frdly Away Belmont (Upton) P – P

26 Dec Frdly Home Plaistow 8 – 2 Scorers unknown

28 Dec Frdly Home West Ham Church Inst. 1 – 0 Oliver

4 Jan Frdly Home Woodville 1 – 1 Scorer unknown

11 Jan Frdly Home Tottenham Hotspur 1 – 1 Scorer unknown
Romford: J.Tetchner;E.H.Hinds(Capt),R.Carter;C.Couzens,H.G.Smith,A.Cornell.Jnr.; W.Wright,R.W.Wedlake,R.Oliver,O.Wheatley,F.Wells.

18 Jan ECC3R Home Leyton Rovers 4 – 1 Amey(3)Pullan
Romford: J.Tetchner;E.H.Hinds(Capt),E.F.Barrow;B.J.Smith,R.Oliver,C.Couzens;
W.Wright,C.G.Pullen,J.Amey,E.J.Ramsey,Fred. Wells.

25 Jan Frdly Home Belmont (Upton) 1 – 1 Wedlake

8 Feb ECCSF Ilford Woodford 2 – 0 Wright,Amey
Romford: J.Tetchner;E.F.Barrow,A.Cornell;C.Couzens,R.Oliver,E.H.Hinds(Capt);
W.Wright,C.G.Pullen,J.Amey,E.J.Ramsey,F.Wells. Referee: Mr.W.Comerford(Crusaders)

1 Mar Frdly Home Woodford 0 – 6
Romford:
Team details unknown but Romford played four men short

8 Mar ECCF Leyton Ilford 0 – 2
Attendance: 1,600
Ilford: H.Hailey;W.King,F.King;E.Markland,H.Porter(Capt),P.A.Read;
E.J.Pracey,H.Watts,H.C.Hinds,J.P.H.Soper,W.J.Somerville.

Romford: J.Tetchner;A.D.Cornell,E.F.Barrow;E.H.Hinds(Capt),R.Oliver,C.Couzens;
C.G.Pullan,W.Wright,J.Amey,F.Wells,E.J.Ramsey.

15 Mar Frdly Home Upton Rovers 0 -11

12 Apr VCH Home F.H.Thirlwall XI 3 – 0 Ramsey,Gibson,Wright
Romford: J.Tetchner, goal; E.F.Barrow and F.J.Burrows, backs; C.Couzens, R.Oliver, and O.Wheatley, half-backs;
E.J.Ramsey, E.H.Hinds(Capt),F.Wells,E.A.Gibson, and W.Wright, forwards.

Mr.Thirlwall's Team: C.Clark, goal;F.Hill and Lawson, backs; W.T.Knowles, Ravenscroft, and V.Howard, half-backs;
F.H.Thirlwall(Capt),E.S.Thirlwall, the Rev.F.W.Hodgson,J.Longden, and J.Dawes, forwards.
Referee: E.Challenor.

SUMMARY OF FIRST TEAM RESULTS OBTAINED SEASON 1889 – 90

					Goals	
	P	W	D	L	For	Ag
ECFA Challenge Cup	5	4	0	1	10	4
Friendly Matches	14	7	4	3	30	31
Victoria Hosp. Fund	1	1	0	0	3	0
Total	20	12	4	4	43	35
A.G.M. Report	21	12	4	5	45	34

CUP RESULTS SEASON 1889 - 90

Essex County F.A. Challenge Cup

Final: Ilford 2 Romford 0

Romford's progress:

1st Round	Away	Grange Park (Leyton)	2 – 0
2nd Round	Home	Upton Excelsior	2 – 1
3rd Round	Home	Leyton Rovers	4 – 1
Semi-Final	Ilford	Woodford	2 – 0
Final	Leyton	Ilford	0 – 2

First Team Appearances Season 1889 – 90

J.Amey	7	E.F.Barrow	8	F.J.Burrows	1	R.Carter	1
A.Cornell.Jnr.	1	A.D.Cornell	2	C.Couzens	9	E.A.Gibson	4
W.Gillett	2	E.H.Hinds	9	W.Jackson	1	F.Jordison	1
W.D.Matthews	3	R.Oliver	9	C.G.Pullen	6	E.J.Ramsey	8
B.J.Smith	5	H.G.Smith	1	J.Tetchner	10	R.W.Wedlake	1
F.Wells	10	O.Wheatley	2	W.Wright	9	Total	110

Few team line-ups are known but the above players definitely played for the first team on one or more occasion, and this summary gives a good idea of the regulars in the team.

First Team Goal Scorers Season 1889 – 90

J.Amey	8	F.Jordison	4	C.G.Pullen	3	F.Wells	3
E.J.Ramsey	3	R.Oliver	1	R.W.Wedlake	1	W.Wright	2
A.E.Gibson	1	Unknown	17	Total	43		

Unfortunately several goal scorers are unknown, due to the poor press coverage.

RESERVE TEAM

Match Details

5 Oct	Frdly	Home	Elgin Rovers Reserves	7 – 1	
12 Oct	Frdly	Home	Woodland Rovers	1 – 1	Challenor

Romford Reserves: E.Titchener;R.Carter,J.F.Burrows;H.R.Pitt,H.G.Smith(Capt),E.Challenor; G.White,R.W.Wedlake,T.Poole,H.Bracknall,T.Turner.

19 Oct	Frdly	Away	Chadwell Heath	1 – 5
26 Oct	Frdly	Home	Tottenham Hotspur Reserves	1 - 2
2 Nov	Frdly	Away	Ilford Park Reserves	3 – 3
9 Nov	Frdly	Home	West Ham Church Inst.Reserves	3 – 1
23 Nov	Frdly	Home	Woodville Reserves	0 – 2
23 Nov	Frdly	Away	Manor Park Reserves	2 – 1
26 Dec	Frdly	Home	Romford St. Andrew's	0 – 2
4 Jan	Frdly	Away	Woodville Reserves	P – P

Romford unable to field a team

1 Feb	Frdly	Home	Manor Park Reserves	3 – 0
15 Feb	Frdly	Home	Ilford Park Reserves	0 – 4
22 Feb	Frdly	Away	Upton Rovers Reserves	1 – 3
20 Mar	Frdly	Home	Chadwell Heath	4 – 0

Very few details of the reserve team goal scorers were reported in the local press.

SUMMARY OF RESERVE TEAM RESULTS OBTAINED SEASON 1889 – 90

					Goals	
	P	W	D	L	For	Ag
All Friendly Matches	13	5	2	6	26	25

Post-Season Summary Season 1889 – 90

Romford began the season with a 4-1 away victory at Buckhurst Hill, and on 19th October played the first home game against Barking Rovers who were beaten 3-2. There followed a fine 0–0 draw against Tottenham Hotspur away. On 2nd November Romford were at home to Ilford Park and won 2-0. A week later they suffered a setback with their first defeat of the season, away to West Ham Church Institute who triumphed by five goals to three. On 16th November Romford travelled to Leyton to play Grange Park in the Essex Challenge Cup 1st Round and progressed with a 2-0 victory. The following week they won two nil in an away friendly against Upton Excelsior.

On 30th November Romford played their first home game for four weeks when they entertained Buckhurst Hill and obtained a 4-1 victory. Two weeks later they returned to cup action in the 2nd Round of the Essex Challenge Cup and defeated Upton Excelsior at the Recreation Ground by two goals to one. On Boxing Day Romford entertained Plaistow, obtaining an emphatic 8-2 victory. Two days later they obtained their sixth victory in a row with a 1-0 home win against West Ham Church Institute.

Romford started the New Year with a couple of home 1–1 drawn games against Woodville and Tottenham Hotspur. In their next game, centre forward Amey recorded a hat-trick in a 4-1 win against Leyton Rovers in the 3rd round of the County Cup competition. On 25th January they drew the home game against a nine-man Belmont (Upton) team. The following day came the sad news of the death of Mr.George Humphrey, a former club secretary and representative to the County Association.

A week later and the much anticipated County Cup Semi-Final tie against the strong Woodford team at Ilford. Romford proved the better side in a fine 2-0 victory, with Amey again among the goals. The team came down to earth the following week when Woodford gained revenge in a friendly game at Romford, running out easy winners by six goals to nil. But it is fair to state that the problem of missing players reared its head again, Romford fielding only seven men! Perhaps the players' minds were tuned in to the forthcoming Essex Senior Cup Final against Ilford at Leyton on 8th March. Romford were hoping to lift the trophy for the first time, whereas Ilford, in the final for the third year running, were anticipating a hat trick of victories, a feat achieved by Old Foresters in the previous three seasons. Alas, two Ilford goals put paid to Romford's high hopes, and the wait to lift this handsome trophy had to be put on hold.

The disappointment obviously hit home, and in front of their own supporters a week later, Romford were trounced 11-0 by Upton Rovers. The composition of the Romford team is unknown, but this was certainly a humiliation for the club. On 12th April Romford were at home to Francis Thirlwall's select eleven for the Victoria Cottage Hospital Cup which Romford won 3-0 with goals from Ramsey, Gibson and Wright.

The season on the whole, was of course a successful one with only four defeats from their twenty matches and the honour of reaching the final of the County Cup.

Annual Dinner
(as reported in the *Essex Times*, Saturday 17th May 1890)

The annual dinner of the Romford Football Club was held at the Golden Lion, on Thursday evening 15th May. Mr.J.Ramsey of Gidea Hall, who presided, was supported by Mr.W.F.Laing and Mr.F.Wilson. The vice-chair was taken by Mr.W.D.Matthews, the popular captain of the Club, who was supported by Mr.E.H.Hinds, the esteemed hon.sec. The company included several members and friends of the Club. An excellent spread was provided by host Reynolds.

The CHAIRMAN gave "The Queen and the Royal family," followed by the "Army, Navy and Reserve Forces," to which Brigd. Arm. – Sergt. G.Weston replied. The VICE-CHAIRMAN, in giving "The President, Vice-Presidents, and supporters," said the President (Mr.G.Theobald. M.P.) was a staunch, good man. They had several vice-presidents who favoured them with their presence upon the field but none more so than the vice-president who occupied the chair that evening. The supporters of the club were numerous, but he trusted that they would increase, for it was by their help that the committee were enabled to carry on the club.

MR.W.P.LAING, in replying, said he had recently heard an opinion expressed that everyone ought to pay for their own sport. That was an opinion he did not agree with. He knew that the clubs in his early days were pleased to have the support of honorary members, and so they were now. He trusted that those who had the means to support the national sport would continue to do so.

The CHAIRMAN, in giving "success to the Romford Football Club," said it was a toast he had pleasure in proposing, for he had the success of the club at heart. Having been one of its vice-presidents for some years, he had taken a deep interest in it. Some said that football was a rough game; but to those who knew how to play it, and played under Association rules, it was not a rough game. Of course there was a danger in everything – cricket, football or hunting. A man walking across the road might fall and sustain an injury, but when football was played under the Association rules, it could not be said to be a dangerous game. If a man slipped during frosty weather in crossing the road, it might be as well said that it was dangerous to have frosty weather. (Laughter).

With respect to the club it would become a success if each one tried to make it so. He regretted that the club did not win the cup. The old Foresters won it three years running; that was due to their combination and system of playing together. Having won it three years they gracefully retired and left the cup to the Essex clubs. The Ilford club which then won it, also showed combination in passing, and he should like to see the Romford club adopt the same combination. If they would only take it to heart they would win the cup, for the club was as good as the Ilford club, but in competition Ilford beat them. He should have been pleased to see them win the cup this year, and he had no doubt that if they took the advice he had given them they would win it next year.

Mr.E.H.HINDS, in replying, said the club had had a successful season. As a team their only fault was a want of combination. This was due to the fact that the players did not turn up to play at ordinary matches. They would go when there was a cup tie to be decided, but they ought to do the same at ordinary matches. During the season the first team had played 21 matches, of these they won twelve, lost five, and four were drawn; 45 goals were scored, against 34 by their opponents. Their second eleven had not done so well, for the first eleven had at times found it necessary to draw upon them, owing to some of the first eleven not turning up. They hoped, however, to do better another season. The result of the matches on behalf of the Cottage Hospital funds was that £5.15s.6d had been paid to the Hon.Secretary of the committee.

The club had lost a member – Mr. Humphrey – whose place he did not know who would fill. Although not a playing member Mr. Humphrey took a great interest in the club, in fact more interest than a playing member. The financial position of the club was satisfactory. The year commenced with a balance of £8.17s.5d. in hand. The subscriptions had reached £23.13s.6d. and although the gate money had been reduced to 2d, yet it amounted to £15.14s.9d. making the total receipts £53.15s.8d. The expenditure which included £14 for rent, amounted to £34.9s.1d., thus leaving them with a balance of £15.9s.4d. Thus the club was in a prosperous position as compared with other clubs in the town and he had no doubt the cricket club would like to have the balance.

The vice-chairman having proposed "The health of the Chairman" and the toast having been replied to, the CHAIRMAN proposed "The health of the Vice-Chairman," In the course of his reply Mr.MATTHEWS gave some interesting details in connection with the club. It was started in 1876, and he found that the first subscription paid was by their late friend, Mr. Grimston Smith. The club was then joined, by other gentlemen who had now gone over to the majority.When he became secretary in 1883, the year closed with a balance of £2.6s.9d., which in the second year became £6.4s.0d., but was afterwards reduced to £4.3.7d.

Very little interest was, however, taken in the club at the time, and a year or two passed without any matches being played. In April 1888, the young club known as the Buffaloes joined them. New life was thus infused into the club, and they had heard from the hon.secretary how the balance had increased. Their late member Mr. Humphrey was one of the club's staunchest supporters. It was a pleasure to hear the testimony to his worth which was given at the recent cyclists' meeting at Chelmsford. He was pleased to say that the entertainment on behalf of the widow and children, was successful, and that he was in a position to hand them £45.7s.6d.

Mr.F.WILSON responded on behalf of the visitors. The other toasts were, "The Ladies," "The Press," and "The Host and Hostess." During the evening harmony was contributed by Messrs. Harding, "Honor," Burrows, Hardy, Poel, Pink, Reynolds, &c. Mr. Pike presided at the piano.

Annual General Meeting
(as reported in the *Essex Times*, Saturday 6 September 1890)

The annual meeting of the Romford Football Club took place at the Golden Lion Hotel, on Tuesday, 2nd September. Mr.W.D.Matthews presided and there was a good attendance of members. The Hon.Secretary Mr.E.H.Hinds read his annual report which showed that the past season had been a very successful one for the club, both financially and also as regarded the results of matches. The first eleven played 21 matches, twelve of which were won, five lost and four drawn. The reserve team had played thirteen matches winning five, losing six and two were drawn.

The Hon.Treasurer, Mr.W.D.Matthews submitted his report, which showed that the balance to the credit of the club, was £14.5s 5d. On the motion of Mr.Gibson the report and balance sheet were unanimously adopted. Mr.J.Theobald was re-elected president and the vice-presidents were re-elected en bloc. It was resolved to invite the following gentlemen to become vice-presidents: Major Holmes, Major Compton, Messrs. H.H. Raphael, E.Bryant, D.Hill, L.Ide, H.J. Cameron, J.Sands and H.Whitmere. The chairman stated that it had been considered expedient to have two grounds and Mr.Reynolds had given them permission to play in the Church Lane Meadow at a rental of three pounds per annum. Mr.E.H.Hinds was re-elected Hon.Secretary, and Mr.F.Wells was appointed as Assistant Secretary. Mr.W.D. Matthews was re-elected Hon.Treasurer, and Mr.E.J.Ramsey and Mr.R.Oliver were chosen captain and vice-captain respectively for the ensuing season. A good list of matches has been arranged for the coming season.

As we have seen, Victorian football was not the well regulated game of today. Kick-off times were rather casual. On many occasions the home team were ready to play but only three or four of the visitors had arrived, causing a delay of as much as an hour and resulting in bad light setting in and the match ending some half an hour or so early.

Although Romford ran a reserve team and managed to field three teams on 23rd November, it can be seen from the team line-ups that the club often played with only nine or ten men in the side. It must be remembered that these were not professional footballers but had to fit the game around their full-time jobs, and could be forced to pull out at short notice because of work commitments. Communication in those days relied on the post and the telegram. It is no surprise that football clubs only lasted for a few seasons and then folded, only to restart perhaps two or three years later.

VICTORIAN ERA FOOTBALL AT ROMFORD

A match played on the Recreation Ground, off Victoria Road. The photo is undated but judging by the players' clothing appears to be late 1880s or early 1890s
Havering Libraries - Local Studies

It is believed that this photograph may have been taken by Arthur Cornell who, as well as playing for Romford, had a keen interest in photography. It was among his possessions now held by the Havering Local Studies collection at Romford Library. (For more about his life, see page 333).
This match may have been a Romford FC game, but a good number of the County Cup semi-finals and finals were played at the Recreation Ground, off Victoria Road, during this period, and it is possible that this may have been one of them as the size of the crowd seems to be bigger than the usual Romford attendances.
The houses in the background run along George Street, whilst the pavilion seen behind the goal stood to the rear of Richmond Road. (See also the street plan showing the ground on page 65). The spectators stand on the cycle track that encompassed the football pitch.

Season 1890 – 91

ROMFORD FOOTBALL CLUB

Chairman: Mr.J.Ramsey **Vice-Chairman:** Mr.D.Hill

Hon.Secretary: Mr.E.H.Hinds **Hon.Treasurer:** Mr.W.D.Matthews

Captain: Mr.E.J.Ramsey **Vice-Captain:** Mr.R.Oliver (As elected at the Annual General Meeting)

Headquarters: Golden Lion Hotel, Romford **Ground:** Recreation Ground, Victoria Road, Romford

COMPETITIONS ENTERED

Essex County F.A. Challenge Cup
Friendly Matches

Match Details

4 Oct Frdly Home Brentwood 1 – 0 Pitt
Romford: J.Tetchner;H.Izatt,E.H.Hinds(Capt);J.F.Burrows,R.Oliver,H.R.Pitt;
W.Wright,E.H.White,E.W.Brixley,F.Wells.

11 Oct Frdly Away Ilford Park P – P
Romford unable to raise a team and scratched.

18 Oct Frdly Home Grange Park 2 – 1 Gibson,Wright
Romford: J.Tetchner;H.Izatt,E.H.Hinds(Capt);G.Stevenson,W.Halson,C.Couzens;
W.Wright,Hills,R.Oliver,F.Wells,E.A.Gibson.

25 Oct Frdly Away Woodford P – P
Romford short of players so scratch game was played with nine men each, the result is not known.

1 Nov Frdly Home Buckhurst Hill 2 – 0 Ramsey,White
Romford:
Teams details unknown

8 Nov Frdly Away Tottenham Hotspur 2 – 2 White, one unknown
Romford: J.Tetchner;E.H.Hinds(Capt),H.Izatt;R.Oliver,J.F.Burrows,H.R.Pitt;
W.Wright,E.H.White,F.Wells,Substitute.

15 Nov Frdly Home Dulwich 1 – 0 Wells
Romford: J.Tetchner;H.Izatt,E.H.Hinds;R.Oliver,J.F.Burrows,H.R.Pitt;
W.Wright,E.A.Gibson,E.W.White,F.Wells,E.J.Ramsey.

6 Dec ECC2R Home Manor Park 2 – 1 # Wells,Ramsey
Attendance: 400
Romford: J.Tetchner;H.Izatt,E.H.Hinds(Capt);H.R.Pitt,R.Oliver,C.Couzens;
E.H.White,W.Wright,E.J.Ramsey,F.Wells,E.A.Gibson.

24 Jan ECCRep Home Manor Park 5 – 1 White(2),E.J.Ramsey(2)Oliver
Romford: G.W.Ramsey.Jnr;H.Isatt,E.H.Hinds;R.Oliver,C.Couzens,H.R.Pitt;
W.Wright,E.H.White,E.J.Ramsey,E.A.Gibson,F.Wells.

31 Jan ECC3R Home Leyton Rovers 3 – 0 Ramsey,White,Oliver
Romford: G.W.Ramsey;H.Izatt,E.H.Hinds;R.Oliver,C.Couzens,H.R.Pitt;
W.Wright,E.H.White,E.J.Ramsey,E.A.Gibson,F.Wells.

14 Feb ECCSF Witham Harwich & Parkeston 3 – 3 Ramsey(2)Gibson
Attendance: 400
Romford: J.Tetchner;H.Izatt,E.H.Hinds;J.Jones,R.Oliver,C.Couzens;
W.Wright,E.H.White,E.A.Gibson,E.J.Ramsey,F.Wells.

21 Feb ECCRep Chlfd Harwich & Parkeston 1 – 1 A scrimmage
Attendance: 500
Romford: G.W.Ramsey;E.H.Hinds,H.Izatt;H.R.Pitt,R.Oliver,C.Couzens;
W.Wright,E.H.White,F.Wells,E.A.Gibson,E.J.Ramsey.

28 Feb ECCRep Witham Harwich & Parkeston 0 – 2
Attendance: 500
Romford: G.W.Ramsey;H.Izatt,E.H.Hinds;C.Couzens,H.R.Pitt,Richard Oliver;
E.W.White,W.Wright,E.A.Gibson,F.Wells,E.J.Ramsey.

Re-played after Manor Park lodged a protest. Referee arrived late and darkness set in as Manor Park kicked off. (Extract from the local newspaper of January 1891).

SUMMARY OF FIRST TEAM RESULTS OBTAINED SEASON 1890 – 91

					Goals	
	P	W	D	L	For	Ag
Friendly Matches	5	4	1	0	8	3
ECFA Challenge Cup	5	2	2	1	12	7
ECFA Chal. Cup (void)	1	1	0	0	2	1
Total	11	7	3	1	22	11
A.G.M. Press Report	12	7	3	2	22	14

CUP RESULTS SEASON 1890 – 91

Essex County F.A. Challenge Cup

Final: Clapton 7 Harwich & Parkeston 0

Romford's progress:	2nd Round	Home	Manor Park	2 – 1 #
	Replay	Home	Manor Park	5 – 1
	3rd Round	Home	Leyton Rovers	3 – 0
	Semi-Final	Witham	Harwich & Parkeston	3 – 3
	Replay	Ch'ford	Harwich & Parkeston	1 – 1
	2nd Replay	Witham	Harwich & Parkeston	0 – 2

Manor Park protested match declared void and a replay was ordered

First Team Appearances Season 1890 – 91

E.W.Brixley	1	J.F.Burrows	3	C.Couzens	6*	E.A.Gibson	7*
W.Halson	1	Hills	1	E.H.Hinds	9*	H.Izatt	9*
J.Jones	1	R.Oliver	9*	H.R.Pitt	7*	E.J.Ramsey	6*
G.W.Ramsey	4	G.Stevenson	1	J.Tetchner	5*	F.Wells	9*
E.H.White	8*	W.Wright	9*	Substitute	1	Total	95

Despite intense searches, team line-ups for two games have not been discovered.
* Also played in the cup tie against Manor Park that was declared void.

First Team Goal Scorers Season 1890 – 91

E.J.Ramsey	7	E.W.White	5	Fred. Wells	2	R.Oliver	2
E.A.Gibson	2	H.R.Pitt	1	W.Wright	1	Unknown	2
Total	22						

THE ESSEX FOOTBALL ASSOCIATION
(as reported in the *Essex Times*, Saturday 24th January, 1891)

A PROTEST SUSTAINED

Manor Park had lodged a protest against their tie with Romford in the second round being awarded to Romford on the ground that, owing to the late arrival of the referee, play began so late that the match was finished in semi-darkness, and that towards the close they obtained a second goal and equalised the Romford score, but that the referee wrongly disallowed the goal. - Mr. Cook stated that Mr. Vasey, the referee, distinctly reported that the ball went over. – After hearing Mr. Cosburn for Manor Park, and Mr. E. H. Hinds for Romford, the committee decided the match to be replayed at Romford, tomorrow (Saturday).

Owing to being engaged last Saturday in the London Junior Cup Competition, Belmont failed to send a team to play off their tie with Leyton Rovers, who claimed the match. Belmont asked that the time should be extended. – Mr. Cook explained that the application for an extension of time came so late that the Leyton Rovers, having made all arrangements, declined to accede to a postponement. – It was decided that the match be awarded to Leyton Rovers.

RESERVE TEAM

Match Details

4 Oct	Frdly	Home	St. Edward's Ch. Inst.	0 – 0
11 Oct	Frdly	Home	Ilford Park Reserves	0 – 3
18 Oct	Frdly	Away	Leyton Rovers	2 – 2
25 Oct	Frdly	Home	Woodford	2 – 7
1 Nov	Frdly	Home	Woodland Rovers	2 – 2
8 Nov	Frdly	Home	Tottenham Hotspur Reserves	3 – 0

Romford Reserves: H.Tetchner;H.G.Smith,W.Halson;R.Carter,C.Couzens,E.Challenor; F.L.Poole,P.W.Smith,A.Wiffen,R.W.Wedlake,O.Wheatley.

15 Nov	Frdly	Away	Chadwell Heath	2 – 0
22 Nov	Frdly	Home	Manor Park	3 – 1
7 Feb	Frdly	Away	St. Edward's Church Institute	9 – 1
14 Feb	Frdly	Home	Leyton Rovers Reserves	7 – 1
14 Mar	Frdly	Home	Belmont (Upton) Reserves	0 – 4

SUMMARY OF RESERVE TEAM RESULTS OBTAINED SEASON 1890 – 91

					Goals	
	P	W	D	L	For	Ag
All Friendly Matches	11	5	3	3	30	21
*A.G.M. Report	11	5	5	1	29	8

*Note: We have discovered two more defeats for the reserve team, but have no details of an additional two drawn games.

Reserve Team Appearances and Goal Scorers

Due to the very poor coverage of the reserve team games in the local press, a summary of appearances and goal scorers is not possible.

Post-Season Summary Season 1890 – 91

Romford commenced their season on 4th October. With only ten men in their team, they managed to defeat local rivals Brentwood by one goal to nil. A week later Romford were due to play away to Ilford Park, but the match was cancelled as Romford were unable to raise a team. The following week a full team turned out and were successful in the home game with Grange Park.

On 25th October Romford were again unable to raise a team to fulfil the fixture away to Woodford and so a scratch game was played with nine players each side, but no details are to hand. The next week Romford defeated Buckhurst Hill by two goals to nil, but no team details are available. On 8th November, Romford played Tottenham Hotspur at Northumberland Park and drew two all, but despite enlisting a substitute from the crowd, Romford again played with only ten men. The following week a full team defeated Dulwich by one goal to nil.

The next six games were all in the Essex Senior Cup. The full eleven turned out against Manor Park, and a 2-1 win was secured. Unfortunately for Romford, Manor Park protested on the grounds that the referee was late arriving and he did not award them a late equaliser. The County Committee declared the match void and ordered a replay. Severe frost persisted for seven weeks and the replay was not played until 24th January, when Romford recorded a fine 5-1 victory. In the third round Romford had a comfortable home win by three goals to nil against Leyton Rovers and reached the semi-final of the competition.

On 14th February, before a crowd of 400 at Witham, a thrilling game ended three all against the strong Harwich & Parkeston team. Romford then declined to play extra time. A week later and another exciting game at Chelmsford again saw the two teams draw, this time with one goal each. Romford again declined to play extra time, provoking, we are told, a hostile demonstration! The second replay took place a week later before an attendance of 500 at Witham, and this time Romford were eliminated by a two goal to nil margin and thus wound up the season in disappointment. It seems that once eliminated from the latter stages of the County Cup, the team went into hibernation until the following season!

Annual General Meeting
(as reported in the *Essex Times,* Saturday 5th September 1891)

The annual general meeting of the Romford Football Club was held at the Golden Lion Hotel on Thursday evening, 3rd Sept., Mr.W.D.Matthews presiding. The hon. sec., Mr.E.H.Hinds read his report, which was of a very satisfactory nature. – The treasurer's report, read by the chairman, showed a balance in hand of £10.3s.4d. – The subscriptions amounted to £31.9s.6d, and the gate money to £11.3s.11d. – On the proposition of Mr.G.Barnes, seconded by Mr.G.White, the report and balance sheet were unanimously adopted. Mr.James Theobald, M.P. was re-elected president, and Mr. Alfred Harvey's name was added to the list of vice-presidents. Officers were appointed as follows.- Captain. Mr.E.J.Ramsey; vice-captain, Mr.H.Izatt; reserve team captain, Mr.J.F.Burrows; reserve team vice-captain, Mr.H.R.Pitt; secretary, Mr.E.H.Hinds; assistant secretary, Mr.C.A.Wilson.

Season 1891 – 92

ROMFORD FOOTBALL CLUB

President: Mr.JamesTheobald.M.P.

Hon.Secretary: Mr.E.H.Hinds **Hon.Asst. Secretary:** Mr.C.A.Wilson **Hon.Treasurer:** Mr.W.D.Matthews

Captain: Mr.E.J.Ramsey **Vice-Captain:** Mr.H.Izatt

Reserve Team Captain: Mr.J.F.Burrows **Reserve Team Vice-Captain:** Mr.H.R.Pitt

Headquarters: Golden Lion Hotel, Romford **Ground:** Recreation Ground, Victoria Road, Romford

COMPETITIONS ENTERED

Essex County F.A. Challenge Cup
Friendly Matches
Club did not compete in the F.A. Cup

Grays Challenge Cup
Friendly Matches

Goal nets were introduced for this season, although it was not compulsory to have them.

Practice Match

12 Mar Romford Present 8 Romford Past 0
E.J.Ramsey,C.Brady,J.Brady(2),Own goal(1) unknown(3)
Romford Past (The Old Crocks): F.H.Thirlwall(Capt),E.Champness,C.Clark,A.Cornell,C.Couzens,T.K.Gayford, J.E.Macfarlane(in goal),W.D.Matthews,R.Oliver,G.Stevenson,W.Wright.
Romford Present: E.J.Ramsey(Capt),S.L.Anderson,C.Brady,J.Brady,E.H.Hinds,H.Izatt, H.Knight,H.R.Pitt,G.W.Ramsey,F.Shackell,F.Wells.
Referee: Mr.Frank Webster. Linesman: Mr.Burrows and Arthur Clark.

Match Details

3 Oct Frdly Home Olympic (Upton Park) 0 – 7
Romford: J.Tetchner;E.H.Hinds(Capt),H.Izatt;C.Brady,J.F.Burrows,H.R.Pitt; J.F.Anderson,A.E.Gibson,F.Wells,R.Partridge,Stokes.

17 Oct Frdly Home Vulcans (Willesdon) 1 – 2 Scorer unknown
Romford:
Team details unknown

24 Oct Frdly Home Buckhurst Hill 3 – 2 Scorers unknown
Romford:
Team details unknown

7 Nov ECC1R Home Upton Park 1 – 2 A scrimmage!
Romford: E.W.Ramsey;E.H.Hinds(Capt),H.Izatt;C.Brady,H.R.Pitt,H.G.Smith; R.Partridge,J.F.Anderson,E.J.Ramsey,F.Wells,E.H.White.

14 Nov Frdly Home St. Edward's Church Institute 4 – 2 Scorers unknown

21 Nov Frdly Home Woodford 5 – 0

28 Nov Frdly Away Upton Park 1 – 1 Scorer unknown

5 Dec Frdly Home West Ham Church Institute5 – 1 Scorers unknown

12 Dec Frdly Home Leyton Rovers 0 – 2

19 Dec	Frdly	Home	Upton Rovers	1 – 1	Scorer unknown
2 Jan	Frdly	Home	2nd Leicestershire Regiment	3 – 2	Scorers unknown
23 Jan	Frdly	Home	Dulwich	3 – 0	Shackle,Wells,Knight

Romford: F.Kelly;E.H.Hinds,W.Knight;C.Brady,F.Hills,H.R.Pitt;
F.Wells,H.Knight,F.Shackell,J.Brady.

30 Jan	Frdly	Home	2nd Leicestershire Regiment	2 – 2	Scorers unknown
13 Feb	Frdly	Home	Buckhurst Hill	3 – 0	J.Brady,Wells,White

Romford: F.Kelly;H.Izatt,W.Knight;H.R.Pitt,E.H.Hinds(Capt),C.Brady;
F.Wells,H.Knight,J.Brady,E.H.White,E.A.Gibson.

27 Feb	Frdly	Away	Manor Park	1 – 4	Scorer unknown
5 Mar	Frdly	Home	Upton Rovers	1 – 2	Scorer unknown
26 Mar	Frdly	Away	Romford St. Andrews	1 – 2	Scorers unknown

SUMMARY OF FIRST TEAM RESULTS OBTAINED SEASON 1891 – 92

					Goals	
	P	W	D	L	For	Ag
ECFA Challenge Cup	1	0	0	1	1	2
Friendly matches	16	7	3	6	34	30
Total	17	7	3	7	35	32
A.G.M. Report	17	7	3	7	37	36

CUP RESULTS SEASON 1891 – 92

Essex County F.A. Challenge Cup

Final: Ilford 3 Colchester 1

Romford's progress: 1st Round Home Upton Park 1 – 2

First Team Appearances Season 1891 – 92

We regret that due to the lack of details in the local press we are unable to give a full summary of the match appearances by players, but the following are known to have played for the first team.

J.F.Anderson	S.L.Anderson	C.Brady	J.Brady
J.F.Burrows	A.Gibson	F.Hills	E.H.Hinds
H.Izatt	F.Kelly	H.Knight	W.Knight
R.Partridge	H.R.Pitt	E.J.Ramsey	G.W.Ramsey
F.Shackell	H.G.Smith	Stokes	J.Tetchner
F.Wells	E.H.White		

First Team Goal Scorers Season 1891 - 92

Due to the lack of information in the local press reports, a listing of goal scorers is not possible.

RESERVE TEAM

Match details

10 Oct	Frdly	Home	Leytonstone United	2 – 8	Scorers unknown
17 Oct	Frdly	Home	Vulcans (Willesdon) Reserves	0 – 3	

Romford: Played with only nine men.

24 Oct	Frdly	Home	Woodland Rovers	5 – 2	Scorers unknown
31 Oct	Frdly	Away	St. Edward's Church Inst. Reserves	4 – 2	Scorers unknown
14 Nov*	Frdly	Away	Old St. John's(Upton Park)	1 – 2	Scorer unknown
14 Nov*	Frdly	Away	Rochford Hundreds Reserves	2 – 4	Scorers unknown

Romford: Played with only seven men
Two men injured early in game, the team struggled on with only five fit men.

5 Dec	Frdly	Away	Elgin Rovers (Tottenham)	0 – 2	
12 Dec	GCC1R	Home	Forest Gate Victoria	0 – 3	
9 Jan	Frdly	Home	West Ham Church Inst. Reserves	0 – 4	
26 Mar	Frdly	Home	St. Edward's Church Inst. Reserves	1 – 2	Scorer unknown

* Played two games on the same day.

RESERVE TEAM SUMMARY OF RESULTS SEASON 1891 – 92

					Goals	
	P	W	D	L	For	Ag
Friendly Matches	9	2	0	7	15	29
Grays Challenge Cup	1	0	0	1	0	3
Total	10	2	0	8	15	32
A.G.M. Press Report	15	5	3	7	32	38

We regret that we have been unable to trace any details for six matches apparently played by the reserve team.

Post-Season Summary Season 1891 – 92

Romford commenced their season with a shocking 7-0 home defeat at the hands of Olympic of Upton Park, followed up with a 2-1 loss to the Vulcans. A couple of narrow victories came next, with the Essex County Cup defeat by Upton Park on 7th November in between. In the Essex Cup tie, Gibson was injured in the warm-up before the game, and withdrew from the team. To add to Romford's tale of woe, Izatt hit the post from a penalty kick and Romford lost by two goals to one.

On 21st November Woodford were only able to put out a scratch team at Romford, and were soundly beaten 5-0. A drawn game against Upton Park followed, and then came a 5-1 victory over West Ham Church Institute. On 12th December Romford were beaten at home 2-0 by Leyton Rovers, but it must be pointed out that Romford had only eight men!

Then came five home games without defeat, starting with a one all draw against Upton Rovers and a 3-2 victory over 2nd Leicestershire Regiment. Then came a win against Dulwich (with only 10 men) by three goals to nil. On the 30th January a return game (also at home) to the 2nd Leicestershire Regiment ended in a 2-2 draw. Next was another home game, this time against Buckhurst Hill, who were beaten by three goals to nil. A 4-1 defeat away to Manor Park followed, and Upton Rovers came to Romford and went away with a 2-1 victory.

Then on 12th March there was an interesting practice game against 'The Old Crocks', a team of Romford players from the past, including Francis Thirlwall, Elijah Champness and Clifford Clark, who had all appeared in the club's first season back in 1876-77. Unsurprisingly, the old boys were overcome by eight goals to nil.

The club wound up the season with another 2-1 away defeat to Romford St. Andrew's. The season could be considered an average one, with the team obtaining seven victories and seven defeats from their seventeen games, although they found it difficult to field a full team on many occasions. Romford did not enter the F.A. Cup or Amateur Cup.

The reserve team had an average sort of year, recording five victories from their fifteen matches. The reserve team played two matches on 14th November, but could only muster seven men for the game against Rochford Hundred Reserves, two of whom were injured early in the game. Playing most of the game with only five fit men, the team did well to suffer only a four goal to two defeat!

Fred Wells and Frank Wells were one of the many sets of brothers who played for the Romford club. Fred, who was often referred to as Wells Snr., would be a regular member of the first team in the years to come. The players' initials were often omitted by the sports writers anyway in their team line-ups, but with both Wells having the initial 'F' it is often uncertain which one played in particular matches. It was much more helpful when both played in the same match! Similarly we are not 100% sure of the appearances of the individual Andersons, Knights or Ramseys (the brothers Ernest and George Ramsey, who played for Romford this season, were the sons of Mr John Ramsey of Gidea Hall). We have shown the initials as and where shown in the press reports.

Annual General Meeting
(as reported in the *Essex Times, Saturday 27th August 1892)*

The annual general meeting of the Romford Football Club, was held at the Golden Lion, on Thursday evening 25th August, 1892, Mr.F.H.Thirlwall presiding. – Mr. E.H.Hinds (hon.sec.) said the annual report was not so favourable as one could wish, but this was accounted for partly by the club having been engaged with stronger clubs, and to the disadvantage they had suffered in having to supplant several old members by new ones. Consequently the combination of the club was somewhat broken for a time.

The team, however, at the latter part of the season, made great improvements and should develop into a first class team. The first eleven played seventeen matches, won seven, lost seven and three were drawn. The second eleven played fifteen matches, won five, lost seven, and three were drawn. The first team obtained 37 goals and 36 were conceded, and the reserves scored 32 and conceded 38. Although not successful in the Essex Cup match, which was won by Upton Park by two goals to one, mainly owing to the Romford club having to make changes at the last moments through accidents, yet the club had the best of the game. A good list of matches had been arranged for the coming season, and it was hoped that members would do their best by playing regularly, whether it was for the first or reserve team.

The balance sheet, submitted by Mr.W.D.Matthews, treasurer, showed a balance in hand at commencement of the year, £10.3s.4d.; subscriptions, £29.6s.6d.; gate money, £20.8s.6d.; season ticket, 5s.0d.; total, £60.3s.4d. The expenditure included rent of grounds, £16, and various other items amounting to £41.19.6d., leaving a balance of £18.3s.10d. – The report and balance sheet were adopted. –

Mr.J.Theobald.M.P., was re-elected president; several gentlemen were added to the list of vice-presidents. Mr.C.Brady was elected captain of the first eleven, and Mr. F.Wells, vice-captain. Mr.T.Hinds was elected captain of the second eleven, and Mr. B.Pitt, vice-captain. Mr.E.H.Hinds was again appointed hon.sec. and Mr.W.D. Matthews also consented to act as treasurer. Mr.A.Wiffen was elected assistant hon.sec.

Mr.Hinds submitted a list of 24 matches – chiefly with prominent clubs – and it was approved. – Votes of thanks to the chairman, hon. sec., and treasurer closed the proceedings.

Season 1892 – 93

ROMFORD FOOTBALL CLUB

President: Mr.J.Theobald.M.P.

Hon.Secretary: Mr.E.H.Hinds **Hon.Asst.Secretary:** Mr.A.Wiffen **Hon.Treasurer:** Mr.W.D.Matthews

First Team Captain: Mr.C.Brady **First Team Vice-Captain:** Mr.Fred.Wells

Reserve Team Captain: Mr.T.Hinds **Reserve Team Vice-Captain:** Mr.B.Pitt

Headquarters: Golden Lion Hotel, Romford

Ground: Recreation Ground, Victoria Road, Romford

Reserve Team Ground: Cricket Ground, Romford Station. The Club reach agreement with Romford Cricket Club allowing the reserves to play on the cricket ground at Romford Station.

COMPETITIONS ENTERED

Essex County F.A. Challenge Cup
Friendly Matches
The club did not compete in the F.A. Cup

Grays Challenge Cup
Friendly Matches

Match Details

1 Oct Frdly Home St. Luke's 1 – 0 Fred. Wells
Romford: W.R.Cosburn;W.H.Hawkins,F.Shackell;H.R.Pitt,E.H.Hinds,C.Brady(Capt);
J.Brady,S.L.Anderson,H.Harris,Fred. Wells.

8 Oct Frdly Home Leicestershire Regiment 7 – 3 J.Brady(4)F.Wells(2)Anderson
Romford: W.R.Cosburn;W.H.Hawkins,F.Shackell;E.H.Hinds,H.R.Pitt,W.Knight;
J.Brady,S.L.Anderson,J.Harris,H.Knight,Fred.Wells(Capt).

15 Oct Frdly Home Gravesend 1 – 0 Pitt
Attendance: 300
Romford: W.R.Cosburn;F.Shackell,W.H.Hawkins;E.H.Hinds,H.R.Pitt,S.L.Anderson;
J.Brady,H.E.Magson,J.Harris,H.Knight,F.Wells(Capt).

22 Oct Frdly Away Buckhurst Hill 6 – 0 Scorers unknown
Romford: W.R.Cosburn;F.Shackell,W.H.Hawkins;H.Izatt,E.H.Hinds,H.R.Pitt;
J.Brady,H.E.Magson,Frank Wells,H.Knight,Fred.Wells(Capt).

29 Oct Frdly Home Old Foresters 9 – 0 Harris(3)Megson(3)J.Brady(2)Isatt
Romford: W.R.Cosburn;F.Shackell,W.H.Hawkins;H.Izatt,E.H.Hinds,H.R.Pitt;
J.Brady,H.E.Magson,J.Harris,H.Knight,F.Wells(Capt).

5 Nov ECC1R Home Upton United 8 – 0 Harris(4)Wells(3)Magson
Romford: W.R.Cosburn;F.Shackell,W.H.Hawkins;C.Brady,E.H.Hinds(Capt),H.Izatt;
J.Brady,H.E.Magson,J.Harris,W.Knight,F.Wells.

19 Nov Frdly Home 2nd Coldstream Guards 1 – 1 Harris

26 Nov Frdly Away Upton Park 0 – 0 #

3 Dec ECC2R Home Woodville 3 – 1 Fred.Wells(3)
Romford: W.R.Cosburn;W.H.Hawkins,F.Shackell;C.Brady,E.H.Hinds(Capt),H.Izatt;
J.Brady,H.E.Magson,J.Harris,W.Knight,Fred.Wells.

10 Dec Frdly Away Old Salways (Leyton) 0 – 2
Romford:
Team details unknown.

17 Dec Frdly Home Brentwood 3 – 0 C,Brady,J.Brady,Knight
Romford: C.Brady
J.Brady,W.Knight. Remainder of team unknown.

24 Dec Frdly Away Ilford 0 – 1
Attendance: 400
Romford: W.R.Cosburn;F.Shackell,W.H.Hawkins;H.Izatt,C.Brady(Capt),E.H.Hinds;
J.Brady,H.E.Magson,J.Harris,E.J.Ramsey,F.Wells.

26 Dec Frdly Home Upton Park P – P Pitch flooded

21 Jan Frdly Home Vulcans (Willesdon) 4 – 2 Scorers unknown
Romford: W.R.Cosburn;H.R.Pitt,W.H.Hawkins;C.Brady(Capt)E.H.Hinds,H.Izatt;
J.Brady,H.E.Magson,J.Harris,H.Knight,Fred.Wells.

28 Jan Frdly Home Middlesex Hospital 5 – 0 Scorers unknown
Romford:
Team details unknown

4 Feb Frdly Away West Herts (at Watford) 1 – 2 Scorer unknown

11 Feb ECCSF Witham Colchester 5 – 5 J.Brady(2)Knight(2)Harris
Romford: W.R.Cosburn;F.Shackell,W.H.Hawkins;C.Brady,E.H.Hinds,H.Izatt;
J.Brady,H.E.Magson,J.Harris,H.Knight,Fred. Wells(Capt),

18 Feb ECCRep Witham Colchester 2 – 0 Own goals (2)
Romford: W.R.Cosburn;F.Shackell,W.H.Hawkins;C.Brady,E.H.Hinds(Capt),H.Izatt;
J.Brady.H.E.Magson,J.Harris,H.Knight,E.J.Ramsey.

25 Feb Frdly Home Woodville 1 – 1 Scorer unknown
Romford: W.R.Cosburn;W.H.Hawkins,F.Shackell;C.Brady(Capt),H.Izatt,E.H.Hinds;
J.Brady,S.L.Anderson,Frank Wells,H.Knight,J.Harris.

4 Mar* Frdly Home Carpenters Institute 1 – 2 Scorer unknown
Romford: Team details unknown.

4 Mar* Frdly Away Gravesend 1 – 3 Scorer unknown
Romford: Team details unknown.

11 Mar ECCF Leyton Chelmsford 0 – 3
Attendance: 2,500
Chelmsford: F.Ashton;T.L.Nelson,H.Brown;R.L.Whitaker,E.E.Rice,A.B.Smith;
E.C.Gray(Capt),H.H.Harris,R.I.Sheldrake,B.Copland,C.M.Williams.
Romford: A.Cornell(in place of Cosburn who was suspended);F.Shackell,W.H.Hawkins;H.Izatt,E.H.Hinds(Capt),C.Brady;
J.Brady,H.E.Magson,J.Harris,H.Knight,E.J.Ramsey.
Referee: Mr.W.Comerford(Crusaders) Linesmen: Messrs.R.J.Johnson(Braintree) and H.G.T.Lee(Grange Park).

* Played two games on the same day.
\# Abandoned after twenty minutes.

SUMMARY OF FIRST TEAM RESULTS SEASON 1892 – 93

					Goals	
	P	W	D	L	For	Ag
ECFA Challenge Cup	5	3	1	1	18	9
Friendly matches*	15	8	2	5	41	17
Total	20	11	3	6	59	26
A.G.M. Report	20	11	4	5	59	35

* The above summary does not include the abandoned friendly match against Upton Park on 26th November.

CUP RESULTS SEASON 1892 – 93

Essex County F.A. Challenge Cup

Final: Chelmsford 3 Romford 0

Romford's progress: 1st Round Home Upton United 8 – 0
2nd Round Home Woodville 3 – 1
Semi-Final Witham Colchester 5 – 5
Replay Witham Colchester 2 – 0
Final Leyton Chelmsford 0 – 3

First Team Appearances Season 1892 – 93

It is regretted that due to the lack of some team details in the local press it is not possible to give a complete listing regarding the match appearances by players, but the following list gives a fair indication of the more regular players. We are not one hundred per cent certain who played regarding Harris, Knight and Wells but have indicated the initials as printed in the press reports.

S.L.Anderson	4	C.Brady	10	J.Brady	14	A.Cornell	1
W.R.Cosburn	12	H.Harris	1	J.Harris	11	W.H.Hawkins	13
E.H.Hinds	13	H.Izatt	10	H.Knight	9	W.Knight	4
H.E.Magson	10	H.R.Pitt	6	E.J.Ramsey	3	F.Shackell	13
Frank Wells	2	Fred. Wells	10			Total	146

First Team Goal Scorers Season 1892 – 93

Once again it is regretted that due to the lack of details reported in the local press it is not possibleto give any details regarding a goal scoring record.

RESERVE TEAM

Match Details

1 Oct	Frdly	Home*	Old St. John's (Upton Park)	4 – 6
15 Oct	Frdly	Home	Squirrels Heath	4 – 3
22 Oct	Frdly	Home	Hornchurch	2 – 0
29 Oct	Frdly	Home	Leytonstone Reserves	9 – 0
12 Nov	Frdly	Home	Hammond & Sons	6 – 0
19 Nov	Frdly	Home	West Ham Church Institute	8 – 2
26 Nov	Frdly	Home	Leyton Rovers	1 – 4
10 Dec	Frdly	Away	Acorn (Snaresbrook)	1 – 1
14 Jan	Frdly	Home	West Ham Church Institute	3 – 0
	GCC1R			Bye
28 Jan	Frdly	Home	Hare Street	2 – 2
18 Feb	GCC2R	Home	Squirrels Heath	6 – 3
25 Feb	Frdly	Home	West Ham Church Institute	2 – 2
11 Mar	GCCSF	Away	Grays Greyhounds	0 – 1

* First game at the cricket ground

SUMMARY OF RESERVE TEAM RESULTS OBTAINED SEASON 1892 – 93

					Goals	
	P	W	D	L	For	Ag
Friendly Matches	11	6	3	2	42	20
Grays Challenge Cup	2	1	0	1	6	4
Total	13	7	3	3	48	24
A.G.M. Report	15	8	2	5	50	27

Post Season Summary Season 1892 – 93

Romford commenced the season in sensational form, winning their first six matches and scoring 32 goals in the process, including eight against Upton United and nine against Old Foresters. In the first game of the season, a 1-0 victory over St. Luke's, Romford played with only ten men. The 2nd Coldstream Guards were due to visit Romford on 12th November, but the game was postponed due to the army men catching the train to Loughton by mistake! They did turn up a week later and enjoyed a one all draw. The following week Romford had two goals disallowed away to Upton Park, but the match was abandoned after only twenty minutes due to fog.

On 3rd December Romford defeated Woodville by three goals to one in the second round of the Essex Cup, but the rest of the month was a difficult time. For the next two games against Old Salways (0-2) and Brentwood (3-0) Romford could only field nine men on each occasion. In the match against Brentwood, a few minutes before time, Quennel fouled Izatt and a free kick awarded, but Brentwood declined to accept the decision and immediately quit the field!

A full complement turned out for the one nil loss to Ilford on Christmas Eve, but two days later the friendly at home to Upton Park was cancelled due to a flooded pitch.

It was nearly four weeks before the next game, at home against Vulcans of Willesdon. Again there was controversy when an unpleasant incident marred the game. One of the visitors shoved Wilfrid Cosburn, Romford's goalkeeper, when he was not in possession of the ball. Cosburn unwisely retaliated by striking his opponent in the mouth. The visitors threatened to leave the ground unless Cosburn was ordered off the pitch, so, by arrangement between the captains, the offender retired, Romford playing ten men for the last twenty minutes. – By the evening harmony was restored between the teams, when a smoking concert was held at the Golden Lion Hotel, Mr.R.Hales (captain of Vulcans) presiding!

After a couple of friendly matches, Romford met Colchester in an astonishing Essex Cup semi-final at Witham which ended in a five all draw! In the replay, again at Witham, the Colchester team was weakened by the absence of Lavar, a surgeon, who was called to an emergency at Colchester Hospital. The Colchester press reported that 'Romford started off with rough play and after only ten minutes three Colchester players were left limping, and to make matters worse Dace was so badly injured he is doubtful to play for the rest of the season'. To add to Colchester's woes, two own goals gave Romford a 2-0 passage into the final. Romford next met Woodville in a friendly and recorded a one each draw.

On 4th March Romford played two friendly matches on the same day against Carpenter's Institute and Gravesend, both resulting in defeat. The team details are unknown but perhaps these games served as a trial for possible future team selection.

A week later Romford wound up the season in the Essex Cup Final at Ilford against old foes Chelmsford. Unfortunately goalkeeper Cosburn was suspended for this match. Old stalwart Arthur Cornell took his place, but could not prevent a three goal to nil defeat.

The reserve team's first home game on the 1st October was the first to be played on the Cricket Ground. The reserves enjoyed a fairly successful season, losing only three of the thirteen games they are known to have played. It is not known if other games were played, due to the lack of information in the local papers in respect of some of these junior matches.

Annual General Meeting
(as reported in the *Essex Times,* Wednesday 13th September 1893)

The annual meeting of the Romford Football Club was held at the Golden Lion Hotel, on Monday evening, 11th September, when Mr.F.H.Thirlwall presided over a numerous attendance of members.

Mr.E.H.Hinds (the indefatigable hon.sec.) read his annual report, which showed that the past season was highly successful, though the club had been very unfortunate, in not bringing home the Essex Cup. The first team played 20 matches, of which they had won 11 and lost five, while four were drawn; scoring 59 goals to their opponents' 35. The reserve team were unfortunate in not securing the Grays and District Cup (succumbing to Grays, the ultimate winners in the semi-final round by the narrow margin of a goal), but they had had a very encouraging season. They had played 15 matches – won 8, lost 5, and drawn 2, scoring 50 goals to 27.

Mr.W.D.Matthews, the popular hon. treasurer, read his balance sheet, which showed that they had a balance in hand of £18.3s.10d. at the commencement of the season, but owing to the heavy expenditure, caused principally by railway fares to Witham on the occasion of the replayed tie with Colchester (which will be obviated in future, the Essex Association having resolved to pay the expenses of teams engaged in replayed semi-final ties – thanks to the Romford representatives) the balance had decreased to £7.4s.3d. The gate receipts amounted to £22.8s.8d.

Mr.J.Theobald.M.P., was re-elected president. The Vice-Presidents were re-elected, and several additions were made to the list. Mr.C.Brady was elected captain and Mr.F.Wells vice-captain of the first team; Mr.H.R.Pitt was chosen captain of the reserves, and Mr.H.Rushbrooke vice-captain; Mr.G.Stevenson captain of the Victoria team, and Mr.A.B.Pollett vice-captain. Mr.W.D.Matthews was re-elected hon. treasurer, with thanks for past services; and Mr.E.H.Hinds hon.sec.

Mr.Hinds was complimented and thanked by the chairman and all present for the manner in which he had conducted the secretarial department, a post he has held for some years to the entire satisfaction of the members. Messrs.W.D.Matthews and E.H.Hinds were re-elected representatives on the Essex Association. Over 30 new members were enrolled. It was decided to enter for the Essex Senior and Essex Junior Cup competitions. The first team play the opening match versus St. Luke's at Tufnell Park on Saturday.

The reserve team were being spoiled by the erection of a "commodious pavilion", as reported in the same issue of the *Essex Times:*

The pavilion which has recently been erected on the ground of the Romford Cricket Club at Romford Station and was opened on Saturday 9th September, by Mrs. Mackenzie, in the presence of a large company. Mr.F.H.Thirlwall, the captain of the club, acknowledged the assistance he had received from Mr.G.Barnes, the hon.sec., and the members of the committee, in raising fund for the erection of the pavilion, and said the club were also indebted to Mr.G.Rich, the occupier. And Mr.J.Roynon, the agent to the owner, for the facilities they had given, and everybody would admit that the building did great credit to Messrs. Hammond and Son, the builders.

About £20 remained to be raised to meet the cost, but he had no doubt this would be forthcoming. – Mrs. Mackenzie, in the course of a neat little speech, then formally declared the pavilion open, and was afterwards presented by Mr.Thirlwall with a charming bouquet of roses. –

The pavilion was designed and built by Messrs.J.S.Hammond and Son at a cost of about £80. It is a very elegant timber structure, with white plaster panels, in Queen Anne style, the base measuring about 24 feet by 28 feet. The roof is of plain red tiles, and the centre gable is surmounted by a small bell cot, rising to a height of 27 feet. An enclosed platform, three feet high, runs along the front, and is approached by steps at either end. The interior is of stained matchboarding. The pavilion portion will seat about 70 visitors. At the rear is a commodious dressing room, and also a retiring-room for visitors, both containing every convenience.

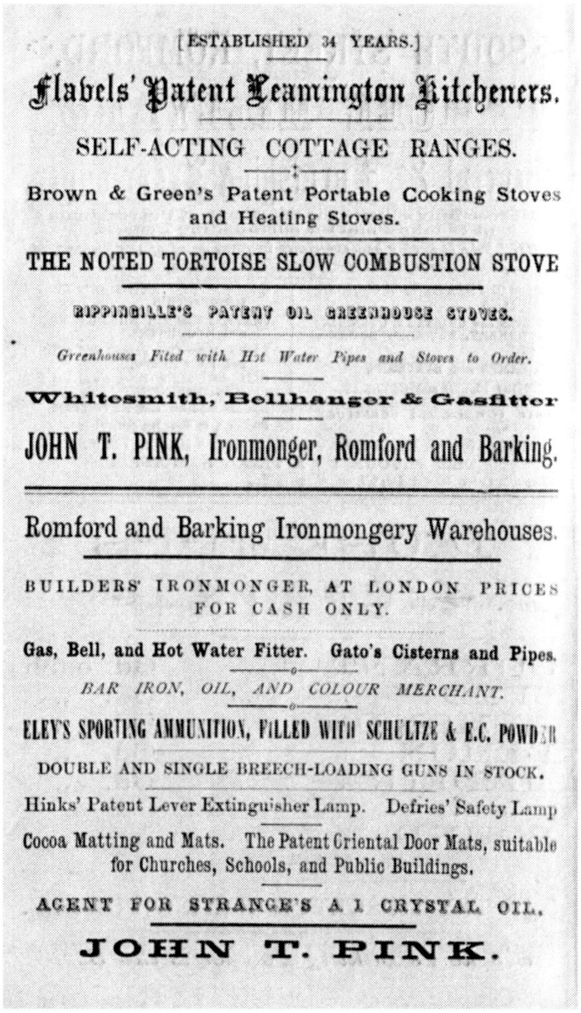

Season 1893 – 94

ROMFORD FOOTBALL CLUB

President: Mr.J.Theobald.M.P.

Hon.Secretary: Mr.E.H.Hinds **Hon.Treasurer:** Mr.W.D.Matthews

Captain: Mr.C.Brady **Vice-Captain:** Mr.Fred.Wells

Reserve Team Captain: Mr.H.R.Pitt **Reserve Team Vice-Captain:** Mr.H.Rushbrooke

Victoria Captain: Mr.G.Stevenson **Victoria Vice-Captain:** Mr.A.B.Pollett

County Representatives: Messrs.W.D.Matthews and E.H.Hinds

Headquarters: Golden Lion Hotel, Romford

Ground: Recreation Ground, Victoria Road, Romford **Reserve Team:** Cricket Ground, Romford Station

COMPETITIONS ENTERED

Essex County F.A. Senior Cup
Friendly Matches
The Club did not compete in the F.A. Cup or Amateur Cup (this being its first season).

Essex County F.A. Junior Cup
Friendly Matches

Match Details

16 Sept Frdly Away St. Luke's 4 – 1 C.Heard,J.Brady,Knight,Shockley

23 Sept Frdly Away Tottenham Hotspur 2 – 2 Scorers unknown
Romford: F.Shackell,C.Brady(Capt) and H.L.Shockley showed up prominently for Romford.
Remainder of team unknown

30 Sept Frdly Home Olympic (Upton Park) 3 – 1 Fred.Wells,Frank Wells,H.L.Shockley
Romford: Frank Wells,H.L.Shockley,Fred.Wells.
Remainder of team unknown.

7 Oct Frdly Home Upton Park 6 – 1 Shockley(2)C.Brady,J.Brady,Hinds,Fred Wells
Romford: W.R.Cosburn;F.Shackell,P.Key;C.Brady(Capt),E.H.Hinds,H.Izatt;
J.Brady,H.E.Magson,H.L.Shockley,W.Harris,Fred.Wells.

14 Oct Frdly Home 2nd Coldstream Guards 3 – 6 J.Brady(2)Key
Romford: J.Brady,P.Key.
Remainder of team unknown.

21 Oct Frdly Home 3rd Grenadier Guards 0 – 3

28 Oct Frdly Away Slough 0 – 0

18 Nov Frdly Away Spartan Harriers 1 – 0 Scorer unknown

25 Nov Frdly Home Norfolk Regiment 2 – 1 Magson(2)
Romford: J.Little;F.Shackell,E.Jones;H.Izatt,P.Key,C.Brady(Capt);
J.Brady,H.E.Magson,J.Harris,W.Harris,Fred.Wells.

2 Dec Frdly Away Chelmsford 4 – 1 J.Harris(2)W.Harris(2)
Romford: J.Little;F.Shackell,E.Jones;H.Izatt,E.H.Hinds,C.Brady(Capt);
J.Brady,Frank Wells,J.Harris,Fred.Wells,W.Harris.

16 Dec Frdly Home Woodville 2 – 5 Scorers unknown

23 Dec Frdly Home Leytonstone Atlas 1 – 2 Scorer unknown

13 Jan ESC1R Home Chelmsford 6 – 2 J.Brady(2)C.Roberts(3)Fred Wells
Romford: J.Little;E.P.Jones,F.Shackell;C.Brady(Capt),H.Izatt,E.H.Hinds;
J.Brady,J.Theobald,J.Harris,C.Roberts,Fred.Wells.

20 Jan ESC2R Away Woodford 0 – 2
Romford: J.Little;E.P.Jones,F.Shackell;C.Brady(Capt),H.Izatt,E.H.Hinds;
J.Brady,J.Theobald,J.Harris,C.Roberts,Fred.Wells.

27 Jan Frdly Home Bexleyheath 2 – 0 Scorers unknown

3 Feb Frdly Home Woodville 2 – 4 Scorers unknown
Romford: J.Little;F.Shackell,E.P.Jones;H.Izatt,E.H.Hinds,C.Brady(Capt);
J.Brady,J.Theobald,J.Harris,C.Roberts,Fred.Wells.

10 Feb Frdly Away 2nd Norfolk Regiment 2 – 4 J.Harris, One own goal
Romford: J.Little;F.Shackell,E.P.Jones;H.Izatt,E.H.Hinds,W.H.Hawkins;
J.Brady,J.Theobald,J.Haris,C.Roberts,Fred.Wells.

17 Feb Frdly Away Olympic (Upton Park) 0 – 3

24 Feb Frdly Away Bexleyheath 2 – 0 Scorers unknown
Romford: E.Burgess;F.Shackell,E.P.Jones;H.Izatt,E.H.Hinds,W.H.Hawkins;
J.Brady,J.Theobald,J.Harris,C.Roberts,Fred.Wells.

3 Mar Frdly Home Slough 2 – 1 Fred.Wells,J.Brady
Romford: F.G.Cosburn;F.Shackell,E.P.Jones;H.Izatt,E.H.Hinds,C.Brady;
J.Brady,W.Harris,J.Harris,Fred.Wells,C.Roberts.

17 Mar Frdly Away Sheppey United 0 – 5

SUMMARY OF FIRST TEAM RESULTS OBTAINED SEASON 1893 – 94

					Goals	
	P	W	D	L	For	Ag
Essex Senior Cup	2	1	0	1	6	4
Friendly Matches	19	9	2	8	38	40
Total	21	10	2	9	44	44

No details of matches played during the season were reported at the Annual General Meeting and the above summary is related to games that have been confirmed.

CUP RESULTS SEASON 1893 – 94

Essex County Senior Cup#

Final: Woodville 5 Braintree Gordon 1

Romford's progress: 1st Round Home Chelmsford 6 – 2
2nd Round Away Woodford 0 – 2

\# Formerly the Essex Challenge Cup

First Team Appearances Season 1893 – 94

C.Brady	8	J.Brady	10	E.Burgess	1	F.G.Cosburn	1
W.R.Cosburn	1	J.Harris	8	W.Harris	4	W.H.Hawkins	2
E.H.Hinds	8	H.Izatt	9	E.P.Jones	8	P.Key	3
J.Little	6	H.E.Magson	2	C.Roberts	6	F.Shackell	10
H.L.Shockley	3	J.Theobald	5	Frank Wells	2	Fred.Wells	10
Total	107						

Note: The players recorded in the above listing are known to have played for the first team during the season but with the local newspapers seemingly showing little interest in the club, the listing is incomplete.

First Team Goal Scorers Season 1893 – 94

J.Brady	6	Fred Wells	4	H.L.Shockley	3	C.Roberts	3
H.E.Magson	2	J.Harris	3	W.Harris	2	Frank Wells	1
C.Brady	1	E.H.Hinds	1	P.Key	1	O.G.	1
Unknown	12	Total	40				

Note: Due to the lack of press coverage many goal scorers are unknown.

RESERVE TEAM

Match Details

7 Oct	Frdly	Home	Woodville Reserves	3 – 3
14 Oct	Frdly	Away	Grays Reserves	1 – 3
21 Oct	Frdly	Home	Spartan Rovers	0 – 4
28 Oct	EJC1R	Home	Woodgrange	0 – 1
11 Nov	Frdly	Away	Brentwood St. Thomas	0 – 2
18 Nov	Frdly	Away	Fermain Hare Street	2 – 2
25 Nov	Frdly	Home	Romford Victoria	6 – 0
2 Dec	Frdly	Home	Woodville Reserves	5 – 0
9 Dec	Frdly	Home	University College Reserves	3 – 3
16 Dec	Frdly	Away	All Saints (Squirrels Heath)	0 – 0
23 Dec	Frdly	Home	Hare Street & Fermain	2 – 7
20 Jan	Frdly	Home	Dulwich Reserves	3 – 0
3 Feb	Frdly	Home	Romford Victoria	5 – 4
24 Feb	Frdly	Home	Woodgrange Reserves	3 – 5
17 Mar	Frdly	Away	Forest Gate	1 – 2
24 Mar	Frdly	Home	Fermain Hare Street	1 – 3

SUMMARY OF RESERVE TEAM RESULTS OBTAINED SEASON 1893 – 94

					Goals	
	P	W	D	L	For	Ag
Reserve Team Friendlies	15	4	4	7	35	38
Essex Junior Cup	1	0	0	1	0	1
Total	16	4	4	8	35	39

RESERVE TEAM CUP RESULTS SEASON 1893 – 94

Essex Junior Cup

(New competition)

Final: Matlock Swifts 4 Witham 1

Romford's progress: 1st Round Home Woodgrange Reserves 0 – 1

Reserve Team Appearances and Goal Scorers Season 1893 – 94

No details of team line-ups or goal scorers have been traced.

Post-Season Summary Season 1893 – 94

Once again the club got away to a good start, beginning with a 4-1 victory over St. Luke's and an amazing 2-2 draw away to Tottenham Hotspur before a large crowd. There followed home wins against Olympic (3-1) and Upton Park (6-1) followed by a 6-3 defeat against 2nd Coldstream Guards. A week later and the army were in town again and this time the 3rd Grenadier Guards went away with a 3-0 win.

A nil-nil draw at Slough and a 1-0 victory at Spartan Harriers showed an improvement. Soldiers came to town yet again, this time from the Norfolk Regiment, and Romford secured a 2-1 victory. Then a fine 4-1 away win at Chelmsford, followed by two defeats from Woodville (2-5) and Leytonstone Atlas (1-2). Next came another meeting with Chelmsford, this time at home in the Essex Senior Cup 1st Round and a satisfactory 6-2 victory. A week later Romford's hopes were dashed when they lost the second round tie 2-0 at Woodford.

A week later Bexleyheath were beaten 2-0 in a friendly, and then came four goals to two defeats in successive matches against Woodville and the 2nd Norfolk Regiment. On 17th February away to Olympic Romford lost by three goals to nil. Romford's fortune changed with two victories against Bexleyheath and Slough. In the game against Slough, Frank Cosburn, brother of the previous year's regular goalkeeper Wilfrid, played in goal. The Cosburn brothers, incidentally, were from a family of stonemasons - a far cry from the office clerks who formed the majority of the Romford team.

In March came the shocking news that the club's President, Romford MP James Theobald, had been killed after slipping between a train and the track at Romford Station. Romford's final game of the season was played on 17th March when they travelled to Sheppey United only to suffer a five nil defeat. Romford did not enter the F.A. Cup or Amateur Cup, but it is not known whether they failed to apply or were turned down. The reserve team had a below-average season with only four victories from the fifteen results we have to hand. This season was not very well reported by the local press, and team line ups and scorers have proved difficult to find.

Annual General Meeting
(as reported in the *Essex Times,* Wednesday 15th August 1894)

The annual general meeting of the Romford Football Club was held at the Golden Lion Hotel on Friday evening, 10th August 1894, Mr.F.H.Thirlwall presided, and among those present were : Messrs. W.Baker, J.R.Roynon, R.Carter, R.B.Pollett, F.H.Rotherham, G.F.White, F.Wells, C.Brady, F.Shackell, W.Hynds, H.W.Burrows, E.Burgess, E.H.Hinds, hon.sec., W.D.Matthews, hon.treasurer, &c. – Mr.W.D.Matthews submitted the statement of accounts for the past year. The receipts totalled up to £63.14s.1d., including a balance of £7.4s.3d. from the previous year; subscriptions, £29.18s.6d. ; Gate money, £25.16s.4d. ; and season tickets 15s. The expenditure amounted to £62.8s.3d., leaving a balance in hand of £1.5s.10d. There were several subscriptions to be got in.

It was decided to invite Mr.A.Money-Wigram,M.P. to accept the presidency of the club, in succession to the late Mr.J.Theobald.M.P. The vice-presidents were re-elected with exception of two gentlemen who have left the neighbourhood, and the names of Major Tye, Mr.W.G.Yound, Mr.E.Farman, Mr.Shirwood, and Mr.F. Collier were added to the list. Mr.C.Brady was re-elected captain for the ensuing year, and Mr.Fred. Wells, vice-captain. Mr.R.Carter and Mr.Burgess were elected captain, and vice-captain of the reserve team respectively. Mr.G.F.White was re-elected captain of the Victoria team, Mr.H.W.Burrows, vice-captain, and Mr.A.B. Pollett, secretary.

Mr.W.D.Matthews was re-elected treasurer to the club, the Chairman referring in terms of commendation to his past services. Mr.E.H.Hinds said it was with regret that he had to announce that he was compelled to resign the secretaryship of the club, as he found himself quite unable to do the work connected with the office. – The Chairman was sure they could not do without Mr.Hinds, and he must reconsider his decision. (Hear,hear). Considerable pressure was brought to bear by those present to induce Mr.Hinds to continue in the office, but without avail.

Eventually it was proposed by Mr.F.H.Rotherham, and seconded by Mr.Burrows, that Mr.F.H. Thirlwall be secretary, and notwithstanding that gentleman's protests, he was unanimously elected, amid great applause. – The Chairman he was sure they were all sorry Mr.Hinds was retiring. He had worked very hard for the club, and brought it to its present proud position. (Hear, hear). The office was not all "beer and skittles" but they must agree that Mr.Hinds had done his best to please everybody, and they could not do less than pass a hearty vote of thanks to him for his past services. (Applause). – The proposition was seconded by Mr.Roynon, and carried by acclamation.

Mr.W.D.Matthews was elected to represent the club on the association. The Committee were elected as follows: Messrs. G.Barnes, E.G.Bratchell, E.Chaloner, E.Champness, E.A.Gibson, T.J.Hare, E.H.Hinds, C.Hollebone, W.Hynds, J.Roynon, F.Shackell, H.L. Shockley, R.J.Slaughter, H.G.Smith, G.Stevenson, O.Wheatley, F.Willsmer, C.A.Wilson, and W.Wright.

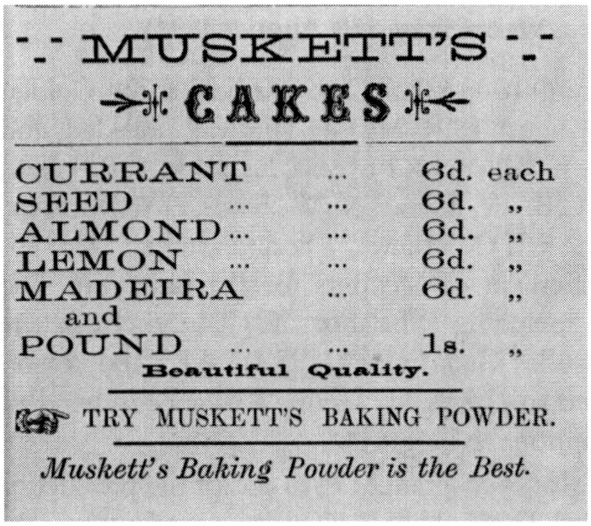

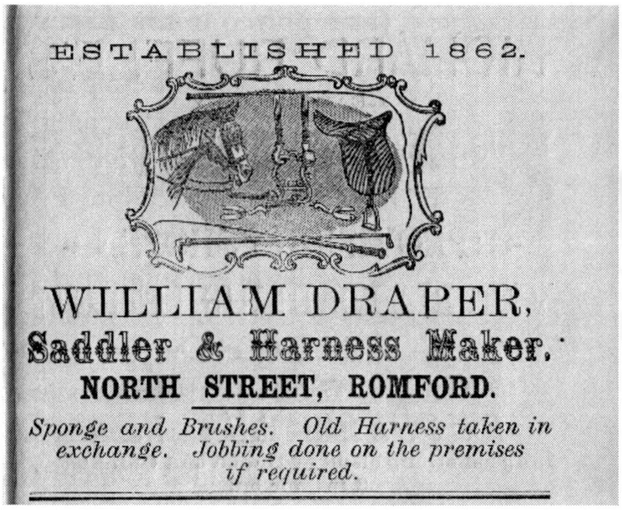

Season 1894 – 95

ROMFORD FOOTBALL CLUB

President: Mr.A.Money-Wigram.M.P. **Hon.Secretary:** Mr.F.H.Thirlwall **Hon.Treasurer:** Mr.W.D.Matthews

First Team Captain: Mr.C.Brady **First Team Vice-Captain:** Mr.Fred. Wells

Reserve Team Captain: Mr.R.Carter **Reserve Team Vice-Captain:** Mr.Burgess

Committee: Messrs.G.Barnes, E.G.Bratchell, E.Challenor, E.Champness, E.A.Gibson, T.J.Hare
E.H.Hinds, C.Hollebone, W.Hynds, J.Roynon, F.Shackell, H.L.Shockley, R.J.Slaughter
H.G.Smith, G.Stevenson, O.Wheatley, F.Willsmer, C.A.Wilson and W.Wright

Headquarters: Golden Lion Hotel, Romford **Ground:** Recreation Ground, Victoria Road, Romford

COMPETITIONS ENTERED

F.A. Amateur Cup
Essex Senior Cup
Friendly Matches
It is unknown why the Club did not compete in the F.A. Challenge Cup

Essex Junior Cup
Friendly Matches

Match Details

22 Sept Frdly Away Slough 2 – 4

29 Sept Frdly Away Kildare (Acton) 1 – 2 Unknown

6 Oct Frdly Away Vampires (Norbury) 1 – 0 Danks
Romford: G.Stevenson;F.Shackell,E.P.Jones;E.H.Hinds,C.E.McCabe,C.Brady(Capt);
J.Brady,A.B.MacDonnell,F.Danks,Fred.Wells,A.Ford.

13 Oct Frdly Home Woodville 2 – 4 J.Brady,MacDonnell

20 Oct Frdly Home Millwall Athletic 2 – 1 Danks(2)
Romford: G.Stevenson;F.Shackell,E.P.Jones;C.Brady(Capt),C.E.McCabe,E.H.Hinds;
A.B.MacDonnell,J.Brady,F.Danks,F.Donn,H.Price.

27 Oct Frdly Away Old Foresters (Snaresbrook) 6 – 0 Price(2)Danks(2)MacDonnell,Wells
Romford: H.Price,F.Danks,A.B.MacDonnell,Fred.Wells
Remainder of team unknown.

3 Nov Frdly Away Robin Hood (Tottenham) 0 – 4

10 Nov AC2Q Home Woodville 1 – 5* MacDonnell
Romford: G.Stevenson;E.H.Hinds,F.Shackell;C.Brady(Capt),C.E.McCabe,F.Adams;
S.W.Sulman,A.B.MacDonnell,F.Danks,Fred.Wells,H.Price.

17 Nov ACRep Home Woodville 2 – 2 Danks(2)
Romford: C.Burgess;E.Jones,A.C.Fellows;C.Brady(Capt),E.H.Hinds,F.Shackell;
E.J.Ramsey,S.W.Sulman,F.Danks,A.B.MacDonnell,J.Brady.

24 Nov ACRep Home Woodville 3 – 1 Price,Wells,one unknown
Romford: C.Burgess,F.Shackell,E.Jones;A.E.Fellows,E.H.Hinds,C.Brady(Capt);
J.Brady,A.B.MacDonnell,S.W.Sulman,H.Price,Fred.Wells.

1 Dec AC3Q Home Tottenham Hotspur 0 – 8
Romford:
Team details unknown

8 Dec ESCP Away Ilford 2 – 1 C.Brady,MacDonnell
Romford: C.Brady,A.B.MacDonnell.
Remainder of team unknown.

15 Dec ESC1R Home Woodville 1 – 0# MacDonnell
Romford: A.B.MacDonnell.
Remainder of team unknown.

22 Dec Frdly Home Upton Park 3 – 1 Scorers unknown

29 Dec ESCRep Home Woodville 2 – 2 Adams,MacDonnell
Romford: G.Stevenson;F.Shackell,E.P.Jones;F.Adams,E.H.Hinds,C.Brady(Capt);
A.B.MacDonnell,S.W.Sulman,J.Harris,A.D.Stanton,J.Mercer.

5 Jan ESCRep St.Lukes Woodville 0 – 1
Romford: G.Stevenson;E.J.Ramsey,F.Danks,J.Harris
Remainder of team unknown

19 Jan Frdly Home 1st Grenadier Guards 2 – 2 Scorers unknown

23 Feb Frdly Away Upton Park 4 – 5 Scorers unknown

16 Mar Frdly Home 1st Suffolk Regiment 4 – 0 Price(2)C.Brady,J.Brady

23 Mar Frdly Home Slough 3 – 2 Scorers unknown

30 Mar Frdly Home Dulwich 2 – 0 Scorers unknown

6 Apr Frdly Home Woolwich Arsenal Reserves 1 – 4 Scorer unknown

* Abandoned after 75 minutes due to bad light.
\# Replayed after protest because Frank Wells was cup tied and ineligible to play.

SUMMARY OF FIRST TEAM RESULTS OBTAINED SEASON 1894 – 95

					Goals	
	P	W	D	L	For	Ag
Friendly Matches	14	7	1	6	33	29
F.A. Amateur Cup	3	1	1	1	5	11
Essex Senior Cup	3	1	1	1	4	4
F.A. Amateur Cup (Aban)	1	0	0	1	1	5
Essex Senior Cup (void)	1	1	0	0	1	0
Total	22	10	3	9	44	49
A.G.M. report	24	11	4	8	49	51

The A.G.M. on this occasion did not include the reserve team games in the summary of results for the season as they often had in previous years, and regrettably we appear to be missing further first team games despite all the efforts made in this respect. It unknown whether the abandoned game was included in the AGM report.

CUP RESULTS SEASON 1894 – 95

F.A. Amateur Cup

Final: Middlesbrough 2 Old Carthusians 1

Romford's progress: 1st Qual Bye
2nd Qual. Home Woodville 1 – 5*
Replay Home Woodville 2 – 2
2nd Replay Home Woodville 3 – 1
3rd Qual Home Tottenham Hotspur 0 – 8

* Abandoned after 75 minutes due to bad light.

Essex Senior Cup

Final: Upton Park 2 Harwich & Parkeston 1

Romford's progress:	Prel.Round	Away	Ilford	2 – 1
	1st Round	Home	Woodville	1 – 0#
	Replay	Home	Woodville	2 – 2
	2nd Replay	St.Luke's	Woodville	0 – 1

Match void Fred.Wells ineligible and a replay ordered on neutral ground.

First Team Appearances Season 1894 – 95

F.Adams	1*	C.Brady	7*	J.Brady	6	C.Burgess	2
F.Danks	5*	F.Donn	1	A.E.Fellows	2	A.Ford	1
J.Harris	2	E.H.Hinds	5*	E.P.Jones	5	A.B.MacDonnell	8*
C.E.McCabe	2*	J.Mercer	1	H.Price	4*	E.J.Ramsey	2
F.Shackell	5*	A.D.Stanton	1	G.Stevenson	4*	S.W.Sulman	3*
Fred.Wells	3*					Total	70

* Also played in the abandoned cup tie against Woodville.
Note: Frank Wells and A.B.MacDonnell also played in the cup tie against Woodville that was declared void.

First Team Goal Scorers Season 1894 – 95

F.Danks	7	H.Price	5	A.B.MacDonnell	4*	Fred.Wells	2
C.Brady	2	J.Brady	2	F.Adams	1	Unknown	15
Total	38						

* The above summary does not include goals scored by MacDonnell against Woodville in the abandoned and void cup ties.

Once again information was sadly missing in the local newspapers, due, it is believed, because the club had failed to pay the ten shillings subscription for a season's coverage. For this reason it is regretted that it is not possible to give full details of appearances and goal scorers.

Essex County Football Association
(as reported in the *Essex Times,* Saturday 22 December 1894)

A meeting of the Executive Committee of the Essex County Football Association was held at the White Hart Hotel, Chelmsford, Mr.H.Craske, of Colchester, presiding, and there were also present Messrs. C.H.Dixon, Woodville F.C.; W.D. Matthews, Romford F.C.; and Mr.R.Cook,Hon.Sec.

The first business was to consider a protest of the Woodville Football Club against the Romford Football Club on the ground that in the Essex Senior Cup match the previous Saturday, they had played two men, Messrs. Frank Wells and A.C.Fellows, who were not qualified according to the rules of the Association.

In the case of Mr.Wells, the allegation was that he had played this season for Woodgrange against Matlock Swifts in the Junior Cup Competition on October 20th, thereby becoming disqualified to play for any other club in the Senior Cup Competition, as rule 6 with regard to the Junior Cup Competition expressly states that a player who has competed may play in the season in the Senior Cup Competition, but only for the club he played for in the junior competition.

As to Mr. Fellows, it was put forward by the Woodville Committee that he had not resided continuously in the county for two years. Mr.Dixon stated the facts. In the list of players forwarded by the assistant secretary of the Matlock Swifts club, the name of Wells occurred without any initial. Mr.Wells argued that this need not be the Wells referred to. Mr. Dixon stated that he saw the secretary of the Woodgrange club on Saturday, and asked him whether Wells had played with their team in the Junior Cup Competition. The secretary refused to tell him, remarking that he was not going to 'give his club mate away'. Mr.Matthews maintained that there was no proof that Wells played in the Junior Cup competition, but he had not himself made inquiries on the point.

Mr. Dixon: It is a fact that he did play. Mr. Dixon then drew attention to rule six, with regard to the Junior Cup competition. Mr.Matthews contended that this was not applicable to the case in point, stating that the junior cup competition rules had nothing whatever to do with the senior cup competition rules. The match between Woodville and Romford was a senior cup match. As regarded the case of Mr.Fellows, the Chairman read a letter from that player, which showed that he had resided in the county for over two years.

The meeting decided to allow the protest against Mr.Wells, but considered that Mr. Fellows was eligible to play for Romford. The Chairman pointed out that the rules regulating the two competitions and the bye-laws of the county association were to be taken as one whole set of bye-laws. The match Woodville v. Romford was ordered to be played on December 29th, the latter club to have choice of ground.

On Friday 15th February the Executive Committee again met at Chelmsford to discuss the Woodford F.C. protest against Woodville F.C. Again it was a successful outcome for Woodville, but they lost to Upton Park in the semi-final without protest! At the same meeting Romford protested against 'illegal action' of the Committee in dealing with the protest of Woodville versus Romford. The matter was left over for a general council meeting, but no details are to hand of the final outcome.

RESERVE TEAM

Match Details

22 Sept	Frdly	Away	Romford Buffs	1 – 3
6 Oct	Frdly	Home	Woodville Reserves	0 – 3
20 Oct	EJC1R	Away	Romford St. Andrews	1 – 13
22 Oct	Frdly	Home	Havering	4 – 0
3 Nov	Frdly	Home	Olympic Reserves	0 – 0
15 Dec	Frdly	Away	Hornchurch	0 – 10
5 Jan	Frdly	Away	Romford Victoria	2 – 5
19 Jan	Frdly	Home	Romford Buffs.	0 – 4
26 Jan	Frdly	Home	Woodville Reserves	3 – 0
2 Mar	Frdly	Away	Squirrels Heath	0 – 14

SUMMARY OF RESERVE TEAM RESULTS OBTAINED SEASON 1894 – 95

	P	W	D	L	Goals For	Goals Ag
Essex Junior Cup	1	0	0	1	1	13
Friendly Matches	9	2	1	6	10	39
Total	10	2	1	7	11	52

No reference was made at the Annual General Meeting regarding the reserve team results, and it is unknown if any results are missing. Reference was made at the A.G.M. to the lack of players turning up for the reserves and this no doubt explains some of the heavy defeats.

CUP RESULTS SEASON 1894 – 95

Essex Junior Cup

Final: Barking Excelsior 3 Saffron Walden 0

Romford's progress: 1st Round Away Romford St. Andrew's 1 – 13

Post-Season Summary Season 1894 – 95

During the close season, prominent player and committee member Livingstone ('Tony') Clark died aged only 34 after a short illness. A former club captain and one of four brothers to play for the club, he would be greatly missed.

Romford commenced the season with seven friendly matches and met with mixed success, losing three of their first four matches. The lone victory was against Vampires at Norbury who were beaten by one goal to nil. Next came two fine wins: against Millwall Athletic at home (2-1) and 6-0 over Old Foresters at Snaresbrook. There followed a 4-0 defeat away to the Robin Hood team at Tottenham.

Then came four successive Amateur Cup ties after Romford had received a bye through the 1st Round, three of which were against Woodville! In the first game Romford were saved from a heavy 5-1 defeat when the game was abandoned after 75 minutes. The two teams fought out a 2-2 draw in the replay, then the third encounter saw Romford go through with a 3-1 victory.

Supporters were looking forward to the third round and a home tie against Tottenham Hotspur. Alas, the formidable Spurs won by eight goals to nil. In their next game, a 2-1 win over neighbours Ilford in the Preliminary Round of the Essex Senior Cup, the newspaper report stated that Romford's Frank Wells took his knee out of the socket!

Next came the Essex Senior Cup 1st Round and Romford had to play Woodville once more. On this occasion Woodville lost by one goal to nil. However they protested that Frank Wells was ineligible to play for Romford. The County Association ordered a replay of the tie, and the match ended in a two all draw. Romford lost the second replay 1-0, amid controversy regarding the poor condition of the neutral St. Luke's ground.

Romford rounded off the season with six more friendly matches winning three, losing two and drawing one. The final game was a home defeat to Woolwich Arsenal Reserves. The reserve team had a disastrous season, winning only a few matches and suffering 13–1, 11–0 and 14–0 defeats. On the whole, it was not a very satisfactory year for the club.

Annual General Meeting
(as reported in the *Essex Times,* Wednesday 28th August 1895)

The annual meeting of the Romford Football Club took place at the Golden Lion Hotel on Friday evening 23rd August. Mr.George Barnes presided over a large attendance, amongst those present being Messrs. R.Adams, L.Barrett, C.Brady, H.Burrows, E.Challenor, L.Davis, H.A.Griggs, H.C.Griggs, E.H.Hinds, W.Hynds, A.Johnson, E.Jones, A.Lawton, A.Mallinson, T.Mallinson, F.Mumford, A.B.Pollett, T.W.Sharpe, E.W.Smith, F.Wells, O.Wheatley, G.W.White & F.H.Thirlwall, hon.sec. The Hon. Sec. reported that the past season had been a fairly successful one. The first team played 24 matches, winning 11 and losing 8. Four were drawn, and one was stopped owing to darkness setting in. Forty-nine goals were won and 51 lost. After playing Woodville several times, the team was beaten on St. Lukes' ground, in the Essex Cup match. The defeat was owing partly to the wretched state of the ground, and also to their opponents playing men who did not belong to the club, which was proved by their being disqualified later on. Romford won one match against Woodville, but the latter protested against Frank Wells playing, their protest being allowed. Most of the old team were available for the coming season. He was sorry that Mr.Wells, who had done good service for them in the past – (Hear, hear) – would be unable to play again – at any rate for some time – through an accident to his knee. Mr.A.C.Fellowes, another prominent member of the team, had removed from the town and they were still in want of a good goalkeeper.

The reserve team, owing to its members turning up in such small numbers, played few matches. Three of these were won, but many had to be scratched owing to the inability to raise an eleven. The long frosts interfered considerably with the matches of both teams. If they were play a reserve team this season he must have some support from the members. He had arranged a good list for the first team, every Saturday except two being already filled up. For the reserves only a few had at present been arranged. It was ridiculous to send three or four men to a match; they must have a good strong reserve and plenty of material to choose from. He could not help thinking that in Romford there were too many clubs for the size of the place. (Hear, hear). When he first came to the town no club existed, and he well remembered the establishment of the Romford club, twenty years ago that month, he being one of the chief starters – (Hear, hear) – now there were he could not say how many clubs. He thought it would be a good thing if two or three of them could amalgamate and form a thoroughly good strong Romford club. (Applause).

Referring to the coming season he said the club had entered for two cups, the National and the Amateur, and he hoped the meeting would resolve to enter for the Essex Cup. At several meetings the question of doing so had been discussed, and he was strongly in favour of it. They had not been well served in the past, but he certainly thought they ought to enter this year. He was glad to say they had several new members – and playing ones – but they wanted some more, and would like more local men. The club were greatly indebted to Mr. Peter Reynolds, who had allowed them the use of a room for all their meetings free of charge. (Applause). In conclusion he hoped the coming season would be a successful one for the club. (Hear, hear).

The financial statement, presented by Mr.E.W.Smith, showed a balance to hand of £1.15s.8d., slightly in excess of the balance brought forward. – The report and balance sheet were unanimously adopted. – The arrangements for the dinner in conjunction with the cricket club were left in the hands of a joint sub-committee. The advisability of entering for the Essex Cup was next discussed. – Mr. Thirlwall said he felt very strongly about the matter. All were well aware that they were not treated properly; he was certain that if they had been they would have brought the cup home. (Hear, hear). It had been suggested that they should not enter this year, but he strongly urged them to do so and to try to win it this season. Mr. Wheatley was not in favour of the club entering, remarking that they had never had fair treatment. – After further discussion it was decided to enter, on the proposal of Mr.Wells, seconded by Mr.Barrett. Mr.Brady suggested that if they were drawn to play on the St. Luke's ground they should ask the Association to send a representative to inspect it.

The usual votes of thanks to the various officers was passed; also one to Mr.P.Reynolds. – Mr.A.Money-Wigram.M.P., was re-elected president, and it was decided to ask Messrs. E.Bryant, V.Castellan, H.Compton, A.Harris, E.Lawton, H.B. Mitchell, H.H.Raphael, and H.Stone to become vice-presidents. The officers were elected as follows: Captain 1st Team, Mr.C.Brady; vice-captain, Mr.E.H.Hinds; captain, reserves, Mr.A.Lawton; vice-captain, Mr.Hugh Griggs; captain Victoria team, Mr.G.W.White; vice-captain, Mr.Ralph Adams; hon.sec. Victoria team, Mr.A.B. Pollett; treasurer, Mr.W.D.Matthews; hon.sec.. Mr.F.H.Thirlwall. The committee members were re-elected, with one or two alterations. Mr.W.D. Matthews was re-elected representative to the associations. The arrangements for a second ground were briefly discussed and referred to the committee. Eight new members joined the club.

VICTORIA FOOTBALL CLUB

Secretary: Mr.A.B.Pollett

Captain: Mr.G.F.White **Vice-Captain:** Mr.H.W.Burrows

Note: The above details were all reported at the Romford Football Club's AGM and it is believed the Victoria team had a vague connection to the Romford FC but not in an official capacity. They apparently held joint meetings.

Romford Market Place in 1895
Havering Libraries - Local Studies

Season 1895 – 96

ROMFORD FOOTBALL CLUB

President: Mr.A.Money-Wigram.M.P.

Hon.Secretary: Capt.F.H.Thirlwall **Hon.Treasurer:** Mr.W.D.Matthews

First Team Captain: Mr.C.Brady **First Team Vice-Captain:** Mr.E.H.Hinds

Reserve Team Captain: Mr.A.Lawton **Reserve Team Vice-Captain:** Mr.Hugh Griggs

Committee: The Committee was re-elected with one or two alterations, details unknown

Headquarters: Golden Lion Hotel, Romford **Ground:** Recreation Ground, Victoria Road, Romford

COMPETITIONS ENTERED

F.A. Challenge Cup
F.A. Amateur Cup
Essex Senior Cup
Friendly Matches

Essex Junior Cup
Friendly Matches

Match Details

21 Sept Frdly Away Marlow 2 – 5 MacDonnell,one unknown
Romford: T.W.Sharpe;E.P.Jones,F.Shackell;E.H.Hinds(Capt),W.S.Triggs,A.Lawton;
S.W.Sulman,A.B.MacDonnell,E.G.Leal,H.Price,J.Mercer.

28 Sept Frdly Away Forest Swifts 0 – 1
Romford: W.H.Kelly;F.Shackell,E.P.Jones;C.Stromeyer,E.H.Hinds(Capt),Taylor;
A.B.MacDonnell,Linnard,E.Barnes,R.Ormford,H.Price.

5 Oct Frdly Away Civil Service (Denmark Hill) 1 – 3 MacDonnell
Romford: G.Stevenson;F.Shackell,E.H.Hinds;C.Brady(Capt),C.Stromeyer,W.S.Triggs;
A.B.MacDonnell,S.W.Sulman,J.Brady,E.Barnes.

12 Oct FAC1Q Home Royal Engineers Training Battn. 1 – 2 Sulman
Romford: W.H.Kelly;F.Shackell,E.P.Jones;C.Brady(Capt),C.Stromeyer,E.H.Hinds;
A.B.MacDonnell,S.W.Sulman,J.Brady,W.S.Triggs,E.Barnes.

19 Oct AC1Q Home Colchester 3 – 1* Barnes(2)Price
Romford: W.H.Kelly;F.Shackell,E.P.Jones;C.Brady(Capt),C.Stromeyer,E.H.Hinds;
A.B.MacDonnell,H.Price,S.W.Sulman,Frank Wells,E.Barnes.

26 Oct ACRep Away Colchester 0 – 1
Romford: W.H.Kelly;F.Shackell,E.P.Jones;W.S.Triggs,E.H.Hinds,C.Brady(Capt);
A.B.MacDonnell,W.McKechnie,S.W.Sulman,H.Price,E.Barnes.

2 Nov Frdly Home Olympic (Upton Park) 1 – 1 Scorer unknown

9 Nov Frdly Home Chelmsford 0 – 0
Romford: W.H.Kelly;F.Shackell,E.P.Jones;C.Brady(Capt),C.Stromeyer,W.S.Triggs;
A.B.MacDonnell,S.W.Sulman,V.Castellan,H.Price,E.Burgess.

16 Nov Frdly Home Fulham 1 – 1 Scorer unknown

30 Nov Frdly Home Slough 1 – 2 Scorer unknown

7 Dec ESC1R Away Leyton 1 – 1 Scorer unknown

14 Dec Replay Home Leyton 2 – 0 Triggs,one unknown
Romford: W.H.Kelly;F.Shackell,E.P.Jones;C.Brady,C.Stromeyer,E.H.Hinds(Capt);
A.B.MacDonnell,S.W.Sulman,W.S.Triggs,J.Mercer,E.Barnes.

21 Dec Frdly Home Upton Park 4 – 0 Scorers unknown

11 Jan Frdly Away Leyton 2 – 5 Scorers unknown

18 Jan ESC2R Away Barking Woodville 1 – 1 Barnes
Attendance: 1,000
Romford: W.H.Kelly;F.Shackell,E.P.Jones;C.Brady(Capt),C.Stromeyer,E.H.Hinds;
A.B.MacDonnell,S.W.Sulman,D.Hill,J.Mercer,E.Barnes.

25 Jan Replay Home Barking Woodville 1 – 3 Barnes
Romford: W.H.Kelly;F.Shackell,E.P.Jones;C.Brady(Capt),C.Stromeyer,E.H.Hinds;
A.B.MacDonnell,J.Mercer,D.Hill,W.S.Triggs,E.Barnes.

1 Feb Frdly Away Upton Park 2 – 2 Scorers unknown

15 Feb Frdly Away Suffolk Regiment 1 – 2 Scorer unknown

22 Feb Frdly Away Ilford 1 – 1 Scorer unknown

14 Mar Frdly Home Leyton 0 – 3
Romford: W.H.Kelly;F.Shackell,E.P.Jones;C.Brady(Capt),C.Stromeyer,E.H.Hinds;
A.B.MacDonnell,W.G.Benson,W.S.Triggs,D.Evans,E.Barnes.

21 Mar Frdly Home London Welsh 6 – 4 Scorers unknown

28 Mar Frdly Away Slough 2 – 1 Scorers unknown

25 Apr Frdly Home Old Stagers 4 – 2 Scorers unknown
Romford: T.W.Sharpe;F.Shackell,E.P.Jones;C.Brady(Capt),E.H.Hinds,
C.Stromeyer,B.Trimmer,S.Mercer,W.H.Kelly.
Old Stagers: Had 16 players, no details available.

* After Extra Time. Abandoned after 113 minutes.

SUMMARY OF FIRST TEAM RESULTS SEASON 1895 – 96

					Goals	
	P	W	D	L	For	Ag
F.A. Challenge Cup	1	0	0	1	1	2
F.A. Amateur Cup	1	0	0	1	0	1
F.A. Am.Cup.Aban.Void	1	1	0	0	3	1
Essex Senior Cup	4	1	2	1	5	5
Friendly matches	16	4	5	7	28	33
Total	23	6	7	10	37	42

CUP RESULTS SEASON 1895 – 96

F.A. Challenge Cup

Final: Sheffield Wednesday 2 Wolverhampton Wanderers 1

Romford's progress: 1st Qual Home Royal Engineers Trng. Battn. 1 – 2

F.A. Amateur Cup

Final: Bishop Auckland 1 R.A. Portsmouth 0

Romford's progress: 1st Qual Home Colchester 3 – 1 *
Replay Home Colchester 0 – 1

* Abandoned in extra time

Essex Senior Cup

Final: Barking Woodville 2 Woodford 0

Romford's progress: 1st Round Away Leyton 1 – 1
Replay Home Leyton 2 – 0
2nd Round Away Barking Woodville 1 – 1
Replay Home Barking Woodville 1 – 3

First Team Appearances Season 1895 – 96

E.Barnes	8*	W.G.Benson	1	C.Brady	9*	J.Brady	2
E.Burgess	1	V.Castellan	1	D.Evans	1	D.Hill	2
E.H.Hinds	10*	E.P.Jones	10*	W.H.Kelly	9*	E.G.Leal	1
Linnard	1	A.Lawton	1	A.B.MacDonnell	9*	McDougal	1
W.McKetchnie	1	J.Mercer	4	S.Mercer	1	R.Ormford	1
H.Price	4*	F.Shackell	11*	T.W.Sharpe	2	G.Stevenson	1
C.Stromeyer	9*	S.W.Sulman	7*	Taylor	1	Trimmer	1
W.S.Triggs	8	Frank Wells	1			Total	119

* These players also played in the abandoned amateur cup tie against Colchester on 19th October.

Note: Due to the lack of press coverage during the second half of the season the above summary is incomplete but it does show the more prominent members of the team.

First Team Goal Scorers Season 1895 – 96

Due to the sparse coverage by the local press it is regretted that no detailed summaries can be made for goal scorers for this season.

RESERVE TEAM

Match Details

n/k	Frdly	Away	Romford Excelsior	1 – 2
2 Nov	EJC1R	Home	Romford St. Andrew's Reserves	0 – 4
14 Dec	Frdly	Away	Romford Excelsior	0 – 1

Romford Reserves: T.W.Sharpe;Luard,D.Hill;Skuse,V.Castellan,E.C.Humphries(Capt); C.W.Hill,S.Mercer,Berkley,B.Macey,H.Burrows.

29 Feb	Frdly	Away	Barking Woodville III	0 – 0
11 Apr	Frdly	Home	Romford Excelsior	2 – 3
	Frdly	Home	Romford St. Andrews	0 – 6
	Frdly	Away	Hartland	3 – 0
	Frdly	Home	Woodville Reserves	0 – 0
	Frdly	Home	Billericay	3 – 0
	Frdly	Away	Peckham	1 – 2
	Frdly	Home	Salway United	0 – 6

SUMMARY OF RESERVE TEAM RESULTS OBTAINED SEASON 1895 – 96

					Goals	
	P	W	D	L	For	Ag
Friendly Matches	10	2	2	6	10	20
Essex Junior Cup	1	0	0	1	0	4
Total	11	2	2	7	10	24

CUP RESULTS SEASON 1895 – 96

Essex Junior Cup

Final: Barking Woodville "A" 2 Colchester Crown 2
Replay: Barking Woodville "A" 2 Colchester Crown 0

Romford's progress: 1st Round Home Romford St. Andrew's Reserves 0 – 4

Post-Season Summary Season 1895 – 96

Romford opened the season with a string of defeats, and once more their problems in putting out a full team came to the surface in the 3-1 loss to Civil Service at Denmark Hill. They were quickly despatched from the F.A. Cup, but held a 3-1 lead over Colchester in the Amateur Cup only for the match to be abandoned with seven minutes left to play of extra time. To add to Romford's woes, Colchester won the replay 1-0.

Four home friendlies followed, with Romford failing to secure a single victory, but hopes were raised when they defeated Leyton 2-0 in the Essex Senior Cup replay after a one all draw. In the second round Romford came up against Barking Woodville, and before a crowd of 1,000 obtained an away one all draw, but lost the home replay 3-1.

Once again the team were left to end the season with a string of friendly matches, without much success. They did record six goals against London Welsh, but the visitors managed to score four!

1896 was the club's 20th anniversary year, so it was appropriate that the final game of the season was the current first team against the Old Stagers, a line-up of former Romford players. It appears that the first team played with only nine men and the Old Stagers used sixteen players (presumably a team of eleven and using substitutes).

We have only been able to find a couple of friendly victories for the reserves, and several defeats, including a 4-0 reverse against St. Andrews Reserves in the Essex Junior Cup. On the brighter side, at the end of the season E.Barnes was awarded his Essex Senior Badge for three or more appearances in the County team.

Annual General Meeting
(as reported in the *Essex Times, Wednesday 22nd July 1896*)

The annual meeting of the Romford Football Club was held at the Golden Lion on Friday evening, 17th July, Mr.G.Barnes presiding.- Mr.F.H.Thirlwall, the hon.sec., in submitting the annual report for 1895-96, said the season did not commence favourably, the club having lost the first six matches. But it should be borne in mind that the clubs played were very strong. The English cup match, in which they had to play the R.E. Training Battalion was lost two goals to one. In the match for the Amateur Cup Colchester were the opponents; five goals to one were obtained, but the game was stopped for the want of light. When replayed their opponents won by one goal to nil. For the Essex Cup, the first match was against Leyton, and resulted in a draw – one to one. It was replayed at Romford, and won, two to one. They then had to play Woodville at Barking; the result was again a draw, but when replayed at Romford their opponents won, three to one.

Having referred to the South Essex League Cup, Mr.Thirlwall said he had to thank the committee for their assistance. He had no doubt that when he mentioned that there was an average of 15 at each meeting, those present would agree with him that the committee had the welfare of the club at heart. He had arranged matches for the first eleven with the exception of two dates for the whole of the season, and several for the second eleven. The club had again been entered for the cups, and he trusted the meeting would approve of the same. It was not often he took notice of anonymous communications, but there had appeared a letter stating that there were good men in Romford who had not been asked to play. He replied to the letter, and could only repeat that if any would come forward they should be glad to give them a trial. He still considered that there were too many clubs in the town, and that it would be better if one combined club could be formed and so enable the very best men to be selected, and to run as often as could be, a third eleven.

Mr.W.D.Matthews, hon.treasurer, submitted the balance sheet, from which it appeared the subscriptions for the year were £38.3s.0d., gate money £49.16s.7d., gate money received from opponents £11.8s.0d., which, with other small items, made a total of £102.6s.7d. The three chief items of expenditure were rents £20, travelling expenses £20.0s.6d., paid to opponents as gate money, £15.2s.7d. After defraying the whole of the expenses the balance in hand was £5.8s.1d., against £1.15s.8d. with which the season commenced. Mr.A.Money Wigram.M.P., was re-elected president. The vice-presidents were re-elected, and it was resolved to invite others to become vice-presidents. Mr.C.Brady was elected captain, first eleven. Messrs.W.H.Kelly and C.Stromeyer were proposed as vice-captains. The result of the ballot was that there were 13 votes for each, and the chairman gave his casting vote to the former. Mr.A.Lawton was elected captain of the second eleven, and Mr.T.Sharp vice-captain.

The question of the Victorian team gave rise to some considerable discussion. – Mr.Kelly urged that the title "Victorian" be struck out. – Mr.Matthews said if this was done the club would often be able to run three elevens.- Mr.Follett said the Victorian were willing to be available for the first eleven, but not for the second. – Mr.Kelly said the outside public considered it a distinct club. – Mr.Thirlwall did not wish to throw cold water upon the Victorian team. The question of equal to the first eleven or the second eleven was not the real question. It was a distinct club, therefore to have the title Victorian in connection with that club was a mistake. – Mr.Kelly proposed, and Mr.Lawton seconded, that the title "Victorian" be struck out. – In reply to Mr.Pollett, Mr.Matthews said the Victorian team had cost the club about 30s., while they had brought in from £3.15s.0d. to £4. – The resolution was adopted by 12 to 3. – Mr.Thirlwall was re-elected hon.sec., Mr.Matthews hon.treasurer, Mr.Kelly was elected assistant secretary. Upon the election of the committee, which formerly consisted of 20 members, Mr.Kelly moved that the number be reduced to 12. – This was carried against an amendment to re-elect a committee of 20. – The following were elected: Messrs. Barnes, Burrows, Champness, Challenor, Hill, Hynds, Hinds, Roynon, Smith, Stevenson, Stromeyer, and Wheatley.

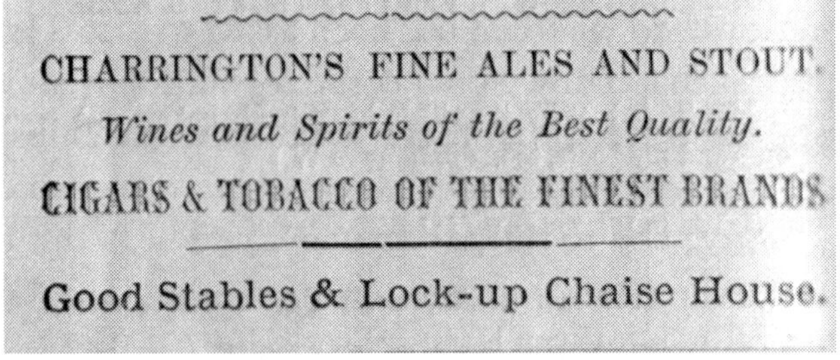

Season 1896 – 97

ROMFORD FOOTBALL CLUB

President: Mr.A.Money Wigram.M.P **Hon. Secretary:** Capt.F.H.Thirlwall

Hon.Asst.Secretary: Mr.W.H.Kelly **Hon.Treasurer:** Mr.W.D.Matthews

Captain: Mr.C.Brady **Vice-Captain:** Mr.W.H.Kelly

Reserve Team Captain: Mr.W.A.Lawton **Reserve Team Vice-Captain:** Mr.T.W.Sharpe

Committee: Messrs. E.Barnes, W.F.Burrows, E.Champness, E.Challenor, D.Hill, W.Hynds E.H.Hinds, J.Roynon, E.W.Smith, G.Stevenson, C.Stromeyer, and O.Wheatley

Headquarters: Golden Lion Hotel, Romford **Ground:** Recreation Ground, Victoria Road, Romford

COMPETITIONS ENTERED

South Essex Football League Division One
F.A. Challenge Cup
F.A. Amateur Cup
Essex Senior Cup
West Ham Charity Competition
Victoria Cottage Hospital Fund

South Essex Football League Division Two
Essex Junior Cup

Match Details

5 Sept Frdly Away Grays United 3 – 4 Two from scrimmages,Sulman
Romford: E.W.Smith;C.Adams,H.W.Brown;R.D.Taylor,C.Brady(Capt),E.H.Hinds;
G.W.Benson,S.W.Sulman,E.Barnes,Trimmer,H.E.Hillman.

19 Sept SEL1 Away Leytonstone 1 – 5 Kelly
Attendance: 1,100
Romford: E.Challenor;F.Mitchell,S.W.Sulman;T.Wiffen,R.Baker,R.D.Taylor;
H.E.Hillman,E.Barnes,F.Robinson,G.W.Benson,W.H.Kelly(Capt).

26 Sept SEL1 Away Leyton 2 – 9 Scorers unknown
Attendance: 800

3 Oct SEL1 Home St. Luke's* 2 – 3# Scorers unknown

10 Oct FAC1Q Home Sittingbourne 3 – 3 Brady,Sulman,Barnes
Romford: W.H.Kelly;F,Mitchell,E.P.Jones;C.Brady(Capt),W.G.Thompson,R.D.Taylor;
A.B.MacDonnell,S.W.Sulman,E.Barnes,Davie.Evans,H.E.Hillman.

14 Oct Replay Away Sittingbourne 2 – 2 Scorers unknown
Romford:
Team details unknown.

17 Oct 2Rep Sittingbourne Scratched w/o

24 Oct SEL1 Away South West Ham 2 – 1 MacDonnell,Sulman
Romford: W.H.Kelly;H.W.Brown,E.P.Jones;R.D.Taylor,W.G.Thompson,C.Brady(Capt);
A.B.MacDonnell,S.W.Sulman,G.W.Benson,E.Barnes,H.E.Hillman.

31 Oct FAC2Q Home Dartford 1 – 4 Barnes
Attendance: 500
Romford: W.H.Kelly;H.W.Brown,E.P.Jones;R.D.Taylor,W.G.Thompson,C.Brady(Capt);
A.B.MacDonnell,S.W.Sulman,E.Barnes,G.W.Benson,H.E.Hillman.

7 Nov Frdly Home Forest Swifts 0 – 1
Romford: W.H.Kelly;W.G.Thompson,E.P.Jones;R.D.Taylor,E.H.Hinds,C.Brady(Capt);
F.Robinson,S.W.Sulman,G.W.Benson,D.Evans,E.Barnes.

14 Nov SEL1 Home Woodford 2 – 1 MacDonnell(2)
Attendance: 400
Romford: W.H.Kelly;W.G.Thompson,E.P.Jones;R.D.Taylor,E.H.Hinds,C.Brady(Capt);
A.B.MacDonnell,S.W.Sulman,G.W.Benson,D.Evans,E.Barnes.

21 Nov AC3Q Away Leytonstone 2 – 4 Scorers unknown
Romford: W.H.Kelly;H.W.Brown,E.P.Jones;R.D.Taylor,W.G.Thompson,C.Brady(Capt);
A.B.MacDonnell,S.W.Sulman,D.Evans,E.Barnes,G.W.Benson.

28 Nov ESC1R Away Manor Park 0 – 1
Romford: W.H.Kelly;H.W.Brown,C.Adams;R.D.Taylor,E.H.Hinds,C.Brady(Capt);
A.B.MacDonnell,S.W.Sulman,D.Evans,G.W.Benson,E.Barnes.

5 Dec Frdly Away Squirrels Heath 1 – 4

12 Dec SEL1 Home Manor Park 6 – 1 Barnes(2)Hillman(2)Hinds,Thompson
Romford: Team details unknown

19 Dec Frdly Home Upton Park 2 – 2 Sulman,Hillman
Attendance: 200
Romford: W.H.Kelly(Capt);C.Adams,E.P.Jones;R.D.Taylor,E.H.Hinds,W.G.Thompson;
A.B.MacDonnell,S.W.Sulman,E.Barnes,D.Evans,H.E.Hillman.

26 Dec Frdly Home Ilford 3 – 2 Scorers unknown

2 Jan SEL1 Away Woodford P – P Fog

9 Jan SEL1 Home Brentwood 6 – 0 Scorers unknown

16 Jan Frdly Home Walthamstow Holborn 4 – 0 Scorers unknown

30 Jan VCH Home Romford St.Andrew's 1 – 0 Scorer unknown
Romford: W.H.Kelly;H.W.Brown,E.P.Jones;R.D.Taylor,E.H.Hinds,C.Brady(Capt);
A.B.MacDonnell,S.W.Sulman,E.Barnes,W.G.Thompson,H.E.Hillman.

6 Feb SEL1 Away Woodford 3 – 2 Scorers unknown
Romford team details unknown

13 Feb WHC1R Home Upton Park 5 – 1 Scorers unknown
Attendance: 300
Romford: W.H.Kelly;H.W.Brown,E.P.Jones;R.D.Taylor,E.H.Hinds,C.Brady(Capt);
A.B.MacDonnell,D.Evans,E.Barnes,H.E.Hillman,W.G.Thompson.

20 Feb SEL1 Home Leytonstone 4 – 2 MacDonnell(2)Barnes,Sulman
Romford: W.H.Kelly;C.Adams,E.P.Jones;R.D.Taylor,E.H.Hinds,C.Brady;
A.B.MacDonnell,H.Hillman,E.Barnes,S.W.Sulman,W.G.Thompson.

27 Feb SEL1 Away Manor Park 3 – 2 Scorers unknown

6 Mar WHCSF Home* West Ham Garfield 1 – 3 Scorer unknown
Attendance: 800
Romford: W.H.Kelly;W.H.Brown,E.P.Jones;R.D.Taylor,E.H.Hinds,C.Brady;
A.B.MacDonnell,W.G.Thompson,E.Barnes,S.W.Sulman,H.Hillman.

13 Mar SEL1 Home Leyton 1 – 7 Scorer unknown
Romford: W.H.Kelly;C.Adams,E.P.Jones;C.Brady,E.H.Hinds,A.Romper;
H.E.Hillman,W.G.Thompson,E.Barnes,S.W.Sulman,A.B.MacDonnell.

20 Mar SEL1 Away Brentwood 6 – 0 Scorers unknown

27 Mar SEL1 Home South West Ham 2 – 0 Scorers unknown

17 Apr Frdly Away Ilford 0 – 10
\# St. Luke's withdrew from the league, their record expunged and this match was declared void.
* Played at the Cricket Ground, Romford Station

SUMMARY OF FIRST TEAM RESULTS OBTAINED SEASON 1896 – 97

	P	W	D	L	Goals For	Goals Ag	Pts
South Essex Football Lge.	12	9	0	3	38	30	18
S.Essex Lge. Void	1	0	0	1	2	3	
F.A. Challenge Cup	3	0	2	1	6	9	
F.A. Amateur Cup	1	0	0	1	2	4	
Essex Senior Cup	1	0	0	1	0	1	
West Ham Charity Comp.	2	1	0	1	6	4	
Victoria Cott. Hosp. Fund	1	1	0	0	1	0	
Friendly Matches#	7	2	1	4	13	23	
Total	28	13	3	12	68	74	
A.G.M. Press Report	28	13	5	10	71	64	

South Essex League Division One
Final Table

	P	W	D	L	Goals For	Goals Ag	Pts
Leyton	12	10	1	1	68	20	21
Romford	**12**	**9**	**0**	**3**	**38**	**30**	**18**
South West Ham	12	6	2	4	40	23	14
Leytonstone	12	5	1	6	30	28	11
Manor Park	12	4	1	7	19	42	9
Woodford	12	4	0	8	26	38	8
Brentwood	12	1	1	10	4	44	3

St. Luke's and Thames Ironworks both withdrew from the league and their records were expunged. Thames Ironworks later became West Ham United.

CUP RESULTS SEASON 1896 – 97

F.A. Challenge Cup

Final: Aston Villa 3 Everton 2

Romford's progress: Prel.Round Home Sittingbourne 3 – 3
Replay Away Sittingbourne 2 – 2
2nd Rep. Home Sittingbourne w/o*
1st Qual Home Dartford 1 – 4
* Sittingbourne scratched

F.A. Amateur Cup

Final: Old Carthusians 1 Stockton 1
Replay: Old Carthusians 4 Stockton 1

Romford's progress: 3rd Qual Away Leytonstone 2 – 4

Essex Senior Cup

Final: Leyton 4 Yorks and Lancashire Regt. 0

Romford's progress: Prel.Round Away Manor Park 0 – 1

West Ham Charity Cup

Winners: West Ham Garfield

Romford's progress:	1st Round	Home	Upton Park	5 – 1
	Semi-Final	Away	West Ham Garfield	1 – 3

Victoria Cottage Hospital Fund

Romford 1 Romford St. Andrew's 0

First Team Appearances Season 1896 – 97

C.Adams	5	R.Baker	1	E.Barnes	15	G.W.Benson	8
C.Brady	13	H.W.Brown	8	E.Challenor	1	D.Evans	7
H.E.Hillman	11	E.H.Hinds	10	E.P.Jones	11	W.H.Kelly	14
A.B.MacDonnell	12	F.Mitchell	2	F.Robinson	2	A.Romper	1
E.W.Smith	1	S.W.Sulman	14	R.D.Taylor	14	G.W.Thompson	12
Trimmer	1	T.Wiffen	1			Total	164

Goal Scorers Season 1896 – 97

Due to the very poor coverage of games in the local press, details of the goal scorers cannot be compiled.

RESERVE TEAM

Match Details

26 Sept	Frdly	Away	Ilford Excelsior	0 – 5
3 Oct	SEL2	Away	St. Lukes Reserves	0 – 1#
10 Oct	Frdly	Home	Ilford Grange	0 – 1
17 Oct	Frdly	Home	Excelsiors	0 – 4
24 Oct	EJC1R	Away	Brentwood Reserves	3 – 2
31 Oct	Frdly	Home	Forest Gate	2 – 0
7 Nov	EJC2R	Away	Grays Anchor	0 – 6
14 Nov	SEL2	Away	Woodford Reserves	Lost+
21 Nov	SEL2	Home	East Ham United	0 – 1
	Frdly	Home	Romford Excelsior	4 – 0
5 Dec	Frdly	Away	Squirrels Heath	0 – 5
	Frdly	Away	Clapton 3rd XI	1 – 5
	SEL2	Away	East Ham United	2 – 4
	SEL2	Home	Woodford Reserves	Romford scratched
	SEL2	Away	Leytonstone Reserves	1 – 3
16 Jan	Frdly	Away	Tilbury	0 – 3
	SEL2	Home	Leytonstone Reserves	Lost+
	SEL2	Away	Leyton Reserves	Romford scratched
	SEL2	Home	Leyton Reserves	Romford scratched
6 Feb	SEL2	Away	Woodford Swifts	1 – 2
	SEL2	Home	Woodford Swifts	Lost+

\# St. Luke's withdrew from the league and their record was expunged.

\+ The three games lost where results are not known indicate that Romford scored one goal and conceded eleven in these matches.

SUMMARY OF "A" TEAM (RESERVES) RESULTS OBTAINED SEASON 1896 – 97

	P	W	D	L	For	Ag	Pts
South Essex League Div.2	7	0	0	7	4+	10+	0
S.E. League (void)	1	0	0	1	0	1	
Essex Junior Cup	2	1	0	1	3	8	
Friendly matches	8	2	0	6	7	23	
Total	18	3	0	15	14	42	
A.G.M. Press Report	19	5	2	12			

\+ It is known that the team lost away to Leytonstone Reserves and Woodford Reserves and at home to Woodford Swifts in the South Essex League but the actual scores are not known, therefore the goals record in the above summary is incomplete.

South Essex League Division Two
Final Table

	P	W	D	L	Goals For	Goals Ag	Pts
*Woodford Reserves	9	8	1	0	25	13	19
#Leyton Reserves	7	3	3	1	17	10	13
Leytonstone Reserves	9	4	2	3	21	16	10
East Ham United	10	3	2	6	15	19	8
Woodford Swifts	10	3	2	6	15	19	8
Romford Reserves	7	0	0	7	5	21	0

* Woodford awarded two points owing to failure of Romford Reserves
\# Leyton awarded four points owing to failure of Romford Reserves.

Leyton and Leytonstone were unable to play their second game owing to the referee not turning up on the last day of the season.

Note: St. Luke's Reserves withdrew from the league and their record was expunged.

RESERVE TEAM CUP RESULTS SEASON 1896 – 97

Essex Junior Cup

Final: Saffron Walden 1 Leytonstone United 1
Replay: Saffron Walden 6 Leytonstone United 0

Romford's progress: Prel.Round Home Brentwood reserves 3 – 2
1st Round Away Grays Anchor 0 – 6

ROMFORD "B"
Believed to be all Friendly Matches

3 Oct	Away	Leytonstone United Reserves	2 – 3
10 Oct	Home	Woodgrange Athletic	2 – 0
17 Oct	Home	Burdett Wanderers	2 – 1
24 Oct	Home	Victoria Dock Swifts	1 – 4
31 Oct	Away	Brentwood Grammar School	1 – 10
14 Nov	Away	Plaistow United	0 – 2
21 Nov	Home	Squirrels Heath	0 – 8
5 Dec	Home	Brentwood Grammar School	4 – 4

SUMMARY OF "B" TEAM RESULTS OBTAINED SEASON 1896 – 97

					Goals	
	P	W	D	L	For	Ag
All Friendly Matches?	8	2	1	5	12	32
A.G.M. Press Report	14	2	3	9	n/k	n/k

THE HARRY W. BROWN INTER-CLUB DISPUTE

Harry W.Brown, known as 'Drummer' Brown, was a player with a promising reputation who joined Romford in November 1896 amid much controversy. He had played a few games for Romford when his previous club, Brentwood, had no fixtures. The Brentwood club held a committee meeting on Saturday 29th November to consider the matter. During the deliberations a letter was received from Mr. Brown tendering his resignation not only from the captaincy, but from the Club. The resignation was accepted, and steps were taken to appoint a successor.

The *Essex Times* reported that 'The captaincy of the Brentwood club this season had been very unfortunate. At the outset Mr. Brown absolutely declined to resume the position, and it was only after considerable pressure that he ultimately accepted the captaincy'.

A letter to the press accused Romford of using inducements to make Mr. Brown desert his own club. Mr.W.D. Matthews (Hon.Treasurer) replied stating that 'the only inducements Mr. Brown has had from Romford is the pleasure of paying his own railway fares!'

Bad blood between Romford and Leytonstone!

In November, Francis H.Thirlwall sent the following indignant letter in response to what he saw as unfair reporting in the Leytonstone local press:

ROMFORD V LEYTONSTONE

As hon. secretary of the Romford Football Club, in justice to same, I cannot allow the report of the Romford versus Leytonstone match, which was played on 21st inst., at Leytonstone, and an account of which appeared in your issue of the 25th last, to pass without a few comments.

I was myself present at the match, as well as many supporters of the club. In the first place, I consider it a very unfair report. The following paragraphs are perfectly untrue, viz.: "Romford quite losing their tempers, played a very foul game, and it was a relief to them when the interval arrived with the score sheet reading one all," also "the visitors were now displaying cruel tactics, but Referee Sans kept a tight rein on them". We seldom have an account of our matches reported in your paper, but I know you would like justice done on both sides. I saw the game, and I emphatically say that these two paragraphs are totally wrong. One fact alone will be sufficient to prove the report very partial. No mention whatever is made of one of the Leytonstone players being cautioned and afterwards ordered off the field by the referee.

Francis H. Thirlwall, Hon. Secretary, Romford Football Club, November 30th.

Post-Season Summary Season 1896 – 97

The team were strengthened as the local side Buffaloes had folded, with almost all of their players joining Romford. The season opened with Romford playing three successive away games in the first month when a total of 24 goals were scored! Alas, Romford scored only six of them and lost all three matches. In the first game against Grays United Romford's goalkeeper William Herbert Kelly failed to arrive, but committee-man and former goalkeeper E.W.Smith filled his boots.

In the 5-1 defeat by Leytonstone, the local press recorded that 'The corner kick was well taken and the ball was passing rapidly towards the goal when one of the Romford forwards fisted it away. The referee saw the little game, and, of course, a penalty kick was allowed. The kick was entrusted to Snazell and he placed the ball into the net well out of the goalkeeper's reach'. Next came a couple of South Essex League games: a best forgotten 9–2 defeat at Leyton and a three two defeat by St. Luke's (as St. Luke's later withdrew from the league the result was expunged).

Then came the F.A. Cup and Romford forced a three all draw at home to Sittingbourne. The replay was also drawn, this time with two goals each. Sittingbourne had had enough by this time and scratched from the competition, so Romford 'progressed' to the second round. Romford then defeated South West Ham 2–1 in the South Essex League. In the second round of the F.A. Cup Romford entertained Dartford before a crowd of 500, but this support failed to inspire the locals, who were beaten 4-1. Ironically after losing to Squirrels Heath by four goals to one in a friendly game Romford then defeated Manor Park in a South Essex League game by six goals to one.

After a friendly game against Forest Swifts, Romford secured a narrow league victory over Woodford before embarking on the Amateur Cup trail. The trail was very short, as Romford were beaten 4-2 away to Leytonstone. The next game was the Essex Senior Cup first round away to Manor Park, which Romford lost 1-0 in controversial circumstances. Romford protested on the grounds that full time was not played. Various opinions regarding time played were considered by the Essex County Committee, and the referee Mr.H.F.Smith stated that full time was played. The committee disallowed the protest and Romford were out of another cup. Ironically Romford then defeated Manor Park in a South Essex League game by six goals to one.

A two all draw at home to Upton Park in a friendly match was followed by eight successive victories. The first of these was a friendly against the powerful Ilford side who were beaten by three goals to two, then came big wins over Brentwood and Walthamstow Holborn. Next was a one goal to nil victory over Romford St. Andrews to win the Victoria Cottage Hospital Cup and a South Essex League win over Woodford in a game described as "a mudlark". Romford then reached the final of the West Ham Charity Cup by defeating Upton Park by five goals to one in the semi-final. Leytonstone and Manor Park were then beaten in league games before the fine run came to an end. On the Cricket Ground at Romford Station, West Ham Garfield defeated them by three goals to one in the West Ham Charity Cup Final.

The final games of the season saw a heavy seven goals to one defeat from Leyton then victories over Brentwood by six nil and South West Ham two nil all in league encounters. The last game of the season was a humiliating ten goals to nil loss away to Ilford in a "friendly" fixture. At the close of the season S.W.Sulman, Evan Pashley Jones and Charles F.Brady were each awarded the Essex Senior Badge for three or more appearances in the County team.

Annual General Meeting
(as reported in the *Essex Times,* Wednesday 21st July 1897)

The annual general meeting of the Romford Football Club was held at the Golden Lion Hotel, on Friday 16th July, Mr.J.R.J.Roynon presiding over a good attendance. The report of the Hon.Secretary, Major Thirlwall, stated that last season 28 matches were played by the first team, 13 being won, ten lost and five drawn. They scored 71 goals and lost 64. The "A" team won five matches, lost 12, and drew two. The "B" team won two, lost nine, and drew three.

The thanks of the club were due to Mr. Peter Reynolds for lending a room free of charge for committee meetings. The report concluded with a statement that Major Thirlwall had determined to resign. – On the motion of Mr.E.W.Smith, seconded by Mr.E.H.Hinds, the report was adopted. – Mr. W.D.Matthews, the treasurer, presented the financial statement showing that the receipts amounted to £111.1s.3d., and included balance from last season, £5.8s.1d.; subscriptions, £33.19s.0d.; and gate money at home matches, £58.4s.11d. The expenditure amounted to £111.0s.1d., thus leaving a balance on the right side of 1s.2d. –

The accounts were passed, subject to being audited by Messrs.E.J.Burgess and L.Fletcher. – On the motion of Mr.Hinds, seconded by Mr.C.Wilson, Mr. H.H.Raphael,J.P., was unanimously elected president of the club; and Messrs. Louis Sinclair, M.P., J.Roynon, E.Murray Ind. (High Sheriff), Thomas Bird, J.P.,C.C., and A.Porter were elected vice-presidents. – Mr.Charles Brady was elected captain; Mr.Evan Jones, vice-captain; Mr.C.Harris, captain, and Mr.E.J.Burgess, vice-captain of the reserves; Mr.W.D.Matthews, hon.treasurer; Mr.W.H.Kelly, hon.secretary; and Mr.R.D.Taylor, assistant secretary. The old committee were re-appointed, with the exception of Mr.R.D.Hill, and with the addition of Major Thirlwall and Messrs. L.Fletcher and T.W.Sharpe. – It was decided to enter for the English, Amateur, and Essex County cups.

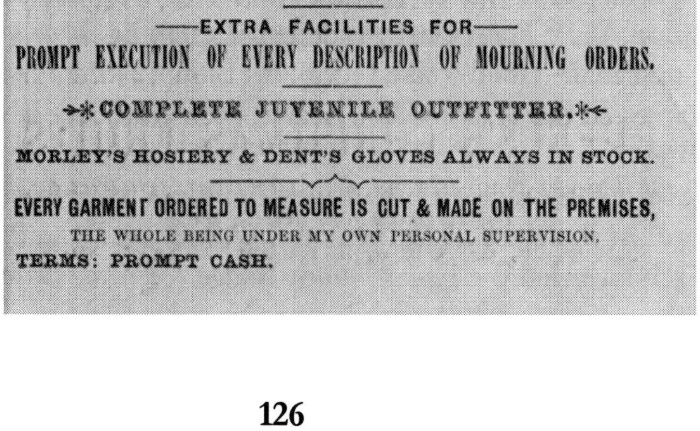

Season 1897 – 98

ROMFORD FOOTBALL CLUB

President: Mr.H.H.Raphael, J.P. **Hon.Secretary:** Mr.W.H.Kelly

Hon.Treasurer: Mr.W.D.Matthews **Hon.Assistant Secretary:** Mr.R.D.Taylor

Vice-Presidents: Messrs.Louis Sinclair, M.P., J.Roynon, E.Murray Ind (High Sheriff), Thomas Bird, J.P., C.C., and A.Porter

Captain: Mr.Charles Brady **Vice-Captain:** Mr.Evan Jones

Reserve Team Captain: Mr.C.Harris **Reserve Team Vice-Captain:** Mr.E.J.Burgess

Committee: Messrs. E.Barnes, W.F.Burrows, E.Champness, E.Challenor, W.Hynds, E.H.Hinds, Roynon, E.W.Smith, G.Stevenson, C.Stromeyer, O.Wheatley, Major F.H.Thirlwall, L.Fletcher and T.W.Sharpe

Headquarters: Golden Lion Hotel, Romford **Ground:** Recreation Ground, Victoria Road, Romford

COMPETITIONS ENTERED

South Essex Football League Division One
F.A. Challenge Cup
F.A. Amateur Cup
Essex Senior Cup
West Ham Charity Cup
Friendly Matches

Match Details

18 Sept Frdly Home Marcians 3 – 2 Scorers unknown

25 Sept FAC1Q Home Swanscombe 2 – 2 E.Barnes,Davie Evans

29 Sept Replay Away Swanscombe 0 – 4

2 Oct Frdly Away Chelmsford# void

2 Oct Frdly Home Romford St. Andrews 6 – 1

9 Oct Frdly Home 1st Essex Regiment 3 – 2

16 Oct AC1Q Away Barking Woodville 1 – 3 Hillman
Attendance: 1,000
Romford: F.Walker;H.W.Brown,Arthur Yates;W.Riley,E.H.Hinds,C.Brady(Capt); A.B.MacDonnell,D.Evans,W.Lamb,E.Groves,H.E.Hillman.

23 Oct SEL1 Away South West Ham 0 – 3

30 Oct SEL1 Home Woodford 3 – 1 Hillman,A.E.Jones,Evans
Romford: F.Walker;H.W.Brown,E.P.Jones; W.Riley,E.H.Hinds,C.Brady(Capt); A.B.MacDonnell,A.E.Jones,J.Fraser,D.Evans,H.E.Hillman.

6 Nov Frdly Home 1st Essex Regiment 3 – 1 Hines(2)E.Jones

13 Nov Frdly Home Askeans 5 – 1 Hillman(2)A.Jones,Evans,MacDonnell
Romford: W.H.Kelly;H.W.Brown,E.P.Jones;W.Riley,E.H.Hinds,C.Brady; A.B.MacDonnell,A.E.Jones,F.Wells,D.Evans,H.E.Hillman.

20 Nov SEL1 Home Manor Park 1 – 1*

27 Nov Frdly Away Chelmsford 1 – 1

4 Dec ESC1R Away Grays United 0 – 2**

n/k SEL1 Away West Ham Garfield 1 – 2

26 Dec Frdly Away Ipswich Town 0 – 9
Romford: W.H.Kelly;H.W.Brown,Forester;W.Riley,Jupp,C.Brady(Capt);
Cox,Lee,J.Fraser,H.E.Hillman,E.Barnes.

1 Jan Replay Away Grays United w/o

1 Jan Frdly Away Grays United 1 – 3

8 Jan Frdly Home Bow 3 – 0 A.E.Jones(2)E.P.Jones

15 Jan SEL1 Home Manor Park 1 – 1 Fraser
Romford: F.Walker;H.W.Brown,E.P.Jones;W.Riley,E.H.Hinds,C.Brady(Capt);
A.B.MacDonnell,A.E.Jones,J.Fraser,D.Evans,H.E.Hillman.

22 Jan SEL1 Away Manor Park 1 – 1

29 Jan ESC2R Away Ilford 4 – 1 MacDonnell(2)D.Evans,A.E.Jones(pen)
Romford: F.(Hookey)Walker;H.W.Brown,Evan P.Jones;W.Riley,E.H.Hinds,C.Brady(Capt);
A.B.MacDonnell,A.E.Jones,J.Fraser,D.Evans,H.E.Hillman.

5 Feb Frdly Home Manor Park 1 – 1

12 Feb SEL1 Away Woodford 0 – 3
Romford: W.Riley;W.Crossley,H.W.Brown;Clayton,Taylor,Harris;
A.B.MacDonnell,W.Lamb,J.Fraser,E.Barnes,D.Evans.

19 Feb ESC3R Home Manor Park 3 – 2 Jones(2)(1pen)Fraser
Romford: F.Walker;H.W.Brown,E.P.Jones;W.Riley,E.H.Hinds(Capt),E.Barnes;
A.B.MacDonnell,A.E.Jones,J.Fraser,D.Evans,H.E.Hillman.

24 Feb WHCSF Sp.Dog West Ham Garfield 0 – 2

26 Feb SEL1 Home South West Ham 4 – 1 A.Jones(2)Hinds,Evans
Romford: F.Walker;H.W.Brown,E.P.Jones;W.Riley,E.H.Hinds,E.Barnes;
A.B.MacDonnell,A.E.Jones,J.Fraser,D.Evans,H.E.Hillman.

5 Mar SEL1 Home West Ham Garfield 1 – 1 A.Jones(pen)

12 Mar SEL1 Away Leytonstone 1 – 2
Attendance: 1,000
Romford: F.Walker;H.W.Brown,F.Brown;W.Pain,E.Barnes,W.Riley;
A.B.MacDonnell,A.E.Jones,J.Fraser,D.Evans,H.E.Hillman.

19 Mar ESCSF Witham Heybridge 2 – 0 MacDonnell(2)
Attendance: 450
Romford: F.Walker;H.W.Brown,E.P.Jones; W.Riley,E.H.Hinds,C.Brady(Capt);
A.B.MacDonnell,A.E.Jones,J.Fraser,D.Evans,H.E.Hillman.

26 Mar SEL1 Home Leytonstone 0 – 3***
Romford: W.H.Kelly;H.W.Brown,F.Brown;W.Riley,E.H.Hinds,W.Crossley;
A.B.McDonnell,A.E.Jones,J.Fraser,H.Hillman.

2 Apr Frdly Home Romford St. Andrew's 6 – 2

11 Apr ESCF Leyton Leyton 0 – 3
Attendance: 6,090
Leyton: T.Stirling;J.Allen,J.H.Inns;E.Fincham,W.Sproston,B.Cartwright;
W.Thompson,E.Russell,A.Russell,H.Massey,S.Carr.

Romford: F.Walker;H.W.Brown,E.P.Jones;W.Riley,E.H.Hinds(Capt),C.Brady(Capt);
E.Barnes,A.E.Jones,J.Fraser,D.Evans,H.E.Hillman.

Referee: S.R.Carr. R.A.

Chelmsford unable to field a team
* Abandoned due to fog. Match void
** Abandoned due to bad light. (See Post Season Summary)
*** Abandoned after Romford walked off the pitch! Points awarded to Leytonstone but no goals included in the table.

SUMMARY OF FIRST TEAM RESULTS OBTAINED SEASON 1897 – 98

	P	W	D	L	Goals For	Goals Ag	Pts
South Essex Football Lge.	10	2	3	5	12	18	7
F.A. Challenge Cup	2	0	1	1	2	6	
F.A. Amateur Cup	1	0	0	1	1	3	
Essex Senior Cup	4	3	0	1	9	6	
Essex Snr.Cup Aban.Void	1	0	0	1	0	2	
West Ham Charity Comp.	1	0	0	1	0	2	
Friendly Matches	11	7	2	2	32	23	
Total	30	12	6	12	56	60	
A.G.M. Press Report	30	12	6	12			

South Essex League Division One
Final Table

	P	W	D	L	Goals For	Goals Ag	Pts
Leytonstone	10	7	1	2	28	15	15
Woodford	10	6	2	2	26	14	14
Manor Park	10	3	4	3	16	16	10
West Ham Garfield	10	3	4	3	11	11	10
Romford	**10**	**2**	**3**	**5**	**12**	**18**	**7**
South West Ham	10	1	2	7	15	34	4

CUP RESULTS SEASON 1897 – 98

F.A. Challenge Cup

Final: Nottingham Forest 3 Derby County 1

Romford's progress: 1st Qual. Home Swanscombe 2 – 2
Replay Away Swanscombe 0 – 4

F.A. Amateur Cup

Final: Middlesbrough 2 Uxbridge 1

Romford's progress: 1st Round Home Barking Woodville 1 – 3

Essex Senior Cup
Final: Leyton 3 Romford 0
(at Leyton)

Romford's progress: 1st Round Away Grays United 0 – 2#
Replay Grays United scratched
2nd Round Away Ilford 4 – 1
3rd Round Home Manor Park 3 – 2
Semi-Final Witham Heybridge 2 – 0
Final Away Leyton 0 – 3

Abandoned due to bad light. Match void
See also the Post Season Summary for full details.

West Ham Charity Cup

Final: West Ham Garfield 1 Ilford 0

Romford's progress: Semi-Final Clapton West Ham Garfield 0 – 2

First Team Appearances Season 1897 – 98

E.Barnes	6	C.Brady	8	F.Brown	1*	H.W.Brown	12*
Clayton	1	Cox	1	W.Crossley	1*	D.Evans	11
Forester	1	J.Fraser	10*	E.Groves	1	Harris	1
H.E.Hillman	11*	E.H.Hinds	9*	A.E.Jones	9*	E.P.Jones	8
Jupp	1	W.H.Kelly	2*	W.Lamb	2	Lee	1
A.B.MacDonnell	10*	W.Pain	1	W.Riley	12*	Taylor	1
F.Walker	9	F.Wells	1	Arthur Yates	1	Total	132

Note: Despite the lack of team details for many games, the above summary gives a good idea of the first team regulars.

First Team Goal Scorers Season 1897 – 98

Once more due to the very poor press coverage no goal scoring record is possible.

RESERVE TEAM

Match Details

2 Oct	Frdly	Away	Burdett Wanderers	2 – 8
9 Oct	Frdly	Away	Clapton Reserves	0 – 1
6 Nov	Frdly	Home	Burdett Wanderers	1 – 1
20 Nov	Frdly	Home	St. Edwards Church Institute	2 – 1
27 Nov	Frdly	Home	Northumbrians of Canning Town	0 – 0
4 Dec	Frdly	Home	Buxton Rovers of Millwall	0 – 2
11 Dec	Frdly	Home	Clapton Reserves	0 – 2

SUMMARY OF RESERVE TEAM RESULTS OBTAINED SEASON 1897 – 98

	P	W	D	L	For	Ag
All Friendly Matches	7	1	2	4	5	15

Note: It is unknown how many games were actually played by the reserve team due to the lack of information in the local press and no details were announced at the annual general meeting.

CUP RESULTS

Essex Junior Cup Final: Leigh Town 2 Colchester Crown 1

Not known whether Romford Reserves entered this competition

Post -Season Summary Season 1897 – 98

Romford opened the season with a 3-2 home victory in a friendly fixture with the Marcians, but were brought down to earth with a heavy defeat in the F.A. Cup, when Swanscombe won a replay by four goals to nil.

On 2nd October Romford's away friendly at Chelmsford was cancelled because the home team were unable to field a full line-up, and Romford won a friendly game against Romford St. Andrew's by six goals to one. Before 1,000 spectators at Barking, Romford were eliminated from the F.A. Amateur Cup at the first attempt when Barking Woodville won 3-1.

On 20th November Romford's home game with Manor Park was brought to a premature end when the sudden arrival of thick fog caused the game to be abandoned.

In their first tie of the Essex Senior Cup Competition, on 4th December, Romford were losing 2-0 against Grays United when the match was abandoned due to bad light. The replay, a week later, was not played. Due to severe flooding and fog Romford arrived late, and the referee awarded the tie to Grays.

On Boxing Day Romford made the journey to Portman Road to play a friendly game with Ipswich Town. Alas, the word 'friendly' proved to be far from the truth, as there was trouble ahead. The local press described events as follows:

> I very much regret to have received complaints of the conduct of Romford players in the second half of the Boxing Day match with Ipswich Town. The allegations are of deliberate kicking and fouling by Romford players because things were going badly for them and eventually Mr.Norcutt who is always an indulgent referee stopped the game to caution and take the name of Romford right back Harry Brown. As that player was afterwards going to the Station Hotel to dress, a demonstration was made against him and two police officers went to form an escort.

This made upsetting reading just after the season of Peace and Goodwill!

The County Football Association stepped in to overturn the referee's decision regarding the Essex Senior Cup tie and ordered a replay on 1st January, but Grays United scratched from the competition and the two teams played a friendly game which Grays United won 3-1. Romford were thus given a walkover into the next round. It is not known why the Grays United team even turned up if their intention was to withdraw!

Romford thrashed Ilford 4-1 in the next round and qualified to meet old friends Manor Park for the fifth time this season. Romford were again successful with a 3-2 victory, and reached the semi-final. They were denied another trophy when West Ham Garfield defeated them 2-0 in the semi-final of the West Ham Charity Cup competition.

Romford defeated South West Ham 4-1, drew one each with West Ham Garfield and lost by two goals to one at Leytonstone before an attendance of one thousand, in the next three games. They then travelled to Witham to meet Heybridge in the Essex Senior Cup semi-final and secured a fine 2-0 victory and were thus in the final once more.

On 26th March Romford were at home to Leytonstone in a South Essex league fixture, commenced the game with only 10 men and Leytonstone scored 3 early goals during a heavy snowstorm! The Romford captain withdrew his team and the game was abandoned. The match was awarded to Leytonstone, but no goals were allocated to the playing record. On 2nd April in a warm up for their impending Cup Final, Romford entertained Romford St. Andrews and easily defeated them by six goals to two.

The next game was the eagerly-awaited Essex Senior Cup Final against Leyton at Ilford. Unfortunately, it was not to be Romford's day. Before over 6000 spectators, Leyton proved to be too strong for Romford and won easily by three goals to nil.

Only seven results are known involving the reserve team and Romford won one, drew two and lost four.

At the end of the season A.B. MacDonnell was awarded his County Senior Cap for six or more matches in the County team.

Annual General Meeting
(as reported in the *Essex Times*, Wednesday 10th August 1898)

The annual general meeting of the Romford Football Club was held at the Golden Lion on Friday evening 5th August, Mr.C.F. Fitch presiding over a good attendance. – The annual balance sheet, submitted by Mr.W.D.Matthews, showed receipts £110.7s.8d., which included £36.19s.6d subscriptions; £43.4s.1d. gate money on home matches, and £25.5s.7d. gate money on out matches; while the expenditure was £119.4s.2d., thus leaving a balance due to the treasurer of £9.14s.6d. – The balance sheet, subject to audit, was adopted. –

Mr.W.H.Kelly, hon.sec., submitted a list of 30 matches played, of which 12 were won, 19 lost, and six drawn – a record which Mr.Kelly attributed to the club not having been able always to place the best team in the field. – Mr.Raphael, J.P. C.C., was re-elected president. The Vice-presidents were also re-elected, with the addition of Messrs. A.R.Wright, E.H.Jones, Egerton Tower, J.Grainger, J.W.Parrott, A. Hammond, Richmond, and Docwra (Havering). Mr.W.D.Matthews, the popular treasurer, and Mr.W.H.Kelly the energetic secretary, were re-elected. Mr.A.B. MacDonnell was elected captain, and Mr.A.E.Jones vice-captain.

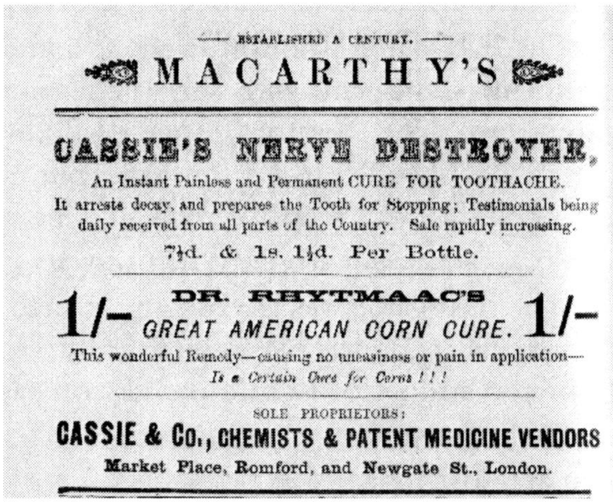

Season 1898 – 99

ROMFORD FOOTBALL CLUB

President: Mr.H.H.Raphael.J.P.,C.C. **Hon.Secretary:** Mr.W.H.Kelly

Mr.Kelly resigned end of November replaced by Mr.E.H.Hinds and Mr.W.D.Matthews.

Hon.Treasurer: Mr.W.D.Matthews

First Team Captain: Mr.A.B.MacDonnell **First Team Vice-Captain:** Mr.A.Jones

Reserve Team Captain: Mr.G.Cornell **Vice-captain:** Mr.R.Adams

Headquarters: Golden Lion Hotel, Romford **Ground:** Recreation Ground, Victoria Road, Romford

COMPETITIONS ENTERED

South Essex Football League Division One
F.A. Challenge Cup
F.A. Amateur Cup
Essex Senior Cup

Romford & District Football League
Essex Junior Cup

Match Details

17 Sept FACPR Away Brighton United 2 – 8 Bilsby,D.Evans
Romford: H.W.Smith;H.W."Drummer" Brown,A.Kittle;H.Clayton,G.Boorman,W.Riley;
A.B.MacDonnell(Capt),A.E.Jones,Davie Evans,J.Bilsby,H.E.Hillman.

24 Sept Frdly Away Lower Clapton 0 – 1

15 Oct SEL1 Away Ilford 0 – 1

22 Oct Frdly Home# 1st Essex Regiment 0 – 3

29 Oct AC2Q Away Harrow Athletic 0 – 12

12 Nov SEL1 Away Manor Park 0 – 5

19 Nov SEL1 Home Leyton 0 – 1
Romford: H.W.Smith;H.W.Brown,E.P.Jones;W.Riley,G.Willis,H.McMillan;
W.Pain,A.B.MacDonnell(Capt),H.E.Hillman.

26 Nov Frdly Home Manor Park 3 – 1$ Day,McMillan,Willis(pen)
Romford: H.W.Smith;A.Kittle,E.P.Jones;G.Willis,E.P.Barnes,W.Day;
W.Pain,A.B.MacDonnell(Capt),A.E.Jones,H.McMillan,H.E.Hillman.

3 Dec SEL1 Home Woodford 3 – 2 Scorers unknown

10 Dec Frdly Home Croydon Park 1 – 2 Scorer unknown

17 Dec SEL1 Away Leyton 2 – 6 Hillman,McMillan
Attendance: 800
Romford: W.Riley;A.Kittle,W.Day;C.T.Townley,A.Jupp.G.Willis;
E.Hopper,A.E.Jones(Capt),H.McMillan,A.Bridge,H.E.Hillman.

24 Dec SEL1 Away Leytonstone 0 – 4

25 Dec Frdly Home Romford & District League XI 3 – 0 Scorers unknown

31 Dec	SEL1	Away	West Ham Garfield	4 – 2##	Scorers unknown
7 Jan	Frdly	Away	1st Essex Regiment	0 – 1	
14 Jan	SEL1	Home	Barking Woodville	1 – 3###	Hillman
21 Jan	SEL1	Home	West Ham Garfield	2 – 2	A.E.Jones,Day
28 Jan	Frdly	Away	Crouch End Vampires (The Bats)	1 – 8	Scorer unknown
n/k	ESC1R			Bye	
4 Feb	ESC2R	Away	Leyton	0 – 6	

Romford: H.W.Smith;R.Ball,A.Kittle;C.T.Townley,A.Jupp,H.Bartlett; H.E.Hillman,F.L.Field,W.Day,A.Bright,A.E.Jones.

11 Feb	SEL1	Away	Barking Woodville	1 – 2	Scorer unknown
18 Feb	SEL1	Away	Woodford	0 – 7	
4 Mar	SEL1	Home	Manor Park	1 – 1	Thompson

Romford: W.Riley;A.E.Jones(Capt),A.Kittle;H.Bartlett,A.Bright,C.T.Townley; W.Thompson,B.Toser,H.McMillan,D.Evans,H.E.Hillman.

11 Mar	SEL1	Home	Ilford	3 – 3	Carter(2)McMillan
18 Mar	Frdly	Home	Marcians	2 – 1	Scorers unknown
25 Mar	SEL1	Home	Leytonstone	1 – 0*	Scorer unknown

Attendance: 400
Romford: T.W.Sharpe;J.L.Field,W.Riley,
A.E.Jones,W.Pain, Remainder of team unknown.

* Aban. 65 mins due to fighting. Match was not replayed and Romford played only 13 league games.

$ Match should have been a South Essex League fixture but due to fog, it was agreed to play a friendly match and this was called off before full time.

Played at Warley Barracks

Played at Recreation Ground at the request of West Ham Garfield.

Played on the cricket ground, Romford Station.

SUMMARY OF FIRST TEAM RESULTS OBTAINED SEASON 1898 – 99

					Goals		
	P	W	D	L	For	Ag	Pts
South Essex League*	13	2	3	8	17	39	7
F.A. Challenge Cup	1	0	0	1	2	8	
F.A. Amateur Cup	1	0	0	1	0	12	
Essex Senior Cup	1	0	0	1	0	6	
Friendly Matches#	8	3	0	5	10	17	
Total	25	5	3	16	29	82	
AGM Report	28	7	3	18			

* The above summary does not include the abandoned game versus Leytonstone at the end of the season.

Does not include the abandoned game against Manor Park on 26th November.

South Essex League Division One
Final Table

	P	W	D	L	Goals For	Goals Ag	Pts
Barking Woodville	14	13	1	0	33	10	27
Leyton	14	10	1	3	41	13	21
Ilford	14	6	3	5	30	31	15
Leytonstone	13	6	2	5	25	17	14
Manor Park	14	5	2	7	23	22	12
Woodford	14	5	0	9	30	36	10
Romford*	**13**	**2**	**3**	**8**	**17**	**39**	**7**
West Ham Garfield	14	0	2	12	15	44	2

(South West Ham withdrew from the League)

* The abandoned Romford versus Leytonstone game was not replayed.

CUP RESULTS SEASON 1898 – 99

F.A. Challenge Cup

Final: Sheffield United 4 Derby County 1

Romford's progress: Prel.Round Away Brighton United 2 – 8

F.A. Amateur Cup

Final: Stockton 1 Harwich & Parkeston 0

Romford's progress: 2nd Qual. Away Harrow Athletic 0 – 12

Essex Senior Cup

Final: Harwich & Parkeston 2 Leytonstone 0

Romford's progress: 1st Round Bye
2nd Round Away Leyton 0 – 6

First Team Appearances Season 1898 – 99

R.Ball	1	H.Bartlett	2	E.P.Barnes	1	J.Bilsby	1
G.Boorman	1	A.Bridge	1	A.Bright	2	H.W.Brown	2
Carter	1	H.Clayton	1	W.Day	4	D.Evans	2
F.L.Field	2	H.E.Hillman	7	E.Hopper	1	A.E.Jones	7
E.P.Jones	2	A.Jupp	2	A.Kittle	5	A.B.MacDonnell	3
H.McMillan	5	W.Pain	3	W.Riley	5	T.W.Sharpe	1
H.W.Smith	4	W.Thompson	1	B.Toser	1	C.Townley	3
G.Willis	3					Total	74

The above players are known to have played during the season but due to the lack of press coverage full details are not possible.

First Team Goal Scorers Season 1898 – 99

H.McMillan	2	H.E.Hillman	2	Carter	2	J.Bilsby	1
D.Evans	1	W.Day	1	A.E.Jones	1	W.Thompson	1
Unknown	12					Total	23

Note: The above summary does not include the goals scored in the abandoned games against Manor Park on the 26th November and against Leytonstone on 25th March.

RESERVE TEAM
Ground: Recreation Ground, Victoria Road
One game played on the cricket ground

Match Details

1 Oct	RDL	Home	St Edwards Institute	0 – 3
8 Oct	Frdly	Home	Plaistow United	3 – 2
22 Oct	EJCPR	Home	Squirrels Heath	9 – 0
29 Oct	Frdly	Home	Thorncliffe	2 – 0
5 Nov	RDL	Away	Romford St. Andrew's	3 – 1
12 Nov	RDL	Away	Dagenham	P – P#
12 Nov	Frdly	Away	Dagenham	5 – 1*
19 Nov	RDL	Away	Oakley Swifts	1 – 1
26 Nov	EJC2R	Away	Chingford	1 – 1
3 Dec	EJCRep	Home	Chingford	1 – 0
10 Dec	RDL	Home	Chadwell Heath	2 – 0
31 Dec	RDL	Away	St Edwards Institute	0 – 2
7 Jan	RDL	Away	Chadwell Heath	3 – 0##
14 Jan	EJC3R	Home	Harlow	1 – 2
21 Jan	RDL	Home	Romford St. Andrew's	1 – 1
28 Jan	RDL	Home	Oakley Swifts	7 – 1
4 Feb	RDL	Home	Squirrels Heath	3 – 1
18 Feb	Frdly	Home	Hornchurch	4 – 0
4 Mar	RDL	Home	Dagenham	1 – 1
11 Mar	RDL	Away	Squirrels Heath	0 – 0

Dagenham had only seven players, Romford awarded points, no goals recorded and a friendly game played.
Chadwell Heath scratched Romford awarded 3 – 0 win.

* Played on the Cricket Ground.

SUMMARY OF RESERVE TEAM RESULTS OBTAINED SEASON 1898 – 99

					Goals		
	P	W	D	L	For	Ag	Pts
Romford & Dist.Lge.	12*	6	4	2	21	11	15
Essex Junior Cup#	4	2	1	1	12	3	
Friendly Matches	4	4	0	0	14	3	
Total	20	12	5	3	47	17	
AGM Report	24	13	8	3			

***** The team actually played only eleven league games. The game against Dagenham was due to have been played on 12th November, but the points were awarded to Romford.

\# The first round opponents and score is unknown, unless the club received a bye.

Romford & District Football League
(Up to and including 11th March)

					Goals		
	P	W	D	L	For	Ag	Pts
Romford St. Andrews	12	9	1	2	32	9	19
St. Edward's Institute	10	8	1	1	25	8	17
Romford Reserves	**11**	**6**	**3**	**2**	**21**	**11**	**15**
Oakley Swifts	11	3	3	5	20	27	9
Squirrels Heath	10	2	1	7	11	26	5
Chadwell Heath	11	1	3	7	9	35	5
Dagenham	9	0	3	6	11	17	3

Romford & District Football League
Final Table

	P	W	D	L	Goals For	Goals Ag	Pts
St. Edwards Institute	12	10	1	1			21
St. Andrews (Romford)	12	9	1	2	32	9	19
Romford Reserves	**12**	**6**	**4**	**2**	**21**	**11**	**16**
Oakley Swifts	12	4	3	5			11
Squirrels Heath	11	2	2	7	11	26	6
Chadwell Heath	12	2	2	8			6
Dagenham	11	0	3	8			3

Note: The Dagenham versus Squirrels Heath game was not played.

RESERVE TEAM CUP RESULTS SEASON 1898 – 99

Essex Junior Cup

Final: Leyton "A" 7 Coggeshall 1

Romford's progress: Prel.Round Home Squirrels Heath 9 – 0
1st Round Home Dagenham or Manor Park Res. won
2nd Round Away Chingford 1 – 1
Replay Home Chingford 1 – 0
3rd Round Home Harlow 1 – 2

Post-Season Summary Season 1898 – 99

The season opened with a devastating away defeat in the F.A. Cup by Brighton United, who routed Romford by eight goals to two. What a start! The club went on to lose their next six games without scoring a single goal. After a couple of friendly losses and a league defeat by Ilford, Harrow Athletic netted twelve times without reply to oust the locals from the Amateur Cup. Next came a five goals to nil defeat away to Manor Park in the league when Romford fielded only nine men! A week later Romford lost narrowly to Leyton also in a league game, but yet again only nine men in the team. The season was becoming a disaster for the club, especially with the apparent lack of support from their own players. On 26th November Romford were beating Manor Park by three goals to one in a friendly when the game was called off early due to fog. This game was scheduled to be a league encounter but due to the fog, under the circumstances it was agreed to play the game as a friendly match.

On Thursday 1st December, Essex versus Middlesex was played at Romford and the teams drew one goal each. Romford players H.W.Smith (in goal), and H.E.Hillman (outside left) were in the Essex team. At the end of the season Hillman and Smith were each awarded their Essex Senior Badge for three or more appearances in the County team.

Romford then gained their first victory of the season, a home 3-2 victory over Woodford before losing a further three games in a row, conceding a dozen goals in the process. On Christmas Day Romford provided some festive cheer by defeating the Romford & District League eleven by three goals to nil.

Next up was a game against West Ham Garfield, who requested the match be played at the Recreation Ground. Romford agreed and scored a good victory, and also got a point in the return game, also held at Romford a couple of weeks later. An 8-1 thrashing away to Crouch End Vampires in a friendly fixture was followed by more humiliation in the Essex Senior Cup when they succumbed to Leyton, who netted six times without reply.

There followed two South Essex League defeats, firstly away to Barking Woodville (1-2) and then to Woodford (0-7), before Romford got a point in the 1-1 draw at home to Manor Park and another with a 3–3 draw against Ilford. They then recorded a friendly win against the Marcians by two goals to one.

Finally, the last game of the season, an appalling home league encounter with Leytonstone, was abandoned by the referee after 65 minutes, due to fighting on the pitch. The match was called off but spectators continued fighting all along South Street. The match was never replayed and thus the terrible season ended.

Annual General Meeting
(as reported in the *Essex Times,* Wednesday 7th June 1899)

The annual meeting of the Romford Football Club was held at the Golden Lion Hotel on Monday evening June 5th, Mr.C.F.Fitch presiding over a large attendance. – Mr. W.D.Matthews, the secretary, in presenting the twenty third annual report stated that his feeling in presenting the report could hardly be described as one of unalloyed pleasure, for of the first nine matches played eight were lost. That appeared so disheartening to their then secretary, Mr.Kelly, that he tendered his resignation, and the duties were taken over by Mr.E.H.Hinds and himself. He could assure them that it was no light task to pick up the broken threads of the club in the midst of the season after such a hard-working hon. secretary.

After referring to various changes which had taken place in the playing officials of the club, the report stated that of 28 matches played seven were won, eighteen lost, and three drawn. During the first two months of the season the club lost eight and won one match; and during the remaining four and a half months the club lost ten, won six, and drew three matches, whilst during the last month they did not lose a single match. With regard to the reserve or "A" team they played twenty four matches, won 13, lost three, and drew eight.

They had heard lately, the report continued, of an opposition club that had been floated in the town, but he did not think it had much backbone, and he sincerely hoped that the promoters would very soon see the error of their judgement, and then throw in their lot heart and soul with the mother club. – The report was received and adopted. - Mr.Matthews also presented the financial statement, which showed that the last year commenced with a balance due to the treasurer of £8.16s.6d. The receipts amounted to £136.0s.5d., the items including £34.17s.6d. subscription; £40.12s.2d. gate money for home matches; and £56.16s.9d. gate money for out matches, the expenditure amounted to £128.8s.9d., leaving a balance in hand of £7.11s.8d. As showing the line and progress of the club he might mention that the cash book showed that in the first year's existence of the club (1876) the receipts amounted to £20.16s.11d. The balance sheet was passed subject to being audited. – Mr.Matthews announced that 19 matches had been arranged for the next season and the club had entered for the English cup, the amateur cup, and the Essex cup.

Several new members were elected. – Mr.H.H.Raphael, J.P.,C.C., was unanimously re-elected president. – It was decided to invite Messrs. Gibb, Watson and Hinds to become vice-presidents. – Mr.Matthews reiterated his previously expressed intention of resigning the post on hon.secretary and treasurer after a term of sixteen years. – The Chairman remarked they were all very thankful to Mr.

Matthews for the service he had rendered the club during the past year. He had pulled them out of difficulties landed them in a fair way towards success, and left the club in a straightforward position for the new secretary. – Mr.L.Field was unanimously elected hon.secretary and Mr.Matthews consented to again act as treasurer for the year – The Chairman said Mr.Matthews had in the most sportsmanlike manner come forward again to serve the club and coach the new secretary, and was deserving of thanks and consideration of the club. (Applause). Mr.A.Kittle was elected captain, and Mr.Riley vice-captain. – Messrs. G.Cornell and R.Adams were re-elected captain and vice-captain respectively of the reserves.

It was resolved that the committee be reduced from 15 to 12 members. – Mr. Matthews was appointed representative on the Essex Football Association for the coming season. – A vote of thanks was accorded to Messrs. Hinds and Matthews for their services to the club. – Mr.Matthews briefly responded.

ROMFORD V. LEYTONSTONE, 25th March, 1899
The match was abandoned after 65 minutes due to fighting

"WARS AND RUMOURS OF WARS"
(as reported in a Leytonstone local newspaper)

According to the rumour, Leytonstone who had journeyed to Romford on Saturday were slaughtered and the remains of the team brought back to Leytonstone in ambulances, this was one yarn. Another was that the Brewery Boys had copped it. No one knew if the game had been finished and the search parties sent out to find the referee, returned with no sightings of that official. These conflicting stories naturally aroused a great deal of comment, and speculation was rife as to what caused the row if there was one. As far as I have learned nobody knows anything other than the half time score which found Romford leading by the narrow margin of one goal to nil, after that several bouts with the fives were in abundance involving players and spectators, it looks as though the Tipperary christening was outdone.

ESSEX COUNTY FOOTBALL ASSOCIATION COMMITTEE DECISION
(as reported in the ***Essex Times,*** Saturday 15th April, 1899**)**

The scene at Romford – Mr.C.R.Boyle, referee in the South Essex League match Romford v. Leytonstone, reported that he was obliged to bring the match to an abrupt termination owing to the conduct of certain of the Leytonstone players. In the first few minutes of the game he had to caution W.Read of Leytonstone, for rough and illegal play, and fouls on the part of Leytonstone were so frequent that he called the majority of the players together, and pointed out the serious consequences that must ensue if the game was continued in such a manner. After penalising V.Taylor, of Leytonstone, for charging the Romford goalkeeper whilst in an offside position, he found the same player Taylor threatening to fight the goalkeeper. After starting the second half one of the linesmen informed him that while he was following the players, Price, of Leytonstone, had struck Field, one of the Romford players. Complaint was made that Read had struck on of the Romford players (Riley), and a row immediately ensued among the players, which became so heated and the crowd so excited, that he deemed it advisable to leave Read to be

In a game full of disreputable play not one foul was given against the Romford players, whose forbearance was admirable. Taylor and Read were the worst offenders, and although the play of the Leytonstone captain was unobjectionable he made no effort to restrain the violence of his team. – A letter was read from the Leytonstone Club stating that this report was most prejudiced and biased against Leytonstone, and that had the referee from the commencement of the game shown the necessary degree of firmness in dealing with the players, no disturbance would have occurred. – In reply to the Chairman, Mr. Boyle said he did all he could to stop the rough play, but as he did not himself see any blows struck he did not feel that he would be justified in ordering any player off the ground. –

Riley, one of the Romford players, said that after he passed the ball to one of his side, Read knocked him down and struck him in the ear. – Mr. Burford denied this on behalf of Leytonstone Club, stating that he witnessed what took place, Riley, being the first on his feet, squared up to Read, but no blows were struck. – Mr.G.Barnes, the Romford Linesman, said he saw Read strike Riley, who bore traces of the blow for an hour afterwards. – Mr.W.D.Matthews said he also saw blows struck. – Taylor denied striking any player, but admitted squaring up to the goalkeeper. – Sharpe, the Romford goalkeeper, said that after he had cleared the ball Taylor came and deliberately kicked him. He remonstrated, and Taylor then challenged him to fight. – Price, of Leytonstone, admitted striking Field, but said he put his hand up simply to stop the other man who was coming at him. – Field said Price jumped in front of him, and then accused him of kicking him, following this accusation up by striking him in the jaw. He had lost a tooth from the blow. – Mr.F.Skinner, the Leytonstone captain, said this was the first complaint made against him since he had been captain. The referee told him that if he would turn Read off the field he (the referee) would see that Riley went off too, but immediately after speaking, recognising that he had made a mistake, he stopped the game.

The committee ordered Read, Taylor, and Price to be suspended for the remainder of the season.

It appears that no action or punishment was taken against the Romford Football Club, and perhaps wisely the match was never replayed! The following season the two teams again met in the South Essex League, Leytonstone winning by four goals to one in both fixtures which were, it appears, played without any unsavoury incidents.

The first-ever games between the two clubs had been friendly matches in 1888–89, each team securing a 2-0 win on their own ground, with no indication of any trouble. They did not meet again until eight years later, this time in the South Essex League, and again each team won on their own ground. A third match, in the Amateur Cup was the first indication of trouble. It was reported that Romford quite losing their tempers, played a very foul game and in the second half used 'cruel tactics' although the referee kept a tight rein on things. A Leytonstone player was cautioned and later sent off. The Romford secretary wrote a letter of protest to the newspaper regarding what he considered an unfair report. The following season Romford commenced their home game with only ten men and conceded three early goals scored in a snowstorm. The match was abandoned after Romford walked off the pitch and Leytonstone were awarded the points. The following season ended as described in the Essex County Meeting above.

Season 1899 – 1900

ROMFORD FOOTBALL CLUB

President: Mr.H.H.Raphael.J.P.,C.C. **Hon.Secretary:** Mr.L.Field **Hon.Treasurer:** Mr.W.D.Matthews

Captain: Mr.A.Kittle **Vice-Captain:** Mr.Riley

Reserve Team Captain: Mr.G.Cornell **Reserve Team Vice-Captain:** Mr.R.Adams

Mr.W.D.Matthews appointed representative to the Essex County Football Association

Headquarters: Golden Lion Hotel, Romford **Ground:** Recreation Ground, Victoria Road, Romford

COMPETITIONS ENTERED

South Essex Football League Division One
F.A. Challenge Cup
F.A. Amateur Cup
Essex Senior Cup

Romford & District League
Essex Junior Cup

Match Details

16 Sept SEL1 Away Grays United 0 – 5
Romford: T.W.Sharpe;A.Kittle(Capt),J.L.Field;Flowers,C.Rees,W.Berridge;
W.Day,Bryant,H.McMillan,Bartlett.

23 Sept FACPR Away Ilford 0 – 6
Romford: T.W.Sharpe;A.Kittle(Capt),R.O.Reeves;W.Riley,G.Willis,H.Barker;
W.Day,A.McNaughton,C.McMillan,F.Tait,J.L.Field.

30 Sept Frdly Home Park Swifts 3 – 1

7 Oct SEL1 Home Ilford 1 – 4 Willis
Romford: T.W.Sharpe;A.Kittle(Capt),C.Rees;Bright,Townley,Berridge;
G.Lazell,G.Willis,H.McMillan,W.Day,J.L.Field.

14 Oct AC1Q Home Ware 1 – 3 Willis
Attendance: 150
Romford: T.W.Sharpe; A.Kittle(Capt),R.O.Reeves; A.Bright,C.T.Townley W.Berridge.;
G.Lazell,W.Day,H.McMillan,G.Willis,J.L.Field.

21 Oct Frdly Away Upton Park 4 – 2

28 Oct SEL1 Home Woodford 0 – 10

4 Nov Frdly Away Essex Regiment 2 – 9

11 Nov SEL1 Home Leyton 1 – 4 Meager

25 Nov Frdly Home North West Ham 9 – 0

2 Dec SEL1 Away Leytonstone 1 – 4

9 Dec SEL1 Away Ilford 0 – 2
Attendance: 400

16 Dec ECWF Home Romford St. Andrew's 1 – 1

23 Dec	SEL1	Away	Manor Park	P – P#	
30 Dec	SEL1	Home	West Ham Garfield	2 – 0	Thompson(2)

Romford: W.Riley;A.Kittle(Capt),R.O.Reeves;A.Bright,W.Day,G.Willis; W.Thompson,Elms,Hickey,G.Lazell,Meager.

6 Jan	Frdly	Home	Upton Park	3 – 1
13 Jan	Frdly	Home	Romford & District League	4 – 0
	ESC1R		Romford received a	Bye
	ESC2R		Romford received a	Bye
20 Jan	ESC3R	Home	Woodford	0 – 9
27 Jan	SEL1	Away	Barking Woodville	0 – 7

Romford: T.W.Sharpe;A.Kittle(Capt),
Remainder of team unknown.

3 Feb	SEL1	Away	Manor Park	1 – 6
24 Feb	SEL1	Away	West Ham Garfield	2 – 2
3 Mar	SEL1	Home	Barking Woodville	0 – 2

Romford: W.Riley;
C.Rees, Remainder of the team unknown.

17 Mar	SEL1	Home	Grays United	0 – 4
24 Mar	SEL1	Home	Manor Park	0 – 3
31 Mar	SEL1	Home	Leytonstone	1 – 4*

Attendance: 400
Romford: T.W.Sharpe;A.Kittle(Capt),W.Burridge;A.Bright,W.Riley,WDay; Bryant,J.L.Field,Webb,Gladwin,A.Cornell.

7 Apr	SEL1	Away	Woodford	0 – 7
13 Apr	SEL1	Away	Leyton	0 – 8
14 Apr	SEL1	Home	Commercial Athletic	1 – 3
16 Apr	SEL1	Away	Commercial Athletic	1 – 2

* Played at Leytonstone as Recreation Ground being used for the Essex Senior Cup Semi-final
\# Romford failed to turn up, the first club in the history of the South Essex League to do so.

SUMMARY OF FIRST TEAM RESULTS OBTAINED SEASON 1899 – 1900

					Goals		
	P	W	D	L	For	Ag	Pts
South Essex League	18	1	1	16	11	77	3
F.A. Challenge Cup	1	0	0	1	0	6	
F.A. Amateur Cup	1	0	0	1	1	3	
Essex Senior Cup	1	0	0	1	0	9	
Essex Cty.War Fund	1	0	1	0	1	1	
Friendly Matches	6	5	0	1	25	13	
Total	28	6	2	20	38	109	
AGM Press Report	31	6	3	22	38	115	

South Essex League Division One

Final Table

					Goals		
	P	W	D	L	For	Ag	Pts
Leyton	18	12	4	2	58	22	28
Grays United	18	13	2	3	58	17	28
Woodford	18	12	2	4	67	23	26
Leytonstone	18	9	3	6	47	33	21
Barking Woodville	18	9	3	6	32	23	21
Ilford	18	9	3	6	44	38	21
Commercial Athletic	18	5	3	10	30	38	13
West Ham Garfield	18	3	4	11	19	42	10
Manor Park **	18	4	1	13	33	86	7
Romford	**18**	**1**	**1**	**16**	**11**	**77**	**3**

** Two points deducted for breach of Rules.

South Essex League Division One

Championship Decider:
Leyton 2 Grays United 0 at Leytonstone.

Note: The Romford first team withdrew from the South Essex League at the end of the season.

CUP RESULTS SEASON 1899 – 1900

F.A. Challenge Cup

Final: Bury 4 Southampton 0

Romford's progress: Prel Round Away Ilford 0 – 6

F.A. Amateur Cup

Final: Bishop Auckland 5 Lowestoft Town 1

Romford's progress: 1st Qual Home Ware 1 – 3

Essex Senior Cup

Final: Leyton 5 Colchester Town 1

Romford's progress: 1st Round Bye
2nd Round Home Woodford 0 – 9

First Team Appearances Season 1899 – 1900

H.Barker	W.Berridge	A.Bright	Bryant
A.Cornell	W.Day	Elms	J.L.Field
Flowers	Gladwin	Hickey	A.Kittle
G.Lazell	Meager	H.McMillan	A.McNaughton
C.Rees	R.O.Reeves	W.Riley	T.W.Sharpe
F.Tait	W.Thompson	C.T.Townley	Webb
G.Willis			

Note: Due to the lack of detail in the press reports full details of players appearances in the first team are not to hand, but it is known that the above named did play during the season.

First Team Goal Scorers Season 1899 – 1900

Due to the lack of information in the local press regarding goal scorers no details can be provided. The team's poor playing record no doubt contributed to the lack of interest from the local press!

RESERVE TEAM

Match Details

n/k	Frdly	Home	Park Swifts	0 – 1
30 Sept	Frdly	Home	West Ham Hawthorne	0 – 3
7 Oct	Frdly	Home	Allies	0 – 3
n/k	Frdly	Home	Wanstead Oaks	4 – 0
n/k	Frdly	Home	Borough Polytechnic	9 – 0
n/k	Frdly	Home	Essex Wanderers	2 – 2
21 Oct	EJC1R	Home	St. Edward's Institute	1 – 5*
28 Oct	EJCRep	Home	St. Edward's Institute	2 – 8
4 Nov	RDL	Away	Oakley Swifts	0 – 3
11 Nov	RDL	Home	Romford St. Andrew's	0 – 3
18 Nov	RDL	Away	Brentwood St. Thomas	2 – 10
25 Nov	RDL	Away	St. Edward's Institute	0 – 6
2 Dec	RDL	Away	Romford St. Andrew's	0 – 5
14 Dec	Frdly	Home	Upton Excelsior	2 – 1
16 Dec	RDL	Away	Chadwell Heath	1 – 7
30 Dec	RDL	Home	Brentwood St. Thomas	0 – 10
20 Jan	RDL	Away	Ilford Alliance	P – P#
27 Jan	RDL	Home	Oakley Swifts	0 – 9

* Abandoned due to fog
\# Romford fail to turn up and are fined two shillings and sixpence.

SUMMARY OF RESERVE TEAM RESULTS OBTAINED SEASON 1899 – 1900

					Goals		
	P	W	D	L	For	Ag	Pts
Essex Junior Cup#	1	0	0	1	2	8	
Romford & Dist. Lge.	8	0	0	8	3	53	0
Friendly Matches	7	3	1	3	17	10	
Total	16	3	1	12	22	71	

\# The above detail does not include the abandoned game at home to St. Edward's Institute.

Romford & District League
Up to and including April 7th

					Goals		
	P	W	D	L	For	Ag	Pts
Romford St. Andrew's	14	11	2	1	62	11	24
St. Edward's Institute	14	10	1	3	39	9	21
Dagenham	12	8	1	3	33	12	17
Ilford Alliance	14	7	3	4	38	12	17
Oakley Swifts	16	7	3	6	29	19	17
Squirrels Heath	15	5	1	9	15	41	11
Brentwood St. Thomas	15	5	0	10	40	53	10
Chadwell Heath	11	1	1	9	6	44	3
Romford Reserves	**8**	**0**	**0**	**8**	**3**	**53**	**0**

Note: The Romford Reserves withdrew from the Romford & District League on 10th February.

RESERVE TEAM CUP RESULTS SEASON 1899 – 1900

Essex Junior Cup

Final:	Clacton Town	0	Barking Institute	0
Replay:	Clacton Town	4	Barking Institute	1

Romford's progress:	1st Round	Home	St. Edward's Institute	1 – 5#
	Replay	Home	St. Edward's Institute	2 – 8

Match abandoned due to fog

Reserve Team Appearances and Goal Scorers Season 1899 – 1900

Due to the lack of information no details can be listed regarding player appearances or goal scorers for this season.

Post-Season Summary Season 1899 – 1900

Romford commenced their league programme with an away defeat at Grays United who scored five times without reply. Riley missed his train connection and Romford were obliged to play with only ten men. This was just the start to what was to become one of the worst-ever seasons for the Romford team. Odd victories were obtained in friendly matches, but some devastating results took place in South Essex League and the cup encounters.

Ilford despatched Romford from the F.A. Cup by six goals to nil and recorded a 4-1 victory in the league, before Ware ousted them from the Amateur Cup. A four goal to two win against Upton Park in a friendly encounter raised Romford supporters' hopes, but Woodford netted ten times without reply in a league game and the Essex Regiment won 9–2 in a friendly match. This was followed with Leyton winning 4–1 in the South Essex League. Romford won a meaningless friendly against North West Ham by nine goals to nil before things got back to normal with league defeats away against Leytonstone and Ilford.

On 16th December a friendly fixture in aid of the Essex County War Fund (the Boer War was now taking place in South Africa) was played against Romford St. Andrew's, which ended in a 1-1 draw and raised £3 for the cause. Then followed another disaster a week later, when Romford failed to turn up for the league game against Manor Park, the first South Essex League game to be called off in such circumstances. The club were handed a fine for their non-appearance.

Romford then gained three successive victories, only one of which was a league game, against West Ham Garfield. The others were friendly matches against Upton Park and versus a Romford & District League eleven. There was then controversy and many complaints when Romford received byes in the first two rounds of the Essex Senior Cup competition. Perhaps justice was done when Romford were well beaten by the so-called 'team of brothers', Woodford, who knocked them out of the County Cup with a nine goal to nil thrashing. The Farnfield brothers were amongst the goal scorers.

Barking Woodville and Manor Park kept up the barrage against Romford in league games, with 7-0 and 6-1 victories respectively. In the Barking Woodville game the newspaper report stated Romford's back, Kittle, 'played well but should keep his hands down!' Romford then picked up a point in a two all draw with West Ham Garfield. In their next game, Romford's Rees fell and injured his ankle and was carried off for medical attention, and the team lost 2-0 against Barking Woodville.

This truly disastrous season for the club came to an end with a further seven successive defeats, in which they scored only a total of only 3 goals and conceded 31!

The reserve team fared no better, recording few victories and twice having ten goals scored against them in league matches. They ended their season with a 9-0 thrashing from Oakley Swifts on 27th January. The previous week the reserves had failed to turn up for the game against Ilford Alliance and were fined two shillings and sixpence! The team withdrew from the Romford and District League on 10th February due to the lack of playing members.

At the end of January 1900 Romford reserve W.Hyett volunteered to fight in the Boer War. The one good aspect was at the end of the season when Arthur Bright was awarded his Essex Senior Badge for three or more appearances in the County team.

Annual General Meeting

(as reported in the *Essex Times,* Wednesday 11th July 1900)

The annual meeting of the Romford Football Club was held at the Golden Lion Hotel, on Friday evening July 6th, Mr.J.A.Fraser presiding over a large attendance. Mr.T.W.Sharpe, the assistant hon. secretary, in presenting the report for the past season, said they regretted having lost the services of their hon.secretary on account of his serious illness at the commencement of the year. Another disaster was that they had had to disband the reserve team. The first team played 31 matches, of which they won 6, lost 22, and drew 3. Thirty eight goals were scored for the club, while 115 had been scored against them. The question of amalgamation had been brought forward, and they had approached St. Edward's Institute Football Club with success.

The Chairman said that for the past nine years they had been troubled with the multiplicity of clubs in the town. He had always felt that if the junior clubs joined together – and they had a splendid lot of fellows – they could turn out a team in Essex second to none. (Hear, hear). His only regret was that more clubs had not seen their way to amalgamate.

Mr.W.D.Matthews endorsed the chairman's remarks. In submitting the balance sheet, he said the year commenced with a balance in hand of £7.11s.8d. The receipts amounted to £86.19s.0d., the items including £34.13s.6d. in subscriptions, and gate money £44.10s.9d. The expenditure amounted to £92.18s.1d., leaving an adverse balance of £3.19s.1d. There were several subscriptions yet to be paid, which would enable them to start the season with a clean sheet. (Applause). The accounts were passed subject to audit.

Mr.Matthews proposed, and Mr.Fletcher seconded, that the name of the joint clubs be the Romford Football Club, with St. Edward's Institute as headquarters, and that no member be eligible for election as a player unless residing within a three miles radius of Romford (Great Eastern Railway) station. This was agreed to. It was resolved that the colours of the club be blue and black.

Mr.H.H.Raphael, J.P.,C.C., was unanimously elected president; and Messrs. A.B. Pollett, R.T.Pratt, J.W.Lasham, Ernest Winmill, S.H.Haynes, J.G.Broodbank, D.Young, Dr.C.Green, and the Rev.H.Godefroy were added to the list of vice-presidents. At this stage a letter was read by Mr.Matthews, intimating that the Victoria Football Club intended to amalgamate. (Applause).

Mr.Richard Ball was elected captain, and Mr.Riley vice-captain, Mr.F.W. Jeffes was appointed captain of the reserve team, and Mr.J.A.Nixon vice-captain. Mr.T.W.Sharpe and Mr.Winmill were elected joint hon.secretaries. Mr.Matthews said that, having held the office of treasurer for sixteen years, circumstances would not permit him to continue in the office any longer. Mr.F.J.Amey was appointed treasurer. Mr.Sharpe moved a vote of thanks to the late treasurer for his past services, which was carried by acclamation. Mr. Matthews, in reply, said his heart and soul must have been thoroughly in the work, looking at the adverse circumstances they had at times suffered. He stuck to it, feeling sure some day to see the advent of amalgamation.

The committee was elected as follows: - Messrs. G.Barnes, C.Ryle, W.Berridge, E.Moore, E.Day, E.Bailey, C.Adams, L.Fletcher, L.Green, F.H.Thirlwall, F.Champness, and R.Pratt. Mr.Matthews was elected representative on the Association.

A discussion ensued as to the desirability of entering for various cups. Mr.Sharpe explained that St. Edward's Institute had already entered for the Romford and District League, and of course the amalgamated clubs would play in that competition. Eventually it was resolved to enter for the Essex Junior Cup Competition only. The usual vote of thanks concluded the proceedings.

Waterloo Road, Romford, in the early 1900s, with Brewery buildings in the distance
Havering Libraries - Local Studies

Season 1900 – 01

ROMFORD FOOTBALL CLUB

President: Mr.H.H.Raphael.J.P.,C.C. **Hon.Secretaries:** Messrs. T.W.Sharpe and George Winmill

Hon.Treasurer: Mr.F.J.Amey (Resigned Sept) Mr.L.J.Field (former secretary) accepted the post

Captain: Mr.R.Ball **Vice-Captain:** Mr.W.Riley

Reserve Team Captain: Mr.F.W.Jeffes **Reserve Team Vice-Captain:** Mr.J.A.Nixon.

Committee: Messrs.G.Barnes, C.Ryle, W.Berridge, E.Moore, E.Day, E.Bailey, C.Adams, L.Fletcher, L.Green, F.H.Thirlwall, F.Champness, and R.Pratt

Club Colours: Blue and Black Stripes **Headquarters:** White Hart Hotel, Romford

Ground: Recreation Ground, Victoria Road, Romford **Reserve Team:** Brooklands, Romford

COMPETITIONS ENTERED

Romford & District Football League Division One
Essex Senior Cup
Essex Junior Cup

Romford & District Football League Division Two

Match Details

22 Sept Frdly Home Coverdale 2 – 0 Hyslop(2)
Romford: Hunwicks;R.Ball(Capt),W.Berridge;Lasham,E.Champness,E.Bacon;
R.Pratt,Bailey,J.J.Hyslop,A.Ball,J.A.Nixon.

13 Oct RDL1 Away Dagenham 3 – 3 Davis(2),F.Adams
Romford: Hunwicks;R.Ball,W.Berridge;V.Davis,C.Adams,W.Riley;
F.Adams,H.Bryant,A.Ball,.

20 Oct EJC1R Home Ilford Alliance 4 – 1 Davis,Bird,Pratt,F.Adams
Romford: Hunwicks;R.Ball,E.Champness,V.Davis,C.Adams,W.Riley;
F.Adams,Bird,H.Bryant,R.Pratt,

27 Oct Frdly Away Brighton & Hove Rangers 2 – 3

3 Nov EJC2R Home Harlow & Burnt Mill 1 – 2* A.Ball
Romford: Hunwicks;R.Ball(Capt),E.Champness,E.Bacon,
A.Ball, Remainder of team unknown.

10 Nov RDL1 Home South Weald 3 – 1 A.Ball,F.Adams,Berridge
Romford: T.W.Sharpe;R.Ball,W.Berridge;;V.Davis,E.Bacon,W.Riley;
R.Pratt,Lasham,F.Adams,H.Bryant,A.Ball.

17 Nov ESC2R Away Walthamstow Town 1 – 6 Scorer unknown
Romford:
Team details unknown.

24 Nov RDL1 Home Brentwood 2 – 1 Bryant,Bacon
Romford: E.Bacon,
Bryant. Remainder of team unknown.

1 Dec Frdly Home Radner 1 – 0 Scorer unknown
Romford:
Team details unknown.

8 Dec RDL1 Home Oakley Swifts 5 – 1 Pratt(2)A.Ball,Berridge(pen), one (og)
Romford: W.Berridge,
R.Pratt,A.Ball, Remainder of team unknown.

15 Dec RDL1 Home Dagenham 6 – 0 Forward(4),Pratt,C.Adams(pen)
Romford: C.Adams,
R.Pratt,Forward, Remainder of team unknown.

29 Dec RDL1 Home Romford St. Andrew's 1 – 4 Hyslop
Romford: W.Riley;R.Ball(Capt),W.Berridge;A.Kittle,E.Bacon,Lasham;
R.Pratt,H.Bryant,J.J.Hyslop,F.Adams,Bird.

5 Jan RDL1 Away Oakley Swifts 7 – 1 Scorers unknown
Romford:
Team details unknown.

26 Jan RDL1 Away Brentwood 6 – 1
Bryant(2)F.Adams,Bacon,Reynolds,Forward
Romford: E.Bacon,
H.Bryant,Reynolds,Forward,F.Adams. Remainder of team unknown.

16 Feb Frdly Away Oakley Swifts 2 – 2 Scorers unknown
Romford:
Team details unknown.

23 Feb RDL1 Away Romford St. Andrew's 1 – 2 Berridge(pen)
Romford: W.Riley;R.Ball(Capt),W.Berridge;A.Kittle,E.Bacon,Lasham;
R.Pratt,H.Bryant,J.J.Hyslop,Baxter,J.L.Field.

2 Mar RDL1 Away South Weald 2 – 0 A.Ball,Forward
Romford:
Forward,A.Ball, Remainder of team unknown.

16 Mar Frdly Home Romford St. Andrew's 1 – 2 Scorer unknown
Romford:
Team details unknown.

* Abandoned after 96 minutes.

SUMMARY OF RESULTS OBTAINED SEASON 1900 – 01

					Goals		
	P	W	D	L	For	Ag	Pts
Romford & Dist. Lge.	10	7	1	2	36	14	15
Essex Senior Cup	1	0	0	1	1	6	
Essex Junior Cup*	1	1	0	0	4	1	
Friendly Matches#	5	2	1	2	8	7	
Total	17	10	2	5	49	28	
AGM Press Report	23	12	5	6	n/k	n/k	

* This summary does not include the abandoned Essex Junior Cup Tie against Harlow & Burnt Mill.

Note: It appears that Romford, although only a junior team, entered both the Essex Senior and Junior Cup Competitions!

Romford & District League Division One
Final Table

					Goals		
	P	W	D	L	For	Ag	Pts
Romford St Andrews	10	10	0	0	47	9	20
Romford	**10**	**7**	**1**	**2**	**36**	**14**	**15**
South Weald	10	3	1	6	14	12	7
Dagenham	9	2	3	4	10	36	7
Brentwood	10	2	1	7	14	26	5
Oakley Swifts	9	2	0	7	10	34	4

CUP RESULTS SEASON 1900 – 01

Essex Senior Cup

Final: Leyton 4 Woodford 3

Romford's progress: 2nd Round Away Walthamstow Town 1 – 6

Essex Junior Cup

Final: Leigh Town "A" 3 Halstead 1

Romford's progress: 1st Round Home Ilford Alliance 4 – 1
2nd Round Home Harlow & Burnt Mill 1 – 2*

* Abandoned after 96 minutes.
Romford unable to raise a team for the replay

West Ham Charity Cup

Winners: Woodford

Romford did not compete

First Team Appearances Season 1900 – 01

Due to the fact that there was very little detail in the local newspapers, a comprehensive listing is not possible, but the following players definitely played during the season.

C.Adams	F.Adams	E.Bacon	Bailey
A.Ball	R.Ball	Baxter	W.Berridge
Bird	H.Bryant	Champness	V.Davis
J.L.Field	Forward	Hunwicks	J.J.Hyslop
A.Kittle	Lasham	J.A.Nixon	R.Pratt
Reynolds	W.Riley	T.W.Sharpe	

First Team Goal Scorers Season 1900 – 01

Forward	6	R.Pratt	4	F.Adams	4	V.Davis	3
J.J.Hyslop	3	H.Bryant	3	A.Ball	3	E.Bacon	2
W.Berridge	2	Bird	1	C.Adams	1	Reynolds	1
Own Goals	2	Unknown	12			Total	47

RESERVE TEAM
(Ground: Brooklands, Romford)

Match Details

6 Oct	RDL2	Away	South Weald Reserves	2 – 1
13 Oct	RDL2	Away	Brentwood Reserves	3 – 1
20 Oct	RDL2	Home	Heath Park	4 – 0
3 Nov	RDL2	Away	Hornchurch	0 – 3
10 Nov	RDL2	Home	Ilford Park	1 – 1
17 Nov	RDL2	Away	Dagenham Reserves	0 – 1
24 Nov	RDL2	Away	Romford Victoria	1 – 2
1 Dec	RDL2	Home	Romford St. Andrew's Reserves	2 – 1
8 Dec	RDL2	Home	South Weald Reserves	2 – 0
15 Dec	RDL2	Home	Harold Wood	5 – 1

22 Dec	RDL2	Away	Oakley Swifts	P – P#
22 Dec	Frdly	Away	Oakley Swifts	2 – 3
26 Dec	RDL2	Away	Barking Ivydale	0 – 2
5 Jan	RDL2	Away	Romford St. Andrew's Reserves	3 – 2
19 Jan	RDL2	Home	Brentwood Reserves	5 – 1
26 Jan	RDL2	Away	Harold Wood	8 – 0
16 Feb	RDL2	Home	Hornchurch	4 – 1
23 Feb	RDL2	Away	Heath Park	4 – 1*
2 Mar	RDL2	Home	Dagenham Reserves	4 – 1
9 Mar	RDL2	Away	Ilford Park	0 – 1
30 Mar	RDL2	Home	Romford Victoria	1 – 1
6 Apr	RDL2	Home	Barking Ivydale	0 – 4

Referee arrived late played as a friendly match. Oakley Swifts withdrew from league, record expunged.

* Played at Romford

SUMMARY OF RESERVE TEAM RESULTS OBTAINED SEASON 1900 – 01

					Goals		
	P	W	D	L	For	Ag	Pts
Rfd. & Dist. Lge. Div2	20	12	2	6	49	25	26 #
Friendly Match	1	0	0	1	2	3	
Total	21	12	2	7	51	28	
AGM Press Report	22	13	2	7	n/k	n/k	

The referee ordered this game to be regarded as a friendly match but the result was originally included in the next league table. Oakley Swifts however withdrew from the league and their record was expunged from the table but the goals for and against remained in Romford's record!

ROMFORD AND DISTRICT FOOTBALL LEAGUE DIVISION TWO
Final Table

	P	W	D	L	Pts
Ilford Park	20	15	5	0	35
Barking Ivydale	20	16	1	3	33
Hornchurch	20	13	2	5	28
Romford Reserves	**20**	**12**	**2**	**6**	**26**
Romford Victoria	19	8	3	8	19
Dagenham Reserves	18	7	3	8	17
Heath Park	20	7	1	12	15
*South Weald Reserves	20	6	4	10	14
St. Andrew's Reserves	20	6	2	12	14
Harold Wood	20	4	1	15	9
Brentwood Reserves	19	2	1	16	5

Note: *Two points deducted for playing an ineligible man.
Oakley Swifts Reserves resigned from the league and their record was expunged.

"A" TEAM
Known as old crocks, older players and young players

Match Results

3 Nov	Frdly	Home	Brentwood Grammar School	4 – 4	Scorers unknown

Post-Season Summary Season 1900 – 01

Romford Football Club amalgamated with St. Edward's Institute and came nominally under the control of the latter, with the club's headquarters now at the St. Edward's Institute in Laurie Square (though there is no evidence of any club meetings taking place at this venue). It became a local club, registering only players who resided within a three-mile radius of Romford Railway Station.

The first team took St Edward's Institute's place in the Romford and District League Division One. The League was enlarged and formed a Division Two in which Heath Park and Romford Victoria competed along with Romford Reserves, who played their home games at Brooklands. The first team continued to play at the Recreation Ground, but by the end of the season the club had lost the ground as the land had been obtained for building development, and in the second half of the season all matches were played on away grounds.

Among the Romford team to play Coverdale in their opening game of the season was forward James Hyslop, son of Andrew Hyslop, manager of the Romford branch of the London and County Bank in South Street. James, who worked as a compositor in the printing trade, was both deaf and dumb, which did not prevent him from scoring both goals! In their first Romford and District League game the following week, Romford secured a 3-3 draw away to Dagenham, apparently playing with only nine men, and followed up with a four goal to one win over Ilford Alliance in the Essex Junior Cup.

On 27th October Romford travelled to the seaside to play Brighton and Hove Rangers and lost by three goals to two. A week later, in the 2nd round of the Essex Junior Cup, the game was abandoned after 96 minutes when Romford were losing by two goals to one against Harlow and Burnt Mill. Romford were unable to raise a team for the replay, and scratched from the competition.

On 10th November Romford defeated strong local rivals South Weald by three goals to one in the Romford & District League, and according to the line-up in the local press, played with only nine men. A week later Romford were beaten 6-1 away to Walthamstow Town in the Essex Senior Cup. It is unknown how they were allowed to enter both Essex County cup competitions!

Next came a run of four successive victories, three of them in the League, when Brentwood, Oakley Swifts and Dagenham conceded thirteen goals between them! The fourth game was a friendly match at home to Radner, which Romford won by one goal to nil.

On Boxing Day Romford were due to play a home friendly against Grays Alliance but we have been unable to find a result for this match. Four days later Romford were soundly defeated at home to eventual league champions Romford St. Andrew's, by four goals to one.

Stung by this reverse, Romford came back strongly with two big away wins against Oakley Swifts (7-1) and Brentwood (6-1) to improve their league position. There was heavy snow across Essex at this time. Queen Victoria died aged 81 on 22 January 1901, and football was suspended until after her funeral. Normal business was resumed on 16th February with a 2-2 draw at Oakley Swifts.

Another defeat by Romford St. Andrew's sealed the league championship, and although the town club beat South Weald in their final league game of the season they had to accept second place in the final table to St. Andrew's, who inflicted even more misery on Romford on 16th March with a two one defeat in a friendly game.

The season was altogether a successful one compared to previous seasons, apart from the County cup competitions, Romford losing only five of their seventeen recorded matches.

Annual General Meeting
(as reported in the *Essex Times,* Wednesday 11th September 1901)

The annual meeting of the Romford Football Club was held at the White Hart Hotel on Friday evening, 6th September, Mr. George Barnes presiding over a good attendance.

Mr.T.W.Sharpe, the energetic hon. secretary, reported that of the 23 matches played by the 1st eleven they won 12, lost 6 and drew 5. They were the runners-up in the 1st division of the Romford and District League, having obtained 15 points out of a possible 20. The second eleven – a promising lot of juniors – played 22 matches, 13 of which were won, 2 being drawn. They obtained 26 points in the second division of the league. A suitable ground had now been offered. The loss of the recreation ground put the club to considerable inconvenience and expense in consequence of the matches having had to be played away.

The accounts submitted by the hon. treasurer (Mr.L.J.Field) showed receipts £40.11s.0d and expenditure £36.15s.1d. The outstanding liabilities were £14.16s.0d., while unpaid subscriptions amounted to £22.9s.0d. When these were paid up there would be a substantial balance in hand. (Applause). The report was adopted subject to audit.

Mr.H.H.Raphael was re-elected president for the ensuing season. It was decided to ask Mr.R.H.Lyon, Mr.H.L.Pocock, Mr.C.D.Green, Mr.W.C.Clifton, Mr. Victor Castellan, Mr.C.E.Sheffield, Mr.J.Craig, Mr.Hansen, Mr.Harrison, and Mr.Hyslop to become vice-presidents.

Mr.R.Ball was elected captain of the 1st eleven and Mr.Walter Riley vice-captain. Mr.George Winmill and Mr.J.Nixon were elected captain and vice-captain respectively of the reserves. Mr.W.D.Matthews was chosen representative on the Association. Messrs.T.W.Sharpe and F.W.Jeffes were appointed joint hon. secretaries, and Mr.L.J.Field was re-elected treasurer. Messrs. C.Ryle and Braund were elected auditors. Several new members were enrolled.

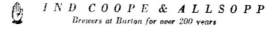

Season 1901 – 02

ROMFORD FOOTBALL CLUB

President: Mr.H.H.Raphael. C.C. **Joint Hon.Secretaries:** Mr.T.W.Sharpe and Mr.F.W.Jeffes

Hon.Treasurer: Mr.L.J.Field **Committee:** Members unknown

Vice-Presidents: Messrs.R.H.Lyon, H.L.Pocock, C.D.Green, W.C.Clifton, Victor Castellan
C.E.Sheffield, J.Craig, Hanson, Harrison, Hyslop
Note: The above named were invited to become Vice-Presidents at the AGM
It is not known whether they all accepted the invitation!

First Team Captain: Mr.R.Ball **First Team Vice-Captain:** Mr.W.Riley

Reserve Team Captain: Mr.George Winmill **Reserve Team Vice-Captain:** Mr.J.Nixon

Auditors: Messrs. C.Ryle and Braund

Club Colours: Blue and Black Stripes **Headquarters:** White Hart Hotel, Romford

Grounds: First Team: Cricket Ground, Romford Station Reserve Team: Brooklands, Romford

COMPETITIONS ENTERED

Romford & District Football League Division One
Essex Junior Cup

Romford & District Football League Division Two

Match Details

28 Sept	Frdly	Home	Ilford Alliance "A"	0 – 1
5 Oct	Frdly	Home	Grays Tricolor	0 – 4
19 Oct	EJC1R	Home	St. John's (Leytonstone)	4 – 1
26 Oct	RDL1	Away	Ilford Balfour	2 – 1
2 Nov	EJC2R	Home	Chingford United	6 – 2
9 Nov	RDL1	Home	Brentwood	6 – 1
16 Nov	RDL1	Away	Hornchurch	2 – 1
7 Dec	RDL1	Home	Ilford Park	1 – 2
14 Dec	RDL1	Away	Romford St. Andrew's	0 – 4
4 Jan	RDL1	Home	South Weald	1 – 3
11 Jan	RDL1	Away	Dagenham	3 – 0*
18 Jan	RDL1	Home	Hornchurch	2 – 1
25 Jan	RDL1	Home	Romford St. Andrew's	0 – 2
1 Feb	RDL1	Home	Ilford Balfour	4 – 0
8 Feb	RDL1	Away	South Weald	0 – 8
15 Feb	RDL1	Away	Brentwood	1 – 1

22 Feb	RDL1	Home	Dagenham	2 – 0*
8 Mar	RDL1	Away	Ilford Park	1 – 1

* The first game against Dagenham was stopped 15 minutes from time due to bad light. The League ruled that the game remain unfinished until the return fixture at Romford, when the remaining 15 minutes was played prior to commencement of the second game – meaning that the original fixture lasted 42 days!!

SUMMARY OF RESULTS OBTAINED SEASON 1901 – 02

					Goals		
	P	W	D	L	For	Ag	Pts
Romford & Dist. Lge.	14	7	2	5	25	25	16
Friendly Matches	2	0	0	2	0	5	
Essex Junior Cup	2	2	0	0	10	3	
Total	18	9	2	7	35	33	
AGM Press Report	20	10	2	8	38	34	

Two results have not been traced, of which one was won and one lost, it is not known of course whether these were friendly matches or competitive games. The scores in the Essex Junior Cup Ties are also not known.

Romford & District League Division One

					Goals		
	P	W	D	L	For	Ag	Pts
Romford St Andrews	14	11	3	0	64	11	25
South Weald	13	7	5	1	40	13	19
Ilford Park	14	7	3	4	26	17	17
Romford	**14**	**7**	**2**	**5**	**25**	**25**	**16**
Brentwood	13	3	2	8	20	42	8
Dagenham	10	4	0	6	14	26	8
Ilford Balfour	13	3	2	8	15	40	8
Hornchurch	13	1	1	11	13	43	3

FIRST TEAM CUP RESULTS SEASON 1901 – 02

Essex Junior Cup

Final: Halstead 2 Chingford United 0

Romford's progress:	1st Round	Home	St. John's Athletic	4 - 1
	2nd Round	Home**	Chingford United	6 - 2
	3rd Round		Scratched	

** It is known that Romford played their first team for this game and the Essex County ordered the tie to be replayed but Romford decided to scratch from the competition.

West Ham Charity Cup

Winners: Clapton Orient

Romford did not compete

First Team Appearances Season 1901 – 02

F.Adams	D'Eath	F.L.Fletcher	A.Hunwicks
S.Partridge	W.Powter	B.Raund	W.Riley
W.Swallow			

The above players are known to have played during the season, but as no actual team line-ups have been printed in the local press, full details are not possible!

First Team Goal Scorers Season 1901 – 02

The local newspapers failed to report goal scorers for any of the first team or reserve team games throughout the season and the leading scorers are a mystery!

Press Coverage

The following message was printed in the *Essex Times* during the late 1890's and early 1900's and it possibly explains the poor coverage that the team received over these years. Due to the lack of funds did the club not pay the ten shillings fee!

TO FOOTBALL CLUBS

"We cannot GUARANTEE the insertion of Matches and Lists of matches to come, unless paid for in advance, at the rate of 10s. for the season, or 1s. each match".

RESERVE TEAM

Match Details

9 Nov	RDL2	Away	Romford St. Andrew's Reserves	2 – 3
Romford: Hunwicks;				
16 Nov	RDL2	Home	Chadwell Athletic	3 – 1
23 Nov	RDL2	Away	Ilford United	2 – 0
30 Nov	RDL2	Home	Romford Alliance	won
14 Dec	RDL2	Away	Heath Park	1 – 0
21 Dec	RDL2	Away	South Weald Reserves	2 – 4**
26 Dec	Frdly	Home	Clare Athletic	5 – 1
28 Dec	RDL2	Away	South Weald Reserves	3 – 0
11 Jan	RDL2	Home	Brentwood Reserves	3 – 2
18 Jan	RDL2	Away	Harold Wood	6 – 0
25 Jan	RDL2	Home	Heath Park	2 – 5
1 Feb	RDL2	Home	Romford St. Andrew's Reserves	2 – 0
15 Feb	RDL2	Away	Chadwell Athletic	n/k
22 Feb	RDL2	Home	South Weald Reserves	5 – 0
1 Mar	RDL2	Away	Romford Alliance	0 – 2
8 Mar	RDL2	Away	Brentwood Reserves	3 – 2
n/k	RDL2	Home	Ilford United	n/k
n/k	RDL2	Home	Harold Wood	won
n/k	RDL2	Home	Romford Victoria	n/k
n/k	RDL2	Away	Romford Victoria	n/k

** This result was declared void due to South Weald fielding an ineligible player, and the match was replayed a week later to Romford's advantage!

SUMMARY OF RESERVE TEAM RESULTS OBTAINED SEASON 1901 – 02

					Goals		
	P	W	D	L	For	Ag	Pts
Romford & Dist. Lge	18	12	3	3	43	19	27
Friendly Match	1	1	0	0	5	1	
Total	19	13	3	3	48	20	
AGM Press Report	25	16	5	4	67	31	

Note: The above summary does not include the void match versus South Weald Reserves, and six results not known.

Romford & District League Division Two
Final Table

					Goals		
	P	W	D	L	For	Ag	Pts
Romford Alliance 18	15	0	3			30	
Romford Reserves	**18**	**12**	**3**	**3**	**43**	**19**	**27***
Romford Victoria	17	10	4	3			24
Ilford United	18	9	2	7			20
Heath Park	18	9	0	9			18
Romford St.Andrews Res.	18	6	4	8			16
Brentwood Reserves	18	6	2	10			14
South Weald Reserves	18	4	5	9			13
Chadwell Athletic 16	2	6	8			10	
Harold Wood	17	2	0	15			4

* At the AGM it was reported that the reserves obtained twenty five league points.
It is possible that the club may have been deducted two points for a rule infringement.

Reserve Team Appearances and Goal Scorers Season 1901 – 02

Due to the very poor press coverage it is not known who played or scored for the reserves during the season!

Post-Season Summary Season 1901 – 02

Romford Football Club held a meeting with Romford Thursday Football Club regarding a possible merger between the clubs, but nothing further came from it. (Thursday was the town's early closing day, giving many locals the afternoon off work).

The team commenced the season with two defeats in friendly matches, but started their league programme in fine form with three successive victories against Ilford Balfour, Brentwood and Hornchurch. However, in the Essex Junior Cup Romford unsportingly fielded their first team, and obtained two victories. Their opponents protested and the game against Chingford United was ordered to be replayed by the County Association. Romford reacted by scratching from the competition, thus allowing Chingford to meet Wanstead Amateurs in the third round.

Romford's next game at home to South Weald on 23rd November was postponed due to the South Weald club being suspended pending an investigation into the club books.

In late November rumours were rife that Romford were going to merge with Romford St. Andrew's Football Club, but again this came to nothing.

Romford's next three games were all defeats. The first of these was against Ilford Park, then the powerful Romford St. Andrew's team inflicted a 4-0 defeat, and finally South Weald won 3-1 at Romford and Romford slipped to mid-table. During this period the first team suffered as a result of illness brought on by the smallpox vaccination.

THE GAME THAT LASTED FOR 42 DAYS!

On 11th January 1902 Romford were away to Dagenham in a Romford & District League Division One fixture, and were winning comfortably by three goals to nil when the game was brought to an end 15 minutes early due to bad light. The League Committee in their wisdom decided to leave the result in abeyance until the return fixture at Romford on 22nd February. It was decided that the remaining fifteen minutes of the first game should be played before the start of the second game, and this was duly completed without any addition to the score. Thus the original fixture was finally completed after 42 days!

Post-season summary (continued)

Meanwhile, on 18th January 1902, Romford had defeated local rivals Hornchurch again by two goals to one, before suffering yet another reverse against St. Andrew's. On 1st February Romford returned to form with a fine 4-0 defeat of Ilford Balfour. Alas, we have to record that the Balfour played with only seven men! The following week saw a rude awakening as Romford came back from South Weald after an eight goal to nil beating.

Romford wound up the season with an away draw at Brentwood, a 2-0 win over Dagenham and a draw against Ilford Park. Before the Dagenham game the 15 minutes mentioned earlier were played without any further goals being scored, and the original 3-0 victory was included in the league table. Romford ended the season in a mid-table position and rarely produced the form of the previous season.

The reserve team enjoyed a fine season in the Romford and District League Division Two, finishing in second place behind Romford Alliance. They lost only three of their eighteen league games and scored over 40 goals. In the Essex Junior Cup Romford defeated St. John's Athletic (Leytonstone) and in the second round beat Chingford United. Unfortunately in the Chingford game Romford played their first team and the match was ordered to be re-played as this was not in keeping with tradition! Perhaps by way of retribution, Romford scratched from the competition for the second year in a row!

The Romford Cricket Club again offered Romford the use of the Cricket Ground for the next season.

Essex County Football Association

(from the *Essex Times*, Saturday 16th November 1901)

A meeting of the Council of the Essex County Football Association was held at the White Hart Hotel, Chelmsford on Wednesday evening 13th November, Alderman F. Chancellor presiding. Chingford United protested that on going to play a Romford 2nd XI in the Essex Junior Cup they had to meet several senior players. – Mr.W.D.Matthews, Romford, said the members of the team complied with the bye-laws, and were registered as Junior players. – The match was ordered to be replayed at Chingford by a bona-fide 2nd XI from Romford. Romford scratched from the competition.

Annual General Meeting

(as reported in the *Essex Times,* Wednesday 18th June 1902)

The annual general meeting of the Romford Football Club was held on Friday evening 13th June at the White Hart Hotel, when there was a good attendance. Mr.G.Barnes was elected to the chair, in the absence of the Rev. H.L.Pocock, who had been announced to preside.

The secretary (Mr.T.W.Sharpe) read his report, which showed that the club's first team played twenty matches during last season, of which they won 10, lost 8, and drew 2, gaining sixteen points in the Romford and District Football League, which placed them fifth in the tables. They scored 38 goals against 34. The reserves played 25 matches, winning 16, losing 5, drawing 4, and they obtained 25 points in the league; goals scored 67, against 31. With regard to next season, the Secretary stated that the first and second teams had entered Divisions I, and II, of the South Essex League.

Mr. Sharpe apologised for the absence of Mr.L.J.Field (the treasurer), and stated that there was a balance on the wrong side of about £15, owing to unpaid subscriptions. Were all the subscriptions paid there would be a balance in hand of £3.15s.0d. After discussion, it was decided to receive the treasurer's statement at the next committee meeting.

Mr.H.H.Raphael was re-elected President of the club for the ensuing year. The Vice-presidents were re-elected, and it was decided to ask the following to become vice-presidents: Messrs. G.Burrows, G.Cummings, W.K.James, and W.Stevenson. Five new members were elected. Mr.R.Ball was re-elected captain of the first team, and Mr.W.Hunter vice-captain. Mr.G.Winmill was re-elected captain of the second team, and Mr.F.Winmill vice-captain. Mr.W.D.Matthews was re-elected to represent the club at various association meetings.

Major Thirlwall was asked to accept the office of treasurer, but said he already had so many offices to fill. Mr. Barnes and Mr. Matthews also declined. Ultimately the appointment was left over for the next committee meeting. Mr.Sharpe said he could no longer act as secretary. He liked the work, but really could not give the time to it. He had served four years as secretary. Mr.Ball said Mr.Swallow would accept office if the club could not get another secretary. With regard to Mr.Sharpe leaving the post, he had done the best he could under hard circumstances. The appointment of match secretary for the first team was adjourned to the next committee meeting.

During the evening medals were presented to Messrs. Jeffes and Doy, and there was one for Mr.Field. A committee was also appointed.

Essex County Football Association

Romford secretary Mr.T.W.Sharpe wrote to the Essex County Football Association apparently withdrawing the Romford Football Club from membership of the county association sometime during the season as a protest against their treatment in the Essex Junior Cup regarding the match against Chingford United.

Season 1902 – 03

ROMFORD FOOTBALL CLUB

President: Mr.H.H.Raphael **Hon.Secretary:** Mr.T.W.Sharpe **Hon.Treasurer:** Mr.L.J.Field

Captain: Mr.R.Ball **Vice-Captain:** Mr.J.B.Hunter

Reserve Team Captain: Mr.G.Winmill **Reserve Team Vice-Captain:** Mr.F.Winmill

Club Colours: Blue and Black Stripes **Headquarters:** White Hart Hotel, Romford

Ground: Cricket Ground, Romford Station Reserve Team: Brooklands, Romford

COMPETITIONS ENTERED

South Essex League Division Two Western
Romford & District Football League Division One
Club did not enter or were not accepted for the F.A., Amateur or Essex Cups

Romford & District Football League Division Two
Romford Charity Cup

Match Details

13 Sept Frdly Home Forest Gate 3 – 4 Scorers unknown
Romford: L.Meloy(Romford St.Andrew's);F.Rowe,E.P.Jones;A.Reeves,J.B.Hunter,R.Ball;
E.Champness,W.Saggers,S.Partridge,Williams,Gibson,W.Derbyshire.

20 Sept Frdly Home Royal Horse Artillery (Woolwich) 3 – 0 A.Jones(2)(1pen),Saggers
Romford: W.Riley;F.L.Fletcher,A.Reeves;J.B.Hunter,R.Ball,L.Gilbert;
Williams,W.Saggers,S.Partridge,A.E.Jones,Reynolds.

27 Sept Frdly Home Goldsmith Institute 4 – 2 A.Jones(4)
Romford:
Team details unknown.

4 Oct RDL1 Away Grays Town 0 – 2
Romford: W.Riley;R.Ball,J.B.Hunter;F.Rowe L.Gilbert,
E.Champness,S.Partridge,Reynolds,H.Day,W.Derbyshire.

11 Oct SEL2W Home Ascension (Custom House) 3 – 2 A.Jones,Saggers,GK(og)
Romford: W.Riley;R.Ockendon,E.P.Jones;F.Rowe,R.Ball,A.Reeves;
J.B.Hunter,W.Saggers,S.Partridge,A.E.Jones,H.Day.

18 Oct Frdly Home Olympic 6 – 1 Arthur Reeves(2)Saggers(2)Rowe,A.Jones
Romford: W.Riley;R.Ockendon,E.P.Jones;F.Rowe,A.Reeves,R.Ball;
W.Derbyshire,W.Saggers,S.Partridge,A.E.Jones,H.Day.

25 Oct SEL2W Away Wanstead Amateurs 7 – 1 E.Jones(4)(1pen)A.Jones(3)
Romford: W.Riley;R.Ockendon,E.P.Jones;A.Reeves,R.Ball,F.Rowe;
S.Partridge,A.E.Jones,W.Saggers,E.Edwards,H.Day.

1 Nov RDL1 Home Ilford Balfour 4 – 1 Scorers unknown
Romford: W.Riley;R.Ockendon,E.P.Jones;F.Rowe,A.Reeves,R.Ball;
E.Edwards,W.Saggers,S.Partridge,J.B.Hunter,H.Day.

8 Nov SEL2W Away Ascension (Custom House) 1 – 3 Scorer unknown
Romford: W.Riley;R.Ockendon,E.P.Jones;F.Rowe,A.Reeves,R.Ball;
E.Edwards,W.Saggers,S.Partridge,J.B.Hunter,H.Day.

15 Nov SEL2W Home Leytonstone Reserves 7 – 1 A.Jones(3)J.Hunter(2)Saggers,Ball
Romford: W.Riley;R.Ockendon,E.P.Jones;F.Rowe,A.Reeves,R.Ball;
E.Edwards,W.Saggers,S.Partridge,J.B.Hunter,A.E.Jones.

22 Nov SEL2W Home Barking 2 – 0 Saggers(2)
Attendance: 400
Romford: W.Riley;R.Ockendon,E.P.Jones;F.Rowe,A.Reeves,R.Ball;
A.E.Jones,W.Saggers,S.Partridge,J.B.Hunter,A.B.MacDonnell.

29 Nov RDL1 Away Ilford Reserves 5 – 1 Scorers unknown
Romford: W.Riley;R.Ockendon,E.P.Jones;F.Rowe,A.Reeves,R.Ball;
E.Edwards,W.Saggers,A.E.Jones,J.B.Hunter,F.Spackman.

6 Dec RDL1 Home Romford St. Andrew's 1 – 2 A.Jones
Romford: W.Riley;R.Ockendon,E.P.Jones;F.Rowe,A.Reeves,R.Ball;
W.Saggers,A.E.Jones,J.B.Hunter,A.B.MacDonnell,F.Spackman.

13 Dec SEL2W Away Romford St. Andrew's 3 – 0 Hunter,Saggers,Spackman
Romford: W.Riley;R.Ockendon,E.P.Jones;A.Reeves,J.B.Hunter,R.Ball;
E.Edwards,A.E.Jones,S.Partridge,W.Saggers,F.Spackman.

20 Dec SEL2W Home Newportonians 4 – 2 Edwards(2)Reeves,A.Jones
Romford: W.Riley;R.Ockendon,E.P.Jones;A.Reeves,J.B.Hunter,R.Ball;
E.Edwards,A.E.Jones,S.Partridge,F.Spackman,F.Rowe.

25 Dec Frdly Home Millwall St. Luke's 8 – 1 Scorers unknown
Romford:
Team details unknown.

26 Dec Frdly Home Royal Artillery 10 – 1 Scorers unknown
Romford:
Team details unknown.

3 Jan RDL1 Away South Weald 2 – 1 Saggers, one (og)
Romford: W.Riley;R.Ockendon,E.P.Jones;F.Rowe,R.Ball,E.Edwards;
W.Saggers,S.Partridge,A.E.Jones,J.B.Hunter,F.Spackman.

10 Jan Frdly Home London Caledonians "A" 7 – 0 A.Jones(4)Partridge,Saggers, one (og)
Romford: W.Riley;R.Ockendon,E.P.Jones;F.Rowe,R.Ball,E.Edwards;
W.Saggers,S.Partridge,A.E.Jones,J.B.Hunter,F.Spackman.

17 Jan RDL1 Home Ilford Reserves 6 – 0 Saggers(3)A.Jones(2)(1pen)Edwards
Romford: W.Riley;R.Ockendon,E.P.Jones;F.Rowe,R.Ball,E.Edwards;
W.Saggers,S.Partridge,A.E.Jones,J.B.Hunter,A.Reeves.

24 Jan Romford were temporarily suspended from playing football (see above).

31 Jan SEL2W Home Romford St. Andrew's 3 – 1 Fletcher,Saggers,A.Jones
Romford: W.Riley;R.Ockendon,E.P.Jones;J.B.Hunter,F.Rowe,W.Saggers;
A.E.Jones,A.Reeves,F.Spackman,S.Partridge,F.L.Fletcher.

7 Feb SEL2W Away Leytonstone Reserves 8 – 0 Fletcher(4),Saggers(4)
Romford: W.Riley;R.Ockendon,E.P.Jones;A.Reeves,J.B.Hunter,F.Rowe;
S.Partridge,A.E.Jones,W.Saggers,F.L.Fletcher,F.Spackman.

14 Feb RDL1 Home South Weald 1 – 2 A.Jones
Romford: W.Riley;R.Ockendon,E.P.Jones;A.Reeves,J.B.Hunter,F.Rowe;
S.Partridge,A.E.Jones,W.Saggers,F.L.Fletcher,F.Spackman.

21 Feb SEL2W Home Wanstead Amateurs 6 – 0 Scorers unknown
Romford: W.Riley;R.Ockendon,E.P.Jones;R.Ball,J.B.Hunter,F.Rowe;
S.Partridge,A.E.Jones,W.Saggers,F.L.Fletcher,F.Spackman.

28 Feb SEL2W Home Wanstead 2 – 1 Scorers unknown
Romford: W.Riley;R.Ockendon,E.P.Jones;J.B.Hunter,R.Ball,A.Reeves;
A.E.Jones,F.L.Fletcher,A.B.MacDonnell,W.Saggers,F.Spackman.

7 Mar SEL2W Away Barking 2 – 0 A.Jones(2)
Romford: W.Riley;R.Ockendon,E.P.Jones;R.Ball,J.B.Hunter,A.Reeves;
A.E.Jones,A.B.MacDonnell,W.Saggers,F.L.Fletcher,F.Spackman.

14 Mar RDL1 Home Grays Town 1 – 2 Scorer unknown
Romford:
Team details unknown.

21 Mar SEL2W Away Newportonians 4 – 3 Saggers(2)Unknown(2)
Romford:
Team details unknown.

28 Mar Frdly Home West Ham Garfield 6 – 1 Scorers unknown
Romford:
Team details unknown.

4 Apr RDL1 Away Ilford Balfour 11 – 1 Scorers unknown
Romford:
Team details unknown.

11 Apr SEL2W Away Wanstead 3 – 2 Fletcher(2)A.Jones
Attendance: 300 travel from Romford to cheer on the Black and Blues.
Romford: W.Riley;R.Ockendon,E.P.Jones;J.B.Hunter,R.Ball,A.E.Jones;
W.Saggers,F.L.Fletcher,S.Partridge,F.Spackman,A.Reeves.

13 Apr RDL1 Away Romford St. Andrew's 2 – 1 Scorers unknown
Romford:
Team details unknown.

25 Apr SELPO Away Southend Athletic 2 – 1 A.Jones(2)
Romford: W.Riley;A.Reeves,E.P.Jones;R.Ball,J.B.Hunter,F.Rowe;
S.Partridge,A.E.Jones,W.Saggers,F.L.Fletcher,F.Spackman.

SUMMARY OF FIRST TEAM RESULTS OBTAINED SEASON 1902 – 03

	P	W	D	L	Goals For	Goals Ag	Pts
South Essex League Div. 2W	14	13	0	1	55	16	26
South Essex League Play Off	1	1	0	0	2	1	
Romford & Dist. League Div. One	10	6	0	4	33	13	
Friendly Matches	8	7	0	1	47	10	
Total	33	27	0	6	137	40	

South Essex League Division Two West
Final Table

	P	W	D	L	Goals For	Goals Ag	Pts
Romford	**14**	**13**	**0**	**1**	**55**	**16**	**26**
Wanstead	14	10	2	2	47	16	22
Ascension	14	8	3	3	37	20	19
Barking	14	7	2	5	32	20	16
Newportonians	14	6	3	5	39	30	15
Wanstead Amateurs	14	2	2	10	12	52	6
Leytonstone Reserves **	14	1	3	10	13	42	3
Romford St. Andrews	14	0	3	11	7	46	3

** Two points deducted for breach of Rules.

Romford & District League Division One
Latest known Table

	P	W	D	L	Goals For	Goals Ag	Pts
Grays Town	9	7	2	0	35	7	16
South Weald Reserves	10	6	2	2	27	13	14
Romford	**10**	**6**	**0**	**4**	**33**	**13**	**12**
Romford St. Andrew's	9	2	1	6	17	20	5
Ilford Reserves	8	2	1	5	11	29	5
Ilford Balfour	8	1	0	7	5	47	2

First Team Appearances Season 1902 – 03

R.Ball	22	E.Champness	2	H.Day	6	W.Derbyshire	3
E.Edwards	10	F.L.Fletcher	9	Gibson	1	L.Gilbert	2
J.B.Hunter	23	E.P.Jones	23	A.E.Jones	21	A.B.MacDonnell	5
L.Meloy	1	R.Ockendon	21	S.Partridge	21	A.Reeves	20
Reynolds	2	W.Riley	24	F.Rowe	20	W.Saggers	24
F.Spackman	14	Williams	2			Total	276

Note: Team details are not available for several matches but the above summary shows the more regular members of the team during the season.

First Team Goal Scorers Season 1902 – 03

A.E.Jones	29	W.Saggers	20	F.L.Fletcher	7	E.P.Jones	4
J.B.Hunter	3	A.Reeves	3	E.Edwards	3	F.Rowe	1
R.Ball	1	F.Spackman	1	S.Partridge	1	Own Goals	3
Unknown!	61					Total	137

Due to the lack of detail in the local press reports a large number of goal scorers are not known.

RESERVE TEAM

Match Details

27 Sept	Frdly	Away	Goldsmith Reserves	0 – 2
n/k	RDL2	Away	South Weald	0 – 2
n/k	RDL2	Away	Shenfield & Hutton	4 – 0
11 Oct	Frdly	Away	Thorncliffe	2 – 2
18 Oct	Frdly	Home	East Ham Crescent	3 – 2
1 Nov	Frdly	Away	East Suburban Banks	6 – 2
n/k	RDL2	Home	Romford St. Andrew's Res.	0 – 0
15 Nov	RDL2	Home	Romford Alliance	5 – 2
n/k	RDL2	Home	Brentwood St. Thomas	7 – 0
29 Nov	Frdly	Home	Wanstead St.James	2 – 1
6 Dec	RDL2	Home	Harold Wood	6 – 0
20 Dec	Frdly	Home	Tottenham Wesleyans	1 – 0
31 Jan	RDL2	Away	Heath Park	2 – 5

Romford Selected Team: E.Foster;Buddery,E.Hunwicks;J.Tarry,E.West,W.Derbyshire; P.Wright,E.Champness,J.Edwards,W.Kittle,J.J.Hyslop.

21 Feb	RCC1R	Home	Chadwell Heath	1 – 1
12 Mar	Replay	Away	Chadwell Heath	3 – 2*
	RCCSemi Final			Bye
25 Apr	RCCF	Neut#	Heath Park	2 – 2
30 Apr	Replay	Neut##	Heath Park	3 – 4
n/k	RDL2	Home	South Weald	1 – 3
n/k	RDL2	Away	Chadwell Heath	1 – 6
n/k	RDL2	Home	Heath Park	2 – 0
n/k	RDL2	Home	Chadwell Heath	1 – 0
n/k	RDL2	Away	Harold Wood	0 – 4
n/k	RDL2	Away	Romford St. Andrew's Res.	3 – 0
n/k	RDL2	Away	Romford Alliance	4 – 0
n/k	RDL2	Away	Brentwood St. Thomas	not played
n/k	RDL2	Home	Shenfield	4 – 1

* After extra time

\# At Romford St. Andrew's ground

\## At Romford Alliance ground (Squirrels Heath)

SUMMARY OF RESERVE TEAM RESULTS OBTAINED SEASON 1902 – 03

					Goals		
	P	W	D	L	For	Ag	Pts
Romford & Dist. League	15	9	1	5	40	23	19
Romford Charity Cup	4	1	2	1	9	9	
Friendly Matches	6	4	1	1	14	9	
Total	25	14	4	7	63	41	

Romford & District League Division Two
Final Table

					Goals		
	P	W	D	L	For	Ag	Pts
South Weald Reserves	16	13	1	2			27
Chadwell Heath	16	12	1	3			25
Heath Park	16	11	2	3			24
Romford Reserves	**15**	**9**	**1**	**5**	**40**	**23**	**19**
Romford Alliance	16	6	1	9			13
Brentwood St. Thomas	15	5	0	10			10
Harold Wood	16	5	0	11			10
Romford St. Andrews Res.	15	3	2	10			8
Shenfield & Hutton	15	2	0	13			4

Note: Brentwood St. Thomas versus Romford Reserves and Romford St. Andrew's Reserves versus Romford Alliance matches were not played.

RESERVE TEAM CUP RESULTS SEASON 1902 – 03

Essex Junior Cup

Final: Wanstead 7 Maldon 1

Romford Reserves did not enter the competition

Romford Charity Cup (First Season)

Final: Heath Park 2 Romford 2
(at Romford St. Andrew's Ground)

Replay: Heath Park 4 Romford 3 (at Romford Alliance Ground (Squirrels Heath)

Romford's progress:	1st Round	Home	Chadwell Heath	1 – 1
	Replay	Away	Chadwell Heath	3 – 2*
	Semi-Final		Bye	
	Final	Neut#	Heath Park	2 – 2
	Replay	Neut##	Heath Park	3 – 4

* After extra time
# At Romford St. Andrew's ground
At Romford Alliance ground (Squirrels Heath)

Post-Season Summary Season 1902 – 03

Romford commenced the season with three friendly matches, winning two and losing one. Arthur Edwin Jones, nicknamed 'Diddy' (younger brother of Romford player Evan Pashley Jones) was in fine form, scoring four goals against Goldsmith's Institute. The first Romford & District League game was lost away to Grays Town by two goals to nil, but a win was recorded a week later against Ascension of Custom House in the more important South Essex League. The winning goal was secured by the Ascension goalie accidentally kicking the ball into his own net!

The following three matches ended in big wins for the locals, with the Jones brothers scoring all seven goals in the game against Wanstead Amateurs in the South Essex League. The match report stated that Arthur Jones only played for 30 minutes, then went off injured! On 8th November Ascension gained revenge on their own ground with a 3-1 victory, inflicting Romford's first defeat in five games.

There then followed three more very good wins, with Arthur Jones and Saggers among the goals. The first two games in December were both against Romford St. Andrews. Romford lost the Romford and District League encounter, but the following week's South Essex League win against their near neighbours was the start of a string of nine successive victories. 51 goals were scored during this run. During this time Romford were temporarily suspended from playing football by the County Association (see next page for details). Romford's next game was against a strong South Weald team who won the Romford & District League game by two goals to one.

Next, it was back to the South Essex League and three successive victories against Wanstead Amateurs, Wanstead and Barking. The game against Wanstead Amateurs on 21st February was marred because during the match a thief entered the Romford club's dressing room and stole money from the pockets of players' clothing. Sums ranging from 9d. to 19s.3d. and totalling £2.5s.0d., were stolen. There had been no one in charge of the dressing room, which was left unlocked.

Next they met Grays Town who beat them by two goals to one, before the Romford team ended the season with six successive victories and a goal haul of twenty eight, including an 11-1 mauling of Ilford Balfour.

There was no Cup excitement for the team as the club was either not accepted or failed to apply for all the cup competitions. They did, however, succeed in winning the South Essex League Division Two West championship by a margin of four points, and defeated Southend Athletic (East section winners) by two goals to one in the playoff for the Championship at Southend.

The reserve team enjoyed a fairly successful season, finishing mid-table in the Romford & District League Division Two and reaching the final of the Romford Charity Cup competition losing the final by four goals to three against Heath Park.

An interesting thing happened in the game on 17th January against Ilford Reserves when Referee Mr.H.Lomas forgot the new rule regarding penalties, and as he couldn't see the old penalty line which used to run the full width of the pitch. He therefore ordered a penalty kick to be taken from the eighteen yard line, but 'Diddy' Jones still scored with ease!

One disappointing occurrence was when Frederic Spackman was condemned by the Committee for pulling out of a game to go ice skating! We are told that 'The question of his loyalty was remarked upon'.

ESSEX COUNTY FOOTBALL ASSOCIATION
(as reported in the *Essex Times*, Saturday 17th January 1903)

On 13th Jan. the Executive Committee of the Essex County Football Association met with Mr.F.J.Bloom Presiding. The Romford Town Club having withdrawn from the Association last season, the hon.sec. Mr.T.W.Sharpe, wrote asking that the Committee should treat the Club as defaulters in their subscription only. If this could not be done, the Club wished to be affiliated to the Association.

Mr.W.D.Matthews, of Romford, wrote supporting the application, and asking that the letter written by Mr.Sharpe on behalf of the Club last season might be considered withdrawn. The Hon.Secretary said the Club had withdrawn from the Association, and their connection with it had entirely ceased.

The consideration of the application was adjourned. Romford Football Club suspended temporarily.

A few days later Mr.James T. Clark (Hon.Secretary) advised that 'The Committee of the Romford F.C., having apologised to this Association for withdrawing their membership during the past season, and having expressed their regret, their apology has been accepted, and the Club has been re-affiliated to the Association by the unanimous vote of the Executive Committee'.

Annual General Meeting

(as reported in the *Essex Times,* Wednesday 8th July 1903)

The annual general meeting of the Romford Football Club was held at the White Hart Hotel on 3rd July, under the presidency of Mr.W.D.Matthews, when there was a large attendance.

The Hon. Secretary, Mr.T.W.Sharpe, presented a favourable account of the club's performances during the past season. The premier team only lost one match in the South Essex League, and won their way from the Second to the First Division. The second team also did well in the Romford and District League, securing a creditable position. Mr.W.H.Kelly remarked that though the premier club had got into the First Division, they would be playing the same clubs as last year. He was of opinion that the South Essex League had treated the Romford club disgracefully.

Mr.G.Barnes reminded the members that they still had an opportunity of gaining the object of their ambition – the championship of the league. If they could climb to the head of their section they would be able to play the other top clubs for this honour, and he hoped they would be able to do it. Mr. Kelly said the club's grievance was that they would have to meet inferior clubs, and the "gates" would suffer in consequence. He would rather the club met five good than 14 mediocre elevens. The Chairman remarked that the discussion was a mere waste of time. The matter was entirely one for the South Essex League to consider – they could do nothing by talking. Personally, he was quite disgusted when he saw they were not playing the clubs they thought they would. The report was adopted.

The Hon. Treasurer, Mr.L.J.Field, stated that the bulk of the financial work had fallen to Mr. Sharpe, who deserved their best thanks. (Hear, hear). Mr.Sharpe said though they had done well, he would have been better pleased if they had done better. The gate money amounted to £61, and on the year's working there was a balance in hand of £2.0s.1d. The Chairman, in congratulating the club, said Mr.Sharpe could never be satisfied, but he thought the accounts were, so far, satisfactory, especially when it is remembered that the debt on the club had been reduced from £22 to £6, which was a large amount to work off in one year. (Hear, hear).

The Hon. Secretary said there was one nasty point to which he would like to draw attention. It cost them £1 to put up a protection to prevent the ball going out of the field so frequently. They had to put 6d. into Mr.Loder's Cottage Hospital box every time the football went into his garden, and they had paid 11s. away in this manner. Thanks to Mr.G.Barnes, this matter had been up at the annual meeting of the Romford Cottage Hospital, and it had been aired in the Press and the club's thanks were due to Mr.Barnes. He (Mr.Sharpe) hoped to see Mr.Loder "knocked on the head about it," for it had been a confounded nuisance. (Laughter). They had not paid their sixpences into the box because they liked it, but simply to have a quick return of the ball! He had had a strong correspondence with Mr. Loder, who persisted in keeping the ball until he got the sixpence. (Laughter).

The following officers were elected to act during the ensuing year: - President, Mr.L.Sinclair.M.P.; new vice-presidents, Messrs. W.Stevenson, H.Durrant, W.G. Reynolds, and W.H. Kittle; captain, Mr.Arthur Jones; vice-captain, Mr.J.B.Hunter; reserves captain, Mr.Derbyshire; reserves vice-captain, Mr.Champness; representative to the Association, Mr.W.D.Matthews; hon.treasurer, Mr.R.Ball; hon.secretaries, Messrs. T.W.Sharpe and Derbyshire; committee, Messrs. Hearn, Kelly, G.Barnes, L.Fletcher, F.H.Thirlwall, A.Reynolds, Wallis, Simmons, Buddery, Field, V.Davis and F.Fletcher.

Mr.Jones accepted the captaincy on the understanding that the three miles radius was removed, as he considered it necessary to draw playing members from a wider area if the strength of the club and its supremacy were to be maintained. Mr.F.H.Thirlwall said playing "foreigners" had been the downfall of the club. In old days there were two Romford players, and the remaining men, whom they only saw on Saturdays, came from Timbuctoo, Leytonstone and other remote places. On the proposition of Mr.Jones, the rule confining the choice of players to a three mile radius was rescinded, notwithstanding the strong protests of the chairman and Mr.Thirlwall.

An advertisement in the *Essex Times* from this period. This animal hospital was situated near the Brooklands Sports Ground

Season 1903 – 04

ROMFORD FOOTBALL CLUB

President: Mr.L.Sinclair.M.P.

Hon.Secretary: Messrs. T.W.Sharpe and Derbyshire **Hon.Treasurer:** Mr.R.Ball

Captain: Mr.A.E.Jones **Vice-Captain:** Mr.J.B.Hunter

Reserve Team Captain: Mr.Derbyshire **Reserve Team Vice-Captain:** Mr.Champness

Representative to the Essex County Football Association: Mr.W.D.Matthews

Vice-Presidents: New vice-presidents elected at the AGM were Messrs. W.Stevenson, H.Durrant, W.G.Reynolds and W.H.Kittle. Original members who were in office the previous season are unknown.

Committee: Messrs. Hearn, Kelly, G.Barnes, L.Fletcher, F.H.Thirlwall, A.Reynolds, Wallis, Simmons, Buddery, Field, V.Davis and F.Fletcher.

Club Colours: Blue and Black Stripes **Headquarters:** Coach and Bell Hotel, Romford

Grounds: Cricket Ground, Romford Station Brooklands Sports Ground, Romford

COMPETITIONS ENTERED

South Essex Football League Division One B
Romford & District Football League Division One
F.A. Challenge Cup
Essex Senior Cup
Romford either failed to apply or were not accepted for the F.A. Amateur Cup

Romford & District Football League Division Two
Essex Junior Cup
Romford Charity Cup

Match Details

12 Sept Frdly Home# Forest Gate 5 – 1 Scorers unknown
Romford:
Team details unknown

19 Sept FACPR Away Leytonstone 0 – 5
Romford:
Team details unknown

26 Sept RDL1 Home Tilbury 2 – 0 Saggers(2)
Romford: T.W.Sharpe;P.J.Anderson,E.P.Jones;F.Rowe,J.B.Hunter,F.Roberts;
F.L.Fletcher,J.Buddery,S.Partridge,W.Saggers,A.Dennis.

3 Oct Frdly Home West Ham Garfield 4 – 0 Scorers unknown
Romford: W.Riley;R.Ball,F.Rowe;A.Reeves,J.B.Hunter,F.Roberts;
F.L.Fletcher,Reynolds,H.W.Biner,W.Saggers,A.Dennis.

10 Oct SEL1B Away Barking 3 – 3 Roberts,A.E.Jones,Saggers
Romford: W.Riley;P.J.Anderson,E.P.Jones,F.Rowe,A.Reeves,J.B.Hunter;
F.Roberts,F.L.Fletcher,A.E.Jones,W.Saggers,A.Dennis.

17 Oct SEL1B Home Southend Athletic 2 – 4 Scorers unknown
Romford: W.Riley;P.J.Anderson,E.P.Jones;F.Rowe,A.Reeves,F.Roberts;
F.L.Fletcher,F.Champness,H.W.Biner,W.Saggers,A.Dennis.

24 Oct ESC1R Home Grays Town 4 – 2 A.Jones(3)Biner
Attendance: 600
Romford: T.W.Sharpe;P.J.Anderson,E.P.Jones;R.Ball,A.Reeves,F.Roberts;
J.B.Hunter,F.L.Fletcher,A.E.Jones,H.W.Biner,A.Dennis.

31 Oct RDL1 Away Grays Town 2 – 0 Fletcher,Saggers
Romford: T.W.Sharpe;P.J.Anderson,E.P.Jones;R.Ball,A.Reeves,J.B.Hunter;
F.Roberts,F.L.Fletcher,Millbank,W.Saggers,A.Dennis.

7 Nov Frdly Home Olympic 4 – 0 Scorers unknown
Romford: T.W.Sharpe;P.J.Anderson,E.P.Jones;A.Reeves,F.Roberts,
A.E.Jones,Crudgington,H.W.Biner,W.Saggers,A.Dennis.

14 Nov ESC2R Home Barking 5 – 1 Saggers(2)A.Jones,Roberts,Dennis
Attendance: 700
Romford: T.W.Sharpe;P.J.Anderson,E.P.Jones;A.Reeves,J.B.Hunter,R.Ball;
A.E.Jones,F.Roberts,W.Saggers,H.W.Biner,A.Dennis.

21 Nov SEL1B Home South Weald 1 – 2 Dennis
Romford: F.W.Sharpe;P.J.Anderson,E.P.Jones;J.B.Hunter,A.Reeves,F.Roberts;
F.L.Fletcher,A.E.Jones,W.Saggers,H.W.Biner,A.Dennis.

28 Nov Frdly Home Old Holloway Collegians 4 – 1 A.Jones,Saggers,Roberts,Biner
Romford: T.W.Sharp;P.J.Anderson,R.Ball;A.Reeves,F.Roberts,F.L.Fletcher;
A.E.Jones,H.W.Biner,L.Pounds,W.Saggers,F.Spackman.

5 Dec Frdly Away Leyton 1 – 3 A.Jones
Attendance: 400
Romford: T.W.Sharpe;P.J.Anderson,R.Ball;A.Reeves,J.B.Hunter,F.Roberts;
F.L.Fletcher,A.E.Jones,H.W.Biner,W.Saggers,A.Dennis.

12 Dec RDL1 Away Romford St. Andrew's 4 – 1 Scorers unknown
Romford: T.W.Sharpe;P.J.Anderson,E.P.Jones;A.Reeves,J.B.Hunter,F.Roberts;
F.L.Fletcher,A.E.Jones,L.Pounds,W.Saggers,A.Dennis.

19 Dec SEL1B Home South West Ham 6 – 2 Scorers unknown
Romford: T.W.Sharpe;P.J.Anderson,J.B.Hunter;E.P.Jones,A.Reeves,F.Roberts;
F.L.Fletcher,A.E.Jones,L.Pounds,W.Saggers,A.Dennis.

26 Dec Frdly Home Romford St. Andrew's 3 – 1 A.Jones(pen) Unknown(2)
Romford: T.W.Sharpe;P.J.Anderson,E.P.Jones;A.Reeves,J.B.Hunter,V.Davis;
F.L.Fletcher,A.E.Jones,L.Pounds,W.Saggers,A.Dennis.

2 Jan RDL1 Away South Weald 0 – 2
Romford: T.W.Sharpe;Millbank,E.P.Jones;R.Ball,J.B.Hunter,F.Roberts;
F.L.Fletcher,A.E.Jones,L.Pounds,W.Saggers,A.Dennis.

9 Jan SEL1B Away Wanstead 6 – 2 Barter(2)A.Jones(2)Pounds,Dennis
Romford: T.W.Sharpe;E.P.Jones,P.J.Anderson;E.Barter,F.L.Fletcher,V.Davis;
F.Roberts,W.Saggers,A.E.Jones,L.Pounds,A.Dennis.

16 Jan RDL1 Home Romford St. Andrew's 8 – 1 A.Jones(3)unknown(5)
Romford: T.W.Sharpe;P.J.Anderson,E.P.Jones;F.Roberts,F.L.Fletcher,V.Davis;
A.E.Jones,L.Pounds,E.Barter,W.Saggers,A.Dennis.

23 Jan RDL1 Home Grays Town 5 – 1 Fletcher,A.Jones,Saggers(2),Barter
Attendance: 400
Romford: T.W.Sharpe;R.Ball,E.P.Jones;F.Roberts,F.L.Fletcher,V.Davis;
A.E.Jones,L.Pounds,E.Barter,W.Saggers,A.Dennis.

30 Jan SEL1B Away South Weald 1 – 0 Dennis
Romford: T.W.Sharpe;R.Ball,E.P.Jones;F.Roberts,F.L.Fletcher,V.Davis;
A.E.Jones,L.Pounds,E.Barter,W.Saggers,A.Dennis.

6 Feb ESC3R Away Leyton P – P

13 Feb SEL1B Home Wanstead 1 – 0 A.Jones
Romford: T.W.Sharpe;J.B.Hunter,E.P.Jones;F.Roberts,F.L.Fletcher,V.Davis;
A.E.Jones,L.Pounds,E.Barter,W.Saggers,A.Dennis.

20 Feb ESC3R Away Leyton 1 – 8 Scorer unknown
Romford: T.W.Sharpe;R.Ball,E.P.Jones;F.Roberts,V.Davis,F.L.Fletcher;
A.E.Jones,L.Pounds,F.Barter,W.Saggers,A.Dennis.

27 Feb SEL1B Home Barking 2 – 1 A.Jones,Fletcher
Romford: T.W.Sharpe;,E.P.Jones,A.Reeves;J.B.Hunter,F.Roberts,V.Davis;
F.L.Fletcher,A.E.Jones,L.Pounds,E.Barter,A.Dennis.

5 Mar SEL1B Away South West Ham 2 – 1 Barter(2)
Romford: W.H.Kelly; ? ,E.P.Jones;A.Reeves,J.B.Hunter,F.Roberts;
A.E.Jones,E.Barter, ? , ? , ? .

12 Mar SEL1B Home Boleyn Castle 2 – 0 A.Jones,Dennis
Romford: T.W.Sharpe;P.J.Anderson,E.P.Jones;F.Roberts,F.L.Fletcher,V.Davis;
A.E.Jones,L.Pounds,W.Saggers,E.Barter,A.Dennis.

19 Mar Frdly Home# Upton Park 7 – 2 A.Jones(4)Roberts,Saggers,Pounds
Romford: T.W.Sharpe;P.J.Anderson,J.Buddery;J.B.Hunter,F.Roberts,F.Champness;
F.L.Fletcher,A.E.Jones,L.Pounds,E.Barter,W.Saggers,A.Dennis.

26 Mar RDL1 Away Tilbury 1 – 0 Barter
Romford: T.W.Sharpe; ? ,F.Champness; ? , ? ,F.Roberts;
? ,L.Pounds,E.Barter,W.Saggers,A.Dennis.

2 Apr SEL1B Away Southend Athletic 0 – 1
Romford: T.W.Sharpe;K.Prentise,Robinson;A.Reeves,F.L.Fletcher, ? ;
A.E.Jones,L.Pounds,W.Saggers, ? , ? .

4 Apr SEL1B Away Boleyn Castle 0 – 4
Romford:
Team details unknown.

16 Apr Frdly Home London Caledonians 6 – 0 A.Jones(4)Fletcher(2)(1pen)
Romford: T.W.Sharpe;P.J.Anderson, ? ;J.B.Hunter,F.Roberts, ? ;
F.L.Fletcher,A.E.Jones, ? ,Merritt, ? .

23 Apr RDL1 Home# South Weald 2 – 0 Fletcher, one (og)
Romford: T.W.Sharpe,P.J.Anderson,Rayner;Robinson, F.Roberts,F.L.Fletcher;
A.E.Jones,L.Pounds,E.Barter,W.Saggers,A.Dennis.

30 Apr SELPO Warley South Weald 2 – 1 Barter,Fletcher
Romford: T.W.Sharpe;P.J.Anderson,A.Reeves;J.B.Hunter,F.Roberts,F.L.Fletcher;
A.E.Jones.L.Pounds,E.Barter,W.Saggers,A.Dennis.

At Brooklands as cricket ground not available.

SUMMARY OF RESULTS OBTAINED SEASON 1903 - 04

					Goals			
	P	W	D	L	For	Ag	Pts	Pos.
South Essex Lge.Div.IB	12	7	1	4	26	20	15	
Sth.Essex Lge. Play-Off	1	1	0	0	2	1		
Romford & Dis.Lge. Div.1	8	7	0	1	24	5*	14	
F.A. Challenge Cup	1	0	0	1	0	5		
Essex Senior Cup	3	2	0	1	10	11		
Friendly Matches	8	7	0	1	34	8		
Total	33	24	1	8	96	50		
A.G.M. Press Report	33	24	1	8	97	55		

* Final League table indicates six goals conceded.

South Essex League Division One B
Final Table

	P	W	D	L	Goals For	Goals Ag	Pts
Southend Athletic	12	8	3	1	29	15	19
Romford	**12**	**7**	**1**	**4**	**26**	**20**	**15**
South Weald	12	6	3	3	23	19	15
Wanstead	12	5	2	5	27	25	12
Barking	12	4	1	7	15	21	9
Boleyn Castle	12	2	4	6	15	22	8
South West Ham**	12	2	2	8	9	22	4

** Two points deducted for breach of Rules.

Romford & District League Division One
Latest available table

	P	W	D	L	Goals For	Goals Ag	Pts
Romford	**8**	**7**	**0**	**1**	**24**	**6**	**14**
South Weald	7	6	0	1	21	6	12
Tilbury	6	3	0	3	17	6	6
Grays Town	7	2	0	5	13	13	4
Romford St. Andrew's	8	0	0	8	2	46	0

The official league table shows that Romford conceded six goals, but actual results of matches obtained shows goals conceded as five.

CUP RESULTS SEASON 1903 – 04

F.A. Challenge Cup

Final: Manchester City 1 Bolton Wanderers 0

Romford's progress: Prel.Round Away Leytonstone 0 – 5

F.A. Amateur Cup

Final: Sheffield 3 Ealing 1

Romford either did not enter or were not accepted for this competition

Essex Senior Cup

Final: Ilford 7 South Weald 0

Romford's progress: 1st Round Home Grays Town 4 – 2
2nd Round Home Barking 5 – 1
3rd Round Away Leyton 1 – 8

West Ham Charity Cup

Winners: Clapton

Romford did not compete

First Team Appearances Season 1903 – 04

P.J.Anderson	20	R.Ball	10	E.Barter	13	H.Biner	8
J.Buddery	2	F.Champness	3	Crudgington	1	V.Davis	9
A.Dennis	26	F.L.Fletcher	26	J.B.Hunter	18	A.E.Jones	25
E.P.Jones	21	W.H.Kelly	1	Merritt	1	Millbank	2
S.Partridge	1	L.Pounds	18	K.Prentise	1	Rayner	1
A.Reeves	17	Reynolds	1	W.Riley	3	F.Roberts	28
Robinson	2	F.Rowe	4	W.Saggers	26	T.W.Sharpe	26
F.Spackman	1					Total	315

Note: Due to a lack of detail in some team line ups, the above record is incomplete but clearly shows the regular members of the team.

First Team Goal Scorers Season 1903 - 04

A.E.Jones	25	W.Saggers	10	E.Barter	7	F.L.Fletcher	7
A.Dennis	5	F.Roberts	4	H.Biner	2	L.Pounds	2
Own Goals	1	Unknown	33			Total	96

Due to the lack of detail in the local press reports such a large number of goal scorers are not known.

RESERVE TEAM

Match Details

3 Oct	RCC1R	Home	Brentwood St. Thomas	1 – 3
14 Nov	EJC1R	Away	Heath Park	1 – 2
	RDL2	Home	Brentwood St. Thomas	2 – 12
	RDL2	Away	Brentwood St. Thomas	0 – 8
	RDL2	Away	Chadwell Heath	0 – 9
	RDL2	Home	Chadwell Heath	2 – 2
	RDL2	Home	Harold Wood	2 – 2
	RDL2	Home	Romford St. Andrew's Reserves	6 – 1
	RDL2	Home	Romford United	2 – 0
	RDL2	Away	Shenfield & Hutton	4 – 2
	RDL2	Away	South Weald Reserves	0 – 2

RESERVE TEAM SUMMARY OF RESULTS OBTAINED SEASON 1903 – 04

					Goals		
	P	W	D	L	For	Ag	Pts
Romford & Dist. League	9	3	2	4	18	38	8
Essex Junior Cup	1	0	0	1	1	2	
Romford Charity Cup	1	0	0	1	1	3	
Total	11	3	2	6	20	43	

Romford & District Football League Division Two

(Up to and including 16th January)

					Goals		
	P	W	D	L	For	Ag	Pts
Brentwood St. Thomas	11	8	2	1			18
Chadwell Heath	9	6	3	0			15
Romford United	9	5	2	2			12
Heath Park	8	6	2	0			14
Romford Alliance	9	6	0	3			12
South Weald Reserves	9	3	5	1			11
Shenfield & Hutton	9	3	3	6			9
Romford Reserves**	**9**	**3**	**2**	**4**	**18**	**38**	**8**
Harold Wood	12	1	1	10			3
St. Andrew's Reserves	11	1	0	10			2

** Romford reserves withdrew from the league after the game played on 16th January.

RESERVE TEAM CUP RESULTS SEASON 1903 – 04

Essex Junior Cup

Final: Chelmsford Arc Works 0 Tilbury 0
Replay: Chelmsford Arc Works 1 Tilbury 0

Romford's progress: 1st Round Away Heath Park 1 – 2

Romford Charity Cup

Final: n/k

Romford's progress: 1st Round Home Brentwood St. Thomas 1 – 3

Post-Season Summary Season 1903 – 04

Romford commenced the season with a friendly match against Forest Gate, played at Brooklands as the cricket ground was not available, and secured a 5-1 win. A week later they were dismissed from the F.A. Cup by a powerful Leytonstone team who won 5-0. Next there was a very unusual occurrence in the Romford & District League fixture against Tilbury. Romford's James B. ('Jimmy') Hunter sent in a long shot and both Saggers and Dennis went hard for goal. Both fell hard into the net, bringing down the upright, which had to be shored up for the game to continue! This didn't stop Romford winning 2-0.

Romford picked up a point from a 3-3 draw away to Barking in the newly-formed South Essex League Division One B, but came unstuck with a four goal to two reverse against Southend Athletic. The next two fixtures were both against Grays Town, and Romford were successful on both occasions. The first game saw the local side progress in the Essex Senior Cup competition by winning four goals to two. In the second round Romford defeated Barking 5-1. During the game Barking's Morgan kicked the ball in 'Diddy' Jones's eye, causing injury.

The following week Romford lost to South Weald in a South Essex League encounter, but 'Diddy' Jones's eyesight may still have been affected, as he missed a penalty which would have earned the team a point. On 28th November in the home friendly against Old Holloway Collegians there were complaints that netting around the pitch had been removed, allowing spectators to encroach. The following week Romford should have played Leyton in the Essex Senior Cup, but the referee was fogbound. Both captains agreed to play a 30 minutes each way friendly match to entertain the 400 crowd and to split the gate receipts.

On 12th December in the Romford & District League Romford defeated Romford St. Andrew's by four goals to one but also had four goals disallowed! A week later, in the 6-2 South Essex League win over South West Ham, Evan Pashley Jones was outstanding. Evan had made his debut a few years previously when Romford were a man short. He was at the ground and was recruited to play but had no kit with him. So he wore his ordinary clothes and played a blinder. (Presumably the missing player still had the his team kit!) Boxing Day brought St Andrew's across town for a friendly which Romford won 3-1.

January was notable as Romford won four out of five league encounters, scoring twenty goals. The only defeat was a 2-0 loss at South Weald. The biggest victory was the home Romford League game against St Andrew's, the homesters winning 8-1. Romford then gained a timely victory over local rivals South Weald by one goal to nil.

The following week Romford were due to play Leyton in the Essex Senior Cup 3rd Round. The Football Association ordered this tie to be played at the County Ground, Leyton, but this ground was unplayable. Romford complained that it should have been played on Romford's pitch, which was in good condition, but to no avail. Two weeks later the game was played at the County Ground, but Romford must have wished it had not been as they were soundly thrashed 8-1!

Romford then went on to have a run of five victories in league and friendly matches. They were then brought down to earth with another defeat from Southend Athletic (in a South Essex League match that drew a record crowd for the Southend club), one goal to nil, and alas 'Diddy' Jones again missed a penalty.

Two days later, on Easter Monday, Romford were well beaten in a South Essex League game away to Boleyn Castle by four goals to nil. A couple of weeks later in a friendly at home to London Caledonians, which Romford won 6-0, they gave Merritt (ex-Clapton Orient) a first game for the club. A week later the Cricket ground was not available for the Romford & District League game against South Weald, and the match was played at Brooklands. Evan Pashley Jones, now approaching 30 years of age, announced his retirement at this game after many years of loyal service to the club, who gave him a good send-off with a two-nil win.

The final game of the season was a South Essex League second place playoff against South Weald which Romford won 2-1. There was an admission charge of sixpence for this match, with each Club and the League taking a one third share each.

The reserve team had a very poor season in league fixtures, suffering several very heavy defeats. They withdrew from the Romford & District League Division Two after the game played on 16th January. They were dismissed from the Essex Junior and Romford Charity Cups by Heath Park and Brentwood St. Thomas respectively.

Thomas William Sharpe, the Romford secretary, was suspended by the County Football Association for a year from 1st June and Mr.E.G.Wallis took over his duties pro. Tem.

Essex County Football Association Executive Meeting (as reported in the *Essex Times,* Saturday 4th June 1904)

On Thursday evening 2nd June, 1904 a meeting of the Executive Committee of the Essex County Football Association was held at the Rising Sun Hotel, Mr.E.Gordon Stuart presiding. The business was to deal with a complaint by the South Essex League with reference to a match between South Weald and Romford on January 30th, and a protest against South Weald on the ground that they had not returned a certain player as having taken part in the match on the ordinary result card. Two points had been deducted from South Weald, and the club had been fined a guinea and censured. The question was considerably involved, and took a long while to investigate.

It was urged that South Weald played J.Harris under a false name, that the player being ineligible at that time; and that F.Wellings, the South Weald secretary, and T.W.Sharpe, the Romford secretary, agreed not to report the matter to the League unless the position of the Romford club ultimately became affected by the result. There were denials that anything improper had been done; it was stated that the return sent in was the selected team. In the end the Committee decided that T.W.Sharpe and F.Wellings should not be allowed to take part in any football or football management for twelve months ending June 1905; that Wellings be not allowed on the ground of the South Weald Club during the same period; that J.Harris be suspended from playing during September 1904; that B.Wellings be censured for the unsatisfactory manner in which he filled up the result card; and that the two clubs jointly pay the expenses of the executive meeting.

Annual General Meeting
(as reported in the *Essex Times,* Wednesday 6th July 1904)

The annual general meeting of the Romford Football Club was held at headquarters, The Coach and Bell Hotel on Friday evening 1st July, Mr. W.D.Matthews presiding over a good attendance. Mr.E.G.Wallis (secretary pro tem) presented his annual report, which was as follows:-

"In presenting the annual report for the past season, the members are to be congratulated on the successful results. The first team played in 33 matches, winning 24, losing 8, 1 drawn, and scoring 97 goals against their opponents 55. The first eleven were entered for the Association and Essex Cups. They were defeated in the first round of the former by Leytonstone and in the third round of the Essex by Leyton. They were also entered for the South Essex and Romford Leagues. In the South Essex, runners up medals were secured, and in the Romford League they tied with South Weald for first place, becoming joint holders of the cup with that team. As regards to the reserves, failure has to be admitted. After every endeavour to keep an eleven running, the Committee were at length compelled to withdraw the Reserves from the Romford League (second division) and to scratch the remaining matches of the season – a result unfortunate in the extreme.

"A new venture by the club last season was the concert held to assist the club funds. It was successful in every way and the sub-committee and others who arranged and worked this concert are to be heartily congratulated on the result of their efforts.

"The club lodged a protest against the South Weald team for playing an illegible man, with the results that South Weald were fined and censured and lost two points. Arising out of this protest, it came to the notice of the League that the then two secretaries of these two clubs had known that this man had been played long before the matter was officially brought forward. The question was referred to the Essex Association, and their decision was that the two secretaries concerned be suspended for twelve months from the 1st June, 1904, from playing or taking any active part in football management.

"The gates showed a marked increase over those of the previous season, and this fact, with the results achieved by the first team, go a long way to prove that the club is speedily working its way back to its old position as one of the best in the county. The matters of the second eleven and late secretary are the only two discordant notes of the season, and on the whole I think it may safely be said that the members of the Romford Football Club are to be congratulated on the results of season 1903 – 04". The Chairman thought the report was very satisfactory, and it was unanimously adopted.

Mr.R.Ball (the treasurer) presented the financial statement, which showed that the club had a balance in hand of £13.14s.5d. (Applause). However, members' subscriptions were £2.10s.0d less than the previous season, but there was an increase in the vice-presidents' subscriptions of £3.1s.6d. He acknowledged the assistance he had received from Messrs. C.Ryle, G.Heron, and T.W.Sharpe. The Chairman said it was a pleasure to hear that the club was once more out of debt, and had a substantial and quite sufficient balance in hand for any amateur club. He congratulated the officers on this satisfactory state of affairs, and moved the adoption of the balance sheet, which was unanimously passed. The Chairman then proposed a vote of thanks to the retiring officers, each of whom deserved their warm thanks. (Applause). This was seconded, and carried with acclamation.

The secretary named 14, and Mr.W.H.Kelly 13 new members, and these with two additions were unanimously elected. Mr.L.Sinclair, M.P., was re-elected president. The Vice-presidents were re-elected, excepting Mr.Hyslop, who had left the neighbourhood, and the following were added:- Lord O'Hagan, The Vicar of Romford (the Rev. R.H.Whitcombe), Messrs. W.Harris, C.E.Sheffield, W.Stevenson, A.Maclaren, and H.L.Pope.

The Chairman stated, as regards the captaincy, Mr.A.E.Jones had expressed his desire not to be re-elected owing to the illness of his father. They all regretted this very much. On the proposition of Mr.W.H.Kelly, seconded by Mr.R.Ball, Mr.Fred. Fletcher was elected captain with enthusiasm. Mr.J.Anderson was unanimously elected vice-captain. The selection of captain and vice-captain of the reserve team was referred to the Committee.

The Chairman said, through very unfortunate circumstances, the club lost Mr. T.W. Sharpe as hon.secretary. He hoped the Essex Association would, after they had a summer's airing, see their way clear to rescind the terrible sentence passed upon him. He (the Chairman) had pleasure in proposing Mr.C.Heard as hon.secretary. This was seconded, and carried unanimously.

Mr.Heard thanked the meeting for the confidence placed in him, and gave the assurance that he would do all he could for the club. Mr.A.J.Dodsworth was elected hon.assistant secretary. Mr.R.Ball was unanimously elected hon.treasurer amid applause. A strong committee was appointed. Mr.H.A. Hants, one of the Executive of the South Essex League, presented medals to the members of last year's team, who were runners up in their division of that League.

Meeting August 1904
(as reported in the *Essex Times*)

The Romford Football Club have decided to re-engage the Cricket Club ground for the coming season, subject to certain terms and conditions, at a cost of £4 in excess of last year's rental. The question of the Brooklands ground has been deferred, the club being unable to agree terms with the tenant. A small sub-committee has been appointed to go round the district with a view to finding a suitable permanent ground for the club to be leased for a certain number of years, as it has become known that the Great Eastern Railway Company will soon require their ground for the extension of the goods sheds.

Several guarantee matches have been arranged by the secretary, Mr.C.T.Heard, and it is also decided to endeavour to arrange fixtures with the Old Carthusians, Old Westminsters, the Casuals, and the Woodford Clubs. Black and blue jerseys are to be obtained for the first team, and the secretary is instructed to obtain estimates of the cost of same. A suggestion has been made that the team make a holiday tour of the Eastern Counties.

Romford withdrew the first team from the Romford and District League Division One and joined the South Essex League once more. The reserves took their place in the Romford and District League Division One. Due to the Cricket Ground being unavailable Romford played the last match of the season on the Heath Park club's ground which was situated opposite the Cricket Ground in Hornchurch Road (now South Street) and known, due to its shape, as the Shoulder of Mutton Ground.

ROMFORD AND DISTRICT LEAGUE DIVISION ONE WINNERS 1903-4

?? Reynolds P.Champness Kyle ??
?? ?? J.Hunter T.Sharp D.Fletcher Anderson
Rogers D.Jones Baxter B.Saggers A.Dennis A.Reeves(Trainer)
Note: The names are as written in pencil on the back of the original photograph
Authors' collection (originators unknown)

It is not known exactly when this picture was taken, but it must have been after the league title was won. The team played only one game after the final Romford & District League match, and the line-up against South Weald was slightly different to the players shown above. The photo may, of course, have been taken in the following season. The player second left front is certainly Arthur E. 'Diddy' Jones, and the goalkeeper Thomas W.Sharpe. It is probable that the player named as Baxter was actually Edgar Barter. No trace has been found of Rogers playing any first team games at all for the club during the season. Could this player be Roberts?

Season 1904 – 05

ROMFORD FOOTBALL CLUB

President: Mr.L.Sinclair.M.P. Mr.C.F.Fitch presided at the A.G.M.

Hon.Secretary: Mr.C.T.Heard (Suspended by Essex County F.A. until 8th Dec). He tendered his resignation as secretary on 28th Nov., but this was not accepted.

Hon.Asst.Secretary: Mr.A.J.Dodsworth **Hon.Treasurer:** Mr.R.Ball

Captain: Mr.Fred.L.Fletcher **Vice-Captain:** J.Anderson

Vice-Presidents: The Vice-Presidents were all re-elected, with the exception of Mr.Hyslop who had left the neighbourhood. The following were added: Lord O'Hagan, Rev.R.H.Whitcombe (Vicar of Romford) Messrs. W.Harris, C.E.Sheffield, W.Stevenson, A.Maclaren and H.L.Pope.

Auditors: Mr.C.J.Wallis and Mr.F.W.Jeffes

Club Colours: Blue and Black Stripes **Headquarters:** Rising Sun Hotel, Romford

Grounds: Cricket Ground, Romford Station Reserve Team: Brooklands, Romford

COMPETITIONS ENTERED

South Essex League Division One
F.A. Challenge Cup
F.A. Amateur Cup
Essex Senior Cup
West Ham Charity Cup

Romford & District League Division One
Essex Junior Cup
Romford Charity Cup

Match Details

3 Sept Frdly Home** New Brompton Amateurs 4 – 2 Fry(2)unknown(2)
Romford: Sandford;P.J.Anderson,Baker;J.B.Hunter,F.L.Fletcher,J.Lovett; F.Roberts,J.Roberts,A.V.Frisby,Fry,A.Dennis.

10 Sept Frdly Home Walthamstow Town 5 – 0 Fry(2)Fletcher(2)Frisby
Romford: Sandford;P.J.Anderson,Field;J.B.Hunter,F.L.Fletcher,Stannard; F.Roberts,F.Champness,A.V.Frisby,Fry,A.Dennis.

17 Sept Frdly Home Shepherds Bush 3 – 1 Fry,Roberts,Dennis
Romford: Sandford;P.J.Anderson,J.B.Hunter;F.L.Fletcher,J.Lovett,Stannard; F.Roberts,A.V.Frisby,Fry,W.Saggers,A.Dennis.

24 Sept SEL1 Away South West Ham 1 – 3 Fry
Romford: J.Runacres;J.B.Hunter,J.Lovett;Stannard,F.L.Fletcher(Capt),L.Pounds; F.Roberts,Fry,E.Barter,A.V.Frisby,A.Dennis.

1 Oct FAC1Q Home Southend Athletic 8 – 0 Fletcher(2)(1pen),Fry(2)Eden(3)Roberts
Romford: McCorkingdale;P.J.Anderson,J.B.Hunter;F.L.Fletcher(Capt),J.Lovett,E.Barter; F.Roberts,A.V.Frisby,Fry,J.Eden,A.Dennis.

8 Oct AC1Q Home Woodford 1 – 1 Dennis
Romford: McCorkingdale; P.J.Anderson,J.B.Hunter;F.L.Fletcher(Capt),J.Lovett,E.Barter; F.Roberts.A.V.Frisby,J.Eden,Fry,A.Dennis.

15 Oct FAC2Q Away Grays United 0 – 3
Romford: McCorkingdale;P.J.Anderson,J.B.Hunter;F.L.Fletcher(Capt),J.Lovett,F.Roberts;
A.V.Frisby,B.G.Aston,J.Eden,E.Barter,A.Dennis.

22 Oct ACRep Away Woodford 0 – 4
Romford: McCorkingdale;P.J.Anderson,J.B.Hunter;F.L.Fletcher(Capt),J.Lovett,E.Barter;
F.Roberts,B.G.Aston,J.Eden,Fry,A.Dennis.

29 Oct WHC1R Home Upton Park 3 – 1 Aston(2)Eden
Romford: McCorkingdale;Starr,J.B.Hunter;J.Lovett,F.Roberts,
Fry,A.V.Frisby,B.G.Aston,J.Eden,A.Dennis.

5 Nov SEL1 Home Barking 5 – 0 Aston(5)
Romford: MacCorkingdale;J.B.Hunter,E.Barter;J.Lovett,F.L.Fletcher(Capt),V.Davis;
A.V.Frisby,A.Dennis,B.G.Aston,F.Roberts,Fry.

12 Nov ESC1R Away Felstead (Custom House) 0 – 1
Romford: McCorkingdale;J.B.Hunter,E.Barter;J.Lovett,F.L.Fletcher(Capt),V.Davis;
A.V.Frisby,A.Dennis,B.G.Aston,F.Roberts,Fry

19 Nov SEL1 Home Chelmsford 8 – 1 Eden(4)Aston(2)Roberts, one o.g.
Romford: MacCorkingdale;J.Wayland,J.B.Hunter;J.Lovett,F.L.Fletcher(Capt),V.Davis;
A.V.Frisby,J.Eden,B.G.Aston,F.Roberts,A.Dennis.

26 Nov Frdly Home Dartford 4 – 1 Roberts,Davis,Lansdale,Eden
Romford: McCorkingdale;J.Wayland,P.J.Anderson;F.L.Fletcher,J.Lovett,V.Davis;
F.Roberts,A.V.Frisby,J.Eden,Lansdale,A.Dennis.

3 Dec Frdly Home Upton Park 0 – 4
Romford: McCorkingdale;P.J.Anderson,J.Wayland;J.B.Hunter,F.L.Fletcher,V.Davis;
F.Roberts,A.V.Frisby,J.Eden,A.Dennis,Fry.

10 Dec SEL1 Away Wanstead 1 – 3 Dennis
Romford: MacCorkingdale;J.B.Hunter,P.J.Anderson;F.L.Fletcher(Capt),J.Lovett,E.Barter;
A.Dennis,J.Eden,B.G.Aston,Fry,F.Roberts.

17 Dec SEL1 Away Leytonstone 1 – 5 Eden
Romford: MacCorkingdale;J.B.Hunter,P.J.Anderson;V.Davis,F.L.Fletcher(Capt),J.Lovett;
A.Dennis,J.Eden,B.G.Aston,F.Roberts,Fry.

24 Dec Frdly Home West Brixton P – P ###

26 Dec Frdly Home Price's Athletic 1 – 1 Frisby
Romford: McCorkingdale;P.J.Anderson,J.B.Hunter;Stanton,J.Lovett,F.L.Fletcher;
A.V.Frisby,B.G.Aston,J.Eden,E.Barter,A.Dennis.

27 Dec Frdly Home Woodford Albion 1 – 0 Fry
Romford: Shepherd;Powter,Bryan;Williams,Peacock,Millbank;
V.Davis,Fry,A.V.Frisby,B.G.Aston,J.Eden.

31 Dec Frdly Home Wanstead 1 – 3 Scorer unknown
Romford:
Fielded a scratch team.

7 Jan SEL1 Home Ilford Alliance 4 – 0 Fletcher(2)Dennis,Aston
Romford: MacCorkingdale; P.J.Anderson,J.Wayland;A.V.Frisby,J.B.Hunter,J.Lovett;
F.L.Fletcher(Capt),Fry,B.G.Aston,J.Eden,A.Dennis.

14 Jan Frdly Home Clapham 0 – 1
Romford: McCorkingdale;P.J.Anderson,J.B.Hunter;V.Davis,J.Lovett,F.L.Fletcher;
F.Roberts,Fry,A.V.Frisby,B.G.Aston,J.Eden.

19 Jan WHC2R Home Leytonstone 3 – 2* A.Jones(3)(1 pen)
Romford:
Team details unknown.

21 Jan SEL1 Home South Weald 3 – 1 Aston,Eden,Dennis
Romford: McCorkingdale;P.J.Anderson,J.B.Hunter;J.Wayland,F.L.Fletcher(Capt),F.Roberts;
Fry,A.V.Frisby,B.G.Aston,J.Eden,A.Dennis.

28 Jan SEL1 Home South West Ham 5 – 1 Dennis(2)Fry(2)Roberts
Romford: McCorkingdale;P.J.Anderson,J.B.Hunter;F.Roberts,A.V.Frisby,F.L.Fletcher(Capt);
J.Lovett,Fry,B.G.Aston,J.Eden,A.Dennis.

4 Feb Frdly Home Croydon Wanderers 6 – 0 Aston(2)Roberts(2)Fry,Eales
Romford: McCorkingdale;P.J.Anderson,J.B.Hunter;A.Reeves,F.L.Fletcher,F.Roberts;
Fry,A.V.Frisby,B.G.Aston,Eales,A.Dennis.

11 Feb SEL1 Away Barking 0 – 0
Romford: McCorkingdale;J.B.Hunter,J.Lovett;A.V.Frisby,F.L.Fletcher(Capt),V.Davis;
F.Roberts,B.G.Aston,Fry,J.Eden,A.Dennis.

16 Feb WHCSF Home Woodford 4 – 2 Aston(3)(1 pen),A.Jones
Romford: B.Goodman;P.J.Anderson,J.B.Hunter;J.Lovett,F.L.Fletcher,F.Roberts;
A.E.Jones,A.V.Frisby,B.G.Aston,J.Eden,J.Miller.

18 Feb SEL1 Home Southend Athletic 0 – 1
Romford: McCorkingdale;P.J.Anderson,V.Davis;J.Lovett,F.L.Fletcher(Capt),F.Roberts;
A.Hyett,A.V.Frisby,Fry,B.G.Aston,J.Eden.

25 Feb Frdly Home Civil Service 2 – 0 Aston,Hyett
Romford: McCorkingdale;P.J.Anderson,J.B.Hunter;A.V.Frisby,F.L.Fletcher,J.Lovett;
Pates,F.Roberts,B.G.Aston,J.Eden,A.Hyett.

4 Mar SEL1 Away Wanstead 1 – 2 Dennis
Romford: McCorkingdale;P.J.Anderson,J.B.Hunter;J.Lovett,F.L.Fletcher(Capt),A.V.Frisby;
A.Dennis,J.Eden,B.G.Aston,Pates,E.Barter.

11 Mar Frdly Home The War Office 2 – 1 Dennis,Aston
Romford: McCorkingdale;P.J.Anderson,V.Davis;A.V.Frisby,F.L.Fletcher, ? ;
F.Roberts,B.G.Aston,E.Barter,J.Eden,A.Dennis.

18 Mar SEL1 Away South Weald 2 – 4 A.Jones(2)
Attendance: 800
Romford: V.Davis;P.J.Anderson,E.Barter;J.Lovett,Milbank,F.Roberts;
A.V.Frisby,A.E.Jones,J.Eden,B.G.Aston,A.Dennis.

25 Mar SEL1 Home Leytonstone 1 – 1 Aston
Romford: McCorkingdale;P.J.Anderson, J.B.Hunter;A.V.Frisby,F.L.Fletcher(Capt),J.Lovett;
F.Roberts,B.G.Aston,E.Barter,Pates,A.Dennis.

1 Apr WHCF Away Clapton 2 – 0 Aston,Dennis
Attendance: 3,000
Romford: B.Goodman;P.J.Anderson,J.B.Hunter; ? ,F.L.Fletcher,E.Barter;
A.E.Jones,B.G.Aston,J.Eden, ? ,A.Dennis.

8 Apr SEL1 Away## Ilford Alliance 2 – 1 Hunter(pen)Milbank
Romford: McCorkingdale;P.J.Anderson,Hughes;E.Barter,J.B.Hunter,A.V.Frisby;
J.Lovett,Burrell,Milbank,J.Eden,A.Dennis.

15 Apr SEL1 Away Chelmsford 2 – 2 A.Jones,Aston
Romford: McCorkingdale;P.J.Anderson,J.B.Hunter;J.Lovett,F.L.Fletcher(Capt),A.V.Frisby;
E.Barter,A.E.Jones,B.G.Aston,J.Eden,A.Dennis.

22 Apr SEL1 Away Southend Athletic 1 – 0 A.Jones
Attendance: 2,000
Romford: McCorkingdale;J.Wayland,Burrell;P.J.Anderson,J.B.Hunter,J.Lovett;
E.Barter,A.V.Frisby,A.E.Jones,B.G.Aston,A.Dennis.

24 Apr Frdly Away Guildford 1 – 2 Scorer unknown
Romford: McCorkingdale;P.J.Anderson,J.B.Hunter;J.Lovett,F.L.Fletcher,A.V.Frisby;
Fry,Burrell,B.G.Aston,V.Davis,A.Dennis.

* After extra time.
** Played at Brooklands as the Cricket ground was not available.

West Brixton sent a wire to say they were fogbound.
Played at Heath Park as the Ilford Alliance ground was not available.
West Brixton fogbound and match postponed.

SUMMARY OF RESULTS OBTAINED SEASON 1904 – 05

					Goals		
	P	W	D	L	For	Ag	Pts
F.A. Challenge Cup	2	1	0	1	8	3	
F.A. Amateur Cup	2	0	1	1	1	5	
South Essex League	16	7	3	6	37	25	17
Essex Senior Cup	1	0	0	1	0	1	
West Ham Charity Cup	4	4	0	0	12	5	
Friendly Matches	13	8	1	4	30	16	
Total	38	20	5	13	88	55	
AGM Press Report	39	20	5	14	90	58	

South Essex League Division One

Final Table

					Goals		
	P	W	D	L	For	Ag	Pts
Southend Athletic	16	10	5	1	40	13	25
Wanstead	16	10	5	1	41	20	25
Leytonstone	16	8	3	5	35	17	19
South Weald	16	9	1	6	34	25	19
Romford	**16**	**7**	**3**	**6**	**37**	**25**	**17**
South West Ham	16	5	4	7	33	37	14
Barking	16	4	5	7	21	30	13
Chelmsford	16	3	3	10	23	60	9
Ilford Alliance	16	0	3	13	14	53	3

Southend Athletic beat Wanstead 1 – 0 in the championship play-off.

First Team Appearances Season 1904 – 05

P.J.Anderson	29	B.G.Aston	27	Baker	1	E.Barter	17
Bryan	1	Burrell	3	F.Champness	1	V.Davis	13
A.Dennis	31	Eales	1	J.Eden	26	Field	1
F.L.Fletcher	31	A.V.Frisby	32	Fry	22	B.Goodman	2
Hughes	1	J.B.Hunter	31	A.S.Hyett	2	A.E.Jones	5
Lansdale	1	J.Lovett	29	McCorkingdale	28	Milbank	3
Miller	1	Pates	3	Peacock	1	L.Pounds	1
Powter	1	A.Reeves	1	F.Roberts	27	J.Roberts	1
Runacres	1	W.Saggers	1	Sandford	3	Shepherd	1
Stannard	3	Stanton	1	Starr	1	Wayland	6
Williams	1					Total	392

First Team Goal Scorers Season 1904 – 05

B.G.Aston	21	Fry	12	J.Eden	11	A.Dennis	10
A.E.Jones	8	F.Roberts	7	F.L.Fletcher	6	A.V.Frisby	2
V.Davis	1	Lansdale	1	Eales	1	A.S.Hyett	1
Millbank	1	J.B.Hunter	1	Own Goals	1	Unknown	4
Total	88						

CUP RESULTS SEASON 1904 – 05

F.A. Challenge Cup

Final: Aston Villa 2 Newcastle United 0

Romford's progress: 1st Qual Home Southend Athletic 8 – 0
2nd Qual Away Grays United 0 – 3

F.A. Amateur Cup

Final: West Hartlepool 3 Clapton 2

Romford's progress: 1st Qual Home Woodford 1 – 1
Replay Away Woodford 0 – 4

Essex Senior Cup

Final: Leytonstone 3 Chelmsford 1

Romford's progress: 1st Round Away Felstead (Custom House) 0 – 1

West Ham Charity Cup

Final: Clapton 0 Romford 2

Romford's progress: 1st Round Home Upton Park 3 – 1
2nd Round Home Leytonstone 3 – 2
Semi-Final Home Woodford 4 – 2
Final Away Clapton 2 – 0

The Old "Spotted Dog," Upton.

From the Essex Times (Wilson and Whitworth, Publishers)

THE WEST HAM CHARITY CUP COMES TO ROMFORD

Romford defeated the powerful Clapton team at their Spotted Dog ground to bring the much-coveted West Ham Charity Cup back to the market town. During the evening players were seen in local hostelries drinking from the magnificent trophy.

RESERVE TEAM

Match Details

17 Oct	Frdly	Away	Dagenham St. Paul's	1 – 3
*	Frdly	Home	Heath Park	1 – 3
*	RDL1	Home	Brentwood St.Thomas	n/k
*	RDL1	Away	Brentwood St.Thomas	n/k
*	RDL1	Home	Chadwell Heath	1 – 6
*	RDL1	Away	Chadwell Heath	n/k
*	RDL1	Home	Heath Park	0 – 4
Romford: Anderson in goal; Starr,Williams,Kittle.				
*	RDL1	Away	Heath Park	1 – 3
*	RDL1	Home	Little Heath	n/k
*	RDL1	Away	Little Heath	n/k
*	RDL1	Home	Romford United	3 – 0
*	RDL1	Away	Romford United	3 – 2
*	RDL1	Home	Tilbury	n/k
*	RDL1	Away	Tilbury	0 – 4
*	EJC1R			Bye
*	EJC2R	Away	Cranbrook Park	2 – 6
*	RCC1R	Home	Little Heath	3 – 3*
*	RCCRep	Away	Little Heath	Lost

* Dates of matches unknown.

SUMMARY OF RESERVE TEAM RESULTS SEASON 1904 – 05

					Goals	
	P	W	D	L	For	Ag
Romford & Dist. League	11	2	2	7		
Essex Junior Cup	1	0	0	1	2	6
Romford Charity Cup	2	0	1	1	3	3
Total	14	2	3	9		

Note: Due to the large number of unknown results a comprehensive summary cannot be produced

Romford & District Football League Division I

Latest available league table

					Goals		
	P	W	D	L	For	Ag	Pts
Chadwell Heath	10	7	1	2			15
Heath Park	9	6	2	1			14
Tilbury	7	6	1	0			13
Brentwood St.Thomas	8	4	2	2			10
Romford Reserves	**11**	**2**	**2**	**7**			**6**
Little Heath	8	3	0	5			6
Romford United	10	0	0	10			0

RESERVE TEAM CUP RESULTS

Essex Junior Cup

Final: Leigh Ramblers 4 Braintree Manor Works 1

Romford's progress:	1st Round			Bye
	2nd Round	Away	Cranbrook Park	2 – 6

Romford Charity Cup

Final: n/k

Romford's progress:	1st Round	Home	Little Heath	3 – 3*
	Replay	Away	Little Heath	Lost

* After Extra Time

Post-Season Summary Season 1904 – 05

On 7th July 1904, Mr. Evan Jones, father of Arthur 'Diddy' and Evan Pashley Jones, died at the age of 67. He was a keen sportsman and excelled at cricket, being known as 'Romford's Grace'. He never wore pads and was never known to be out leg before wicket!

On Saturday 26th August 1904 it was reported in the *Essex Times* that 'Footballers will note with satisfaction that the Romford club has entered in the London Senior Cup Competition'. No trace has been found of any games having been played by Romford in this competition, other than the controversy relating to the Union Club during the 1880's.

As usual, the Cricket Ground was not available for the opening friendly match, and Romford defeated New Brompton Amateurs by four goals to two at Brooklands. A week later, back where they belonged on the Cricket Ground, Romford celebrated with an outstanding 5-0 victory against Walthamstow Town, and followed with a three goal to one win against Shepherd's Bush, both friendly matches.

The first league encounter was away to South West Ham, where Romford lost by three goals to one. This was followed by a resounding eight goals to nil victory over old friends Southend Athletic in the F.A. Cup. In this tie Romford full back P.J. Anderson kicked the ball out of the ground into a passing laundry van which disappeared down the road. It is not known whether the ball was ever recovered!

Romford next drew one all with Woodford in the Amateur Cup, but were eliminated from the F.A. Cup a week later by Grays United, and then lost the replay against Woodford by four goals to nil. Cup success came a week later when they defeated Upton Park in the first round of the West Ham Charity Cup. On November 5th, fireworks! Romford defeated Barking in a league game by five goals to nil, with B.G. Aston netting all five goals.

A week later, Romford were out of the Essex Senior Cup due to a 1-0 defeat away to Felstead of Custom House. Romford were stung by these top cup exits and took their revenge on local rivals Chelmsford with an eight goal to one hiding in a league game.

A couple of friendly matches followed, and between the two games Charles T. Heard tendered his resignation as secretary at the Committee Meeting on Monday, 28th November, owing to his having brought 'disgrace' on the club by causing as alleged the recent suspension of Aston and himself. However, this was not accepted by the Committee. Then followed two successive league defeats at the hands of Wanstead and Leytonstone.

The following week Romford were due to play a home friendly against West Brixton, but their opponents sent a 'wire' to say that they were fog-bound. The match was postponed, and Romford supporters left the ground very disappointed. On the last day of the year Romford, fielding a scratch team, were beaten by Wanstead by three goals to one in a friendly match.

Romford opened the New Year with an outstanding 4-0 home league victory against Ilford Alliance, and a week later lost to Clapham in a home friendly. On 19th January they beat Leytonstone by three goals to two after extra time in the second round of the West Ham Charity Cup. 'Diddy' Jones netted a hat-trick, including one goal from the penalty spot. On the 21st January Romford beat South Weald 3-1 in the South Essex League. They then defeated South West Ham and drew with Barking in league games, before beating Woodford by four goals to two in the semi-final of the West Ham Charity Cup.

Three successive league defeats followed before Romford picked up a point in a one all draw against Leytonstone. In the middle of these games Romford's Dennis scored straight from the kick-off in a South Essex League game against Wanstead, but they were defeated by two goals to one.

On 1st April Romford picked up the handsome West Ham Charity Cup by defeating Clapton at the Spotted Dog ground in the final tie. Unfortunately for Clapton, Gilbert Farnfield broke his leg in the first minute and they played the remaining 89 minutes with only ten men. Romford then defeated Ilford Alliance at Heath Park, drew with Chelmsford and beat Southend Athletic 1-0 in their final South Essex league games. The team ended their long season with a two goal to one loss away to Guildford in a friendly match.

At the Annual General Meeting, held on 18th May it was stated that 'As regarded the second eleven, they had failed lamentably, and the less said about them the better'. Only six league results have been traced for the reserve team, and in view of the above quote it is not surprising that all results were not published. Suffice to say that the League table indicates that a further five games were played, of which two were drawn and three were lost, and the final match may not have been played. In view of the comments made at the A.G.M. regarding the reserve team difficulties, it is surprising that the committee eventually agreed to run a reserve team for 1905-06.

Annual General Meeting
(as reported in the *Essex Times,* Saturday 20th May 1905)

The annual general meeting of the Romford Football Club took place at the Sun Hotel on Thursday evening 18th May, Mr.C.F.Fitch presiding over a large attendance. Others also present included Messrs. C.T.Heard (hon.secretary), R.Ball (hon.treasurer), W.D.Matthews, S.Stebbings, A.Turvey, F.Roberts, W.R.Carter, L.Green, C.A.Wilson, Evan Jones, H.W.Wilson, W.Powter, J.Anderson, E.Barter, F.Fletcher, W.H.Kelly, J.Hunter, W.Simmons, C.Ryle, E.J.Wallis, Smith, Hale, V.Davis, C.Spencer, and Fry.

Mr.Heard said he had great pleasure in submitting his first report. The first eleven had played 39 games, won 20, lost 14, and drawn 5. The goals for numbered 90, and those against 58. (Applause). They secured fifth position in the South Essex League, and won the West Ham Charity Cup.

He thought that was satisfactory considering the strength of the opposition, but there might be some of the members who might think they ought to have done better. He could assure them they would have done so if accidents had not intervened, but he was pleased to say they made amends for their shortcomings in the league tourney by winning the West Ham Charity Cup, which came as a great surprise to the football community. In securing that trophy the team created a record in the annals of Romford football. The splendid performance they achieved in attaining that trophy spoke for themselves, and it would be as well if he repeated them. They defeated Upton Park at Romford 3-1; Leytonstone at Leytonstone, 3-2; Woodford at Woodford 4-2; and last, but not least, they had the audacity to knock out Clapton on their own ground by 2-0.

In the Football Association Cup they had but a very short career, being defeated in the second round by a professional club, Grays United, at Grays by 2-0. They did not cover themselves with glory in the Amateur Cup, as they were defeated by Woodford at the memorial Ground, Canning Town, by 4-0, after a drawn game at Romford. In the County Cup Competition they received the coup de grace at the hands of Felstead (Custom House), in the first round, by 1-0.

Their team when at full strength, had proved themselves a very capable lot, and their best thanks were due to them for the admirable way in which they had upheld the prestige of the club, especially McCorkingdale, who had proved a very capable custodian; also to captain Freddie Fletcher, who had done his work admirably as a player and also officially. B.G.Aston had proved himself to be the best shot in the team – (hear, hear) - by scoring 23 goals, which was a very good record. (Applause). He was very pleased to say their team had proved themselves thorough sportsmen and men of principle.

As regarded the second eleven, they had failed lamentably, and the less said about them the better. He would like to take that opportunity of thanking Messrs. Champness, Williams, Burrell, and Milbank for their services in such trying times. In conclusion, Mr. Heard thanked the committee for the very excellent service he had received at their hands. The Chairman thought that was a very satisfactory report.

Mr.Ball presented his financial statement, which showed that while the receipts had gone up something like £75, there had also been increased expenditure. The receipts totalled £212.13s.6d., and the balance in hand was one of £15.10s.11d. There were several small accounts to be paid, but he had no doubt when some little items in the way of receipts had come in, they would finish up with a balance on the right side. He thought, as the club was getting so large, they might appoint a kind of Finance Committee to control the expenses during the season. It would be a great help in bringing them out on the right side. The report and balance sheet were adopted.

The Chairman said he thought the secretary's and treasurer's reports, after the meeting he had the honour to preside over a fortnight ago, when he heard an account of their doings – eminently satisfactory. They had met that night for the purpose of electing officers, and also new members.

After the successful record of last year, it was highly probable that they would have some strong challenges. The club was on the upward bound. It had surprised itself, and might have surprised several clubs in the county and put them on their mettle. He, therefore, thought it behove them to strengthen their team in every way, so as to be in readiness to meet any challenges which might be extended to them. He thought the team had been well managed by Captain Freddie Fletcher. There did not appear to be any suggestion of a second eleven. He heard from their secretary that they were not up to the mark. If they could have a second eleven, to feed their team, it would be as well, and the more money there would be in the way of subscriptions.

He saw they had gone to an expense of £70 to £80 over travelling expenses but he did not think that a very big item for a club like that. They must be prepared to keep up their record. They would thus excite greater interest in the town and get better gates. The financial work in connection with a club like that was no small thing, and, considering the secretary and treasurer were both honorary officers, it would be as well if two or three members were appointed to form a Financial Committee and help in the detail work.

With regard to the receipts, they appeared to be very much larger. Last year their gate money amounted to £107, and that year it reached £158. They had made greater stridesthat year than in the previous twelve months, and probably the interest excited in town would bring bigger gates, but he was pleased to see they had a surplus to hand, and he must congratulate the secretary and treasurer and all of them upon such a winding up. He should like to see more playing members. There were many young fellows, sound in wind and limb, who only watched the game.

The following new members were elected: Messrs. W.A.Smith, C.Spencer, H.W.Wilson, J.W.Braund, H.Brooks, A.Pay, W.H.Kelly, H.J.Merrick, T.A. Herbertson, C.Rudkin, H.D.Warner, E.Corrin, L.M.Wells, J.J.Danby, H.Carter, and C.Pitt.

On the proposition of Mr. Anderson, seconded by Mr. Barter, Mr. Fitch was unanimously elected president of the club. The Chairman said he was very much obliged to them for the honour they had conferred upon him. If he had known he would not have offered to take the chair. It had not given him a moment to consider the matter, although, of course, he took a very deep interest in the club. But there were other vice-presidents, and he hardly knew what to say. If they desired that he should occupy the position he would do his best to fill it. (Applause).

The vice-presidents, with certain alterations, were re-elected, and the following were added to the list:- Lord.O'Hagan, Sir Montague Turner, Mr.F.Mullis, Dr.Upwood, Mr. D.S.L.Archibald, Mr.Frederick Wilson, Mr.A.Barber, Mr.A.A. Tween, the Rev. Woodman, Col.Woodforde Finden, Mr.Causton, Mr.F.Bassett, and Mr.S.Simonds.

The chairman observed that the major part of the work and responsibility devolved upon the secretary, and it was now their duty to appoint one. He need hardly say anything with regard to their late secretary, because they knew how well he had served them. Mr.Matthews said he had the honour last year of proposing Mr.Heard, and anyone who knew what he had done would congratulate the club upon its choice. He proposed that Mr.Heard should be asked to again fill the office. Mr.Ball seconded the motion, which was cordially received, and Mr.Heard said after their kind remarks he could not but accept the post.

The Chairman said their treasurer had conducted the financial business in an admirable manner. He proposed the re-election of Mr.Ball. Mr.Anderson seconded. Mr.Carter and Mr.Matthews were proposed for the position, and the former remarked that when they had such a good man as Mr.Ball he thought they should keep him. Mr.Ball said he did not think he could again undertake the duties; he had not the time to give to the work.

Mr.Matthews supported the election of Mr.Carter. The chairman was sure they all regretted very much that Mr.Ball had resigned the treasurership. He had given evidence of ability to manage the finances of the club. He knew Mr.Carter personally, and had no doubt they would find him a worthy successor to Mr.Ball. Mr.Carter was elected to the position, and said he would do his best for the club.

Mr.Kelly proposed Mr.Anderson for the post of captain. Mr.Heard thought, after the services they had received from Mr. Fletcher, they could not do better than give that gentleman another run. (Hear,hear). Mr. Anderson remarked that he should very much like to see their captain in his old place. He withdrew. Mr.Fletcher was then voted to the position, and, in reply, said he hoped they would have two cups next year. (Applause). In proposing Mr.Anderson as vice-captain, Mr.Matthews said last year he and the captain worked very amicably together. The proposition was heartily carried.

An 1890s photograph of the Victoria Cottage Hospital, Romford, which received the proceeds of the Romford Charity Cup
Havering Libraries - Local Studies

Season 1905 – 6

ROMFORD FOOTBALL CLUB

President: Mr.C.F.Fitch.C.C. **Hon.Secretary:** Mr.C.T.Heard **Hon.Treasurer:** Mr.R.Ball

Hon.Asst.Secretary: Mr.H.J.Merrick (Resigned in August and replaced by Mr.W.H.Kelly)

Captain: F.L.Fletcher **Vice-Captain:** Mr.J.Anderson

Committee: Messrs. E.Barter, Evan Jones, J.Hunter, C.Wilson W.H.Kelly, A.Parrish
H.Webb, H.J.Merrick, F.Roberts, N.Davey, L.Green, V.Davis

Auditors: Mr.C.J.Wallis and Mr.F.W.Jeffes **Club Colours:** Blue and Black Stripes

Headquarters: Rising Sun Hotel, Romford **Ground:** Cricket Ground, Romford Station

COMPETITIONS ENTERED

South Essex League Division One
F.A. Challenge Cup
F.A. Amateur Cup
Essex Senior Cup
West Ham Charity Cup

Romford & District League Division One
Essex Junior Cup

Match Details

2 Sept Frdly Away Leytonstone 1 – 2 Aston
Romford: B.Goodman;Barter.Jnr.,J.B.Hunter;F.L.Fletcher(Capt),E.Barter,E.Doy;
J.Lovett,A.Miller,B.G.Aston,A.S.Hyett,A.Dennis.

9 Sept Frdly Home Grenadier Guards 3 – 0 Miller(2),plus one unknown
Romford: B.Goodman;J.W.Wayland,J.B.Hunter;F.L.Fletcher(Capt),A.V.Frisby,E.Barter;
E.Doy,A.E.Jones,A.Miller,B.G.Aston,A.S.Hyett.

16 Sept Frdly Home 3rd Kent RGA 3 – 0 Jones(2)Howes
Romford: B.Goodman;J.W.Wayland,Pearson;Howes,A.V.Frisby,J.Lovett;
A.E.Jones,A.Miller,B.G.Aston,H.Hughes,W.Church.

23 Sept Frdly Home Hampstead 4 – 1 Jones(2)Aston(2)
Romford: B.Goodman;P.J.Anderson,J.B.Hunter;L.R.Day,F.L.Fletcher(Capt),A.V.Frisby;
A.E.Jones,A.Miller,B.G.Aston,A.S.Hyett,W.Church.

30 Sept Frdly Home Wanstead 2 – 2 Scorers unknown
Romford: B.Goodman;P.J.Anderson,J.W.Wayland;Venner,F.L.Fletcher(Capt),J.Lovett;
Pearson,A.Miller,B.G.Aston,A.S.Hyett,W.Church.

7 Oct FAC1Q Home Enfield 4 – 1 Hyett,Eden,Jones(2)
Attendance: 1,500
Romford: B.Goodman;P.J.Anderson,J.B.Hunter;A.V.Frisby,F.L.Fletcher(Capt),J.Lovett;
A.E.Jones,A.S.Hyett,B.G.Aston,J.Eden,W.Church.

14 Oct AC1Q Away Chelmsford 3 – 2 Jones(2)Fletcher
Romford: B.Goodman;P.J.Anderson,J.B.Hunter;A.V.Frisby,F.L.Fletcher(Capt),J.Lovett;
A.S.Hyett,A.E.Jones,B.G.Aston,J.Eden,W.Church.

21 Oct SEL1 Home Southend Athletic 0 – 0
Romford: B.Goodman,P.J.Anderson,J.B.Hunter,A.V.Frisby,F.L.Fletcher(Capt),J.Lovett,
E.Barter,A.E.Jones,J.Eden,H.Hughes,A.S.Hyett.

28 Oct FAC2Q Home Wanstead 2 – 1 Aston(2)
Romford: B.Goodman;P.J.Anderson,J.B.Hunter;A.V.Frisby,F.L.Fletcher(Capt),J.Lovett;
A.S.Hyett,A.E.Jones,B.G.Aston,J.Eden,W.Church.

4 Nov AC2Q Home Harwich & Parkeston 6 – 0 Jones(2)Aston,Eden,Frisby,Hyett
Attendance: 800
Romford: B.Goodman;H.Hughes,J.B.Hunter;A.V.Frisby,F.L.Fletcher(Capt),J.Lovett;
A.S.Hyett,A.E.Jones,B.G.Aston,J.Eden,W.Church.

11 Nov ESC1R Home Felstead (Custom House) 5 – 1 Aston(2)A.Jones,Eden,Hyett
Romford: B.Goodman;P.J.Anderson,J.B.Hunter;F.L.Fletcher(Capt),J.Lovett,A.V.Frisby;
A.S.Hyett,A.E.Jones,B.G.Aston,J.Eden,W.Church.

18 Nov FAC3Q Home South Weald 0 – 1
Attendance: 2,000
Romford: B.Goodman;P.J.Anderson,J.B.Hunter;A.V.Frisby,F.L.Fletcher(Capt),J.Lovett;
A.S.Hyett,A.E.Jones,B.G.Aston,J.Eden,W.Church.

25 Nov AC3Q Home South Weald 2 – 1 Aston,Eden
Attendance: 2,000
Romford: B.Goodman;P.J.Anderson,J.B.Hunter;E.Barter,F.L.Fletcher(Capt),J.Lovett;
A.S.Hyett,A.E.Jones,B.G.Aston,J.Eden,W.Church.

2 Dec ESC2R Home Southend Athletic 2 – 0 Aston,Eden
Attendance: 1,000
Romford: B.Goodman;P.J.Anderson,J.B.Hunter;A.V.Frisby,F.L.Fletcher(Capt),J.Lovett;
A.S.Hyett,A.E.Jones,B.G.Aston,J.Eden,W.Church.

9 Dec Frdly Home Croydon Wanderers 3 – 2 Eden(2)Barter
Attendance: 400
Romford: B.Goodman;P.J.Anderson,J.B.Hunter;A.V.Frisby,F.L.Fletcher(Capt),E.Barter;
A.E.Jones,J.Eden,B.G.Aston,A.S.Hyett,Colebatch.

16 Dec AC4Q Away King's Lynn 1 – 1 Jones
Romford: B.Goodman;P.J.Anderson,J.B.Hunter;A.V.Frisby,F.L.Fletcher(Capt),J.Lovett;
A.S.Hyett,A.E.Jones,B.G.Aston,J.Eden,W.Church.

23 Dec ACRep Home King's Lynn 3 – 1 Hyett(2),Jones
Attendance: 1,600
Romford: B.Goodman;P.J.Anderson,J.W.Wayland;A.V.Frisby,F.L.Fletcher(Capt),E.Barter;
A.S.Hyett,A.E.Jones,B.G.Aston,J.Eden,W.Church.

26 Dec Frdly Home Luton Clarence 2 – 1 Jones(2)
Romford:
Team details unknown

30 Dec SEL1 Home Woodford 2 – 1 Hyett,Jones
Romford: B.Goodman,P.J.Anderson,J.B.Hunter,A.V.Frisby,Biddell,EdgarBarter;
A.S.Hyett,A.E.Jones,J.Eden,B.G.Aston,W.Church.

6 Jan ESC3R Away Leytonstone (holders) 3 – 0 Jones(pen)Aston(2)(1pen)
Romford: B.Goodman;P.J.Anderson,J.B.Hunter;A.V.Frisby,F.L.Fletcher(Capt),E.Barter;
A.S.Hyett,A.E.Jones,B.G.Aston,J.Eden,W.Church.

13 Jan SEL1 Home Chelmsford 5 – 2 Jones(4)Aston
Romford: B.Goodman,P.J.Anderson,J.B.Hunter,J.Lovett,F.L.Fletcher(Capt),E.Barter,
A.E.Jones,J.Eden,B.G.Aston,A.S.Hyett,W.Church.

20 Jan AC1R Home Ipswich Town 4 – 2 Eden(2)Aston,Hyett
Romford: B.Goodman;P.J.Anderson,J.B.Hunter;A.V.Frisby,F.L.Fletcher(Capt),E.Barter;
A.S.Hyett,A.E.Jones,B.G.Aston,J.Eden,W.Church.

27 Jan SEL1 Away Woodford P – P Flooded pitch

3 Feb SEL1 Home Barking 1 – 0 Fletcher
Attendance: 700
Romford: B.Goodman,P.J.Anderson,J.B.Hunter,J.Lovett,F.L.Fletcher(Capt),E.Barter,
W.Church,A.V.Frisby,B.G.Aston,Griffiths,A.S.Hyett.

10 Feb AC2R Home Eastbourne 6 – 3 Aston(4)Jones,Church
Attendance: 1,800
Romford: B.Goodman;P.J.Anderson,J.B.Hunter;A.V.Frisby,F.L.Fletcher(Capt),J.Lovett;
A.S.Hyett,A.E.Jones,B.G.Aston,E.Barter,W.Church.

17 Feb ESC4R Away Barking 3 – 0 Aston(2)Dennis
Romford: B.Goodman;,P.J.Anderson,J.B.Hunter;A.V.Frisby,F.L.Fletcher(Capt),J.Lovett;
A.S.Hyett;E.Barter, J.Eden,B.G.Aston,A.Dennis.

24 Feb AC3R Home New Crusaders 0 – 0*
Attendance: 3,336 Record attendance with receipts of £75.
Romford: B.Goodman;P.J.Anderson,J.B.Hunter;A.V.Frisby,F.L.Fletcher(Capt),J.Lovett;
A.S.Hyett,A.E.Jones,B.G.Aston,J.Eden,W.Church.

3 Mar ACRep Away New Crusaders 1 – 1* Church
Attendance: 3,000
Romford: B.Goodman;P.J.Anderson,J.B.Hunter;A.V.Frisby,F.L.Fletcher(Capt),J.Lovett;
A.S.Hyett,A.E.Jones,B.G.Aston,J.Eden,W.Church.

7 Mar ACRep Neut.# New Crusaders 1 – 4 Aston
Attendance: 5,000
Romford:
Team details unknown

10 Mar Frdly Home Upton Park 2 – 2 Scorers unknown
Romford:
Team details unknown

15 Mar WHCSF Home Wanstead 1 – 1 Scorer unknown
Romford:
Team details unknown

17 Mar SEL1 Home Wanstead 0 – 3
Romford: B.Goodman,P.J.Anderson,J.B.Hunter,J.Lovett,Griffiths,E.Barter,
W.Church,J.Eden,B.G.Aston,A.S.Hyett,A.E.Jones.

22 Mar WHCRp Neut## Wanstead 0 – 1
Romford:
Team details unknown

24 Mar ESCSF Neut## South Weald 0 – 2
Attendance: 2,000
Romford: B.Goodman;P.J.Anderson,J.B.Hunter;J.Lovett;G.T.Mason,A.V.Frisby;
A.E.Jones,Plested,B.G.Aston,A.S.Hyett,W.Church.

31 Mar SEL1 Home South Weald 1 – 2 Frisby
Romford: B.Goodman,P.J.Anderson,J.B.Hunter,J.Lovett,Lewis,A.V.Frisby;
A.S.Hyett,A.Miller,W.Church,J.Eden,Powell.

7 Apr SEL1 Away Woodford 2 – 6 Hyett,Eden
Romford: B.Goodman,P.J.Anderson,J.B.Hunter,J.Lovett,Lewis,A.V.Frisby,
A.S.Hyett,A.Miller,W.Church,J.Eden,Powell.

13 Apr SEL1 Away Barking 0 – 1
Attendance: 500
Romford:
Team details not available, and with virtually a reserve side Romford put up a spirited performance.

14 Apr SEL1 Away Southend Athletic 0 – 2
Romford: B.Goodman,P.J.Anderson,J.B.Hunter,J.Lovett,Lewis,A.V.Frisby,
A.S.Hyett,A.Miller,W.Church,J.Eden,Powell.

16 Apr SEL1 Away Chelmsford 1 – 1 Scorer unknown
Romford:
Team details unknown.

19 Apr SEL1 Away South Weald 0 – 1
Romford:
Team details unknown, but comprised of reserve team players.

21 Apr SEL1 Away Wanstead 0 – 3
Romford: B.Goodman,P.J.Anderson,A.S.Hyett,Powell plus seven reserve team players.

* After extra time
\# At Stamford Bridge
\#\# At Spotted Dog Ground, Clapton.

SUMMARY OF FIRST TEAM RESULTS OBTAINED SEASON 1905 – 06

					Goals		
	P	W	D	L	For	Ag	Pts
South Essex League	12	3	2	7	12	22	8
F.A. Challenge Cup	3	2	0	1	6	3	
F.A. Amateur Cup	10	6	3	1	27	15	
Essex Senior Cup	5	4	0	1	13	3	
West Ham Charity Cup	2	0	1	1	1	2	
Friendly matches	8	5	2	1	20	10	
Total	40	20	8	12	79	55	
AGM Press Report	40	20	8	12	79	55	

South Essex League Division One
Final Table

					Goals		
	P	W	D	L	For	Ag	Pts
South Weald	12	9	1	2	30	10	19
Wanstead	12	7	2	3	33	10	16
Southend Athletic	12	7	2	3	17	11	16
Barking	12	5	3	4	17	16	13
Romford	**12**	**3**	**2**	**7**	**12**	**22**	**8**
Chelmsford	12	3	1	8	22	44	7
Woodford	12	2	1	9	15	33	5

Note: Individual match results found show Romford's goals against as 19, but league table goals totals tally.

CUP RESULTS SEASON 1905 – 06

F.A. Challenge Cup

Final: Everton 1 Newcastle United 0

Romford's progress: 1st Qual. Home Enfield 4 – 1
2nd Qual. Home Wanstead 2 – 1
3rd Qual. Home South Weald 0 – 1

F.A. Amateur Cup

Final: Oxford City 3 Bishop Auckland 0

Romford's progress: 1st Qual. Away Chelmsford 3 – 2
2nd Qual. Home Harwich & Parkeston 6 – 0
3rd Qual. Home South Weald 2 – 1
4th Qual. Away King's Lynn 1 – 1
Replay Home King's Lynn 3 – 1
1st Round Home Ipswich Town 4 – 2
2nd Round Home Eastbourne 6 – 3
3rd Round Home New Crusaders 0 – 0*
Replay Away New Crusaders 1 – 1*
2nd Replay Stam.Brdge. New Crusaders 1 – 4

Essex Senior Cup

Final: Wanstead 2 South Weald 0

Romford's progress: 1st Round Home Felstead(Custom House) 5 – 1
2nd Round Home Southend Athletic 2 – 0
3rd Round Away Leytonstone 3 – 0
4th Round Away Barking 3 – 0
Semi-Final Clapton South Weald 0 – 2

West Ham Charity Cup

Winners: Wanstead beat Clapton

Romford's progress: Semi-Final Home Wanstead 1 – 1
Replay Clapton Wanstead 0 – 1

First Team Appearances Season 1905 – 06

P.J.Anderson	29	B.G.Aston	28	E.Barter	15	Barter.Jnr	1
Biddell	1	W.Church	27	Colehatch	1	L.R.Day	1
A.Dennis	2	E.Doy	2	J.Eden	24	F.L.Fletcher	24
A.V.Frisby	26	B.Goodman	33	Griffiths	3	Howes	1
H.Hughes	3	J.B.Hunter	29	A.S.Hyett	32	A.E.Jones	25
Lewis	3	J.Lovett	25	G.T.Mason	1	A.Miller	8
Pearson	2	Plested	1	Powell	4	Venner	1
J.W.Wayland	4					Total	356

Note: The above details are not a complete record, as several team line ups have not been traced. It is a good illustration of the most regular players who played during the season.

First Team Goal Scorers Season 1905 – 06

A.E.Jones	22	B.G.Aston	21	J.Eden	10	A.Hyett	8
A.Miller	2	F.L.Fletcher	2	W.Church	2	A.V.Frisby	2
Howes	1	E.Barter	1	A.Dennis	1	Unknown	8
Total	80						

Due to the lack of information in the local press, we are unable to give a more accurate listing of goal scorers.

AMATEUR CUP COMMITTEE MEETING (as reported in the *Essex Times*, Saturday 17th March 1906)

14 Mar The F.A.Amateur Cup Committee met to discuss the complaint by New Crusaders that they had been "kicked off the park" in the drawn game at Sidcup. F.L.Fletcher (captain and centre half) and P.J.Anderson (right back) were named as the offenders. New Crusaders were represented by Mr.Farnfield Snr. and W.D. Matthews represented Romford. Fletcher was accused of deliberately fouling A.J. Farnfield and Anderson for fouling H.V.Farnfield.

Fletcher was unable to attend, being away on business, but he forwarded a letter in his defence and Anderson appeared before the committee. The Committee heard that the referee failed to see Fletcher's foul and the linesman saw the foul but was unable to identify the player. After four hours the Committee came to the conclusion that the charge against Fletcher was proved, and he was suspended for the remainder of the season. The charge against Anderson could not be sustained, and the Committee further decided not to accept Romford's entry for next season.

This decision seemed to affect the Romford team, who failed to win any of their remaining twelve games!

Two humorous (and anonymous) poems concerning the Romford vs New Crusaders controversy, printed in the *Essex Times.* The second may be proof that the rural Essex accent was still to be heard in Romford in the early 20th century!

LINE UP ROMFORD

Come on again, Crusaders, not yet have you beaten the Blues,
'Twas only an error of judgement that has saved you from a lose.
We don't blame the ref. for the goal disallowed, but one of the linesmen we do,
He was in a position and must have seen Cook play the ball before Jones put through

We played a foul game, so the papers say, and the papers are never wrong;
But of footballers can't take a charge or two they'd far better play ping pong.
A two hours' game, and no one hurt, I think I'm right if I say,
That there wouldn't have been many Crusaders left in the Brothers Walters day.

We've played on a ground that was heavy and slow, and on ground that was fast and true;
Home and away, with extra time, yet the struggle must start anew.
If Crusaders win or Romford win, or the match be drawn again,
It goes to show that the Romford team were not beaten by a name.
So line up again, my bonny Blues, and gird yourselves for the fray;
It's an even chance, not six to one, whatever the critics say.
Should you make an excited charge or two, I can't see where's the blame,
For football as played on the garden lawn is no good in a cup-tie game.

FIRST MATCH

I must a bin barmy on the thatch,
Wen I went ter see der bonny blues
Play agin a team, a clarsey sort of team,
Well dressed, an wearing curly lever shoes;
Well, wen dey landed ere, dey must a smelt der beer,
Cause day walked on der field a looking dawn;
As Romford goes an breaves on em, a course dat means a fowl;
An dere shore to git a free kick if yer frown.

RESERVE TEAM
(Ground: Cricket Ground)

Match Details

16 Sept	Frdly	Home	Leytonstone Reserves	0 – 4
23 Sept	Frdly	Away	Leyton Granville	1 – 2
7 Oct	RDL1	Away	Tilbury	Lost
14 Oct	EJC1	Home	Heath Park	2 – 3
21 Oct	Frdly	Away	Leytonstone Reserves	2 – 2
	RDL1	Home	Barley Hall	Lost
	RDL1	Away	Barley Hall	n/k
	RDL1	Home	Brentwood St.Thomas	Won
	RDL1	Away	Brentwood St.Thomas	Drew
	RDL1	Home	Romford United	n/k
2 Dec	RDL1	Away	Romford United	0 – 9
	RDL1	Home	Tilbury	n/k
	RDL1	Home	Wouldham Athletic	0 – 0
	RDL1	Away	Wouldham Athletic	n/k

SUMMARY OF RESERVE TEAM RESULTS SEASON 1905 – 06

Due to the lack of information in the newspapers a summary cannot be compiled.

CUP RESULTS SEASON 1905 – 06

Essex Junior Cup

Final: Barking Victoria 3 Braintree Manor Works 1

Romford's progress: 1st Round Home Heath Park 2 – 3

Post-Season Summary Season 1905 – 06

The club installed raised standing boards (an early form of terracing) around the perimeter of the pitch to make viewing easier for spectators. The season began with five friendly matches, three of which were won, one drawn and one lost. The first two competitive matches were both cup ties. First Romford defeated Enfield 4-1 in the F.A. Cup and then beat Chelmsford in the Amateur Cup. For the latter match it was reported that 'Through the generosity of the Great Eastern Railway Company, cheap fares at the rate of 1s 6d will be issued, but as the club have guaranteed a certain number, it is hoped that all those interested in the club's doings will make the journey!'

Their first league game did not take place until 21st October, when a 0-0 draw was played with old friends Southend Athletic. This was followed with further success against Wanstead in the F.A. Cup and a 6-0 win over Harwich & Parkeston in the Amateur Cup. A third successive cup victory was obtained against Felstead (of Custom House, not Felsted in Essex!) in the Essex Senior Cup. Next came another cup tie, but this time our heroes lost at home to South Weald before 2,000 supporters, and they were out of the F.A. Cup. The following week drew another 2,000 attendance and another visit by South Weald, who left with a narrow defeat in the Amateur Cup tie. Romford then defeated Southend Athletic by two goals to nil in the Essex Senior Cup.

Cup football was interrupted by a friendly match against Croydon Wanderers which was won by three goals to two. Next came the long trip to Norfolk to meet King's Lynn in the Amateur Cup and a well-earned one one draw. It was reported that the Great Eastern Railway attached a saloon carriage to the mail train to Liverpool Street Station to accommodate the team, and a large throng of supporters were on the platform to see them off on the Friday evening. In the match itself, W.'Connie' Church was the outstanding player.

The replay at the Cricket Ground drew a crowd of 1,600 who enjoyed a fine Romford victory by three goals to one. Next was a home victory over Luton Clarence in a friendly match. This was followed at last by a South Essex League game and Woodford were defeated by two goals to one.

Romford then defeated Leytonstone (the holders) on their own ground in the Essex Senior Cup, before taking both points in the home league game with Chelmsford who played with only ten men. Next, in the first round proper of the Amateur Cup, Romford won at home to the strong Ipswich Town team by four goals to two. At right back for Ipswich was Baxter, a former Romford player.

The following week's fixture away to Woodford was postponed due to a flooded playing surface. Romford complained to the League that they were only notified late on Friday that the game was off, when it was obvious on Thursday that the game could not be played!

Romford next defeated Barking 1-0 in a league encounter before 700 spectators, and then beat Eastbourne in the Amateur Cup in front of a crowd of 1,800. Romford then had an outstanding win by three goals to nil over Barking in a league game and followed it up with a thrilling 0-0 draw after extra time against the powerful New Crusaders in the Amateur Cup. This match attracted a record attendance at the Cricket ground of 3,336 with record receipts of £75. These figures indicate the importance of making good progress in the cup competitions.

Romford were then required to travel to Sidcup for the replay and again the match ended in a draw after extra time, but 'Diddy' Jones had a goal disallowed close to the end of normal time. The attendance was 3,000. The following Wednesday Romford travelled to Stamford Bridge where 5,000 spectators watched the epic second replay. Alas, it was not Romford's day and they were beaten 4-1. The New Crusaders were known as the Farnfield Troupe, having the former Woodford brothers in their team. As we have seen, New Crusaders had protested at the alleged 'rough play' of the Romford team in the match at Sidcup.

After a 2-2 draw with Upton Park, Romford played Wanstead three times in eight days! The first was a home drawn game in the West Ham Charity Cup Semi-Final, followed by a 3-0 home defeat in a league match. The third game also ended in defeat, this time by one goal to nil in the Charity Cup replay. Two days later Romford failed to score for a third time and were beaten 2-0 in the Essex Senior Cup semi-final by local rivals South Weald.

It was proving to be a disastrous end to the season, as Romford drew one and lost six of their last seven league games. In the league games away to Barking and South Weald during April Romford fielded a reserve team, probably due to the large number of games to be played by the season's end. After exiting the Amateur Cup at Stamford Bridge, Romford failed to win a single one of their last twelve games!

The reserve team again had a very poor season and we have traced only one victory, although we do not know the score, and a large number of results are unknown. After the season ended 'Diddy' Jones was awarded his Essex Senior Cap, having played six or more games for the County team.

Annual General Meeting
(as reported in the *Essex Times,* Saturday 19th May 1906)

The annual meeting of the Romford Football Club was held at the Rising Sun Hotel on Thursday evening 17th May, Mr.C.F.Fitch (President) occupying the chair. There was a large attendance of members.

The hon.treasurer (Mr.W.R.Carter), in presenting the balance sheet, said they would agree with him it was the best which had ever been presented to that club. The balance in hand last year was £7.5s.7d.; president and vice-presidents' subscriptions amounted to £12.10s.0d; and members subscriptions to £13; gate money and guarantees came to £470.10s.2d. Total receipts, £504.10s.5d. The principal items on the expenditure side were: Guarantees and half gates £137.18s.10d. Materials and repairs £34.18s.5d. groundsmen and assistance £20.8s.9d; printing, bill-posting etc. £20.5s.2d; referees' and linemen's expenses £17.6s.2d; and team's travelling and players' expenses £116.19s.2d. Referring to the last mentioned item Mr.Carter said considering the distances they had had to go for some matches, and the large number of matches they had played, he thought it was satisfactory as compared with some other clubs. (Hear, hear).

The balance at the bank amounted to £90.2s 3d (Applause). In addition to that they expected a grant from the Essex County Football Association by reason of playing in the semi-final versus South Weald. The Chairman said he was sure it was a satisfactory report. He had been in the chair when they had had worse ones. (Laughter and applause). Mr.W.D. Matthews observed that he should have great pleasure in proposing the accounts should be passed, subject to audit. It must be gratifying to every townsman that Romford had at last a good balance on the right side. The proposition was heartily carried.

Mr.Heard said, in submitting his report, he thought they must congratulate themselves on the splendid financial position of the club, notwithstanding the great drawback they experienced in coming under the ban of the Football Association during the latter part of the season. Their record for all matches was as follows: Played 40, won 20, lost 12, and drawn 8. Goals scored 70, against 55 (Applause). The chief goal getters were Aston 22, Jones 22, Eden 10, Hyett 8. In the Football Association Cup they were ousted in the third round, but it was in the Amateur Cup that their team excelled, as they reached the third round of the competition proper, and were only defeated by the New Crusaders at the third time of asking. That in itself was a really remarkable performance – he should say, one of the best ever performed by the club, and it had no doubt placed them amongst the first flight of amateur clubs. (Applause). Mr.Heard here stated that the club had secured a requisition, signed by 20 clubs, to re-open the New Crusaders incident and an Extraordinary Meeting would take place on May 31st. In the County Cup they reached the semi-final, and they got knocked out of the West Ham Charity Cup in the semi-final. In regard to the South Essex League, they performed very indifferently, only securing fifth position.

He felt reluctantly compelled to refer to the New Crusaders incident, which without doubt was a severe blow to the club in more respects than one. Not only did it cause the suspension of their captain F.L.Fletcher, but the drastic sentence seemed to affect the whole of the players. The part of the sentence which they felt most was the barring of the club from competing in the Amateur Cup next season. That placed a great slur upon the club, but he could assure them they had done their level best to get that stigma removed.

To give them some idea of how the suspension affected their team he gave the following statistics: Before the suspension they had played 29 matches, of which they had won 20, lost 3, and drawn 6. Afterwards 11 matches were played, of which they won none, lost 9 and two were drawn games. Those figures spoke for themselves. (Hear,hear). But, besides the suspension referred to, he must point out that they experienced very bad luck with their players during the latter part of the season, as Jones, Church and Aston were seriously injured, and Barter was indisposed, but he was pleased to say they had practically recovered.

He took the opportunity of thanking the team for the sportsmanlike manner in which they kept with them, and also the way in which they had upheld the prestige of the club; and he sincerely hoped they would be able to command their services next season. (Hear, hear). He must make special mention of their goalkeeper, B.Goodman, who played in every match, which he considered a unique performance. In conclusion he thanked his fellow officers for the great assistance he had received from them, and said, if re-elected as their hon.secretary, he would do his utmost to keep the club in the position it now held in the football world.

The Chairman thought that, with the exception of the little incident relating to the Crusaders, that was one of the most interesting and satisfactory reports which had ever been submitted to the club at its annual meeting. They had a round sum of nearly £100 to their credit; a very good prospect before them, nothing of which they were ashamed in the past – nothing had been left undone so far as they knew to play a fair manly game – and they had placed the club in the front rank of amateur players. (Applause). Several of the members had been picked to play for the county. The last member picked was, he believed, their recent martyr & late captain. He had no doubt he was selected by those competent to judge for what they considered fair play, and that was one of the best answers which could be made to what had been said against him.

Referring to Mr.Heard, the Chairman said they all felt that the services which had been rendered by their secretary were invaluable. (Hear,hear). There was a great deal of work attached to the position of secretary of so large a club as that, and the man discharging the duties had often anxious moments in respect to the right men being on the field. They all owed Mr.Heard a debt of gratitude for his voluntary services and the work he had put in. Nothing had given him greater pleasure than to hear Mr.Heard's remark that he would be pleased to continue in the position. He was sure Mr.Heard could not do more than he had done. So highly did the members think of his services that it was thought some slight recognition might be made him.

On behalf of the members he asked Mr.Heard to accept a small honorarium of five guineas as a slight token of the appreciation in which they held his services. (Applause). Mr.Heard said the words failed to express his pleasure in accepting, but he did not think he deserved it. ("Yes"). He could assure them he would do his best for them next season. The report was adopted. 15 new members were elected.

Mr.Matthews proposed that Mr.C.F.Fitch should be asked to honour them by again becoming their president. Mr.C.Wilson seconded, observing that some of the members hardly know how much Mr.Fitch had helped them….The proposition was unanimously carried. The Chairman, in reply, remarked that he was afraid it was no use for him at that stage to say he could not accept the presidency. He was extremely obliged to them for the very kind and flattering terms in which they had proposed his re-election, but he felt that there were many names on the list of vice-presidents, and they might have looked round. Personally he could assure them it had been a great pleasure to him to be president. He had the pleasantest recollections of meetings there, which would ever remain in his memory, and it would be ungracious if he did not accept the compliment they had paid him. He accepted with pleasure, and hoped they would retrieve what they had lost owing to the discouragement and disheartening of last year. (Applause).

With certain exceptions the vice-presidents we re-elected en bloc, and the following were added to the list: Mr.George White, Mr.V.Cawdrey, Mr.J.H. Bethell.M.P., and Mr.E.Pilling. Mr.Matthews said he had a little proposition to make. He made it two years ago, when it was unanimously accepted, and again last year, and he was proud to hear Mr.Heard say that if elected he would again serve. He (the speaker) was sure no one it that room would desire to submit another name for the post of hon.secretary. Mr.T.Meadsmore seconded. The Chairman put the motion in the following shape: "That our very popular secretary whom we cannot afford to lose, shall be re-elected". (Applause). It was unanimously carried, and Mr.Heard briefly responded.

The Chairman said he should take the liberty of proposing the re-election of their treasurer, Mr.Carter. He was sure it would be very difficult to find anyone who would fill the post to a better manner. Mr.Carter had had the pleasure of presenting the finest balance sheet which had ever been placed before the members.He (the chairman) hoped he would never present a smaller balance than had been the case that night, when they came within a little of one of three figures. (Applause). Mr.Carter was proposed for re-election to the post of treasurer. Mr. Robarts seconded the motion which was unanimously carried.

The Chairman said, as they knew, they had lost a very good captain, and they were anxious to get another good one. Mr.C.Wilson said he had great pleasure in proposing someone who was well known to all of them, and he thought it was very desirable that the captain should reside in the town. He submitted the name of Mr.J.Hunter. (Applause). Mr.Reeves seconded. There were no other nominations. The Chairman said he had seen Mr.Hunter play and he had seen him at the festive board – (laughter) – and thought a very wise selection had been made. The proposal was unanimously carried. Mr.Hunter thanked them for the honour they had done him, and said he would do his best. (Applause). Mr.Carter proposed Mr.Bert Aston as vice-captain. Mr.Jones seconded. The Chairman he did not hear a murmur of disapproval in the room, and he did not expect to hear it. He wished to endorse the choice they had made. It would be difficult to find a better player in the county. The motion having been heartily carried, Mr.Aston thanked them.

The following were appointed on the committee: Messrs. P.J.Anderson, E.Barter, Evan Jones, A.Reynolds, F.Robarts, C.Wilson, T.W.Sharp, W.H.Kelly, G.Smith, T.Meadmore, E.J.Wallis, and C.Ryle. Messrs. F.W.Jeffes and Geo. Winmill were elected auditors. After some discussion it was decided, on the proposition of Mr.Smith, seconded by Mr.Booth, to run a second team.

Mr.Smith said he had a very pleasant duty put into his hands – to propose a vote of thanks to the officers for what they had done for them last season. Mr.H.W.Wilson, in seconding, said he did not think any words from him were necessary in eulogy of the excellent work which had been done. (Applause). The motion was heartily carried. It was resolved that the secretary should apply for admission to the London League. Mr.Carter proposed that a letter should be written to Mr.A.Reynolds conveying the thanks of the club. He mentioned that at he beginning of the season Mr.Reynolds decided to charge them £5 as rent for the reserve ground, but when asked to send in his account he said he would make them a present of the amount. (Loud,applause)…

Mr.Smith said that was the first occasion upon which he had had the pleasure of being under the chairmanship of their president, and he hoped Mr.Fitch would preside over many future gatherings. (Applause). He proposed a hearty vote of thanks to their chairman. Mr.Matthews seconded the proposal, which was received with musical honours. The chairman said he was extremely obliged to them. He could congratulate the team on having had a very good year, with the exception of one little incident. They had lost their captain, but had replaced him by the election of another good man. He (the chairman) had watched most of the games, and had been present at most of the club's social functions. He valued very highly his connection with the club, and it would always give him pleasure to help them in any way. He hoped there were many more meetings before them. Everything looked bright for next year, and he hoped Romford would then give a good account of itself.

ROMFORD FOOTBALL CLUB: Extraordinary General Meeting (as reported in the *Essex Times,* Saturday 9th June 1906)

At a meeting of the committee of the above club held on Wednesday evening, June 6th, at the headquarters, the Rising Sun, Mr.Evan Jones presiding, a letter was read from the Romford United Football Club, stating they were desirous of amalgamating with the town club. It was felt that this would greatly help the town club, having in view the splendid success of the United Club last season, they having won the Grays and District League Challenge Cup, and they were runners up in the Tilbury Hospital Cup competition.

Romford will now have a strong, purely local reserve team playing on the fine Church Lane Ground of Romford United, and it has been decided to enter in the following competitions:- Essex Junior Cup, Romford and District League, Grays and District League, Tilbury Hospital, and Romford Charity Cups.

The election of officers for the reserve team resulted in Mr.A.Bayley being elected captain; Mr.H.Mayes, vice-captain; and Mr.F.G.Rice, assistant hon.secretary. Mr. W.D. Matthews was re-elected a shareholder on the Football Association, and also representative to Essex County Football Association. It was unanimously resolved to make Mr.Fred. Mullis an honorary life member of the club in appreciation of his services to the club in connection with the recent Amateur Cup. Mr.W.D.Matthews, the club's representative at the Association meeting called in connection with the Romford Crusaders fiasco, gave a report, and hopes were expressed that Romford's entry would eventually be accepted.

This old postcard of Romford Station shows the Rising Sun to the right, for some years headquarters of the Romford Football Club
Havering Libraries - Local Studies

Season 1906 – 7

AMALGAMATION OF CLUBS

Evan Jones, the Romford secretary, received a letter from his counterpart at Romford United, stating that his club was desirous of amalgamating with the town club. The matter was fully discussed and it was decided to agree to the amalgamation. It was felt that this would greatly help the town club having in view the splendid success of the United club the previous season, having won the Grays and District League £25 Challenge Cup and been finalists in the Tilbury Hospital Cup. Romford would now have through this amalgamation a strong purely local reserve team.

ROMFORD FOOTBALL CLUB TEAM 1906-07

No names are given for this photo, but W.G.Smith can be identified as the goalkeeper, with Arthur 'Diddy' Jones to the left of him. The player seated centre front appears to be A.S. Hyett (perhaps he was captain that particular day). *Authors' collection (originators unknown)*

ROMFORD FOOTBALL CLUB

President: Mr.C.F.Fitch.C.C. **Hon. Secretary:** Mr.C.T.Heard

Hon. Treasurer: Mr.W.R.Carter **Asst.Hon.Secretary:** Mr.F.G.Rice

Committee: Messrs. P.J.Anderson, E.Barter, Evan Jones, A.Reynolds, F.Robarts, C.Wilson, T.W.Sharp, W.H.Kelly, G.A.Smith, T.Meadmore, E.J.Wallis, and C.Ryle.

Captain: A.V.Frisby

Reserve Team Captain: Mr.A.Bowley **Reserve Team Vice-Captain:** Mr.H.Mayes

Club Colours: Blue and Black Stripes **Headquarters:** Rising Sun Hotel, Romford

Ground: Cricket Ground, Romford Station Reserve Team ground: Church Lane, Romford

1906-07

COMPETITIONS ENTERED

South Essex League Division One
F.A. Challenge Cup
Essex Senior Cup
West Ham Charity Cup
Romford were suspended from the Amateur Cup

Romford & District League Division One
Essex Junior Cup
Romford Charity Cup
Grays & District League

Match Details

1 Sept Frdly Home Plumstead 1 – 3 Scorer unknown
Romford:
Team details unknown

8 Sept Frdly Home Page Green Old Boys 5 – 1 Wilson(2)Aston,Jones,Ehrenfried
Romford: W.G.Smith;W.Hayman,Nettledon;A.V.Frisby(Capt),A.Bowley,L.Pounds;
G.Wilson,A.E.Jones,B.G.Aston,A.S.Hyett,Ehrenfried.

15 Sept Frdly Away Tottenham Hotspur 0 – 17
Romford:
Team details unknown

22 Sept. FACPR Home Barking 3 – 2 Aston,Beaumont(2)
Romford: W.G.Smith;W.Hayman,Nettledon;A.V.Frisby(Capt),Gibson,O.Pearson;
Beaumont,A.E.Jones,B.G.Aston,A.S.Hyett,Ehrenfried.

29 Sept SEL1 Away Wanstead 1 – 1 Hunter(pen)
Romford: W.G.Smith;W.Hayman,Nettledon;A.V.Frisby(Capt),Gibson,J.B.Hunter;
E.Baldwin,O.Pearson,B.G.Aston,A.S.Hyett,Ehrenfried.

6 Oct FAC1Q Away Woodford 1 – 2 Frisby
Romford: W.G.Smith;W.Hayman,Nettledon;A.V.Frisby(Capt),Gibson,O.Pearson;
Wallage,B.G.Aston,S.C.Squier,A.S.Hyett.Ehrenfried.

13 Oct Frdly Home Leyton Reserves 1 – 7 Scorer unknown
Romford:
Team details unknown

20 Oct SEL1 Home Wanstead 3 – 1 Riley,Unknown(2)
Romford: W.G.Smith;Nettledon,Wallage;A.V.Frisby(Capt),Gibson,E.Baldwin;
A.E.Jones Franks,W.Riley,A.S.Hyett,Beaumont.

27 Oct Frdly Home Upton Park 1 – 1 Beaumont
Romford: W.G.Smith;W.Hayman,Nettledon;A.V.Frisby(Capt),Gibson,E.Baldwin;
A.E.Jones,Beaumont,B.G.Aston,A.S.Hyett,S.C.Squier.

3 Nov SEL1 Home South Weald 4 – 5 Frisby,Beaumont,Jones(pen)Coxhead(o.g)
Romford: W.G.Smith;Nettledon,Wallage;A.V.Frisby(Capt),Gibson,E.Baldwin;
A.E.Jones,Franks,W.Riley,Beaumont,S.C.Squier.

10 Nov Frdly Away Clapton 1 – 3 Scorer unknown
Romford: W.G.Smith;Mowbray,Wallage;A.V.Frisby(Capt),R.Ball,Gibson;
A.E.Jones,Lazell,Edwards,Beaumont,S.C.Squier.

17 Nov SEL1 Home Leigh Ramblers 3 – 2 Hyett,Ball,Beaumont
Romford: T.W.Sharpe;Mowbray,Wallage;E.Baldwin,R.Ball,Morren;
W.Riley,A.V.Frisby(Capt),A.S.Hyett,A.E.Jones,Beaumont.

22 Nov WHC2R Home Barking 1 – 1 Hyett
Romford:
Team details unknown

24 Nov Frdly Home New Brompton Amateurs 5 – 2 Scorers unknown
Romford: T.W.Sharpe;Mowbray,A.Finch;Hills,Gibson,E.Baldwin;
A.E.Jones,W.Riley,Beaumont,A.S.Hyett,S.C.Squier.

1 Dec SEL1 Home Chelmsford 3 – 1 Squier,Hyett,Mowbray
Romford: W.G.Smith;Mowbray,A.Finch;Hills,Gibson,E.Baldwin;
A.E.Jones,Franks,Beaumont,A.S.Hyett,S.C.Squier.

6 Dec WHCR Away Barking 1 – 3 Scorer unknown
Romford:
Team details unknown

8 Dec Frdly Away Ilford 1 – 5 Scorer unknown
Romford:
Team details unknown

15 Dec Frdly Home Wanstead 3 – 0 Squier,Beaumont,Jones
Romford: W.G.Smith;Mowbray,J.B.Hunter;Hills,Gibson,E.Baldwin;
A.E.Jones,Franks,Beaumont,A.S.Hyett,S.C.Squier.

22 Dec Frdly Home Upton Park 0 – 2
Romford: W.G.Smith;Mowbray,Hills;J.Hunter,Gibson,E.Baldwin;
A.E.Jones,Franks,Beaumont,A.S.Hyett,Ehrenfried.

26 Dec Frdly Home Erith Town 1 – 0 Scorer unknown
Romford:
Team details unknown

5 Jan ESC3R Home Chadwell Heath 3 – 2 Riley(2)Gibson
Romford: W.G.Smith;W.Saggers,Bond; A.V.Frisby(Capt),Gibson,G.Wilson;
A.D.Cornell,W.D.Matthews,W.Riley,A.S.Hyett,S.C.Squier.

12 Jan SEL1 Home Woodford 3 – 0 Squier(2)Hyett
Romford: W.G.Smith;Mowbray,A.Finch;A.V.Frisby(Capt),Hills,E.Baldwin;
G.Wilson,Beaumont,A.S.Hyett,S.C.Squier,Ehrenfried.

19 Jan SEL1 Away South Weald 2 – 4 Beaumont(2)
Romford: W.G.Smith; Mowbray, A.Finch A.V.Frisby(Capt),G.T.Mason,Hills;
Beaumont,G.Wilson,W.Riley,A.S.Hyett,Ehrenfried.

26 Jan ESC4R Home Walthamstow Grange 0 – 4
Romford:
Team details unknown

2 Feb SEL1 Home Southend Athletic 1 – 2 Clarke
Romford: E.Baldwin;Mowbray;Evans;Hills,A.V.Frisby(Capt),G.T.Mason;
Beaumont,G.Wilson,A.S.Hyett,D.Clarke,S.C.Squier.

9 Feb SEL1 Away Barking 0 – 4
Romford: W.G.Smith;Mowbray,A.Finch;Hills,A.V.Frisby(Capt),E.Baldwin;
Ehrenfried,G.T.Mason,D.Clarke,Evans,A.Dennis.

16 Feb SEL1 Away Chelmsford 2 – 2 Jones,Frisby
Romford: W.G.Smith;A.Finch,Hills;A.V.Frisby(Capt),D.Clarke, ? ;
G.Wilson,Beaumont,A.E.Jones,A.S.Hyett,S.C.Squier.

23 Feb Frdly Home Woodford 7 – 2 Jones(4)Hyett(2)Knight
Romford:
A.E.Jones,A.S.Hyett,Knight.

2 Mar Frdly Home Page Green Old Boys 0 – 0
Romford: F.H.Kittle (from Squirrels Heath)
Remainder of team unknown.

7 Mar Frdly Home 2nd Life Guards Battalion 6 - 1
Romford:
Team details unknown

9 Mar Frdly Home Walthamstow Grange 4 – 3 Clarke(3)Hyett
Romford: W.G.Smith;Rowberry,Hills;A.V.Frisby(Capt),E.Baldwin,Beaumont;
A.E.Jones,D.Clarke, ? ,A.S.Hyett,S.C.Squier.

16 Mar SEL1 Away Southend Athletic 1 – 2 Hyett
Attendance: 200
Romford: W.Smith;A.Finch,Hills;Beaumont,E.Baldwin,A.V.Frisby(Capt);
S.Squier,D.Clarke,A.E.Jones,A.S.Hyett,G.Wilson.

23 Mar SEL1 Away Woodford 4 – 2 Hyett(2),Jones,one unknown
Romford: W.Smith;Moore,Hills;Beaumont,E.Baldwin,A.V.Frisby(Capt);
A.Finch,A.E.Jones,A.S.Hyett,Gibson,F.H.Kittle.

29 Mar Frdly Away Lynn Town 1 – 3 Ives
Romford:
B.Ives,

30 Mar SEL1 Home Barking 2 – 2 Jones(2)
Romford:
A.E.Jones, remainder of the team unknown.

1 Apr Frdly Away Great Yarmouth Town 1 – 1 Hyett
Romford:
A.S.Hyett,

4 Apr Frdly Home London & Provincial Bank won
Romford:
Team details unknown

13 Apr SEL1 Away Leigh Ramblers 2 – 1 Jones(2)
Romford: W.Smith;A.V.Frisby(Capt), ?? ;Hills, ? ,F.H.Kittle;
A.E.Jones,B.G.Aston, ? ,S.C.Squier,A.S.Hyett.

20 Apr Frdly Away Stansted 0 – 0*
Romford:
Team details unknown

* Abandoned after 20 minutes.

SUMMARY OF FIRST TEAM RESULTS OBTAINED SEASON 1906 – 07

	P	W	D	L	Goals For	Goals Ag	Pts
F.A. Challenge Cup	2	1	0	1	4	4	
South Essex Lge. Div.One	14	6	3	5	31	29	15
Essex Senior Cup	2	1	0	1	3	6	
West Ham Charity Cup	2	0	1	1	2	4	
Friendly Matches	18*	8	3	7	38*	51*	
Total	38	16	7	15	78	94	
AGM Press Report	37	14	7	16	76	96	

Note: The above summary does not include the abandoned game against Stansted
* One match was won but the score is not known.

South Essex League Division One
Final Table

	P	W	D	L	Goals For	Goals Ag	Pts
South Weald	14	13	0	1	63	16	26
Wanstead	14	7	3	4	33	22	17
Romford	**14**	**6**	**3**	**5**	**31**	**29**	**15**
Leigh Ramblers	14	6	2	6	31	41	14
Barking	14	4	3	7	31	31	11
Southend Athletic **	14	6	1	7	17	37	11
Chelmsford	14	4	2	8	31	36	10
Woodford	14	3	0	11	24	49	6

** Two points deducted for breach of Rules.

CUP RESULTS

F.A. Challenge Cup

Final: Sheffield Wednesday 2 Everton 1

Romford's progress: Prel. Home Barking 3 – 2
1st Qual. Away Woodford 1 – 2

F.A. Amateur Cup

Final: Clapton 2 Stockton 1

Romford F.C. suspended from the competition

Essex Senior Cup

Final: South Weald 5 Harwich & Parkeston 0

Romford's progress: 3rd Round Home Chadwell Heath 3 – 2
4th Round Home Walthamstow Grange 0 – 4

West Ham Charity Cup

Winners: Clapton

Romford's progress: 2nd Round Home Barking 1 – 1
Replay Away Barking 1 – 3

First Team Appearances Season 1906 – 07

B.G.Aston	6	E.Baldwin	15	R.Ball	2	Beaumont	16
Bond	1	Bowley	1	D.Clarke	5	A.Cornell	1
A.Dennis	1	Edwards	1	Ehrenfried	9	Evans	2
A.Finch	8	Franks	5	A.V.Frisby	19	Gibson	12
W.Hayman	5	Hills	13	J.B.Hunter	3	A.S.Hyett	22
A.E.Jones	17	F.H.Kittle	3	Knight	1	Lazell	1
G.T.Mason	3	W.D.Matthews	1	Moore	1	Morren	1
Mowbray	10	Nettledon	7	O.Pearson	3	L.Pounds	1
W.Riley	6	Rowberry	1	W.Saggers	1	T.W.Sharpe	2
W.G.Smith	20	S.C.Squier	14	Wallage	7	G.Wilson	8
Total	255						

Note: The above detail is not complete due to several team line ups having not been traced.

First Team Goal Scorers Season 1906 – 07

A.E.Jones	13	A.S.Hyett	11	Beaumont	8	S.C.Squier	4
D.Clarke	4	W.Riley	3	A.V.Frisby	3	G.Wilson	2
B.G.Aston	2	Ehrenfried	1	J.B.Hunter	1	R.Ball	1
Mowbray	1	Gibson	1	Knight	1	B.Ives	1
Coxhead (o.g)	1	Unknown	14			Total	72

RESERVE TEAM

Match Details

10 Nov	EJC2R	Home	Squirrels Heath	2 – 1
8 Dec	Frdly	Away	Mawney United	won
22 Dec	EJC3R	Home	Plashet	2 – 0
19 Jan	EJC4R	Home	Richmond Athletic	1 – 5#
26 Jan	EJCRep	Home	Richmond Athletic	3 – 0
2 Feb	RCC1R	Away	Squirrels Heath	lost
21 Feb	Frdly	Home	Romford Thursday	1 – 2
	RDL1	Home	Barley Hall	n/k
	RDL1	Away	Barley Hall	0 – 5
	RDL1	Home	Beaconstone	n/k
	RDL1	Away	Beaconstone	1 – 2
	RDL1	Home	Dagenham St. Paul's	0 – 1
	RDL1	Away	Dagenham St. Paul's	1 – 2
	RDL1	Home	Grays Athletic	n/k
	RDL1	Away	Grays Athletic	0 – 0
	RDL1	Home	Hornchurch	3 – 3
	RDL1	Away	Hornchurch	n/k
	RDL1	Home	Purfleet	0 – 2
	RDL1	Away	Purfleet	1 – 3
	RDL1	Home	Squirrels Heath	n/k
	RDL1	Away	Squirrels Heath	1 – 1
	GDL	Home	Tilbury	0 – 2
	GDL	Away	Tilbury	0 – 5
	GDL	Home	Beaconstone	n/k
	GDL	Away	Beaconstone	n/k
	GDL	Home	Grays "A"	n/k
	GDL	Away	Grays "A"	n/k
	GDL	Home	Purfleet	n/k
	GDL	Away	Purfleet	n/k

Abandoned after 77 minutes due to fog.

SUMMARY OF RESERVE TEAM RESULTS OBTAINED SEASON 1906 – 07

					Goals		
	P	W	D	L	For	Ag	Pts
Romford & Dist.Lge.	14	3	4	7			10
Grays & Dist. Lge.	8	n/k	n/k	n/k			
Essex Junior Cup*	2	2	0	0	4	1	
E.Junior Cup (Void)#	2	1	0	1	4	5	
Romford Charity Cup	1	0	0	1			
Friendly Matches	2	1	0	1	1	2	
Total	29	7	4	10			
AGM Press Report	28	11	6	11	34	39	

* The above summary does not include the abandoned game against Richmond Athletic.
# Following a protest by Richmond Athletic, Romford were struck out of the competition.

Romford and District League Division One
Final Table

	P	W	D	L	Pts
Barley Hall*	15	13	0	2	26
Grays Athletic*	15	11	2	2	24
Purfleet	14	6	6	2	14
Beaconstone	14	6	1	7	13
Dagenham St. Paul's	14	5	1	8	11
Romford Reserves	**14**	**3**	**4**	**7**	**10**
Squirrels Heath	14	3	3	8	9
Hornchurch	14	3	1	10	7

Note: The above league table includes the play-off game won by Barley Hall by three goals to two.

Grays & District League
Final Table!!

	P	W	D	L	Pts
Tilbury	8	n/k	n/k	n/k	n/k
Purfleet	8	n/k	n/k	n/k	n/k
Beaconstone	8	n/k	n/k	n/k	n/k
Grays "A"	8	n/k	n/k	n/k	n/k
Romford Reserves	**8**	n/k	n/k	n/k	n/k

Note: Two defeats by Tilbury are the only results we have been able to find.

CUP RESULTS

Essex Junior Cup

Final: Custom House "A" 1 Chelmsford Swifts 0

Romford's progress:

1st Round			Bye
2nd Round	Home	Squirrels Heath	2 – 1
3rd Round	Home	Plashet	2 – 0
4th Round	Home	Richmond Athletic	1 – 5#
Replay	Home	Richmond Athletic	3 – 0##

\# Abandoned due to fog.
\## Richmond Athletic protested that Mason was not eligible and Romford were struck out of the competition.

Romford Charity Cup

Final: Mawney Institute 1 Harold Wood 0

Romford's progress: 1st Round Away Squirrels Heath lost

Reserve Team Summary of appearances and goal scorers.

Due to the lack of information in the local press it is not possible to compile any details.

THE CHURCH LANE GROUND, ROMFORD

The reserve team ground was situated in the open area top left of picture (the Market Place is in the centre)
Havering Libraries - Local Studies

Essex County Football Association Executive Meeting
Tuesday 5th Feb., 1907 at White Hart Hotel, Chelmsford

A protest was read from the Richmond Athletic F.C. against Romford 2nd XI in the fourth round of the Junior Cup on the ground that G.T.Mason was ineligible, he having played in more than 2 senior competitions the previous season, contrary to rule 6 of the junior cup rules. The protest was allowed and the protest fee lodged by the Richmonds Athletic F.C. was ordered to be returned, and the Romford 2nd XI was ordered to be struck out of the competition.

(The *Essex Times*, Sat.9th February 1907)

Post-Season Summary Season 1906 – 07

Romford commenced the season with the usual series of friendly matches, starting with a home three goal to one loss against Plumstead. They then defeated Page Green Old Boys by five goals to one. The third game was a very attractive one at White Hart Lane against Tottenham Hotspur. The Spurs proved very hot indeed, and our heroes lost by seventeen goals to nil!

Next came a home F.A. Cup tie against Barking, who were defeated by three goals to two. A league point was obtained at Wanstead before the team was ousted from the F.A. Cup with a 2-1 defeat at Woodford, followed by a seven goals to one thrashing at home to Leyton Reserves in a friendly match.

In the next two league encounters Romford beat Wanstead 3-1 and lost a thriller against powerful local rivals South Weald by four goals to five! The next game was an away friendly against Clapton which Romford lost 3-1. It was reported that 'goalkeeper Smith was injured and he had been performing brilliantly. Romford will need him back as soon as possible'.

Romford then defeated Leigh Ramblers in a South Essex League game, drew with Barking in the West Ham Charity Cup and defeated New Brompton Amateurs 5-2 in a friendly. On 1st December Smith was back in goal and Romford defeated Chelmsford 3-1 in a league fixture, which was followed by two more defeats. The first came against Barking in the West Ham Charity Cup replay by three goals to one, and then came a 5-1 beating from Ilford in a friendly match. A couple of wins and a defeat in friendly games ended the year.

Next up was the Essex Senior Cup tie on 5th January. Chadwell Heath, who forfeited home advantage, were defeated 3-2 at the Cricket Ground. Then in South Essex League games Romford gained revenge on Woodford with a 3-0 victory, only to again lose 4-2 to South Weald. Club officials presented popular player B.G.Aston with a wedding gift.

On 26th January Romford were knocked out of the Essex Senior Cup at home to Walthamstow Grange by four goal to nil. With the club suspended from the Amateur Cup and in a mediocre league position, there was now very little to play for over the rest of the season.

Successive league defeats by Southend Athletic and Barking was not helpful, but a point was picked up in the away fixture at Chelmsford. Romford had several players injured or away on business for the Barking encounter. There then followed a few friendly matches, including a seven goal to two home win over Woodford with the evergreen 'Diddy' Jones notching four.

Three more friendly games were played at the start of March, the first a nil nil draw with Page Green Old Boys. Romford then entertained the Army Champions the 2nd Life Guards Battalion, and secured a six goals to one victory. The third game was a 4-3 win over old friends Walthamstow Grange. Romford then lost to Southend Athletic before again beating Woodford in league games. Romford's 4-2 win against Woodford saw two local juniors, full back Moore and outside left Frank H. Kittle, make their first appearances in place of D.Clarke and Stuart Squier. This victory was Romford's first away league win for two years!

Romford had then arranged friendly matches in Norfolk over the Easter period, but the South Essex League insisted that they play Barking on the Saturday. In order not to let their Norfolk friends down, Romford made the double trip and played games against Lynn Town and Yarmouth. Barking were held to a two all draw in the game in between.

Romford next beat London Provincial Bank in a friendly fixture arranged by Jimmy Hunter (who worked for the bank), and then Leigh Ramblers in a league game, before meeting Stansted in what was supposed to be a friendly. This match turned out to be a disaster for the club to end the season with. It was reported in the local press that 'From the kick-off referee E.Glasscock warned the Romford players about their rough play but these warnings went unheeded and with twenty minutes gone he abandoned the game!'

The reserve team experienced an average season and finished in a lowly position in the Romford & District League with only three victories to their name but in the Grays & District League we have been only able to find a couple of results. They won three games in the Essex Junior Cup and were then thrown out of the competition by the Executive Committee following a protest from Richmond Athletic.

The Romford United committee members decided to sever their connection with Romford Football Club, feeling that they had not been fully supported by the senior club. They re-established themselves as an independent club, reverting from Romford Reserves back to Romford United playing on their Church Lane Ground. After this decision the United club lasted only one year before disbanding due to lack of support. Romford in turn decided against funding or running a reserve team.

Annual General Meeting
(as reported in the *Essex Times,* Wednesday 15th May 1907)

The Annual General Meeting of the Romford Football Club was held on Monday 13th May at the Rising Sun Hotel, South Street, Romford. Mr.C.F.Fitch,C.C. (the President) occupied the chair. There was a large attendance of Members including: Messrs. W.D. Matthews, A. Reynolds, A.Page, C.T.Heard (Hon.Secretary), A.E. Jones, W.R.Carter (Hon.Treasurer), J.F.Pilling, G.A.Smith, H.W.Wilson, J.Tarry, W.H.Kelly, A.Turvey, H.Smith, C.Spencer, A.V.Frisby (Captain), F.Robarts, T.W.Sharpe, F.W.Jeffes, L.Fletcher and J.King.

Mr.W.R.Carter said he was sure they would not consider the balance sheet which he had to present to them as very satisfactory, the balance having decreased by over two thirds. There was only one reason: the decision to run a reserve team which was arrived at at the last annual general meeting, and which had resulted in a loss of about £40. As they knew, they had a balance in hand at the beginning of the season of £90.2s.3d.: they received a grant of £5 for playing in the Essex semi-final; the president and vice-presidents' subscriptions amounted to £17.5s.6d.; members' subscriptions, £10.5s.0d.; gate money and guarantees, £222.16s.8d.; a total of £345.9s.5d. On the other side, the items included guarantees and half gates, £44.10s.9d.; team's travelling and players' expenses, £121.2s.3d.; groundsmen and assistance, £19.16s.6d. materials and repairs, £18.18s.3d.; poor childrens' breakfast fund, £1.; Romford Cottage Hospital, £2.8s.4d.; West Ham Charity Cup competition, £4.10s.0d., printing £26.0s.3d.,; doctor's fees £9.12s.0d.; Postages, telegrams etc., £12.10s.8d. The balance at the bank amounted to £24.2s.5d.

Mr.Matthews remarked that, as Mr.Carter had explained, the gate money had fallen short by about £200, but then they had not had a Crusader match and had not been able to run up in the cups as they did in the previous season, which was phenomenal. Never before had they touched such an amount….They were also fortunate in having nearly all the draws at home, which was not likely to occur another year. But he did not think they should be at all downhearted. If they could give them anything like the run of the year before last they would bring the gate money up to what it had been.

The Chairman, in moving the adoption of the statement said, as Mr. Matthews had very lucidly explained, the reason was in a nutshell. They rose to fame very suddenly, but at the same time it was not less than they deserved, but, as Mr. Matthews had put it, they had a Crusader match played three times, which aroused a very great deal of interest, both at Romford, Sidcup, and Stamford Bridge. He found that the gate money and guarantees for the season before last amounted to £470, and probably £200 was netted as a result of the interest taken in that particular match. Otherwise he did not see that there was any great falling off in the funds of the club. Subscriptions seemed to him to have kept up to past records, in fact, to have increased. They were left with a balance of something like £25, whereas for the year before they had a balance of £90. But £25 was greater than they had had in previous years. It was something to be left with a balance on the right side.

Of course, it was for them to go into the matter of the reserve team, but he thought on the whole they might congratulate themselves on having had a fairly successful year. If they had, as he hoped they might, good luck next season, it would not take them long to make up the £60. They must not be downhearted if they had to take the ups and downs of life as others had, and perhaps found themselves a little bit short. Of course, they had been shut out of some competitions owing to no fault of their own, but perhaps he might say to a rather hard and narrow minded decision on the part of those who might have taken a wider view of the matter, given a fairer decision, and the benefit of the doubt...Mr.Matthews seconded, and said, in his opinion, a £25 balance was as much as any amateur club wanted. It was a great mistake for amateur clubs to have very large balances in hand. It led to extravagance, and questions by other clubs as to what had been done with it. So long as they paid their way and had a small balance to the good they should feel satisfied. (Applause). The proposition was heartily carried.

Mr.Heard read his report as follows: "In submitting my report for the past season I regret we cannot congratulate ourselves on having had a successful one. Our record stands:- First Team: Played 37, won 14, lost 16, drawn 7; goals for 76, against 96. Reserve Team: Played 28, won 11, lost 11, drawn 6; goals for 34, against 39. I do not wish to bore you with explanations as to the cause of this unsatisfactory state of affairs, but I feel I must comment somewhat on the matter, otherwise you may think your committee have not done their work to the best of their ability; but allow me at once to assure you that, in my opinion, they have.

"First of all, on the very eve of commencing the season Bert Goodman (goalkeeper) informed that he was leaving the country on a sea trip, and then J.Hunter (our captain-elect) told me he was not available, as he would have to assist his bank. This in itself was a terribly bad start, but, fortunately, we secured at once a worthy successor to Goodman in W.G.Smith, who has been a tower of strength in goal during the season. But in the other case we were not so fortunate. We secured the services of J.H.Hayman, late of Wanstead F.C., but here again we were doomed to disappointment, as he was only with us a short time before he badly sprained his ankle, necessitating his retirement from the game.

"In addition to these serious drawbacks, we have had to contend, as usual, with accidents to the players. A.E.Jones, our old and esteemed player, was away from the team for some time owing to injury, this happening at a very critical period. Aston, hero of the season 1905-06, was practically useless owing to the effects of his bad accident; Wallage, who was showing good form, also met with a serious accident while at work, which prevented his playing for a very long time; and many others could be mentioned. With regard to our performance in cups, etc. we finished third in the South Essex League, were dismissed from the County Cup in the fourth round, and from the West Ham Charity Cup in the first round. Without doubt our poor show in the Essex Senior Cup was brought about owing to our usual backs not possessing the necessary qualification to enable them to assist us.

As to our position in the League, I think you will all agree with me that it was nothing but sheer bad luck that prevented us from being runners up and without doubt the same remark applies to the West Ham Charity Cup.

"Our thanks are due to all the players who assisted us during the season. It would take up too much of your time were I to mention each player separately, but I must say that great praise is due to Mr.Frisby (who acted as captain of the team) for his excellent services. Our principal scorers were Jones and Hyett, 17 each, Beaumont 12, Squier 5. In conclusion, I take this opportunity of thanking the Committee for their valuable assistance, and especially Mr.Carter for his help at the most critical times, which I have highly appreciated".

Mr.G.A.Smith thought the report a most eloquent record of what the Committee had had to go through. They no sooner picked a team than some of the men were crocked or business engagements prevented them playing. He proposed that the report should be adopted. Mr.Kelly seconded, and agreed with what Mr.Smith had said. Personally, he thought they started too late in the season to get players. If they did not get them in May or June they would not in September. That was the primary cause of their non-success last season. The report was adopted. Fifteen new members were enrolled.

Mr.Carter said the question was again raised as to whether it was advisable to run a reserve team. From what he had seen and knew of them he said it was not advisable. Last year there was a loss of £40 on the reserve team, and they had also to look at the fact that when the first team was short they could hardly ever get a man. They scarcely ever got a man who was good enough for the first team. Those were his reasons for moving that they should not run a reserve team that year. Mr.C.Spencer seconded.

Mr.G.A.Smith said he spoke up for a reserve team more than anyone else last year for the simple reason that he was hoping they might be able to foster local talent. No one was more astounded than he was to hear that the reserve team had cost them £40. He had thought they might be out of pocket to the extent of about £20, but £40 was rather stiff. He agreed that the majority of the second team were not of the class for the first team, and the unfortunate thing was that once having played a man in the first team he became ineligible for the reserves in respect to certain competitions. While that state of things existed it seemed to him impossible to carry on a reserve team, for the simple reason that they were spoiling both.

Mr.A.Page thought they should not drop the reserve team after one year's trial. They should not take a sordid view of pounds, shillings and pence. There were many people in Romford with limited incomes who could not afford to follow the club, and when the first team were playing away they were left with nothing at all. One of the things he had heard levelled against the club was the absence on certain occasions of a match on the ground. Mr.Fletcher was also in favour of a second team being run. Mr.Carter said he should like to point out to Mr.Page that the club had run a second team in previous years, and with the same disastrous fate. Mr.Page said he meant to say after a number of years. Mr.G.A.Smith said it seemed to him if they continued with a reserve team they would soon not have a balance of £25. Nine were in favour of a second team being run and thirteen against.

The Chairman said the next item on the agenda was the election of a president, and as he had occupied the position during the past year he proposed to leave the chair. Mr.Matthews remarked that he thought it was only a question of shifting chairs for two minutes. He was sure there was no one in the room who would propose an amendment to the resolution he had to submit, namely, that they should ask Mr.Fitch to again act as their president. (Hear,hear). He could only repeat what he had said on two previous occasions – that during the whole of his experience of the club they had never had a president who had come up to the present one. He proposed that they ask Mr.Fitch to again fill the post. Mr.H.W.Wilson seconded the proposition, which was unanimously carried.

Mr.Fitch, on again taking the chair, said he was very much obliged for the confidence they had shown in him. That was the third year he had acted as president. Last year they kindly honoured him with re-election, and he made a remark which he was going to repeat – that there were vice-presidents, and it would be advisable if they spread their favours. He need hardly say he was very proud of having been elected president for the third time…There was not so favourable a record that year as he should have liked to see, but as sportsmen they must not feel down on what they had done on the field. What they had accomplished in the past they could do again, and he hoped they would have a better record for next year. He thanked them cordially for re-electing him as their president.

The vice-presidents, with certain exceptions, were re-elected, and the following were added to the list: Mr.H.E.Crane, Mr.W.Baker, Mr.C.Burgess, Mr.G.St.Croix, Mr. F.E.Cuming, Mr.R.H.Cumine, Mr.G.F.Daldy, Mr.F.J.Hunt, Mr.S.C.Norton, the Rev. G.Vernon Smith, the Rev.C.Steer, Mr.Hugh Kemsley, Mr.J.Spencer, Mr.W.Young, Mr.A.E.Williams, Mr.E.Winmill.J.P., Mr.J.Squier, Mr.P.J.Weston, Mr.T.Adams.

Mr.A.Reynolds proposed, and Mr.J.Tarry seconded, that Mr.C.T.Heard should be re-elected hon.secretary The Chairman said Mr.Heard had served them well, faithfully, and energetically in the past. He was sure it required no words of his at that stage; it was a resolution which would meet with cordial and hearty acceptance at their hands. They were indebted very deeply to Mr.Heard for his services. As they knew, everything depended upon the secretary in putting the right men in the field and being responsible for the whole of the working and management of the club during the year. During the years Mr.Heard had filled the position they had gone from one success to another, and he thought if they re-elected him that night he would add to his already long list of successes. The motion was unanimously carried.

Mr.Heard observed that he must say he was rather surprised at that, (Laughter). He had come up there intending to give the position up, because he was under the impression – in fact, he had been told as much – that several of their members and subscribers were not altogether satisfied with the way in which he had discharged the duties. And that it was time they had another man. He would do his best, as he had always done. The Chairman said perhaps it would not be out of place if he proposed the re-election of Mr.Carter as hon.treasurer. They all knew what a very deep interest he took in the club, and last year he presented a report which was the best the club had had since its inception. It was through no fault of his that the present financial report was not so good, but there was no reason why last year's report should not be repeated. They could not value too highly the services of a gentleman who was resident in the town. He had spoken that night and given his views, which were very practical and valuable, in regard to the reserve team, and the voting showed that they accepted his opinion. He had great pleasure in moving his re-election.

They regretted very much that during the year Mr.Carter had been somewhat out of health, and trusted that, if not fully restored to health, the present season would find him so. Mr.Frisby seconded, and said Mr.Carter took an interest in the players, and had always done his best to further the interests of the club. The proposition was unanimously carried, and Mr.Carter thanked them for that renewal of their confidence, assuring them he should do his best to advance the club's interests.

Mr.Kelly said they elected a captain and a vice-captain at the last annual meeting, but as it turned out they were not able to take the positions. He thought the matter should be left with the players and not dealt with by the general meeting. Mr.C.Wilson seconded, because he thought it was in the interests of the club that the captain should know something of the composition of the team. Mr.Matthews thought it would be creating a very bad precedent if they did not elect their captain at the general meeting. He should like to propose that Mr.Arthur Jones should be asked to take the position of captain. Mr.J.Terry seconded. Mr.Frisby said it was recognised in Romford that the captain should be a Romford man. He (the speaker) should like to play under the captaincy of Mr.Jones, who was undoubtedly the senior member of the team, and the man who should fill the position. (Applause).

The proposal met with a cordial reception, and Mr.Jones replying, said with the secretary, treasurer, and committee they should be able to get a team between them. He would do the best he could. (Applause). On the proposition of Mr.Robarts, seconded by Mr.Spencer, Mr.Frisby was elected vice-captain, and suitably thanked them. Mr.Kelly proposed that the committee should consist of 7 members exclusive of ex-officio members, instead of 12 as heretofore. Mr.Jones seconded. Mr.Fletcher proposed, and Mr.Robarts seconded, that the number should remain as at present. Mr.G.A.Smith spoke in favour of this. Mr.Kelly's proposal was carried. Mr.Wilson asked whether those nominated for the committee could not be asked to give a guarantee that they would attend the away matches. The Chairman, who agreed that such support should be given, thought Mr.Wilson's remarks on the subject would be sufficient; they had been heard by everyone.

Those nominated for the committee were: Messrs. T.H.Randall, L.Fletcher, E.Currie, G.Winmill, W.Simmons, E.P.Jones, W.H.Kelly, T.Meadmore, A.Reynolds, F.Robarts, T.W.Sharpe, G.A.Smith and J.Tarry. Messrs. T.H.Randall, A.Reynolds, G.Winmill, G.A.Smith, W.H.Kelly, E.Currie and E.P.Jones were elected. Messrs. F.W.Jeffes and E.J.Wallis were elected honorary auditors. A proposition to run a Thursday team was lost by a large majority.

Mr.Page proposed a vote of thanks to the officers for their past services, remarking that none but those who had served on the committees of football and athletic clubs realised the disappointments which were experienced, and the great amount of work to be done. Mr.H.W.Wilson seconded, and said he was sure they felt very pleased at the manner in which the officers had carried out their duties. Mr.Heard had done remarkably well, and he knew he had often had to run after a player. He also spoke of the work which the treasurer had done, and said they must not forget the president and vice-presidents. Their president had frequently helped them in the matter of their teams. Mr.Heard suitably responded.

Mr.Smith proposed a similar compliment to the Chairman, observing that he never wished to sit under a better. Mr.Heard seconded, and said they had little idea of what Mr.Fitch had done for the club. Only on Friday he had an interview with Mr.Fitch on football matters, and on Saturday he asked him to do a favour for the club. The motion met with an enthusiastic reception. The Chairman thanked them for the cordial manner in which they had received the proposition. It was always a pleasure to him to come there and meet them, as he took a very deep interest in the club. He was afraid the value of the little he had done had been rather over estimated.

Regarding the ground, they were entering into an agreement with the Great Eastern Railway Company. He thought the ground had been obtained on favourable terms, and made the fortunes of the club secure for three years. He again thanked them for their vote of thanks, and hoped he should meet them on many future occasions, and that the club had a successful time in front of it. (Applause).

Letter from a former Romford player

R.M.S. Paparos,
October 27th, 1906.

Dear "Jack Horner", - How are the "Bonnie Blues" getting on this season? I sincerely trust they will have a good season, and prove to be better than they were last year. There is one department on the field where I noticed a decided improvement on last year, and that is in goal, and I feel sure if Smith keeps up the reputation he made, in my mind he will be one of the best goalkeepers in Essex by the time you receive this letter. I am feeling much better and having a good time. Nobody can imagine the fun there is on board ship when the weather is fine. I am on the committee (sports), and take an active part in all the sports. We have played several cricket matches against the officers and crew, also a match England v. New Zealand, and Colonials winning by four wickets. It was great fun.

Wishing you all a happy Christmas and prosperous new year, although, perhaps rather previous, and a jolly successful season.

Yours very sincerely, BERT GOODMAN

Note: The writer Bert Goodman had been Romford's goalkeeper the previous season!

A couple of little items of interest from the Press

"It is with pleasure I beg to draw our readers' attention to the subscription lists in the town in order to give our little wonder of last season, B.G.Aston, a suitable wedding gift, and hope his many friends and admirers will come forward liberally." (Jack Horner, *Essex Times*, 19th Jan.)

23 Mar: In the Chelmsford Swifts versus Saffron Walden game B.Ackland the Walden goalkeeper in getting rid of the ball carried it according to the referee, for three steps out of his goal. A free kick was awarded and a very "soft" goal was scored.

Season 1907 – 8

ROMFORD FOOTBALL CLUB

President: Mr.C.F.Fitch,C.C. **Hon.Secretary:** Mr.C.T.Heard **Hon.Treasurer:** Mr.W.R.Carter

Captain: A.E.Jones **Vice-Captain:** A.V.Frisby

Committee: Messrs. E.Currie,E.P.Jones,W.H.Kelly,T.H.Randall,A.Reynolds,G.A.Smith,G.Winmill.

Hon. Auditors: Messrs. F.W.Jeffes and E.J.Wallis **Club Colours:** Blue and Black Stripes

Headquarters: Rising Sun Hotel, Romford **Ground:** Cricket Ground, Romford Station

COMPETITIONS ENTERED

South Essex League Division IA
F.A. Challenge Cup
F.A. Amateur Cup
Essex Senior Cup
West Ham Charity Cup
King's Lynn Hospital Cup

Reserve Team disbanded

Match Details

7 Sept Frdly Away Leytonstone 1 – 4 Jones
Romford: W.G.Smith;P.H.Rowberry,W.M.Turner;A.V.Frisby,A.Denny,G.Wilson;
F.H.Kittle,A.E.Jones(Capt),F.C.Moule,J.Welch,A.S.Hyett.

14 Sept Frdly Home Plumstead 4 – 0 Hyett(2)Jones,Moule
Attendance: 500
Romford: W.G.Smith;P.H.Rowberry,G.Drury;A.V.Frisby,A.Denny,J.Hunter;
G.Wilson,A.E.Jones(Capt),F.C.Moule,A.W.Asater,A.S.Hyett.

21 Sept FACPR Home Woodford 10 – 1 A.E.Jones(5)Hyett(3)Wilson,Moule
Romford: W.G.Smith;P.H.Rowberry,W.M.Turner;G.Drury,A.Denny,G.Wilson;
F.H.Kittle,A.E.Jones(Capt),F.C.Moule,J.Welch,A.S.Hyett.

28 Sept SEL1A Away Chelmsford 1 – 4 Hyett
Romford: W.G.Smith;P.Rowberry,W.M.Turner;A.V.Frisby(Capt),A.Denny,G.Wilson;
F.H.Kittle,A.W.Asater,F.C.Moule,A.S.Hyett,S.C.Squier.

3 Oct WHC1R Home 2nd Grenadier Guards w/o **The Guards failed to arrive!**

5 Oct FAC1Q Away Clapton Orient 3 – 6 Jones,Denny,Wilson
Attendance: 4,000 at Homerton
Romford: W.G.Smith;P.H.Rowberry,W.M.Turner;A.V.Frisby,A.Denny,G.Wilson;
F.H.Kittle,A.E.Jones(Capt),F.C.Moule,F.A.Stevens,S.Squier.

12 Oct SEL1A Home 4th King's Royal Rifles 2 – 1 Wilson(2)
Romford: W.G.Smith;P.H.Rowberry,W.M.Turner;A.V.Frisby(Capt),A.Denny,G.Wilson;
F.H.Kittle,A.E.Jones(Capt),F.C.Moule,J.Welch,S.C.Squier.

19 Oct Frdly Away** Tottenham Hotspur Reserves 1 – 4 Asater
Romford: W.G.Smith;P.H.Rowberry,W.M.Turner;A.V.Frisby,A.Denny,G.Wilson;
F.H.Kittle,A.E.Jones(Capt),F.C.Moule,S.Cartwright,S.C.Squier.

26 Oct SEL1A Away South Weald 2 – 3 Squier,Moule
Romford: W.G.Smith;P.H.Rowberry,W.M.Turner;A.V.Frisby,A.Denny,G.Wilson;
F.H.Kittle,A.E.Jones(Capt),F.C.Moule, ? ,S.C.Squier.

2 Nov Frdly Home Page Green Old Boys 4 – 3 Jones(2)Wilson,Drury
Romford: W.G.Smith;P.H.Rowberry,W.M.Turner;G.Drury,E.Baldwin,A.Denny;
G.Wilson,F.H.Kittle,A.E.Jones(Capt),F.C.Moule,Mace.

9 Nov Frdly Home Coldstream Guards 1 – 1 Jones
Romford: W.G.Smith;P.H.Rowberry, ? ; ? , ? ,G.Wilson;
F.H.Kittle,A.E.Jones(Capt),S.Cartwright,A.W.Asater,S.C.Squier.

16 Nov Frdly Home Upton Park 5 – 2 Jones(4)Wilson
Romford: W.G.Smith;P.H.Rowberry,W.M.Turner;E.Baldwin,A.Denny,G.Wilson;
F.H.Kittle,A.E.Jones(Capt),S.Cartwright,F.C.Moule,S.C.Squier.

23 Nov ESC2R Home Leigh Ramblers 7 – 0 Jones(3)(1pen)Cartwright(2)Moule(2)
Romford: W.G.Smith; P.H.Rowberry,W.M.Turner;E.Baldwin,A.Denny,G.Wilson;
F.H.Kittle,A.E.Jones(Capt),S.Cartwright,F.C.Moule,S.C.Squier.

30 Nov Frdly Home Leigh Ramblers P – P #

7 Dec Frdly Home Leytonstone 4 – 1 Jones(4)
Romford: W.G.Smith;P.H.Rowberry,W.M.Turner;E.Baldwin, ? ,G.Wilson;
F.H.Kittle,A.E.Jones(Capt),D.H.Clark,F.C.Moule,S.C.Squier.

14 Dec SEL1A Home Wanstead 5 – 0 Jones(3),Frisby,Moule
Romford: W.G.Smith;P.H.Rowberry,W.M.Turner;A.V.Frisby,A.Denny,E.Baldwin;
F.H.Kittle,A.E.Jones(Capt),G.Wilson,F.C.Moule,A.W.Asater.

19 Dec WHC2R Home East Ham w/o ##

21 Dec Frdly Home Clapton 1 – 0 Moule
Attendance: 500
Romford: W.G.Smith;P.H.Rowberry,A.V.Frisby;E.Baldwin,A.Denny,G.Wilson;
F.H.Kittle,A.E.Jones(Capt),F.C.Moule,B.Ives,A.W.Asater.

25 Dec Frdly Home Wanstead 2 – 1 Wilson(pen),Ives
Romford: G.Wilson,
B.Ives, Remainder of team unknown.

26 Dec Frdly Home South Weald 2 – 2 Moule,Mongford
Attendance: 900
Romford: W.G.Smith;P.H.Rowberry,W.M.Turner;A.V.Frisby(Capt), ? , ? ;
F.H.Kittle,Mongford,F.C.Moule,B.Ives,A.W.Asater.

28 Dec Frdly Home 1st Scots Guards 3 – 0 Moule,Ives,Wilson
Romford: W.G.Smith;P.H.Rowberry,W.M.Turner;A.V.Frisby(Capt),A.Denny, ? ;
G.Wilson, ? ,F.C.Moule,B.Ives,S.C.Squier.

4 Jan AC1R Away Ilford 1 – 3 Moule
Attendance: 2,000
Romford: W.G.Smith;P.H.Rowberry,W.Turner;A.V.Frisby,A.Denny,G.Wilson;
F.H.Kittle,,A.E.Jones(Capt),S.CartwrightF.C.Moule,S.C.Squier.

11 Jan ESC3R Home Leytonstone 8 – 0 Jones(3)Moule(3)Wilson(2)
Romford: W.G.Smith;P.H.Rowberry,W.M.Turner;F.H.Kittle,A.Denny,G.Wilson;
A.E.Jones(Capt),D.H.Clark,S.Cartwright,F.C.Moule,S.C.Squier.

18 Jan SEL1A Home Barking 6 – 2 Jones(3),Clarke,Ives,Moule(pen)
Romford: W.G.Smith;P.H.Rowberry,W.M.Turner;F.H.Kittle,A.Denny,G.Wilson;
A.E.Jones(Capt),D.H.Clark,F.C.Moule,B.Ives,A.W.Asater.

25 Jan SEL1A Home South Weald 3 – 2 Jones(2pens)Wilson
Attendance: 1,500
Romford: W.G.Smith;P.H.Rowberry,W.M.Turner;F.H.Kittle,A.Denny,G.Wilson;
A.E.Jones(Capt),D.H.Clark,F.C.Moule,B.Ives,A.W.Asater.

1 Feb SEL1A Home Walthamstow Grange 1 – 1 Ives
Romford: W.G.Smith;D.H.Clark,W.M.Turner;A.V.Frisby,A.Denny,G.Wilson;
F.H.Kittle,A.E.Jones(Capt),F.C.Moule,B.Ives,A.W.Asater.

8 Feb ESC4R Away Walthamstow Grange 1 – 2 Scorer unknown
Romford: W.G.Smith; Remainder of team unknown.

15 Feb SEL1A Away Walthamstow Grange 4 – 1 Jones(2)(1pen),Scotton,Ives
Romford: S.Poulter;P.H.Rowberry,W.M.Turner;D.H.Clark,A.Denny,G.Wilson;
F.H.Kittle,A.E.Jones(Capt),F.C.Moule,B.Ives,W.Scotton.

20 Feb WHC3R Home Manor Park Albion 4 – 3 Jones(3)Scotton
Romford: J.L.McNair;Giles,
A.E.Jones,W.Porter,W.Scotton.

22 Feb SEL1A Away Barking 3 – 2 Jones,Denny,Scotton
Attendance: 600
Romford: R.Heath;P.H.Rowberry,W.M.Turner;D.H.Clark,A.Denny,G.Wilson;
F.H.Kittle,A.E.Jones(Capt),F.C.Moule,W.Scotton,S.C.Squier.

29 Feb SEL1A Away Wanstead 5 – 1 Scorers unknown
Romford: J.L.McNair;P.H.Rowberry,W.M.Turner;D.H.Clark,A.Denny,G.Wilson;
F.H.Kittle,F.C.Moule,B.Ives,W.Scotton,S.C.Squier.

7 Mar Frdly Home Upton Park 3 – 0 Scorers unknown
Romford:
Team details unknown.

14 Mar Frdly Away Clapton 3 – 3 Jones(2)Moule
Romford: J.L.McNair;P.H.Rowberry,W.M.Turner;D.H.Clark,A.Denny,F.H.Kittle;
A.E.Jones(Capt),F.C.Moule,B.Ives,W.Scotton,S.C.Squier.

21 Mar WHCSF Home Woodford Albion 4 – 3 Scorers unknown
Romford:
Team details unknown.

28 Mar SEL1A Home Chelmsford 1 – 1 Moule
Romford: J.L.McNair;P.H.Rowberry,W.M.Turner;D.H.Clark,A.Denny,G.Wilson;
F.H.Kittle,A.E.Jones(Capt),F.C.Moule,B.Ives,S.C.Squier.

4 Apr WHCF Away Clapton 3 – 4* Jones(2)Moule
Romford:
A.E.Jones(Capt),F.C.Moule, Remainder of team unknown.

11 Apr KLCSF Neut Norwich St James 5 – 1 Jones,Purvis,Ives,Fitchie,Wilson
Romford: G.Wilson,
Purvis,A.E.Jones(Capt),T.Fitchie,B.Ives, Remainder of team unknown.

17 Apr SEL1A Home Leigh Ramblers 8 – 0 Scorers unknown
Romford: J.L.McNair;P.H.Rowberry,W.M.Turner;A.V.Frisby,A.Denny,G.Wilson;
F.H.Kittle,A.E.Jones(Capt),F.C.Moule,B.Ives,W.Scotton.

18 Apr SEL1A Away Leigh Ramblers 2 – 2 Moule,Clarke
Romford: J.L.McNair;P.H.Rowberry;W.M.Turner,A.V.Frisby,A.Denny,D.H.Clark;
F.H.Kittle,A.E.Jones(Capt),F.C.Moule,W.Scotton,S.C.Squier.

23 Apr SEL1A Away 4th King's Royal Rifles 1 – 2### Scorer unknown
Romford: Team details unknown

25 Apr KLCF Away Lynn Town 2 – 6 Jones,Clark
Romford:
A.E.Jones(Capt),D.H.Clark, Remainder of team unknown.
'Diddy' Jones scores his fiftieth goal of the season.

29 Apr SEL1A Away 4th King's Royal Rifles 0 – 4
Romford:
Team comprised all reserve team players, names unknown.

* After extra time.
** Played at White Hart Lane.

Leigh Ramblers failed to turn up, amid rumours that they had folded, leaving disgruntled Romford supporters with no game.
East Ham sent a telegram saying they were unable to raise a team and scratched from the competition.
The match was abandoned 20 minutes from time due to snow, by this time two Romford players had already left the field suffering from the cold. When the referee stopped the game the soldiers pleaded to carry on, but by this time the Romford team had left the ground!

SUMMARY OF RESULTS OBTAINED SEASON 1907 – 08

	P	W	D	L	Goals For	Goals Ag	Pts
South Essex League	14	8	3	3	43	24	19
F.A.Challenge Cup	2	1	0	1	13	7	
F.A. Amateur Cup	1	0	0	1	1	3	
Essex Senior Cup	3	2	0	1	16	2	
West Ham Charity Cup	3	2	0	1	11	10	
King's Lynn Hosp. Cup	2	1	0	1	7	7	
Friendly Matches	13	8	3	2	34	21	
Total	38	22	6	10	125	74	

Note: The above record does not include the abandoned game against 4th King's Royal Rifles.

South Essex League Division One "A"

Final Table

	P	W	D	L	Goals For	Goals Ag	Pts
4th King's Royal Rifles	14	9	3	2	63	15	21
Romford	**14**	**8**	**3**	**3**	**43**	**24**	**19**
South Weald	14	8	2	4	35	35	18
Walthamstow Grange	14	6	4	4	29	20	16
Barking	14	7	1	6	30	30	15
Chelmsford	14	6	2	6	30	28	14
Wanstead	14	2	1	11	12	41	5
Leigh Ramblers	14	0	4	10	11	60	4

Note: The final league game was abandoned and the replayed game saw Romford take the field with no first team players in the team due to being away on holiday or business!

CUP RESULTS

F.A. Challenge Cup

Final: Wolverhampton Wanderers 3 Newcastle United 1

Romford's progress: Prel.Round Home Woodford 10 – 1
1st Qual Away Clapton Orient 3 – 6

F.A. Amateur Cup

Final: Depot Battalion Royal Engineers 2 Stockton 1

Romford's progress: 1st Round Away Ilford 1 – 3

Essex Senior Cup

Final: Ilford 3 Walthamstow Grange 0

Romford's progress: 2nd Round Home Leigh Ramblers 7 – 0
3rd Round Home Leytonstone 8 – 0
4th Round Away Walthamstow Grange 1 – 2

West Ham Charity Competition

Final: Clapton 4 Romford 3

Romford's progress: 1st Round Home 2nd Grenadier Guards w/o #
2nd Round Home East Ham w/o ##
3rd Round Home Manor Park Albion 4 – 3
Semi-Final Home Woodford Albion 4 – 3
Final Away Clapton 3 – 4*

* After extra time

\# 2nd Grenadier Guards failed to arrive.

\## East Ham scratched via a telegram!

King's Lynn Hospital Cup

Final: Lynn Town 6 Romford 2

Romford's progress:	Semi-Final	Neut.	Norwich St. James	5 – 1
	Final	Away	Lynn Town	2 – 6

South Essex League Appearances Season 1907 – 08

A.Asater	9	E.Baldwin	6	S.Cartwright	6	D.H.Clark	12
A.Denny	26	G.Drury	3	T.Fitchie	1	A.V.Frisby	15
Giles	1	R.Heath	1	J.Hunter	1	A.S.Hyett	4
B.Ives	13	A.E.Jones	29	F.H.Kittle	27	Mace	1
J.L.McNair	6	Mongford	1	F.Moule	29	W.Porter	1
S.Poulter	1	Purvis	1	P.H.Rowberry	28	W.Scotton	7
W.G.Smith	23	S.C.Squier	17	F.A.Stevens	1	W.Turner	26
A.Welch	3	G.Wilson	28			Total	327

Note: The final league game was abandoned and the replayed game saw Romford take the field with no first team players in the team due to being away on holiday or business! The players who did play are unknown and these appearances are of course missing from the above summary. A number of team line ups are unknown or incomplete and this affects the above summary.

First Team Goal Scorers Season 1907 – 08

A.E.Jones	43	F.C.Moule	17	G.Wilson	12	A.S.Hyett	6
B.Ives	6	W.Scotton	3	D.H.Clark	3	S.Cartwright	2
A.Denny	2	A.W.Asater	1	S.C.Squier	1	G.Drury	1
A.V.Frisby	1	Mongford	1	Purvis	1	T.Fitchie	1
Unknown	24					Total	125

Note: The above record does not include the goal scored in the abandoned fixture against 4th King's Royal Rifles. Due to the fact that the scorers of 25 goals are not known, the above record is unfortunately far from complete. It is understood that "Diddy" Jones scored his 50th goal of the season in the away game against Lynn Town.

RESERVES

Match details

9 Nov	Frdly	Home	Hoffmann Athletic	2 – 0

Post-Season Summary Season 1907 – 08

The season opened with two friendly matches, first a defeat against Leytonstone by four goals to one and then a 4-0 victory over Plumstead. Then came a 10-1 thrashing for poor old Woodford in the F.A. Cup, with 'Diddy' Jones netting on five occasions. This was followed by defeat in the first South Essex League game of the season by Chelmsford.

Romford then made progress in the West Ham Charity Cup without kicking a ball! The club received a walkover due to the non-appearance of the 2nd Grenadier Guards. Two days later Romford were despatched from the F.A. Cup when Clapton Orient won 6-3. Romford then picked up two league points with a 2-1 victory over 4th King's Royal Rifles and lost 4-1 to Tottenham Hotspur Reserves in a friendly. Local rivals South Weald then took the league points with a 3-2 home win and this was followed by three more meaningless friendly encounters.

On 23rd November, amid rumours in the local press that Arthur 'Diddy' Jones was to join Portsmouth, Romford defeated Leigh Ramblers 7-0 in the Essex Senior Cup. Jones got a hat-trick! A week later Leigh Ramblers were due at the Cricket Ground for a friendly but they failed to turn up amid rumours that they had folded, leaving disgruntled Romford supporters with no game. December began with 'Diddy' Jones denying that any approach had been received from Portsmouth, and Romford beat Leytonstone in a friendly match in which he scored all four goals.

Jones recorded a hat-trick in his next game against Wanstead in the league, won by five goals to nil. The following Thursday East Ham sent a telegram and scratched from the West Ham Charity Cup, putting Romford through to the third round without playing a game! December was definitely Romford's month. They won five and drew one of the six games played, albeit that five were friendlies.

The New Year started with a swift exit from the Amateur Cup away to Ilford, but the following week progress was made in the Essex Senior Cup at the expense of Leytonstone, who were soundly trounced by eight goals to nil with Jones and Fred Moule each getting a hat-trick. Jones scored another three goals in the next match when Romford defeated Barking 6-2 in a South Essex League game. It was reported that John Lamont McNair, Barking's goalkeeper and captain, chose to defend the Railway End.

Next was a home league fixture against old friends South Weald which Romford won by the odd goal in five. This was also a benefit match for long-time favourite Albert Hyett, tickets being sold for sixpence each. Romford then played Walthamstow Grange in three successive games, the first of which was a home one all draw in the league. Grange knocked Romford out of the Essex Senior Cup the following week at Walthamstow. The *Essex Times* received numerous letters criticizing goalkeeper Smith for his performance in this game, and he left the club immediately. A week later, with Poulter in goal, Romford won 4-1 away to Grange and two league points were in the bag.

On 20th February, Romford borrowed three players (J.L.McNair, Giles and W.Porter) from their friends at Barking, when they entertained and beat Manor Park Albion in the West Ham Charity Cup with 'Diddy' Jones recording yet another hat-trick.

The following week Romford won at Barking in a league fixture amid much controversy. It was reported that a Romford player punched a Barking player full in the face, the Barking man retaliated and both were sent off. As the Barking player was walking back to the changing room, a Romford supporter attacked him. This apparently caused a wholesale stampede and it took some time to clear the ground!

A week later Romford beat Wanstead by five goals to one in a league game. We do not know the scorers, but Jones happened to be absent playing for Luton Town in the Southern League! A couple of friendly matches were then played, followed by the West Ham Charity Cup semi-final tie against Woodford Albion which was won by four goals to three. Romford picked up a league point at Chelmsford, but disappointingly lost to the powerful Clapton team by the odd goal in seven after extra time in the West Ham Charity Cup final.

The following week Romford defeated Norwich St. James 5-1 in the King's Lynn Charity Cup. Scottish International T.Fitchie guested for the club and scored one of the goals. Romford then met Leigh Ramblers in two league games, recording an eight goal to nil win at home and a two two draw away. In the latter game Jones missed his train and arrived with 20 minutes played and Romford losing 0-2.

On 23rd April there was more controversy! Romford were losing 2-1 away to 4th King's Royal Rifles when the match was abandoned 20 minutes from time due to snow. By this time two Romford players had already left the field suffering from the cold. When the referee stopped the game the soldiers pleaded to carry on, but by this time the Romford team had left the ground! Two days later Romford travelled to Norfolk to meet Lynn Town in the King's Lynn Charity Cup and were beaten by six goals to two.

The final game of the season was the replay of the 4th King's Royal Rifles league game and this would decide the outcome of the league title. Romford's senior players were all on holiday and no first team members took part in the game. The composition of the team is unknown. Romford lost by four goals to nil and finished as runners up!

During the season the following players all left the club for pastures new: Albert V. Frisby (Dulwich Hamlet), B.Ives (Crystal Palace), P.H.Rowberry (West Norwood and later Wanstead), W.G. Smith (Woodford) and G.Wilson (Leytonstone). J.Welch, who played for the first team at the start of the season and once or twice later on, was employed by P. & O. Liners and often had to work on a Saturday. The club did not run a reserve team this year. Finally, D.H.Clark and Fred Moule were both awarded their Essex Senior Badge for three or more appearances in the County team.

Annual General Meeting
(as reported in the *Essex Times,* Wednesday 3rd June 1908)

The annual general meeting of the Romford Football Club was held at the Rising Sun, Hotel on Monday evening June 1st the popular president (Mr.C.F.Fitch C.C.) occupying the chair. There was a large attendance of members. Mr.Carter referred to a statement contained in a circular issued by the Committee, that only members who produced their membership tickets would be admitted to the meeting. That had not been enforced, and he thought there should be some explanation. He produced a copy of the rules, which stated that members' subscriptions should become payable on September 1st. The Chairman, after looking at the copy, said the rules were evidently very old because he saw that the subscription was down as 2s 6d., and he believed it was now 5s 0d. He did not see anything in the rules with regard to the latter clause in the circular which had been sent out. He thought it meant that no one was entitled to his membership card until he had paid his subscription. He did not know whether it was the wish of any in the room that he should ask those who were not members to withdraw.

The Hon.Secretary (Mr.C.T.Heard) said last year sixteen new members were made and only four paid their subscriptions. That was why they issued the poster. They were not the only club to do so. If people came there and made application for membership, they should pay. Mr.Carter said that his point was the Committee had no right to alter the rules. Rule 9 said they could not be altered, except by notice at the annual meeting, or at a special meeting convened for the purpose.

Mr.A.Page claimed that a member did not become a full member until he had paid his subscription. They would not admit a man to the ground until he had paid his subscription. He could not see that there had been any alteration to the rules. A man who had paid his subscription was a member up to the 1st September. Mr.Carter said he should like to point out that of 172 old members only about 30 had paid. The Chairman said Mr.Carter had pertinently put an important point, and if only 30 of 170 old members paid their subscriptions last year, the new members elected that night should undertake to pay their subscriptions when they became due.

Mr.Carter said he was satisfied with the Chairman's ruling that a member elected that night should not have to at once put his hand into his pocket. Mr.W.H. Kelly suggested that those proposing new members should guarantee that the subscriptions would be paid. The Chairman did not think that they could ask for a guarantee, but he could not see how they could conduct the club if the members did not pay the very small subscription demanded. It seemed to him the rules were not quite definite enough. He thought they ought to be re-drafted. Mr.W.D. Matthews moved that anyone not a full member that night should be asked not to vote until his subscription had been paid. Mr.Bowley seconded Mr. Matthews' motion. Mr.Carter moved as an amendment that the subscriptions of those elected members that night should become due on September 1st. Mr. Matthews said his only object was to help them get on with the business. Mr.H. Small seconded the amendment, which was carried. The following new members were then elected: Messrs. C.Buckridge, W.Abrahams, Geo.Burrows, C.J.Russell, O.Deane, F.Wilson, F.J.Bescoby, J.Emberson, F.Spencer, H.D.Warner, W.H. Stephens, P.Harvey, H.Phelp, C.Davis, H.Hawkins, H.Brooks, H.Lamb, and A.E.Bramble.

The Hon.Secretary submitted the financial report, from which it appeared the receipts had amounted to £377.10s.2d. and there was a balance at the bank of £25.17s.5d. and in his hands of 5s.0d. The gates with guarantees came to £320; President and Vice-Presidents' subscriptions to £14.1s.0d, & members' subscriptions to £10.15s.0d. The team's travelling and players' expenses totalled £125.13s.7d. The benefit match for Mr.A.S.Hyett realised £11.10s.2d. Mr.Matthews proposed that the balance sheet be adopted. This was seconded by Mr.Kelly and carried.

The Annual Report was submitted by the Hon.Secretary and read as follows: "In submitting my report, I have very great pleasure in stating we have had a very successful season, both financially and playing. We played 40 matches, won 23, lost 10 and drew 7, scored 125 goals with 77 against. It is with regret I have to inform you that although our team acquitted themselves so creditably, we did not secure any trophies, although we had some exciting events. We reached the final of the West Ham Charity Cup, and after a most arduous and exciting struggle (which no doubt you all remember), Clapton beat us by 4-3. In the South Essex League we experienced very hard luck, as we were ordered to replay the Fourth King's Royal Rifles, of Colchester, on a Wednesday, this match to decide the championship. Unfortunately, we were unable to command the services of our team, in fact we only mustered nine men, with the result we lost the match and the championship of the League.

"In the F.A.Cup tie, we were defeated, but not disgraced, by Clapton Orient in the first round and in the Amateur Cup we were exempted from the qualifying rounds, but succumbed to our near neighbours, Ilford F.C. in the first round competition proper. In the Essex Senior Cup we were unluckily defeated in the third round. I must congratulate the team on their brilliant performances during the season, and also thank them for the most consistent manner in which they turned up, in fact, with the exception of the mid-week matches, the team was very little trouble. I must make special reference to our worthy captain, Mr.A.E.Jones, to whom we owe a great debt of gratitude for his services on and off the field. I can assure you he has done a lot for the club in more ways than one. With regard to our goal scorers, our captain heads the list with 40 to his credit, F.Moule 21, Wilson 14, and Ives 10.

"It is with great regret I have to refer to the great loss the club sustained in losing the services of Mr.A.S.Hyett early in the season, owing to an injury which turned to blood poisoning. He lay in a very critical state for a long time, and his family had many anxious moments, but I am glad to say he has quite recovered. I have no hesitation in saying that his absence from the team lost us at least one or two cups. With the exception of the foregoing, I am pleased to say we have been very free from injuries this season. I take this opportunity of thanking my committee for their able assistance during the season. In conclusion, I feel somewhat reluctantly to tender you my resignation as hon.secretary".

The Chairman said the remark that Mr.Heard was going to retire would not meet with all their approval. He had acted as pilot and guide during the years he (the Chairman) had been connected with the club. They were indebted to him for the voluntary work he had done for the good of the club. In future he hoped it would not be left to the secretary or chairman to make references to non-payment of subscriptions. They must not think because they found themselves at the end of the year with £25 in hand that there was no need to pay subscriptions. The report seemed to him to compare very favourably with other reports. Mr.H.Currie moved the adoption of the report, which was agreed to.

Mr.Matthews took the chair, and proposed that they again ask Mr.Fitch to take the position of president. During his long experience of the club they had never had a president who had taken a more wholehearted interest in its doings than Mr.Fitch had done. (Hear,hear). He proposed his re-election. Mr.Heath seconded, and said they could not do better. The proposition was unanimously carried. It was also agreed that an appreciation of Mr.Fitch's services should be recorded on the minutes.

Mr.Fitch, on again taking the chair, said he had to thank them for the confidence they had again reposed in him. That made the third year he had been their president. He could not but feel gratified, and so long as he lived in Romford he should take an interest in sport, more particularly in the football club. (Applause). It had made a good name, and it was his wish that it should always retain it.

The vice-presidents, with some exceptions, were re-elected. The Chairman said they deeply regretted the loss during the year of two vice-presidents, who had been liberal supporters of the club. He referred to the late Mr.Fredk.Wilson and the late Mr. W.M.Lusby. He was sure they would like to express their regret by passing a vote on condolence with the families. This was agreed to. Mr.Percy W.Wilson was unanimously elected a vice-president.

Mr.C.A.Wilson proposed Mr.W.H.Kelly for the post of hon.secretary. Mr.Kelly had done a great deal of the hard work for the club, and he thought the time had come when they should promote him. Mr.Pring seconded. Mr.Page asked if Mr.Heard would reconsider his decision and again act. He proposed that he should be pressed to reconsider his decision, and Mr.Heard was again re-elected. Heard offered his thanks for the loyal support.

Mr.C.E.Spencer proposed Mr.W.R.Carter as hon.treasurer, and this was seconded by Mr.Heard, but Mr.Carter said his health would not allow him to take the post. Mr.Evan Jones and Mr.A.E.Jones were also proposed, and the former was eventually elected, and expressed his willingness to act. Mr.Arthur Jones was unanimously re-elected captain, on the proposition of Mr.Turner, seconded by Mr.Moule. Mr.A.S.Hyett was unanimously re-elected as vice-captain, on the proposition of Mr.Asater, seconded by Mr.Kittle. The auditors, Messrs.F.W.Jeffes and E.J.Wallis, were re-elected. The following were appointed on the Committee:- Messrs. G.A.Smith, E.Currie, L.Fletcher, S.Dowsing, J.Robarts, A.Reynolds, and R.Heath. Mr.W.H.Kelly was proposed, but desired that his name should not be voted upon.

The Chairman presented the medals which had been won by the club, as runners-up in the South Essex League. Those receiving them were: Messrs. E.Baldwin, D.Clarke, G.Wilson, W.Smith, A.E.Jones, P.Robery, A.Denny, S.C.Squier, L.McNair, A.V.Frisby, S.W.Asater, W.Turner, F.Kittle, F.Moule, and B.Ives. A vote of thanks to the officers was proposed by Mr.A.Page, and heartily accorded, and the Chairman replied. On the proposition of Mr.Smith, seconded by Mr.Matthews, it was resolved to ask the Hon.secretary's acceptance of an honorarium of five guineas. A vote of thanks to Mr.Fitch for presiding brought the proceedings to a close.

Letter to the editor of the *Essex Times*:

FOOTBALL CLUB MANAGEMENT

Having been connected with football management before I came to reside in Romford, I cannot understand the wording of the notice sent out to members of the Town club, who are asked to attend the annual meeting next Monday. In that notice I take exception to the words "only those who produce their cards of membership can gain admission". May I ask the hon.secretary what is to be said or done to those who are not already members, but are willing to become same for season 1908-09? Are they to be refused admission unless they pay their subscription? If so, why should they be asked to pay their subscription at this meeting when last year's members were allowed till October 1st, and, in some cases, after that date? Has the club any guarantee that all last year's members are going to pay their subscriptions? Having paid last year's subscriptions they are entitled to vote, although they may not have any idea of being members this season. The scheme is too open to deceive right-minded people, and I trust all those who have the interest of the Romford club at heart will attend the meeting, and if not already members, will become same on that night, and by the rules of the club no secretary or any other official can refuse them admission."

W.H.PRING. "St. Dunstans" 9, Medora Road, Romford. 25th May 1908.

The above letter was the forerunner to the uprising at the following year's meeting on 14th July 1909, when Mr.Pring was to be elected hon.secretary in controversial circumstances!

West Ham Hospital Charity Match

The following players were selected to play against West Ham United at Boleyn Castle on Thursday next, 30th April:-
L.McNair(Romford);J.J.Bayley(Clapton),W.C.Millward(Woodford);D.H.Clark(Romford),
C.Fairweather(Leytonstone),J.E.Olley(Clapton);W.Church(Leytonstone),O.Papineau(Upton Park),
A.E.Jones(Romford),C.Purnell(Clapton), and F.Jackson(Custom House).
Referee, Mr.J.T.Tappin. Kick-off 5.30 p.m.

Season 1908 – 9

ROMFORD FOOTBALL CLUB

President: Mr.C.F.Fitch.C.C. **Hon. Secretary:** Mr.C.T.Heard **Hon. Treasurer:** Mr.E.P.Jones

Captain: A.E.Jones **Vice-Captain:** A.S.Hyett

Club Colours: Blue and Black Stripes

Committee: Messrs. G.A.Smith, E.Currie, L.Fletcher, S.Dowsing, J.Robarts, A.Reynolds, and R.Heath

Auditors: Messrs. F.W.Jeffes and E.J.Wallis

Headquarters: Rising Sun Hotel, Romford **Ground:** Cricket Ground, Romford Station

COMPETITIONS ENTERED

South Essex League Division One
F.A. Challenge Cup
F.A. Amateur Cup
Essex Senior Cup
West Ham Charity Cup
Ilford Hospital Cup

The Club committee decided not to run a reserve team for this season.

Match Details

5 Sept Frdly Away# Southend United Reserves 2 – 9 Scorers unknown
Attendance: 1,500
Romford: Selected team J.L.McNair;A.M.Baker(late of Chelmsford),W.Turner;D.H.Clark,J.C.Doggett,F.H.Kittle;
W.A.Porter,F.C.Moule,A.E.Jones(Capt),B.Ives,J.Dadswell.

12 Sept Frdly Home Southend United Reserves 1 – 4 Porter
Romford: J.L.McNair;A.M.Baker,W.Turner;D.H.Clark,B.G.Aston, ?? ;
W.A.Porter,F.C.Moule,A.E.Jones(Capt), ?? ,A.C.Potter.

19 Sept FACPR Away Leyton 0 – 1
Attendance: 3,000
Romford; J.L.McNair;A.M.Baker,W.Turner;B.G.Aston,J.C.Doggett,F.H.Kittle;
W.A.Porter,F.C.Moule,Corbett,A.S.Hyett(Capt),A.C.Potter.

26 Sept SEL1 Away 4th King's Royal Rifles 4 – 0 Corbett,Jones(2)Porter
Romford: J.L.McNair;A.M.Baker,W.Turner;A.C.Potter,J.C.Doggett,F.H.Kittle;
W.A.Porter,F.C.Moule,A.E.Jones(Capt),Corbett,A.S.Hyett.

3 Oct Frdly Home Leyton Reserves 3 – 2 Moule,Porter,Jones
Romford: J.L.McNair;A.M.Baker,W.Turner;B.G.Aston,J.C.Doggett,F.H.Kittle;
W.A.Porter,F.C.Moule,A.E.Jones(Capt),Corbett,A.S.Hyett.

10 Oct SEL1 Home Custom House 1 – 1 Scorer unknown
Romford: J.L.McNair;A.M.Baker,W.Turner;B.G.Aston,J.C.Doggett,F.H.Kittle;
W.A.Porter,F.C.Moule,B.Hibbert,Corbett,A.S.Hyett(Capt).

17 Oct SEL1 Away Wanstead 1 – 0 Aston
Romford: J.L.McNair,T.Davies,W.Turner;A.C.Potter,J.C.Doggett,F.H.Kittle;
B.G.Aston,F.C.Moule,A.E.Jones(Capt),Corbett,A.S.Hyett.

24 Oct Frdly Home Gresham 4 – 0 Scorers unknown
Romford:
Team details unknown

31 Oct ESC1R Away Shoeburyness Garrison 3 – 3 Hyett(2)Potter
Romford: J.L.McNair;A.M.Baker,W.Turner;A.C.Potter,J.C.Doggett,F.H.Kittle;
W.A.Porter,F.C.Moule,B.Hibbert,Corbett,A.S.Hyett(Capt).

7 Nov ESCRep Home Shoeburyness Garrison 3 – 1 Moule(2),Corbett
Romford: J.L.McNair;A.M.Baker,W.Turner;A.C.Potter,J.C.Doggett,F.H.Kittle;
W.A.Porter,F.C.Moule,D.Clarke,Corbett,A.S.Hyett(Capt).

14 Nov SEL1 Away Barking 3 – 4 Jones(2)Dadswell
Attendance: 900
Romford: J.L.McNair;A.M.Baker,W.Turner;F.H.Kittle,J.C.Doggett,B.G.Aston;
J.Dadswell,Corbett,A.E.Jones(Capt).A.S.Hyett,A.C.Potter.

21 Nov ESC2R Home Newportonians 1 – 1 Jones
Romford: J.L.McNair;A.M.Baker,W.Turner;F.H.Kittle,J.C.Doggett,A.S.Hyett;
W.A.Porter,W.Scotton,A.E.Jones(Capt),Corbett,A.C.Potter.

28 Nov ESCRep Away Newportonians 2 – 3 Jones,Porter
Romford: J.L.McNair;A.M.Baker,W.Turner;D.H.Clark,J.C.Doggett,F.H.Kittle;
W.A.Porter,W.Scotton,A.E.Jones(Capt),Corbett,A.C.Potter.

5 Dec SEL1 Home Shoeburyness Garrison 3 – 1 Hyett(2)Jones
Romford: J.L.McNair;A.M.Baker,W.Turner;B.G.Aston,J.C.Doggett,F.H.Kittle;
W.A.Porter,F.C.Moule,A.E.Jones(Capt),A.S.Hyett,A.C.Potter.

12 Dec SEL1 Home Woodford 5 – 0 Hyett,?? others
Romford: J.L.McNair;A.M.Baker,W.Turner;B.G.Aston,J.C.Doggett,F.H.Kittle;
W.A.Porter,F.C.Moule,A.E.Jones(Capt),A.S.Hyett,A.C.Potter.

19 Dec Frdly Home Upton Park 2 – 2 Jones,Hyett
Romford: J.L.McNair;A.M.Baker,W.Turner;P.J.Moore,J.C.Doggett,F.H.Kittle;
W.A.Porter,A.E.Jones(Capt),F.C.Moule,B.Hibbert,A.S.Hyett.

25 Dec Frdly Home Wanstead 3 – 1 Jones,Hyett,Porter
Romford: J.L.McNair;A.M.Baker,W.Turner;P.J.Moore,J.C.Doggett,F.H.Kittle;
A.E.Jones(Capt),F.C.Moule,B.Hibbert,A.S.Hyett,W.A.Porter.

26 Dec Frdly Home Foots Cray 1 – 2 Moule
Romford:
Team details unknown

2 Jan SEL1 Home South Weald 7 – 3 Porter(3),Hyett(2)Squier,Jones
Romford: J.L.McNair;A.M.Baker,W.Turner;B.G.Aston,J.C.Doggett,F.H.Kittle;
W.A.Porter,F.C.Moule,A.E.Jones(Capt),A.S.Hyett,S.C.Squier.

9 Jan AC1R Away Ilford 4 – 4 Porter,Kittle(2)Hyett
Attendance: 2,500 Receipts: £57
Romford: J.L.McNair;A.M.Baker,W.Turner;B.G.Aston,J.C.Doggett,F.H.Kittle;
W.A.Porter,F.C.Moule,A.E.Jones(Capt),A.S.Hyett,A.C.Potter.

16 Jan ACRP Home Ilford 0 – 1
Attendance: 2,000 Receipts: £44
Romford: J.L.McNair;A.M.Baker,W.Turner;B.G.Aston,J.C.Doggett,F.H.Kittle;
Willy Porter,Fred.Moule,Arthur E.Jones(Capt),Albert S.Hyett,J.Dadswell.

23 Jan SEL1 Away South Weald 3 – 3 Jones,two others unknown
Romford: J.L.McNair;A.M.Baker,W.Turner;B.G.Aston,J.C.Doggett,F.H.Kittle;
W.A.Porter,F.C.Moule,A.E.Jones(Capt),J.Dadswell,A.C.Potter.

30 Jan SEL1 Away Custom House 1 – 1 Scorer unknown
Romford: J.L.McNair;A.M.Baker,W.Turner;B.G.Aston,J.C.Doggett,F.H.Kittle;
W.A.Porter,F.C.Moule,A.E.Jones(Capt),J.Dadswell,A.C.Potter.

6 Feb WHCSF Home Wanstead 3 – 2 Jones(2)Hyett
Romford: J.L.McNair;A.M.Baker,W.Turner;B.Hibbert,J.C.Doggett,F.H.Kittle;
J.Dadswell,B.G.Aston,A.E.Jones(Capt),A.S.Hyett,S.C.Squier.

13 Feb SEL1 Home 4th King's Royal Rifles 2 – 5 Porter(2)
Romford: J.L.McNair;A.M.Baker,W.Turner;B.G.Aston,J.C.Doggett,F.H.Kittle;
W.A.Porter,F.C.Moule,A.E.Jones(Capt),J.Dadswell,S.C.Squier.

20 Feb Frdly Home 1st Scot's Guards 2 – 3 Scorers unknown
Romford: J.L.McNair;A.M.Baker,W.Turner;A.C.Potter,J.C.Doggett,F.H.Kittle;
W.A.Porter,A.E.Jones(Capt),F.C.Moule,Metzier,B.Hibbert.

27 Feb SEL1 Away Chelmsford 2 – 4 Moule(2)
Romford: J.L.McNair;A.M.Baker,W.Turner;B.G.Aston,J.C.Doggett,F.H.Kittle;
B.Hibbert,F.C.Moule,J.Dadswell,S.C.Squier.

6 Mar Heavy Snow No game

13 Mar SEL1 Home Wanstead 2 – 3 Moule,one unknown
Romford: J.L.McNair;A.M.Baker,W.Turner;B.G.Aston,J.C.Doggett,F.H.Kittle;
W.A.Porter,F.C.Moule,A.E.Jones(Capt),B.Hibbert,A.S.Hyett.

20 Mar SEL1 Away## Woodford 5 – 0 Moule(2)Porter,Jones,Hyett(pen)
Romford: J.L.McNair;A.M.Baker,W.Turner;B.G.Aston,J.C.Doggett,F.H.Kittle;
W.A.Porter,F.C.Moule,A.E.Jones(Capt),A.S.Hyett.S.C.Squier.

25 Mar ICCSF Away Ilford 1 – 4 Phillips
Romford: J.L.McNair;A.M.Baker,P.J.Moore(Roneo);Hardy(Wanstead), ?? ,F.H.Kittle;
A.S.Hyett,Phillips,Brown(Roneo), ?? , ?? . (Three reserves)

27 Mar SEL1 Home Chelmsford 4 – 1 Jones(3)Hyett
Romford: J.L.McNair;A.M.Baker,W.Turner;B.G.Aston,J.C.Doggett,F.H.Kittle;
Head,F.C.Moule,A.E.Jones(Capt),A.S.Hyett,S.C.Squier.

3 Apr WHCF Clapton Leytonstone 4 – 1 Jones(3)Hyett
Romford: J.L.McNair;A.M.Baker,W.Turner;B.G.Aston,J.C.Doggett,F.H.Kittle;
W.A.Porter,F.C.Moule,A.E.Jones(Capt),A.S.Hyett,Stewart C.Squier.

9 Apr Frdly Away Halesworth 3 – 2 Scorers unknown
Romford:
Team details unknown

10 Apr Frdly Away Gorleston 3 – 0 Scorers unknown
Romford:
Team details unknown

12 Apr Frdly Away Leiston 1 – 0 Scorer unknown
Romford:
Team details unknown

15 Apr SEL1 Home Barking 2 – 3 Hyett,Moule
Romford; J.L.McNair;A.M.Baker;A.W.Asater,B.G.Aston,F.H.Kittle;
B.Hibbert,F.C.Moule,A.E.Jones(Capt),,A.S.Hyett,A.C.Potter.

17 Apr SEL1 Away Shoeburyness Garrison 1 – 4 Scorer unknown
Romford: J.L.McNair;A.M.Baker,W.Turner;A.W.Asater,B.G.Aston,F.H.Kittle;
B.Hibbert,F.C.Moule,A.S.Hyett(Capt),A.C.Potter.

\# Played at Roots Hall, Southend

\## Match played at Romford

SUMMARY OF FIRST TEAM RESULTS OBTAINED SEASON 1908 – 09

					Goals		
	P	W	D	L	For	Ag	Pts
South Essex Lge. Div.1	16	7	3	6	46	33	17
F.A.Challenge Cup	1	0	0	1	0	1	
F.A. Amateur Cup	2	0	1	1	4	5	
Essex Senior Cup	4	1	2	1	9	8	
West Ham Charity Cup	2	2	0	0	7	3	
Ilford Charity Cup	1	0	0	1	1	4	
Friendly Matches	11	6	1	4	25	25	
Total	37	16	7	14	92	79	

South Essex League Division One
Final Table

	P	W	D	L	Goals For	Goals Ag	Pts
4th King's Royal Rifles	16	12	2	2	56	22	26
Barking	16	10	1	5	34	27	21
Shoeburyness Garrison	16	9	2	5	51	30	20
Romford	**16**	**7**	**3**	**6**	**46**	**33**	**17**
Chelmsford	16	7	3	6	49	36	17
South Weald	16	7	2	7	45	45	16
Wanstead	16	4	5	7	31	36	13
Custom House	16	5	3	8	22	14	13
Woodford	16	0	1	15	8	79	1

CUP RESULTS

F.A. Challenge Cup

Final: Manchester United 1 Bristol City 0

Romford's progress: Prel.Round Away Leyton 0 – 1

F.A. Amateur Cup

Final: Clapton 6 Eston United 0

Romford's progress: 1st Round Away Ilford 4 – 4
Replay Home Ilford 0 – 1

Essex Senior Cup

Final: King's Royal Rifles 4 Barking 0

Romford's progress: 1st Round Away Shoeburyness Garrison 3 – 3
Replay Home Shoeburyness Garrison 3 – 1
2nd Round Home Newportonians 1 – 1
Replay Away Newportonians 2 – 3

West Ham Charity Cup

Final: Romford 4 Leytonstone 1
(at Spotted Dog, Clapton)

Romford's progress: Semi-Final Home Wanstead 3 – 2
Final Clapton Leytonstone 4 – 1

Ilford Charity Cup

Final: n/k

Romford's progress: Semi-Final Away Ilford 1 – 4

First Team Appearances Season 1908 – 09

A.W.Asater	2	B.G.Aston	22	A.M.Baker	30	Brown	1
D.H.Clark	3	Corbett	10	T.Davies	1	J.Dadswell	7
J.C.Doggett	27	Hardy	1	Head	1	B.Hibbert	10
A.S.Hyett	23	A.E.Jones	24	F.H.Kittle	30	J.L.McNair	31
Metzier	1	Fred. Moule	26	P.J.Moore	3	Phillips	1
Willie A. Porter	23	A.C.Potter	17	W.Scotton	2	S.C.Squier	8
W.Turner	29					Total	333

Note: Team line ups are not known for five friendly matches and some other line ups are incomplete, all of which affects the above summary.

First Team Goal Scorers Season 1908 – 09

A.E.Jones	21	A.S.Hyett	15	W.A.Porter	12	Fred.C.Moule	10
Corbett	2	F.H.Kittle	2	B.G.Aston	1	A.C.Potter	1
S.C.Squier	1	Phillips	1	J.Dadswell	1	Unknown	25
Total	92						

Post-Season Summary Season 1908 – 09

Romford's season commenced with a best-forgotten away friendly match at Roots Hall against Southend United Reserves, who achieved a resounding 9-2 win. The following week the return match was played at Romford, but the seasiders were again victorious, this time by four goals to one.

Romford's first competitive game was in the F.A. Cup, when 3,000 spectators saw them defeated 1-0 at Leyton. Leyton played a Southern League fixture on the same day and Romford protested that the home club had fielded a reserve team. The Leyton club were censured and fined £40, but the result was allowed to stand and Romford were out of the competition.

In their next game, a South Essex League match away to 4th King's Royal Rifles, Romford goalkeeper McNair saved two penalties and the team won 4-0. Then came a friendly match against Leyton Reserves which Romford won 3-2. This was followed by the first home league game of the season, in which Romford had to be content with a point in the one all draw with Custom House. Next came a 1-0 victory away to Wanstead giving Romford two more league points, followed up with a comfortable win over Gresham in a friendly fixture.

On 31st October Romford drew 3-3 away to old foes Shoeburyness Garrison in the first round of the Essex Senior Cup, and scored a three goal to one victory in the replay a week later. Next came a thriller at Barking in the league where Romford met their first league defeat of the season by three goals to four. In the second round of the Essex Senior Cup Romford drew 1-1 at home to Old Newportonians and in the replay, also played at home, Romford were knocked out by three goals to two in a disappointing game.

Early December and there were two fine home league victories, against Shoeburyness Garrison and Woodford, with Romford notching up eight goals in the process. Three friendly matches wound up the year. Romford opened 1909 with a tremendous 7-3 thrashing of local rivals South Weald and collected two more league points. A week later they were again among the goals with four away to Ilford in the Amateur Cup. However, 'Diddy' Jones missed a penalty and Romford had to settle for a drawn game. 2,000 spectators were at the Cricket Ground for the replay, but Romford disappointed them by losing 1-0.

The following week Romford picked up a league point at South Weald with a three all draw. Then came another draw at Custom House and a 3-2 win in the West Ham Charity Cup semi-final against Wanstead. Romford had to play without Fred Moule in this tie, as he took the day off to get married!

Next came a tough home league game against 4th King's Royal Rifles and Romford were defeated by five goals to two. Then came defeat in a friendly against 1st Scots Guards, followed by much controversy on 27th February. Jones and Porter missed the away match against Chelmsford after being telephoned by an unknown person saying the match was called off! Romford played with only ten men, losing 4-2.

The following week snow prevented any game being played, then there followed more disappointment for the local supporters when Romford were defeated at home against Wanstead by three goals to two.

The following week's away league game against Woodford was played at Romford at Woodford's request and Romford celebrated with a 5-0 victory. The following Thursday Romford played away to Ilford in the Ilford Charity Cup and included a couple of guest players and three reserves. Unsurprisingly, Ilford won 4-1. Next came two four goals to one victories, firstly gaining revenge against Chelmsford in the league and then a fine win against powerful Leytonstone in the West Ham Charity Cup final at the Spotted Dog Ground.

A very pleasant period followed over Easter with a trip to Suffolk and three good wins, all against Suffolk teams. The first match was against Halesworth which was won 3-2, followed by victories over Gorleston (3-0) and Leiston (1-0). Then back to Essex with a bump, as two South Essex League defeats cost Romford the runners-up spot. They lost their final two fixtures by three goals to two against Barking and four goals to one against Shoeburyness Garrison. However, Romford played with only ten men in both games!

Despite winning the West Ham Charity Cup it was only a very average season for the club and things took a dramatic turn at the Annual General Meeting. Full details are given in our Annual General Meeting report. On the brighter side, consistent performances by the club's goalkeeper, J.L.McNair, were rewarded when he was awarded his County Senior Badge for three or more appearances in the County team.

FOOTBALL ASSOCIATION COMMITTEE

The F.A. Committee met at Holborn on Monday 28th September to consider Romford's protest. The match in question drew an £80 "gate", and was won by Leyton 1-0. On the same day Leyton also played a Southern League fixture at Luton, and it may be mentioned that the Southern League and the Cup rules agree in demanding the best available teams. For Leyton, Mr. E.E.Alexander maintained, with the assistance of Sandy Tait, that they did play the full available strength on that day, and produced figures showing that Romford did not suffer through playing an alleged reserve team. Romford were not, through Mr.Matthews called upon to prove their contention, and after a meeting lasting over an hour and a half the verdict was given as follows:

> "The Committee are of opinion that the Leyton Club did not play their full available strength in the Cup-tie against Romford, in accordance with Cup rule 4. The club was censured, and fined £40, and ordered to pay the Romford club the sum of £10 as compensation."

Letter printed in the *Essex Times*, January 1909: "Romford F.C. and its critics"

For many years past 'Jack Horner's' criticisms in the *Essex Times* have always commanded the respect of the Romford F.C., even when those criticisms may have been adverse to the club. This season, however, your correspondent has – and there is no gainsaying the fact – taken strong objection to practically everything in connection with the club, and his unwarranted remarks from time to time have caused much annoyance to players and officials alike.

His latest 'grievance' (sic) is that would-be players are prevented from joining the club because of their inability to obtain registration forms. This 'rub' is undoubtedly intended for the club management in general, and myself in particular. Your correspondent knows – no one better – that the proper course for a player desirous of joining a club to pursue is for him to communicate with the hon.secretary; and should this letter catch the eye of any class player anxious to assist the Town Club he may be assured that his request will receive prompt attention by addressing it to yours truly,

C.T.HEARD, hon.secretary, Romford F.C., Ivydene, Brentwood Road, Romford. –

P.S.: Meanwhile let your correspondent do 'his' part in assisting the club."

Proposed new football club
(from the *Essex Times,* Saturday 10th May 1909)

Thursday 8th May 1909 a meeting was held at The Coach and Bell, Romford, in connection with the proposed new senior football club for Romford. Mr.W. Robshaw, who presided, said that he and two colleagues were prepared to find all necessary monies to see the club through its first season. They were in touch with several good professional and amateur players, who said they were willing to join the proposed new club. He felt uneasy regarding the ability of the club to get into a good league competition.

He was hopeful that the club might gain admittance to the 2nd Division of the Southern Football League. A letter had been received from Mr.Alexander (Secretary to the sub-committee) who felt sure that providing the club was stable and gained strong support they should be able to achieve their object. A ground quite close to the railway station could be secured at an annual rental of twenty five pounds, and this would enable two matches to be played at the same time. The meeting was adjourned pending further investigations.

About a month later Mr. Robshaw stated the he and his colleagues had abandoned the idea of forming a new professional club for the town, at least for the following season, as the suggested ground had been sold for the erection of public buildings.

Annual General Meeting
(as reported in the *Essex Times,* Saturday 23rd June 1909)

The Annual General Meeting of the Romford Football Club was held on Monday 21st June 1909, at the Rising Sun Hotel. Mr.C.F.Fitch.C.C. the President was in the chair, and there was an unusually large attendance. Among those present were Messrs. W.D. Matthews, A.Page, L.Fletcher, P.Roughton, H.W.Wilson, F.J.Dulley, C.E.Spencer, G.A. Smith, R.Carter, F.Lawrence, P.W.Wilson, J.C.Doggett, B.G. Aston, W.Boyes, F.H. Kittle, C.Russell, B.Hibbert, C.Ryle, R.Heath, G.Pearson, C.A.Wilson, A.Turvey, A.J.Joice, F.Milbank, A.Partridge, A.C.Potter, S.Dowsing, F.Robarts, A.Jarvis, H.J. Emberson, H.L.Pope, J.King, W.H.Pring, H.W.Brown, F.Rice, and J.Pearson, with Mr. C.T.Heard (Hon.Secretary) and Mr. Evan P.Jones (Hon.Treasurer). Mr.W.D.Matthews took the chair while Mr.Fitch was unanimously re-elected to President.

The Hon.Secretary presented his annual report, which stated the club had a fairly successful season, both from a playing point of view and financially. The record for the season was:- Played, 37; won, 16; lost, 14; drawn, 7; goals for, 92; against, 79. The worthy captain (Mr.A.E.Jones) once again headed the list of goal scorers, with 26 to his credit; while his deputy (Mr.A.S.Hyett) followed him closely with 21, Mr.W.A.Porter was third with 14, and Mr.F.C.Moule fourth with 13. The principal event of the season was the final of the West Ham Charity Cup, in which

Romford defeated Leytonstone and secured the handsome cup. In the F.A.Cup Romford succumbed to Leyton in the preliminary round, and in the Amateur Cup their neighbours Ilford ousted them at Romford after a drawn game at Ilford. The Essex Cup defeat by the Newportonians in the second round was a severe blow to the club, as consequently the "gates" suffered considerably. Romford finished fourth in the South Essex League – a very humble position considering the ability of the team. Several good excuses could be put forward to explain the team's poor show in the League, but he would not take up time in quoting them, as no good purpose would be served, but he felt it his duty to refer to the Chelmsford telephone incident, which deprived the club of the valuable services of Messrs. A.E.Jones and W.A.Porter.

He thanked the committee for their great assistance, as considerable trouble had been experienced from many sources, but he was pleased to say, through their energy and tact, the club had emerged successfully from a very trying season. He would like to point out that Mr. Smith, chairman of the committee, did not miss a committee meeting throughout the season. This, he thought, constituted a record, and spoke volumes for the interest Mr.Smith had taken in the club. He also thanked the players, whose valuable services during the season had so ably upheld the prestige of the club. He could also assure them that the committee had done their very best in the interests of the club. (Applause). On the proposition of Mr.W.D.Matthews, seconded by Mr.H.W.Wilson, the report was adopted.

The Hon.Treasurer presented the financial statement, which showed receipts amounting to £358.13s.1d., against £377.10s.2d last year, and a credit balance of £26.8s.6d. The Chairman proposed the adoption of the balance sheet, and said the hon.treasurer had told them the reason why the total was somewhat less than last year. He thought that was fully accounted for by the hoax at Chelmsford.The club now had their field on a three years agreement, of which one year had expired. This was the first year they had been able to recoup themselves by subletting for cricket, so they had really got the whole of the rent back. It redounded to the credit of the club that they had given a donation of £7.10s.0d. to Romford Cottage Hospital and £2.10s.0d to the Poor Children's Free Breakfasts Fund. (Hear, Hear). While they were in full health and strength they had not forgotten the suffering and the needy, and it was very creditable that they had made such handsome donations. (Applause).

He was pleased to see such a very crowded meeting. It was the largest meeting of the club he had ever attended, and it showed not only the success of the club, but the very deep interest which was taken in it by all their members. In winning the West Ham Cup, they had added to their laurels, and the play of the team seemed to have been, if possible, better than in previous years. He trusted they would do as well in the future as they had done in the past. The club seemed to march on to greater success every year. (Applause). The Romford Football Club was one of the principal clubs in Essex, and financially it held its own, because after giving liberal donations to good objects, there was a substantial balance in hand. (Applause). Mr.A.Page seconded the proposition. Mr.P.W.Wilson pointed out that the amount of the vice-presidents' subscriptions showed that a good many of the vice-presidents had not supported the club financially. The Chairman said he thought a successful club should not look to the vice-presidents to subscribe as freely as in the past. The time had come when the vice-presidents might have a rest, and he felt sure their help would be forthcoming in the future if it became necessary. The Hon. Treasurer said that the vice-presidents who did not subscribe would not be put on the list next year. The balance sheet was unanimously adopted.

Mr.W.D.Matthews took the chair during the election of the new president. He said he felt sure, from his experience, that they could not have a better president than Mr.Fitch. (Applause). Mr.H.W.Wilson proposed the re-election of Mr.Fitch as president, saying he felt quite confident there would be no opposition, and that no other name would be put forward. (Hear, Hear). Mr.J.King seconded the proposition, which was carried unanimously, amid hearty applause. Mr.Fitch again took the chair, and expressed his thanks for the very kindly terms in which they had alluded to his services. It had been a great pleasure in the past to do all he possibly could for the club. He hoped that during this year he would acquit himself to their satisfaction.

The Hon. Treasurer reported that 18 vice-presidents had not replied to his letters, and their names would not appear on the card next year. The vice-presidents were re-elected, and it was resolved to notify those who had not sent subscriptions that they would be expected to subscribe.

The Chairman read a letter from Mr.W.H.Kelly, who asked why the hon.treasurer had returned his annual subscription, and stated that Mr.Jones was entirely wrong when he said that he (Mr.Kelly) had resigned his membership. It was true that he had sent in his resignation, but he afterwards re-considered it when he was requested to do so. He thought the action of the treasurer was very arbitrary. The Chairman said he understood that the subscription had been returned in accordance with rule 5. Mr.Heard had told him that Mr.Kelly was asked to re-consider his resignation, but did not do so, and therefore he ceased to be a member of the club. Mr.Heard said Mr.Kelly declined to withdraw his resignation. Mr.Carter contended that Mr.Kelly had not received fair treatment, and proposed his election as a member. Mr.Brown seconded the proposition. The Chairman said there was nothing to prevent Mr.Kelly being elected at that meeting. After some further discussion it was agreed to proceed with the election of officers.

Mr.A.Page proposed the re-election of Mr.C.T.Heard as Hon.Secretary, and highly eulogised the services of Mr.Heard to the club. The Chairman seconded the proposition. Mr.C.A.Wilson proposed, as an amendment and as a protest against the treatment that Mr.Kelly had received, that Mr.W.H.Kelly should be elected hon. secretary. Mr.Brown seconded the amendment. The Chairman ruled the amendment out of order, and, in reply to questions, said Mr.Heard was a member of the club. Mr.Carter proposed Mr.Pring as hon. secretary. Mr.Dennison seconded the amendment, and a large number of hands were held up in favour of Mr.Pring. The election took place by ballot, & after the papers had been collected it was announced that they numbered 81, although there were only 74 members present. Mr.W.D. Matthews, one of the scrutineers, said some members had been unsportsmanlike enough to vote twice. Voices: A lot have gone out. The Chairman said there must be a fresh ballot. Mr.Matthews said there were six spoilt papers among the 81.

A second ballot took place, and eventually the Chairman announced that there were 73 papers collected. The votes recorded for Mr.Pring numbered 44, and for Mr.Heard 28. There was one spoilt paper. He declared Mr. Pring to be elected. (Cheers, cries of "Rotten!" and booing). A member questioned the legality of the voting. It was eventually agreed to take a third ballot, and this resulted in 42 votes for Mr.Pring,18 for Mr.Heard and four spoiled papers. The Chairman declared Mr.Pring to be elected as hon. secretary. Mr.Pring, Thank you, gentlemen; thank you. Mr.W.R. Carter was proposed as Hon.Treasurer. Mr.Evan P.Jones declined to stand for re-election and Mr.Carter was declared elected. The following were elected as the committee:- Messrs.D.Mead, F.W.Bridgen, C.E.Spencer, T.Twine, H.W.Brown, A.Ball and P.W.Wilson.

Mr.A.Page proposed a vote of thanks to the retiring officers and committee. He hoped the gentlemen who had been elected to fill the positions appreciated the work that was expected of them. The position of an officer of a football club was no sinecure, but entailed a vast amount of work. In the past the work had been done gladly and in the interests of the club, and all the officials were deserving of a very hearty vote of thanks for the success they had brought to the club. (Applause). Mr.Brown seconded the proposition, which was heartily carried. The Chairman briefly returned thanks. The election of a captain and a vice captain was left over to a meeting of the committee.

On the proposition of Mr.G.A.Smith, seconded by Mr.Hodson, an honorarium of £5.5s.0d. was voted to Mr.Heard for his services as hon.secretary. Mr.Heard returned thanks, and said he wished the new hon. secretary and committee every success. (Applause). The meeting ended with a vote of thanks to the Chairman.

From the same issue:
Editorial comment on the events at the Annual General Meeting

Electricity was in the air at the annual meeting of the Romford Football Club, and the unusually large gathering of members participated in discussions that were as heated as the atmosphere of the room in which the meeting was held, and that is saying a great deal. The highly satisfactory report on the achievements of last season, and the equally gratifying financial statement, met with unanimous approval.

The meeting were also at one in their selection of Mr.C.F.Fitch.C.C., to continue in the office of president. It was when the time came for the election of the other officers that the fireworks began. Discussions that became exceptionally animated arose over some questions that were raised, and it must be said in spite of all the heat engendered, the questions were really left unsettled. The majority of those present were decidedly in favour of a change of officials, and the club now has a new hon. secretary, a new hon.treasurer and a brand new committee, and the selection of a captain and vice-captain has been left to the new officers….

The club is an important and a prosperous one, and all its supporters will hope that under the new management, its prestige will be maintained and increased. Already several really good class players have expressed their willingness to throw in their lot with the Romford club.

From the same issue:
Formation of a new football club

Subsequent to the meeting of the Romford Football Club on Monday evening, at which new officers and a new committee were elected, a meeting of the supporters of the old officials and players was held. Mr.G.A.Smith, late chairman of the Committee presided over an attendance of nearly 40. Mr.C.T.Heard said the majority of the old players had asked him to run another club, to be called Romford Wanderers. Personally, he did not know whether to do so or not, but they would not let him say "No", and he had, therefore, called them together to consider the matter, and to see if they could undo the cliquism of the Romford Football Club. (Hear, hear).

The Chairman said it behoved them to do something to upset the conspiracy by several influential persons in the town, and if there were a possible chance of running a Wanderers Club he would heartily support it. (Applause). Replying to questions, Mr.Heard said it was doubtful whether the new club could enter the South Essex League, but they would be in time to enter for the Amateur, West Ham Charity, Essex Senior, and Ilford Charity Cups. The question of a ground was raised, and the Chairman said he had heard that a professional club was to be formed, but a ground could not be got; and the promoters had now come and ousted that club. Mr.A.Page suggested that endeavours should be made to get a ground just outside Romford, in the metropolitan area, and they could then enter competitions which were not open to the Romford club. In the meanwhile a Wanderers club without a ground was a good suggestion.

Mr.Evan P.Jones suggested that a deputation should wait upon Mr.Gay, of Brentwood Road, with a view to getting the use of the White Star ground. Mr.J.Doggett, an old player, proposed and Mr.J.Frank Pilling seconded, that a club should be formed. This was carried, Mr.C.T.Heard being elected hon. secretary. A further meeting is to be held this (Saturday) evening, to go into the question of Name, ground, etc. The meeting will be held at the Rising Sun Hotel at 8.30 p.m.

THE ADJOURNED MEETING
(as reported in the Essex Times, Wednesday 30th June 1909)

An adjourned meeting was held on Saturday evening 26th June to further consider the question of forming a new football club, in accordance with a decision arrived at after the annual meeting of Romford Football Club, at which a new hon. secretary, hon. treasurer, and committee were elected. Mr.G.A.Smith was elected Chairman and those present included Messrs. C.T.Heard, E.P.Jones, A.Hodson, S.Dowsing, A.Page, A.E.Jones, F.C.Moule, W.D.Matthews, G.Barnes, C.F.Russell, J.C.Doggett, W.J.Emberson, P.V.Wright, E.E.Carter, S.Bescoby, A.M.Baker, F.H.Kittle, R.Heath, A.C.Potter, F.Robarts, E.R.Hyett, W.H.Hyett, T.Small, H.Small, J.Collis, A.Asater, G.Maddocks, A.Saltwell, J.Moore, S.Stebbings, P.Roughton, W.A.Stephenson, and Arthur Drury.

The Chairman said that, as they all knew, the meeting was an outcome of what he might say was – (Voices: "The clique"):- one had to be very careful what one said– (Voices: "A conspiracy") – the turning out of the committee and other officers of the club at the annual meeting. They all felt it deeply, and they felt they did not deserve it,because they thought they had gone through a successful season and their secretary had done his work very efficiently, so that it was an insult for him to be ousted from office. (Hear, hear). It was no use crying over spilt milk, and the only thing to do was to see whether they should support the old club, or form a new club and go against the old one.

He should be very sorry to go against the old club, but if they decided to do it they must get to work at once, because unless they started successfully it would be very difficult to end successfully. (Applause).

Mr.C.T.Heard said that after the Romford Football Club's annual meeting an informal meeting was held, and it was decided to call that meeting, and to invite anyone who cared to attend, to see what they could do as a protest against the cliquism of the Romford Football Club. Mr.E.P.Jones and himself had discussed the matter thoroughly, and he was going to lay three suggestions before the meeting...The three suggestions were:- (1) That owing to the old players resenting the manner in which the new management gained office, they decline to assist the club under the new regime, but agree to a deputation, consisting of three gentlemen to be selected at this meeting on their behalf, to confer with a deputation of the new management, with a view to certain alterations being made. In the event of no satisfaction being obtained by the conference, a new club to be formed at once as a protest. (2) That we run a new club as a protest against the unsportsmanlike action of a certain clique of the members, and the manner in which they gained office. (3) That we pocket all differences, and let the new management run for a season, and see the result. (Voices: "No fear" "No").

In support of the first suggestion, he would like to point out the following facts. First of all, he thought they would all agree with him that the new officers and committee gained possession of the old club in an unfair manner. (Hear, hear). They simply scoured Romford to get new members, and he thought he was correct in saying that 30 of these new members joined within two months of the end of the season. They had no interest in sport or in the club, but they simply paid their subscriptions, or had their subscriptions paid for them, so that they might attend the meeting and out-vote the oldest members of the club.

In adopting the first suggestion he thought they would be doing something open and straightforward, and nothing that was underhand. (Hear, hear). If the other side refused the suggestion, then those present could go on their own sweet way. If they formed a new club he thought they would get all the support they had last season. Only one club would be able to live – that was to say, the old club must die. If they acted on the first suggestion they would be acting quite straightforwardly and honourably. (Applause).

The Chairman said he considered it was a very fair way of treating the old club. It was not doing anything underhand. The suggestion showed the way to obtain peace with honour, and without in any way caving in. They ought to see whether they could not come to terms with the other side in order to keep the old club running. They could not run two good clubs, and a new club would be simply running against the old club all through the season.

Mr.Page asked whether the suggestion indicated the views of the players. Mr.Heard said the suggestion was that if the old players were willing to play for the old club on certain conditions, those present should support them. Mr.A.E.Jones asked what the suggested alterations were to be. Mr. Heard said he took it that the suggestions would be made by the players, and would be supported by that meeting.

Mr.Page asked what the players wanted. Did they want the old officials re-instated? If they were going to ask the other people to cut their throats, they might as well do away with the deputation. Mr.A.E.Jones, speaking on behalf of the players, said he would like to hear the suggestions of the meeting. Mr.Tatam said he would suggest that the deputation should ask that the late hon.secretary, Mr.C.T.Heard, should be again placed in office. (Hear, hear)...Mr.Small said that after such a vile conspiracy he should not approach the other side at all. Let them stew in their own juice. Mr.A.E.Jones said he thought that meeting was proof that the players were not disaffected. They were there to back up the old executive. The Chairman said he did not say the players were disaffected.

Mr.W.D.Matthews said that, while he thought something could be done in the way of getting over the trouble, he was strongly opposed to the methods that were adopted at the Romford Football Club's annual meeting. But he saw rocks ahead of them if they formed another club. There would the difficulty of getting a ground and the difficulty of entering leagues. If some suggestion like that put forward could be adopted, and they could meet the new executive of the old club – it was difficult to find words to identify who was old and who was new – they could have a chat together, and he thought the trouble might be overcome. He did not say that he altogether approved of it, but of the two evils they should choose the least. There was a chance of the difficulty being met by the retirement of some of the new officials and the election of old ones in their place. This might be a way of getting over the trouble – that was, if the players would be loyal to such an arrangement. If the players said they would not play under the new arrangements it would be no use to approach the other side. They did not want to crawl under. It was a heavy blow; it was engineered well and successfully. He had been to Chelmsford that afternoon, and all the talk there was that they never heard of such things that were enacted at Romford last Monday. If some oil could be thrown on the troubled waters he thought it would be better for the interests of football in Romford. (Applause).

Mr.H.Small said he thought it would be perfectly useless to approach Mr.Kelly's family. He did not think they would compromise. Mr.Page said it seemed to him that they were going to ask the other side to entirely stultify what they did on Monday, and they might as well not have a deputation. A Voice: No white flag. Mr.Heard said that in the event of an arrangement being made he would pocket his pride to a certain extent, and do what he could for the old club. If they formed a new club he believed they would smash the Romford Club, and then the good name of Romford would be gone, but if they could in any way save the name of the Romford Football Club he thought they ought to do it.

Mr.H.J.Emberson suggested that they should ask for the annual meeting to be held over again. Mr.Matthews said a very prominent member of the opposition had asked him to attend that meeting and see what he could do, saying he was sure the new executive would be willing to fall in with any suggestions that might be made. Mr.H.Small said he thought that the other side had cut more than they could eat. He would like to see them get on with their job. They were showing weakness in approaching the supporters of the old officers already. Why should that meeting submit to the dirty tactics? Mr.Heard said the Romford Football Club was formed

36 years ago, and it seemed hard that they should wipe out a good name when there was a possibility of overcoming the difficulty. If they ran a new club, which without a doubt would smash the old club, they would lose the good old Romford name.

Mr.A.E.Jones said that meeting was an appreciation of the old secretary, treasurer and committee. On behalf of the players, he would say that whatever the meeting decided to do, the players would follow. If the meeting liked to join that estimable club the Mawneys Institute, the players would play for that club. (Laughter, and hear, hear). Whatever the meeting decided to do the players would chance their luck and follow them. (Applause).

Mr. Heard proposed the adoption of the first suggestion. Mr.J.Doggett proposed, as an amendment, that the deputation should ask that the old secretary, the old treasurer, and three of the old committee, should be re-instated. (Hear, hear). Mr.Bescoby seconded the amendment, Mr.E.P.Jones seconded the proposition to adopt the first suggestion. Mr.H.Small proposed as a further amendment that the meeting should ignore the present executive of the Romford Football Club, and should start a new club to be called the Romford Wanderers, or whatever name might be decided upon. Mr.Drynan seconded this amendment, and urged that there should be no compromise, and no concessions with a view to a compromise. Mr.Emberson pressed his suggestion, saying that at another general meeting the balance might be more even. At the last meeting there was a regular flood on the other side. The proposition to adopt the first suggestion was carried.

Mr.Hodson suggested that the first thing the deputation should ask for should be the re-instatement of the old treasurer and the old secretary. It was proposed and seconded that the old treasurer and the old secretary should be asked for, and that the deputation should get what they could with regard to representation on the committee. Mr.Heard said he would be quite willing to do his best with the new committee, but at the same time he should feel more at home if he had some of the old committee to work with. Mr.Doggett proposed that the deputation should definitely ask for the re-instatement of the old secretary, and the old treasurer, and should get as many of the old committee as they could, with a minimum of three. This should be an ultimatum to the new executive. Unless they could get these concessions all negotiations should stop. (Hear, hear). This was carried unanimously.

Mr.Heard said that Mr.C.F.Fitch,C.C., the president of the Romford Football Club, was quite willing to go to the conference and act as peacemaker. They would agree that Mr.Fitch was a thorough sportsman. He was very much disgusted with the state of affairs at the present time, and he hoped something would be done to smooth over the difficulties. It was resolved that the deputation should consist of Messrs. W.D.Matthews, G.Barnes, and A.Hodson...

Mr.Heard proposed that, in the event of no satisfaction resulting from the conference, a new club should be formed at once. Mr.Doggett seconded the proposition, which was carried unanimously. On the proposition of Mr.Page, seconded by Mr.Bescoby, it was resolved that the conference should take place on or before Wednesday evening, and that the meeting should stand adjourned until Friday at 8.30 p.m., to receive the report of the deputation.

Mr.Heard proposed a vote of thanks to all who had supported them, and to the chairman for presiding. He said the meeting showed that there was a feeling of confidence in the old officers, and that they did all that was required last season.

ADJOURNED MEETING
(as reported in the Essex Times, Wednesday 7th July 1909)

The adjourned meeting of the supporters of the old executive of the Romford Football Club was held on Friday night, 2nd July, at the Rising Sun Hotel, to receive the report of the deputation appointed to wait of the new executive of the club, with a view to the re-instatement of the former hon.secretary and hon.treasurer, and some members of the committee, and to the amicable settlement of the differences that had arisen. Mr.A.Page was elected to the chair. There was a large attendance, including Messrs. G.A.Smith, E.Hodson, W.D.Matthews, G.Barnes, C.Heard, E.P. Jones, A.E. Jones, S.Dowsing, G.Page, E.E.Carter, F.W.Robarts, C.F.Russell, A.Drury, F.H. Kittle, H.Small, J.Frank Pilling, W.Tatam, H.Turvey, H.W.E. Stephenson, A.Viney, H.Hibbert, H.Curley, H.Parsons, H.J.Bramble, J.Collis, J.Moore, A.Hunwicks, T.Small, C.Webb, H.Drynan, and H.H.Hinds.

The Chairman said that at the last meeting a deputation was appointed to try to effect a comprise, and in the event of non-success in this object it was resolved to form a new club at once. Mr.C.T.Heard, the late hon.secretary, read a letter from Mr.C.F.Fitch, president of the club, which had been published in full in the *Essex Times*. Mr. W.D.Matthews for the deputation said the whole result of the conference was embodied in Mr.Fitch's letter. After a great deal of discussion the new executive sent the deputation back with absolutely nothing more than that they assured the deputation of the good wishes of the new executive, and hoped the members who were opposed to them would re-consider their decision and fall into line and lovally support them. That was all they could offer the deputation. They did not even offer to give one seat on the committee, or anything. So he was afraid the deputation must consider themselves an absolute failure. They simply did nothing.

Mr.G.Barnes said he was afraid he was the fighting member of the deputation. He got rather angry. After a great deal of discussion which led to nothing, it came to the question whether they would let Mr.Heard go back, and they absolutely refused. They said they had been elected by a large majority. He could not help asking how they got the majority, and whether it was a fair majority. (Hear, hear and laughter). Mr.Hodson said the deputation did all they could, and nothing further could be done to get the new executive to give some concessions. They would not give way in anything. The deputation tried to find out why Mr.Heard was turned out. For a long time they could get no answer, but eventually it was said that there was a rumour that the club had not been properly managed. A Voice:- "Most unsatisfactory".

The Chairman asked whether the meeting would adhere to their decision to form a new club. Mr.Heard said he would like to hear comments on Mr.Fitch's letter. Mr.Fitch was very strongly against promoting a new club. Mr. Matthews recapitulated the difficulties in the way of forming a new club, but said he was sure a new club would get the most support, because many people in Romford thought the old executive had been treated in a hard and harsh manner. (Hear, hear).

Mr.Heard said there were nine of the old players who would absolutely play for the new club. (Hear, hear). There would be no trouble about a ground. He could get a ground at any moment, and that was the Shoulder of Mutton field. He would be very pleased to do what he could as secretary of the new club, if he were elected. (Applause). Mr.E.P.Jones said he would like to see a new club formed. (Applause). Mr.A.E.Jones said he was surprised that only nine players were certain. Personally he thought all players were agreed that they would play for the new club. Mr.Heard said he had not included the goalkeeper and S.Squier.

Mr.G.A.Smith proposed that a new club should be formed, to be called the Romford Town Football Club. He was rather of opinion that the new club would succeed, and as there could be only one club the old club would have to go under, & the Romford Town F.C. could easily revert to the old name & drop the "Town" out of their title. Mr A.E.Jones seconded the proposition which was carried unanimously. Officers were elected as follows:- Hon.secretary, Mr.C.T.Heard; hon.treasurer, Mr.E.P.Jones; committee, Messrs.G.A.Smith, E.Hodson, R.Heath, F.W.Robarts, L.Fletcher, H.Small, and S.Dowsing; captain, Mr.A.E.Jones; vice-captain, Mr.A.S. Hyett. The question of the election of a president was deferred. The Chairman said he believed that the club would get greater support than the most optimistic of them expected. When they saw what support they got they could elect a president.

Messrs. F.W.Jeffes and E.J.Wallis were elected auditors. It was resolved that the headquarters of the club should be the Rising Sun Hotel. The annual subscription was fixed at a minimum of 5s.0d. A large number of those present gave in their names for membership, and paid their subscriptions. The question of club colours was left for consideration by the committee.

No details of any further meetings are to hand, but the club did go ahead under the name of Romford United (a club defunct since 1908) in direct opposition to the old Romford Football Club.

From the same issue:

AN OPEN LETTER

The threatened split in the Romford Football Club will come, I am sure, as a surprise to many, and will be regarded with dismay by all true lovers of the game. As president of the club, I venture at this critical juncture of its affairs to appeal to the members to avoid adopting a course which cannot fail, if persisted in, to have disastrous results eventually to a club which has come to be regarded as one of the best in the county, and which has been so successful in the past.

A brief resume of the events which have led up to the present impasse will probably not be out of place here, and may help to clear the issues. At the last Annual General Meeting on the 21st., which some 70 or 80 members attended (about 30 of whom had recently joined), after adopting the treasurer's and secretary's reports, the motion for the election of officers came on. The late secretary (Mr.Heard) was nominated for re-election, and Mr.Pring, another member,was also nominated. On a ballot being taken, Mr.Pring was found to be, and was, duly declared elected by 48 votes to 18. The rejection of the late secretary by the meeting appears for some reason to have given dire offence to a number of the members, including all the players, and the late treasurer and committee declining to stand, a new treasurer and committee were consequently elected. Since then the dissentient members, if I may so term them, have held amongst themselves several meetings, the outcome of which has been the delivery of an ultimatum to the Executive Committee of the club, demanding, as the condition of their continued allegiance, the resignation of the present secretary and treasurer, and the re-instatement of the old ones, and also the resignation of at least three members of the committee, to be replaced by three members to be nominated by them – in my opinion, an unreasonable demand. In the alternative, they threaten to cut themselves adrift, and form at once a new club in opposition. The Executive Committee very properly decline to accede to such unreasonable and unwarrantable demands, and a deadlock has arisen in consequence.

I am sure I shall be voicing the sentiments of all well wishers of the club if, at this stage, and before it is too late, I ask the members to reflect, sink their differences, and come into line, and give the new committee and officers the same measure of loyalty and support as they have hitherto accorded in the past to their predecessors, in the sporting interest of themselves, their club, and the town.

No good can possibly come of splitting the club in two. There will be then, in that event, two grounds required; the expense will be doubled; financial support will be diverted or withheld; the gates, which are mainly relied on for expenses, will be diminished, to say nothing of the difficulties which will arise in arranging matches, entering leagues etc. The whole ground of the dispute is too trivial and petty to justify disruption, and I make this final appeal to the best sporting instincts of the members to preserve the unity and good fellowship of the club intact, and maintain its strength and reputation unimpaired.

C.F.Fitch, Elmhurst, Romford June 30th 1909.

Thus the Romford Football Club continued under a virtually new management and new players, while members of the old committee and most of the players formed the Romford United Football Club. The two were set to compete against each other in the new season.

This undated photograph of a team in the Romford strip was given to one of the authors but came with no other details. It possibly shows the original club with its new Committee and players after the split in 1909.

Authors' collection (originators unknown)

Season 1909 – 10

ROMFORD FOOTBALL CLUB
"The Blues"

President: Mr.C.F.Fitch.C.C.

Hon. Secretary: Mr.W.H.Pring From November Mr.W.H.Kelly **Hon.Treasurer:** Mr. W.R.Carter

Committee: Messrs. D.Mead, F.W.Bridgen, C.E.Spencer, T.Twine, H.W.Brown, A.Ball and P.W.Wilson.

Club Colours: Blue and Black Stripes

Headquarters: The Golden Lion Hotel **Ground:** Cricket Ground, Romford Station (see map on page 343)

COMPETITIONS ENTERED

F.A. Challenge Cup
Amateur Cup
South Essex League Division Two B
Essex Senior Cup
West Ham Charity Cup

Most of the previous season's players having left to assist the newly-formed Romford United, the old club advertised for playing members and received 137 applications. Most of these proved to be not up to the standard required, but the following players made it to the first team: J.H. de Meza (Leyton), G.Olley (Clapton), W.Giles (Barking), F.Prout (Fulham), F.Walters (Stoke), C.Parmenter (Newportonians), W.Waterfall (Herts and Oxford County) W.J.Evans and G.W. Baldwin (Millwall), A.Edwards (West Bromwich Albion) and P.Brien (Connaught Rangers).

Match Details

4 Sept Frdly Away Enfield 2 – 1 Walters,Prout
Romford: J.H.de Meza;G.Olley,S.Sheppey;J.Webb,W.Olley,C.E.Peers;
A.Mann,C.Parmenter,F.Walters,F.Prout,P.Brien.

11 Sept Frdly Away Wealdstone 3 – 2 Scorers unknown
Romford:
Team details unknown

18 Sept FACPR Home Shoeburyness Garrison 1 – 4 Scorer unknown
Romford: J.H. de Meza;G.Olley;R.Boulton,J.Webb,W.Olley,D.Clark;
E.Bassett,F.Prout,F.Walters,C.Parmenter,W.Waterfall,

25 Sept SEL1 Home Grays Athletic 7 – 1 Clark(3)Walters(2)Prout(2)
Romford: J.H. de Meza;G.Olley,R.Boulton;F.Abrams,J.Webb,E.Baldwin;
F.Prout,D.Clark,F.Walters,C.Parmenter,W.Waterfall.

2 Oct SEL1 Away Grays Athletic 0 – 1
Romford: J.H. de Meza;G.Olley,W.Davis;F.Abrams,J.Webb,E.Baldwin;
F.Prout,Willmore,F.Walters,C.Parmenter,W.Waterfall.

9 Oct SEL1 Home Shoeburyness Garrison 2 – 4 Walters,Prout
Romford: J.H. de Meza;G.Olley,W.Martin;F.Abrams,J.Webb,E.Baldwin;
F.Prout,Willmore,F.Walters,C.Parmenter,W.Waterfall.

16 Oct Frdly Home Luton Town 1 – 3 Walters
Romford: J.H. de Meza;W.Dickerson,G.Olley;F.Abrams,R.Boulton,E.Baldwin;
F.Prout,F.C.Moule,F.Walters,J.Webb,W.Waterfall.

21 Oct Frdly Home Cricklewood 1 – 4
Romford:
No team details available.

23 Oct SFL2B Home South Farnborough 1 – 2 Parmenter
Attendance: 700
Romford: J.H. de Meza;W.Dickerson,G.Olley;T.W.Carter,Ray Boulton,E.Baldwin;
F.Prout,F.C.Moule,F.Walters,C.Parmenter,W.Waterfall.

30 Oct ESCPR Home Dagenham St. Paul's 0 – 1
Romford: Hoare;W.Dickerson,F.C.Moule,C.Parmenter;
Plus seven players from Norfolk Regiment, based at Warley Barracks.

6 Nov SEL1 Away Wanstead 1 – 0 Parmenter
Romford: J.H. de Meza;A.J.Gallagher,G.Olley;Shackland,A.Edwards,T.W.Carter;
F.Prout,H.Wilkins,F.Walters,C.Parmenter,W.Waterfall.

13 Nov SFL2B Home Kettering 1 – 4 Prout
Romford: J.H.de Meza;A.J.Gallagher,A.Jones;W.Dickerson,A.Edwards,T.W.Carter;
P.Brown,F.Prout,Ray Boulton,F.Walters,W.Waterfall.

20 Nov SEL1 Away South Weald 1 – 6 Prout
Romford: J.H. de Meza;A.J.Gallagher,J.Webb;Mooney,A.Edwards,T.W.Carter;
P.Brien,F.Prout,J.Lloyd-Evans,F.Walters,W.Matthews.

27 Nov Frdly Home Walthamstow Grange 2 – 0 Scorers unknown
Romford: J.H. de Meza;A.Jones,A.J.Gallagher;W.Dickerson,A.Edwards,T.W.Carter;
P.Brien,F.Prout,J.Lloyd-Evans,F.Walters,W.Matthews.

4 Dec SEL1 Away Barking 2 – 1 Matthews,Lloyd-Evans
Romford: J.H. de Meza(Capt);A.J.Gallagher,A.Jones;W.Dickerson,A.Edwards,T.W.Carter;
P.Brien,F.Prout,J.Lloyd-Evans, F.Walters, W.Matthews.

11 Dec SEL1 Home South Weald 2 – 4 Matthews,Brien
Romford: J. H.de Meza;A.J.Gallagher,A.Jones;W.Dickerson,A.Edwards,T.W.Carter;
P.Brien,F.Prout,J.Lloyd-Evans, F.Walters,W.Matthews.

18 Dec SFL2B Away South Farnborough 1 – 5 Walters
Romford: W.Martin;A.J.Gallagher,A.Jones;T.W.Carter,W.Giles,Clarke;
P.Brien,F.Prout,A.Edwards,F.Walters,W.Matthews.

1 Jan SEL1 Away Romford United 0 – 2
Romford: W.Martin;A.J.Gallagher,W.Dickerson;,A.Edwards,T.W.Carter,W.Meares;
P.Brien,F.Prout,J.Lloyd-Evans,F.Walters,W.Matthews..

8 Jan AC1R Away Tufnell Park 0 – 2#
Romford: F.Prout;A.J.Gallagher,W.Dickerson,A.Edwards,T.W.Carter;
P.Brien,F.Walters,J.Lloyd-Evans,W.MatthewsW.Waterfall.

15 Jan SFL2B Home Chesham 2 – 4 Scorers unknown
Romford: J.H. de Meza;A.J.Gallagher,W.J.Giles;W.Dickerson,A.Edwards,T.W.Carter;
F.Prout,D.H.Clark,J.Lloyd-Evans,F.Walters,W.Matthews.

20 Jan ACRep Away Tufnell Park 0 – 1##
Romford:
Team details unknown

22 Jan SEL1 Home Romford United 0 – 1
Romford: J. H.de Meza;A.J.Gallagher(Capt),W.J.Giles;W.Dickerson,A.Edwards,T.W.Carter;
P.Brien,F.Prout,J.Lloyd-Evans,F.Walters,W.Waterfall.

5 Feb SEL1 Away Custom House 0 – 1
Romford: J.H. de Meza;A.J.Gallagher(Capt),W.J.Giles;W.Dickerson,A.Edwards,T.W.Carter;
P.Brien,F.Prout,J.Lloyd-Evans,F.Walters,W.Waterfall.

12 Feb Frdly Away South Weald 1 – 5 Lloyd-Evans
Romford: J.H. de Meza;A.J.Gallagher(Capt),W.J.Giles;W.Dickerson,A.Edwards,A.Jones;
P.Brien,F.Prout,Woolf,J.Watson,J.Lloyd-Evans.

19 Feb SEL1 Home Barking 1 – 2** Walters
Romford: J. De Meza;A.J.Gallagher,W.J.Giles;W.Dickerson,A.Edwards,T.W.Carter;
W.J.Evans,F.Prout,J.Webb,F.Walters,J.Lloyd-Evans.

19 Feb SFL2B Away Kettering 0 – 11**
Romford:
Team comprised of nine soldiers from Royal Norfolk Regiment based at Warley Barracks.

26 Feb SEL1 Away Shoeburyness Garrison 2 – 3 Webb(2)
Romford: W.Martin;A.J.Gallagher,W.J.Giles;W.Dickerson,A.Edwards,T.W.Carter;
W.J.Evans,F.Prout,J.Webb,F.Walters,J.Lloyd-Evans.

5 Mar SFL2B Home Hastings & St. Leonards 0 – 2
Romford:
Team details unknown

12 Mar SEL1 Home Chelmsford 5 – 4 Prout(2)Brien,Webb,Walters
Romford: W.Martin;A.J.Gallagher,W.J.Giles;W.Dickerson,A.Edwards,T.W.Carter;
D.Clark,P.Brien,F.Prout,J.Webb,F.Walters.

17 Mar WHCSF Home Romford United 1 – 2 Bassett(pen)
Romford: W.Martin;A.J.Gallagher,W.H.Clark;W.Dickerson,A.Edwards,T.W.Carter;
P.Brien,D.Clark,F.Prout,J.Lloyd-Evans,E.Bassett.

19 Mar SEL1 Home Wanstead 2 – 1 D.Clark,Walters
Romford: W.Martin;A.J.Gallagher;W.Dickerson,A.Edwards,T.W.Carter,
F.Prout,J.Webb,D.Clark,F.Walters,P.Brien.

25 Mar SFL2B Home Peterborough City 0 – 1
Romford: W.Martin,A.J.Gallagher,W.Dickerson;F.K.Milbank,A.Edwards,T.W.Carter;
F.Prout,J.Webb,J.Lloyd-Evans,F.Walters,P.Brien.

26 Mar SFL2B Away Chesham 0 – 3
Romford:
Team details unknown

28 Mar SFL2B Away Peterborough City 1 – 2 Bassett
Romford: W.Martin;A.J.Gallagher,F.K.Milbank;W.Dickerson,A.Edwards,T.W.Carter;
Brown,F.Prout,J.Webb,E.Bassett,P.Brien.

29 Mar SEL1 Home Custom House 0 – 1
Romford: W.Martin;A.J.Gallagher,F.K.Milbank;W.Dickerson,A.Edwards,T.W.Carter;
F.Prout,D.Clark,P.Brien,J.Webb,F.Walters.

16 Apr SEL1 Away Chelmsford 3 – 2 Walters(2)Webb
Romford: W.Martin;A.J.Gallagher,F.K.Milbank;W.Dickerson,A.Edwards,T.W.Carter;
F.Prout,D.Clark,P.Brien,J.Webb,F.Walters.

SFL2B Away Hastings & St. Leonards Not played (unable to find a suitable date).

Romford appeal as Tufnell Park fielded two Sunday players and the tie was ordered to be re-played.

A London newspaper gave this result as 0 – 2.

** Romford had a home South Essex League fixture arranged against Barking but the Southern League insisted this match be played. The first team played against Barking and Romford enlisted nine soldiers from The Royal Norfolk Regiment at Warley Barracks and played the game with nine men only!

SUMMARY OF FIRST TEAM RESULTS OBTAINED SEASON 1909 – 10

					Goals		
	P	W	D	L	For	Ag	Pts
Southern League Div.2B	9	0	0	9	6	34	0
South Essex Lge. Div.1	16	6	0	10	28	34	12
F.A.Challenge Cup	1	0	0	1	1	4	
F.A. Amateur Cup	1	0	0	1	0	2	
Essex Senior Cup	1	0	0	1	0	1	

West Ham Charity Cup	1	0	0	1	1	2
Friendly Matches	6	3	0	3	10	15
Total	35	9	0	26	46	92

Note: The above record does not include the void Amateur Cup Tie versus Tufnell Park.

AGM Press Report	31	8	0	23	41	71

Southern Football League Division Two B
Final Table

					Goals		
	P	W	D	L	For	Ag	Pts
Hastings & St Leonards#	9	6	3	0	27	11	15
Kettering	10	6	0	4	34	19	12
Chesham	10	5	2	3	25	25	12
Peterborough City	10	4	2	4	16	23	10
South Farnborough	10	4	1	5	23	19	9
Romford#	**9**	**0**	**0**	**9**	**6**	**34**	**0**

Final match not played as unable to find a suitable date.
Note: Romford F.C. withdrew from the Southern League at the end of the season.

South Essex League Division One
Final Table

					Goals		
	P	W	D	L	For	Ag	Pts
South Weald	16	14	1	1	61	12	29
Custom House	16	11	2	3	24	20	24
Shoeburyness Garrison	16	8	2	6	48	29	18
Barking	16	8	2	6	33	28	16**
Romford United	16	6	2	8	35	35	14
Grays Athletic	16	5	3	8	27	38	13
Chelmsford	16	6	1	9	29	43	13
Romford	**16**	**6**	**0**	**10**	**28**	**34**	**12**
Wanstead	16	1	1	14	13	56	3

** Two points deducted for breach of Rules.

CUP RESULTS

F.A. Challenge Cup

Final: Newcastle United 1 Barnsley 1
Replay: Newcastle United 2 Barnsley 0

Romford's progress: Prel.Round Home Shoeburyness Garrison 1 – 4

F.A. Amateur Cup

Final: R.M.L.I. (Gosport) 2 South Bank 1

Romford's progress: 1st Round Away Tufnell Park 0 – 2#
Replay Away Tufnell Park 0 – 1##

Essex Senior Cup

Final: South Weald 1 Leytonstone 0

Romford's progress: Prel.Round Home Dagenham St. Paul's 0 – 1

West Ham Charity Cup

Final: Leytonstone 4 Romford United 0

Romford's progress: Semi-Final Home Romford United 1 – 2

\# Romford protest replay ordered
\## One newspaper gives this result as two nil.

First Team Appearances Season 1909 – 10

F.Abrams	4	E.Baldwin	5	E.Bassett	3	R.Boulton	5
P.Brien	17*	P.Brown	2	T.W.Carter	21*	D.Clark	6
D.H.Clark	1	W.H.Clark	1	Clarke	1	W.Davis	1
J.De Meza	18	W.Dickerson	21*	A.Edwards	21*	W.J.Evans	2
A.J.Gallagher	21*	W.Giles	8	Hoare	1	A.Jones	6
J.Lloyd-Evans	13*	A,Mann	1	W.Martin	11	W.Matthews	7*
W.Meares	1	F.K.Milbank	4	Mooney	1	F.C.Moule	3
G.Olley	8	W.Olley	2	C.Parmenter	8	C.E.Pears	1
F.Prout	28*	Shackland	1	S.Sheppey	1	F.Walters	25*
J.Watson	1	W.Waterfall	10*	J.Webb	15	H.Wilkins	1
Willmore	2	Woolf	1				

* Also played in the void amateur cup tie against Tufnell Park.

First Team Goal Scorers Season 1909 – 10

F.Walters	11	F.Prout	8	D.Clark	4	J.Webb	4
C.Parmenter	2	S.Matthews	2	J.Lloyd-Evans	2	P.Brien	2
Bassett	2	Unknown	8			Total	45

TRIAL GAMES

Match Details

16 Sept.	Home	Romford Thursday	9 – 0	Scorers unknown
26 Feb	Home	Mawney Institute	1 – 0	Scorers unknown

Post-Season Summary Season 1909 – 10

Romford Football Club began their season with two friendly victories, but yet again met with a heavy defeat in their first competitive fixture, going down 4-1 to Shoeburyness Garrison in the F.A. Cup. Ray Boulton made his debut for Romford after joining from Clapton. In their next game, against Grays Athletic in the South Essex League, there was great interest in the return of Dave Clark to the side. Romford celebrated in fine style with a resounding 7-1 victory.

Clark was not in the team again until January, however, and Romford lost 1-0 to Grays in the return game. Another home defeat was inflicted by Shoeburyness Garrison and Romford had surrendered two more league points, despite including Bert Martin from West Ham United at left back. Next up was a home friendly against Luton, which was lost by three goals to one.

On 23rd October Romford opened their Southern League programme with a home game against South Farnborough and included another new player in T.W.Carter from Fulham, but were beaten 2-1. It was to prove an unhappy season in the new league. Romford ended October with another disaster, losing 1-0 at home to Dagenham St. Paul's in the prestigious Essex Senior Cup competition.

Romford, with only three of their regular team qualified to play in the competition, had included seven players from the Norfolk Regiment who were stationed at Warley Barracks. The following week the club included three more new players, A.Gallagher and H.Wilkins from Shepherds Bush and A.Edwards from West Bromwich Albion, and achieved a 1-0 victory over Wanstead in the South Essex League.

There then followed a disastrous couple of weeks in which ten goals were conceded. The first loss was against Kettering in the Southern League by four goals to one. It was followed by a 6-1 thrashing from South Weald in the South Essex League despite the inclusion of another new signing at centre forward in J.Lloyd-Evans from Norwood. The newly-constituted committee were finding it very difficult to get a settled and successful team.

Romford defeated Walthamstow Grange in a friendly and beat Barking 2-1 in a South Essex League game, but success was short-lived. A home defeat in the South Essex League by South Weald was followed by a Southern League thrashing away to South Farnborough by five goals to one, with W.Martin in goal.

Romford opened the New Year with a South Essex League fixture against their newest (and fiercest!) rivals Romford United and were beaten by two goals to nil. A week later Romford played in the Amateur Cup, losing 2-0 to Tufnell Park. With Martin injured, Romford had no goalkeepers available and Prout played in goal for the first half with another forward, Waterfall, going between the posts for the second half. It also appears from the team line-ups that Romford only had nine players. Romford lodged an appeal as Tufnell Park included two players who were also Sunday players, and the match was ordered to be replayed.

The next week Romford's Southern League misery continued with a home defeat from Chesham by four goals to two, despite including two new players in the experienced Giles who joined from Barking and D.H.Clark of Tottenham Hotspur. Romford then suffered three consecutive one nil defeats! First was the replay against Tufnell Park which was lost by one goal to nil (although one newspaper reported it as two nil) followed by a further two one nil defeats against local rivals Romford United and Custom House in South Essex League games.

More disaster followed with a 5-1 defeat by South Weald and a 2-1 defeat by Barking in the South Essex League on 19th February. Romford were ordered to play a Southern League game on the same day as the Barking match, and they were forced to enlist the help of the Norfolk Regiment to play the match against Kettering. Romford lost by eleven goals to nil! Two further league defeats followed against Shoeburyness Garrison (South Essex) and Hastings & St. Leonards (Southern League).

After 13 successive defeats Romford at last achieved a win. Essex rivals Chelmsford were the victims in a 5-4 victory in the South Essex League. The following Thursday they crashed at home against Romford United in the West Ham Charity Cup Semi-final by two goals to one. Next was a second successive South Essex League win against Wanstead by two goals to one. The ten-man bogey hit Romford again as Watson missed the train!

Success was short lived, as three consecutive Southern League defeats followed against Peterborough City (twice) and Chesham. Romford wound up the season with two South Essex League games: firstly against Custom House at home which they lost by one goal to nil, and then away to Chelmsford where they were successful in securing a 3-2 victory. This proved to be the last match of a very poor season, as no date could be found for the return Southern League game against Hastings & St. Leonards.

Annual General Meeting

(as reported in the *Essex Times,* Saturday 2nd July 1910)

The annual meeting of the Romford Football Club was held at the Golden Lion Hotel on Wednesday evening, 29th June, Mr. C.F.Fitch presiding over a good attendance. The Chairman announced that the hon.secretary (Mr.W.H.Pring) had resigned, in consequence of his having left the district. Mr.W.H.Kelly, in presenting the secretarial report, alluded to the pluck of those who had stuck to the club in spite of the somewhat disastrous season. For the ensuing season the club had entered, for the English Cup, the Amateur Cup, the South Essex League, and probably they would also enter for the Chelmsford and West Ham Charity Cups.

The report prepared by Mr.W.H.Pring stated; "We played 31 matches, of which we only won 8, and lost 23, with 41 goals scored for and 71 against. This is not exactly a flattering result, but we played in the Southern League against teams a great deal better than those in the South Essex League. These teams were, with exception of Romford, all professional teams. Of the matches lost, 11were lost by the bare margin of a goal, and 6 with a margin of two goals. The two chief scorers were F.Prout and F.Walters, with 11goals each".

The Hon.Treasurer read the financial report stating that he thought it was a very fair one considering that they had practically no balance in hand at the commencement of the season, and had had a very heavy initial expense in building up a new team. The receipts totalled £247.17s.6d. including vice-presidents' subscriptions, £12.1s.0d.; members subscriptions £7.5s.0d.; gate receipts, £105.8s.10d.; guarantees and half gates, £14.14s.2d.;Southern League subsidy £28, given by the committee, £30.17s.3d.

The principal item on the expenditure side – the team having to travel long distances in the Southern League competition – was £120.0s.5d. for travelling expenses and teas. Rent, rates and taxes accounted for £28.0s 5d.; referees' expenses £8.9s.2d., subscriptions to cups and leagues, £19.14s.6d.; honorarium to Mr.C.T. Heard, £5.5s.0d.; wedding present to Mr.A.M.Baker, £2.; materials and repairs, £6.5s.1d.; laundry, £2.11s.8d.; billposting, £1.0s.9d.; Mrs.Loder,2s.; postages and telegrams £4.12s.4d.; groundsman, assistance, etc. £17.6s.2d.; and incidentals 12s.0d. The balance due to the treasurer was £2.5s.5d. In addition there were two or three outstanding accounts, but the greater portion of this money had been subscribed by gentlemen residing in the neighbourhood. Mr. J. Butterfield thought the balance sheet was of a very satisfactory character. The Chairman said the deficit, which amounted to about £6 or £7, would probably be wiped out by subscriptions, etc. The lease of the ground would run out in September, and he presumed it would be renewed for another three years. Both reports were then adopted.

On the proposition of Mr.H.W.Brown, seconded by Mr.C.A.Wilson, Mr.Fitch was re-elected president. The vice-presidents were re-elected, with the addition of several gentlemen who have lately come to reside in the town. Mr.W.H.Kelly was elected hon.secretary; Mr.W.R.Carter was re-elected hon. treasurer; and the committee was appointed as follows;- Messrs. H.W.Brown, G.Bridgen, W.H.Pring, A.Parrish, J.Tetchner, F.Laurence, J.Robinson, and H.Barkham. The Chairman then announced several donations, stating that the liabilities had been reduced to 30s.0d. (Applause). It was stated that practically the whole of last season's team would be available including A.J.Gallagher, W.Millbank, T.W.Carter, A.Edwards, W.Dickerson, J.Lloyd-Evans, F.Prout, J.Webb, F.Walters, and C.Watson. In addition, negotiations are proceeding with several other players, including C.F.Browne, an amateur centre forward of some repute.

The draw for the English Cup had resulted in South Weald having to play Romford on the Town ground (Cricket Field, Romford Station), on September 17th.

Note: It is not known if the Chairman referred to was in fact Mr.C.F.Fitch the president or some other person.

Romford fined and censured

(as reported in the *Recorder*, Friday, November 26th, 1909)

The Romford F.C. were reported under Rule 14 by South Weald for having, as it was alleged, played a man who had not discharged his financial liabilities, to his previous club, and was played in spite of a telegram sent by the hon.secretary of the Association telling Romford not to play him. A good deal of evidence was heard, and one of the Romford witnesses said the telegram referred to was thought to be a hoax. Romford evidently thought that as the man in question was playing in a Southern League game the Essex F.A. Rule did not apply. The player told the committee that after the question was raised he offered South Weald his subscription, but it was refused. He had since sent the money. – Romford were fined £1, and the club was censured. – Notice of appeal was given by a Romford official.

The *Golden Lion*, for several years headquarters of the Romford Football Club, as portrayed by Alfred Bennett Bamford in 1889

Havering Libraries - Local Studies

Season 1909 – 10

ROMFORD UNITED

Adjourned meeting held at the Rising Sun Hotel, Friday, 2nd July 1909

The new Club was formed following the old committee being voted out of office at the previous AGM. Various names were considered including Romford Wanderers and Romford Town, but it was finally agreed as Romford United (using the title of the former local junior team which had become defunct a year earlier). The new Club joined the South Essex League and the Romford and District League, in direct opposition to the old Romford team now under new management.

GENERAL MEETING

(as reported in the *Essex Times,* Wednesday 2nd September 1909)

A general meeting of the newly formed Romford United Football Club was held on Saturday 29th August at the Rising Sun Hotel.Mr. John Bassett.J.P. President of the Club, was in the chair supported by Messrs.J.J.Prentice, G.A.Smith, H.Small, E.Hodson, T.N.Davey, F.Robarts, H.S.Hibbert, H.H.Hinds, A.C.Potter, A.W.Asater, R.Heath, F.H.Kittle, H.Hanch, L.P.Pratt, E.A.Stalley, R.R.Pratt, A.Buckeridge and J.Smith; with Mr.E.P.Jones (Hon.Treasurer) and Mr.C.T.Heard (Hon.Secretary).

The Hon.Secretary reported that the Committee had obtained possession of the Shoulder of Mutton Field, on the corner of Victoria Road and Hornchurch Road. The following officers were elected for the reserve team which would play in the Ilford & District League. Hon.Secretary: Mr.C.Russell, Captain: Mr.A.Drury, Vice-Captain: Mr.G.Ball. Messrs. E.Currie and A.Farrant were added to the Committee.

Mr.E.H.Hinds of Hong Kong, a former Romford player, had written to say he would be pleased to be nominated as a vice-president. Messrs.B.Keith Green, J.J.Prentice and E.Hodson had also consented to become vice-presidents.

The Shoulder of Mutton Field, so-called because of its shape (clearly seen on the map on page 343), was owned by Mr. W.Poel junior. On the north-west corner of the field stood the Cosy Corner Theatre of Varieties, a prefabricated-type building constructed from wood and canvas. The new ground took its name from this venue, and the Romford United Football Club received a share of the theatre's profits on match days.

Season 1909 – 10

ROMFORD UNITED

President: Mr.J.Bassett,J.P. **Chairman:** Mr.G.A.Smith

Hon.Secretary: Mr.C.T.Heard **Hon.Treasurer:** Mr.Evan P.Jones.

Committee: Messrs.G.A.Smith,E.Hodson,R.Heath,F.W.Robarts,L.Fletcher,H.Small and S.Dowsing

Captain: Mr.A.E.Jones **Vice-Captain:** Mr.A.S.Hyett

Reserve Team Hon.Secretary: Mr.C.Russell

Reserve Team Captain: Mr.A.Drury **Reserve Team Vice-Captain:** Mr.G.Ball

Auditors: Messrs.F.W.Jeffes and E.J.Wallis **Club Colours:** Royal Blue Jerseys, White Knickers

Essex County F.A. Executive Committee Member: Mr.W.D.Matthews

Headquarters: Rising Sun Hotel, Romford

Ground: Cosy Corner Ground (known also as the Shoulder of Mutton Field), Hornchurch Road
(see map on page 343)

COMPETITIONS ENTERED

South Essex League Division One
F.A. Amateur Cup
Essex Senior Cup
West Ham Charity Cup
Chelmsford Charity Cup

Ilford & District League
Romford & District League Division One
Essex Junior Cup
Romford Charity Cup

Match Details

4 Sept Frdly Home South Weald 1 – 1 Scorer unknown
Attendance: 500
Romford United: J.L.McNair;A.M.Baker,W.M.Turner;W.Harvey,J.C.Doggett,F.H.Kittle;
J.Chapman,B.G.Aston,A.E. "Diddy" Jones(Capt),A.S.Hyett,J.Collar.

11 Sept Frdly Home Deptford Invicta 3 – 2 Hyett(2)Own goal
Romford United: J.L.McNair;A.M.Baker,W.M.Turner;B.G.Aston,J.C.Doggett,F.H.Kittle;
J.Chapman,F.C.Moule,A.E.Jones,A.S.Hyett,J.Collar.

18 Sept SEL1 Away Custom House 1 – 2 Chapman
Attendance: 400
Romford United: L.McNair;A.M.Baker,W.M.Turner;B.G.Aston,J.C.Doggett;F.H.Kittle;
J.Chapman,F.C.Moule,A.E.Jones(Capt),A.S.Hyett,A.J.Collar.

25 Sept. SEL1 Away Barking 2 – 4 Collar,Hyett
Attendance: 1,300
Romford United: L.McNair;A.M.Baker;W.M.Turner;B.G.Aston,J.C.Doggett,F.H.Kittle;
J.Chapman,F.C.Moule,A.E.Jones(Capt),A.S.Hyett,A.J.Collar.

2 Oct SEL1 Home South Weald 1 – 3 Hyett
Romford United: L.McNair;A.M.Baker,P.J.Moore;B.G.Aston,J.C.Doggett,F.H.Kittle;
J.Chapman,A.E.Jones(Capt),A.Gladwin,A.J.Collar,A.S.Hyett.

9 Oct Frdly Home Plumstead St. John's 6 – 0 Robeson,Hyett,Jones(2)Doggett,Hunwicks
Attendance: 150
Romford United: J.L.McNair;A.M.Baker,P.J.Moore;G.Hunwicks,W.Turner,F.H.Kittle;
B.Robeson,A.E."Diddy"Jones(Capt),J.C.Doggett,A.S.Hyett,S.C.Squier.

16 Oct SEL1 Home Wanstead 9 – 2 Asater,Hyett(pen)others(7)
Romford United: L.McNair;A.M.Baker,P.J.Moore;B.G.Aston,J.C.Doggett ,F.H.Kittle;
A.W.Asater,A.E.Jones(Capt) ,A.J.Collar,A.S.Hyett,S.C.Squier.

23 Oct AC2Q Away Wanstead 5 – 2 Jones(2)Doggett,Collar,Taylor(og)
Romford United: J.L.McNair;A.M.Baker,P.J.Moore;B.G.Aston,W.M.Turner,F.H.Kittle;
J.Chapman,J .C.Doggett,A.E.Jones(Capt),A.S.Hyett,A.J.Collar.

30 Oct SEL1 Home Shoeburyness Garrison 4 – 3 Hyett(2)Jones(2)
Romford United: L.McNair;A.M.Baker,P.J.Moore;B.G.Aston,W.Turner,F.H.Kittle;
C.S.Brown,A.E.Jones(Capt),J.C.Doggett,A.S.Hyett,A.J.Collar.

6 Nov AC3Q Home Upton Park 4 – 3 Kittle,Collar,Aston,Chapman
Romford United: J.L.McNair;A.M.Baker,P.J.Moore;B.G.Aston,W.M.Turner,F.H.Kittle;
A.S.Hyett,A.E.Jones(Capt),J.C.Doggett,J.Chapman,A.J.Collar.

13 Nov SEL1 Away South Weald 0 – 5
Romford United: L.McNair;A.M.Baker,P.J.Moore;B.G.Aston,W.M.Turner,F.H.Kittle;
J.Chapman,A.E.Jones(Capt),G.Hunwicks,A.S.Hyett,A.J.Collar.

20 Nov ESC1R Home Custom House 2 – 1 Hyett,Jones
Romford United: L.McNair;A.M.Baker,P.J.Moore;P.Adams,W.M.Turner,F.H.Kittle;
J.Chapman,A.E.Jones(Capt),J.C.Doggett,A.S.Hyett,A.J.Collar.

27 Nov AC4Q Away Custom House 0 – 1
Romford United: J.L.McNair;A.M.Baker,P.J.Moore;B.G.Aston,J.C.Doggett,W.M.Turner;
J.Chapman,A.E.Jones(Capt),S.C.Squier,A.S.Hyett,A.J.Collar.

4 Dec SEL1 Home Grays Athletic 2 – 2 Scorers unknown
Romford United: L.McNair;A.M.Baker,P.J.Moore;B.G.Aston,W.Turner,F.H.Kittle;
J.Chapman,A.E.Jones(Capt),C.S.Brown,A.S.Hyett,A.J.Collar.

11 Dec ESC2R Away Walthamstow Grange 0 – 6 Aban. 82 Mins Bad Light
Romford United: J.L.McNair;A.M.Baker,P.J.Moore;P.Adams,W.M.Turner,F.H.Kittle;
W.A.Porter,A.E.Jones(Capt),J.C.Doggett,A.S.Hyett,A.J.Collar.

18 Dec Frdly Home City of Westminster 4 – 3 Bartlett(og),Collar,Porter,Algar
Romford United: J.L.McNair;A.M.Baker,W.M.Turner;B.G.Aston,J.C.Doggett,F.H.Kittle;
J.Chapman,W.A.Porter,Algar,A.S.Hyett(Capt),A.J.Collar.

25 Dec Frdly Home South Weald 2 – 2 Scorers unknown
Romford United:
Team details unknown

26 Dec Frdly Home Bronze Athletic 3 – 1 Scorers unknown
Romford United: ,W.M.Turner,
J.Chapman, Remainder of the team unknown

1 Jan SEL1 Home Romford 2 – 0 Aston,Harris
Romford United: L.McNair;A.M.Baker,P.J.Moore;B.G.Aston,J.C.Doggett,F.H.Kittle;
J.Chapman,A.E.Jones(Capt),J.Harris,A.S.Hyett,A.J.Collar.

8 Jan ESCRP Away Walthamstow Grange 2 – 1 Harris,Hyett
Attendance: 600
Romford United: J.L.McNair;A.M.Baker,P.J.Moore;W.M.Turner,J.C.Doggett,F.H.Kittle;
J.Chapman,Algar,J.Harris,A.S.Hyett(Capt),A.J.Collar.

15 Jan CCCSF Home South Weald 2 – 2 Jones,Harris
Romford United: J.L.McNair;A.M.Baker,P.J.Moore;B.G.Aston,J.C.Doggett,F.H.Kittle;
J.Chapman,A.E.Jones(Capt),J.Harris,A.S.Hyett,A.J.Collar.

22 Jan SEL1 Away Romford 1 – 0 Harris
Romford United: J.L.McNair;A.M.Baker,P.J.Moore;B.G.Aston,J.C.Doggett,F.H.Kittle;
J.Chapman,A.E.Jones(Capt),J.Harris,S.C.Squier,A.J.Collar.

29 Jan SEL1 Home Chelmsford 1 – 1 Collar
Romford United: L.McNair;A.M.Baker,W.Turner;B.G.Aston,J.C.Doggett,F.H.Kittle;
J.Chapman,A.E.Jones(Capt),J.Harris,A.S.Hyett,A.J.Collar.

5 Feb ESC3R Home Shoeburyness Garrison 7 – 0 Harris scored the first
Romford United: J.L.McNair;A.M.Baker,P.J.Moore;W.M.Turner,J.C.Doggett,F.H.Kittle;
J.Chapman,A.E.Jones(Capt),J.Harris,S.C.Squier,A.J.Collar.

12 Feb Frdly Home East Ham F.C. 4 – 0 Squier,Jones,Chapman,Collar
Romford United:
J.Chapman,A.E.Jones(Capt),S.C.Squier,A.J.Collar rest of team unknown.

19 Feb SEL1 Away Grays Athletic 1 – 4 Collar
Romford United: W.M.Turner;A.M.Baker,B.G.Aston,J.C.Doggett,F.H.Kittle,
J.Chapman,A.E.Jones(Capt),J.Harris,A.S.Hyett,A.J.Collar.

26 Feb ESCSF C'ford South Weald 0 – 3
Attendance: 1,600
Romford United: J.L.McNair;A.M.Baker,
A.E.Jones(Capt). Remainder of the team unknown

3 Mar WHC2R Home Custom House 3 – 0 Scorers unknown
Romford United:
Team details unknown

5 Mar Frdly Home Grays Athletic 1 – 4 Aston
Romford United: W.Champness;A.M.Baker,G.Hunwicks;P.Adams,J.C.Doggett,F.H.Kittle(Capt);
J.Chapman,J.Harris,A.J.Collar,B.G.Aston,A.Bowley.

12 Mar SEL1 Away Shoeburyness Garrison 2 – 4 Squier,Collar
Romford United: L.McNair;A.M.Baker,P.J.Moore;B.G.Aston,J.C.Doggett,F.H.Kittle;
J.Chapman,A.E.Jones(Capt),J.Harris,S.C.Squier,A.J.Collar.

17 Mar WHCSF Away Romford 2 – 1 Harris(2)
Romford United: J.L.McNair;A.M.Baker,P.J.Moore;W.M.Turner,J.C.Doggett,F.H.Kittle;
W.Matthews,A.E.Jones(Capt),J.Harris,A.S.Hyett,A.J.Collar.

19 Mar SEL1 Away Chelmsford 1 – 3 Hyett
Romford United: L.McNair;A.M.Baker,P.J.Moore;B.G.Aston,J.C.Doggett,F.H.Kittle;
J.Chapman,A.E.Jones(Capt),J.Harris,A.S.Hyett,A.J.Collar.

25 Mar Frdly Home Woolwich 5 – 2 Scorers unknown
Romford United:
Team details unknown

26 Mar Frdly Home 1st Grenadier Guards 2 – 2 Harris(2)
Romford United: J.L.McNair;A.M.Baker,P.J.Moore;Partridge,J.C.Doggett,G.W.Squier;
J.Chapman,A.E.Jones(Capt),J.Harris,G.Hunwicks,A.J.Collar.

28 Mar Frdly Home Hitchin Blue Cross 5 – 1 Scorers unknown
Romford United:
Team details unknown

2 Apr WHCF Clapton Leytonstone 0 – 4
Attendance: 4,000
Romford: J.L.McNair;A.M.Baker,P.J.Moore;B.G.Aston,J.C.Doggett,F.H.Kittle;
J.Chapman,A.E.Jones(Capt),J.Harris,S.C.Squier,A.J.Collar.

9 Apr SEL1 Home Barking 1 – 2 A.E.Jones.
Romford United: L.McNair;A.M.Baker,P.J.Moore;B.G.Aston,J.C.Doggett,F.H.Kittle;
J.Chapman,A.E.Jones(Capt),J.Harris,G.Hunwicks,A.J.Collar.

14 Apr CCCRP Home South Weald 2 – 1 Jones,S.C.Squier
Romford: J.L.McNair;A.M.Baker,P.J.Moore;P.Adams,Creswell,F.H.Kittle;
G.Hunwicks,S.C.Squier,A.E.Jones(Capt),G.W.Squier,T.Ball.

16 Apr SEL1 Away Wanstead (at Romford) 4 – 0 Aston,Jones,Kittle,Doggett
Romford United: L.McNair;A.M.Baker,P.J.Moore;P.Adams,J.C.Doggett,F.H.Kittle;
J.Chapman,A.E.Jones(Capt),B.G.Aston,S.C.Squier,A.J.Collar.

23 Apr SEL1 Home Custom House 3 – 0 Scorers unknown
Romford United: L.McNair;A.M.Baker,P.J.Moore;P.Adams,J.C.Doggett,F.H.Kittle;
J.Chapman,A.E.Jones(Capt),B.G.Aston,Croxall,A.J.Collar.

30 Apr CCCF Away Chelmsford 0 – 4
Attendance: 1,000
Romford United: J.L.McNair;A.M.Baker,P.J.Moore; ? , ? , ? ;
J.Chapman, ? ,A.E.Jones, ? , ? .

SUMMARY OF RESULTS OBTAINED SEASON 1909 – 10

	P	W	D	L	Goals For	Goals Ag	Pts
South Essex League	16	6	2	8	35	35	14
F.A. Amateur Cup	3	2	0	1	9	6	
Essex Senior Cup	4	3	0	1	11	5	
West Ham Charity Cup	3	2	0	1	5	5	
Chelmsford Charity Cup	3	1	1	1	4	7	
Friendly Matches	11	7	3	1	36	18	
Total	40	21	6	13	100	76	
AGM Press Report	41	21	6	14	100	81	

Note: It appears from the Annual General Meeting report that one result is missing from the summary and it could be that the A.G.M report included the the Essex Senior Cup match against Walthamstow Grange (0-6) which was abandoned.

South Essex League Division One
Final Table

	P	W	D	L	Goals For	Goals Ag	Pts
South Weald	16	14	1	1	61	12	29
Custom House	16	11	2	3	24	20	24
Shoeburyness Garrison	16	8	2	6	48	29	18
Barking **	16	8	2	6	33	28	16
Romford United	**16**	**6**	**2**	**8**	**35**	**35**	**14**
Grays Athletic	16	5	3	8	27	38	13
Chelmsford	16	6	1	9	29	43	13
Romford	16	6	0	10	28	34	12
Wanstead	16	1	1	14	13	56	3

** Two points deducted for breach of Rules.

CUP RESULTS

F.A. Challenge Cup

Final: Newcastle United 1 Barnsley 1
Replay: Newcastle United 2 Barnsley 0

Romford United did not enter the competition

F.A. Amateur Cup

Final: R.M.L.I. (Gosport) 2 South Bank 1

Romford's progress: 2nd Qual Away Wanstead 5 – 2
3rd Qual Home Upton Park 4 – 3
4th Qual Away Custom House 0 – 1

Essex Senior Cup

Final: South Weald 1 Leytonstone 0

Romford's progress: 1st Round Home Custom House 2 – 1
2nd Round Away Walthamstow Grange 0 – 6 #
Replay Away Walthamstow Grange 2 – 1
3rd Round Home Shoeburyness Garrison 7 – 0
Semi-Final Ch'frd South Weald 0 – 3

Abandoned after 82 mins. Due to bad light

West Ham Charity Cup

Final: Leytonstone 4 Romford United 0

Romford's progress: 2nd Round Home Custom House 3 – 0
Semi-Final Away Romford 2 – 1
Final Clapton Leytonstone 0 – 4

Chelmsford Charity Cup

Final: Chelmsford 4 Romford United 0

Romford's progress: Semi-Final Home South Weald 2 – 2
Replay Home South Weald 2 – 1
Final Away Chelmsford 0 – 4

First Team Appearances Season 1909 – 10

P.Adams	5*	Algar	2	A.W.Asater	1	B.G.Aston	25
A.M.Baker	34*	T.Ball	1	Bowley	1	C.S.Browne	2
W.Champness	1	J.Chapman	30	A.J.Collar	31*	Cresswell	1
Croxall	1	J.C.Doggett	29*	A.Gladwin	1	J.Harris	14
W.Harvey	1	G.Hunwicks	6	A.S.Hyett	22*	A.E.Jones	32*
F.H.Kittle	30*	W.C.Matthews	1	J.L.McNair	32*	P.J.Moore	25*
F.C.Moule	3	Partridge	1	W.A.Porter	1*	B.Robeson	1
G.W.Squier	2	S.C.Squier	10	W.Turner	19*	Total	365

* Also played in the abandoned Essex Senior Cup match against Walthamstow Grange.

First Team Goal Scorers Season 1909 – 10

A.E.Jones	12	A.S.Hyett	11	J.Harris	9	J.Collar	8
B.G.Aston	4	J.C.Doggett	3	J.Chapman	2	F.H.Kittle	2
S.C.Squier	3	B.Robeson	1	G.Hunwicks	1	A.W.Asater	1
W.A.Porter	1	Algar	1	Own Goals	3	Unknown	37
Total	100						

"A" TEAM (RESERVES)

Match Details

4 Sept	Frdly	Away	South Weald Reserves	3 – 5	
25 Sept	IDL1	Away	Barking "A"	1 – 3	
2 Oct	RDL1	Away	Beaconstone	1 – 5	Centre forward
Romford United "A": Played with only nine men					
16 Oct	EJC1R	Home	Epping	3 – 1	
30 Oct	IDL1	Home	Barking Orient	1 – 1	
6 Nov	EJC2R	Away	Woodford Crusaders "A"	2 – 3	
20 Nov	Frdly	Away	Mawneys Old Boys	0 – 3	
n/k	RDL1	Away	Mawneys Institute	0 – 1	
n/k	RDL1	n/k	Purfleet	2 – 2	
18 Dec	RDL1	Home	Grays Olympic	1 – 4	
8 Jan	**	Home	Mawneys Institute	1 – 2	
29 Jan	IDL1	Away	North East Ham	0 – 2	
26 Mar	IDL1	Away	Barking Orient	Lost#	
31 Mar	IDL1	Home	North East Ham	5 – 1	
16 Apr	IDL1	Home	Barking "A"	1 – 4	

** This result was reported in the local press as a Romford & District League Division One game, but the result was not included in the league table. It is therefore concluded to be a friendly game.
\# Romford scratched due to having only four men turn up for this game and the points were awarded to Barking Orient and Romford United were fined five shillings.

RESERVE TEAM SUMMARY OF RESULTS OBTAINED SEASON 1909 – 10

	P	W	D	L	Goals For	Goals Ag	Pts
Ilford & District League	6	1	1	4	8	11	3
Rfd. & Dist.Lge.Div.1.	4	0	1	3	4	12	1
Essex Junior Cup	2	1	0	1	5	4	
Friendly Matches	3	0	0	3	4	10	
Total	15	2	2	11	21	37	

Note: This includes the Ilford & District game away to Barking Orient which was not actually played but points awarded to Barking Orient. The reported Romford & District League game lost to Mawney Institute on 8th January but not included in the league records or league table is regarded as a friendly match in the above report.

Ilford & District Football League Division One

Final Table

	P	W	D	L	Goals For	Goals Ag	Pts
Barking Orient	6	4	2	0	8	4	10
Barking "A"	6	3	0	3	13	6	6
North East Ham	6	2	1	3	4	12	5
Romford United Res.	**6**	**1**	**1**	**4**	**8**	**11**	**3**

Note: Due to only four players turning up for the away game with Barking Orient, the points were awarded to Barking Orient. A defeat is recorded against Romford United "A" although this match was not in fact played.

Romford & District Football League Division One

(Table as at 29th January, latest available)

	P	W	D	L	Goals For	Goals Ag	Pts
Mawneys Institute	4	3	1	0	8	2	7
Beaconstone United	5	2	1	2	11	10	5
Purfleet	4	1	3	0	8	5	5
Grays Olympic	3	1	0	2	6	9	2
Romford United "A"	**4**	**0**	**1**	**3**	**4**	**12**	**1**

Note: It is known that all fixtures were completed each team playing eight games, and that Mawneys Institute were the league champions.

At the Annual General Meeting the previous season it had been decided, for travel reasons, to compete in the Ilford & District League rather than the Romford & District League. Possibly due to pressure from the Romford & District League, it was now resolved that the club play in both competitions. It was clear from the beginning that the club was finding it difficult to field a full eleven, as only nine men played in the heavy defeat at Beaconstone. On 26th March only four turned up for the away Ilford & District League game at Barking Orient. The match was awarded to the home team, and Romford United were fined five shillings. They and Barking were warned by the league that they must play their outstanding fixture or risk further fines.

In the first half of the season Romford United played each of their opponents once, as reflected in the league table of 29th January, but a second game against Mawneys Institute on 9th January which Romford United lost 2-1 is not included in that table. Unfortunately no trace has been found of a final league table. It is known that Mawneys Institute were the league champions.

Further research has revealed that Beaconstone United played all their eight fixtures, winning three, drawing two and losing two, but goals for and against are unknown or the club's final position in the table. However as Beaconstone fulfilled their fixtures they must have played Romford United "A" a second time, or had the points awarded!

RESERVE TEAM CUP RESULTS

Essex Junior Cup

Final: Hoffmann Athletic 2 Woodford Crusaders 1

Romford's progress: 1st Round Home Epping 3 – 1
2nd Round Away Woodford Crusaders 2 – 3

Romford Charity Cup

Final: Mawneys Institute 1 Roneo 0

Romford's progress: 1st Round Home Mawneys Old Boys Lost

Post-Season Summary Season 1909 – 10

The newly-formed Romford United club opened the season with two friendly matches, the first of which was a fine 1-1 draw against the powerful South Weald team, followed by a victory against Deptford Invicta. The first South Essex League games were a disappointment, however, as Romford United lost successively away to Custom House and Barking. Worse was to follow when they were defeated 3-1 at home to South Weald. The following week saw a less stressful friendly fixture against Plumstead St. John's, culminating in a 6-0 victory. Encouraged by this result, the team won their next league game at home to Wanstead with their biggest victory of the season by nine goals to two. The following week they were away to Wanstead in the Amateur Cup and achieved a 5-2 win.

Two home 4-3 victories followed, against Shoeburyness Garrison (in the league) and Upton Park (in the Amateur Cup); then a rude awakening away to South Weald and a 5-0 thrashing. Next came home and away games against Custom House in two cup ties, resulting in a home Essex Senior Cup victory followed by an away defeat in the coveted Amateur Cup. Early December saw a home 2-2 draw against Grays Athletic, followed by an extraordinary piece of good fortune! Romford United were losing 6-0 against Walthamstow Grange in the Essex Senior Cup when the match was abandoned eight minutes from the end due to bad light. There followed three friendly matches to end the year.

New Year's Day 1910 and a home league fixture against the old Romford club. Referee Mr.J.R.Schumaker, anticipating trouble, requested the league to give him assistance by appointing two neutral linesmen. The press commented that 'It is to be hoped that the game will be contested in a sportsmanlike manner, and the referee will undoubtedly put a stop to any attempt at rough play!' United enjoyed a 2-0 victory over their rivals.

The following week Romford United defeated Walthamstow Grange by two goals to one in the replayed Essex Senior Cup tie. After a 2-2 Chelmsford Charity Cup semi-final draw with South Weald, it was the return league game with 'Them Over the Way' (Romford Football Club) resulting in a 1-0 victory for the United, Harris doing the needful. January was rounded off undefeated with a 1-1 draw in the home league game with Chelmsford.

February started on a high with a 7-0 romp against Shoeburyness Garrison in the Essex Senior Cup and a friendly win against East Ham Football Club. Two heavy defeats followed, by Grays Athletic in the league and South Weald in the Essex Senior Cup semi-final at Chelmsford. A West Ham Charity Cup second round victory against Custom House was followed by a friendly reverse at Grays Athletic by four goals to one.

There followed a disastrous game away to Shoeburyness Garrison in the South Essex League. Not only did the team lose 4-2, but Aston was sent off and seven players were booked. There was some consolation the following week when they again defeated the old Romford team 2-1 in the semi-final of the West Ham Charity Cup, Harris scoring both. Then came a 3-1 defeat at Chelmsford in the league followed by a measure of success in three friendly matches. Bitter disappointment was to follow when before 4,000 spectators at the

Spotted Dog Ground, Clapton, Romford United were defeated 4-0 in the final of the West Ham Charity Cup by the powerful Leytonstone team. Another league defeat came next, by 2-1 at home to Barking.

Three successive victories followed to give the team a useful mid-table league position and a place in the Chelmsford Charity Cup Final. Alas, the season ended when before 1,000 spectators at the King's Head Meadow ground, Chelmsford (Walters, Clover and Turrall(2)) gained a 4-0 victory. The newspaper report describes Walters of 'Romford Town' scoring the first goal for Chelmsford, but he of course played for Romford during the season, there being no Romford Town! The reserve team met with little success, finishing bottom of Ilford and District League Division One with only one win from their six games.

During the season the following players joined Romford United: W.M.Turner (Custom House), J.Chapman and W.Harvey (South Weald), J.C.Doggett (Old Newportonians), P.J.Moore (Roneo Athletic) and finally Algar who joined from Cullum College, Reading. S.Hibbert and A.Potter left Romford United to join Mawney Institute.

At the end of the season, at the Essex County Football Association concert, United's players A.M.Baker, James Charles Doggett and Arthur S. Hyett were awarded their Essex Senior Caps for six or more appearances in the County team.

PROTESTS AND MORE PROTESTS!
(as reported in the *Essex Times*)

A joint Commission of the Essex and London Football Associations met on Thursday 23rd December, 1909 to consider a protest by Romford United against Walthamstow Grange relating to the Essex Senior Cup tie played on 11th December. The Romford club protested that several players in the Walthamstow Grange team had also participated in Sunday Football. The players in question had also played for Red Lion against The Horns on 12th December. The players admitted the offence and the Commission decided that a number of players and officials of the Walthamstow Grange Club should be suspended sine die from football and football management. At the same meeting, A.E.Jones, the Romford United captain, was suspended for six days for alleged foul play in the same cup tie.

Essex County Football Association
Entry in Minute Book Friday 22nd April 1910

The F.A. having requested this Association to deal with complaints Colchester Town v South Weald and Romford v Romford United, the Hon. Sec. stated that he intended summoning the "South Essex" members for that purpose at an early date.

Romford v Romford United

The conduct of some officials and playing members of the Romford United F.C. on the occasion of the Southern League match, Romford v Peterboro', having been reported to the F.A., that body authorised the Essex Association, to enquire into, and deal with the matter. Mr. Wilson (Romford) and Mr. Smith (Romford United) were examined, and the Romford F.C. withdrew any imputation of officials of Romford United F.C. having been the cause of the disturbance.

The Commission found:- "The four players of the Romford United F.C. who admitted "scrambling coppers" were cautioned as to their future conduct". The action of the referee (Mr.J.Foster), in reporting the case to the Southern League instead of the Association, and then only on his being asked for his report 12 days after the occurrence, was ordered to be brought to the notice of the Football Association, together with the above findings of the Commission.

(Mr.W.D.Matthews did not adjudicate in the above matter).

Annual General Meeting
(as reported in the *Essex Times,* Saturday 2nd July 1910)

The annual general meeting of the Romford United Football Club was held on Wednesday evening 29th June, at the Rising Sun Hotel. Mr.John Bassett (president) was in the chair, and those present included Messrs.A.J.Smith, J.Currie, E.E.Carter, W.Drynan, W.Hyett, R.Heath, H.W.E.Stephenson, A.Drury, H.Small, E.Carter, L.P.Pratt, F.G.Padgham, R.R.Pratt, O.Hanck, C.King, A.MacDonald, T.G. Galdwin, F.Robarts, C.Webb, P.Moore, J.Chapman, A.Hunwicks, W.D.Matthews, R.Bramble, W.Tatam, A.Asater, E.Crossall, E.J.Johnson, C.H.Jones, H.Turvey, E.T.Smee, T.Hodson, L.Fletcher, A.Page, Geo.A.Smith, A.M.Baker, and P.Adams; with Mr.C.T.Heard (hon.secretary) and Mr.E.P.Jones (hon.treasurer). The Chairman said he was very glad to see so many present – (hear,hear) – but he was sorry that they could not put a better financial statement before them. He might say that the balance sheet showed the worst side of the case, and it would be better to hear the hon.treasurer's report before making any comments. – (hear,hear).

The hon.secretary (Mr.C.T.Heard) said it was with pleasure he presented the first annual report, which he considered very satisfactory in every way. The club's record stood: Played 41, won 21, lost 14, drawn 6, goals for 100, against 81. The principal goal scorers were: A.E.Jones 20, J.Harris 17, A.S.Hyett 16, and J.Collar 13. In the Amateur Cup competition the club were defeated in the fourth round by Custom House, away, by the narrowest of margins – 1-0 – and in the Essex Senior Cup the club reached the semi-final stage, only to be vanquished by their old friends, South Weald by 3-0.

It was only fair to the team to say they were severely handicapped through their esteemed goalkeeper Mr.L.McNair being incapacitated through injury, thus being prevented from showing his good form throughout the match. The club won its way into the finals of the West Ham and Chelmsford Charity Cups, only to be well beaten by Leytonstone and Chelmsford respectively. With regard to the South Essex League, he regretted to say the club did not come up to expectations, but ultimately reached fifth position.

He would like to thank the whole of the players for their services, but he thought special reference should be made to their worthy captain Mr.A.E.Jones. (Applause). It was Mr.Jones' intention to retire from the game at the end of the season 1908-09, but, owing to circumstances, he unhesitatingly accepted the captaincy of the new club. He thought he was correct in stating that, although Mr.Jones would not play regularly next season, he would assist the club occasionally if required.

There appeared to be some misunderstanding between Mr.A.S.Hyett (the vice-captain) and the committee, which led the player to assist Ilford F.C. during the latter part of last season. This had caused considerable consternation among the spectators as to what Mr. Hyett intended to do, but it was his (the secretary's) sincere hope that Mr.Hyett would give the club his valuable services next season. (Hear,hear). It was with regret that he had to report the retirement of another player, their old friend, Mr.F.Kittle, but no doubt he would be like their captain, and give the club his valuable services if required. (Hear,hear). The committee had attended meetings remarkably well, and the Chairman (Mr.G.A.Smith) had never missed a meeting, which spoke volumes for the interest he took in the club. He thanked the committee for the great assistance they had given him, and said it had been a great pleasure to work with them. (Hear,hear). The reserves came in very useful several times last season, and he thought it would be a great pity to let them slide.

Mr.E.P.Jones presented the financial statement, saying the balance sheet had not turned out so well as they hoped. The balance sheet was as follows:-

Receipts: Presidents and vice-presidents' subscriptions £15.4s.0d.; members' subscriptions £19.15s.0d.; gate receipts £170.13s.0d.; stand receipts £11.1s.6d.; guarantee and share of gates £18.7s.5d.; profit on whist drives, £7.17s.2d.; sundry, 5s.6d.; balance due to hon.secretary, £8.9s.3d.; Total £251.12s.10d.

Expenditure: Rent, £20; guarantees and share of gates. £53.12s.3d.; players' travelling expenses, £47.10s.11d.; players' teas £85.9s.4d.; referees' expenses £9.1s.8d.; subscriptions to leagues, associations, cup etc. £7.2s.8d.; groundsman £13.0s.3d.; assistance in pay-box, £3.5s.0d. ground expenses £30.11s.11d.; police £7.0s.6d.; printing etc. £3.14s.0d.; postage and telegrams £6.13s.6d.; laundry £1.6s.0d.; players' outfits £7.5s.0d.; incidental expenses £5.15s.2d.; cash at bank, 3s 4d.; total £251.12s.10d.; Liabilities: amount due to hon.secretary £8.9s.3d.; unpaid accounts £26.7s.6d. total, £34.16s.9d.

Mr.Jones said that since the accounts had been prepared they had received a profit on Cosy Corner of £4.12s.0d. That practically left them with £5.1s.0d. to carry on the club. Mr.Hodson said there were assets which would reduce the deficit to £16.6s.0d. This was very satisfactory, considering that they started with nothing in hand. (Hear,hear).

In reply to questions, it was stated that the grand stand had not been brought into the balance sheet, it being a private concern. Mr.Drynan said he thought that the position was very satisfactory, considering how they started. There was a good deal of outlay at the start. The chairman said the cost of players' travelling expenses and teas seemed to be excessive. The Hon.Secretary said the cost only came out at about £2 a match. He considered this was reasonable. The Chairman said the matter had been mentioned to him outside. He thought the meeting was the proper place to say what they had got to say. (Hear,hear). The balance sheet was adopted on the proposition of Mr.Drynan, seconded by Mr.Tatam.

Mr.G.A.Smith proposed the re-election of Mr.Bassett as president, and said he hoped Mr. Bassett would long continue to be their president, and to show the interest in the club which he had shown since the start. Mr.Hodson seconded the proposition, which was unanimously carried.

The Chairman, in returning thanks, said he had always taken a great interest in football and more particularly in the Romford United Club after what had occurred last year. He would impress on them not to talk about little quibbles outside, but to settle matters inside, and then they could go on a clear course. (Hear,hear). The vice-presidents were re-elected, with the addition of Messrs.E.P.Jones, C.T.Heard, G.A.Smith, A.J.Smith, H.Small, E.Currie, H.W.E. Stephenson, A.S.Hyett, R.R.Pratt, F.G.Padgham, A.Page, L.P.Pratt, W.D. Matthews, L.Fletcher, S.Dowsing, H.D.Warner, H.Turvey, W.P.Griggs,J.P.,C.C., O.Hanck, R.Heath, F.Chipperfield, W.Stevens, J.M.Evett, W.Adams, W.Weir, E.G. Pearsons, A.S.Maskelyne, P.J.Anderson, G.Barnes, G.C.Eley, A.E.Jones, J.Suckling, N.T. Moore, and F.O.Rush. Mr.C.T.Heard was heartily re-elected hon.secretary, on the proposition of Mr.Tatam, seconded by Mr.Drynan. Mr.Heard said he would do his very best for the club, and he hoped that this time next year they would be happier than they were at the present time. Mr.Drynan: We are happy enough now. (Hear,hear).

Mr.E.P.Jones was heartily re-elected hon.treasurer and he said he would forego the amount he advanced for the grand stand. (Applause). Mr.Drynan: There is nothing like following a good example, and I'll do the same. (Applause). The Chairman: Any other volunteers? (Laughter). The Hon.Secretary said the following players would play next season: Messrs. A.M.Baker, P.J.Moore, J.C.Doggett, J.Collar, S.C.Squier, B.G.Aston, P.Adams, and J.Chapman. Mr.A.S.Hyett* was elected captain, and Mr.A.M.Baker*, vice-captain, it being understood that if Mr.Hyett declined the captaincy Mr.Baker* shall be captain, and the vice-captain shall be appointed by the committee.

The Hon.Secretary proposed that a reserve team should be run, the same as last season. Mr.Fletcher seconded the proposition which was carried. Mr.A.Drury was elected hon.secretary of the reserve team; Mr.P.Adams, captain; and Mr.A.Hunwicks, vice-captain. The committee was elected as follows:- Messrs. G.A.Smith, E.Currie, S.Dowsing, L.Fletcher, R.Heath, F.Robarts, H.Small, E.T.Smee, and L.P.Pratt. Messrs. F.W.Jeffes and E.J.Wallis were re-elected auditors.

Mr.A.Page proposed a vote of thanks to the officers, and eulogised the work of the committee and other officials, whom he heartily congratulated on the season's result. Mr.H.W.E.Stephenson seconded the proposition, which was heartily carried.

The Hon.Secretary replying to Mr.Tatam, said he thought they were all aware of the fact that the club was not entered for the English Association Cup. The reason of this was that he was unfortunately ill at the time the entry should have been made, and when he was able to attend to things the time in which entries had to be made had passed....The omission was absolutely due to his illness and he deeply regretted it. In the circumstances they would have to forgive him. (Hear,hear). They could not summon him for it (Laughter). He had entered the club for the Amateur Cup. He applied for exemption, but had not got it, and they had to go through the qualifying rounds. The explanation was considered thoroughly satisfactory. Three new members were elected.

* Note: Mr.Hyett did not play for the club in the following season, and it is believed that Mr.P.J.Moore was the captain. It is unknown who became vice-captain.

Season 1910 – 11

ROMFORD FOOTBALL CLUB

President: Mr.C.F.Fitch **Chairman:** Mr.G.Bridgen

Hon. Secretary: Mr. W.H.Kelly, "Patna," Brooklands Road, Romford Mr.H.Barkham w.e.f. 12th November

Hon. Treasurer: Mr. W.R.Carter

Committee: Messrs.H.W.Brown, G.Bridgen, W.H.Pring, A.Parrish, J.Tetchner, F.Laurence, J.Robinson and H.Barkham

Headquarters: Golden Lion Hotel, Romford **Ground:** Cricket Ground, Romford Station

COMPETITIONS ENTERED

South Essex League Division One
F.A. Challenge Cup
Amateur Cup
Essex Senior Cup
West Ham Charity Cup

Match Details

3 Sept SEL1 Away Shoeburyness Garrison 0 – 6
Romford: W.H.Nurthen; F.Milbank,A.J.Gallagher;W.Dickerson,T.W.Carter,M.C.Farrant; F.Prout,A.E.Denyer,C.S.Browne,H.Hobbs,S.Flaxman.

10 Sept Frdly Away Ilford 0 – 4
Romford: W.H.Nurthen;F.Milbank,A.J.Gallagher;R.Boulton,T.W.Carter,M.C.Farrant; W.Dickerson,F.Prout,C.S.Browne,J.Harris,S.Flaxman.

17 Sept FAC1Q Home South Weald 0 – 2
Romford: W.H.Nurthen;E.Marsh,A.J.Gallagher(Capt);W.Dickerson,Ray Boulton,T.W.Carter; J.Harris,M.C.Farrant,C.S.Browne,F.Prout,S.Flaxman.

24 Sept Frdly Away Tooting Graveney 2 – 0 C.Steele(2)
Romford: C.Steele,
Team details unknown

1 Oct SEL1 Away Grays Athletic 1 – 1 Browne
Romford: W.H.Nurthen;F.Milbank,A.J.Gallagher;W.Dickerson, R.Boulton,T.W.Carter; F.Prout,S.Flaxman,C.S.Browne,A.E.Denyer,M.C.Farrant.

8 Oct Frdly Away Bedford Town 4 – 8 Smith(2)Prout,Browne
Romford: W.H.Nurthen; ? ,A.J.Gallagher(Capt);W.Dickerson,R.Boulton, ? ; F.Prout, ? ,C.S.Browne,S.Flaxman,A.Smith.

15 Oct SEL1 Away Southend United Reserves 0 – 2
Romford: W.H.Nurthen;W.Dickerson,A.J.Gallagher(Capt);M.C.Farrant,R.Boulton,T.W.Carter; C.Steele,C.S.Browne,J.Harris,A.Smith,S.Flaxman.

22 Oct AC2Q Home Shoeburyness Garrison 2 – 5 Scorers unknown
Romford: W.H.Nurthen;W.Dickerson,A.J.Gallagher(Capt);M.C.Farrant,Mildmay,T.W.Carter; J.Casey,C.Steele,J.Harris,C.S.Browne,S.Flaxman.

29 Oct SEL1 Home Grays Athletic 2 – 1 Bennett,Browne
Romford: W.H.Nurthen; W.Dickerson,A.J.Gallagher(Capt);M.C.Farrant,R.Boulton,T.W.Carter; J.Harris,C.Steele,C.S.Browne,J.Casey,H.Bennett.

5 Nov Frdly Away Hoddesdon Town 4 – 1 Browne(2)Unknown(2)
Romford: W.H.Nurthen;A.J.Gallagher(Capt),W.Dickerson; Half backs all reserves; ? , ? ,C.S.Browne, ? ,S.Casey.

19 Nov ESC1R Away Grays Athletic 1 – 3 Harris
Romford: W.H.Nurthen;
A.E.Denyer,J.Harris, remainder of the team reserve team players.

26 Nov SEL1 Home Wanstead 3 – 2## Browne,Harris(2)(1pen)
Romford: W.H.Nurthen;A.J.Gallagher(Capt),F.Denyer;T.W.Carter,A.Edwards,J.Casey;
H.Bennett,A.E.Denyer,J.Harris,C.S.Browne,F.Prout.

10 Dec SEL1 Away South Weald 0 – 8
Romford: W.H.Nurthen;T.Ball,A.Gallagher;H.Bradshaw,plus eight reserves.

17 Dec SEL1 Home Chelmsford 0 – 3
Romford: W.H.Nurthen;A.J.Gallagher(Capt),T.Ball;T.W.Carter,A.Edwards,W.Dickerson;
J.Casey,H.Bennett,C.S.Browne,A.E.Denyer,J.Harris.

24 Dec SEL1 Home South Weald 1 – 9** Harris
Romford: W.H.Nurthen;A.M.Baker,A.Miser;A.Dearman,C.Russell,H.Bennett;
C.S.Browne,F.Walters,A.E.Denyer,C.Steele,J.Harris.

26 Dec SEL1 Away Colchester Town 0 – 2
Romford: W.H.Nurthen;A.M.Baker,A.J.Gallagher;W.Dickerson,A.Edwards,T.W.Carter;
F.Walters,J.Harris,A.E.Denyer,C.Steele,J.Casey.

31 Dec Frdly Away Metrogas 0 – 3
Romford:
Team details unknown.

14 Jan Frdly Home 1st Grenadier Guards 5 – 0
Romford: W.H.Nurthen;A.M.Baker,A.J.Gallagher(Capt);W.Dickerson,A.Edwards,J.Casey;
F.Walters,C.S.Browne,C.Steele,J.Harris,A.E.Denyer.

21 Jan Frdly Home Bronze Athletic 4 – 1 Dearman(2)Harris,Steele
Romford: W.H.Nurthen;A.M.Baker,T.Ball;W.Dickerson,A.Edwards,T.W.Carter;
J.Casey,A.Dearman,C.Steele,J.Harris,A.E.Denyer.

28 Jan. Frdly Away Barking 2 – 1 Harris(2)
Attendance: 800
Romford: W.Saggers;A.M.Baker,A.J.Gallagher(Capt);W.Dickerson,A.Edwards,T.W.Carter;
J.Casey,A.Dearman,F.Prout,C.Steele,J.Harris.

4 Feb SEL1 Home Colchester Town 3 – 1 Prout(2),Harris
Romford: W.H.Nurthen;A.J.Gallagher,W.Biles;W.Dickerson,A.Edwards,T.W.Carter;
F.Prout,J.Harris,A.E.Denyer,J.Casey,C.Steele.

18 Feb SEL1 Home Shoeburyness Garrison 0 – 3
Romford: W.H.Nurthen;A.J.Gallagher,W.Biles;W.Dickerson,A.Edwards,T.W.Carter;
J.Casey,F.Prout,J.Harris,A.E.Denyer,C.Steele.

23 Feb WHC2R Home Custom House 2 – 1 Harris,Denyer
Romford: C.Poulter;A.Edwards,B.Wilding;D.Chike,L.Burn,A.Hunwicks;
C.Russell,A.E.Denyer,J.Harris,A.Smith,A.Parker.

25 Feb Frdly Away Kilburn 2 – 3 Dickerson,Denyer
Attendance: 2,500
Romford: W.Dickerson,
A.E.Denyer. Remainder of the team unknown.

4 Mar SEL1 Home Southend United Reserves 0 – 2
Romford: W.H.Nurthen;A.J.Gallagher,W.Biles;W.Dickerson,A.Edwards,T.W.Carter;
J.Casey,F.Walters,J.Harris,A.E.Denyer,C.Steele.

11 Mar Frdly Away Harwich & Parkeston 1 – 3 Casey
Romford:
Only three first team players travelled due to illness and business commitments.

Romford were expelled from the League on 16th March for falling foul of F.A. Regulations, and this proved to be the Club's last ever game.

** Romford deducted two points for playing C.Russell who was ineligible to play.
Wanstead expelled from the league on 12th January record expunged. Match void.

SUMMARY OF FIRST TEAM RESULTS OBTAINED SEASON 1910 – 11

	P	W	D	L	Goals For	Goals Ag	Pts
South Essex League	11	2	1	8	7	38	3
S.E.League (expunged)	1	1	0	0	3	2	
F.A. Challenge Cup	1	0	0	1	0	2	
F.A. Amateur Cup	1	0	0	1	2	5	
Essex Senior Cup	1	0	0	1	1	3	
West Ham Charity Cup	1	1	0	0	2	1	
Friendly Matches	10	5	0	5	24	24	
Total	26	9	1	16	39	75	

South Essex League Division One
Final Table

	P	W	D	L	Goals For	Goals Ag	Pts
Custom House	14	9	3	2	30	12	21
South Weald	14	9	2	3	56	18	20
Southed United Reserves	14	8	3	3	33	18	19
Shoeburyness Garrison	14	8	1	5	26	18	17
Romford United	14	4	4	6	18	29	12
Grays Athletic **	14	3	4	7	20	33	8
Colchester Town **	14	4	1	9	22	46	7
Chelmsford **	14	1	2	11	19	50	2
Romford ##	**11**	**2**	**1**	**8**	**7**	**38**	**3**

** Two points deducted for breach of Rules.
Romford expelled from the league and record expunged. Four points deducted on 16th March.

12 Jan Wanstead expelled from the league and record expunged.

CUP RESULTS

F.A. Challenge Cup

Final: Bradford City 0 Newcastle United 0
Replay: Bradford City 1 Newcastle United 0

Romford's progress: 1st Qual Home South Weald 0 – 2

F.A. Amateur Cup

Final: Bromley 1 Bishop Auckland 0

Romford's progress: 2nd Qual Home Shoeburyness Garrison 2 – 5

Essex Senior Cup

Final: Custom House 3 South Weald 1

Romford's progress: 1st Round Away Grays Athletic 1 – 3

West Ham Charity Cup

Final: Romford United 1 South Weald 0

Romford's progress: 2nd Round Home Custom House 2 – 1
Semi-Final Romford United*

* Due to have been played on 25th March, but the Romford Club folded a few days earlier.

First Team Appearances Season 1910 - 11

A.M.Baker	5	T.Ball	3	H.Bennett	3*	W.Biles	3
Ray Boulton	6	H.Bradshaw	1	C.S.Browne	12*	L.Burn	1
T.W.Carter	14*	J.Casey	11*	D.Chike	1	A.Dearman	3
A.E.Denyer	12*	F.Denyer	0*	W.Dickerson	18	A.Edwards	9*
M.C.Farrant	7	S.Flaxman	7	A.J.Gallagher	17*	J.Harris	16*
H.Hobbs	1	A.Hunwicks	1	F.Marsh	1	F.Milbank	3
Mildmay	1	A.Miser	1	W.H.Nurthen	19*	A.Parker	1
C.Poulter	1	F.Prout	8*	C.Russell	2	W.Saggers	1
A.Smith	3	C.Steele	12	F.W.Walters	4	B.Wilding	1
Total	209						

* Also played in the void South Essex League game against Wanstead.

First Team Goal Scorers Season 1910 – 11

J.Harris	9	C.S.Browne	6	C.Steele	3	F.Prout	3
A.Smith	2	A.Dearman	2	A.Denyer	2	H.Bennett	1
W.Dickerson	1	J.Casey	1	Unknown	9	Total	39

Post-Season Summary Season 1910 – 11

The Great Eastern Railway Company agreed to allow the original Romford team to play at the Cricket Ground, although extensive building work was taking place modernising Romford Station.

The season opened in disastrous fashion as the team met with three successive defeats and failed to score a goal! A 6-0 loss was suffered at Shoeburyness Garrison in the opening league fixture, then a four nil friendly defeat by Ilford was followed by an early exit from the F.A. Cup with a home defeat by South Weald by two goals to nil. All of this was followed by a 2-0 win away to Tooting Graveney in a friendly.

A week later away to Grays Athletic there was a very large attendance, because Romford were billed (unauthorised) as playing their professional team. The result was a fine 1-1 draw. There followed another appalling defeat in an away friendly match against Bedford by eight goals to four. Some mitigation could be claimed as both Steel and Carter missed the train. Two unknown players were picked up en route, but they played poorly.

Southend United Reserves gained a 2-0 league victory and Shoeburyness Garrison ousted the club from the Amateur Cup by virtue of a five goals to two thrashing. On 29th October a good home win by two goals to one against Grays Athletic was marred by the sending off of Dickerson. Next an away win in a friendly game against Hoddesdon by four goals to one suggested the team were on the up.

A week later Romford forfeited home advantage and played with only Nurthern, Denyer and Harris plus eight reserves in the Essex Senior Cup tie with Grays Athletic. Due to an oversight, eight regular first team men were not qualified to play in the competition. No surprise, then, that they were defeated 3-1. Hopes were raised by a 3-2 win against Wanstead in the league, but this victory was expunged as Wanstead withdrew from the league!

Next came a devastating period when the team suffered five successive defeats, the first of which was an 8-0 mauling away to South Weald followed by a 3-0 reverse at home to Chelmsford. South Weald repeated the dose in the return fixture, this time by nine goals to one. A.M.Baker, former Romford United captain, made his unhappy debut and to add to the club's misery they were deducted two points for playing Charlie Russell who was ineligible. Defeats by Colchester Town (League) and Metrogas (Friendly) completed this sad few weeks.

Suddenly there was a revival with four wins in a row, although three of these were only friendly matches. One was a game against Barking when Saggers played in goal as Nurthern played for Portsmouth on that day and made a good impression in front of a crowd of 3,000. Romford managed to score fourteen goals in these four games, including three against Colchester Town in the South Essex League.

Next came another defeat by Shoeburyness Garrison in the league but the team secured a fine 2-1 victory in the West Ham Charity Cup against Custom House to earn a place in the semi-finals. Alas no date could be found to meet Romford United and the tie was never played!

Three more defeats rounded off the season. The first, a friendly against Kilburn, of the London League, by three goals to two, was followed by a 2-0 reverse at home to Southend United Reserves in the league. The final game was a friendly away to Harwich & Parkeston on 11th March which was lost 3-1. Only three first team players travelled to Harwich, citing illness, business commitments or a journey too far! This proved to be the club's last-ever game. On 16th March 1911, Romford were expelled from the South Essex League for continued breaches of rules and some committee members were suspended by the Essex County F.A.

ESSEX COUNTY FOOTBALL ASSOCIATION COMMISSION (as reported in the *Essex Times*)

The above Committee met at the General Havelock, Ilford on Thursday 2nd March to consider a protest from Woodford Crusaders regarding the eligibility of A.C.Potter to play for Mawney Institute in the Essex Junior Cup. It was alleged that Potter was a senior player having played on two occasions for the Romford Town [sic] Football Club. The protest was dismissed and the protest fee returned to the Woodford Club.

THE BEGINNING OF THE END.....

INVESTIGATION INTO THE ROMFORD FOOTBALL CLUB AFFAIRS

(as reported in the *Essex Times*)

An investigation into the affairs of the Romford F.C. was undertaken, after consultation with the F.A. by a commission, consisting of Messrs. A. Porter, (Chair), M. A. Wants, A. M. Andrews, and Jas. T. Clark, (Hon.Sec.). Meetings were held at the General Havelock Hotel, Ilford, on Jan. 19th and 26th 1911, at which the whole of the books, vouchers, etc., submitted by the club, were examined.

A further meeting was held at the Y.M.C.A. rooms, Romford, on Feb. 3rd 1911, at which various officials, of the club were examined. A final meeting, for the taking of evidence, was held at Winchester House, Old Broad Street, E.C., on February 14th 1911, when a large number of players were examined as to the various charges they had made for "expenses" .

At a meeting, at the Railway Hotel, Grays, on February 22nd 1911, the whole of the evidence was reviewed, and the appended findings and decisions arrived at. These were submitted to the F.A., for confirmation, and, upon being approved by that body, were duly promulgated.

FINDINGS

(A) The Romford F.C. has not been carried on in accordance with the Rules and regulations of the Football Association.

(B) The accounts for season 1909 – 10, submitted at the Annual Meeting in June 1910, have not been audited, nor is there any record shown of the Assets and Liabilities of the club at the end of the season.

(C) From October 1st to November 7th 1910, the club was entirely managed by Mr. W. H. Kelly, who received all monies, and made all payments. There is no record in the Minute Book of any meetings of the club having been held from Sept. 19th to November 7th 1910 and Messrs. Carter (Treasurer), and Bridgen (Chairman), decline to state why they failed to discharge the obligations of their respective offices during that period.

(D) The club has made a practice of ordering teas for a number of people other than the players, but there is no record of any money having been received from such persons, although, on the other hand, there is a large sum still owing for teas supplied to the club. (Mr. Carter stated that all players stayed to tea, but many of the players stated they charged for tea in their expenses, as they did not stay).

(E) So far as can be ascertained no check whatever has been kept upon the gate receipts of the club, and there is no record of tickets sold.

(F) Several members of the club are to have first advanced a sum of £30:17:3 as a loan to the club, and afterwards to have waived the right of repayment, the amount appearing in the 1909 – 10 A/Cs as "Given by the Committee". No record of the transaction, however, can be found in the Minute Book, nor can the counterfoils of the receipts for the amounts making up the total be found in either of the three Receipt Books.

(G) There is no item for "printing" in last season's A/Cs. But Mr. Carter explained that Messrs. Wilson and Whitworth had done this gratuitously. The Minute Book contains no reference to this matter, despite the fact that the item must have been a considerable one.

(H) The club has received, through the signatories to the agreement notice to be quit from the ground by April 4th next, owing to two quarters arrears of rent, and the G.E.R. Coy. Have put men in possession, at the ground, on occasions.

(I) Payments have been made to players for which no receipts have been obtained, and it has not been the custom for the club to observe Rule 28 of the Football Association, in the matter of players' expenses.

(J) The various allegations and statements made by Mr. C. F. Fitch are substantially correct.

DECISION

(1) That the club be severely censured and ordered to forthwith reconstitute itself to comply with the requirements of the Football Association.

(2) That Mr. G. Bridgen be permanently removed from football and football management and be debarred till Sept. 1st 1912, from entering the ground of the Romford F.C. during the time matches are in progress.

(3) That Mr. W. R. Carter be suspended from March 1st 1911 till Sept. 1st 1912.

(4) That Mr. W. H. Kelly be suspended from March 1st 1911 till Sept. 1st 1912.

(5) That Mr. W. H. Pring be suspended from March 1st 1911 till Sept. 1st 1911.

(6) That the club pay, within fourteen days of date, the sum of two guineas, (£2:2:0), towards the cost of the enquiry.

(7) That the club be ordered to submit its books to the Association in June next, prior to the holding of the Annual General Meeting.

(8) That Mr. C. F. Fitch be thanked for his services to the commission.

(9) That all papers and documents in connection with the case, be impounded.

SOUTH ESSEX FOOTBALL LEAGUE

At a specially convened Meeting of the South Essex Football League, held at the Pigeons, Stratford, on Thursday 16th March, under the presidency of Mr. Thomas H. Kirkup, secretary of the London Football Association, the Romford Football Club, one of the oldest amateur organisations in the county, was expelled from membership for breaches of the rules of the competition, and the record of the club was expunged from the League table. The result of this decision is that the League match between Romford and Romford United for March 25th will not take place.

Annual General Meeting

Due to the club being expelled from the South Essex League in March and the decision to close down the club, it is believed that no annual general meeting was ever held.

R.I.P.

11th March Romford played a friendly match and were defeated at Harwich & Parkeston by three goals to one.

16th March and Romford were expelled from the South Essex League.

This was the unhappy ending of the original Romford Football Club, but the town name was to be carried for a further eight years by Romford United, later known as Romford Town.

Season 1910 – 11

ROMFORD UNITED

President: Mr.John Bassett J.P. **Chairman:** Mr.G.A.Smith

Hon. Secretary: Mr.C.T.Heard, 18 King Edward Road, Romford

Reserve Team Hon.Secretary: Mr.A.Drury **Hon. Treasurer:** Mr.E.P.Jones

Captain: Mr.P.J.Moore

Reserve Team Captain: Mr.P.Adams **Reserve Team Vice-Captain:** Mr.A.Hunwicks

Committee: Messrs. E.Currie,S.Dowsing,L.Fletcher,R.Heath,L.P.Pratt, F.Robarts,H.Small,E.T.Smee and G.A.Smith (Chairman)

Colours: Royal Blue Shirts, White Shorts **Headquarters:** Rising Sun Hotel, Romford

Ground: Cosy Corner, (also known as the Shoulder of Mutton Field), Hornchurch Road, Romford

COMPETITIONS ENTERED

South Essex League Division One
F.A.Amateur Cup
Essex Senior Cup
Romford Charity Cup
West Ham Charity Cup
Chelmsford Charity Cup

Due to the secretary's illness the club failed to apply for entry into the F.A. Challenge Cup

Ilford & District League Division One
Essex Junior Cup

Match Details

3 Sept Frdly Home City of Westminster 3 – 3
Romford United:
Team details unknown

10 Sept Frdly Home South Weald 3 – 3 Knight(3)
Romford United: H.A.Bown;A.M.Baker,P.J.Moore;F.A.Hance,J.C.Doggett,C.Millington; W.A.Porter,J.Knight,S.A.Cartwright,J.Graves,A.J.Collar.

17 Sept SEL1 Away Southend Utd. Reserves 1 – 1 Squier
Romford United: W.Watkins;A.M.Baker,P.J.Moore;F.A.Hance,J.C.Doggett,F.H.Kittle; J.Chapman,J.Knight,S.A.Cartwright,S.C.Squier,A.J.Collar.

24 Sept SEL1 Home Grays Athletic 3 – 1 Cartwright(2)Collar
Romford United: W.Watkins;A.M.Baker,P.J.Moore;F.A.Hance,J.C.Doggett,F.H.Kittle; J.Chapman,J.Knight,S.A.Cartwright,S.C.Squier,A.J.Collar.

1 Oct SEL1 Away Wanstead## 5 – 1 Cartwright(2)Harvey(2)Squier
Romford United: W.Watkins;A.M.Baker,P.J.Moore;F.A.Hance,J.C.Doggett,F.H.Kittle; W.Harvey,J.Graves,S.A.Cartwright,S.C.Squier,A.J.Collar.

8 Oct AC1Q Home Upton Park (Scratched) w/o

8 Oct Frdly Home Bronze Athletic 2 – 4 Cartwright,A.E.Jones
Romford United: R.Heath;A.M.Baker,P.J.Moore;F.A.Hance,J.C.Doggett,F.H.Kittle; A.E.Jones,Guy Squier,S.A.Cartwright,S.C.Squier,A.J.Collar.

22 Oct AC2Q Away Grays Athletic 3 – 6 Cartwright(2)Squier
Romford United: W.Watkins;A.M.Baker,P.J.Moore;F.A.Hance,J.C.Doggett,B.G.Aston;
J.Chapman,B.S.Ruggles,S.A.Cartwright,S.C.Squier,A.J.Collar.

29 Oct SEL1 Away South Weald (void) 1 – 5# Squier
Romford United: W.Watkins;A.M.Baker,P.J.Moore;F.A.Hance,J.C.Doggett,F.H.Kittle;
J.Chapman,B.S.Ruggles,S.A.Cartwright,S.C.Squier,A.J.Collar.

5 Nov Frdly Home QPR Reserves 1 – 4 C.Doggett
Romford United: W.Watkins;A.M.Baker,P.J.Moore;F.A.Hance,J.C.Doggett,F.H.Kittle;
C.Doggett,W.Matthews,S.A.Cartwright,S.C.Squier,A.J.Collar.

12 Nov SEL1 Home Chelmsford 2 – 1 C.Doggett,Squier
Romford United: W.Watkins;A.M.Baker,P.J.Moore;F.A.Hance,J.C.Doggett,F.H.Kittle;
C.Doggett,A.White,J.Graves,S.C.Squier,A.J.Collar.

19 Nov Frdly Home West Norwood 2 – 2 Collar,Graves
Romford United: H.A.Bown;A.M.Baker,P.J.Moore;F.A.Hance,J.C.Doggett,F.H.Kittle;
J.Chapman,C.Doggett,A.White,J.Graves,A.J.Collar.

26 Nov Frdly Home Woodford Albion 2 – 0
Romford United:
Team details unknown

3 Dec SEL1 Home Wanstead## 2 – 1 Graves(2)
Romford United:
Team details unknown

10 Dec Frdly Away Leytonstone 2 – 7 Graves(2)
Romford United:
Team details unknown

17 Dec Frdly Home Plumstead St. John 3 – 1
Romford United:
Team details unknown

20 Dec SEL1 Away South Weald 0 – 5
Romford United: W.Watkins;A.M.Baker,P.J.Moore;O.Hance,J.C.Doggett,F.H.Kittle;
W.Harvey,A.W.Asater,S.A.Cartwright,F.Woolley,A.J.Collar.

31 Dec Frdly Home East Ham F.C. 3 – 0 Jones,Squier,Mackay(pen)
Romford United: H.A.Bown;W.M.Turner,P.J.Moore;F.A.Hance,J.C.Doggett,F.H.Kittle;
G.E.Mackay,A.E.Jones,J.Graves,S.C.Squier,A.J.Collar.

7 Jan SEL1 Home Custom House 0 – 0
Romford United: H.A.Bown;A.W.Asater,P.J.Moore;F.A.Hance,J.C.Doggett,F.H.Kittle;
F.Woolley.S.A.Cartwright,J.Graves,S.C.Squier,A.J.Collar.

14 Jan SEL1 Away Grays Athletic 1 – 3 J.C.Doggett
Romford United: H.A.Bown;A.W.Asater,P.J.Moore;F.A.Hance,J.C.Doggett,F.H.Kittle;
F.Woolley,G.E.Mackay,J.Graves,S.C.Squier,A.J.Collar.

21 Jan SEL1 Away Custom House 1 – 2 Collar
Romford United: H.A.Bown;A.W.Asater,P.J.Moore;F.A.Hance,J.C.Doggett,F.H.Kittle;
F.Woolley,G.E.Mackay,J.Graves,S.C.Squier,A.J.Collar.

28 Jan SEL1 Home South Weald 2 – 2 Wooding,Collar
Romford United: H.A.Bown;*A.Reading,P.J.Moore;F.A.Hance,*H.B.West,*E.Taylor;
A.W.Asater,*Wooding,G.E.Mackay,J.Graves,A.J.Collar.
*These players ex defunct Wanstead team

4 Feb ESC3R Away Grays Athletic 1 – 1 Graves
Romford: H.A.Bown;A.W.Asater,P.J.Moore;F.A.Hance,J.C.Doggett,F.H.Kittle;
B.S.Ruggles,W.Rushbrook,J.Graves,S.C.Squier,A.J.Collar.

11 Feb ESCRP Home Grays Athletic 4 – 1 Ruggles(3)Collar
Romford: H.A.Bown;A.W.Asater,P.J.Moore;F.A.Hance,J.C.Doggett,J.B.Hunter;
B.S.Ruggles,W.Rushbrook,J.Graves,S.C.Squier,A.J.Collar.

18 Feb SEL1 Away Chelmsford 2 – 1 Squier,Taylor
Romford United: H.A.Bown;A.W.Asater,P.J.Moore;F.A.Hance,J.C.Doggett,F.H.Kittle;
A.Reading,H.B.West,E.Taylor,S.C.Squier,A.J.Collar.

25 Feb SEL1 Away Shoeburyness Garrison 0 – 4
Romford United: H.A.Bown;A.Reading,P.J.Moore;F.A..Hance,J.C.Doggett,F.H.Kittle;
F.Woolley,H.B.West,E.Taylor,J.Graves,S.C.Squier.

4 Mar ESCSF Ch'ford South Weald 1 – 3 Ruggles
Attendance: 2,000
Romford: H.A.Bown;J.B.Hunter,P.J.Moore;F.A.Hance,J.C.Doggett,H.C.Massey;
B.S.Ruggles,G.E.Mackay,J.Graves,S.C.Squier,A.J.Collar.

11 Mar SEL1 Home Colchester Town 2 – 1 Collar,Squier
Romford United: H.A.Bown;A.Reading,P.J.Moore; A.W.Asater,J.C.Doggett,Wooding;
F.Woolley,G.E.Mackay,H.B.West,S.C.Squier,A.J.Collar.

18 Mar SEL1 Home Southend Utd. Reserves 0 – 2
Romford United: H.A.Bown;A.Reading,P.J.Moore;A.W.Asater,J.C.Doggett,H.E.Massey;
W.Harvey,E.Taylor,A.E.Jones,H.B.West,S.C.Squier.

25 Mar WHCSF Romford Void*

1 Apr WHCCF Clapton Leytonstone 3 – 2 Kittle(2)Rushbrook
Attendance: 4,000
Romford United: H.A.Bown;A.Reading,P.J.Moore;A.W.Asater,J.C.Doggett,F.H.Kittle;
B.S.Ruggles,G.E.Mackay,W.Rushbrook,E.Taylor,S.C.Squier.

8 Apr Frdly Home Barking 3 – 2 Eldridge(2)Moore(pen)
Romford United: ?? ;P.J.Moore,
Eldridge. Remainder of the team unknown.

15 Apr SEL1 Home Shoeburyness Garrison 3 – 3 Hance,Knight,Woolley
Romford United: H.A.Bown;A.W.Asater,P.J.Moore;F.A.Hance,F.H.Kittle,J.Knight;
Eldridge,E.Taylor,H.B.West,F.Woolley,A.J.Collar.

19 Apr CCCSF Away Chelmsford 0 – 1
Romford United:
Team details unknown

22 Apr SEL1 Away Colchester Town 1 – 3 Squier
Romford United: H.A.Bown;A.W.Asater,P.J.Moore;F.A.Hance,F.H.Kittle,J.Knight;
Eldridge,E.Taylor,H.B.West,S.C.Squier,A.J.Collar.

29 Apr RCCF Home South Weald 1 – 0 Willats
Romford United: H.A.Bown;A.Reading,P.J.Moore;H.B.West,J.C.Doggett,F.H.Kittle;
Willats,E.Taylor,W.Rushbrook,Eldridge,F.Walters.

Aban. 86 Mins(Bad light) void
##Expelled from league 12 Jan
* Not played due to Romford Football Club folding.

SUMMARY OF FIRST TEAM RESULTS OBTAINED SEASON 1910 – 11

	P	W	D	L	Goals For	Goals Ag	Pts
South Essex League	14	4	4	6	18	29	12
S.E.League (Expunged)	2	2	0	0	8	3	
F.A. Amateur Cup	1	0	0	1	3	6	
Essex Senior Cup	3	1	1	1	6	5	
West Ham Charity Cup	1	1	0	0	3	2	
Chelmsford Charity Cup	1	0	0	1	0	1	
Romford Charity Cup	1	1	0	0	1	0	
Friendly Matches	10	4	3	3	24	26	
Total	33	13	8	12	63	72	

Note: The above summary does not include the match against South Weald on 29th October which was abandoned.

South Essex League Division One
Final Table

					Goals		
	P	W	D	L	For	Ag	Pts
Custom House	14	9	3	2	30	12	21
South Weald	14	9	2	3	56	18	20
Southed United Reserves	14	8	3	3	33	18	19
Shoeburyness Garrison	14	8	1	5	26	18	17
Romford United	**14**	**4**	**4**	**6**	**18**	**29**	**12**
Grays Athletic **	14	3	4	7	20	33	8
Colchester Town **	14	4	1	9	22	46	7
Chelmsford **	14	1	2	11	19	50	2
Romford##	11	3	1	7	11	37	7

** Two points deducted for breach of Rules.

The Romford club was expelled from the league at a meeting on 16th March and their record expunged. Wanstead were expelled on 16th Jan. and their record was expunged.

CUP RESULTS

F.A. Challenge Cup

Final: Bradford City 0 Newcastle United 0
Replay: Bradford City 1 Newcastle United 0

Romford United did not enter the competition

F.A. Amateur Cup

Final: Bromley 1 Bishop Auckland 0

Romford's progress: 1st Qual Home Upton Park w/o
2nd Qual Away Grays Athletic 3 – 6

Essex Senior Cup

Final: Custom House 3 South Weald 1

Romford's progress: 3rd Round Away Grays Athletic 1 – 1
Replay Home Grays Athletic 4 – 1
Semi-Final Chelmsford South Weald 1 – 3

West Ham Charity Cup

Final: Romford United 3 Leytonstone 2

Romford's progress: Semi-Final Romford Void*
Final Clapton Leytonstone 3 – 2

Chelmsford Charity Cup

Final: n/k

Romford's progress: Semi-Final Away Chelmsford 0 – 1

Romford Charity Cup

Final: Romford United 1 South Weald 0

Romford's progress: Final Home South Weald 1 – 0

* Due to have been played on 25th March, but the Romford Club folded a few days earlier.

First Team Appearances Season 1910 - 11

A.W.Asater	13	B.G.Aston	1	A.M.Baker	9*	H.A.Bown	18
S.A.Cartwright	8*	J.Chapman	4*	A.J.Collar	21*	C.Doggett	3
J.C.Doggett	22*	Eldridge	4	J.Graves	12*	O.Hance	21*
W.Harvey	2*	Heath	1	J.B.Hunter	2	A.E.Jones.	3
F.H.Kittle	18*	J.Knight	5	G.E.Mackay	7	H.C.Massey	2
W.Matthews	1	C.Millington	1	P.J.Moore	26*	W.A.Porter	1
A.Reading	7	B.S.Ruggles	5*	W.Rushbrook	4	G.Squier	1
S.C.Squier	19*	E.Taylor	8	W.M.Turner	1	F.Walters	1
W.Watkins	6*	H.B.West	8	A.White	2	Willats	1
Wooding	2	F.Woolley	7			Total	277

* These players also played in one or more of the void games versus Wanstead and South Weald.

First Team Goal Scorers Season 1910 – 11

S.C.Squier	8	C.Cartwright	7	A.J.Collar	6	J.Graves	4
J.Knight	4	B.S.Ruggles	4	J.Harvey	2	C.Doggett	2
A.E.Jones	2	F.H.Kittle	2	Eldridge	2	G.E.Mackay	1
J.C.Doggett	1	Wooding	1	E.Taylor	1	W.Rushbrook	1
P.J.Moore	1	O.Hance	1	F.Woolley	1	Willats	1
Unknown	11					Total	63

Note: Stuart Squier also scored the goal in the abandoned game against South Weald.

"A" TEAM (RESERVES)

Match Details

17 Sept	Frdly	Home	Clapton "A"	3 – 3
15 Oct	EJC1R	Home	Barking Reserves	1 – 3
	IDL1	Home	Bow Argyle	2 – 2
	IDL1	Away	Bow Argyle	Lost#
	IDL1	Home	Forest Gate	6 – 1
	IDL1	Away	Forest Gate	0 – 3
	IDL1	Home	Hornchurch Territorials	1 – 1
	IDL1	Away	Hornchurch Territorials	1 – 2
	IDL1	Home	Ilford Reserves	2 – 1
	IDL1	Away	Ilford Reserves	Lost#
	IDL1	Home	Mawney Institute	1 – 2
	IDL1	Away	Mawney Institute	0 – 2
	IDL1	Home	Rainham	0 – 2
	IDL1	Away	Rainham	0 – 2

\# Romford scratched from these games and the points awarded to their opponents.

SUMMARY OF RESERVE TEAM RESULTS OBTAINED SEASON 1910 – 11

	P	W	D	L	Goals For	Goals Ag	Pts
Ilford & Dist.Lge.Div.1	12	2	2	8	13	18#	6
Essex Junior Cup	1	0	0	1	1	3	
Friendly Matches	1	0	1	0	3	3	
Total	14	2	3	9	17	25	

\# Romford scratched from two matches and both opponents were awarded the points, no goals allocated.

Ilford & District League Division I
Final Table

	P	W	D	L	Goals For	Goals Ag	Pts
Bow Argyle	12	10	1	1	44	8	21
Ilford Reserves	12	7	0	5	14	19	14
Rainham	12	6	1	5	20	17	13
Forest Gate	12	5	1	6	24	24	11
Hornchurch Ter.	12	4	2	6	17	34	10
Mawney Institute	12	4	1	7	12	24	9
Romford United "A"	**12**	**2**	**2**	**8**	**13**	**18**	**6**

CUP RESULTS

Essex Junior Cup

Final: Colchester Athletic 3 Southend Amateur 3
Replay: Colchester Athletic 2 Southend Amateur 1

Romford's progress: 1st Round Home Barking "A" 1 – 3

Post-Season Summary Season 1910 – 11

The team opened the season with two 3–3 home drawn friendly matches before commencing the league programme. A fine 1-1 draw away to Southend United Reserves gave Romford United their first league point, and successive victories over Grays Athletic and Wanstead added to the total. The following week should have been an F.A. Amateur Cup tie at home to Upton Park, but the latter scratched from the tie and Romford United moved into the next round. Instead of the cup tie United played a friendly match against Bronze Athletic, which was lost. R.Heath, formerly of Barking, was in goal. 'Diddy' Jones returned and was partnered in the team by Guy Squier (brother of long-standing Romford player Stuart Squier).

The team's progress in the Amateur Cup was soon halted as they lost 6-3 away to Grays Athletic. The next game in the league, on 29th October at South Weald, was full of incident and abandoned after 86 minutes. Three footballs burst, causing considerable delay, and darkness set in before the game could be completed. United were losing 5-1 at the time! In their next league games they beat Chelmsford 2-1 and another victory was secured against Wanstead (later expunged). December again saw mainly friendly matches and only one league game. This was the replayed match against South Weald, when our heroes were soundly beaten 5-0.

The new year opened with a home draw against Custom House, followed by defeats by Grays Athletic and Custom House, severely denting the team's league hopes. To add to their sorrows, Wanstead were expelled from the league, their record expunged and Romford United lost the four points which they had got from Wanstead! On the plus side, Reading, West, Taylor and Wooding all joined the team from the now-defunct Wanstead, and they helped United to a 2–2 draw against South Weald in a league game. The following week the team drew with Grays Athletic in the Essex Senior Cup. In the replay they scored a thrilling 4-1 victory and followed with a 2-1 win over Chelmsford in the league. The following week United were thrashed 4-0 by Shoeburyness Garrison, Frank Kittle was sent off and Graves missed a penalty! Worse was to follow when South Weald scored a 3-1 win in the Essex Senior Cup Semi-Final at Chelmsford, with Bown also saving a penalty from Freeman.

A special commission of the Essex County Football Association suspended Kittle for a fortnight as a result of him being ordered off the field at Shoeburyness Garrison on 25th February, during a South Essex League match. On 11th March Romford United beat Colchester Town 2-1 in the league, but failed to win any of their last three league games. Cup success did come, however. Although they lost to Chelmsford 1-0 in the semi-final of the Chelmsford Charity Cup, Romford United defeated Leytonstone and South Weald in the finals of the West Ham Charity and Romford Charity Cups.

The reserve team had a poor season, winning it seems only a couple of matches, although one of these was a 6-1 win over Forest Gate in the Ilford and District League. It appears that the team also competed in the Romford & District League, but only no results have been found. Their Essex Junior Cup hopes were dashed by Barking reserves, who secured a 3-1 win in the first round.

The season, however, could be regarded as a good one for the recently-formed club, which achieved a mid table league place and won two cups. At the end of the season, John Collar was awarded his Essex Senior Badge for making three appearances in the County team.

Annual General Meeting
(as reported in the *Essex Times,* Wednesday 14th June 1911)

The annual general meeting of the Romford United Football Club was held on Monday evening 12th June at the Rising Sun Hotel, Romford, Mr.J.Bassett (President) occupying the chair. The Hon. Secretary (Mr.C.T.Heard) read his report, showing that the last season's record was as follows:- Matches played 36, won 13, lost 13, drew 10; goals for 66, against 77. The season had been a fairly satisfactory one from the players' point of view. They had won the West Ham and Romford Charity Cups, which proved they had a very capable side. The members' best thanks were due to the players, who had so ably upheld the prestige of the club, both on and off the field; and the hon. secretary thanked the players for their past services, and hoped they would turn out for the club in the ensuing season.

Mr.Evan P.Jones presented the statement of accounts for the past season, as follows:- Receipts: Cash at bank 4s.8d.; president and vice-presidents' subscriptions £31.7s.0d.; members' subscriptions £12.15s.0d.; Gate receipts, £103.9s.6d.; stand receipts, £6.16s.3d.; share of gates, £41.10s.11d.; sundry receipts, £7.11s1d.; due to hon.secretary, £8.0s.9d.; due to assistant hon. secretary, £1.15s.0d. total £213.10s.2d. Expenditure: £25,; guarantees and share of gates, £32.3s.1d.; players' expenses, £45.1s.10d.; players' teas, £32.16s.5d.; referees' expenses, £6.7s.5d.; subscriptions to leagues etc., £5.13s.5d.; groundsman, £12.3s 0d.; assistance in paybox, £2.12s.6d.; ground expenses, £4.12s.9d.; police account, £4.15s.0d.; stamps, telegrams, etc., £7.13s.2d.; laundry, £5.3s.11d.; printing, £9.19s.7d.; wedding present (J.Collar) £2.8s.9d.; 2nd eleven expenses, £5.15s.0d.;

sundries, £9.14s.10d.; cash at bank, £1.9s.6d.: total £213.10s.2d. Outstanding liabilities season 1909-10, £34.16s.9d., less paid of £17.15s.1d.; outstanding liabilities, season 1910-11, £22.19s.6d.; due to hon. secretary £8.0s.9d.; due to assistant hon. secretary, £1.15s.0d.; total £49.16s.11d.: Cash at bank £1.9s.6d.; excess of expenditure over income, £48.7s.5d. To meet this expenditure the club has assets consisting of goal posts, nets, marker, canvas, footboards, wire, etc., estimated worth to the club as a going concern, £15. The report and statement of accounts were adopted.

Mr.G.A.Smith proposed the re-election of Mr.J.Bassett as president of the club. Mr.Bassett had been of great assistance to them on many occasions throughout the season; he had not only presided at the meetings, but he had given his whole-hearted support by attending every match the club had played on its own ground, and had occasionally gone to see the team play away when the distance had not been too great. (Applause). The proposition was seconded and carried unanimously. The Chairman, in acknowledging his re-election, said he been able to attend only a few meetings of the club, but when the place of matches was at all get-at-able he liked to honour the team with his presence, which he thought was what a president should do, and so encourage others to support the club.(Applause).

In proposing the re-election of the hon. secretary, Mr.W.D.Matthews said he thought he had had the honour for two or three years of proposing the re-election of Mr.C.T.Heard. He had brought the club through stormy and troublous times, and he (the speaker) hoped they would now be sailing through smoother waters. In the past Mr.Heard had put an enormous amount of work into the club; he had given a great deal of time to it; and had attended to the work to the satisfaction of every member; and he had much pleasure in proposing Mr.Heard's re-election. Mr.Smith seconded the proposition, which was carried unanimously. The Chairman said that from what he knew and had seen of Mr.Heard he did not think the club could have a better gentleman to fill the position. (Applause). Mr.Heard, in acknowledging his re-election, promised to do all he could to further the interests of the club. The club had entered for the English Cup, and were drawn against Barking, at Romford.

On the proposition of Mr.F.Robarts, seconded by Mr.Carter, Mr.Evan P.Jones was re-elected hon. treasurer. Mr. Jones said he intended having a rest, but seeing the club was in debt he thought it was his duty to assist them in getting the deficit wiped out and a balance on the right side. (Hear, hear). He would double his subscription for the ensuing year if anyone else would follow his example. Mr.Smith: You can put me down the same Mr.Treasurer. Seven of the retiring members of the Committee were re-elected, and Messrs. G.H.Maddocks and F.Walters were elected to the two seats which had been declared vacant (R.Heath and L.Fletcher). It was agreed to run a reserve team. Mr.A.Drury was asked to accept the hon. secretaryship of that team, but said he was unable to undertake the duties. Ultimately Mr.A.Parsons was elected to the office.

The next business was the election of captain of the first team. Mr.Smith said that it was a mistake for the general meeting to elect the captain. It should be done, he thought, by the players, with the consent of the committee. The hon. secretary pointed out that the rule provided that the general meeting should do this.

Four names were put forward for the captaincy, and the voting, which was by ballot, resulted in Mr.Kittle receiving the largest number of votes...Mr.Reading was elected vice-captain, and Mr.G.Hunwicks was elected captain to the reserve team, and Mr.F.Woolley vice-captain.

The Vice-Presidents were re-elected en bloc, with Messrs. J.E.Castle and T.Small elected to fill vacancies. Mr.F.H.Kittle was elected captain of the first team and Mr.Reading Vice-Captain. Mr.G.Hunwicks was elected reserve team captain, and Mr.F.Woolley Vice-captain. Messrs. F.W.Jeffes and E.J.Wallis were re-elected auditors. On the proposition of Mr.E.E.Carter, seconded by Mr.Walters, a vote of thanks was passed to the auditors, committee, and officers for their past services.

The next item on the agenda was the alteration of Rule 1, to read "Romford Town F.C." Mr.Heard said was a strong recommendation through the committee to have the name altered. The reason for this recommendation was that, as they were aware, the Romford F.C. was now defunct, and therefore if they did not change the name of their club, not necessarily to Romford, but to Romford Town, they left a loophole for any other club to spring up and take that name, and therefore take the badge of the premier club of the town. He moved that the club in future be called the Romford Town F.C. Mr.Smith seconded the proposition. Mr.Matthews proposed as an amendment that the club be called the Romford F.C. The amendment was seconded. Mr.Small said he thought that if they took the name Romford F.C., they would take over the liabilities of the old club.

Mr.Matthews said he disagreed with Mr.Small on that point. Had they amalgamated with the Romford F.C. they would have taken over their liabilities, but the Romford F.C., had been expunged from the books of the association, and was dead. Their club would have no responsibility whatever. After some discussion, Mr.Matthews withdrew his amendment, and the proposal to rename the club "Romford Town F.C." was carried. The next question for consideration was the change of colours, and it was decided that the colours should be Black and Blue striped jerseys.

Referring to the statement of accounts, the Chairman said they were in rather low water, and he suggested they should adopt some measure to alter that. They might have subscription cards prepared, and each member should do his utmost to collect funds. They might raise a fair amount by small subscriptions. The Hon. Secretary said the committee had discussed this matter, and they thought it would be a good idea to open a public subscription list. They might get their intimate friends to subscribe and so help to wipe out the deficit...Mr.Matthews said that without a counter attraction next season they ought to get a bigger "gate", and, with an eye on the expenses, they should do better. It was decided to issue a subscription list with the view of assisting to place the club on a sound financial basis.

Announcement: A GOLD WATCH FOR NOTHING

"Cosy Corner" is being exceptionally well patronised under the new and able management of Mr. Adams. The whole of the present week (23rd July, 1911) there has been full houses and some good turns have been provided. Next week there will be an entirely new company and on Friday, the proceeds will be given to the Romford United Football Club. For that evening special numbered tickets will be issued, and the fortunate possessor of the lucky ticket (the number will be selected by two well known sportsmen, Messrs. Frank Pilling and W. Lewis, and placed in a sealed envelope three days previously), will receive either a gentleman's or lady's gold, dust proof, chromatic watch.

FIRE AT ROMFORD'S FOOTBALL GROUND

On Friday, 11th August, 1911, the fence enclosing Romford Football ground at the Cosy Corner caught fire, causing slight damage to the stand.

COSY CORNER,
MILL PATH, VICTORIA ROAD,
ROMFORD.
Grand Illuminated Al fresco Concerts
Every Evening.
DAN THOMAS'S POPULAR PIERROTS.
Funny Comedians. Instrumental and Vocal Solos. Laughable Sketches, etc.
Doors open 7.30. Commence 8 o'clock.
ADMISSION 2d. CHAIRS 6d. and 3d.
Afternoon Performances Thursday and Saturday at 3.
x57-30

This advertisement promoted the Cosy Corner Theatre which held regular concerts in and out of doors. The al fresco concerts were held on the football pitch to the rear of the building. These were particularly popular, attracting audiences of around 2,000. The Romford United Football Club, who played on the Cosy Corner ground, benefited from match day takings at the Cosy Corner bar where they were given a share of the profits. Regular fundraising events were organised to benefit the club.

The fire of 11th August must have been alarming, but far worse was to follow, as this cutting from the *Essex Times* of Wednesday 23rd October 1911 reveals:

NOT SO COSY BY THE FIRE

Early on Sunday morning, 20th October, 1911, the "Cosy Corner" Theatre of Varieties, Romford, was totally destroyed by fire. The building which is the property of Mrs. S. Poel, stood on land adjoining the ground of the Romford United Football Club, and consisted of timber and canvas. The total damage is estimated at £900.

The outbreak was first observed shortly after mid-night, and the fire brigade quickly attended, under captain S. Davis. The theatre and two sheds adjoining it were hopelessly involved, but the brigade were able to prevent the fire from spreading to the granaries of Messrs. Whitmore Limited, and the pumping house of Messrs. Ind Coope and Co., both of which were dangerously near. Among the materials destroyed was a marionette show of lay figures, the property of Mr.Arthur Knight, of Wenlock Street, London. This was valued at £20 but was not covered by insurance. The theatre was insured.

There had been a performance on Saturday evening, and the place was locked up just before 11 p.m., by Mr. Hutchings, variety agent, and Mr.Walter Broom, the stage manager. The place appeared to be then alright. Mr.W.Mynott who saw the flames first, stated that they appeared to have started at the stage end. Superintendent Jones, P.S.Watson, and a number of constables were present and rendered valuable help.

Season 1911 – 12

ROMFORD UNITED CHANGED NAME TO ROMFORD TOWN
(Known as the Town of Old Ales)

Associate members of the Football Association
Affiliated to Essex County Football Association

President: Mr.John Bassett J.P. **Chairman:** Mr.G.A.Smith

Hon. Secretary: Mr.C.T.Heard **Hon.Treasurer:** Mr.E.P.Jones

Committee: Mr.G.A.Smith(Chairman)
Messrs. E.Currie,S.Dowsing,G.H.Maddocks,L.P.Pratt,F.Robarts,H.Small,E.T.Smee and F.Walters

Captain: Mr.A.Reading

Colours: Black and Blue striped Jerseys **Headquarters:** Rising Sun Hotel, Romford

Ground: Cosy Corner, (also known as the Shoulder of Mutton Field), Hornchurch Road, Romford

COMPETITIONS ENTERED
South Essex League Division One
F.A. Challenge Cup
F.A. Amateur Cup
Essex Senior Cup
Romford Charity Cup
West Ham Charity Cup
Chelmsford Charity Cup
Titanic Disaster Fund

Ilford & District League Division One
Essex Junior Cup
Romford Charity Junior Cup

Friendly Match

31st August POSSIBLES 1 PROBABLES 0
C.Wilkinson

Probables(Blues): H.A.Bown;Parker,Olney,F.Walters,E.Taylor,Drury,Tongood,Willetts,Smith,Curtis,H.B.West.
Possibles(Whites): W.Saggers,Hunwicks,W.Dickerson,Hunwicks,W.Wilkinson,W.Leach,T.Scarf,Jewers, C.Wilkinson,Burrell.
W.J.Biles(Ex Wanstead),W.Dickerson and F.Walters from the late Romford club, A.Reading(Wanstead), W.Wilkinson(Chelmsford), H.H.W.Druitt(from Wiltshire County) has just joined the staff at St.Edward's School. C.Wilkinson(Chelmsford),T.Scarf(Army International),V.Odgers(South Weald),W.Leach(Hornchurch Territorials).
"F.H.Kittle has informed the club that he will definitely not play again and refused the captaincy".

The club had an abundance of eager players wanting to play for them which augured well for strengthening the team for the forthcoming season, as the club was now the sole senior representative for the town of Romford.

Match Details

2 Sept Frdly Home Waltham 3 – 4 Scorers unknown
Romford Town:
Team details unknown.

9 Sept. FACEP Home Barking 1 – 2 Leach
Romford Town: H.A.Bown;A.Reading(Capt),W.J.Biles;F.Walters,E.Taylor,H.B.West;
V.Odgers,C.Wilkinson,H.H.W.Druitt,C.Seabrooke,W.Leach.

16 Sept Frdly Away South Weald 4 – 6 Druitt,Leach,Unknown(2)
Romford Town: H.A.Bown;H.A.Morgan,W.J.Biles;H.Welham,E.Taylor,W.Dickerson;
T.Scarf,J.Cresswell,H.H.W.Druitt,C.Seabrooke,W.Leach.

23 Sept SEL1 Away Colchester Town 2 – 3** Doggett,Druit
Romford Town: H.A.Bown;A.Reading(Capt),W.J.Biles;W.Dickerson,E.Taylor,J.C.Doggett;
T.Scarff,F.Walters,H.H.W.Druit,C.Campbell,Curtis,W.Leach.

30 Sept Frdly Home East Ham 2 – 0 Clark,Doggett
Attendance: 250
Romford Town: H.A.Bown;A.Reading(Capt),W.J.Biles;H.B.West,E.Taylor,J.C.Doggett;
Clark,H.H.W.Druitt,F.Walters,C.Seabrooke,W.Leach.

7 Oct SEL1 Home Shoeburyness Garrison 0 – 0
Romford Town: H.A.Bown;A.Reading(Capt),W.J.Biles;W.Dickerson,E.Taylor,H.B.West;
S.C.Squier,C.Seabrooke,H.H.W.Druitt,F.Walters,W.Leach.

14 Oct SEL1 Away Chelmsford 3 – 1 Seabrooke,Rashbrook,Simpson
Romford Town: H.A.Bown;A.Reading(Capt),W.J.Biles;W.Dickerson,E.Taylor,H.B.West;
Rashbrook,C.Seabrooke,J.Simpson,F.Walters,W.Leach.

21 Oct AC2Q Home Newportonians 8 – 1 Walters(4)Leach(2)Simpson,Seabrooke
Romford Town: H.A.Bown;A.Reading(Capt),W.J.Biles;W.Dickerson,E.Taylor,H.B.West;
P.C.Phillips,C.Seabrooke,J.Simpson,F.Walters,W.Leach.

28 Oct SEL1 Home Chelmsford 2 – 2 Simpson,Biles(pen)
Romford Town: H.A.Bown;A.Reading(Capt),W.J.Biles;W.Dickerson,E.Taylor,H.B.West;
P.C.Phillips,C.Seabrooke,J.Simpson,F.Walters,W.Leach.

4 Nov AC3Q Home Walthamstow Grange 0 – 1
Romford Town: H.A.Bown;A.Reading(Capt),W.J.Biles;W.Dickerson,E.Taylor,A.W.Asater;
P.C.Phillips,C.Seabrooke,J.Simpson,F.Walters,W.Leach.

11 Nov SEL1 Away South Weald 2 – 3 Osborne,Simpson
Romford Town: H.A.Bown;A.Reading(Capt),W.J.Biles;F.Walters,E.Taylor,A.W.Asater;
P.C.Phillips,C.Seabrooke,J.Simpson,C.Osborne,W.Leach.

18 Nov Frdly Home 1st Coldstream Guards 3 – 3 Biles(3)
Romford Town: H.A.Bown;A.Reading(Capt),W.J.Biles;F.Walters,E.Taylor,W.Dickerson;
P.C.Phillips,C.Seabrooke,J.Simpson,A.S.Hyett,W.Leach.

25 Nov SEL1 Away Grays Athletic 5 – 2 Seabrooke(2)Phillips,Leach,Woolley
Romford Town: H.A.Bown;A.Reading(Capt),W.J.Biles;S.Wilson,E.Taylor,F.Walters;
P.C.Phillips,C.Seabrooke,J.Simpson,F.Woolley,W.Leach.

2 Dec Frdly Home Tufnell Park 1 – 0
Romford Town:
Team details unknown.

9 Dec Frdly Home Deptford Invicta 3 – 0 Leach(2)Looker
Romford Town: H.A.Bown;A.Reading(Capt),W.J.Biles;F.Walters,E.Taylor,H.B.West;
C.S.Steele,Heard,Looker,C.Campbell,W.Leach.

16 Dec SEL1 Home Colchester Town 1 – 0 Leach
Romford Town: H.A.Bown;A.Reading(Capt),W.J.Biles;F.Walters,E.Taylor,H.B.West;
C.S.Steele,C.Seabrooke,J.Simpson,C.Osborne,W.Leach.

23 Dec SEL1 Away Barking 1 – 5 Seabrooke
Romford Town: H.A.Bown;A.Reading(Capt),W.J.Biles;F.Walters,E.Taylor,P.C.Phillips;
C.S.Steele,C.Seabrooke,J.Simpson,C.Osborne,W.Leach.

25 Dec Frdly Home West Ham Thursday K.O.11.30 3 – 1
Romford Town:
Team details unknown

26 Dec Frdly Home South Weald 2 – 0 Hyett,Graves
Romford Town:
J.Graves,A.S.Hyett.

30 Dec RCCSF Home East Ham 1 – 0
Romford Town:
Team details unknown

13 Jan CCCSF Away Hoffmann Athletic 0 – 2
Romford Town:
Team details unknown

20 Jan SEL1 Home South Weald 2 – 2 Seabrooke,Leach
Romford Town: H.A.Bown;A.Reading(Capt),W.J.Biles;F.Walters,E.Taylor,H.B.West;
P.C.Phillips,C.Seabrooke,F.J.Wiles,A.S.Hyett,W.Leach.

27 Jan SEL1 Home Custom House 1 – 2 Seabrooke
Romford Town: H.A.Bown;A.Reading(Capt),W.J.Biles;F.Walters,E.Taylor,H.B.West;
P.C.Phillips,C.Seabrooke,F.J.Wiles,A.S.Hyett,W.Leach.

3 Feb ESC3R Home Custom House 3 – 1 Leach,Seabrooke,Wiles
Romford Town: H.A.Bown;A.Reading(Capt),W.J.Biles;F.Walters,E.Taylor,H.B.West;
A.W.Asater,C.Seabrooke,F.J.Wiles,A.S.Hyett,W.Leach.

10 Feb Frdly Away Kingston 2 – 3 Hyett,Seabrooke
Romford Town:
Team details unknown

17 Feb SEL1 Home Grays Athletic 1 – 1 Walters
Romford Town: H.A.Bown;A.Reading(Capt),W.J.Biles;F.Walters,E.Taylor,H.B.West;
S.C.Squier,C.Seabrooke,F.J.Wiles,A.S.Hyett,W.Leach

24 Feb SEL1 Home Southend Utd. Reserves 1 – 2 Steele
Romford Town: H.A.Bown;A.Reading(Capt),W.J.Biles;F.Walters,E.Taylor,H.B.West;
S.C.Squier,C.Seabrooke,F.J.Wiles,C.S.Steele,W.Leach.

2 Mar ESCSF Barking Grays Athletic 4 – 0 Leach,Squier,Hyett,Seabrooke
Attendance: 2,000
Romford Town: H.A.Bown;A.Reading(Capt),W.J.Biles;F.Walters,E.Taylor,A.W.Asater;
S.C.Squier,C.Seabrooke,F.J.Wiles,A.S.Hyett,W.Leach.

9 Mar SEL1 Away Custom House 0 – 3
Romford Town: H.A.Bown;A.Reading(Capt),W.J.Biles;F.Walters,E.Taylor,A.W.Asater;
P.C.Phillips,C.Seabrooke,C.Osborne,C.S.Steele,W.Leach.

14 Mar WHCSF Home Leytonstone 4 – 1 Hyett(2)Leach,West
Romford Town: H.A.Bown;A.Reading(Capt),W.J.Biles;F.Walters,E.Taylor,H.B.West;
A.W.Asater,F.H.Kittle,A.E.Jones,A.S.Hyett,W.Leach.

16 Mar Frdly Home West Norwood 2 – 1 Seabrooke,Hyett
Romford Town: H.A.Bown;A.Reading(Capt),W.J.Biles;F.Walters,E.Taylor,H.B.West;
A.W.Asater,C.Seabrooke,F.J.Wiles,A.S.Hyett,W.Leach.

23 Mar Frdly Home Woodford Albion 5 – 2 Ockendon(3)Taylor,Reading
Attendance: Smallest gate on record for Romford, twelve shillings only taken at gate.
Romford Town: ?? ;A.Reading(Captain),E.Taylor,
E.Ockendon,

30 Mar SEL1 Away Shoeburyness Garrison 1 – 3 Seabrooke
Romford Town: H.A.Bown;A.Reading(Capt),W.J.Biles;F.Walters,E.Taylor,H.B.West;
A.W.Asater,C.Seabrooke,F.J.Wiles,A.S.Hyett,W.Leach.

5 Apr Frdly Away Clapton 3 – 2 Scorers unknown
Romford Town:
Team details unknown

8 Apr ESCF Ilford South Weald 1 – 0 Hyett
Attendance: 5,000
Romford Town: H.A.Bown;A.Reading(Capt),W.J.Biles;F.Walters,E.Taylor,H.B.West;
A.W.Asater,C.Seabrooke,A.S.Hyett,S.C.Squier,W.Leach.

13 Apr WHCF Clapton Custom House 0 – 2
Attendance: 3,000
Romford: H.A.Bown;A.Reading(Capt),W.J.Biles;F.Walters,E.Taylor,H.B.West;
A.W.Asater,C.Seabrooke, S.C.Squier,A.S.Hyett,W.Leach.

20 Apr. SEL1 Home Barking 0 – 2
Romford Town: H.A.Bown;A.Reading(Capt),W.J.Biles;A.W.Asater,E.Taylor,H.B.West;
F.J.Wiles,C.Seabrooke,A.S.Hyett,S.C.Squier,W.Leach.

25 Apr SEL1 Away Southend Utd. Reserves 0 – 4
Romford Town: H.A.Bown;A.Reading(Capt),W.J.Biles;F.Walters,E.Taylor,H.B.West;
A.W.Asater,C.Seabrooke,F.J.Wiles,A.S.Hyett,W.Leach.

27 Apr RCCF Home South Weald 4 – 1 Leach.Hyett(2),Wiles
Romford Town: H.A.Bown;A.Reading(Capt),W.J.Biles;F.Walters,E.Taylor,H.B.West;
A.W.Asater,C.Seabrooke,F.J.Wiles,A.S.Hyett,W.Leach.

4 May TDF Home Mawney Inst/Roneo Ath 3 – 2 Ockendon,Doggett(2)
Romford Town: J.C.Doggett;E.Ockendon,
Team details unknown.

** The match report indicates that Leach arrived late and took part in the game, but twelve names were given as the team. He must have replaced one of the other players as there is no way they could have played a South Essex League game with twelve men.

SUMMARY OF FIRST TEAM RESULTS OBTAINED SEASON 1911 – 12

	P	W	D	L	Goals For	Goals Ag	Pts
South Essex League	16	3	4	9	22	35	10
F.A.Cup	1	0	0	1	1	2	
F.A. Amateur Cup 2	1	0	1	8	2		
Essex Senior Cup	3	3	0	0	8	1	
West Ham Char. Cup	2	1	0	1	4	3	
Chelmsford Char. Cup	1	0	0	1	0	2	
Romford Char. Cup	2	2	0	0	5	1	
Titanic Disaster Fund	1	1	0	0	3	2	
Friendly Matches	12	8	1	3	33	22	
Total	40	19	5	16	84	70	
A.G.M. Press Report	41	20	5	16	84	70	

South Essex League Division One
Final Table

	P	W	D	L	Goals For	Goals Ag	Pts
Barking	16	11	3	2	47	13	25
Custom House	16	11	2	3	29	19	24
Shoeburyness Garrison	16	8	3	5	23	21	19
Colchester Town	16	7	0	9	38	34	14
Grays Athletic	16	5	2	9	20	25	12
Chelmsford	16	4	4	8	23	43	12
Southend Amateurs **	16	8	1	7	32	32	11
South Weald	16	5	1	10	28	40	11
Romford Town	**16**	**3**	**4**	**9**	**22**	**35**	**10**

** Six points deducted for breach of Rules.

CUP RESULTS

F.A. Challenge Cup

Final: Barnsley 0 West Bromwich Albion 0
Replay: Barnsley 1 West Bromwich Albion 0 a.e.t.

Romford's progress: Ex.Prel Home Barking 1 – 2

F.A. Amateur Cup

Final: Stockton 0 Eston United 0
Replay: Stockton 1 Eston United 0

Romford's progress: 2nd Qual Home Newportonians 8 – 1
3rd Qual Home Walthamstow Grange 0 – 1

Essex Senior Cup

Final: Romford Town 1 South Weald 0

Romford's progress: 3rd Round Home Custom House 3 – 1
Semi-Final Barking Grays Athletic 4 – 0
Final Ilford South Weald 1 – 0

West Ham Charity Cup

Final: Custom House 2 Romford Town 0

Romford's progress: Semi-Final Home Leytonstone 4 – 1
Final Clapton Custom House 0 – 2

Chelmsford Charity Cup

Final: n/k

Romford's progress: Semi-Final Away Hoffmann Athletic 0 – 2

Romford Charity Cup

Final: Romford Town 4 South Weald 1

Romford's progress: Semi-Final Home East Ham Won
Final Home South Weald 4 – 1

Titanic Disaster Fund

Home Mawney Inst/Roneo Ath. 3 – 2

First Team Appearances Season 1911 – 12

A.W.Asater	13	W.J.Biles	30	H.A.Bown	30	C.Campbell	2
Clark	1	J.Cresswell	1	Curtis	1	W.Dickerson	8
J.C.Doggett	3	H.H.W.Druitt	5	J.Graves	1	Heard	1
A.S.Hyett	15	A.E.Jones	1	F.H.Kittle	1	W.Leach	30
Looker	1	H.A.Morgan	1	E .Ockendon	2	V.Odgers	1
C.Osborne	4	P.E.Phillips	10	A.Reading	30	Rushbrook	1
Scarff	2	C.Seabrooke	27	J.Simpson	9	S.C.Squier	7
C.S.Steele	5	E.Taylor	31	F.Walters	28	H.Welham	1
H.B.West	21	F.J.Wiles	11	C.Wilkinson	1	S.Wilson	1
F.Woolley	1					Total	336

First Team Goal Scorers Season 1911 – 12

W.Leach	13	C.Seabrooke	12	A.S.Hyett	9	F.Walters	5
J.Simpson	4	R.Ockendon	4	J.C.Doggett	4	W.J.Biles	4
H.H.W.Druitt	2	F.J.Wiles	2	Clark	1	Rushbrook	1
C.Osborne	1	P.E.Phillips	1	F.Woolley	1	J.Graves	1
C.S.Steele	1	S.C.Squier	1	H.B.West	1	E.Taylor	1
Looker	1	A.Reading	1	Unknown	13	Total	84

RESERVES ("A" Team)

Match Details

9 Sept	Frdly	Away	Clapton "A"	3 – 1
12 Oct	IDL1	Away	Purfleet	0 – 7
14 Oct	EJC1R	Home	Custom House "A"	2 – 3
21 Oct	IDL1	Away	Forest Gate	3 – 6
28 Oct	IDL1	Away	Hornchurch	1 – 1
11 Nov	IDL1	Home	Forest Gate	1 – 1
18 Nov	IDL1	Home	GER Athletic Association	0 – 1
9 Dec	IDL1	Away	St. Bartholomews	2 – 3
23 Dec	IDL1	Home	Mawney Institute	0 – 3
8 Feb	IDL1	Home	Mansfield House	1 – 0
10 Feb	IDL1	Home	Roneo Athletic	1 – 0
17 Feb	IDL1	Away	Mawney Institute	3 – 0
24 Feb	RJCSF	Away	GER Athletic Association	1 – 2
2 Mar	IDL1	Home	Hornchurch	0 – 3
9 Mar	IDL1	Home	Purfleet	0 – 3
16 Mar	IDL1	Away	Roneo Athletic (scratched)	won#
30 Mar	IDL1	Away	Mansfield House	3 – 3
6 Apr	IDL1	Away	GER Athletic Association	2 – 6
13 Apr	IDL1	Home	St. Bartholomews	0 – 7
22 Apr	RJCF*	Home	Mawney Institute	0 – 2

Romford Town "A" awarded the points by default. No goals allocated.

Ilford & District Football League Division 1
Final Table

					Goals		
	P	W	D	L	For	Ag	Pts
Mawney Institute	16	12	2	2	52	19	26
Purfleet	16	12	1	3	51	20	25
St Bartholomews	16	11	1	4	48	25	23
Hornchurch	16	7	1	8	36	40	15
Roneo Athletic	16	5	2	9	24	24	12
Mansfield House	16	3	6	7	19	29	12
GER Athletic	16	5	2	9	29	44	12
Forest Gate	16	3	4	9	20	50	10
Romford Town "A"	**16**	**3**	**3**	**10**	**17**	**44**	**9**

CUP RESULTS

Essex County F.A. Junior Cup

Final: Southend Amateur 2 Maldon 1

Romford's progress: 1st Round Home Custom House "A" 2 – 3

Romford Junior Charity Cup Competition

Final:	Mawney Institute	2	Romford Town "A"	0*
	Mawney Institute	4	GER Athletic	0

Romford's progress: Semi-Final Away GER Athletic Association 1 – 2
Final Home Mawney Institute 0 – 2

* GER Athletic unable to field a team on this date and Romford Town "A" invited to replace them in the final. On an appeal by GER Athletic the match was declared void and GER met Mawney Institute on 27th April.

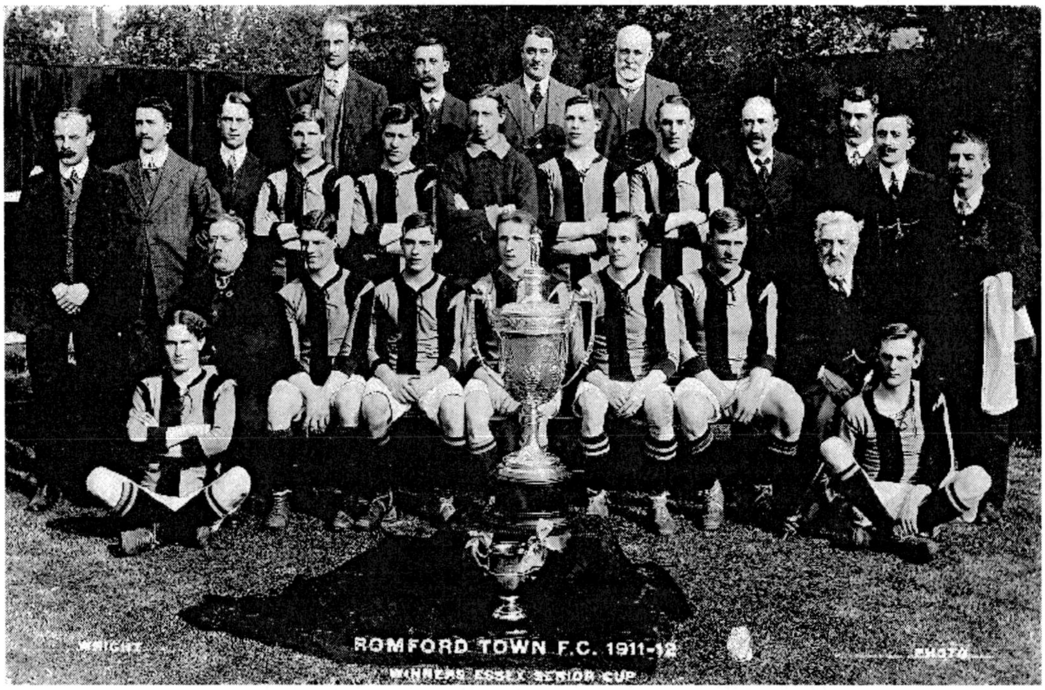

Essex Senior Cup and Romford Charity Cup Winners 1911-12
Authors' collection (originators unknown)
Who's Who? Unfortunately, once again, no list of names is provided!

ROMFORD REDIVIDUS (from the *Romford Times*, 1912)

Although, strictly speaking, the present Romford club has only been in existence three seasons, it is unquestionably a counterpart of the famous organisation founded by that grand old Romford sportsman, Major Francis Hugh Thirlwall, way back in 1876, for which the ever-to-be-regretted incident which culminated in the formation of the present club occurred at the end of season 1908-9. Practically the whole of the gentlemen identified with the old club transferred their allegiance – and rightly so!- to the new concern, which happily developed as rapidly as the other retrogressed, with the result that today there is, once again, a Town Club for Romford.

Long may it flourish under the guidance of such good old stalwarts as W. D. Matthews (who has represented Romford on the council of the Essex County F.A. since the formation of the association 30 years ago), Evan Jones (a county player of the early nineties), and Charles Thomas Heard, who has given the best years of his life to the advancement of the king of winter sports in Romford, and who is hoping that his retirement from the secretaryship of the club at the end of the present season will synchronise with the team's winning the Essex Senior Cup.

Post-Season Summary Season 1911 – 12

Romford Town opened their season with a home friendly match with Waltham, which they lost 4-3. They then, as so often with earlier Romford teams, lost their first competitive game of the season in the F.A. Cup, at home to Barking by two goals to one. Romford wore white sashes for the second half to assist the referee in distinguishing the two sides. Then followed a thrilling friendly against local rivals South Weald, who won 6-4 on their own ground.

Romford's next game was the first South Essex League fixture of the season, away to Colchester Town. The newspaper report mentions that Leach arrived late, but includes him in a team that contains twelve names. It is not known who actually played in the game, but the result was a 3-2 beating for the visitors. Another friendly match saw Romford beat East Ham Borough by two goals to nil. Romford then drew 0–0 at home to Shoeburyness Garrison, and won away to Chelmsford by three goals to one in South Essex League games.

Next up was the Amateur Cup and a big victory over Newportonians by eight goals to one, followed by a 2-2 draw at home to Chelmsford in another league game. 4th November but no fireworks from Romford in the 3rd Qualifying Round of the Amateur Cup as they lost at home to Walthamstow Grange by the only goal scored. More dismay came a week later with a three goals to two league defeat at South Weald. The gloom was lifted by an entertaining home 3–3 draw against 1st Coldstream Guards in a friendly encounter, and a fine five goals to two defeat of Grays Athletic in a South Essex League game.

December commenced with two friendly victories against Tufnell Park (1-0) and Deptford Invicta (3-0) followed by revenge against Colchester Town on 16th December, with a home one goal to nil league victory. On the same day the *Essex Times* printed this appreciative piece about the popular Romford Secretary, Charles T. Heard:

> Though the original Romford Football Club came to grief last March, after a career dating back to 1876, the present organisation is to all intents and purposes a continuation of the old club, although, let it be said it disclaims any connection with the club that came under the ban of the County Association. In Mr. Charles Thomas Heard, Romford Town have a secretary who has played the game and knows the ropes, it is very seldom that he is caught napping. He once served on the executive committee of the Essex F.A., and has been a member of the South Essex League Council for over ten years. In his day he was a cricketer of some repute, and could also swing a racquet. Latterly he has become a convert to the ancient game of bowls, which goes to show he is not as young as he used to be, although "C.T" always was "very thin on the thatch". The present club owes its existence almost entirely to the efforts of Mr.Heard, and it will be a bad day for football in Romford when he decides to retire. The Romford Town team is a good one, and only once this season has it succumbed by more than a goal margin; and one hopes for a continuation of this happy state of affairs in succeeding matches following next Saturday's away match at Barking in a South Essex League fixture.

It was back to earth with a bang on 23rd December, when Barking ran riot with a home five goal to one victory. Romford rounded off the year with a couple of friendly wins and a victory over East Ham by one goal to nil in the Romford Charity Cup semi-final. The first game of the New Year was in the Chelmsford Charity Cup semi-final when Hoffmann Athletic proved to be too strong, winning by two goals to nil.

Two home league games followed, but Romford only picked up one point from the 2–2 draw against local rivals South Weald and lost to Custom House by two goals to one. On 3rd February Romford entered the Essex Senior Cup at the 3rd round stage when they beat Custom House 3-1 to reach the semi-final. The match report described Romford's winger as Mad Mullah Leach, for reasons unknown!

There followed three games without a win, Kingston away (2-3) in a friendly, Grays Athletic at home (1–1) and Southend United Reserves also at home (1–2) both in league games. In the Grays game Fred. Moule, now with Grays, tripped over the ropes entering the pitch, dislocating his elbow, and Grays played with ten men.

The Town team came to life in their next match when they defeated Grays Athletic at Barking by four goals to nil, before 2,000 spectators, in the County Cup semi-final. League affairs were not going well and they lost 3-0 at Custom House. It seems that the team was intent on cup glory, as the following week the strong Leytonstone team were defeated in the semi-final of the West Ham Charity Cup by four goals to one!

Two home friendly victories followed, first against West Norwood by two goals to one and then Woodford Albion by five goals to two. The latter game drew the smallest-ever gate to the ground, and only twelve shillings gate money was taken! In the West Norwood game Romford had only nine men for the first twenty minutes, before Wiles appeared and a little later Doggett relinquished the flag and joined the team until half time. For the second half Biles (who had arrived by then), replaced Doggett with the agreement of the West Norwood Club. There was a very poor attendance for this friendly. More league points went down the drain in the next encounter and Shoeburyness Garrison were the fortunate recipients, but this was followed by a good 3-2 victory over the strong Clapton side in a friendly match.

Two cup finals were next, starting when our favourites secured the coveted Essex Senior Cup at last by virtue of a 1-0 win against South Weald at Ilford. The attendance was 5,000 and Albert Hyett scored the all-important goal. The second game was the West Ham Charity Cup final before 3,000 spectators at the Spotted Dog ground, where the Town team were humbled by two goals to nil by Custom House. Romford failed to score in their next two league games, succumbing to Barking and Southend United Reserves.

Another Cup final and the team came to life again with a 4-1 victory over old rivals South Weald in the Romford Charity Cup Final. The cup and medals were presented by Mrs. W.D.Matthews.

The last game of the season was in aid of the Titanic Disaster Benefit Fund (the disaster had occurred on 12th April that year). Romford met a combined Mawney Institute and Roneo Athletic team and won 3-2. With four players playing for the County team, Romford played with only ten men. The visitors' goals were both scored by old Romford favourite Frank 'Jigger' Kittle, who now played for Mawney Institute. The attendance was very poor, and only £1.8s.9d was raised, but more donations were sent to the hon.secretary during the summer.

Annual General Meeting
(as reported in the *Essex Times,* Wednesday 17th July 1912)

The Annual General Meeting of the Romford Town Football Club was held at the Rising Sun Hotel, Romford, on Saturday, 13th July, Mr.J.Bassett presiding. The secretary, Mr.C.T.Heard, said he had the greatest pleasure in once again reading his report of the season's work. They had had a fairly good season, and their record was: Matches played 41, won 20, lost 16, drawn 5, goals for 84, against 70. Their greatest victory was against South Weald on Easter Monday, when they won the Essex Senior Cup for the first time, after twenty nine years struggling. That was a glorious victory, and he felt a very happy man when they won, because it was one of his weaknesses to hope they would win the cup during his term of office. The best goal scorers were: Leach 17, Seabrooke 14, Hyett 9 and Ockendon 7. Respecting the cup ties, Mr. Heard went on to say they were knocked out far too early in the English cup ties, but they once again secured the Charity Cup, defeating South Weald in the final, but they had to hand over the West Ham Charity Cup to Custom House. He regretted that they finished last in the League, but he must say winning the cup covered a multitude of sins in connection with the League matches. They had joined the Corinthian League for next season, and had been re-entered in the Essex League. Thus they would have plenty of league matches, and friendlies would be conspicuous by their absence. (Hear, hear).

Most of the players had signified their intention of again signing on for the club, and they would form the nucleus of a strong team. Mr. Heard parenthetically remarked that he had had some nasty remarks made about the dinner, and he thought it only fair to say that some of the committee appointed to make the arrangements, resigned about two days before the function came off; and left it all to one, so they could see that they were not to blame. He thanked the officials and players for the excellent manner in which they had worked during the past season, and went on to refer to his retirement from the position of secretary. He had given the matter very careful consideration, and though resigning from the present office he was not severing his connection with the club, and he would still do all in his power for its interests. (Applause).

The balance sheet as printed, was read, showing the total receipts to be £260.13s.4d. There was an excess of expenditure over income of £38.1s.8d. Mr.L.Fletcher called attention to the member's subscriptions, which were £9 this year, against £12.15s.0d last year. This represented 36 members only who had paid their subscriptions, and he thought that was very miserable indeed.

On the other hand, gate receipts were £140.15s.10d, but he believed they had to take out of that the £34 for the Essex Cup, bringing the receipts to a few shillings less than the previous year. He had not much to complain of on the receipts side, but he noticed on the expenses side, the guarantees of gates had gone up £12.10s.0d. The biggest item, in his opinion, was that for the players' teas, which cost £41.4s.3d. This combined with other expenses, he thought much too large an item. Ground expenses, independent of £14 outstanding, were £13.7s.3d., against £4.12s.9d. for the previous year. He did not know what had been done to the ground so far as he had seen.

Mr.E.P.Jones, the hon.treasurer, was not present, and Mr.Heard replied that he could not explain the balance sheet. He did not know what was included in the £13.7s.3d., but the treasurer must have had vouchers, or the auditors would not have passed the accounts. Mr Eley asked if it did not represent something paid off an old account. He understood £5 or £6 for players' teas had been outstanding. Mr.Heard agreed that might be so. On the receipts side they had £16 paid off outstanding accounts, more than was shown on the expenses side. Mr.G.Hodgson asked if the books were there. He presumed they belonged to the club. The Chairman: "Yes. I must say the balance sheet is not explicit enough for me." Mr.W.D.Matthews said they had appointed their auditors and knew them well enough to feel perfectly satisfied that they had seen the vouchers for the expenses or they would not have passed the balance sheet. At the same time he thought it a pity that the treasurer had gone away without leaving the cash book.

Mr. Fletcher asked if the committee had had a balance sheet for the dinner. Mr.Heard "Yes, otherwise they would not be able to show the loss on the dinner." Mr.Fletcher: "There was £2.12s.4d. profit. Did any account against the dinner come in after the balance sheet was struck?". Mr.Heard: "I don't think that is a fair question, Mr.Chairman. The money was handed over to the club". The Chairman ruled that it was quite in order. Mr.Heard then answered in the affirmative, and continued: "If anyone runs a concert and then hands a balance sheet showing a profit of £2.12s.4d., and passes the money to the club, and then, about five or six months afterwards, someone sends in a bill, who is responsible?" He believed the item was something for the Corn Exchange. The deposit had been paid, but the account was for the remainder of the hire, The balance sheet showed the item was paid. Mr.G.A.Smith said the account kept coming to him instead of Mr.A.J.Smith, (secretary of the concert). He saw the latter, who assured him he had a receipt for the money. He alleged it was a mistake on the part of Messrs. Kemsley. The Chairman: "Then I take it they have no claim against the club?- On that statement, no. Mr.Fletcher: "The hall was taken in the name of the club". Mr.Matthews: "Then why was the account sent to Mr.Smith?". Mr.Fletcher: "Because he was secretary for the concert". Mr.Eley said the account had been shown on the balance sheet, so he must have deducted it from the receipts. Mr.Fletcher said if the club instructed Mr.Smith to take the hall he did not want to find fault about it. He just wanted to have things straight. The Chairman: "Quite right, Mr.Fletcher. This is the proper place to bring these things up".

The secretary, in reply to a question, stated that the club had about 60 members last season. The balance sheet only accounted for 36, but Mr.Jones had told him (Mr.Heard), that he had written to many of them and could not get the money. Mr.Matthews thought the balance sheet had been thoroughly thrashed out. And their auditors had been satisfied with the accounts. He moved the balance sheet be adopted. Mr.Hodgson seconded, saying nothing further could be done in the matter. Mr.Turvey asked for an explanation of why players' expenses and teas totalled £87. That was a big item for an amateur club. Mr.Heard, in reply to Mr.Turvey, said they played 41 matches last season, and it cost the club about £2 per match for players' expenses and teas. They would not find a team near London which ran so cheaply as theirs. Mr.Redding said he had heard rumours of 21 and 22 sitting down to tea, Mr.Heard: "That only occurred once. The average number was 14". The balance sheet was adopted.

Mr.Hodgson proposed that Mr.J.Bassett be re-elected president. Mr.Fletcher seconded, and Mr. Bassett was unanimously elected. He thanked them very much for again electing him. He hoped the secretary and other officers and the committee that was formed would attend to their business and have the books and statements there before them, so as to do away with any quibbling. Let them have things done on business lines and it would be better for them all.

All vice-presidents who had paid their subscriptions for last year were re-elected, on the proposition of Mr.Matthews, seconded by Mr.Walters. Mr.Heard remarked that he was resigning the secretaryship but he was not leaving them in the lurch. He was going to ask them to appoint a good man in his place. He had not had a large experience but he could learn, and would take up his duties very quickly. The young man he referred to was Mr.A.Drury. He was very willing, young, and enthusiastic. He proposed Mr.Drury as hon.secretary. Mr. Walters seconded and the motion was carried unanimously. Mr.Drury expressed his thanks, for this honour, and said he fully realised the responsibility placed on his shoulders. He would do all he possibly could to make the appointment a success. He hoped that the supporters would deal with him leniently and not form a judgement until they had heard both sides of the question.

Mr.Drury proposed that Mr.Heard be appointed treasurer. He was sure the two would work hand in glove with each other. Mr.Heard said he would prefer someone else having the position, as he did not wish to hold any position whatever. At the same time, if they could not find anyone else to take the post, he would take it on – only for one season though. Mr.Hodgson thought they ought to have Mr.Heard in some office or on the committee. He was a man who could give them the full benefit of his knowledge and assistance. Mr.Heard was unanimously elected.

Mr.Walters speaking of the appointment of committee, said he did not intend to stand for that year as a committeeman, and he would like to point out that they could not have a better man for chairman than Mr.G.A.Smith, who had all the details at his finger ends. Besides, he did not thimk they ought to have players on the committee. Mr.Matthews differed from Mr.Walters, and said there should be a certain number of players on the committee. A man watching a match could not see all the little ins and outs of the game. Mr.Smith said he would like to be let off as it interfered so much with his business. The committee was ultimately constituted as follows: Messrs.Eddie Dowsett, Byles, Eley, Parsons, Dawson, Maddicks, Walters, Drewitt, L.Fletcher and Matthews.

Messrs.F.W.Jeffes and E.J.Wallis were unanimously re-elected auditors, on the proposition of Mr.Matthews. Mr.Reading declined to accept the captaincy of the first team for the ensuing season, and proposed Mr.A.E. Hyett for the post. Mr.Heard, as an amendment, proposed Mr. H.A.Bown (the vice-captain). He thought it only fair, where possible, for the offices to go round. Mr.Bown was elected. Mr.W.G.Byles was appointed vice-captain. Mr.W.Parsons explained that there had been some trouble relating to the second team. Some of the players had their expenses paid and others wanted their expenses paid. Mr.Matthews pointed out that when a man had played three times for the first team he could not play for the second team. It was resolved to run a second team, members' expenses to be paid. Mr.W.Parsons was appointed assistant secretary.

Mr.Heard suggested that the club should choose an outside finance committee of influential local gentlemen who would take an interest in the club. Messrs. W.D.Matthews, G.Hodgson and G.Hauch were appointed.

Season 1912 – 13

ROMFORD TOWN

President: Mr.John Bassett J.P. **Hon.Secretary:** Mr.A.Drury, 19, Carlisle Road, Romford

Hon.Treasurer: Mr.C.T.Heard, 18 King Edward Road, Romford

Committee: Messrs.E.Dowsing,S.Dowsing,A.Drury,G.C.Eley,L.Fletcher, C.T.Heard,G.H.Maddocks,A.Saville,G.A.Smith and F.Walters.

Finance Committee: Messrs.W.D.Matthews, G.Hodgson and G.Hauch

Captain: Mr.H.A.Bown **Reserve Team Secretary:** Mr.E.R.Walford

Headquarters: Rising Sun Hotel, Romford **Ground:** Shoulder of Mutton Field, Hornchurch Road, Romford

COMPETITIONS ENTERED

South Essex League Division One
Athenian Football League
F.A. Challenge Cup
F.A. Amateur Cup
Essex Senior Cup
West Ham Charity Cup

Ilford & District Football League
Essex Junior Cup

Match Details

7 Sept SEL1 Home Southend Amateurs 2 – 3 Hyett(2)
Romford Town: H.A.Bown(Capt);A.W.Asater,W.J.Biles;C.E.Manning,E.Taylor,H.B.West; C.Seabrooke,A.S.Hyett,C.S.Steele,F.Walters,W.Leach.

14 Sept SEL1 Away Colchester Town 1 – 4 Hyett
Romford Town: H.A.Bown(Capt);A.W.Asater,W.J.Biles;F.Walters,E.Taylor,S.Wilson; E.Ockendon,C.Seabrooke,A.S.Hyett,C.S.Steele,W.Newstead.

21 Sept AFL Away Grays Athletic 1 – 3 Asater
Romford Town: H.A.Bown(Capt);A.W.Asater,W.J.Biles;F.Walters,E.Taylor,H.B.West; C.E.Manning,G.Algar,C.Osborne,C.S.Steele,A.S.Hyett.

28 Sept FACEP Home Walthamstow Grange 2 – 3 C.Steele,G.Algar
Romford Town: H.A.Bown(Capt);A.W.Asater,W.J.Biles;F.Walters,E.Taylor,C.E.Manning; C.Seabrook,G.Algar,A.S.Hyett,C.S.Steele,C.Osborne.

5 Oct SEL1 Home 2nd Middlesex Regiment 1 – 0 Asater
Romford Town: H.A.Bown(Capt);R.E.Going,W.J.Biles;S.Wilson,E.Taylor,C.E.Manning; A.Reading,E.Ockendon,A.W.Asater,F.Walters,W.Newstead.

12 Oct SEL1 Away Southend Amateurs 0 – 2
Romford Town: H.A.Bown(Capt);R.E.Going,W.J.Biles;F.Walters,E.Taylor,C.E.Manning; A.Drury,G.Algar,A.W.Asater,Eldridge,A.S.Hyett.

19 Oct AC1Q Home Grays Athletic 1 – 2 Hyett
Romford Town: H.A.Bown(Capt);A.Reading,H.F.Easton;C.E.Manning,F.Walters,H.B.West; G.Algar,C.S.Steele,A.W.Asater,T.C.Clover,A.S.Hyett.

26 Oct AFL Home Finchley 0 – 1
Romford Town: H.A.Bown(Capt);A.W.Asater,R.E.Going;C.E.Manning,E.Taylor,H.B.West; A.Drury,T.C.Clover,J.Sharpley,S.C.Squier,A.S.Hyett.

2 Nov. SEL1 Away Barking 2 – 2 Bown(pen),Ockendon
Romford Town: H.A.Bown(Capt);A.Reading,A.W.Asater;C.E.Manning,E.Taylor,H.B.West;
F.Walters,E.Ockendon,J.Sharpley,T.C.Clover,W.Newstead.

9 Nov Frdly Home East Ham F.C. 3 – 0 Ockendon,Clover,Hyett
Romford Town: H.A.Bown(Capt);R.E.Going,A.W.Asater;C.E.Manning,E.Taylor,H.B.West;
F.Walters,T.C.Clover,E.Ockendon,A.S.Hyett,W.Leach. A.Drury played for East Ham to complete their team.

16 Nov AFL Away Catford Southend 0 – 1
Attendance: 1,500
Romford Town: H.A.Bown(Capt);R.E.Going,A.W.Asater;C.E.Manning,E.Taylor,H.B.West;
F.Walters,E.Ockendon,A.S.Hyett,T.C.Clover,J.Sharpley.

23 Nov AFL Home Chesham Town 2 – 2 Clover(2)
Romford Town: H.A.Bown(Capt);R.E.Going,A.W.Asater;C.E.Manning,E.Taylor,H.B.West;
F.Walters,E.Ockendon,A.Drury,T.C.Clover,A.S.Hyett.

30 Nov SEL1 Away Custom House 0 – 2
Romford Town: H.A.Bown(Capt);W.Whitehead,A.W.Asater,C.E.Manning,E.Taylor,H.B.West;
T.C.Clover,E.Ockendon,J.Sharpley,F.Walters,W.Leach.

5 Dec WHCSF Away Leytonstone 0 – 1
Attendance: 300
Romford Town: H.A.Bown(Capt);R.E.Going,A.W.Asater;Sanders,E.Taylor,S.Wilson;
F.Walters,Payne,J.Sharpley,T.C.Clover,A.S.Hyett.

7 Dec AFL Home Grays Athletic 1 – 1 Ockendon
Romford Town: H.A.Bown(Capt);R.E.Going,A.W.Asater;C.E.Manning,E.Taylor,H.B.West;
F.Walters,E.Ockendon,W.Whitehead,T.C.Clover,A.S.Hyett.

14 Dec SEL1 Home Chelmsford 3 – 1 Clover(2),Hyett
Romford Town: H.A.Bown(Capt);R.E.Going,A.W.Asater;C.E.Manning,F.Walters,E.Taylor;
A.S.Hyett,S.C.Squier,W.Newstead,W.Whitehead,T.C.Clover.

21 Dec AFL Home Tufnell Park 1 – 2 Scorer unknown
Romford Town: H.A.Bown(Capt);R.E.Going,A.W.Asater;F.Walters,E.Taylor,C.E.Manning;
S.C.Squier,W.Newstead,W.Whitehead,T.C.Clover,A.S.Hyett.

25 Dec AFL Away Chelmsford 1 – 5 Whitehead
Romford Town: H.A.Bown(Capt);R.E.Going,A.W.Asater;F.Walters,E.Taylor,C.E.Manning;
S.C.Squier,E.Ockendon,W.Whitehead,T.C.Clover,A.S.Hyett.

26 Dec AFL Home Chelmsford 1 – 2 Asater
Romford Town: H.A.Bown(Capt);R.E.Going,A.W.Asater;F.Walters,E.Taylor,C.E.Manning;
S.C.Squier,W.Whitehead,A.S.Hyett,A.E.Jones,J.Hunter.

28 Dec SEL1 Home Colchester Town 0 – 2
Romford Town: H.A.Bown(Capt);Fisher,A.W.Asater;C.E.Manning,A.Drury, ? ;
S.C.Squier,B.G.Aston,W.Whitehead,T.C.Clover,A.S.Hyett.

11 Jan SEL1 Home Shoeburyness Garrison 0 – 2
Romford Town: E.R.Walford;R.E.Going,A.W.Asater;C.E.Manning,E.Taylor,H.B.West;
S.C.Squier,B.G.Aston,W.Whitehead,T.C.Clover,A.S.Hyett.

18 Jan AFL Away Finchley 1 – 1 Aston
Romford Town: H.A.Bown(Capt);R.E.Going,A.W.Asater;C.E.Manning,E.Taylor,A.A.Rayner;
W.A.Thorpe,B.G.Aston W.Whitehead,T.C.Clover,A.S.Hyett.

25 Jan ESC3R Home Walthamstow Grange 2 – 0 Rayner(2)
Attendance: 700
Romford Town: H.A.Bown(Capt);R.E.Going,A.W.Asater;C.E.Manning,E.Taylor,H.B.West;
S.C.Squier,B.G.Aston,A.A.Rayner,T.C.Clover,A.S.Hyett.

1 Feb SEL1 Away Grays Athletic 0 – 5
Romford Town: H.A.Bown(Capt);R.E.Going,A.W.Asater;E.Taylor,S.C.Squier,W.A.Thorpe;
W.Whitehead,T.C.Clover,A.Drury.

8 Feb SEL1 Away Chelmsford 1 – 1 Hyett
Romford Town: E.R.Walford;A.Wyles,A.W.Asater;F.Walters,E.Taylor,C.E.Manning;
A.G.Manning,B.G.Aston,W.Whitehead,T.C.Clover,A.S.Hyett.

15 Feb SEL1 Home Grays Athletic 1 – 2 C.Manning
Romford Town: H.A.Bown(Capt);R.E.Going,A.W.Asater;C.E.Manning,S.Wilson,A.G.Manning;
S.C.Squier,B.G.Aston,W.Newstead,T.C.Clover,A.S.Hyett.

22 Feb ESC4R Home# Clapton 1 – 0 Rayner
Attendance: 1,500
Romford Town: H.A.Bown(Capt);R.E.Going,A.W.Asater;F.Walters,E.Taylor,C.E.Manning;
S.C.Squier,B.G.Aston,A.A.Rayner,T.C.Clover,A.S.Hyett.

6 Mar Frdly Home West Ham United Reserves 2 – 3 A.Jones(2)(1pen)
Attendance: 200
Romford Town:
A.E.Jones,

8 Mar AFL Home Enfield 2 – 1 Askew,Taylor
Romford Town: H.A.Bown(Capt);C.E.Manning,R.Smith;A.G.Manning,E.Taylor,H.B.West;
S.Askew,B.G.Aston,F.Walters,T.C.Clover,A.S.Hyett.

15 Mar AFL Away Chesham Town 4 – 1 Aston(2)Hyett,Squier
Romford Town: H.A.Bown(Capt);C.E.Manning,A.W.Asater;A.G.Manning,E.Taylor,S.Askew;
A.Drury,S.C.Squier,B.G.Aston,T.C.Clover,A.S.Hyett.

21 Mar AFL Home Catford Southend 0 – 5
Romford Town:
The reserve team played, due to the Essex Senior Cup Semi-Final to be played the following day.

22 Mar ESCSF Ilford Chelmsford 2 – 2 Taylor,Rayner
Attendance: 3,000
Romford: H.A.Bown(Capt);C.E.Manning,A.W.Asater;F.Walters,E.Taylor,S.Askew;
S.C.Squier,B.G.Aston,A.A.Rayner,T.C.Clover,A.S.Hyett.

24 Mar AFL Away Tufnell Park 1 – 3 Drury
Romford Town: H.A.Bown(Capt) in goal and Club Secretary A.Drury
plus nine players from Mawney Institute.

25 Mar SEL1 Away 2nd Middlesex Regiment 0 – 2
Romford Town: H.A.Bown(Capt);C.E.Manning,A.W.Asater;A.G.Manning,E.Taylor,S.Askew;
F.Walters,S.C.Squier,B.G.Aston,T.C.Clover,A.S.Hyett.

29 Mar ESCRP Barking Chelmsford 1 – 1* Rayner
Attendance: 2,000
Romford Town: H.A.Bown(Capt);R.E.Going,A.W.Asater;F.Walters,E.Taylor,C.E.Manning;
S.C.Squier,B.G.Aston,A.A.Rayner,T.C.Clover,A.S.Hyett.

3 Apr AFL Home Barnet Alston 0 – 3
Romford Town: E.R.Walford;
plus ten soldiers from the Middlesex Regiment.

5 Apr AFL Away Enfield 2 – 2 T.C.Clover(2)
Romford Town: H.A.Bown(Capt);R.E.Going,A.W.Asater;C.E.Manning,E.Taylor,S.Wilson;
G.A.Drury,T.C.Clover,S.C.Squier,A.G.Manning,A.Clover.

12 Apr ESC2RP Leytonstone Chelmsford 1 – 0 Squier
Attendance: 1,500
Romford Town: H.A.Bown(Capt);R.E.Going,A.W.Asater;F.Walters,E.Taylor,C.E.Manning;
S.C.Squier,B.G.Aston,A.A.Rayner,T.C.Clover,A.S.Hyett.

19 Apr. SEL1 Home Barking 0 – 4
Romford Town: Myhill;R.E.Going,A.W.Asater;F.Walters,E.Taylor,S.Wilson;
A.Bissett,B.G.Aston,A.A.Rayner,T.C.Clover,A.S.Hyett.

21 Apr SEL1 Away Shoeburyness Garrison 0 – 5
Romford Town: E.R.Walford;R.E.Going,
Plus nine reserves.

26 Apr ESCF L'stone Ilford 2 – 3 Taylor,Squier
Attendance: 4,000
Romford Town: H.A.Bown(Capt);R.E.Going,A.W.Asater;F.Walters,E.Taylor,C.E.Manning;
S.C.Squier,B.G.Aston,A.A.Rayner,T.C.Clover,A.S.Hyett.

28 Apr SEL1 Home Custom House 4 – 1 Collar,Clover,A.G.Manning,Bissett
Romford Town: H.A.Bown(Capt);R.E.Going,A.Hunwicks;C.E.Manning,A.A.Rayner,F.Walters;
A.J.Collar,W.Newstead,A.G.Manning,T.C.Clover,A.Bissett.

29 April AFL Away Barnet Alston 0 – 7
Romford Town:
Romford represented by the soldiers of the Middlesex Regiment for the second time.

* After extra time

\# As the holders, Romford had choice of venue.

SUMMARY OF RESULTS OBTAINED SEASON 1912 – 13

	P	W	D	L	Goals For	Goals Ag	Pts
South Essex Lge.	16	3	2	11	15	38	8
Athenian League	16	2	4	10	17	40	8
F.A. Challenge Cup	1	0	0	1	2	3	
F.A. Amateur Cup	1	0	0	1	1	2	
Essex Senior Cup	6	3	2	1	9	6	
West Ham Charity Cup	1	0	0	1	0	1	
Friendly Matches	2	1	0	1	5	3	
Total	43	9	8	26	49	93	

South Essex League Division One
Final Table

	P	W	D	L	Goals For	Goals Ag	Pts
Colchester Town	16	11	2	3	32	18	24
Barking	16	9	5	2	38	13	23
*Grays Athletic	16	10	4	2	26	10	22
Chelmsford	16	8	3	5	28	20	19
Custom House	16	8	1	7	25	24	17
Shoeburyness Garrison	16	4	5	7	21	28	13
Southend Amateurs	16	4	1	11	22	36	9
Romford Town	**16**	**3**	**2**	**11**	**15**	**38**	**8**
2nd Batt. Middlx.Regt.	16	3	1	12	13	33	7

* Two points deducted for breach of Rules.

Athenian Football League
Final Table

	P	W	D	L	Goals For	Goals Ag	Pts
Catford Southend	16	11	3	2	50	15	25
Barnet & Alston	16	9	3	4	36	17	21
Tufnell Park	16	8	5	3	25	13	21
Finchley	16	8	4	4	19	11	20
Grays Athletic	16	4	6	6	18	23	14
Chelmsford	16	5	3	8	21	36	13
Enfield	16	3	6	7	18	28	12
Chesham Town	16	3	4	9	21	42	10
Romford Town	**16**	**2**	**4**	**10**	**17**	**40**	**8**

CUP RESULTS

F.A. Challenge Cup

Final: Aston Villa 1 Sunderland 0

Romford's progress: Ex.Prel Home Walthamstow Grange 2 – 3

F.A. Amateur Cup

Final: South Bank 1 Oxford City 1
Replay: South Bank 1 Oxford City 0

Romford's progress: 1st Qual Home Grays Athletic 1 – 2

Essex Senior Cup

Final: Ilford 3 Romford Town 2

Romford's progress: 3rd Round Home Walthamstow Grange 2 – 0
4th Round Home Clapton 1 – 0
Semi-Final Ilford Chelmsford 2 – 2
Replay Barking Chelmsford 1 – 1
2nd Replay Leytonstone Chelmsford 1 – 0
Final Leytonstone Ilford 2 – 3

West Ham Hospital Charity Cup

Final: n/k

Semi-Final Away Leytonstone 0 – 1

First Team Appearances Season 1912 – 13

G.Algar	4	A.W.Asater	35	S.Askew	4	B.G.Aston	15
W.J.Biles	6	A.Bissett	2	H.A.Bown	35	A.Clover	1
T.C.Clover	30	A.J.Collar	1	A.Drury	7	G.A.Drury	1
H.F.Easton	1	Eldridge	1	Fisher	1	R.Going	25
J.Hunter	1	A.Hunwicks	1	A.S.Hyett	31	A.E.Jones	2
W.Leach	3	A.G.Manning	7	C.E.Manning	33	Myhill	1
W.Newstead	7	E.Ockendon	9	C.Osborne	2	Payne	1
A.A.Rayner	9	A.Reading	3	Sanders	1	C.Seabrooke	3
J.Sharpley	5	R.Smith	1	S.C.Squier	18	C.S.Steele	5
E.Taylor	33	W.A.Thorpe	2	E.R.Walford	4	F.Walters	28
H.B.West	13	W.Whitehead	11	S.Wilson	6	A.Wyles	1
Total	212						

First Team Goal Scorers Season 1912 - 13

A.S.Hyett	8	T.C.Clover	8	A.A.Rayner	5	A.W.Asater	3
E.Ockendon	3	B.G.Aston	3	E.Taylor	3	S.C.Squier	3
A.Jones	2	C.Steele	1	G.Algar	1	H.A.Bown	1
W.Whitehead	1	C.E.Manning	1	S.Askew	1	A.Drury	1
A.J.Collar	1	A.G.Manning	1	A.Bissett	1	Unknown	1
Total	49						

RESERVES ("A" Team)

Match Details

8 Oct	Frdly	Away	Carlisle Institute	2 – 4
	EJC1R			Bye
26 Oct	EJC2	Away	West Ham Town	3 – 5
9 Nov	IDL1	Away	East Ham Town	0 – 7
16 Nov	IDL1	Home	G.E.R. Athletic	2 – 3
21 Dec	IDL1	Away	G.E.R. Athletic	2 – 0
4 Jan	IDL1	Away	Wanstead	1 – 2
11 Jan	IDL1	Away	Ilford "A"	2 – 10
1 Feb	IDL1	Away	Barking Curfew	1 – 10
22 Feb	IDL1	Away	Mansfield House	Lost
1 Mar	IDL1	Home	East Ham Town	2 – 4
8 Mar	IDL1	Away	Purfleet	n/k
29 Mar	IDL1	Home	Purfleet	1 – 2
5 Apr	IDL1	Home	Wanstead	1 – 2
	IDL1	Home	Barking Curfew	n/k
	IDL1	Home	Forest Gate	n/k
	IDL1	Away	Forest Gate	n/k
	IDL1	Home	Ilford "A"	n/k
	IDL1	Home	Mansfield House	n/k

Ilford & District Football League Division One

					Goals		
	P	W	D	L	For	Ag	Pts
East Ham Town	16	13	2	1	72	18	28
Purfleet	16	11	2	3	38	18	24
Ilford "A"	16	9	1	6	41	38	19
Forest Gate	16	6	5	5	22	20	17
Barking Curfew	16	7	2	7	42	29	16
Wanstead	16	6	1	9	24	31	13
Romford Town "A"	**16**	**5**	**0**	**11**	**24**	**53**	**10**
G.E.R. Athletic	16	4	1	11	21	48	9
Mansfield House	16	3	2	11	14	43	8

POLICEMAN TOOK OFFENCE!

Friday, 20th December, 1912, master George Box of Richmond Road, was summoned for damaging a fence to the value of five shillings. P.C. Watt said the fence belonged to Mr.W.Poel junior, and it divided the Mill Path from the Romford Football ground, defendant was standing on the fence watching a football match when spoken to by the officer. The youth said he would get down when he liked, in getting down he broke the fence and was fined two shillings and sixpence, damages two shillings and sixpence and costs four shillings.

(as reported in the *Essex Times*)

Post Season Summary   Season 1912 – 13

Romford Town was one of the founder members of the Athenian League, and also competed in the South Essex League for the new season. They opened their campaign with four successive defeats before obtaining a narrow victory. They started off with a narrow 3-2 reverse at home to Southend Amateurs and were well beaten at Colchester Town, both South Essex League games. Romford fared no better in the first Athenian League fixture, losing 3-1 at Grays. Worse was to follow in the fourth game when Walthamstow Grange came to town and ousted the team from the F.A. Cup, a devastating blow to the club's financial hopes. Success came at last when they defeated 2nd Middlesex Regiment by one goal to nil in the South Essex League.

Then followed three more defeats, and the officials must have wondered at their wisdom in entering two top leagues for the season. The team surrendered league points to Southend Amateurs and Finchley, and in between they suffered another severe blow when Grays Athletic knocked them out of the Amateur Cup. W.J.Biles played his last game for the club in the Southend Amateurs match before leaving to join Ilford.

The team obtained a South Essex League draw against Barking and a 3-0 win over East Ham in a friendly match, but just two wins from the first ten games was a dismal start. The club did not fare much better in the next five games, obtaining two draws, in the Athenian League, against Chesham Town and Grays Athletic, but suffering three defeats without scoring a goal. They were perhaps a little unfortunate in the West Ham Charity Cup semi-final away to Leytonstone, who scored the only goal of the game in the 85th minute.

A special meeting of the Athenian League was held on Monday 18th November, Mr.C.D.Crisp presiding. The Committee dealt with the case of Barking's non-fulfilment of a fixture with Romford on 9th November. The Barking club were fined thirty shillings.

Early in December West Ham United informed Romford that they intended to sign their goalkeeper H.A.Bown, but things brightened up with a good home victory over Chelmsford by three goals to one in their first South Essex League victory for over two months. Back down to earth again, as this was followed by five successive league defeats, including two at the hands of Chelmsford. First came a 5-1 Athenian League thrashing at Chelmsford, followed by a two one defeat in the return home game on Boxing Day. Maybe the Christmas Day beating affected some players, as once more the team found themselves with only nine men for the return game. It was fortunate the two old Romford players 'Diddy' Jones and Jimmy Hunter were in the crowd and they made up the team.

After the 2-0 defeat by Shoeburyness Garrison in the South Essex League, Romford picked up an Athenian League point away to Finchley. Then the team met with cup success at last, with a fine two goal to nil win at home to Walthamstow Grange in the Essex Senior Cup before a crowd of seven hundred. Romford picked up only one point, against Chelmsford, from their next three league games and suffered two defeats by Grays Athletic, one by 5-0 when Romford once more had only nine men.

With such a poor record in the league games it seemed that the club was determined to succeed in the Essex Senior Cup competition, and as holders had choice of venue for the fourth round tie against powerful Clapton. Romford rewarded the fifteen hundred spectators with a grand 1-0 victory.

On 6th March Romford met West Ham United in a friendly game at Romford which the homesters lost 3-2. This match was held to repay Romford for loaning goalkeeper H.A.Bown to play in West Ham United Reserves when required. Alas, the attendance was only 200, no doubt due to it being played on a weekday afternoon. Romford's team was made up of Mawney Institute, Roneo Athletic and Town players. Rogers and Blackburn scored for West Ham United, whilst 'Diddy' Jones scored two for the home team.

Romford then secured two Athenian League victories, against Enfield and Chesham Town, but these were followed by a 5-0 home defeat by Catford Southend in the same competition. It is only fair to point out that Romford put out their reserve team, due to the Essex Senior Cup semi-final to be played the following day.

Around this time, Middlesbrough made an enquiry to sign goalkeeper H.A.Bown. The semi-final was played at Ilford before an attendance of 3,000, where Romford earned a replay with a two all draw against Chelmsford. Next came two more league defeats, by Tufnell Park and the 2nd Middlesex Regiment. The following week the Essex Senior Cup replay took place at Barking, and despite extra time Romford and Chelmsford could not be separated and they had to settle for a one all draw.

Two Athenian League games, resulting in a loss to Barnet Alston by three goals to nil and a two all draw at Enfield, were followed with the second replay of the Essex Senior Cup semi-final at Leytonstone. On this occasion Romford were at last able to overcome Chelmsford by one goal to nil. Romford were now in Cup Final mood, but their league form was horrendous, as they suffered heavy league defeats against Barking (0-4) and with a weakened team against Shoeburyness Garrison (0-5).

Then came the great day at Leytonstone against the strong Ilford team in the final of the Essex Senior Cup. Ilford were the winners by three goals to two to the disappointment of Romford supporters. Mr.F.E.Pelly, the old Felsteadian and Corinthian player, presented the cup to Will.H.Martin, the Ilford captain.

Romford rounded off their South Essex League fixtures with a fine 4-1 win over Custom House. The final Athenian League game, away to Barnet Alston, was a disaster. For reasons unknown, no first team players played, and the club was once more represented by the 2nd Middlesex Regiment from Warley, and were soundly beaten 7-0.

The season, despite reaching the Essex Senior Cup Final, was a very disappointing one for Romford. The team were put out of the F.A.Cup and Amateur Cup at the first attempt, finished second from last in the South Essex League, and bottom of the Athenian League. The reserve team finished in a lowly position in the Ilford & District League, and twice conceded ten goals in league games. Before the next season, H.A.Bown left the club altogether and joined Roneo Athletic.

Annual General Meeting
(as reported in the *Essex Times*, Wednesday 2nd July 1913)

The Annual General Meeting of Romford Town Football Club was held on Monday evening, 30th June, at the Rising Sun Hotel, Romford.Mr.J.Bassett president, was in the chair, and there was a fair attendance.

The Hon.Secretary's report, read by Mr.A.Drury, stated that he would like it to have recorded a greater number of successes in the league games. He regretted that it would be his last report, as it was his first. The club played 42 matches, of which they won 10, drew 8 and lost 24. Fifty goals were scored for the club, and 87 against.

Although the record as it stood did not indicate that they had enjoyed a very successful season, yet they could congratulate themselves that their team accomplished many fine performances. In the Essex Cup they won their way to the final, defeating such formidable opponents as Walthamstow Grange, Clapton and Chelmsford. In the final Ilford won by the narrowest of margins after a keen and hard fought battle. On the day's play it was generally admitted that there was little difference between the merits of the two teams. The club were dismissed from the English Cup by Walthamstow Grange by an odd goal, which, by the way, was a penalty goal; and Grays put them out of the Amateur Cup by the odd goal.

Having reviewed the results of other matches, the report stated that Messrs. A.Saville and A.A.Raven had been elected to vacancies on the committee caused by the resignations of Messrs.H.H.W.Druitt and F.Walters. Special thank were due to the captain (Mr. H.A. Bown) and Messrs. A.Asater, A.S.Hyett, E.Taylor, F.Walters, C.Manning, R.E.Going and T.Clover, who played regularly throughout the season with a true sportsmanlike spirit. Other players also rendered invaluable aid.

The reserve team, under the secretaryship of Mr.E.R.Walford, had finished up with a better position in the Ilford League than they had occupied for some time. The team was stronger last season than it had been for some years. Mr.Drury concluded with an assurance that he would have been delighted to have continued as hon.secretary, but under present circumstances it was impracticable. The club had entered this coming season for the English Cup, the Amateur Cup, the Essex Cup, the Athenian League and the South Essex League.

The hon.treasurer (Mr.C.T.Heard) regretted to report a deficit on the year's working of £16.5s.2d. He thought the position would have been better if they had received more fair treatment from the Essex County Football Association. The weather had also been very much against them. The receipts amounted to £221.9s.10d. The expenditure was £209.10s.9d. The amount paid off old accounts was £24.14s.0d. and there was a balance due from the club of £55.19s.2d.

Mr.E.J.Wallis, one of the hon. auditors, made some remarks explanatory of the balance sheet, and expressed regret that the club was in such a parlous financial position. The principal receipts were: President and vice-presidents, £21.19s.6d.; gate receipts, £133.9s.8d.; and grant from Essex County Football Association, £39.3s.4d.

Mr.L.Fletcher said he was not satisfied with the statement of accounts. He would like to know what they owed £55 for. Mr.Wallis said it was not the duty of the auditors to value the club's assets. Mr.Heard said the £55.19s.2d. was owing for printing, fencing, teas etc., and an amount due to officers. Off the old accounts £24.14s.0d. had been paid.

Mr.W.D.Matthews said it was very unfortunate that the club was going downhill financially. They had been very unfortunate in the matter of weather. He proposed the adoption of the report and accounts. Mr.Hodgson seconded the proposition, which was carried. Mr.Matthews said he had suggested to the committee thay they should give as much as they could towards paying off the debt. He would give £2.2s.0d., and would write to the vice-presidents and the members asking them, in the exceptionally adverse circumstances, to give special donations this year. He had been connected with football in Romford for very many years, and it would be a sad day for him if the club had to be wound up.

Mr.Willis expressed appreciation of the offer made by Mr.Matthews, and proposed its acceptance. (Hear, hear). The Chairman said he would do his part, and he would like an effort to be made to reduce expenses. The proposition was carried. Mr.Matthews said the club must be kept in an efficient condition, but it must be possible to effect some saving. It would be very sad if the club met the fate of the Romford Cricket Club, which fell through in its Jubilee year.

Mr.Heard read a letter from Mr.Bassett, who resigned the presidency and asked to have his name removed from the joint tenancy of the ground. He would continue his interest in the club. Mr.Matthews asked Mr.Bassett to withdraw his resignation, and proposed his re-election. Mr.F.Walters seconded the proposition, which was carried unanimously. Mr.Bassett returned thanks, and counselled the players to take the field in a body when playing matches, and not to let their opponents score before the full Romford team was in play.

Mr.Drury, on resignation of the office of hon.secretary, was elected a vice-president. The question of the election of an hon.secretary was left to the committee. Mr.C.T.Heard was re-elected hon.treasurer; and the following committee was elected: Messrs. G.A.Smith, G.Maddocks, S.Dowsing, E.Dowsing, A.Saville, Myhill and A.Asater. Messrs. F.W.Jeffes and E.J.Wallis were re-elected Hon.Auditors.

Mr.Heard said that, with the exception of Mr.Bown, all last year's players would be available next season. Mr.E.Taylor was elected captain and Mr.C.Manning vice-captain.

Mr.Matthews said that, although the club were disappointed at the grant from the Essex County Football Association, the association dealt magnanimously with all the clubs in the final and semi-final, dividing 55.6% of their profits, whereas other associations did not divide more than 33%. It was resolved to run a reserve team. The meeting ended with a vote of thanks to the auditors, committee and officers.

Season 1913 – 14

ROMFORD TOWN

President: Mr.John Bassett J.P.

Hon.Secretary: Mr.O.C.Rolfe, 51, King Edward Road, Romford **Hon.Treasurer:** Mr.C.T.Heard

Captain: Mr.E.Taylor **Vice-Captain:** Mr.C.E.Manning

Committee: Messrs.A.Asater,E.Dowsing,S.Dowsing, G.H.Maddocks,Myhill,A.Saville and G.A.Smith.

Reserve Team Secretary: Mr.E.R.Walford **Auditors:** Messrs.F.W.Jeffes and E.J.Wallis.

Headquarters: Rising Sun Hotel, Romford **Ground:** Shoulder of Mutton Field, Hornchurch Road, Romford

COMPETITIONS ENTERED
South Essex League Division One
Athenian League
F.A. Challenge Cup
F.A. Amateur Cup
Essex Senior Cup
West Ham Charity Cup

Ilford & District League Division One
Essex Junior Cup

Match Details

6 Sept SEL1 Home Custom House 0 – 1
Romford Town: F.W.Newman;A.W.Asater,Powell;A.A.Rayner,E.Taylor(Capt),C.E.Manning;
B.G.Aston,L.Jones,J.T.Lee,T.C.Clover,A.J.Collar.

13 Sept AFL Away Metrogas 2 – 7 Scorers unknown
Attendance: 2,000
Romford Town:
Team details unknown.

20 Sept AFL Away Chesham Town 3 – 2 Scorers unknown
Romford Town:
Team details unknown.

27 Sept FACPR Home Shoeburyness Garrison 4 – 2 Lee(2)Asater,Sawyer
Romford Town: F.W.Newman;F.A.Chadders,A.W.Asater;C.A.Morrison,Eddie.Taylor(Capt),C.E.Manning;
B.G.Aston,H.J.Sawyer,J.T.Lee,T.C.Clover,A.J.Collar.

2 Oct WHCSF Away Clapton (at Spotted Dog) 1 – 4 Clover
Romford Town: F.W.Newman;C.E.Manning,A.W.Asater;L.Jones,E.Taylor(Capt),C.A.Morrison;
E.C.Bissett,H.J.Sawyer,J.T.Lee,T.C.Clover,A.J.Collar.

4 Oct AC1Q Home Walthamstow Grange 2 – 0 Rayner,Lee
Attendance: 1,500
Romford Town: F.W.Newman;C.E.Manning,A.W.Asater;F.Walters,E.Taylor(Capt),A.A.Rayner;
B.G.Aston,H.J.Sawyer,J.T.Lee,T.C.Clover,A.J.Collar.

11 Oct FAC1Q Home Custom House 0 – 2
Attendance: 100
Romford Town: F.W.Newman;C.E.Manning,A.W.Asater;F.Walters,E. Taylor(Capt),A.A.Raynor;
A.Bissett,H.J.Sawyer,J.T.Lee,T.C.Clover,A.J.Collar.

18 Oct AC2Q Home Shoeburyness Garrison 1 – 0# Rayner
Romford Town: F.W.Newman;F.A.Chadders,A.W.Asater;A.A.Rayner,E.Taylor(Capt),C.A.Morrison;
A.G.Manning,H.J.Sawyer,J.T.Lee,T.C.Clover,A.J.Collar.

25 Oct ACRP Away Shoeburyness Garrison 1 – 1* Lee
Romford Town: F.W.Newman;F.A.Chadders,A.W.Asater;A.A.Rayner,E.Taylor(Capt),C.A.Morrison;
B.G.Aston,H.J.Sawyer,J.T.Lee,T.C.Clover,A.J.Collar.

29 Oct AC2RP Barking Shoeburynes Garrison 0 – 0*
Romford Town: F.W.Newman,A.A.Raynor,A.W.Asater;A.G.Manning,E.Taylor(Capt),C.A.Morrison;
B.G.Aston,H.J.Sawyer,J.T.Lee,T.C.Clover,A.J.Collar.

1 Nov AFL Away Enfield 3 – 4 Lee(2)Collar
Romford Town:
Team details unknown.

3 Nov AC3RP Barking Shoeburyness Garrison 3 – 1* Rayner,Lee,Collar
Romford Town: F.W.Newman;F.A.Chadders,A.W.Asater;A.A.Raynor,E.Taylor(Capt),C.A.Morrison;
B.G.Aston,H.J.Sawyer,J.T.Lee,T.C.Clover,A.J.Collar.

8 Nov AC3Q Away Woodford Crusaders 4 – 2 Clover(2)Sawyer,Collar
Romford Town: F.W.Newman;A.A.Raynor,A.W.Asater;S.Wilson,E.Taylor(Capt),C.A.Morrison;
A.S.Hyett,H.J.Sawyer,J.T.Lee,T.C.Clover,A.J.Collar.

15 Nov AFL Home Grays Athletic 4 – 1 Sawyer,Lee,Clover,Taylor
Romford Town: F.W.Newman;A.A.Rayner,A.W.Asater;C.E.Manning,E.Taylor(Capt),C.A.Morrison;
A.S.Hyett,H.J.Sawyer,J.T.Lee,T.C.Clover,A.J.Collar.

22 Nov AC4Q Home Grays Athletic 0 – 0
Attendance: 1,500
Romford Town: F.W.Newman;A.A.Raynor,A.W.Asater;C.E.Manning,E.Taylor(Capt),C.A.Morrison;
A.S.Hyett,H.J.Sawyer,J.T.Lee,T.C.Clover,A.J.Collar.

29 Nov ACRP Away Grays Athletic 2 – 3 Aston,Lee
Romford Town: F.W.Newman;A.A.Raynor,A.W.Asater;C.E.Manning,E.Taylor(Capt),C.A.Morrison;
B.G.Aston,H.J.Sawyer,J.T.Lee,T.C.Clover,A.J.Collar.

6 Dec AFL Home Chelmsford 0 – 1
Romford Town: F.W.Newman;A.A.Rayner,A.W.Asater;C.E.Manning,Hewitt.C.A.Morrison;
B.G.Aston,H.J.Sawyer,J.T.Lee,Channon,A.J.Collar.

11 Dec SEL1 Away Leyton 2 – 1 Scorers unknown
Romford Town:
Team details unknown.

13 Dec SEL1 Away Grays Athletic 2 – 1 Lee,Templar(o.g)
Romford Town: F.W.Newman;A.A.Rayner,A.W.Asater;C.E.Manning,E.Taylor(Capt),C.A.Morrison ;
B.G.Aston,H.J.Sawyer,J.T.Lee,T.C.Clover,A.J.Collar.

20 Dec AFL Home Hastings & St. Leonards 0 – 0
Romford Town: F.W.Newman;Bourne,A.W.Asater;A.A.Rayner,E.Taylor(Capt),C.A.Morrison;
Griffin,H.J.Sawyer,J.T.Lee,Channon,A.J.Collar.

25 Dec AFL Away Grays Athletic 2 – 3 Sawyer(2)
Romford Town:
Team detals unknown.

26 Dec SEL1 Home Grays Athletic 1 – 0 Sawyer
Romford Town:
Team details unknown.

27 Dec. SEL1 Away Barking 0 – 2
Romford Town: Team details unknown.

3 Jan SEL1 Away Woodford Crusaders 2 – 3 Griffin,Morrison
Romford Town: Astley;Bourne,A.W.Asater;A.A.Rayner,E.Taylor(Capt),C.A.Morrison;
Griffin,B.G.Aston,J.T.Lee,H.J.Sawyer,A.J.Collar.

10 Jan SEL1 Home Woodford Crusaders 4 – 2 Rayner(3)(1pen),Morrison
Romford Town: Astley;Bourne,A.W.Asater;Channon,E.Taylor(Capt),C.E.Manning;
J.T.Lee,H.J.Sawyer,A.A.Rayner,C.A.Morrison,A.J.Collar.

17 Jan SEL1 Away Custom House 4 – 1 Rayner(3)Lee
Romford Town: F.W.Newman;Bourne,A.W.Asater;Channon,E.Taylor(Capt),C.E.Manning;
J.T.Lee,H.J.Sawyer,A.A.Raynor,S.C.Squier,A.J.Collar.

24 Jan AFL Home Barnet Alston 3 – 2 Rayner,Sawyer,Squier
Romford Town: F.W.Newman;R.E.Going,A.W.Asater;Channon,E.Taylor(Capt),Griffin;
J.T.Lee,H.J.Sawyer,A.A.Rayner,S.C.Squier,A.J.Collar.

31 Jan ESC3R Away Ilford 2 – 4 Lee,Rayner
Romford Town: F.W.Newman;Channon,A.W.Asater;F.Walters,E.Taylor(Capt),C.E.Manning;
J.T.Lee,H.J.Sawyer,A.A.Rayner,S.C.Squier,A.J.Collar.

7 Feb AFL Away Finchley 1 – 4 Steele
Romford Town: Astley;Bourne,A.W.Asater;Channon,E.Taylor(Capt),C.A.Morrison;
C.E.Manning,H.J.Sawyer,J.T.Lee,C.S.Steele,A.J.Collar.

14 Feb AFL Home Chesham 2 – 1 Rayner,Squier
Romford Town: A.W.Asater;Bourne,J.T.Lee;F.Walters,E.Taylor(Capt),C.A.Morrison;
B.G.Aston,H.J.Sawyer,A.A.Rayner,S.C.Squier,A.J.Collar.

21 Feb SEL1 Away Walthamstow Grange 2 – 7 Lee,Rayner
Attendance: 1,200
Romford Town: Astley;Bourne,A.W.Asater;F.Walters,E.Taylor(Capt),C.A.Morrison;
J.T.Lee,H.J.Sawyer,A.A.Raynor,S.C.Squier,A.J.Collar.

28 Feb AFL Home Catford Southend 2 – 2 Rayner,Squier
Romford Town: Dockrill;Bourne,A.W.Asater;Taylor,E.Taylor(Capt),C.A.Morrison;
J.T.Lee,H.J.Sawyer,A.A.Rayner,S.C.Squier,A.J.Collar.

5 Mar SEL1 Home Leyton 6 – 3 Squier(2)Rayner(2)Chalk,Collar
Romford Town: F.W.Newman;B.G.Aston,A.W.Asater;F.Walters,E.Taylor(Capt),J.T.Lee;
H.J.Sawyer,Chalk,A.A.Rayner,S.C.Squier, A.J.Collar.

7 Mar AFL Home Enfield 3 – 2 Collar,Lee,Squier
Romford Town: F.W.Newman,Bourne,A.W.Asater;Taylor,E.Taylor(Capt),C.A.Morrison;
B.G.Aston,F.Walters,J.T.Lee,S.C.Squier,A.J.Collar.

12 Mar SEL1 Away Shoeburyness Garrison 1 – 3 Scorer unknown
Romford Town:
Team details unknown.

14 Mar AFL Home Finchley 1 – 0 Rayner(pen)
Romford Town: F.W.Newman;Bourne,A.W.Asater;Rolfe,E.Taylor(Capt),C.A.Morrison;
B.G.Aston,J.T.Lee,H.J.Sawyer,A.A.Rayner,A.J.Collar.

19 Mar SEL1 Home Walthamstow Grange 4 – 4 Chalk,Collar,Rayner(pen),Roberts(o.g)
Romford Town: F.W.Newman;Bourne,A.W.Asater;F.Walters,E.Taylor(Capt), ? ;
Chalk,H.J.Sawyer, A.A.Rayner,S.C.Squier,A.J.Collar.

21 Mar AFL Away Luton Clarence 0 – 8
Romford Town:
Romford fielded a reserve team.

28 Mar SEL1 Home Colchester Town 1 – 2 Sawyer
Romford Town: F.W.Newman;Bourne,A.W.Asater;F.Walters,E.Taylor(Capt),C.E.Manning;
B.G.Aston,H.J.Sawyer,A.A.Rayner,S.C.Squier,A.J.Collar.

2 Apr SEL1 Home Shoeburyness Garrison 1 – 1 Scorer unknown
Romford Town: F.W.Newman; ? ,A.W.Asater;Rolfe, ? ,S.Wilson;
Chalk,H.J.Sawyer,Harvey,S.C.Squier,A.J.Collar.

4 Apr AFL Away Catford Southend 2 – 2 Sawyer,Lee
Romford Town:
J.T.Lee,H.J.Sawyer,

10 Apr SEL1 Away Colchester Town 1 – 1 Walters
Romford Town: F.W.Newman,Bourne,A.W.Asater;Taylor,E.Taylor(Capt),C.E.Manning;
B.G.Aston,A.A.Rayner,J.T.Lee,F.Walters,A.J.Collar.

11 Apr SEL1 Home Barking 2 – 2 Walters,Rayner(pen)
Romford Town: F.W.Newman,Bourne,A.Asater;Taylor,E.Taylor(Capt),C.E.Manning;
B.G.Aston,A.A.Rayner,J.T.Lee,F.Walters,A.J.Collar.

13 Apr AFL Away Hastings & St. Leonards 5 – 4 Scorers unknown
Romford Town:
Team details unknown.

16 Apr SEL1 Away Southend Amateurs 0 – 2
Romford Town:
Team details unknown.

18 Apr AFL Away Chelmsford 3 – 4 Rutland(2) and a scrimmage!
Romford Town: Rutland;
Team details unknown.

23 Apr AFL Home Luton Clarence 3 – 3 Scorers unknown
Romford Town:
Team details unknown.

25 Apr SEL1 Home Southend Amateurs 1 – 1 Sawyer
Romford Town: Lewis;Bourne,A.W.Asater;Taylor,E.Taylor(Capt),Williams;
H.J.Sawyer,F.Walters,J.T.Lee,Harvey,A.J.Collar.

27 Apr AFL Home Tufnell Park 3 – 1 Scorers unknown
Romford Town:
Team details unknown.

30 Apr AFL Away Barnet & Alston 1 – 4 Scorer unknown
Romford Town:
Team details unknown.

n/k AFL Away Tufnell Park 0 – 6
Romford Town:
Team details unknown.

n/k AFL Home Metrogas 4 – 4 Scorers unknown
Romford Town:
Team details unknown.

* After extra time

\# Abandoned after 116 minutes due to bad light.

SUMMARY OF FIRST TEAM RESULTS OBTAINED SEASON 1913 – 14

	P	W	D	L	Goals For	Goals Ag	Pts
Athenian League	22	8	5	9	47	65	21
South Essex Lge.Div.1.	18	6	5	7	34	37	17
F.A. Challenge Cup	2	1	0	1	4	4	
F.A. Amateur Cup**	7	3	3	1	12	7	
Essex Senior Cup	1	0	0	1	2	4	
West Ham Charity Cup	1	0	0	1	1	4	
Total	52	18	13	20	100	121	

** This does not include the game against Shoeburyness Garrison which Romford Town were winning by one goal to nil, when it was abandoned.

South Essex League Division One
Final Table

	P	W	D	L	Goals For	Goals Ag	Pts
Shoeburyness Garrison	18	11	4	3	37	19	26
Barking	18	11	4	3	38	21	26
Walthamstow Grange	18	11	3	4	44	24	25
Grays Athletic	18	8	6	4	49	21	22
Romford Town	**18**	**6**	**5**	**7**	**34**	**37**	**17**
Colchester Town	18	5	5	8	27	36	15
Custom House	18	6	2	10	20	29	14
Southend Amateurs	18	5	3	10	21	33	13
Woodford Crusaders	18	5	2	11	22	48	12
Leyton#	18	4	2	12	29	53	8

Two points deducted for breach of Rules.

Athenian Football League
Final Table

	P	W	D	L	Goals For	Goals Ag	Pts
Tufnell Park	22	15	3	4	61	24	33
Luton Clarence	22	15	2	5	64	34	32
Grays Athletic	22	13	3	6	43	27	29
Metrogas	22	11	3	8	62	52	25
Enfield	22	10	3	9	52	37	23
Barnet & Alston	22	9	4	9	32	28	22
Catford Southend	22	7	7	8	35	41	21
Romford Town	**22**	**8**	**5**	**9**	**47**	**65**	**21**
Finchley	22	8	3	11	53	47	19
Hastings & St.Leonards	22	7	2	13	38	59	16
Chelmsford	22	6	1	15	32	68	13
Chesham Town	22	4	2	16	24	61	10

CUP RESULTS

F.A. Challenge Cup

Final: Burnley 1 Liverpool 0

Romford's progress: Prel.Round Home Shoeburyness Garrison 4 – 2
1st Qual Home Custom House 0 – 2

F.A. Amateur Cup

Final: Bishop Auckland 1 Northern Nomads 0

Romford's progress:

1st Qual	Home	Walthamstow Grange	2 – 0
2nd Qual	Home	Shoeburyness Garrison	1 – 0#
Replay	Home	Shoeburyness Garrison	1 – 1*
2nd Replay	Barking	Shoeburyness Garrison	0 – 0*
3rd Replay	Barking	Shoeburyness Garrison	3 – 1*
3rd Qual	Away	Woodford Crusaders	4 – 2
4th Qual	Home	Grays Athletic	0 – 0
Replay	Away	Grays Athletic	2 – 3

Essex Senior Cup

Final: Leytonstone 2 Harwich & Parkeston 2
Replay: Leytonstone 2 Harwich & Parkeston 1

Romford's progress: 3rd Round Away Ilford 2 – 4

West Ham Charity Cup

Romford's progress: Semi-Final Away Clapton 1 – 4

First Team Appearances Season 1913 – 14

A.W.Asater	34	Astley	4	B.G.Aston	17	A.Bissett	1
E.C.Bissett	1	Bourne	15	F.A.Chadders	4	Chalk	3
Channon	7	T.C.Clover	14	A.J.Collar	34	Dockrill	1
R.E.Going	1	Griffin	3	Harvey	2	Hewitt	1
A.S.Hyett	3	L.Jones	2	J.T.Lee	31	Lewis`	1
A.G.Manning	2	C.E.Manning	17	C.A.Morrison	21	F.W.Newman	27
Powell	1	A.A.Rayner	28	Rolfe	2	Rutland	1
H.J.Sawyer	29	S.C.Squier	11	C.S.Steele	1	Taylor	5
E.Taylor	32	F.Walters	12	Williams`	1	S.Wilson`	2
Total	371						

Note: Unfortunately team line-ups were missing from several match reports in the middle and the end of the season and this has affected the above summary.

Goal Scorers Season 1913 – 14

A.A.Rayner	18**	J.T.Lee	15	H.J.Sawyer	10	A.J.Collar	6
S.C.Squier	6	T.C.Clover	4	Chalk	2	C.A.Morrison	2
Rutland	2	F.Walters	2	A.W.Asater	1	E.Taylor	1
B.G.Aston	1	Griffin	1	C.S.Steele	1	Own Goals	2
Unknown	26					Total	100

** Rayner also scored the only goal in the abandoned Amateur Cup Tie against Shoeburyness Garrison.

RESERVES ("A" Team)

Match Details

27 Sept	IDL1	Home	East Ham Town	3 – 2
4 Oct	IDL1	Home	Purfleet	0 – 7
11 Oct	IDL1	Away	G.E.R. (Romford scratched)	Lost*
18 Oct	IDL1	Home	Little Ilford	3 – 1
25 Oct	IDL1	Home	G.E.R.	0 – 1
	EJC1R			Bye
15 Nov	EJC2R	Home	East Ham Town	1 – 8
29 Nov	IDL1	Away	Forest Gate	0 – 2
6 Dec	IDL1	Away	Wanstead	1 – 2
13 Dec	Frdly	Home	Old Kinsonians	2 – 0
3 Jan	IDL1	Home	Ilford "A"	1 – 1##
24 Jan	IDL1	Away	Ilford "A"	1 – 2
21 Feb	IDL1	Home	St. Saviours (Romford scratched)	Lost**
7 Mar	IDL1	Away	St. Saviour's	3 – 5 Rolfe,centre forward(2)
21 Mar	IDL1	Home	Forest Gate	2 – 4##
28 Mar	IDL1	Away	East Ham Town	1 – 4
10 Apr	IDL1	Home	Wanstead	0 – 3
11 Apr	IDL1	Away	Little Ilford	2 – 3
18 Apr	IDL1	Away	Purfleet (Purfleet scratched)	won***

* Match awarded to G.E.R.
** Match awarded to St. Saviours
*** Match awarded to Romford Town
Played at Roneo Ground, Hornchurch Road.
Note: Some matches were awarded to one team as the opponents scratched or failed to arrive.
No goals were allocated and the league tables reflect these decisions.

SUMMARY OF RESERVE TEAM RESULTS SEASON 1913 – 14

	P	W	D	L	Goals For	Goals Ag	Pts
Ilford & District League	16	3	1	12	17	37	7
Essex Junior Cup	1	0	0	1	1	8	
Friendly Match	1	1	0	0	2	0	
Total	18	4	1	13	20	45	

Ilford & District Football League Division One
Final Table

	P	W	D	L	Goals For	Goals Ag	Pts
St. Saviours	16	12	3	1	46	16	27
G.E.Railway	16	7	6	3	32	26	20
Forest Gate	16	8	3	5	40	26	19
Little Ilford	16	7	4	5	38	28	18
Wanstead	16	7	3	6	29	42	17
East Ham Town	16	7	1	8	25	34	15
Purfleet	16	5	1	10	20	31	11
Ilford "A"	16	4	2	10	22	38	8*
Romford Town "A"	**16**	**3**	**1**	**12**	**17**	**37**	**7**

* Two points deducted for breach of rules.

CUP RESULTS

Essex Junior Cup

Final: 1st East Lancashire Regt. "A" 6 Southend Amateur "A" 0

Romford's progress: 1st Round Bye
2nd Round Home East Ham Town 1 – 8

Post-Season Summary Season 1913 – 14

Romford's season opened with a South Essex League defeat at the hands of Custom House, by one goal to nil. Disaster followed in the Athenian League with a 7-2 thrashing by Metrogas. It appears that Romford may have run out of gas! A week later they won away to Chesham Town, also in the Athenian League, and then achieved some much-needed success in the F.A. Cup Preliminary Round by defeating Shoeburyness Garrison 4-2. A week later Romford were well beaten by Clapton at the Spotted Dog Ground in the West Ham Charity Cup Semi-Final. The third cup tie in a row saw Romford defeat Walthamstow Grange in the Amateur Cup by two goals to nil.

Four more cup ties followed this success, but the first was a disappointment as Romford went out of the F.A. Cup due to a 2-0 defeat at home to Custom House. On 18th October Romford were defeating Shoeburyness Garrison 1-0 in the Amateur Cup when the game was abandoned due to bad light in extra time. In the replay the following Saturday, at the end of normal time with the two teams tied at one goal each, both clubs agreed that it was too dark for extra time, but the referee blew the whistle to start the extra period and then he immediately blew again to call it off.

The following Wednesday, 29th October, the two teams tried again for the third time, at Barking, but the game again ended in a draw after extra time. Three days later Romford lost 4-3 away to Enfield in the Athenian League. The next encounter with Shoeburyness Garrison took place at Barking two days later, on Monday 3rd November, when the soldiers got off to a great start with Driver Talfourd scoring in the third minute. Romford, however, were not downhearted, and went on to win by three goals to one. The following Saturday Romford made further progress in the competition by virtue of a 4-2 victory away to Woodford Crusaders.

Next, Romford had three successive fixtures against old rivals Grays Athletic. The first was a home Athenian League game which Romford won easily by four goals to one, and the following week, again at home, they had to settle for a 0–0 draw in the Amateur Cup. A week later Grays won the replay by three goals to two. Romford then lost 1-0 to Chelmsford in the Athenian League. They then achieved two victories by two goals to one in the South Essex League, away at Leyton and Grays Athletic.

A 0–0 draw at Hastings and St. Leonards in the Athenian League was followed by another two games against Grays Athletic. The first of these was on Christmas Day at Grays, which was lost by three goals to two in the Athenian League, and on Boxing Day Romford gained revenge with a one goal to nil win at home in the South Essex League. Romford rounded off the year with a South Essex League game against Barking which they lost 2-0. At about this time Romford's Clover left the club to join Grays Athletic.

Romford started off the New Year with three South Essex League fixtures, the first of which was lost at Woodford Crusaders by three goals to two. Wing half Rayner moved up to centre forward for the next two games and scored a hat-trick in each when Romford beat Woodford Crusaders in the return fixture by four goals to two and then overcome Custom House by four goals to one. Rayner was on the mark the following week when Romford beat Barnet Alston 3-2 in the Athenian League.

A week later he again scored, and Lee got a second goal, but Romford had to bow out away to Ilford by four goals to two in the Essex Senior Cup. Next came two Athenian League games, the first being a four goal to one beating at Finchley. Romford faced a dilemma for the second game as they had no goalkeeper available. Arthur Asater agreed to fill the position, and Romford defeated Chesham by two goals to one. Chesham arrived with the same shirts as Romford and had to send out to purchase different ones, causing a late kickoff, and they were forced to wear what can only be described as white vests.

The next South Essex League appointment was on 21st February when Romford were away to Walthamstow Grange. In a best-forgotten game Romford surrendered by two goals to seven! Romford then got an Athenian League point at home to Catford Southend, and followed this with a 6-3 victory over Leyton in the South Essex League. Romford then collected four Athenian League points from Enfield and Finchley, but in between met with defeat at the hands of Shoeburyness Garrison in the South Essex League.

Next, also in the South Essex League, Romford had a thrilling 4-4 draw with Walthamstow Grange, only for this to be followed with another disaster. For reasons unknown, Romford fielded a reserve team for the away Athenian League fixture against Luton Clarence and were thrashed by eight goals to nil.

A week later came two more South Essex League games, first a defeat by Colchester Town, and then a draw with Shoeburyness Garrison. Three more drawn games followed, before the team secured another Athenian League victory in a five goals to four thriller against Hastings & St.Leonards.

Romford then lost an away South Essex League game to Southend Amateurs, and in another high-scoring game lost by three goals to four against Chelmsford in the Athenian League. Two drawn games followed, against Luton Clarence and Southend Amateurs.

Romford managed a surprising 3-1 victory at home over league champions Tufnell Park, but then suffered two very heavy Athenian League defeats away to Barnet & Alston (1-4) and Tufnell Park (0-6). The team ended the season with another high scoring drawn game against Metrogas, which finished 4-4. Romford finished in a creditable mid-table position in the Athenian League and a similar position in the South Essex League. They had a good run in the Amateur Cup, but fared badly in the other cup competitions.

The reserves had a very poor season, being beaten in their first game in the Essex Junior Cup and finishing in last place in the Ilford & District League, winning only three of their sixteen games.

Annual General Meeting

(as reported in the *Essex Times,*Wednesday 17th June 1914))

The annual meeting of the Romford Town Football Club was held on Monday evening, 15th June 1914 at The Rising Sun Hotel, Romford. Mr.J.Bassett, president, occupied the chair and there was a fairly large attendance. Mr.O.C.Rolfe, hon.secretary, presented his first annual report, saying he was in the happy position to state that from being the "wooden spoonists" of last year, the club had secured places in both the Athenian League and the South Essex League more worthy of a club that had the traditions of the Romford club as regarded cup-ties.

In the English Cup they defeated Shoeburyness Garrison at the first time of asking, only to lose to Custom House in the succeeding round by 2-0. In the Amateur Cup they had a great struggle with the soldiers from Shoeburyness, drawing with them three times before they eventually defeated the soldiers at Barking 3-1. He regretted that, although they won, they suffered financially through the mid-week matches. Following on in the same competition they defeated Woodford Crusaders 4-2, and after a drawn game with Grays Athletic they lost in the replay 3-2. In the Essex Senior Cup they were unable to repeat their success of two former years, for they were drawn against their old opponents and last year's winners – Ilford – who defeated them 4-2..

In the Athenian League they played 22 matches, winning 8, drawing 5, and losing 9. They scored 47 goals to 65. They eventually finished the season eighth out of twelve clubs, this being an improvement on last year. In the South Essex League they played 18 matches, winning 6, drawing 5, and losing 7. They scored 34 goals against 37, finishing up fifth from the top out of ten clubs. In all they played 52 matches, winning 18, losing 20, drawing 13, and one being abandoned. J.T.Lee and A.A.Rayner were the most consistent scorers. Owing to the repeated draws in the cup-ties it was necessary to arrange several mid-week matches, in which, although the club was successful in gaining many points, the gate materially suffered. He was greatly indebted to the committee, and particularly Mr. Heard, without whom he would undoubtedly experienced great difficulty. He thanked them all for the courtesy during his first year of office as hon.secretary.

Mr.C.T.Heard, hon.treasurer, presented the statement of accounts, which showed receipts amounting to £280.12s.9d., including gate receipts £171.11s.6d., and share of gates £48.9s.6d. The expenditure amounted to £280.4s.0d. and unpaid accounts bring the total to £297.7s.5d., or a loss on the season's working of £16.14s.8d. Special donations per Mr.W.D.Matthews towards outstanding accounts for seasons 1911-12 and 1912-13 amounted to £48.6s.0d. thus reducing the amount from £63.6s.0d to £15. The chief items of expenditure were: Players' travelling expenses £104.17s.8d.: Players' Teas £58.7s.2d.: Rent £25.0s.0d: loss on "A" team, £11.18s.8d.: and printing £10.18s.0d. The report and statement of accounts were unanimously adopted, without discussion.

Mr.Bassett said he should retire from the presidency, as he considered the club should have a younger man as its head. Mr.W.D.Matthews refered to the improved financial position, owing to the generosity of those who had so considerably reduced the adverse balance, and said he hoped Mr.Bassett would retain the presidency and see the club out of debt. Mr.Bassett said he intended to retire, but would still support the club as he had done in the past.

Mr.J.Tetchner supported what had been said by Mr.Matthews; and Mr.G.A.Smith appealed to Mr.Bassett to re-consider his decision. Mr.Bassett said they would see him just as often at matches, be he must retire from the presidency. On the proposition of Mr.C.T.Heard, seconded by Mr.Bassett, Mr.W.D.Matthews was unanimously elected president of the club. Mr.Matthews, in responding, said it had been a labour of love to do what he had done in the way of getting donations, because he met with such a ready response. He would do his very best for the club in the high office of president. (Hear, hear).

Messrs.J.Bassett,M.B.Larkin,C.Manning and F.W.Jeffes were elected Vice-Presidents. Mr.O.C.Rolfe was re-elected hon.secretary, and Mr.C.T.Heard, hon.treasurer. Mr.E.Taylor was re-elected captain and Mr.A.Asater vice-captain. The following were elected on the committee: Messrs.G.A.Smith, E.Dowsing, S.Dowsing, S.Stebbings, W.G.Wenn, L.Fletcher, C.E.Manning, J.Tetchner and C.Harvey. Messrs.E.J.Wallis and F.W.Jeffes were re-elected hon.auditors. Mr.S.Stebbings proposed, and Mr.J.Tetchner seconded, a vote of thanks to the hon.secretary and hon.treasurer. The proposition was carried unanimously.

Mr.Tetchner asked whether the committee were empowered to withdraw from the Athenian League without calling a general meeting. Mr.Matthews said the committee had full power either to enter or withdraw from the League. Mr.Heard referred to the rules, and said they gave the committee the requisite power. Mr.Tetchner said he was perfectly satisfied with the information on the subject. Mr.Heard said the club was entered for the London League and the South Essex League, and consequently would have 32 League matches to play next season. The London League would be more beneficial to them financially than the Athenian League.

Messrs. C.E.Manning and W.G.Wenn were elected as a Finance Committee to act with the hon. treasurer. Discussion took place on a suggestion that an "A" team should be formed. Eventually it was decided to try to secure a purely local "A" team. Mr.Heard said it would be possible to enter the "A" team in the Second Division of the South Essex League. Mr.C.Mayer was elected to assist the Honorary Secretary in the work connected with the "A" (reserve Team); and it was decided to enter the team in the South Essex League Second Division, the Essex Junior Cup Competition and the Ilford Charity Cup Competition.

Season 1914 – 15

ROMFORD TOWN

President: Mr.W.D.Matthews

Honorary Secretary: Mr.O.C.Rolfe, 2, Kyme Road, Romford

Over Christmas time appointed Mr.C.W.Mayer, 23,Cromer Road,Romford.

Hon. Treasurer: Mr.C.T.Heard

Committee: Messrs.G.A.Smith,E.Dowsing,S.Dowsing,S.Stebbings, W.G.Wenn,L.Fletcher,C.E.Manning,J.Tetchner and C.Harvey

Captain: E.Taylor **Vice-Captain:** A.Asater

Hon. Auditors: F.W.Jeffes and E.J.Wallis

Headquarters: Rising Sun Hotel, Romford **Ground:** Shoulder of Mutton Field, Hornchurch Road, Romford

COMPETITIONS ENTERED

South Essex League Division One
London League Amateur Division
F.A. Challenge Cup
F.A. Amateur Cup
Essex Senior Cup

South Essex League Division Two
Ilford Hospital Cup
Essex Junior Cup (Competition suspended)

Britain declared war on Germany on 4th August 1914 following Germany's invasion of Belgium. The Athenian League disbanded for the duration of the war, and Romford Town Football Club reverted to Junior Status competing in the South Essex League. They also competed in the London League Amateur Division. The only Club of Senior Status in the area was the G.E.Railway (Romford) side.

Trial Match (reported in the *Essex Times,* Wednesday 2nd September 1914)

The Romford team on Saturday 29th August had a trial match on the Cosy Corner enclosure, many local men being given a trial. Very few of last season's players were to be seen, Collar, A.G.Manning and Graves only taking part. Two teams were got together by the Management, Red and White versus Blue and White, and some good football was seen, the old players showing to advantage. Potter at centre half, and Bramble at outside left, for the Blues, showed considerable skill. Result: Blue and White 3, Red and White 2.

Match Results

5 Sept	LLAD	Home	Page Green Old Boys	2 – 6
12 Sept	LLAD	Away	Walthamstow Grange	1 – 1
19 Sept	LLAD	Home	Walthamstow Grange	2 – 0
26 Sept	LLAD	Home	Charlton Athletic	1 – 2 # Stone
3 Oct	FACPR	Home	Woolwich	w/o

10 Oct FAC1Q Away Walthamstow Grange 0 – 3

24 Oct LLAD Away Charlton Athletic 0 – 2 #

31 Oct SEL1 Home Grays Athletic 4 – 0 Collar,Bennett,Stone(2)
Romford Town: Lewis;A.W.Asater,Bourne;C.E.Manning,E.Taylor(Capt),A.C.Potter;
A.S.Hyett,Stone,Bennett,Plaistow,A.J.Collar.

7 Nov LLAD Away Grays Athletic P – P

7 Nov SEL1 Away Grays Athletic 2 – 9 Bennett(2)
Attendance: 1,500
Romford Town: H.A.Bown;Bourne,A.W.Asater;Rolfe,E.Taylor(Capt),A.C.Potter;
A.Moore,Stone,Bennett,Middleton,A.J.Collar.

14 Nov LLAD Home Catford (Southend) 1 – 4 Stone

21 Nov AC1Q Away Woodford Crusaders 1 – 3 Stone

5 Dec SEL1 Home Walthamstow Grange 1 – 1 Scorer unknown

12 Dec Frdly Home Sportsmen's Battalion 0 – 1
Romford Town: Wright;Bourne,A.W.Asater(Capt);H.C.Bear,A.C.Potter,Chapman;
Finch,Stone,Bennett,Plaistow,A.J.Collar.

19 Dec SEL1 Away Woodford Crusaders 2 – 4 Scorers unknown

25 Dec LLAD Home Grays Athletic P – P Fog

26 Dec LLAD Away Grays Athletic P – P See friendly match below

26 Dec Frdly Away Grays Athletic 0 – 18##

16 Jan SEL1 Home Woodford Crusaders 1 – 1 E.Jones

30 Jan ESC1R Away Newportonians 3 – 0 Bennett,Stone,Potter

6 Feb LLAD Home Barking 2 – 2 Bear,Stone

13 Feb LLAD Away Custom House 2 – 6### Manning, one unknown

13 Feb SEL1 Away Custom House 2 – 6### Manning, one unknown

20 Feb SEL1 Home Custom House 0 – 1###
Romford Town: Dockrill;A.W.Asater(Capt),Bourne;H.C.Bear,A.C.Potter,Chapman;
Brown,Stone,Bennett,C.E.Manning,A.J.Collar.

20 Feb LLAD Home Custom House 0 – 1###
Romford Town: Dockrill;A.W.Asater(Capt),Bourne;H.C.Bear,A.C.Potter,Chapman;
Brown,Stone,Bennett,C.E.Manning,A.J.Collar.

27 Feb ESC2R Home Grays Athletic 0 – 0*
Romford Town: Dockrill;A.W.Asater(Capt),Bourne;H.C.Bear,A.C.Potter,Chapman;
Plaistow,Stone,Bennett,C.E.Manning,A.J.Collar.

6 Mar ESCRP Away Grays Athletic 0 – 8
Romford Town: Dockrill;A.Asater(Capt),Bourne;Chapman,A.C.Potter,Bissett;
Brown,Stone,H.C.Bear,Bennett,A.J.Collar.

13 Mar LLAD Home Finchley Petrels 4 – 1 Manning(2),Bissett,Stone

20 Mar LLAD Away Finchley Petrels 1 – 5 Stone

27 Mar LLAD Away Barking 2 – 1 Stone,Bennett

3 Apr LLAD Away Catford (Southend) Lost**

19 Apr LLAD Away Grays Athletic 0 – 11

22 Apr	LLAD	Home	Grays Athletic	1 – 8	Scorer unknown
24 Apr	SEL1	Away	Walthamstow Grange	0 – 4	
1 May	LLAD	Away	Page Green Old Boys	0 – 2	

Charlton Athletic withdrew from the league and record expunged.
Abandoned
These games were played as double headers, counting for points in both the South Essex and London Leagues.
* After extra time.
**Romford failed to appear , points were awarded to Catford.

SUMMARY OF FIRST TEAM RESULTS OBTAINED SEASON 1914 – 15

					Goals		
	P	W	D	L	For	Ag	Pts
South Essex League Div. One	8	1	2	5	12	26	4
London League Amateur Div.	14	3	2	9	18	48	8
F.A. Challenge Cup	1	0	0	1	0	3	
F.A. Amateur Cup	1	0	0	1	1	3	
Essex Senior Cup	3	1	1	1	3	8	
Friendly Matches	1	0	0	1	0	1	
Total	28	5	5	18	34	89	

Note: Two games were played against Custom House on successive weeks in February. Both these matches were played for South Essex League and London League points, and the actual number of games **played** in the season was 26! This sort of thing was not appreciated by the leagues concerned.

This summary does not include the Boxing Day game against Grays Athletic which was abandoned late on.

South Essex League Division One
Final Table

					Goals		
	P	W	D	L	For	Ag	Pts
Grays Athletic	8	7	0	1	17	6	14
Custom House	8	4	1	3	10	9	9
Walthamstow Grange	8	3	2	3	11	3	8
Woodford Crusaders	8	1	3	4	7	13	5
Romford Town	**8**	**1**	**2**	**5**	**12**	**26**	**4**

The Council of the South Essex League have decided after careful consideration that in deference to the unanimous wish of the clubs still able to muster sufficient players the competition should be continued. Colchester Town retired from the competition.

London Football League Amateur Division
Final Table

					Goals		
	P	W	D	L	For	Ag	Pts
Grays Athletic	12	11	1	0	53	13	23
Walthamstow Grange	12	8	2	2	37	9	18
Catford Southend	14	6	3	5	25	29	15
Page Green Old Boys	14	6	2	6	29	32	14
Custom House	14	5	3	6	27	25	13
Barking	14	3	3	8	28	44	9
Finchley	14	4	0	10	26	43	8
Romford Town	**14**	**3**	**2**	**9**	**18**	**48**	**8**

Grays Athletic and Walthamstow Grange did not play each other at home or away and Charlton Athletic withdrew from the league and their record was expunged.

CUP RESULTS SEASON 1914 – 15

F.A. Challenge Cup

Final: Sheffield United 3 Chelsea 0

Romford's progress:	Prel.Round	Home	Woolwich	w/o
	1st Qual	Away	Walthamstow Grange	0 – 3

F.A. Amateur Cup

Final: Clapton 1 Bishop Auckland 0

Romford's progress:	1st Qual	Away	Woodford Crusaders	1 – 3

Essex Senior Cup

Final: Grays Athletic 2 Clapton 1

Romford's progress:	1st Round	Away	Newportonians	3 – 0
	2nd Round	Home	Grays Athletic	0 – 0*
	Replay	Away	Grays Athletic	0 – 8

First Team Appearances and Goal Scorers Season 1914 – 15

A.W.Asater	H.C.Bear	Bennett	Bissett
Bourne	H.A.Bown	Brown	Chapman
A.J.Collar	Finch	A.S.Hyett	Lewis
C.E.Manning	Middleton	A.Moore	Plaistow
A.C.Potter	Rolfe	Stone	E.Taylor
Wright			

No doubt due to the War, sports reports in the local press were very sparse and the lack of details makes it impossible to compile any tables for match appearances or goal scorers. It is known however that the above named definitely played for the first team at some time during the season.

RESERVES ("A" Team)

Match Details

12 Sept	SEL2	Home	Walthamstow Grange "A"	3 – 1
19 Sept	SEL2	Away	Bromley Reliance	3 – 5
26 Sept	SEL2	Away	Walthamstow St. Andrews	0 – 6
3 Oct	SEL2	Home	G.E.R.	0 – 1
24 Oct	SEL2	Away	Barking "A"	0 – 4
31 Oct	IHC1R	Home	Little Ilford Congregational	w/o
7 Nov	SEL2	Home	St. Andrews	P – P
14 Nov	SEL2	Away	G.E.R.	1 – 2
21 Nov	SEL2	Away	Walthamstow Grange "A"	P – P
28 Nov	IHC2R	Away	Plashet Park	0 – 4#
n/k	SEL2	n/k	Grays/Walth.St.Andrews	0 – 8##

\# Abandoned in 89th minute!
\## Arising out of the league table on 5th December, it is obvious that Romford must have lost a further game by eight goals to nil and it could only have been against one of these teams.

Romford Town "A" withdrew from the League and their record was expunged

South Essex League Divison Two
(Up to and including 5th Dec)

					Goals		
	P	W	D	L	For	Ag	Pts
Grays Athletic "A"	6	6	0	0	21	2	12
Walthamstow St. Andr.	3	3	0	0	17	0	6
Bromley Reliance	3	2	0	1	9	6	4
Barking "A"	4	2	0	2	6	10	4
G.E.Railway	5	2	0	3	5	10	4
Romford Town "A"	**7**	**1**	**0**	**6**	**7**	**27**	**2**
Walthamstow Grange "A"	4	0	0	4	2	12	0

15 Jan Romford Town withdrew from South Essex League. Record expunged

South Essex League Divison Two
Final Table

					Goals		
	P	W	D	L	For	Ag	Pts
Grays Athletic "A"	6	6	0	0	26	1	12
Barking "A"	5	2	2	1	4	11	7
Great Eastern Railway	6	0	3	3	2	14	3
Walthamstow Grange "A"	5	0	3	2	1	7	2

Grays Athletic won the championship for the second season in succession.

Note: In addition to Romford Town "A", Bromley Reliance and Walthamstow St.Andrews must also have withdrawn from the league at some time during the season!

CUP RESULTS

Ilford Hospital Cup

1st Round Home Little Ilford Congregational w/o
2nd Round Away Plashet Park 0 – 4#

Abandoned after 89 minutes.

Essex County F.A. Junior Challenge Cup

Competition suspended by the County Association due to the War.

Post-Season Summary Season 1914 – 15

Romford commenced activities with a trial match but there were very few of the previous season's players present. The first competitive game of the season was a London League match at home to Page Green Old Boys who handed out a 6-2 thrashing for the locals. An away draw and a home win against Walthamstow Grange were encouraging before a fourth London league game saw Charlton Athletic as the visitors. Romford played the first 20 minutes without their captain Eddie Taylor and were already two goals behind when he appeared. Romford managed a goal but were unable to equalise.

Romford were due to entertain Woolwich in the F.A. Cup on 3rd October, but their opponents withdrew and Romford were safely into the next round with a walkover. A week later they met Walthamstow Grange away in the 1st Qualifying Round of the F.A. Cup but were soundly beaten by three goals to nil. Next up was another game against Charlton Athletic who beat them by two goals to nil. The two Charlton results were expunged from the league table following the withdrawal of that club later in the season.

Commencing their South Essex League programme, Romford scored a rare and stunning victory over local rivals Grays Athletic, by four goals to nil. The following week the return fixture was played before 1,500 spectators at Grays, who duly triumphed by nine goals to two! On 14th November Romford were again well beaten, this time at home to Catford (Southend) by four goals to one in a London League game.

Struggling to put out a good side, this became a terrible period for the club as they failed to win another game until 30th January when they defeated Newportonians in the Essex Senior Cup by three goals to nil. Prior to this the Christmas Day home match against Grays Athletic was postponed due to fog, and with conditions much the same the following day only six Romford players and eight Grays Athletic players turned up. The League game was postponed and a friendly match was played, although Grays were not very charitable and they were winning by eighteen goals to nil when the match was called off!

The next game was against Woodford Crusaders and a valuable point was obtained despite Romford fielding only eight men. Then came the aforementioned Essex Senior Cup tie against Newportonians, followed by a home London League game against Barking and a valuable two all draw earned a point.

With the season moving on it was becoming difficult to fit in all the games, and two matches against Custom House were played for both London League and South Essex League points, something which the two leagues were not keen on. Romford were not too happy either as Custom House beat them 6-2 at home (Romford only had nine men) and 1-0 at Romford.

Then came the Essex Senior Cup again, and against all the odds Romford secured a 0-0 draw against old rivals Grays Athletic after extra time. The following week Grays put things straight, from their point of view, with an 8-0 hiding for Romford. Romford then had two vastly contrasting games against Finchley Petrels in the London League with Romford winning by four goals to one at home but then losing five one at Finchley! A week later on 27th March two valuable London League points were obtained with a 2-1 victory over Barking.

The month of April offered no respite. The club failed to provide a team for the return fixture at Catford (Southend), and the match was awarded to their rivals. The next two games were against Grays Athletic, who handed out their usual resounding defeats – by eleven goals to nil at Grays and eight goals to one at Romford in London League games. The season ended with two further defeats, against Walthamstow Grange and Page Green Old Boys.

Despite the lack of playing members, mainly of course due to the war, Romford did commence a league programme in the South Essex League Division Two, starting with a 3-1 victory over Walthamstow Grange reserves. The team struggled on until withdrawing from the league on 15th January 1915. Their final game was in fact on 30th November, when they were beaten 4-0 in the Ilford Hospital Cup away to Plashet Park. This tie was in fact abandoned one and a half minutes from time, but was never replayed. A couple of league games were postponed prior to this, probably due to Romford failing to field a team, but this was of no consequence at their record was expunged from the table following their withdrawal in January.

A year later, on Sunday 20th February 1916, Romford Football Club's pavilion on the Shoulder of Mutton Field was set on fire, the blaze being deliberately started under the joists. A considerable effort was made to minimise the damage.

WOMEN'S FOOTBALL DURING WORLD WAR ONE

Although the vast majority of men's football in Romford and surrounding areas had ceased due to the war, the game was now being played, in front of large crowds, by young women employed in local factories. The following match was reported in the *Essex Times*:

FOOTBALL IN AID OF BLINDED HEROES

EASTER MONDAY 2ND APRIL 1917

At the Great Eastern Railway ground, Romford Station

ROMFORD LADIES 0 HOFFMANN'S LADIES 0

A crowd of more than five hundred spectators was attracted to the Great Eastern Railway Club's ground, Romford, on Easter Monday afternoon, to witness a ladies' football match between teams from Mr.H.N.Brock's Blouse Factory, Mawney Road and the Works of the Hoffmann Manufacturing Company, Chelmsford. In addition to the spectators on the field large numbers occupied other points of vantage, the upper part of the railway slope in particular being inconveniently crowded.

The match was arranged for the benefit of the funds of St. Dunstan's Home for blinded soldiers and sailors, Regents Park. The actual money taken at the gate amounted to five pounds three shillings.

Owing to the fierce snowstorm that prevailed during the latter part of the afternoon, it was not possible to finish the match, to the great disappointment of the players and spectators alike. Although no goals were scored the game was distinctly in favour of the Romford Ladies who played with much skill and showed that they had taken full advantage of the instruction given during the short time they had been at practise. Their exhibition of football did great credit to them and to Mr.Alf.Hunwicks (a former Romford team player), their trainer. The healthy and athletic appearance of the girls excited much favourable comment and was a tribute to the excellent conditions under which they work in the commodious and well appointed factory recently erected by Mr. Brock.

On points the home team were the winners as they pressed their opponents throughout and had much the best of the play. The home team was captained by Miss Starling, who lined up as follows: Goal, Miss.Curtis; Right Back Miss Starling (Captain), Left Back Miss Fletcher, Centre Half Miss Carstairs, Centre Forward Miss Smith, Right Half Miss Burrell, Left Half Miss H. Curtis, Outside Right Miss Weatherall, Inside Left Miss Dack, Inside Right Miss Creasey, Outside Left Miss Carr. Referee Mr. Alf. Hunwicks.

After the match tea was served in the pavilion on the ground. Unfortunately the visitors had to leave early to catch their train to Chelmsford. Mrs. Hunwicks had charge of the fine catering arrangements.

A further game was arranged between both teams at Chelmsford:

21st April, 1917

HOFFMANN'S LADIES 2 ROMFORD LADIES 3

Three years into the war, Romford supporters were shocked to hear that Arthur 'Diddy' Jones, the club's star striker (and still its highest goalscorer even to this day) had been killed in action. He was a corporal in the Royal Warwickshire Regiment, and his service number was 260114. For more on his life, see page 339).

The ***Essex Times*** obituary read as follows:

ARTHUR EDWIN "DIDDY" JONES

It is with deep regret that we announce the death of Corporal Arthur E. Jones on August 29th 1917 of wounds received in action in France. The deceased, who was 37 years of age, was badly wounded on August the 27th and his untimely end will be deplored by all Essex footballers. Without doubt he was the most prominent footballer in the county and was the idol of the Romford crowd, by whom he was affectionally known as "Diddy". As an amateur forward he was probably without an equal for his shooting, and many visiting goal keepers have reason to remember his piledrivers.

On many occasions he represented his County and was considered a valuable acquisition. Other clubs that Jones played for were Romford St. Andrews, Mawney Institute, Ilford and Luton, as well as having a trial with Portsmouth. Despite his prowess he was of an unassuming nature and he died as he would have wished, a hero's death.

When he joined up he had an opportunity of joining a unit removed from the firing line, but characteristic of Jones he remarked. "No, if my country is in for a scrap I am going to be in it". Prior to joining up, Diddy was a painstaking member of the Romford Division of the Essex Special Constabulary.

Much sympathy is felt for his brother and sisters in their bereavement. The Matron of No. 4 C.C.S. Hospital writes:

" 29.8.17. I am very grieved to tell you that Corporal A.E.Jones, 260114 R.W. Regiment was very badly wounded in the leg and hand and although everything possible was done for him he passed away quite peacefully at 2.10 a.m. this morning. He was too ill to realize he was dying and was unconscious at the last. I told him during the afternoon that I was writing to you, and he said to give you his love. He will be buried with Military Honours and be with many of his comrades. The graves are very well looked after and his name and number will be put on the cross with much sympathy".

The trophy-winning Mawney Institute team of 1911-12. Arthur Jones sits behind the shield
(Location of original photograph currently unknown)

The grave of Arthur Jones in Dozinghem Military cemetery, Belgium.
Courtesy of the British War Graves website www.britishwargraves.co.uk

This poem recounts how a company of the East Surrey Regiment dribbled four footballs, the gift of their fallen captain William Nevill, a mile and a quarter into the enemy trenches.

THE GAME

On through the hail of slaughter
Where gallant comrades fall
Where blood is poured like water
They drive the trickling ball.
The fear of death before them
Is but an empty name
True to the land that bore them
The Surreys played the game.

On without check or falter
They press towards the goal
Who falls on freedoms alter
The Lord shall rest his soul
But still they charged the living
Into that hell of flame
Ungrudging in their giving
Our soldiers played the game

And now at last is ended
The task so well begun
Though savagely defended
The lines of death are won.
In this their hour of glory
A deathless place they claim
In England's splendid story
The men who played the game.

("Touchstone," July 1916)

The war ended on 11th November 1918, but just three days after the Armistice another well-known Romford player and former captain fell victim, having been invalided out of the army three months previously. This was 31 year-old Percy John Moore, nicknamed 'Joey'. Son of Nicholas T. Moore, a railway clerk, Percy was a millwright by trade. At the time of the split in 1909 he had joined most of the other players in moving to the new club, Romford United.

During the war he served as a Corporal in the Royal Field Artillery (service number 155305) before being transferred to the Labour Corps (314190). A newspaper obituary gives his cause of death as heart disease, but it must have been a consequence of his war service as his name appears in the Commonwealth War Graves Commission register.

On 19th November Percy's body was removed from his parents' house, at 9 Princes Road, for burial at Crow Lane Cemetery. If he was awarded a military funeral we can imagine the scene as Romfordians took the opportunity of grieving for their own loved ones killed in the war and buried far away.

Season 1919 – 20

In 1919, with four years having passed since Romford Town last kicked a football in anger, it was decided, under the prompting of Mr J.H.Little, to get the club up and running again. He also became the club's secretary. It would need a great effort to restore the interest and enthusiasm which was bestowed upon the town's football club in bygone days. The main problem was that their pre-war ground along Hornchurch Road (now South Street) had been vandalised and then turned over to allotments, with the railings removed to aid the war effort.

It brought about a frantic effort to secure a suitable ground. The officials eventually found a pitch on the Crown Field, London Road (alongside the Crown Public House), but not being fully enclosed it left them no option but to restart proceedings as a junior club in the Romford & District Football League. The club would, however, continue to hold its meetings at the Rising Sun by Romford Station, as it had done before the war.

It was realised that the new club would face stiff opposition, in the desire to attract a good following, from the Great Eastern Railway team who were to compete in the Spartan League against such worthy opposition as St. Albans City and Wycombe Wanderers. Nevertheless, those brave officials decided to go ahead. The team succeeded in winning the Romford & District League title at the first attempt, but sadly the local folk were naturally attracted to the higher grade of football being played across the town. Some of the crowds at Romford's home games were recorded as a 'small gathering'.

ROMFORD TOWN, 1919

Original Post Card photograph dated 13 September 1919
Authors' collection (originators unknown)

H.Everitt,J.Johnson,W.Clements,C.Heard(Jnr),W.Kimber
A.Evans,A.R.Bear,H.Girling
T.Evans,F.Heard,F.Graves,L.Hooper,H.Dennis

The names are as written on the back of the card. C.Heard (son of the former secretary) was the goalkeeper, and the missing name appears to refer to the soldier on the right

Season 1919 – 20

ROMFORD TOWN

Vice-President: Mr.T.Fletcher

Chairman: Mr.C.T.Heard **Hon.Secretary:** Mr.J.H.Little, "Brent Tor", Brentwood Road, Romford

Club colours: black and blue striped jerseys, white knickers

Headquarters: Rising Sun Hotel, Romford **Ground:** Crown Field, London Road, Romford

COMPETITIONS ENTERED
Romford & District Football League Division One
Essex Junior Cup
Romford Charity Cup

Match Results

4 Oct	RDL	Home	Romford Ivyleafers "A"	4 – 0	
11 Oct	RDL	Home	Brentwood Orient	6 – 0	
25 Oct	RDL	Away	Hornchurch DDSS & United	2 – 1	
1 Nov	EJC1R		Bye		
8 Nov	RDL	Home	Emerson Park	5 – 0	
15 Nov	EJC2R	Home	Eagle Park	3 – 2	
22 Nov	RDL	Home	Squirrels Heath "A"	3 - 1	
29 Nov	RDL	Away	Roneo Athletic "A"	7 – 0	
6 Dec	EJC3R	Home	Roneo Athletic	2 – 3 #	Bear(pen),Hooper

Romford Town: C.Heard;

13 Dec	RDL	Away	Brentwood Orient	1 – 2	
20 Dec	RDL	Home	Eagle Park	2 – 1	
27 Dec	RDL	Home	Roneo Athletic "A"	5 – 0	
10 Jan	RDL	Home	Hornchurch DDSS & United	2 – 1	
17 Jan	RDL	Away	GER	2 – 0	
24 Jan	RCC2R	Away	Hornchurch DDSS & United	1 – 2	
31 Jan	Frdly	Away	Eagle Park	1 – 2	
7 Feb	RDL	Away	Emerson Park	3 – 0 ##	
28 Feb	RDL	Away	Romford Baptists	2 – 0	
6 Mar	RDL	Away	Squirrels Heath "A"	3 – 2	
13 Mar	RDL	Home	Chadwell Heath Ivyleafers	2 – 1	
3 Apr	RDL	Away	Romford Ivyleafers "A"	1 – 1	
10 Apr	RDL	Home	Romford Baptist	3 – 2	
17 Apr	RDL	Home	GER	9 – 0	

24 Apr RDL Away Chadwell Heath Ivyleafers 5 – 2

1 May RDL Away Eagle Park 3 – 2 A.H.Bear(2), one unknown
Romford Town: C.Heard;S.Tetchner,W.Clements;A.Evans,A.H.Bear,Haviland;
T.Evans,F.Graves,T.Saggers,A.R.Bear,R.Bear.
Referee: Mr.H.Chapman.

\# Played at Roneo Ground
\## Played at Romford

ROMFORD TOWN ARE LEAGUE CHAMPIONS
(as reported in the *Brentwood Recorder*, Friday 7th May 1920)

On Saturday 1st May Romford Town defeated Eagle Park (present Holders of the Romford Charity Cup) in the Romford and District League by three goals to two and those who had the fortune to witness the final of that cup will readily agree the the Romford Town team had no light task to do so. The Town have now by this well deserved victory secured the Romford and District League Championship, with the splendid record of having lost only one match, the club have battled through the season without support from the townsfolk which makes their achievement all the more remarkable.

It will be recalled that they had hard luck in the Romford Charity Cup losing by the odd goals to Hornchurch DDSS & United in the second round. On Saturday they went all out for victory and by the final whistle deserved the decision. P.Watts the now famous outside right of Eagle Park looked a dangerous customer from the start, but Romford did well tactically in placing Haviland at left half, who carried out his duties to great effect, and kept his man well marked. Tetchner at Right back showed good judgement as did A.H.Bear at centre half who scored two excellent long range goals for the town. To mention all who deserve praise would take up too much space and time as all the Romford men played an equal part and need congratulating on their splendid achievement.

Note: This match was played at Eagle Park's home ground at Selinas Lane, Dagenham.

SUMMARY OF FIRST TEAM RESULTS SEASON 1919 – 20

					Goals		
	P	W	D	L	For	Ag	Pts
Romford & D. Lge	20	18	1	1	70	16	37
Essex Junior Cup	2	1	0	1	5	5	
Romford Charity Cup	1	0	0	1	1	2	
Friendly Match	1	0	0	1	1	2	
Total	24	19	1	4	77	25	

Romford & District League

					Goals		
	P	W	D	L	For	Ag	Pts
Romford Town	**20**	**18**	**1**	**1**	**70**	**16**	**37**
Hornchurch DDSS & Utd.	20	17	1	2	77	15	35
Eagle Park	19	12	4	3	63	23	28
Squirrels Heath "A"	20	11	1	8	78	41	23
Romford Ivyleafers "A"	20	10	3	7	63	49	23
Chadwell Hth.Ivyleafers	19	8	1	10	38	38	17
Brentwood Orient	20	6	2	12	27	54	14
Romford Baptist	20	5	3	12	43	54	13
Roneo Athletic "A"	20	4	3	13	24	25	11
Emerson Park	19	2	4	13	21	66	8
G.E.R	19	3	1	15	15	89	7

Note: Two matches were not played

FIRST TEAM CUP RESULTS SEASON 1919 – 20

Essex Junior Cup

Final: Culver Street Ironworks (Colchester) 1 Grays Athletic "A" 0

Romford's progress:	1st Round			Bye
	2nd Round	Home	Eagle Park	3 – 2
	3rd Round	Home	Roneo Athletic	2 – 3

First Team Appearances and Goal Scorers Season 1919-20

After a considerable amount of research at many libraries it is believed that the results of all of the games have been discovered, but only one team line up has been found, and of course it is not known who were regular players or who scored the goals!

Post Season Summary Season 1919-20

The Romford Town team commenced their league programme in fine style, defeating Romford Ivyleafers and Brentwood Orient by four goals to nil and six goals to nil respectively. They then defeated Hornchurch DDSS & United, a very strong side, by two goals to one. On 8th November they achieved a resounding league victory over Emerson Park 5-0, and a week later played their first Essex Junior Cup tie of the season against Eagle Park who were defeated by three goals to two.

Further big league wins were obtained against Squirrels Heath 'A' and Roneo Athletic 'A' before the team were ousted from the Essex Junior Cup by the Roneo Athletic first team. This was followed by a 2-1 defeat away to Brentwood Orient, which was Romford's only league defeat of the season. Four successive league victories were followed by two defeats by two goals to one, the first against Hornchurch DDSS & United in the Romford Charity Cup and the other a friendly game against old rivals Eagle Park.

The locals rounded off the season by winning eight of their last nine league games and drawing the other, including a 9-0 drubbing of the Great Eastern Railway. Romford won the title, finishing two points ahead of runners up Hornchurch DDSS & United, with both teams well clear of the rest of the pack.

Despite the success of the club, there was much scratching of heads and no doubt sleepless nights due to the parlous state of the club's finances. Great Eastern continued to draw the spectators for their Spartan league games, and few local folk were interested in Romford Town competing at a low level with games against the second teams of Squirrels Heath, Roneo Athletic, Romford Ivyleafers etc.

There were a number of Ivyleafers teams formed around the country, composed mainly of ex-servicemen, thus making it difficult for other teams to attract players at junior level. Meetings were arranged before finally it was agreed that the Romford Town team would merge with the Romford Ivyleafers for the new season.

Annual Dinner and Concert, 15th May 1920

The first Annual Dinner and Concert of the Romford Town Football Club took place on Saturday, Mr.T.Fletcher, vice-president, presiding. The chairman congratulated the club upon being the first winners of the Romford and District League, and said a special meeting would be called for the purpose of distributing the shields and medals. The League had raised £99.9s.0d. for the Cottage Hospital,, and this sum was made up to £100 during the evening. A musical programme was contributed to by Messrs. S.Tetchner, A.Bush, T.Saggers, A.H.Bear, L.Wood, R.Giles and E.Evans.

ROMFORD TOWN FOOTBALL CLUB WATCH COMPETITION

A local jeweller ran a competition to pay sixpence and guess the time that a watch stopped. It was announced that:

> The valuable prize offered, namely, a gentleman's gold watch, has been won by Mr. W. Thomas, 2, Cotleigh Road, Romford. The time the watch stopped was 12h 14m 58s. The watch will be on view at Messrs. T and F Fletcher's, High Street, Romford, until Saturday next 17th July 1920. All profits were donated to the football club. The Management Committee desire to thank the promoter and all who came forward in such a sporting way to enhance the club's funds.

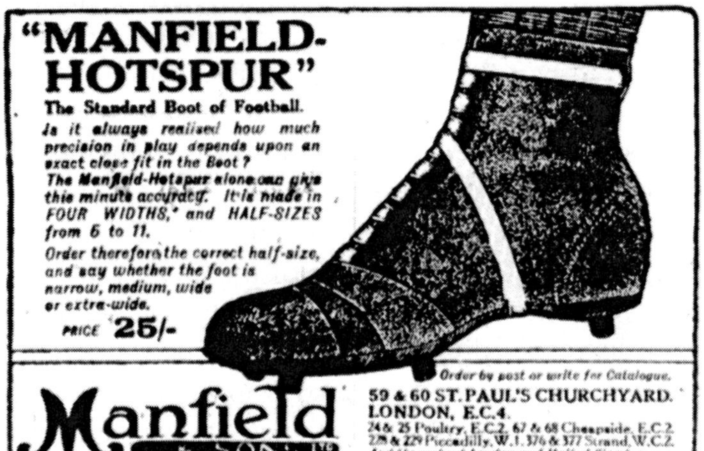

A pair of these boots from 1920 cost 25 shillings (£1.25)

ROMFORD TOWN AND IVYLEAFERS

Season 1920 – 21

Romford Town merged with Romford Ivyleafers to become Romford Town & Ivyleafers, using the Ivyleafers' headquarters at the Coach and Bell Public House in which to hold their meetings. Mr.J.H.Little, Romford Town's secretary, became joint secretary, working alongside the former Ivyleafers' secretary Mr.J.R.Stebbings. The newly-merged club put out a rallying call for help from Romfordians, attempting to raise much-needed cash to keep the club going.

Romford Town Football Club were the reigning Romford & District League champions, but, due to their ground at the Crown Field being out of town, they were struggling to attract the support that had been so loyal to them before the War.

It seems that since the Great Eastern Railway Club, whose ground was next to Romford Station, had risen to the ranks of a senior club and entered the Spartan League, locals were attracted to their matches instead of supporting the town club who had reformed at the lower junior level, using a pitch on Crown Field. The Ivyleafers, who had the previous season been playing on Blackwell's Field, were not faring much better, with most games reportedly watched by a small gathering. The newly-amalgamated town club had secured Brooklands Farm, Medora Road, as their home ground.

The Romford Ivyleafers club contained some former Romford players, and it was probably felt that the two clubs could become more successful by pooling their resources. The new merged club would enter its first team in the South Essex League Division Two, with its 'A' team in the Romford & District League and its 'B' team in the Romford & District League Division Two.

HELP THE BLINDED HEROES!
A Friendly Football Match
will be played between
RONEO ATHLETIC F.C.
AND
ROMFORD TOWN IVYLEAFERS
on the
Roneo Athletic Ground,
Hornchurch Rd., Romford,
On SATURDAY, SEPTEMBER 18th, 1920.
In Aid of St. Dunstan's Hostel.
THEY ARE SPORTSMEN, TOO!

Season 1920 – 21

ROMFORD TOWN & IVYLEAFERS

President: Mr. Percy C. Haydon-Bacon C.C. **Chairman:** Mr. T. Fletcher

Vice-Chairman: Mr. A. S. Giles **Joint Hon. Secretaries:** Messrs J.H.Little and J.R.Stebbings

Hon. Treasurer: Mr. T. Fletcher **Hon. Assistant Secretary:** Mr. W. J. Cumberland

Headquarters: Coach & Bell

Ground: Brooklands Farm, Medora Road, Romford **Reserves Ground:** Heath Park, Romford

COMPETITIONS ENTERED

South Essex League Division II
Essex County F.A. Junior Challenge Cup Competition

Romford & District Football League Division One
Romford Charity Cup Division One

Romford & District Football League Division Two

Match Results

25 Sept SEL2 Home Custom House "A" 1 – 3

2 Oct SEL2 Away London Electric 2 – 3 Palmer,Dearman
Romford Town & Ivyleafers: Tetchner;Hunwicks,Clements;Wood,Fisher,Richardson; Parker,Dearman,York,Palmer,Sawyer.

9 Oct SEL2 Home Tilbury 3 – 0

16 Oct EJC1R Home Emerson Park 5 – 1

23 Oct SEL2 Away Barking "A" 2 – 1

6 Nov EJC2R Away Harold Wood 0 – 2

13 Nov SEL2 Home Squirrels Heath 2 – 4

20 Nov SEL2 Away Roneo Athletic 2 – 6

11 Dec SEL2 Home Walthamstow Avenue "A" 1 – 6

South Essex League Division Two "A"
Table up to 11th December

					Goals		
	P	W	D	L	For	Ag	Pts
Custom House "A"	7	5	0	2	21	11	10
Squirrels Heath	6	4	1	1	15	7	9
London Electric	6	2	2	2	16	10	6
Walthamstow Avenue	6	3	0	3	16	13	6
Roneo Athletic	4	2	1	1	15	7	5
Grays Athletic "A"	3	2	0	1	6	8	4
Tilbury	6	2	0	4	8	19	4
Romford Tn. & Ivylrs.	**7**	**2**	**0**	**5**	**13**	**23**	**4**
Barking "A"	2	1	0	1	3	3	2
Chelmsford "A"	5	1	0	4	5	17	2

24 Dec at the monthly South Essex League Meeting for December Romford Town & Ivyleafers withdrew from the South Essex League.

Essex Junior Cup

Final: Grays Athletic "A" 0 Custom House "A" 0
Replay: Grays Athletic "A" 2 Custom House "A" 1

Romford's progress:	1st Round	Away	Emerson Park	5 – 1
	2nd Round	Away	Harold Wood	0 – 2

SUMMARY OF FIRST TEAM RESULTS OBTAINED SEASON 1920 – 21

					Goals		
	P	W	D	L	For	Ag	Pts
South Essex League	7	2	0	5	13	23	4
Essex Junior Cup	2	1	0	1	5	2	
Total	9#	3	0	6	18	25	

These are the only results that have come to hand and as the club withdrew from the league on 24th December they are probably the only games that were played by the club during the season.

Appearances and Goal Scorers

Due to the very limited coverage by the local press, no comprehensive tables for match appearances or goal scorers can be compiled. Only one team line up has been found and only two goal scorers are known!

RESERVES

ROMFORD TOWN & IVYLEAFERS "A"

Match Results

25 Sept	RDL1	Away	Roneo Athletic "A"	3 – 1 Stone
2 Oct	RDL1	Home	Romford White Star	6 – 4
23 Oct	RDL1	Home	Emerson Park	2 – 4
30 Oct	RCC1	Home	Heath Park Celtic	lost
13 Nov	RDL1	Away	Romford Central	1 – 3
20 Nov	RDL1	Home	GER Stores	5 – 3
27 Nov	RDL1	Home	Brentwood Town	won
4 Dec	RDL1	Home	Records United	2 – 4
11 Dec	RDL1	Away	Romford White Star	lost

Romford & District League Division One

Table as at 18th December

					Goals		
	P	W	D	L	For	Ag	Pts
Records United	10	9	0	1	52	14	18
Depot Essex Regiment	9	6	1	2	31	13	13
Brentwood Town	8	5	1	2	29	21	11
Emerson Park	8	5	1	2	18	11	11
Heath Park Celtic	7	4	1	2	31	25	9
Romford Central	10	4	1	5	21	34	9
Romford Town & Ivyleafers "A"	**8**	**4**	**0**	**4**	**26**	**21**	**8**
Upminster	6	3	0	3	15	15	6
Romford White Star	8	1	2	5	15	25	4
Roneo Athletic "A"	10	1	2	7	14	42	4
G.E.R. Stores	8	1	1	6	21	26	3
Chadwell Heath United	4	0	0	4	3	17	0

Romford withdrew from the league as did Chadwell Heath United on 24th December.

CUP RESULTS

Romford Charity Cup

Romford's progress: 1st Round Home Heath Park Celtic lost

"B" TEAM

Match Results

18 Sept	RDL2	Home	Romford White Star "A"	5 – 1
2 Oct	RDL2	Home	Emerson Park Juniors	12 – 1
16 Oct	RDL2	Home	Rosemount United	3 – 7
23 Oct	RDL2	Away	Upminster Rovers	12 – 3
30 Oct	RCC1R	Home	Chadwell Heath United "A"	Won*
30 Oct	RDL2	Home	Junior Red Triangle	4 – 3
6 Nov	RDL2	Away	Brentwood BB Cadets	7 – 2
13 Nov	RDL2	Home	Shenfield United	3 – 3
20 Nov	RDL2	Away	Rosemount United	3 – 0
27 Nov	RDL2	Home	Upminster Rovers	3 – 1
11 Dec	RDL2	Home	Heath Park Celtic "A"	4 – 1

* Chadwell Heath United "A" scratched from the competition.

Romford & District League Division Two
Table as at 18th December

					Goals		
	P	W	D	L	For	Ag	Pts
Roneo Athletic "B"	9	9	0	0	88	13	18
Rfd.Tn & Ivyleafers "B"	**10**	**8**	**1**	**1**	**56**	**22**	**17**
Records United "A"	9	8	0	1	47	12	16
Romford White Star "A"	12	6	2	4	35	32	14
Brentwood BB Cadets	13	5	4	4	49	26	14
Junior Red Triangle	12	5	2	5	62	27	12
Rosemount United	10	3	5	2	34	26	11
Heath Park Celtic "A"	9	3	1	5	26	25	7
Shenfield United	7	1	2	4	10	22	4
Chadwell Heath Utd "A"	7	0	3	4	6	28	3
Upminster Rovers	10	1	0	9	19	83	2
Emerson Park Juniors	10	0	0	10	8	119	0

Romford Town & Ivyleafers "B" withdrew from the league on 24th December.
Emerson Park "A" took over the Romford Town and Ivyleafers "B" current record and fulfilled the remaining league fixtures.

Chadwell Heath United "A" withdrew from the league.

Romford & District League Division Two
Table as at 22nd January

					Goals		
	P	W	D	L	For	Ag	Pts
Roneo Athletic "B"	12	12	0	0	100	18	24
Records United "A"	12	11	0	1	61	16	22
Emerson Park "A"	12	9	2	1	60	23	20
Brentwood BB Cadets	15	6	4	5	54	36	16
Junior Red Triangle	14	5	2	7	63	36	12
Rosemount United	11	3	5	3	37	31	11
Romford White Star "A"	13	5	1	7	34	43	11
Heath Park Celtic "A"	11	4	1	6	36	34	9
Shenfield United	9	3	1	5	22	30	7
Upminster Rovers	14	1	1	12	26	108	3
Emerson Park Juniors	14	0	1	13	13	133	1

Chadwell Heath United "A" team withdrew from the league and their record was expunged. This appears to have greatly affected the Romford White Star "A" record which has changed dramatically, a win and a draw being deleted and three defeats suffered since 18th December.

Romford Charity Cup Division II

1st Round Home Chadwell Heath "A" scratched

Semi-Final
19 Feb Emerson Park "A" 1 Roneo Athletic "B" 3
(Emerson Park "A" replaced Romford Town & Ivyleafers "B")

Post-Season summary Season 1920 – 21

The newly-constituted club was keen to succeed, and it was decided to run three competitive teams. Competing at a higher level than the previous season, though still at junior level, the team immediately met with a setback, losing the opening game 3-1 at home to Custom House 'A' in the South Essex League Division Two.

They then suffered a three goal to two reverse away to London Electric. There then came a fine league victory over Tilbury by three goals to nil, and a 5-1 thrashing of Emerson Park in the Essex Junior Cup. On the 23rd October a South Essex League victory was obtained against Barking 'A', and any interest in the Essex Junior Cup disappeared with a 2-0 beating away to Harold Wood.

The team then fell apart losing their next three league games, conceding sixteen goals in the process although they scored five goals themselves.

At this stage of the season (mid-December 1920) it was decided to withdraw from all competitions, and the club eventually folded due to serious financial problems. The reserve team had a fairly good season and were in a mid-table position at the time of withdrawal. The third team had played ten matches, losing only one of them, but after their withdrawal Emerson Park "A" took over their playing record and completed the season. It was impossible for the Romford Town and Ivyleafers club to continue activities.

It must have been heartbreak for those fine men who had formed the club and for the players who probably did their best.

R. I. P.

ROMFORD TOWN THURSDAY FOOTBALL CLUB

As we have seen, the original Romford Football Club's history finally ended with the demise of Romford Town and Ivyleafers on Christmas Eve 1920. Alas, lack of funds combined with strong competition from the senior club Great Eastern Railway, who competed in the Spartan League, F.A.Cup, Amateur Cup etc., had brought about this club's abrupt end.

Local football enthusiasts felt that there was a niche for a new Romford club to fill, and it was decided to avoid competition from the Great Eastern Club by having the new club play on a Thursday afternoon (when the town's shops were closed). The club would be called the Romford Town Thursday Football Club, with its headquarters at the Mawney Road Swimming Baths and a pitch secured at Brooklands. It would compete in the West Ham Thursday League.

This club continued playing until just after the formation of the new Romford Football Club in 1929.

THE REST IS HISTORY.....

JOHN HALEY and TERRY FELTON

HALL OF FAME

Biographical notes on some personalities from the early years

Edmund CARTER

Edmund was born in Wickford in 1859, and his family moved to Romford around six years later. He was one of the club's pioneers, playing in the first season at the age of 17. Edmund followed his father's trade as carpenter and joiner and went on to run a successful building business. In 1880 he married Ann Letitia Sapsford and they had one child, Ernest. Edmund Carter died aged 74 at his home, 125 George Street, Romford, on 5 December 1933, and was buried at Crow Lane Cemetery.

Elijah CHAMPNESS

Elijah Champness was born in Bishops Stortford, Herts. He married Kate Martin in 1875 and moved to Romford a year or two later to work at the County Court in South Street, first as a solicitor's clerk and then as bailiff. Another pioneer player for the club, he usually kept goal. His son Frank Elijah Champness later also played for the club. Elijah died in 1932 aged 79 and was buried at Crow Lane Cemetery.

Arthur D. CORNELL

Born around 1858, son of William Cornell, a house painter, and Emma Ellen Stannard. The family lived at 1 Cornell's Cottages, St Andrew's Road, for many years.

Arthur first appeared in the club's second season line-up. He was usually a striker, but as the years went by he often took the role of goalkeeper. Arthur's younger brothers Alf and George also played for Romford.

By 1891 Arthur had become Registrar of Marriages for Romford. From relatively humble beginnings he had become one of the town's most well-known and respected figures. He himself never married, remaining with his mother, sister Alice, and brother-in-law Edward Harrold and their children. At the time of the 1901 census the family are at 1 Main Road, and by 1911 they have moved to 5 Junction Road.

Mr Cornell died 6th January 1921 at his home White Cottage, Main Road, Romford, and was buried at Crow Lane Cemetery five days later. A newspaper obituary stated that:

> In the football field Mr. Cornell was a prominent figure; he was certainly the most capable footballer Romford has produced, taking part in the ever-memorable English Cup-tie when Romford met Blackburn Rovers. He was equally gifted as a cricketer, and was familiarly known to all as 'Doddy'. The musical world will also lose a gifted musician.

As we have seen, some of the early photographs featured in this book were from Mr Cornell's own collection. He was also an enthusiastic local historian, and spent several years compiling a history of Romford and district known as the 'Cornell Manuscript', now in the London Borough of Havering Libraries Local Studies collection.

Percy Meredith EARLE

Born in 1860, Percy was the son of Dr Joseph Earle of the Priory, High Street, Brentwood. He was one of Romford's most regular players during the first half of the 1880s, and also appeared for the Essex County side (see photograph on page 52). After medical training in Edinburgh, Percy seems to have spent his entire working life as a doctor in British Guiana (now Guyana). He and his wife Mary Edith Greene had four children.

Charles Thomas HEARD

Charles was born in Billericay and came to Romford to work as a railway clerk. The 1911 census shows him with his wife Elizabeth and two sons at 18 King Edward Road. He gave many years of service to the club, both as a player and an official. As Hon. Secretary he was responsible for player selection and the club's overall running and management. Ousted from the Secretaryship in the coup of 1909, he was instrumental in founding the new club, Romford United. In retirement he moved to Heath Park Road, and died aged 78 in Harold Wood Hospital in February 1950.

William Darron HEARD

Born in Leighton Buzzard in 1854, William came to Romford to work as a solicitor's clerk. He played in Romford FC's inaugural season. He married Elizabeth Annie Medcalf, daughter of a local oil merchant, and had four children. The family eventually settled at 33 Eastern Road, which William named "Leighton" after his birthplace. He died in November 1933 and was buried at Crow Lane Cemetery.

Edward Harvey HINDS

He was born in Romford in 1866, son of John Hinds, a carpenter and builder of the Market Place. Edward worked as a shipping clerk. He first played for Romford in 1886, and until 1899 was heavily involved as a player, team captain and also for many years its secretary. His brothers Albert and Horace also appeared for the club. Edward married Emily Haylock in 1895 and they had one daughter, Kathleen. He died in November 1943 aged 77.

William HYNDS

William Hynds, born in 1867 at Bengeo, Herts, son of Robert Hynds a miller. He moved to Romford to work as a railway clerk, and was active in the football club as a player and committee member from 1887 to the mid-1890s. In 1901 William and his wife Sarah were living in Victoria Road with their three sons.

William Herbert KELLY

Born in India around 1864, William lived in Leyton before obtaining a post as a clerk at the Romford brewery. He played as goalkeeper for the Romford club from 1896, after keeping goal for several seasons for Forest Swifts of Leytonstone. He had married Minnie Elizabeth Collingwood in 1889, and in 1901 they were living in Victoria Road with their four children.

They later moved to a house in Brooklands Road named 'Patna' after his birthplace in India. Mr Kelly later served as assistant club secretary, and was instrumental in the overthrow of the existing committee at the 1909 A.G.M.

Ralph Harvey LYON

He was born in 1856 in Hare Street, Romford, son of Charles Lyon, a commercial clerk. At 18 Ralph became a clerk at the Romford Brewery, and was eventually promoted to Registrar. He played in the football club's inaugural season, and also undertook the responsibilities of Hon. Secretary and Treasurer in 1877 and 1878.

At the time of the 1901 census Mr Lyon was living at 5 Laurie Square with his wife Agnes and daughter Violet. By 1911 they had moved to 'Eden', 71 North Street. Mr Lyon rose to the rank of Colonel of the local Regiment of Volunteers, and acted as regional recruiting officer during World War One. He died on 19 September 1931 aged 75, and was buried at Crow Lane Cemetery.

William David MATTHEWS

Born around 1859 in Wootton Bassett, Wiltshire, William moved to Romford in the mid-1870s and worked as a cashier in the offices of the Singer Sewing Machine Company. He was an important figure at Romford FC for many years, as a player. Hon. Secretary and Hon. Treasurer. He was one of the leaders of the opposition to the 1909 coup. He lived at various addresses in Romford over the years, and eventually he and his wife Kate settled At 'Kelso' in Eastern Road.

Mr Matthews died 14th May, 1916 aged 57. An obituary stated that 'His bright and pleasant disposition secured his many friends' and that he 'was closely identified with sporting organisations in Romford, and was well known by reason of his association with Essex sport. He was formerly prominent in connection with the Romford cricket and football clubs, and he had much to do with other clubs devoted to sport, besides being a member of the Essex County Cycling and Athletic Association and a delegate to other county associations'.

Harry William PALMER

Another pioneer of the club's first season. Harry was born around 1858 and grew up in South Street, son of Eusebius S Palmer, a brewery foreman. Harry spent his working life as a clerk in the brewery. In the census returns of 1901 and 1911 he is living with his mother and three sisters at 70 Eastern Road.

Charles Shaw PALMER

A younger brother of Harry William Palmer, Charles was born in 1860. He followed Harry into the brewery offices, and in 1877 joined him in the Romford football team. Charles married Emma Kemp in 1889. In 1901 they were living at 91 Eastern Road, and later moved to Kingswood Road in Goodmayes. Charles died in January 1931 aged 70, and was buried at Crow Lane Cemetery.

William John REID

Another teenage player in the very first season of the club. In the 1881 census William is a 22 year-old clerk living in Eastern Road with his widowed mother and younger siblings. All the children are listed as being born in Burma.

Grimston Abel SMITH

Another name from the club's inaugural season. Grimston was born in Enfield in 1843 and came to Romford to work as a cashier in the brewery. He lived in South Street immediately next to the Clark family, whose four sons all played for the club. Grimston married twice and had a large family. He died in 1888 aged 45 and was buried at Crow Lane Cemetery.

Frederick William H. STROMEYER

Frederick also played in the club's first season. He was born in Chelmsford in 1860, the son of F.W. Stromeyer, a music teacher from Frankfurt, Germany. In 1871 the family were living in Eastern Road. By 1881 they had moved to South Street, and Frederick was employed as a merchant's clerk. His younger brother Cyril later also played for Romford.

Francis Hugh THIRLWALL

He was born on August 13th 1857 at 7 Claremont Bank, Shrewsbury, second son of the Rev Thomas J. Thirlwall, vicar of Nantmel, Radnorshire. His mother Agnes died on 3rd March 1859, a few weeks after giving birth to a daughter. His father remarried in 1862 and had a second family.

Francis attended Marlborough College, where he gained a rugby cap. He came to Romford in April 1875 to take a job as a bank clerk and, as we have seen, he initiated the meeting in October 1876 that led to the formation of Romford Football Club. Francis also captained the Romford cricket team and represented the town at rugby.

Mr Thirlwall was a member of the local volunteer reserve force for over 20 years, attaining the rank of Major. In later life he left Romford to work in Halstead, before finishing his career as branch manager for the London County & Westminster Bank in Canterbury.

In 1905 Mr Thirlwall married a widow, Elizabeth Maria Johns (known as Bessie), at St Peter's Church, Eaton Square, London. He died on 27th September 1923 aged 65, while on a visit to Llandrindod Wells. He was buried at Nantmel, where his father had been vicar for 42 years.

William Henry WRIGHT

William was born around 1860 in Shoreditch. He played for Romford Football Club from 1877, including the FA Cup ties against Blackburn and Darwen. William lived at various times at St Andrew's Road and Marks Road, and worked as a postman. He died in September 1908 aged 47 and was buried at Crow Lane Cemetery.

Brothers in arms for the Brewery Boys: the Clarks

Several sets of brothers played for Romford in the early years, but the Clark family produced four! Their parents, Richard George Clark and Eliza Love Osborn, were both English but had married in March 1853 in Boston, Massachusetts. Eliza's father John was in business in the United States a merchant. Richard Clark was working in the audit office of the Great Western Railway in Ontario, Canada. The couple settled in Hamilton, Ontario, where three sons were born. They then returned to England and set up home in South Street, Romford. Richard worked in the offices at the Ind Coope brewery. A fourth son was born to them in Romford.

The eldest boy, **Frederick D'Arcy Richard Clark** (known as Fred) was, as we have seen, chairman of the original meeting which led to the formation of the Romford Football Club in 1876. Fred had been born around 1858, and worked as a bank clerk.

The second son, **Livingstone Eaton Clark** (nicknamed Tony) was about a year younger, and employed as an insurance clerk. The team line-up is not known for Romford's first ever match on 9th December 1876 against Chigwell Grammar School, but both brothers definitely played in the second game on January 6th 1877. They were approximately 18 and 17 years of age.

On 17th February 1877, in the game against Mars, a third member of the family, 16 year-old **Clifford Clark**, made his debut for the team.

In the 1880-81 season the fourth member of the Clark family made his appearance in the first team, on 2nd October away to Pilgrims. This was **Reason Arthur Clark**, playing in the forward line aged only 15! On 4th December 1880 with his brothers Tony and Clifford in the Romford side playing against Union, Reason was unable to secure a place, and it appears that he may have played in goal for the Union team! A further player, W.Clark also played for the club. He was apparently a cousin of the Clark brothers.

Sadly, three of the brothers were to die young. The eldest, Frederick D'Arcy Richard, passed away in December 1885 after an attack of bronchitis, at the age of only 27. A newspaper obituary stated that 'He was of an affable disposition, kind, and generous, and was held in much esteem by his associates in cricketing and football, in both of which pastimes he took a great interest'. He was buried at Crow Lane Cemetery.

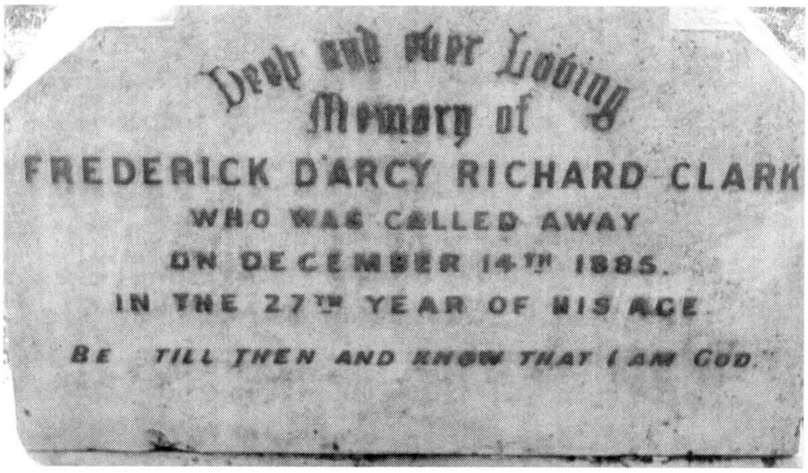

Authors' collection

Fred's brother Livingstone Eaton Clark died in July 1894 aged 34 and was buried in the same grave. An obituary noted that 'He took a great interest in local sports, and was for many years captain of the Romford Football Club'.

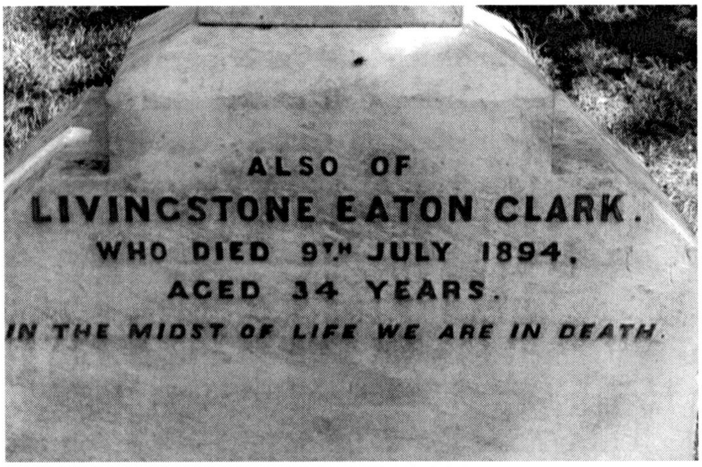

Authors' collection

The youngest brother, Reason Arthur (seemingly known as Arthur), married Eleanor Jane Wilson in 1890, but died 1st January 1896 at the age of only 31. He too was laid to rest at Crow Lane.

The remaining brother, Clifford, led a chequered life. Formerly a clerk with the Phoenix Fire Insurance, he set up in business in the 1890s as an auctioneer and valuer. This probably ended in failure, for by the time of the 1901 census he is a 'Betting bookmaker Comm. Agt' – that is, a horse racing tipster! Clifford ran into trouble several times with the law, including being convicted of failing to maintain his wife and four children.

BIOGRAPHIES BASED ON PEN-PORTRAITS OF FOOTBALLERS PRINTED IN THE *ESSEX TIMES* IN THE EDWARDIAN ERA

James Charles Doggett

Born in Walthamstow in 1881, at 14 James represented West Ham Schoolboys as a centre-forward. His first senior team was Great Eastern Mechanics, for whom he played for two seasons before joining Leyton in 1899. He enjoyed considerable success there, winning many medals and becoming vice-captain before spending two seasons with Croydon. Already an accomplished County player, he secured his badge in 1902-03 and later the coveted County Cap. James joined Romford at the start of the 1908-09 season, and following the big upset in 1909 he moved on to Romford United.

Fred Leslie Fletcher

Born in October 1883, son of Samuel Fletcher, a butcher. The family lived at Victoria House in Romford Market Place. In his junior days Freddie was captain of Romford Victoria for three seasons, before joining Romford in 1901. At the Annual General Meeting in July 1904 he was elected captain. He led his team to success in the 1904-05 season when they beat Clapton in the final of the West Ham Charity Cup.

The following season the club reached the third round of the Amateur Cup only to lose to New Crusaders in a second replay in controversial circumstances. New Crusaders protested that they had Been 'kicked off the park' and their appeal was upheld by the Football Association, resulting in Fletcher being suspended until the end of the season. A carpenter by trade, Freddie emigrated to New Zealand in May 1906 and died there in 1966 aged 83.

Albert Victor Frisby

Known as Jack, he left Forest Gate Football Club to join Romford for the 1904-05 season and was immediately a success in his first year of senior football. He played over 30 matches for the club in his first season and almost as many the following year. With the untimely departure of Fletcher, Frisby was elected Romford's captain for the 1906-07 season, but left for Chelmsford the following year.

Arthur Edwin Jones

Born in Romford in 1880, Arthur lived all his life in Victoria Road and worked as a clerk in the Ind Coope brewery alongside his brother Evan Pashley Jones (also a Romford footballer) and their father Evan Jones senior. Arthur, or 'Diddy' as he was known, learnt his football with Romford Excelsiors, before joining the Romford senior club.

Arthur's first known game for Romford was against Woodford on 30th October 1898 and he continued to play for them for three seasons. He played few games for the club over the following four or five years, and it is believed that he played for Ilford during that period. Returning to Romford, he was elected captain for the 1907-08 season. He was captain again for the following year, but in the upheaval of 1909 he decided to remain loyal to Secretary Charles Heard and joined the newly-formed Romford United. He remained with them a few more years, until nearing the end of his career he joined Mawney Institute. Tragically, Arthur was killed aged 36 in the First World War (see page 318).

Albert S. Hyett

Born at Camberwell in May 1885, he first played for Oakley Swifts, then spent 5 years at Heath Park, a local junior club. In 1904 he joined Romford. He secured his County Badge in the 1905-06 season. In the 1911 census Albert is listed as a 'telegraphist at the General Post Office', and living at Park Villa, Heath Park Road, Romford. Mr Hyett married Alice Brown in 1939, and died 14th November 1941 aged 56. He was buried at Crow Lane Cemetery. A newspaper obituary described him as 'the clever outside-right of the Romford Football Club'.

William Olley

Joined Romford from Leyton at the start of the 1909-10 season, one of the many new signings following the debacle at the A.G.M. earlier in the year. He played in the first game of the season against Enfield along with a G.Olley (ex-Clapton). Only two match appearances have been traced for William, but he was described when this photo was published as captain of Romford Football Club. It is known that A.J.Gallagher captained the team on a number of occasions that season and goalkeeper de Meza did so on at least one occasion. It could be that Olley was made captain at the start and Gallagher took over later in the season.

Frank Henry Kittle

Born in the Brewery Town in May 1886, Frank played for several junior clubs before being persuaded to join the town club from Squirrels Heath early in 1906. He was described as, like his elder brother Albert, 'a robust player who distributes the ball well'. Also an Essex County player, Frank remained loyal to the officials and players who formed Romford United after the split with the old club. Frank died in March 1928, and was buried at Crow Lane Cemetery. A newspaper obituary stated that 'A well-known local sportsman has died in the person of Mr. Frank Henry ("Jigger") Kittle, of 4, Hainault Road, Romford, at the age of 41...He was formerly a prominent member of the old Romford Town F.C., playing at left-half, and was a great favourite among local players and supporters of the game'.

Arthur Reading

Born at Wandsworth in 1899, Arthur was captain of St. Paul's School Stratford for two years. He then joined Hainault Spurs of Leyton, before moving on to Wanstead. When the Wanstead club sadly folded he joined Romford United in February 1911. The following year he was made captain when the club changed its name to Romford Town.

A. J. Gallagher

Born at Preston, Lancashire in 1885, he played for junior sides before coming to London in 1902 where he was at St. Mary's, Hammersmith. He played for the City of Westminster for one season before joining Shepherd's Bush. He played little football for a year due to injury, then joined West Norwood and toured with them in Germany at Easter 1909. He joined Romford around November 1909 and remained until the club folded in March 1911.

J. Lamont McNair

Played for Millwall St. Paul's at fullback as a schoolboy, then joined Little Ilford where he received a bad knee injury. He then became a goalkeeper and played for Southend and Barking before joining Romford in 1907. He was only 5 feet 6 inches tall, but marvellous at judging high shots and crosses.

Charles Edwin Manning

Charles played school football in East Ham before joining East Ham Grange and then becoming a South Weald player in 1909. He transferred his allegiance to Romford Town in September 1912, and immediately became a regular first team player. Nicknamed 'Wag', he was with Romford at the time the First World War commenced and football ceased.

GROUNDS FOR AN EXPLANATION

As the authors of this publication we feel that the players and officials of the old Romford Football Club are like long-lost friends of ours, in what seemed a strange tale of to-ing and fro-ing on the local football scene. It can seem a complicated tale, so for those asking yourselves where the club were playing in this year or that, or where each ground was situated, we have provided as close as possible the locations and era in which each ground was used.

1876 – 1885
Great Mawneys

The ground was actually on Mawneys Farm, where the football club shared a field with the Romford Cricket Club. The pitch was next to the footpath. Through our research we believe the pitch was behind Mawneys farmhouse, in a field adjoining what later became the Brooklands ground. On a modern map this area is enclosed by Mawney Road, Como Street and St. Edward's Way.

1885 – 1902
Recreation Ground, off Victoria Road

On the modern map this area is enclosed by Victoria Road, George Street, Richmond Road and Alexandra Road, with Thurlow Gardens cutting through where the football pitch would have been.

1902 – 1911
Cricket Field, Romford Station

This ground was later named the Great Eastern Railway Athletics Association Sports Ground, and from 1919 was known as the Great Eastern Railway Football Ground. On today's modern map this area is bordered by Romford Station, South Street, Oldchurch Road and the River Rom.

1909 – 1915
Cosy Corner Ground/Shoulder of Mutton Field, Hornchurch Road

The acrimonious split of 1909 saw most of the players and committee leave the club and resurrect the name of Romford United Football Club, a junior club which had folded in 1908. Their new club set up home on a field owned by Mr.W.Poel, Jnr., on Hornchurch Road (now called South Street). This field stood directly opposite the cricket field which had been played on by the original Romford Football Club. On the modern map this area is bordered by Victoria Road, South Street, Alexandra Road and Thurlow Gardens.

1919 – 1920
Crown Field, London Road

After World War One, Romford Town reformed but their Shoulder of Mutton Field had been turned over to allotments and the railings removed to serve the war effort. The club found a new ground at Crown Field, London Road, next to the Crown Public House. Due to this being an open field the club obtained only junior status, and attendances were small. On a modern map, Crown Field is bordered by London Road, Spring Gardens and Jubilee Avenue.

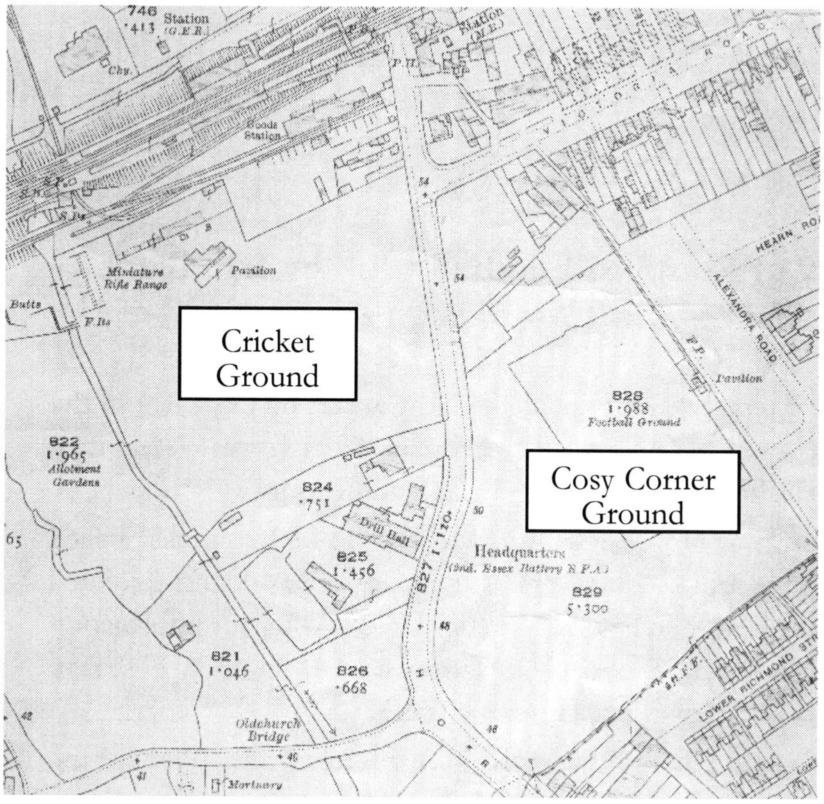

Ordnance Survey map c.1915 showing how close to each other were the grounds used by the rival Romford clubs (Romford and Romford United).

South Street runs from top to bottom of the map. The original Romford club played on the Cricket Ground to the left (west) of South Street until 1911, while the breakaway Romford United club played on the Cosy Corner (Shoulder of Mutton Field) to the right of South Street from 1909 to 1915.

Havering Libraries - Local Studies

1920 – 1921
Brooklands

In a desperate attempt to increase attendances, the Romford Town club merged with the Romford Ivyleafers, who had previously played at Blackwell's Field (which was situated off North Street, to the rear of High Street). The newly-merged club made an agreement with farmer Joseph Linsell to use a field on his farm at Brooklands, Medora Road. On the modern map this area is bordered by Cedar Road, Chesham Close, Willow Street and Brooklands Road. Attendances were no better, however. In mid-December 1920 the club folded through lack of local support.

RESERVE TEAM

1889 – 1890 and 1906 – 1907
Church Lane Ground

On the modern map this area is bordered by Church Lane, Park End Road, The Avenue and North Street.

We hope this has cleared up any confusion you may have encountered, leaving you a happy reader!

APPENDIX

Article on the history of Romford Football Club by J.T. Clark in the *Chelmsford Chronicle*, 1906

At a fairly late stage in our research we located a lengthy article by J.T. Clark in the sports columns of the *Chelmsford Chronicle* of 9th February 1906. It was no less than a survey of the history of the club to mark its thirtieth anniversary.

We were gratified to find that the match statistics that we had compiled tallied exactly with the figures given in the article. However, when we looked at the list (pictured below) of first team captains and Hon. Secretaries and compared it with our information from Annual General Meeting reports and the surviving fixture card of the 1878-79 season (see page 25), we were surprised to discover huge discrepancies!

It is impossible at this stage to establish the reason for this inaccuracy. Perhaps the author was working from memory when he compiled the list, or the compositor had difficulty reading his writing. Who knows? The lesson is that we researchers must always check and double-check our sources!

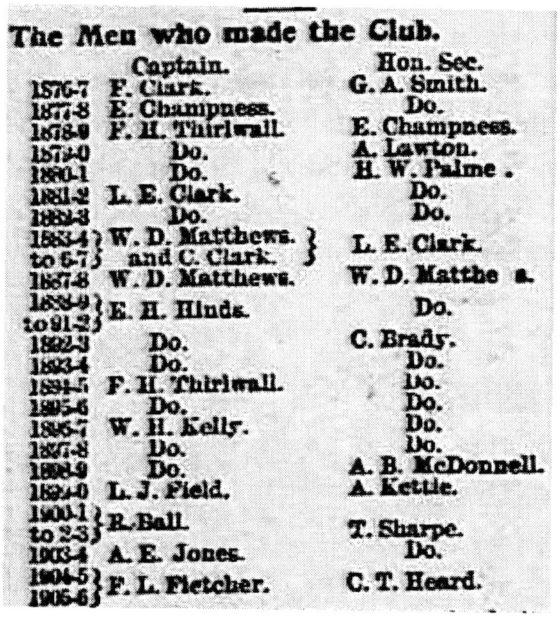

The Men who made the Club.

	Captain.	Hon. Sec.
1876-7	F. Clark.	G. A. Smith.
1877-8	E. Champness.	Do.
1878-9	F. H. Thirlwall.	E. Champness.
1879-0	Do.	A. Lawton.
1880-1	Do.	H. W. Palme .
1881-2	L. E. Clark.	Do.
1882-3	Do.	Do.
1883-4 to 6-7	W. D. Matthews. and C. Clark.	L. E. Clark.
1887-8	W. D. Matthews.	W. D. Matthe s.
1888-9 to 91-2	E. H. Hinds.	Do.
1892-3	Do.	C. Brady.
1893-4	Do.	Do.
1894-5	F. H. Thirlwall.	Do.
1895-6	Do.	Do.
1896-7	W. H. Kelly.	Do.
1897-8	Do.	Do.
1898-9	Do.	A. B. McDonnell.
1899-0	L. J. Field.	A. Kettle.
1900-1 to 2-3	R. Ball.	T. Sharpe.
1903-4	A. E. Jones.	Do.
1904-5 1905-6	F. L. Fletcher.	C. T. Heard.

James T. Clark, author of the article, when Hon. Assistant Secretary of the Essex County Football Association 1902-03
Courtesy of the Essex County Football Association

About the authors

JOHN HALEY

John was born at Gardener's Cottage, Bedfords Park, Havering-Atte-Bower in 1932. He first attended Mawney Road Infants School, then after his family moved to Rush Green he transferred to Rush Green Infants and Junior schools, before passing the scholarship and earning a place at the Royal Liberty Grammar School. John first watched Romford play in 1945 at the Brooklands ground, and at the tender age of 13 was already compiling the club's statistics and researching its history.

The photo shows John as a Romford supporter over 60 years ago. John is fourth from the right, holding the letter "O". His brothers James, (1st left) Eddie (3rd left) and Alf (4th left) also appear. It was taken on 9th February 1952, in the High Street, Crook Town, County Durham, on the occasion of the F.A. Amateur Cup 3rd round tie between Crook Town and Romford, which ended in a 4-all draw.

On leaving school John started work as a clerk with Thomas Moy Limited, (Coal Merchants) in South Street, Romford. He then undertook two years' National Service with the Royal Air Force, before returning to Thomas Moy as manager of their small Upminster Depot for four years. During this time John was contributing pieces about the visiting clubs in the Romford Football Club match programmes.

In 1956 he took up employment with the South Essex Waterworks Company as a Rates Officer. He continued to work on a voluntary basis with the football club, as a member of the advertising and public relations committee, under the chairmanship of Director Glyn Richards. He was mainly concerned with the compilation of the match programmes.

When the Football Club joined the Southern Football League as a semi-professional club in August 1959, John became the official Club Statistician, working on a voluntary basis with Herbert Muskett learning the football administration side and the Limited Company matters.

In April 1964 John took up full-time employment with The Romford Football Club Limited as Football Secretary under the Company's Secretary and Chief Executive Officer Herbert Muskett. When Mr. Muskett retired John replaced him as the Company Secretary and Chief Executive Officer.

John in office as Company Secretary of Romford FC
Authors' collection

John remained with the club until becoming Company Secretary of Bristol Speedway Limited and of Wally Mawdsley Promotions Ltd., moving to Cullompton, Devon in February 1977. Five years later he joined Exeter Health Authority, eventually taking control of the computer system in the Estates Division. John remained with the Health Authority until taking early retirement in 1994.

TERRY FELTON

Terry Felton was heavily involved in the re-formation of Romford Football Club in 1992. He was Vice-Chairman during the 1992-93 season. He writes:

This publication is the end result of a project that was inspired in the very early years of my life. I was born in the early 1960s, the eldest of six. Being the first-born, my grandparents spoiled me rotten to the point where I spent every weekend and school holiday at nan and grandad's.

My grandad, Albert Hanson, was more like a dad to me, involving me in all his little chores and hobbies. He used to tell me about his childhood and wartime dramas and his love of Romford Football Club. He was also a good listener. If I had a question about something he had told me he would answer it. but my interest in Romford Football Club soon became an obsession of which I was asking so many questions Grandad's patience wore a bit thin, so the next step was a visit to Brooklands to watch the Boro play.

I was hooked, and more questions needed answering. Grandad told me the Romford club I had been to watch was not the original club – the first Romford Football Club had been formed in 1876, long before he was born. Plus, he said, there had been another senior club in Romford called the Great Eastern whose ground was next to Romford Station.

I was by this time completely confused, and took myself off to the new library in Romford to ask if they had any information on the history of Romford Football Club. The lady said 'I'm afraid not, but would you like to look through our old local newspapers to see if that can help you?'

I was like a kid loose in a sweet shop, going back to the library day after day, my mum wondering what the hell could be that interesting in a library, and why was I spending so much time there? My biggest mistake was not taking notes of my research. I just read away and absorbed all the information to a point where I was more confused about the history of the local football club than when I started, so eventually the library took a back seat.

I continued going over to Brooklands to watch Romford, amid rumours Brooklands was to be sold – which it eventually was, with the demise of the club following a year later. I always wondered how Brooklands evolved, and started researching the subject. By 1994 I had enough to put together a publication. Things took a different turn when John Haley moved back to Essex from Devon. John had formerly been Secretary of the Romford Football Club for many years. I asked John if he could help me with any information on Brooklands itself. John asked if I had any information on the original 1876 Romford Football Club. The Brooklands book then went on the back burner.

With my research, and John Haley's information and typing expertise put together, those questions I used to ask my grandad have all been answered. I wish he had been here to read what we have unearthed. It's all thanks to those little stories he told me over 40 years ago. Thanks, Grandad!

ACKNOWLEDGEMENTS

Our special thanks are due to:

Simon Donoghue and **Jane Finnett** of the London Borough of Havering Local Studies and Family History Centre at Romford Library, for their unstinting help and support during the course of our research

Phil Sammons (Chief Executive) and **Chris Evans** (Press & Publicity) of the Essex County Football Association

We are also most grateful to the following:

Craig Jobbins for his help with the cover design

John Copleston

The late **Martin Brazier**

Fred Hawthorn

The late **Albert Hanson**

Teresa Trowers of the London Borough of Barking and Dagenham Archives and Local Studies Centre, Valence House

Mick McCann of the British War Graves website (www.britishwargraves.co.uk)

The staff of the **British Library Newspaper Library**, Colindale

Other libraries and archives used during our research included:

The London Borough of Newham Archives and Local Studies Library

Southend Central Library

Colchester Library

Chelmsford Library

Thurrock Local Studies Service, Grays Library

The London Borough of Waltham Forest Archives and Local Studies Library, Vestry House Museum

Other local history books you may enjoy:

The Romford Outrage: the murder of Inspector Thomas Simmons, 1885
by Linda Rhodes and Kathryn Abnett (Pen & Sword 2009)

Foul Deeds and Suspicious Deaths in Barking, Dagenham and Chadwell Heath
by Linda Rhodes and Kathryn Abnett (Pen & Sword 2007)

The Dagenham Murder: the brutal killing of PC George Clark, 1846
by Linda Rhodes, Lee Shelden and Kathryn Abnett (Barking & Dagenham Libraries, 2005). ***Winner of the Crime Writers' Association Gold Dagger award***

Lightning Source UK Ltd.
Milton Keynes UK
UKOW01f0013141013

218975UK00002B/12/P